The Law Against War

The Law against War is a translated and updated version of a book published in 2008 in French (Le droit contre la guerre, Pedone). The aim of this book is to study the prohibition of the use of armed force in contemporary positive international law. Some commentators claim that the field has undergone substantial changes arising especially since the end of the Cold War in the 1990s. More specifically, several scholars consider that the prohibition laid down as a principle in the United Nations Charter of 1945 should be relaxed in the present-day context of international relations, a change that would seem to be reflected in the emergence of ideas such as 'humanitarian intervention', 'preventive war' or in the possibility of presuming Security Council authorisation under certain exceptional circumstances. The argument in this book is that while marked changes have been observed, above all since the 1990s, the legal regime laid down by the Charter remains founded on a genuine jus contra bellum and not on the jus ad bellum that characterised earlier periods. 'The law against war', as in the title of this book, is a literal rendering of the familiar Latin expression and at the same time it conveys the spirit of a rule that remains, without a doubt, one of the cornerstones of public international law.

Volume 4 in the series French Studies in International Law

D1334728

French Studies in International Law

General Editor: Emmanuelle Jouannet (Sorbonne Law School)

French Studies in International Law is a unique new series which aims to bring to the attention of an English-speaking audience the most important modern works by leading French and French-speaking scholars of international law. The books which appear in this series were selected by Professor Emmanuelle Jouannet of the University of Paris 1 (Sorbonne Law School). French Studies in International Law is a books collection of the CERDIN Paris 1 Sorbonne Law School (The Centre of Studies and Research on International Law). The CERDIN is the largest French research centre in international law comprising 11 professors, 3 lecturers, 21 research professors and researchers, and 188 PhD students. CERDIN follows an active policy of collective work around several fields of key research, including: general international law, law of the United Nations, international disputes, international economic and finance law (in particular WTO), international human rights law, theory, philosophy and history of international law and foreign doctrines, international air space law, and the law of the sea.

Volume 1: Ordering Pluralism: A Conceptual Framework for Understanding the Transnational Legal World *Mireille Delmas-Marty translated by Naomi Norberg*

Volume 2: International Law, Power, Security and Justice: Essays on International Law and Relations *Serge Sur*

Volume 3: The Advancement of International Law *Charles Leben*

Volume 4: The Law against War: The Prohibition on the Use of Force in Contemporary International Law *Olivier Corten* (translated by Christopher Sutcliffe)

The Law against War

The Prohibition on the Use of Force in Contemporary International Law

Olivier Corten

With a Preface by Bruno Simma

Translated by Christopher Sutcliffe

·HART·
PUBLISHING

OXFORD AND PORTLAND, OREGON
2012

Published in the United Kingdom by Hart Publishing Ltd
16C Worcester Place, Oxford, OX1 2JW
Telephone: +44 (0)1865 517530
Fax: +44 (0)1865 510710
E-mail: mail@hartpub.co.uk
Website: http://www.hartpub.co.uk

Published in North America (US and Canada) by
Hart Publishing
c/o International Specialized Book Services
920 NE 58th Avenue, Suite 300
Portland, OR 97213-3786
USA
Tel: +1 503 287 3093 or toll-free: (1) 800 944 6190
Fax: +1 503 280 8832
E-mail: orders@isbs.com
Website: http://www.isbs.com

British Library Cataloguing in Publication Data
Data Available

ISBN: 978-1-84113-942-5 (Hardback)
978-1-84946-358-4 (Paperback)

Typeset by Hope Services, Abingdon
Printed and bound in Great Britain by
CPI Antony Rowe Ltd, Chippenham, Wiltshire

Public avec le concours de la Fondation Universitaire de Belgique

Series Editor's Preface

This Series aims to contribute to the dissemination in English of the works of the most eminent international law scholars writing in French. Because these works have not yet been published in English, this scholarship is inaccessible to a great number of potential readers who, due to the language barrier, cannot become acquainted with or discuss it. This is highly regrettable, as it limits the debate on international law to works in English—the *lingua franca* of our contemporary world—and thus primarily to Anglophone scholars.

The publication of these works in English therefore seeks to create the conditions for genuine debate among Francophone and Anglophone international law scholars across the globe, a debate that should ideally be based on the work of both. *Learning* of others' theories through translation is in fact the first essential step towards *acknowledging* the contributions and differences of each. Knowledge and acknowledgement lead to understanding the core of irreducibility, as well as truth, in each legal culture's international law doctrine, its traditions and distinct ideas, as well as each author's way of thinking. They should make it possible to avoid the all-too-frequent misunderstanding of each other's position on international law that results from simple ignorance of each other's work. Between the Francophone and Anglophone worlds, the rule is still too often mutual, even courteous indifference or ignorance, dialogue the exception.

Emmanuelle Jouannet
Professor, University of Paris I (*Sorbonne Law School*)

Foreword

by Bruno Simma

A look at the current state of international law ought to put the representatives of our discipline into a comfortable mood. After all, while until recently
they had to battle against doubts as to the very existence of international law
as genuine law rather than some kind of moral-political philosophy
expressed in legal terms, international lawyers now rather appear to face an
embarras de richesse. So much international law, recognised as such, has
come into being in an ever-wider variety of fields that observers have begun
to diagnose, but also to repair and prevent further, the fragmentation of
(what they considered to have been) a unitary order into a multiplicity of
regimes only insufficiently held together by systematic thinking. Further, the
former much-lamented dearth of international institutions for the settlement
o
f
disputes by impartial third parties has given way to what many scholars
consider to be no less than a 'proliferation' (with all frightening undertones
of this term) of international courts and tribunals. At the same time an
increasing number of scholars are able to view a 'constitutionalisation' of
international law as being on the way: the embodiment of fundamental values shared by an international community, in the true sense of the term, in
hard and hierarchically organised principles and rules. Thus, we are in the
presence of more international law, and more judges guarding it, going into
more different directions, than ever before. So, why, in view of all this, aren't
we more reassured about the capacity of our discipline to make the world a
better place or, at least, to keep it in an orderly state? Because the same international law that is becoming more developed and diversified almost by the
day, is still struggling hard with the most fundamental question of all: that
of the containment of the use of force in international relations. To speak of
a hard struggle in this regard, is anything but an exaggeration. It has even
turned into a fight against an irrationality that we thought had been overcome centuries ago, with leading statesmen of the Western world recently
confessing that their unfortunate decisions to go to war against Iraq had been
inspired directly by the voice of God. . . . To return to the world of the mundane, international legal discourse since 1945 has never witnessed a more

massive onslaught against the system of containment of military force set up in the Charter of the United Nations than at present, particularly in the wake of September 11. Wars have become imaginable, indeed feasible, again. As I regretfully had to say in a Separate Opinion to a recent judgment of the International Court of Justice: more and more, legal justification of the use of force within the system of the Charter is discarded even as a fig leaf, while an increasing number of writers appear to prepare for the outright funeral of international legal limitations on the use of force (ICJ Rep (2003) 328). That some voices have become more guarded in view of the fiasco in Iraq is cold comfort only—the legality or illegality of the use of force cannot depend upon the success of one's armies. And, at the time of writing, not only politicians and strategists but also writers fascinated, indeed blinded, by military power are discussing the prospects of new wars in ways that remind us of the plans of Schlieffen and the rest of European general staffs, as if 1914 had never happened.

At this critical state of affairs, a treatment of the matter displaying the quality of the present work by Olivier Corten is particularly welcome. Corten's book is weighty not just by its size, but above all through the depth and comprehensiveness with which it analyses the entirety of what the author calls the law against war, the *jus contra bellum*—this title already marking the ethos of the work and its anchoring in the United Nations Charter, which after all, was 'to save succeeding generations from the scourge of war, which twice in our lifetime has brought untold sorrow to mankind'. Corten tackles his immense task with a combination of methodical rigour, applying modern positivism and abstaining from constructions of a *lex ferenda*, and great sensibility for the political context and the ensuing possibilities and limitations of the legal regulation of force. He regards as his foremost object not the determination of the countless violations of the respective rules since 1945, but the faithful depiction and interpretation of these rules as they are recognised by the international community of States—still recognised, that is, despite all the breaches. As such, Corten's work also constitutes an exemplary exercise of the application of contemporary positivist theories of customary international law-making (and the conditions of change of international custom, handled in a cavalier fashion by most proponents of the unilateral use of force) and treaty interpretation. What he treats as the outcome of these processes, is a genuine stocktaking of the contemporary law on the matter. State practice and *opinio juris* in the multilateral framework of the United Nations is given pride of place. The contribution of the International Court of Justice is duly, but also critically, acknowledged. Several themes of the book are based on earlier publications of its author, for instance on humanitarian intervention. Personally, I have found myself in disagreement with Corten on a number of points, particularly with regard to his views on the legal consequences of—and the availability of self-defence against—the use of force by non-State actors. But Corten's views have always made me consider, and sometimes re-consider, my own positions.

A great work like the present one will undoubtedly make a contribution by intellectually solidifying its subject-matter and thus creating informed views in the minds also of international law practitioners. Whether legal advice against the use of force will then be heeded, is another matter. What we need to do is to come up with advice as well-founded and convincing as possible. To the attainment of this task Olivier Corten has made a huge contribution.

Acknowledgments

This book has benefited from the assistance of numerous people. First and foremost, I would like to express my deep gratitude to Emmanuelle Jouannet who is at the origin of this project. I am also grateful to Christopher Sutcliffe who had the difficult task of understanding what I had written in the French version of the book. The *Université libre de Bruxelles* and the *Fondation universitaire de Belgique* supplied financial support for the translation. Martyna Falkowska helped me in the finalisation of the text in a very efficient way. Thanks are also due to my friends and colleagues, François Dubuisson, Pierre Klein and Theodore Christakis who made helpful comments along the way. Finally, I would like to express my heartfelt gratitude to Barbara, Martin and Hugo for everything.

Contents

Table of Cases

Introduction

I N LATE APRIL 1965, when just a few months of age, I was with my parents in Santo Domingo, at the height of the civil war between the partisans of an ousted former president and those of the military junta that had overthrown him. With the help of several army units, the rebel forces had taken a part of the city but were under fire from air and naval forces loyal to the authorities, which were actively supported by the United States. We were living in a 'high risk' district and constantly had to take refuge in cellars to escape from what was not always targeted artillery fire or bombing. After a week's fighting, US armed forces invaded the capital, officially to rescue imperilled foreign nationals. In fact the US was coming to the aid of its local allies, who were carrying out indiscriminate attacks and were to regain power a few months later thanks to this outside intervention. In the meantime, our family was evacuated on a US aircraft carrier bound for Puerto Rico and my parents were quite surprised to meet young marines who genuinely believed they were carrying out a humanitarian mission . . .

This anecdote from my childhood may explain why I have always been interested in the use of force, and also my distrust of the official justifications given by the intervening powers. In this sense I no more than anyone else can claim to be absolutely objective in dealing with the subject matter that makes up the substance of this book, a subject that always has been and still is particularly controversial. This does not mean, as I shall set out below, that I am neither willing nor able to follow the rules of scientific method as stringently as possible.[1] However, those rules require that, rather than claiming some unattainable neutrality, one should say from the outset 'where one is coming from'. In this perspective, then, allowance must be made for a sensitivity that I am not trying to hide in any way, even if that sensitivity shall not be evoked any further in the context of the positivist legal reasoning that shall guide the developments that follow.

The aim of this book is to study the prohibition of the use of armed force[2] in contemporary positive international law. Some commentators claim that

---

[1] See below, ch 1, s II.

[2] This book concentrates on armed force and does not extend to economic or political force, for example. I shall not state an opinion as to whether Charter article 2(4) covers all uses of 'force' but shall contemplate military force alone in what follows.

the field has undergone substantial changes arising especially since the end of the Cold War in the 1990s. More specifically, several scholars consider that the prohibition laid down as a principle in the United Nations Charter of 1945 should be relaxed in the present-day context of international relations, a change that would seem to be reflected in the emergence of ideas such as 'humanitarian intervention' and 'preventive war' and in the possibility of presuming Security Council authorisation under certain exceptional circumstances. The argument in this book is that while marked changes have been observed, above all since the 1990s, the legal regime laid down by the Charter remains founded on a genuine *jus contra bellum* and not on the *jus ad bellum* that characterised earlier periods. 'The law against war', as in the title of this book, is a literal rendering of the familiar Latin expression and at the same time it conveys the spirit of a rule that remains, without a doubt, one of the cornerstones of public international law.

The method followed for testing this hypothesis shall be set out in the first chapter, which will show at the same time the diversity of theoretical and epistemological approaches to be found in current doctrine. Generally, it shall be specified from the outset that the specific feature of this study—which is to my knowledge the only work of comparable scope, in French at least—is to base itself essentially on practice and on the positions taken by States,[3] as observed since 1945.[4] To this end, I have analysed both relevant precedents dealt with by the UN's political organs (and especially the Security Council[5]) and the discussions of principle relating to the prohibition of the use of force, especially in the General Assembly. By postulating both the existence of an international law—which is not self-evident in a domain that is often the breeding ground of realist theories—and the possibility of identifying an *opinio juris* in the minds of States, I have attempted to determine the lowest common denominator in their positions.[6] As such, my aim has not been to judge States and make pronouncements as to the lawfulness or otherwise of this or that military intervention. Beyond individual precedents, the aim has been rather to question the common interpretation of the UN Charter that

---

[3] While I have based the argument primarily on documents expressing States' positions, needless to say I have taken account of scholarship, although without being able to claim to have been exhaustive in such a vast and so widely debated a domain. For details of source material, readers should see the selected reading at the end of the book which contains references to the main studies consulted. Sources can be identified from footnotes: a full reference is given for the first occurrence in each chapter.

[4] This book has a historical dimension and refers to many episodes from contemporary history up until December 2009. However, it does not go further back than 1945 and the drawing up of the UN Charter, which, I argue, marks a break with the former international legal order.

[5] Allowance is also made for positions expressed by States in other fora, including within national legal frameworks. See the bibliography for details.

[6] To this end many citations are given in the main text or in the footnotes. I apologise for the cumbersome style that results from this but I felt it was the only way to set out grounds sufficiently clearly as to convince readers of the argument. For further clarifications on States' positions readers might like to consult www.ulb.ac.be/droit/cdi ('cahiers documentaires').

must make it possible to clarify the contemporary meaning of the prohibition of the use of force.

The book is divided into eight chapters arranged into two parts. The first part tries to mark out the contours of the prohibition of the use of force by investigating the methodological issues the rule raises (chapter one), its subject matter (with the definitions of 'force' or 'threat', that make up chapter two), its scope (which raises the question of 'international relations within the meaning of article 2(4) that is the gist of chapter three) and finally its status (the characterisation as *jus cogens* and its consequences being covered in chapter four). In part two I try to identify the limits of the prohibition by investigating the admissibility and scope of justifications traditionally used in the domain of the use of force, be they consent (chapter five), Security Council authorisation (chapter six), self-defence (chapter seven), or the 'right of humanitarian intervention' (chapter eight). For each of these themes, the debates that often divide doctrine are exposited in an attempt to propose an interpretation that seems to me to reflect the position of the UN Member States.

1

A Choice of Method

A T A CONFERENCE on 'the right of humanitarian intervention in contemporary international law', two speakers clash. The first claims that the right of humanitarian intervention arose in the 1990s as a result of the advancement of humanistic values typical of the 'new world order'. The second retorts that the United Nations Charter ('UN Charter') has not been amended and does not recognise the existence of any such right in the positive international legal order. The first speaker then points out that international law can and must evolve informally so as to keep pace with the needs of life in society. The second answers that law cannot admit any informal evolution of the sort unless it is materialised by a treaty revision or, at the very least, by the emergence of a customary rule accepted by the community of States as a whole.

This schematised debate clearly shows that, in the area of the non-use of force perhaps more than in others, legal controversies are often inseparable from deeper issues about the methods, or even the theory, of international law.[1] In the example just set out, the proponent and the opponent of the right of humanitarian intervention plainly do not share the same methodological options. For their discussion to be meaningful, it must therefore extend beyond the analysis of this or that particular source of law (article 2(4) of the UN Charter, the major resolutions of the UN General Assembly on the use of force, such and such a precedent at the time the rule was invoked, and so on) and address the way such sources are apprehended and interpreted. So, and this was borne out by precedents like Kosovo or Iraq, it seems that such controversies cannot be understood without some grasp of the methodological debates and options underpinning them.

The purpose of this first chapter is not to come down on one side or other of the fence by trying to show that one or other option is scientifically valid. It is first to emphasise the width of the methodological divide by identifying two extremes between which commentators can usually be situated (section 1). Only after setting out the terms of the debate shall we be in a

---

[1] L Condorelli, 'Conclusion générale: quelques remarques peu . . . concluantes' in E Cannizzaro and Paolo Palchetti (eds), *Customary International Law On the Use of Force* (Leiden/Boston, Martinus Nijhoff, 2005) 321; E Cannizaro and Paolo Palchetti, 'Customary International Law on the Use of Force . . . at a Time of Perplexity', ibid 1–6.

position to ascertain the methodological options to be followed in the remainder of this book (section 2). These options are the result of a choice; and while no claim is made that it is the only possible choice, it is important to be clear about it from the outset if we are to understand properly the scope of the substantive arguments to be developed in the ensuing chapters.

I The Terms of the Methodological Debate on the Non-Use of Force: the Extensive Versus the Restrictive Approach

The prohibition of the use of force is first and foremost a treaty-based rule, enshrined in the UN Charter and in numerous other treaties of regional scope. However, it is at the same time a rule of customary law, the evolution of which has been at the centre of lively debates, particularly in the last few years. On one side of those debates is the extensive approach; it consists in interpreting the rule in the most flexible manner possible. By this approach, doctrines such as 'preventive self-defence' or the right of 'humanitarian intervention', for example, can be accepted as conforming to the rules. On the other side is what can be categorised as the restrictive approach; it advocates a much stricter interpretation of the prohibition so making it much less likely that new exceptions will be viewed as acceptable.[2] Beyond the validity of the basic arguments advanced by both sides, a review of scholarship reveals that the debate is also, and perhaps above all, about method.[3] The most profound divergences arise over the status and interpretation of the customary prohibition on the use of force. The extensive approach, unlike the restrictive one, tends to favour a highly flexible method when it comes to ascertaining the status and content of the customary rule. In any event, it is this working hypothesis that will be tested in this section. The questions of the status and the constitutive elements of custom will be dealt with in turn in order to illustrate the methodological differences between the two approaches.

Before addressing the first of these two points, it should be noted that, while the arguments that will be presented here are articulated in terms of the two opposite extremes, the diversity of doctrinal opinions that have currency is considerably more complex and nuanced than this might suggest. This, however, shall not prevent us from illustrating the two theoretical

---

[2] These two approaches are well illustrated by comparing the books by TM Franck, *Recourse to Force: State Actions Against Threats and Armed Attacks* (Cambridge, Cambridge University Press, 2002) and C Gray, *International Law and the Use of Force*, 3rd edn (Oxford, Oxford University Press, 2008).

[3] See, in this regard, M Byers, 'The Shifting Foundations of International Law: A Decade of Forceful Measures against Iraq' (2002) 13 *EJIL* 22–23; TJ Farer, 'Humanitarian Intervention before and after 9/11: Legality and Legitimacy' in JL Holzgrefe and RO Keohane (eds), *Humanitarian Intervention: Ethical, Legal and Political Dilemmas* (Cambridge, Cambridge University Press, 2003) 53 *ff*.

extremes by using commentators whose work cannot be reduced to either position, the objective being to present types of argumentation rather than to classify any given author as belonging to one or the other category. It is in this spirit that a sample of works on the use of force has been selected, ranging from the war in Kosovo to that in Iraq. The following table, which will be explained in more detail below, provides us with an overall picture of the debate.

	Extensive approach	Restrictive approach
Status of custom	Privileged source Formal and material source Policy-oriented or objectivist tendencies	Equality between sources Formal source Voluntarist or formalist tendencies
Understanding of the constitutive elements of custom	Practice as the dominant element; the role of political organs 'Instant' or rapidly evolving custom Dominant role of major States	*Opinio juris* as the dominant element; the role of legal discourse Custom evolves gradually Equality between States

Although it is impossible to be anything like exhaustive in this regard, an attempt has nonetheless been made here to cover as wide a range of viewpoints as possible, in particular by integrating 'US' and 'European' works into the analysis alongside those from Third World countries. It may be possible to advance the hypothesis of a schism opposing US scholars to those from the rest of the world, with the former espousing the extensive approach and the latter the restrictive one.[4] In any event, it must be noted that the present author does not claim to be totally neutral in the debate presented here. My personal preference is for the restrictive approach.[5] This, however, need not disqualify me from describing the extensive approach (A) in as objective a manner as possible, before going on to specify the ways in which my own preferred understanding differs from it (B).

A. The Extensive Approach to the Customary Prohibition of the Use of Force

Scarcely any commentators today are prepared to question the importance of custom in the debates surrounding the scope of the prohibition on the use of force. At the core of the controversies besetting the doctrine in terms of 'preventive war', 'implicit authorisation' or 'humanitarian intervention'

---

[4] See, in this regard, M Glennon, 'The UN Security Council in a Unipolar World' (2003) 44 *Virginia JIL* 97–99.

[5] See II below.

are certain precedents that bear witness to the evolution of this rule that is otherwise enshrined in the UN Charter. The extensive approach is charac-terised by the general status that it confers upon custom, seen as a means of adapting international law to the necessities of international life (1). This status implies a particular interpretation of the constituent elements of custom, which brings us back essentially to the practices of certain 'major' States (2).

Custom as a Means of Adapting International Law

Generally speaking, the extensive approach tends to move beyond the formalism of treaty texts in order to view them in relation to the particular factual circumstances of each case.[6] From this perspective, it would be inconceivable to remain confined to the wording of article 2(4) or of article 51 of the UN Charter, or even to UN General Assembly resolutions 2625 or 3314, as do certain commentators variously referred to as 'jurisprudes',[7] 'European formalists'[8] or even 'objective legalists'.[9] Rather, the jurist should take account of each concrete situation; and it is in terms of each such situation that the legal rule takes on its meaning:

> In the end, each use of force must find legitimacy in the facts and circumstances that the States believe made it necessary. Each should be judged not on abstract concepts, but on the particular events that gave rise to it.[10]

A preventive war or a humanitarian intervention can only be judged to be consistent or not with international law on the basis of the specific fea-tures of each case. It is thus necessary to hold to 'the same general rule applicable to all uses of force: necessity to act under the relevant circum-stances, together with the requirement that any action be proportionate to the threat addressed'.[11]

Custom is precisely what enables us to link the abstract legal concept to the particular factual situation; custom, then, enjoys the status of a privi-leged source of law, in particular with regard to treaties.[12] It is easier to eval-uate a situation in terms of comparable precedents than by reference to intractable texts. Rather than, for example, arbitrarily ruling out all forms of 'pre-emptive self-defence' under the pretext that article 51 only comes into

---

[6] AD Sofaer, 'On the Necessity of Pre-emption' (2003) 14 *EJIL* 212–13.

[7] RN Gardner, 'Neither Bush nor the "Jurisprudes"' (2003) 97 *AJIL* 585 *ff*.

[8] M Koskenniemi, 'Iraq and the "Bush Doctrine" of Pre-emptive Self-Defense. Expert analysis', *Crimes of War Project*, 20 August 2002, www.crimesofwar.org/expert/bush-koskenniemi.html.

[9] S Schieder, 'Pragmatism as a Path towards a Discursive and Open Theory of International Law' (2000) 11 *EJIL* 691.

[10] Taft IV and Buchwald, 'Pre-emption, Iraq and International Law' (2003) 97 *AJIL* 557.

[11] AD Sofaer, 'On the Necessity of Pre-emption', above n 6, 220.

[12] MN Schmitt, *Counter-Terrorism and the Use of Force in International Law* (Garmisch-Partenkirchen, George C Marshall European Center for Security Studies, 2002) 2.

play 'if an armed attack occurs', it is better to take into account precedents in which the international community has viewed certain pre-emptive actions as admissible. Moreover, article 51 itself was never intended to jeopardise the 'natural', and thus customary, right to self-defence, either as it existed at the time or as it has evolved since. Custom thus permits us to free ourselves from the text of a treaty, or, at the very least, to interpret it in a very broad manner, and even to amend it while avoiding the need to follow strict procedures.[13] In any event, the 'narrow interpretation has already been modified by the practice of UN members'.[14]

Custom enables us, in this context, to relate the legal rule not merely to the facts of any given case, but also to moral and political values; values that we cannot pretend are excluded from the process of interpretation. In this regard, we can flag notions such as a 'reasonableness standard',[15] 'contextual reasonableness',[16] a 'common sense of value—justice, morality, good sense',[17] a 'reasonable objective',[18] a 'teleological understanding',[19] or even a 'common moral instinct'.[20] It is through recourse to custom that we enable the interpreter to take account of non-legal considerations, and thus to bring together legality and legitimacy[21]—and even to blur the boundaries between *lex lata* and *lex ferenda*.[22] Most importantly, the UN Charter is a convention of a constitutional nature, meaning that allowance must invariably be made for political considerations when interpreting it. Article 2(4) 'is also intended to be perpetually evolving as the seemingly static norms are applied to practical situations through an essentially political process

[13] A Buchanan, 'Reforming the International Law of humanitarian intervention' in JL Holzgrefe and RO Keohane (eds), above n 3, 134.

[14] RN Gardner, 'Neither Bush nor the "Jurisprudes"', above n 7, 589.

[15] AD Sofaer, 'On the Necessity of Pre-emption', above n 6, 213.

[16] TM Franck, 'Interpretation and Change in the Law of Humanitarian Intervention' in JL Holzgrefe and RO Keohane (eds), *Humanitarian Intervention: Ethical, Legal and Political Dilemmas* (Cambridge, Cambridge University Press, 2003) 205.

[17] ibid, 229–30; see also TM Franck, *Recourse to Force. State Actions Against Threats and Armed Attacks*, above n 2, 98.

[18] M Koskenniemi, 'Iraq and the "Bush Doctrine" of Pre-emptive Self-Defense. Expert analysis', above n 8.

[19] R Wedgwood, 'The Fall of Saddam Hussein: Security Council Mandates and Preemptive Self-Defense' (2003) 97 *AJIL* 584.

[20] TM Franck, *Recourse to Force. State Actions Against Threats and Armed Attacks*, above n 2, 229–30.

[21] R Wedgwood, 'The Fall of Saddam Hussein: Security Council Mandates and Preemptive Self-Defense' above n 19, 578; see also P Weckel, 'L'emploi de la force contre la Yougoslavie ou la Charte fissurée' (2000) 104 *RGDIP* 19; TM Franck, *Recourse to Force. State Actions Against Threats and Armed Attacks*, above n 2, 94; R Falk, 'What Future for the United Nations Charter System of War Prevention?' (2003) 97 *AJIL* 596; P Weckel, 'L'usage déraisonnable de la force' (2003) 107 *RGDIP* 387–89; and RB Garcia, 'El Debate sobre la legalidad internacional tras la crisis de Iraq y las Naciones Unidas' (2003) 19 *Annuario de derecho internacional* 56 *ff*.

[22] See, for example, RB Garcia, 'Cuestiones actuales referentes al uso de la fuerza en el Derecho Internacional' (1999) 15 *Annuario de derecho internacional* 14 and 59 *ff*; JE Stromseth, 'Law and Force After Iraq: A Transitional Moment' (2003) 97 *AJIL* 629.

operating to solve real crises, instance by instance'.[23] Moreover, it is for this reason that the Member States conferred very extensive powers upon the political organs, and upon the Security Council in particular 'the practice of a UN organ may be seen to interpret the text and thereby to shape our understanding of it'.[24] It is essential to take into account the decisions of this organ, but also its silences, if we are to specify the meaning of the rule of law: 'the Council enjoys a normative authority that builds coalitions and musters public support'.[25] The fact that certain humanitarian interventions have not been condemned by the Security Council is testament to the legality of this type of intervention, provided that the circumstances are comparable to those of the precedents raised.[26] The opinions and silences of the Secretary-General may also be taken into consideration.[27]

Overall, custom may be considered as both a formal and material source of the international legal order. Of course, there are many different versions and variants of this extensive approach. Nevertheless, it should be noted that these variants can be traced to a common sensitivity that is well illustrated by the following passage:

> [T]he interpretative principles deployed in the application of a constitutive text may also depend on the nature of values and interests at stake—the theology of an instrument as much as its literal form. This is not to deny a claim of objectivity in interpretation, but at minimum, values and interests are likely to influence State practice, which in turn must inform the meaning given to a treaty understanding.[28]

Custom should not be reduced to a purely formal source, but should be viewed as a means of adapting law to the evolving international sphere. The rule must be understood in relation to 'some useful purpose that the rule serves',[29] and the question that must thus be asked is, 'what human goals are at stake, and whether forcible interference is necessary for their preservation?'[30]

Therefore, certain forms of unilateral pre-emptive war must be viewed as acceptable because of their logically necessary character. In its classical

---

[23] TM Franck, 'Interpretation and Change in the Law of Humanitarian Intervention', above n 16, 205.

[24] TM Franck, *Recourse to Force. State Actions Against Threats and Armed Attacks*, above n 2, 174; TM Franck, 'Iraq and the "Bush Doctrine" of Pre-Emptive Self-Defense. Expert Analysis', *Crimes of War Project*, 20 August 2002, www.crimesofwar.org/expert/bush-franck. html.

[25] R Wedgwood, 'NATO's Campaign in Yugoslavia' (1999) 93 *AJIL* 832.

[26] TM Franck, *Recourse to Force. State Actions Against Threats and Armed Attacks*, above n 2, 13 *ff*; TM Franck, 'What Happens Now? The United Nations After Iraq' (2003) 97 *AJIL* 615; R Wedgwood, 'NATO's Campaign in Yugoslavia', above n 25, 830–32.

[27] R Wedgwood, ibid, 831.

[28] R Wedgwood, 'Unilateral Action in the United Nations System' (2000) 11 *EJIL* 352.

[29] M Koskenniemi, 'Iraq and the "Bush Doctrine" of Pre-Emptive Self-Defense. Expert Analysis', above n 8.

[30] R Wedgwood, 'Unilateral Action in the United Nations System', above n 28, 352.

formulation, that is, that characterised by the imminence of the threat and
the absolute necessity of the response, the right of anticipatory self-defence
is not in question. By definition, a State will defend its existence and its survival; this will lead it to make use of all the means within its power to ensure
that an imminent threat facing it will not come to fruition: 'the formalist
position, which insists on the occurrence of an armed attack, seem[s] like a
ludicrous position'.[31] It could not be otherwise: the rule of law here reflects
only a basic necessity of the political order: 'the UN Charter is not a suicide pact'.[32] Above and beyond this classical assumption, pre-emptive
action must also be allowed in situations where the threats are more diffuse:
'a strict reading of Article 51 is no longer tenable in the face of modern terrorism and aggression'.[33] Developments in the international sphere have
illustrated that terrorist groups can commit deadly, surprise attacks with the
active or passive complicity of certain States.[34] It is unthinkable in this context that the States targeted in such attacks should wait patiently for the
threats to materialise.[35] Pre-emptive action then becomes legitimate, and
thus legal, because it is necessary in the light of recent developments in the
international sphere:[36] 'reason suggests that self-help and countermeasures
remain necessary remedies of last resort'.[37] This type of reasoning, which
can be found in the work of very different authors, rests upon an objectivist
theoretical foundation. Positive law can only correspond to objective law,
that is, the rules considered as necessary in a given social context and at a
given historical period.[38] It is logically and objectively impossible to prohibit
pre-emptive anti-terrorist action, and this is in the interests of all. It is not
surprising, then, that States act in this manner, or declare their support
for such an approach, thereby enabling the development of the customary

[31] M Koskenniemi, 'Iraq and the "Bush Doctrine" of Pre-Emptive Self-Defense. Expert
Analysis', above n 8.

[32] E Benvenisti, 'Iraq and the "Bush Doctrine" of Pre-Emptive Self-Defense. Expert
Analysis', *Crimes of War Project*, August 20, 2002, www.crimesofwar.org/expert/bush-
benvenisti.html; TM Franck, *Recourse to Force. State Actions Against Threats and Armed Attacks*,
above n 2, 98.

[33] TM Franck, 'What Happens Now? The United Nations After Iraq', above n 26, 619; see
also R Wedgwood, 'Responding to Terrorism: The Strikes Against Bin Laden', (1999) 44 *Yale
JIL* 559 *ff*.

[34] J Yoo, 'International Law and the War in Iraq', (2003) 97 *AJIL* 575–76; AD Sofaer, 'On
the Necessity of Pre-emption', above n 6, 209–10.

[35] R Wedgwood, 'The Fall of Saddam Hussein: Security Council Mandates and Preemptive
Self-Defense', above n 19, 583; see also Y Dinstein, *War, Aggression and Self-Defense*, 4th edn
(Cambridge, Cambridge University Press, 2005) 204–08.

[36] JE Stromseth, 'Law and Force After Iraq: A Transitional Moment', above n 22, 634;
FA Biggio, 'Neutralizing the Threat: Reconsidering Existing Doctrines in the Emerging War
on Terrorism', (2002) 34 *Case Western Reserve JIL* 1; MN Schmitt, *Counter-Terrorism and the
Use of Force in International Law*, above n 12.

[37] TM Franck, *Recourse to Force. State Actions Against Threats and Armed Attacks*, above
n 2, 110.

[38] See: O Corten, *Méthodologie du droit international public* (Bruxelles, edn Université de
Bruxelles, 2009), 48–57.

rule. Custom appears here as both a formal and a material source of law, with positive law not radically distinguished from the objective law that determines it.

From a related perspective, it can be argued that the 'right of humanitarian intervention' is acceptable in the light of the progress of the humanistic values at the heart of the international community. It is objectively necessary to allow certain unilateral actions in cases in which the collective security mechanisms have not functioned. Unlike the argument in favour of pre-emptive anti-terrorist action, which is often more strictly attached to the notion of social necessity and objective law, that of humanitarian intervention seems to return to certain currents that assume a radical deformalisation of the rule of law, including

> a comprehensive assessment that includes an embrace of complementary norms, as well as an appraisal of what has been done in the name of law and an evaluation of whether preferable policy alternatives were available to those with the authority to make decisions.[39]

The extensive approach here provides an illustration of the theoretical current predominant in the English-speaking world that favours a 'policy-oriented' perspective. Such a perspective tends to justify a very broad range of grounds for the use of force, which, it is accepted, rest upon political considerations: 'one central ingredient is the moral necessity of action—the credible invocation of shared community purposes'.[40] It is therefore necessary to evaluate the legality of military action

> not simply in terms of certain rules, that are supposed to form part of a black-letter code of international law, but in terms of the acceptability of those responses in different contexts, to the contemporary international decision process . . . Trends must then be tested against the requirements of world public order as a means of assessing their adequacy . . . Scholars should take the responsibility of proposing alternative arrangements so that a better approximation of political and legal goals can be achieved in the future.[41]

Without always acknowledging their affinity with this particular approach, many authors seem to share this sensibility; rejecting 'legalism',[42] by reliance on positivist styles of legal appraisal'.[43] Such theorists insist

---

[39] R Falk, 'Kosovo, World Order, and the Future of International Law' (1999) 93 *AJIL* 848–49; TM Franck, 'What Happens Now? The United Nations After Iraq', above n 26, 615 and 619.

[40] R Wedgwood, 'The Fall of Saddam Hussein: Security Council Mandates and Preemptive Self-Defense', above n 19, 578.

[41] M Reisman, 'International Legal Responses to Terrorism' (1999) 22 *Houston JIL* 5–6; M Reisman and O Schachter, 'Coercion and Self-Determination: Construing Charter Article 2(4)', (1984) 78 *AJIL* 642–45; see also MN Schmitt, *Counter-Terrorism and the Use of Force in International Law*, above n 12, 56.

[42] R Falk, 'Kosovo, World Order, and the Future of International Law', above n 39, 852–53.

[43] ibid, 854.

upon the aporia of the positivist, formalist method. In its most radical version, this method implies that a rational interpretation of the legal rule, into which no value judgement enters, is not only possible but also inherent in the scientific character of legal science. This somewhat naïve vision of an absolute distinction between law and politics (or morality) has been called into question by all contemporary legal theories, which view interpretation as a constructive task invariably involving value judgements. In this context, it cannot be claimed that legal interpretation is divorced from political and moral considerations.[44] The only truly objective position, then, consists in assuming a 'policy-oriented' perspective, rather than denying the involvement of such value judgements (which in practice amounts to trying to hide them). There is thus no need to feel uneasy about modifying the texts of treaties by taking into account the values or objectives that supposedly lie behind the rules, or even about referring to natural law notions such as that of the 'just war'.[45] This brings us back to the connection between law and fact, or between law and values, that custom allows us to make. Such a conception of custom carries with it certain consequences when it comes to determining its content.

The Dominant Role of the Practice of Major States

It is traditionally held that custom is composed of two constitutive elements: practice and *opinio juris sive necessitatis*. The extensive approach does not in principle deny this proposition. The second condition, and more specifically the Latin expression *sive necessitatis*, urges allowance to be made for social necessities. These necessities also allow, should the case arise, for justifications of military action based upon a teleological interpretation of the texts of treaties: 'the answer turns on whether the intervention can be reconciled with the purposes that animate the international order'.[46] A more detailed analysis, however, suggests that, in this context, *opinio juris* is not a dominant element of custom, in any event to the extent that the term obliges the interpreter to verify that the international community of States has accepted

[44] TM Franck, 'Interpretation and Change in the Law of Humanitarian Intervention', above n 16, 207–14; TM Franck, *Recourse to Force. State Actions Against Threats and Armed Attacks*, above n 2, 176 *ff*.

[45] RB Garcia, 'Cuestiones actuales referentes al uso de la fuerza en el Derecho Internacional', above n 22, 68; AD Sofaer, 'On the Necessity of Pre-emption', above n 6, 225; JE Stromseth, 'Rethinking humanitarian intervention: the case for incremental change' in JL Holzgrefe and RO Keohane (eds), *Humanitarian Intervention: Ethical, Legal and Political Dilemmas* (Cambridge, Cambridge University Press, 2003) 268; FA Biggio, 'Neutralizing the Threat: Reconsidering Existing Doctrines in the Emerging War on Terrorism', above n 36, 20–22.

[46] BR Roth, 'Bending the law, breaking it, or developing it? The United States and the humanitarian use of force in the post-Cold War era' in M Byers and G Nolte (eds), *United States Hegemony and the Foundations of International Law* (Cambridge, Cambridge University Press, 2003) 256.

the legal character of the customary rule. Thus, rather than embarking upon a textual analysis of certain UN General Assembly resolutions, more emphasis is placed on State practice,[47] and on the practice of certain States in particular: 'State practice remains key to the shaping of legal norms'.[48] It is this practice that demonstrates how social necessities are embedded in and expressed through legal norms.

Essentially, practice is what matters, and not the declarations of principle issued by public authorities. What is crucial is to show that, on the facts, the rule has evolved in such or such a manner. Official speeches are of little import, the only truly legal rule being that which is applied in practice and accepted, willingly or otherwise, by the other actors in the international community: 'the Charter is what the principal organs do'.[49] From this perspective, customary rules can change very rapidly, with the law adapting itself instantaneously to the facts as they evolve. The war against Afghanistan, for example, immediately rendered obsolete the conception by which a military action against another State could be launched only if it could be demonstrated that the other State had participated in an armed attack in a substantial manner. As was demonstrated at the time, action against terrorist groups is legitimate in the territory of any State sheltering them, whether or not that State has participated in an armed attack against another.[50]

Which are the States whose practice more than any others dictates the interpretation of the customary rule? The answer is not always clear, no definitive list having been drawn up.[51] As a minimum, 'major' or 'leading' States are cited; an obvious reference to the United States and some of its allies. The expressions used in this context vary, from 'western governments'[52] to the 'community of democracies'[53] or even the 'civilized world'.[54] As this terminology implies, the decision to confer privileged status upon certain States is based upon a double justification. Firstly, and in conformity with the US notion of 'manifest destiny', it is legitimate that democratic States are recognised as having an enhanced role in the development of

---

[47] AM Weisburd, 'Consistency, Universality, and the Customary Law of Interstate Force' in E Cannizzaro and P Palchetti (eds), *Customary International Law On the Use of Force. A Methodological Approach* (Leiden, Marinus Nijhoff Publishers/Brill Academic, 2005) 31–33.

[48] R Wedgwood, 'NATO's Campaign in Yugoslavia', above n 25, 828.

[49] TM Franck, 'Interpretation and Change in the Law of Humanitarian Intervention', above n 16, 206.

[50] TM Franck, *Recourse to Force. State Actions Against Threats and Armed Attacks*, above n 2, 53–54.

[51] See, however, the examples given by J Yoo, 'International Law and the War in Iraq', above n 34, 573; or M Reisman, 'Kosovo's Antinomies' (1999) 93 *AJIL* 49.

[52] TJ Farer, 'Humanitarian Intervention before and after 9/11: Legality and Legitimacy', above n 3, 80.

[53] M Glennon, 'United Nations: Time for a New "Inquiry"' in *International Law/Forum du droit international* (Leiden, Martinus Nijhoff Publishers, 2003) 286–87; R Wedgwood, 'The Fall of Saddam Hussein: Security Council Mandates and Preemptive Self-Defense', above n 19, 578.

[54] AD Sofaer, 'On the Necessity of Pre-emption', above n 6, 209.

customary rules, which enables them to transpose into law the progress of certain humanistic values.[55] Thus, in order to justify the war against Yugoslavia, emphasis was placed on the practice of the NATO Member States, and the fact that these States were all democracies; the reticence and protests of other States (such as members of the Non-Aligned Movement), on the other hand, were minimised; ignored, even.[56] Furthermore, it is important to notice that these very States are at the same time those with the power to enforce compliance with legal rules.[57] Unless we view international law as being nothing more than empty formal incantations, we must be mindful of the special status of these 'major States'. Put otherwise, between an international law that is formally egalitarian (an equality that results in dictatorships and democracies having the same standing) but not applied, and an international law that is under influence (from democratic States only) but effective, the most elementary realism leaves us with no choice, as 'the operational legal order is the only legal order'.[58] Military interventions are thus justified by reference to the fact that those involved in them are 'highly influential on the international stage',[59] or 'represent a significant cross-section of the international community'.[60] From this perspective, custom is to be found first in concrete and material acts, not in diplomatic statements or in principles detached from all practical application. The rule of law implies sanction, and sanction implies authority. International law does not exist in the abstract; it is rather what States make of it. It is thus both desirable (based on the criterion of democratic legitimacy) and inevitable (through the application of a qualified 'legal realism') that we recognise that 'major States' have a special status in the elaboration of customary law.

One last characteristic of the extensive approach is to acknowledge a certain role for actors other than States in the formation and development of customary rules. As already noted, this is the case of certain political organs such as the UN Security Council or the Secretary-General, and even, it seems, of certain regional organisations like NATO and ECOWAS.[61] It can also be said of legal scholars, with the positions of certain specialists (essentially in the English-speaking world, if we refer back to the sources cited)

[55] JG Castel, 'The Legality and Legitimacy of Unilateral Armed Intervention in an Age of Terror, Neo-Imperialism, and Massive Violations of Human Rights: Is International Law Evolving in the Right Direction?' (2004) 42 *CYIL* 4.

[56] R Wedgwood, 'NATO's Campaign in Yugoslavia', above n 25, 833.

[57] V Lowe, 'The Iraq Crisis: What Now?' (2003) 52 *ICLQ* 863.

[58] TJ Farer, 'Humanitarian Intervention before and after 9/11: Legality and Legitimacy', above n 3, 67.

[59] J Currie, 'Humanitarian Intervention in Kosovo: Making or Breaking International Law?' (1998) 36 *CYIL* 304.

[60] ibid, 325–26.

[61] TM Franck, *Recourse to Force. State Actions Against Threats and Armed Attacks*, above n 2, 155 *ff*; TM Franck, 'Interpretation and Change in the Law of Humanitarian Intervention', above n 16, 223.

being accepted as particularly pertinent in ascertaining the evolution of a rule.[62] In the domain of the 'right of humanitarian intervention', we are also referred occasionally to the positions of certain non-governmental organisations in support of advancement of the doctrine.[63] The whole is sometimes referred to as an 'international jury', the composition of which has never been easy to determine with any accuracy.[64]

Lastly, this very flexible conception of the constitutive elements of custom allows those who favour the extensive approach to justify a large number of unilateral armed actions, whether 'anti-terrorist' preventive wars or 'humanitarian' interventions:

> [A]rtificial rules cannot bear the burden of the real world pressures that underlie use-of-force issues. Today, moreover, the need to enforce rules to advance human rights and to limit the power of tyrants and terrorists is greater than ever. To deprive the international community of a reasoned basis for using force threatens Charter interests and values, rather than supporting and advancing them.[65]

This is without doubt the essential reason this approach is criticised by those who prefer to adopt a more restrictive stance, which leads to an altogether different method of understanding the customary prohibition of the use of force.

B. The Restrictive Approach to the Customary Prohibition of the Use of Force

Those authors who favour the extensive approach often tend to portray the restrictive approach as excessively rigid, consisting in adhering to the letter, and only the letter, of the rule prohibiting the use of force. Scholars preferring the restrictive approach reject this criticism. In their view, it is certainly advisable to take as a point of reference the relevant treaty texts, and in particular articles 2(4) and 51 of the UN Charter; this allows the construction of a 'textually-oriented, hierarchical series of rules set out in Articles 31 and 32 of the Vienna Conventions'.[66] However, the purpose of the rule (which consists in radically altering the regime that existed before 1945 by bringing about a stricter prohibition of the use of force) is also taken into

---

[62] V Lowe, 'The Iraq Crisis: What Now?', above n 57, 859–60.

[63] See: M Iovane, 'The Role of Public Opinion and Non-Governmental Organizations in the Reconstruction of General International Norms on the Use of Force' in E Cannizzaro and P Palchetti (eds), *Customary International Law On the Use of Force. A Methodological Approach* (Leiden, Martinus Nijhoff Publishers/Brill Academic, 2005) 219–31.

[64] TM Franck, *Recourse to Force. State Actions Against Threats and Armed Attacks*, above n 2, 67.

[65] AD Sofaer, 'On the Necessity of Pre-emption', above n 6, 225.

[66] M Byers, 'The Shifting Foundations of International Law: A Decade of Forceful Measures against Iraq', above n 3, 25; see also M Bothe, 'Terrorism and the Legality of Pre-emptive Force' (2003) 14 *EJIL* 229.

consideration, in order to justify its restrictive interpretation.[67] In this context, subsequent developments of the rule, and consequently the role of practice and of the customary prohibition of the use of force, are neither rejected nor even minimised. It is therefore not *a priori* relevant to seek to contrast the two approaches by presenting the first as the only one that is heedful of custom. What is fundamentally different, on the other hand, is the conception of the status of custom (1), and the method used to understand its constituent parts (2).

Custom as a Formal Source of the International Legal Order

From the restrictive perspective, the prohibition of the use of force is viewed as arising from both a treaty regime and a customary rule, with neither source prevailing over the other. While the UN Charter provides clarifications as to the content of the rule, for example by specifying that self-defence can only be relied on in cases of 'armed attack' (article 51), that same provision recognises that it 'shall not impair' the existence of the customary right of self-defence. The only way these two statements can be reconciled is by acknowledging that the customary rule and the treaty rule have the same content[68] excluding the possibility of anticipatory self-defence.[69] Custom does not occupy a position of dominance allowing it to ignore the texts of treaties; indeed, article 103 of the UN Charter could be interpreted as conferring a preferential status upon treaties.[70] However, the UN Charter itself cannot be understood without an awareness of the manner in which the parties to it construe it (article 31(3) of the Vienna Convention on the Law of Treaties), which brings us back to the interpretation of the customary rule. This is the method used by the International Court of Justice in the *Nicaragua* case, to which advocates of the restrictive approach very frequently refer: just as a treaty cannot be interpreted independently of the custom engendered by its enforcement, so a custom cannot be interpreted

---

[67] B Simma, 'NATO, the UN and the Use of Force: Legal Aspects' (1999) 10 *EJIL* 2–3; A Constantinou, *The Right of Self-Defense under Customary International Law and Article 51 of the United Nations Charter* (Brussels, Bruylant, 2000) 22; R Hofmann, 'International Law and the Use of Military Force Against Iraq' (2002) 45 *GYIL* 30; LA Sicilianos, 'L'autorisation par le Conseil de sécurité de recourir à la force: une tentative d'évaluation' (2002) 106 *RGDIP* 47; A Randelzhofer, 'Article 51' in B Simma (ed), *The Charter of the United Nations. A Commentary* 2nd edn (Oxford, Oxford University Press, 2002) 803; M Bothe, 'Terrorism and the Legality of Pre-emptive Force', above n 66, 229; M Byers and S Chesterman, 'Changing the rules about rules? Unilateral Intervention and the Future of International Law' in JL Holzgrefe and RO Keohane (eds), *Humanitarian Intervention: Ethical, Legal and Political Dilemmas* (Cambridge, Cambridge University Press, 2003) 181; T Christakis, 'Vers une reconnaissance de la notion de guerre préventive?' in K Bannelier *et al* (eds), *L'intervention en Irak et le droit international* (Paris, Pedone, 2004) 9–45.

[68] M Bothe, 'Terrorism and the Legality of Pre-emptive Force', above n 66, 232.

[69] A Randelzhofer, 'Article 51', above n 67, 805.

[70] B Simma, 'NATO, the UN and the Use of Force: Legal Aspects', above n 67, 3–4; M Byers, 'The Shifting Foundations of International Law: A Decade of Forceful Measures against Iraq', above n 3, 37–38.

independently of the treaties that define the rule in question and express an *opinio juris*.[71] We thus cannot ignore the texts that define the elements of the rule in an abstract fashion (whether the text of the UN Charter itself, or General Assembly resolutions such as resolutions 2625 or 3314), even if it is obvious that these elements must be taken into consideration along with others, in examining the practices of particular States.[72]

It is inaccurate, then, to claim that custom in particular allows us to make a connection between law and facts (all kinds of particularities), or even between law and values (considerations of justice and politics). Custom is a formal source of the international legal order, with the same standing as treaties, both of which can—and must—be considered from a 'strictly legal perspective'.[73] In each case, we are confronted with a source that, by definition, can only refer back to abstract and general precepts. Whether they are expressly set forth in a treaty or deduced from an examination of existing custom, those precepts must be the subject of interpretation whenever they are to be applied to specific circumstances. It is this interpretation, and not the law itself, that brings about the connection between law and facts. What matters is not the practice itself, but how it is interpreted. In this sense, it is not practice (nor, as a result, custom) in itself that allows us to relate the rule to the facts or values that surround it; rather, it is the reasoning developed by the interpreter of the legal rule.

Interpretation, however, is a highly subjective process. Arguments that pre-emptive self-defence is indispensable as it is 'logically' or 'objectively' necessary pass off as inevitable a solution that has arisen from a political choice. We could equally logically claim that the fight against terrorism necessitates even closer cooperation, whether through traditional international criminal law or through collective security mechanisms.[74] Unilateral pre-emptive action is no more an 'objective' or 'logical' solution than any other.[75] Proponents of the restrictive approach thus distance themselves fundamentally from the objectivist tendencies that often underlie the extensive approach. There is no

---

[71] S Laghmani, 'La doctrine américaine de la "preemptive self-defense": de la guerre par "mesure de prévention" à la guerre par "mesure de précaution"' in R Ben Achour and S Laghmani (eds), *Le droit international à la croisée des chemins* (Paris, Pedone, 2004) 16–17.

[72] A Constantinou, *The Right of Self-Defense under Customary International Law and Article 51 of the United Nations Charter*, above n 67, 120; JI Charney, 'Anticipatory Humanitarian Intervention in Kosovo' (1999) 93 *AJIL* 837; A Randelzhofer, 'Article 2 (4)' in B Simma (ed), *The Charter of the United Nations. A Commentary*, above n 67, 134–35; M Bothe, 'Terrorism and the Legality of Pre-emptive Force', above n 66, 230; see also, more generally, the methodology used by E de Wet, *The Chapter VII Powers of the United Nations Security Council* (Oxford, Hart Publishing, 2004) ch 7, 25 ff.

[73] TD Gill, 'War in Iraq and the Contemporary *Jus ad Bellum*' in *International Law/Forum du droit international* (Leiden, Martinus Nijhoff Publishers, 2003) 245.

[74] O Corten and F Dubuisson, 'Opération 'liberté immuable': une extension abusive du concept de légitime défense' (2002) 106 *RGDIP* 76.

[75] T Christakis, 'Existe-t-il un droit de légitime défense en cas de simple "menace"? Une réponse au "Groupe de personnalités de haut niveau" de l'ONU' in *Les métamorphoses de la sécurité collective. Droit, pratique et enjeux stratégiques* (Paris, Pedone, 2005) 209–11.

'objective law' expressing the social needs or the mutual-support mechanisms characteristic of the international community. It is the interpreter, and the interpreter alone, who gives meaning to what is required in any particular instance to meet those needs or provide that mutual support. This power of the interpreter is even more apparent from a 'policy-oriented' perspective. What is not clear, on the other hand, is why this or that commentator should be more capable than another of determining which political road the international community should go down and of determining the 'requirements of world public order'. On the contrary, 'reasonableness and proportionality are concepts which are difficult to operationalize in the context of a decentralized system. They open the door to arbitrariness and subjectivity'.[76] The appeals to 'common sense', 'logic' or 'reason' simply seek to present subjectively-charged claims as objective. It seems self-evident, from within the restrictive perspective, that recognition of a right of unilateral humanitarian intervention can certainly never objectively represent the advancement of the humanistic values of the international community.[77] The debate is an ethical and political one, and so an open-ended one; and it is difficult to see how the jurist can claim to settle it through the use of authoritarian notions such as 'common sense' or 'reason'. The rhetoric of objectivism or of the 'policy-oriented' perspective (that there is one reasonable, objective solution that the jurist is responsible for discovering, above and beyond the texts themselves) is thus at best naïve, and at worst purely instrumental and strategic—with jurists trying to hide their attempts to legitimate their own particular positions behind appeals to supposedly universal precepts.

This critique of the subjectivism of the extensive approach is much like a critique of natural law theories, to which that approach can ultimately be traced back.[78] Can it be inferred from this, though, that the restrictive approach must for its part be traceable back to some form of legal positivism? In many respects, the answer to this is yes. In denouncing the lack of legitimacy of the interpreter's political leanings we are brought back to the need to abide by the legal rule as it was devised by its creators, which has obvious voluntarist connotations.[79] Moreover, the need to maintain a clear distinction between law and politics or morals is strongly reaffirmed, in keeping with one of the essential characteristics of formal positivism: 'Kelsen's insistence on the strict autonomy of the law . . . constitute[s] an attempt to save the law from destruction through its instrumentalization for

---

[76] M Bothe, 'Terrorism and the Legality of Pre-emptive Force', above n 66, 239; see also J Verhoeven, 'Les 'étirements' de la légitime défense' (2002) 54 *AFDI* 61–62.

[77] O Corten, 'La référence au droit international comme justification du recours à la force: vers une nouvelle doctrine de la "guerre juste"?' in AM Dillens (ed), *La guerre et l'Europe* (Bruxelles, FUSL, 2001) 69–94.

[78] ibid.

[79] JL Holzgrefe, 'The Humanitarian Intervention Debate' in JL Holzgrefe and RO Keohane (eds), *Humanitarian Intervention: Ethical, Legal and Political Dilemmas* (Cambridge, Cambridge University Press, 2003) 36.

political purposes'.[80] From there, one is compelled to endorse the classical argument that 'any specific use of force can be lawful only if it can be based on an exception to this rule which is valid as a matter of law'.[81] That law is autonomous does not mean that it is independent; both the creation and the interpretation of law inevitably give rise to value judgements, and so to a cognitive excursion into the political and moral spheres. Put simply, autonomy refers to the fact that these judgements will only be accepted as legitimate if they are based, methodologically speaking, on a reference to the relevant legal rule as it appears in the formal sources. The diversity of possible interpretations is not denied, but this relativism is limited by the need to justify choices in terms of the common reference framework that positive law constitutes.[82] Legality and legitimacy must be conceptually distinguished.[83] The claims to validity of differing interpretations can then be decided between by procedures that allow for rational debate: 'It is traditional wisdom of legal theory that where substantive law cannot bring about a sufficient degree of legal certainty, procedural rules must be used to obtain results which are socially or politically acceptable'.[84] These procedures have proved to be particularly decisive in the area of the non-use of force in which, most especially, 'the claim of better knowledge, better morals or the like does not create sufficient legitimization in the international legal system'.[85] The rule that any military action can only be legitimate if authorised by a Security Council resolution is based on a form of procedural legitimacy; a just and legal war being one that has been recognised as such as the result of a debate and vote on particular and often opposing conceptions.[86] In this context, the political orientation guiding the enforcement of the rule will not be decided upon by any particular interpreter, but by means of a strongly institutionalised procedure, which alone seems capable of moving towards universality: 'the UN continues to be the only existing forum that can accommodate and protect the diversity of cultures and claims'.[87]

Lastly, the restrictive approach conceives of custom within a very particular framework, refusing to incorporate practice to the exclusion of texts,

---

[80] V Gowlland-Debbas, 'The Limits of Unilateral Enforcement of Community Objectives in the Framework of United Nations Peace Maintenance' (2000) 11 *EJIL* 381.

[81] M Bothe, 'Terrorism and the Legality of Pre-emptive Force', above n 66, 228.

[82] O Corten, 'Les ambiguïtés de la référence au droit international comme facteur de légitimation: Portée et signification d'une déformalisation du discours légaliste' in O Corten and B Delcourt (eds), *Droit, légitimation et politique extérieure: l'Europe et la guerre du Kosovo* (Bruxelles, Bruylant, 2001) 256.

[83] A Cassese, '*Ex iniuria ius oritur*: Are We Moving towards International Legitimation of Forcible Humanitarian Countermeasures in the World Community?' (1999) 10 *EJIL* 25; O Corten and F Dubuisson, 'L'hypothèse d'une règle émergente fondant une intervention militaire sur une "autorisation implicite" du Conseil de sécurité' (2000) 104 *RGDIP* 876.

[84] M Bothe, 'Terrorism and the Legality of Pre-emptive Force', above n 66, 239.

[85] ibid.

[86] ibid, 239–40.

[87] V Gowlland-Debbas, 'The Limits of Unilateral Enforcement of Community Objectives in the Framework of United Nations Peace Maintenance', above n 80, 383.

and, more generally, of the rule of positive law. Custom, like treaties, is a formal legal source, which does not in itself make it easier to take non-legal value judgements into account. Such a conception of custom results in a particular understanding its constituent parts.

The Dominant Role of the *Opinio Juris* of All States

Whereas the extensive approach tends to emphasise the practice of States as the dominant component of custom, the restrictive approach gives precedence rather to *opinio juris*. It is precisely this element that allows for facts, to which practice corresponds, to be transformed into law, and into a full-blown customary rule. The importance of practice is not denied, but practice only takes on significance if and to the extent that we can deduce that States are convinced their acts are in accordance with a legal rule.[88] Similarly, consideration of a rule's object and purpose is fully incorporated into this approach, provided that the object and purpose have been expressed by States in some manner or other, and are not merely subjectively determined by an interpreter.[89] This methodological doctrine is based upon the jurisprudence of the International Court of Justice, specifically the *Nicaragua* case, in which it is affirmed that practice is only significant to the extent that it is accompanied by official legal justifications.[90]

One familiar consequence of this is that a practice contrary to a rule can, paradoxically, serve to reinforce it, provided that the practice is accompanied by legal arguments referring to the rule. Thus, the fundamental issue is to determine

> how the deviant describes and rationalizes its conduct. It may, for instance, attempt to obscure the real nature of its activities. In doing so, the deviant implicitly recognizes the authority of the established interpretation.[91]

In this sense, it can be argued that, in terms of the numerous precedents for military intervention, 'the attempts made by those involved to justify their behaviour by law is the greatest tribute vice can pay to virtue'.[92]

---

[88] F Dubuisson, 'La problématique de la légalité de l'opération "Force alliée" contre la Yougoslavie: enjeux et questionnements' in O Corten and B Delcourt (eds), *Droit, légitimation et politique extérieure: l'Europe et la guerre du Kosovo* (Brussels, Bruylant, 2001) 176; A Randelzhofer, 'Article 2 (4)', above n 72, 130–31; A Lagerwall, 'Kosovo, Afghanistan, Irak: le retour des guerres d'agression' in O Corten and B Delcourt (eds), *Les guerres antiterroristes* (Brussels, Contradictions, 2004) 90.

[89] O Christakis, 'Existe-t-il un droit de légitime défense en cas de simple "menace"? Une réponse au "Groupe de personnalités de haut niveau" de l'ONU', above n 75.

[90] O Corten and B Delcourt, 'La guerre du Kosovo: le droit international renforcé?' (2000) 8 *L'Observateur des Nations Unies* 134.

[91] TJ Farer, 'The Prospect for International Law and Order in the Wake of Iraq' (2003) 97 *AJIL* 622.

[92] Our translation; M Kohen, 'L'emploi de la force et la crise du Kosovo: vers un nouveau désordre juridique international' (1999) 32 *RBDI* 148.

From this perspective, what is important is less the material act itself than the declarations and the legal texts relied on at the time the act was performed. It is necessary 'to look at international law in terms of the language used by States'.[93] General Assembly resolutions, and official State declarations or, indeed, meaningful silences, are thus the dominant elements enabling us to give meaning to each precedent.[94] To underscore the point: a practice is not in itself meaningful or relevant. In order to transform fact into law, the legal position of States is of fundamental importance. For every State declaration, therefore, great care must be taken to distinguish political or moral elements from strictly legal ones.[95] Here again, we find an entirely different perspective from that of the extensive approach, which, as noted above, considers this distinction to be artificial, and that justificatory statements can be determining even if no strictly legal element is apparent. If, for example, a State affirms that it has intervened militarily in order to save the population of another State from inhumane repression, an advocate of the restrictive approach would not necessarily see in this anything to support the recognition of a right of humanitarian intervention.[96] For that to be so, the official discourse would have to be accompanied by a more strictly legal reference, such as an explicit appeal to a 'right of humanitarian intervention', to a 'state of necessity', or to some legal source or institution.[97] A fortiori, the utmost caution must be exercised when seeking to make inferences from the silence of one or more States: 'Is failure to condemn evidence of legality? Not necessarily so, for there are many reasons for a failure to condemn'.[98] Therefore, 'reluctant tolerance does not evidence opinio juris'.[99] On the contrary, 'In order to prove acquiescence, there must be a "consistent and undeviating attitude" a "clear", "definite" and "unequivocal" course of action, showing "clearly and consistently evinced acceptance"', to use the wording of the ICJ on different occasions.[100]

---

[93] C Gray, *International Law and the Use of Force*, 3rd edn, above n 2, 28.

[94] JL Holzgrefe, 'The Humanitarian Intervention debate', above n 79, 47–48.

[95] O Corten and B Delcourt, 'Droit, légitimité et politique extérieure: précisions théoriques et méthodologiques' in O Corten and B Delcourt (eds), *Droit, légitimité et politique extérieure: l'Europe et la guerre du Kosovo* (Brussels, Bruylant, 2001) 26–27.

[96] A Cassese, 'A Follow Up: Forcible Humanitarian Countermeasures and *Opinio Necessitatis*' (1999) 10 *EJIL* 791–95; JI Charney, 'Anticipatory Humanitarian Intervention in Kosovo', above n 72, 836; C Gray, 'From Unity to Polarization: International Law and the Use of Force against Iraq' (2002) 13 *EJIL* 11.

[97] O Corten, 'Les ambiguïtés de la référence au droit international comme facteur de légitimation: Portée et signification d'une déformalisation du discours légaliste', above n 82.

[98] C Gray, *International Law and the Use of Force*, 3rd edn, above n 2, 21.

[99] M Byers, 'The Shifting Foundations of International Law: A Decade of Forceful Measures against Iraq', above n 3, 36; see also A Constantinou, *The Right of Self-Defense under Customary International Law and Article 51 of the United Nations Charter*, above n 67, 22.

[100] M Kohen, 'The Use of Force by the United States after the end of the Cold War, and its impact of International Law' in M Byers and G Nolte (eds), *United States Hegemony and the Foundations of International Law* (Cambridge, Cambridge University Press, 2003) 224.

Taken together, this leads one to disregard official positions unless they reflect the existence of a genuine legal conviction. A number of consequences ensue. First, a State's position must have been expressed freely, thereby excluding positions that are essentially explained by political or diplomatic pressure.[101] In this sense, criticism of an intervention by an ally of the intervening State would have more significance than an absence of criticism, as the latter could easily spring from a political desire not to break the alliance.[102] It has been argued in this context that 'The end of the cold war and the United States's position as the world's sole and unchallenged superpower renders opposition to United States actions even more difficult in the absence of some strong interests motivating other States'.[103] As a result, we can only determine the legal position of any given State by considering many different precedents involving various intervening States, allied or otherwise. It is only if a consistent legal position emerges from this array of facts that we can conclude that an *opinio juris* exists.

One result of all this is that, even if it may be rapid, it is difficult to conceive of the development of custom as instantaneous.[104] To take an example referred to above, the widespread acquiescence to the war against Afghanistan is insufficient to support the conclusion that there has been a relaxation of the definition of indirect aggression in article 3(g) of the definition of aggression annexed to General Assembly resolution 3314. This acquiescence, which resulted in large part from both the emotional climate that followed the attacks of 11 September 2001 and the nearly unanimous political opposition to the Taliban regime, would only become significant in legal terms if it were to be confirmed in other cases.[105] Thus:

> Even if some do not hesitate in appealing to a 'spontaneous' custom, it is difficult to see how a modification of the Charter can seriously be derived from the approval, however widespread, given to one particular action . . . At most, it represents the expression of an interpretation of both fact and law, in a particular case.[106]

This strict interpretation also expresses itself in an inter-State conception of custom. The political organs of the UN, NGOs, scholars or other actors

[101] M Byers, 'The Shifting Foundations of International Law: A Decade of Forceful Measures against Iraq', above n 3, 36.

[102] C Gray, *International Law and the Use of Force*, 3rd edn, above n 2, 20.

[103] J Lobel, 'The Use of Force to Respond to Terrorist Attacks: the Bombing of Sudan and Afghanistan' (1999) 44 *Yale JIL* 557.

[104] M Byers, 'The Shifting Foundations of International Law: A Decade of Forceful Measures against Iraq', above n 3, 33.

[105] O Corten and F Dubuisson, 'Opération "liberté immuable": une extension abusive du concept de légitime défense', above n 74, 53; M Kohen, 'L'emploi de la force et la crise du Kosovo: vers un nouveau désordre juridique international', above n 92, 222; G Espada, 'La 'contaminación' de Naciones Unidas o las Resoluciones 1483 y 1511 (2003) del Consejo de seguridad', (2003) 19 *Annuario de derecho internacional* 76; A Lagerwall, 'Kosovo, Afghanistan, Irak: le retour des guerres d'agression', above n 88, 93.

[106] Our translation; J Verhoeven, 'Les 'étirements' de la légitime défense', above n 76, 64.

certainly play an essential political role in the evolution of the rule, to the extent that they influence official State positions. It is, however, these positions themselves that must be examined when seeking to determine whether or not a custom has evolved.[107] In this context, Security Council resolutions take on significance only in certain well-defined circumstances. Firstly, it is necessary to demonstrate that the Council has expressed itself on a strictly legal basis, which is neither its role nor its habit.[108] Secondly, even if certain strictly legal pronouncements have been made, it must then be demonstrated that the relevant resolutions have gained much more general legal approval: 'the views of the member States are important because it is necessary for interpretations of the Security Council to be generally acceptable to the member States in order to give such interpretations binding force.'[109]

The restrictive approach, unlike the extensive one, does not confer any special status on a group of States in interpreting or elaborating customary rules. In the field of interpretation, in which it is assumed that the rule always has a determinate meaning, application of the principles of interpretation codified in the Vienna Conventions on the Law of Treaties implies that practice must reveal the assent of *all* States parties to the rule in question.[110] If, on the other hand, it is claimed that a rule has evolved, or has been modified by subsequent significant practice, the agreement of 'the international community of States as a whole' must be demonstrated, pursuant to articles 53 and 64 of those same conventions.[111] Those commentators who favour the restrictive approach commonly point out that the prohibition of the use of force is the archetype of a peremptory norm of international law, a *jus cogens*.[112] This status implies not only that any evolution of the rule must be based upon near-unanimous agreement, involving the most varied groups of States,[113] but also that there can be no derogations from the rule. It is thus impossible to conceive of a sort of 'right of humanitarian intervention' or 'pre-emptive self-defence' on a regional or other particular scale, based on

---

[107] See, eg: C Gray, *International Law and the Use of Force*, 3rd edn, above n 2, 28.

[108] V Gowlland-Debbas, 'The Limits of Unilateral Enforcement of Community Objectives in the Framework of United Nations Peace Maintenance', above n 80, 377; M Kohen, 'L'emploi de la force et la crise du Kosovo: vers un nouveau désordre juridique international', above n 92, 217.

[109] N Blokker, 'Is the Authorization Authorized? Powers and Practice of the United Nations Security Council to Authorize the Use of Force by "Coalitions of the Able and Willing"' (2000) 11 *EJIL* 567.

[110] F Dubuisson, 'La problématique de la légalité de l'opération "Force alliée" contre la Yougoslavie: enjeux et questionnements', above n 88, 179.

[111] ibid.

[112] ibid, 173; JI Charney, 'Anticipatory Humanitarian Intervention in Kosovo', above n 72, 837; R Hofmann, 'International Law and the Use of Military Force Against Iraq', above n 67, 11; M Kohen, 'The Use of Force by the United States after the end of the Cold War, and its impact on International Law', above n 100, 228.

[113] ibid, 225; JI Charney, 'Anticipatory Humanitarian Intervention in Kosovo', above n 72, 837; V Gowlland-Debbas, 'The Limits of Unilateral Enforcement of Community Objectives in the Framework of United Nations Peace Maintenance', above n 80, 377.

the claim that these doctrines, if they are not endorsed unanimously or even by a large majority, are nonetheless accepted by certain States.[114] Therefore, all alterations to the rule

> require the support of most, if not all, States, as expressed through their active or passive support, coupled with a sense of legal obligation. Given the public policy and peremptory character of these rules, the threshold for their development is necessarily very high: higher than that for other customary rules.[115]

It is clear from this that nothing is more alien to the restrictive approach than the idea of 'major' or 'leading' States. The *opinio juris* that must be established requires as broad an analysis of State positions as possible; hence the privileged status accorded to the major UN General Assembly resolutions. Moreover, attention needs to be given to the views of certain organisations or groups that boast large memberships; organisations like NATO, but also the 'Group of 77' (more than 130 States), the 'Non-Aligned Movement' (more than 110 States), the 'Organization of the Islamic Conference' (57 States), or even regional organisations or fora such as the OAS, the Rio Group, the European Union, the African Union, ASEAN, etc.[116] In contradistinction, limiting the analysis to powerful States and neglecting or even ignoring the position of those in the Third World has been denounced as a 'hegemonical approach to international relations',[117] with certain States proclaiming themselves to be the sole representatives of the 'international community'.[118] These States can in no way be reduced to those 'whose interests were specially affected' by the customary rule in question. The choice is essentially ideological, as is attested to by the fact that such States are peremptorily characterised as

---

[114] B Simma, 'NATO, the UN and the Use of Force: Legal Aspects', above n 67, 3.

[115] M Byers and S Chesterman, 'Changing the rules about rules? Unilateral Intervention and the Future of International Law', above n 67, 180; M Byers, 'The Shifting Foundations of International Law: A Decade of Forceful Measures against Iraq', above n 3, 35; see also Randelzhofer, 'Article 51', above n 67, 806.

[116] Notably, it is through the application of this method that the Kosovo precedent can be interpreted as in no way affirming the progress of a 'right of humanitarian intervention'; see, eg F Dubuisson, 'La problématique de la légalité de l'opération "Force alliée" contre la Yougoslavie: enjeux et questionnements', above n 88, 180–81; A Lagerwall, 'Kosovo, Afghanistan, Irak: le retour des guerres d'agression', above n 88, 95–97. The same reasoning was also applied to the military operations against Iraq in the 1990s; C Gray, 'From Unity to Polarization: International Law and the Use of Force against Iraq', above n 96, 16; M Kohen, 'The Use of Force by the United States after the end of the Cold War, and its impact on International Law', above n 100, 203–04; O Corten, 'Opération *Iraqi Freedom*: peut-on admettre l'argument de l' "autorisation implicite" du Conseil de sécurité?' (2003) 36 *RBDI* 232–41.

[117] M Byers and S Chesterman, 'Changing the rules about rules? Unilateral Intervention and the Future of International Law', above n 67, 194.

[118] A Lagerwall, 'Kosovo, Afghanistan, Irak: le retour des guerres d'agression', above n 88, 98; P Klein, 'Les problèmes soulevés par la référence à la "communauté internationale" comme facteur de légitimité' in O Corten and B Delcourt (eds), *Droit, légitimation et politique extérieure: l'Europe et la guerre du Kosovo* (Brussels, Bruylant, 2001) 261; see also C Chinkin, 'Kosovo: A "Good" or "Bad" War?' (1999) 93 *AJIL* 846–47.

democracies, while any States opposing the developments are dismissed as dictatorships.[119] Is it to be assumed, for example, that all members of NATO are democracies, whereas those of the Rio Group, which condemned the military intervention against Yugoslavia, are all dictatorships? Can we also present the schism between the advocates and opponents of the war against Iraq from this angle? It is only too obvious that the debate over democracy is neither objective nor, in any event, legally relevant when it comes to establishing the existence of a customary rule; no State can demand a privileged status in this regard. The argument that such a status must be accorded from a realist perspective, that those States capable of enforcing the law must have particular influence over its elaboration, is likewise ruled out. For, by definition, international law can draw its legitimacy only from its autonomy in relation to powerful States, to the extent that the legal order is intended to embody a common language connecting groups of States with different ideologies and cultures.[120] From this standpoint, the doctrine of 'major States' serves, on the contrary, to reduce law to a simple instrument of power and thus, ultimately, to fact. Realism, if it is to be squared with the recognition of a genuine legal order, compels us to acknowledge only that certain rules, even the most fundamental ones, can be violated by powerful States, provided that those violations can be denounced on the basis of law.[121] International law thus essentially fulfils a 'declaratory function'.[122] It is conceived of as a framework of reference that allows for an evaluation of the facts of a given case, and not as the simple translation of those facts into a legitimating legal language: 'After all, law is an intersubjective prescriptive consensus about the world of brute fact'.[123] Even if it encounters limits in terms of its effectiveness, international law 'is a social regulator intended to create a common denominator for behaviour . . . and to prevent to the greatest extent possible the rule of "private justice"'.[124]

Lastly, the extensive approach is criticised as leading to an almost complete conflation of fact and law. The emphasis on practice as the dominant component of custom, the refusal to separate law from non-law formally, and the privileged role accorded to major powers are all factors that lead in

---

[119] O Corten, 'Opération *Iraqi Freedom*: peut-on admettre l'argument de l'"autorisation implicite" du Conseil de sécurité?', above n 116, 25–27 and 86–87.

[120] O Corten, 'Les ambiguïtés de la référence au droit international comme facteur de légitimation. Portée et signification d'une déformalisation du discours légaliste', above n 82, 249.

[121] M Byers and S Chesterman, 'Changing the rules about rules? Unilateral Intervention and the Future of International Law', above n 67, 203; see also Randelzhofer, 'Article 2(4)', above n 72, 136.

[122] C Gray, *International Law and the Use of Force*, 3rd edn, above n 2, 27.

[123] TJ Farer, 'The Prospect for International Law and Order in the Wake of Iraq', above n 91, 622.

[124] Our translation; M Kohen, 'L'emploi de la force et la crise du Kosovo: vers un nouveau désordre juridique international', above n 92, 124.

this direction. Contrary to this, from the restrictive perspective, the auto-nomy of international law dictates a radical separation between the *rule* prohibiting the use of force and the *fact* that this rule is regularly violated.

Criticism of the international legal order, which has become particularly manifest in the context of the Iraq crisis, has focussed essentially on institu-tions, and in particular the UN, which has been denounced as 'inade-quate'.[125] Custom, for its part, is not at the centre of the criticism, unless, of course, it targets international law itself more generally, from a radical realist perspective whereby 'there [is] no international law governing use of force, and in the absence of governing law, it [is] impossible to act unlawfully'.[126] However, within the legal discipline at least, this position seems relatively iso-lated, with authors generally addressing the issue of the interpretation, and not the very existence, of international law.

Beyond this common sensitivity, specialists of international law are radi-cally opposed to one another over method, in particular when it comes to making sense of customary rules. The extensive approach assumes that moral and other non-legal considerations will be taken into account, and emphasises the practice of major States, which are considered better able to satisfy the demands of legitimacy and effectiveness. The restrictive approach denounces this method as subjective, even ideological, preferring instead to insist on the necessity of differentiating law from politics or morality. From this perspective, the customary rule outlawing the use of force can evolve only by means of the explicit acceptance of the inter-national community of States as a whole, the prohibition on the use of force being considered as a foundational rule of the international public order.

It is not surprising that, all other things being equal, the use of the first of these two methods ultimately results in a relatively broad recognition of a certain number of exceptions to the prohibition of the use of force, whereas the second generally leads to a rejection of them. From the same perspective, it can be noted that US commentators tend to situate them-selves more within the first current,[127] the others (most notably the Europeans) within the second.[128] The dividing lines are by no means hard and fast. Some authors who basically defend a restrictive position may

---

[125] M Glennon, 'United Nations: Time for a New 'Inquiry'', above n 53, 283 *ff*; M Glennon, 'The UN Security Council in a Unipolar World' (2003) 44 *Virginia Journal of International Law* 91 *ff*.

[126] ibid, 100.

[127] cp ME O'Connel, 'Taking *Opinio Juris* Seriously, A Classical Approach to International Law on the Use of Force' in E Cannizzaro and P Palchetti (eds), *Customary International Law on the Use of Force. A Methodological Approach* (Leiden, Martinus Nijhoff Publishers/Brill Academic, 2005) 9–30.

[128] cp ME O'Connel, 'La doctrine américaine et l'intervention en Iraq' (2003) 55 *AFDI* 3–16; M Iovane and F De Vittor, 'La doctrine européenne et l'intervention en Iraq' (2003) 55 *AFDI* 17–31.

embrace certain features of a more extensive approach.[129] Moreover, even if it does seem more complex, it is not inconceivable that the adoption of a restrictive approach could lead to an acceptance that the prohibition of the use of force be relaxed, in certain domains at least.[130] Furthermore, certain European authors favour the extensive approach, and some US writers seem to prefer a more restrictive one. More generally, it is possible to question the coherence of several US authors, who seem to adopt an extensive approach in terms of the use of force, but who prefer a more rigorous and classical methodology when engaged in the related debate over the evolution of international criminal law.[131]

Be that as it may, the study of this methodological divide illustrates the advantages of moving beyond the impression of the 'dialogue of the deaf' that characterises the recurrent debates over the legality of military interventions. More precisely, it allows us to frame the debate in terms of method and, moreover, in terms of the theoretical conceptions of international law that are brought into play in debates over the use of force above all:

> [T]he future shape of the international legal system will depend, above all, on how we interpret Security Council resolutions and treaties, on how we create and change rules of customary international law, and on how we understand the relationship between customary international law and treaties.[132]

II Methodological Approach of this Book

In this book we shall try to steer a course between two extremes.

The first extreme is exaggerated formalism whereby the only way to further the prohibition of the use of force, which is primarily a treaty-based rule, would be to revise or amend the UN Charter in keeping with the procedures laid down by that instrument (articles 108 and 109). No trace of such a formalistic extreme is to be found in contemporary doctrine, although some US commentators seemingly claim such formalism prevails in European scholarship.[133]

---

[129] See, in this sense, F Nguyen-Rouault, 'L'intervention armée en Irak et son occupation au regard du droit international' (2003) 107 *RGDIP* 835.

[130] It is possible to interpret in this sense the works of A Pellet, 'Brief Remarks on the Unilateral Use of Force' (2000) 11 *EJIL* 385; PM Eisemann, 'Attaques du 11 septembre et exercice d'un droit naturel de légitime défense' in K Bannelier *et al* (eds), *Le droit international face au terrorisme* (Paris, Pedone, 2002) 239; ME O'Connel, 'Lawful Self-Defense to Terrorism' (2002) 63 *University of Pittsburgh LR* 889 and 'The Myth of Preemptive Self-Defense', *ASIL* August 2002, www.asil.org/taskforce/oconnel.pdf; or SD Murphy, 'Terrorism and the Concept of 'Armed Attack' in Article 51 of the United Nations', (2002) 43 *Harvard ILJ* 41–51.

[131] See, eg: S Estreicher, 'Rethinking the Binding Effect of Customary International Law' (2003) 44 *Virginia JIL* 5–17.

[132] M Byers, 'The Shifting Foundations of International Law: A Decade of Forceful Measures against Iraq', above n 3, 41.

[133] See, eg: RN Gardner, 'Neither Bush nor the "Jurisprudes"', above n 7, 585 *ff*.

The other extreme, to my mind, is that of the almost unlimited flexibility that is found in some doctrines in the English-speaking world such as the policy-oriented perspective. Such doctrines have just been described within the general exposition of what has been referred to as an extensive approach.[134] There is no need to revisit them at this point.

Between these two extremes, we will follow the approach adopted by the International Court of Justice, in particular in its judgment in the case concerning *Military and Paramilitary Activities in and against Nicaragua*:

> The Court does not consider that, for a rule to be established as customary, the corresponding practice must be in absolutely rigorous conformity with the rule. In order to deduce the existence of customary rules, the Court deems it sufficient that the conduct of States should, in general, be consistent with such rules, and that instances of State conduct inconsistent with a given rule should generally have been treated as breaches of that rule, not as indications of the recognition of a new rule. If a State acts in a way prima facie incompatible with a recognized rule, but defends its conduct by appealing to exceptions or justifications contained within the rule itself, then whether or not the State's conduct is in fact justifiable on that basis, the significance of that attitude is to confirm rather than weaken the rule.[135]

Following this approach, we will not ask whether an action which is 'apparently irreconcilable' with the rule either is or is not lawful (question of lawfulness *in casu*), but we will focus rather on the official justifications advanced by the State concerned.[136] From this standpoint, any breach of the rule prohibiting the use of force is not liable as such to undermine or challenge the rule.[137] Although not dismissed, actual practice merely provides an opportunity to ascertain the legal convictions of the States concerned by analysing the discourse to which it gives rise.[138] The Court adds further on that 'Reliance by a State on a novel right or an unprecedented exception to a principle might, if shared in principle by other States, tend towards a modification of customary international law'.[139]

---

[134] Above, s I.

[135] ICJ, *Military and Paramilitary Activities in and against Nicaragua*, [1986] ICJ Rep 98, para 186.

[136] This kind of approach is also adopted by C Gray, *International Law and the Use of Force*, 3rd edn, above n 2, 6 *ff*; see also L Louis Henkin, 'The Reports of the Death of Article 2(4) Are Greatly Exaggerated' (1971) 65 *AJIL* 547.

[137] For a different methodology, see, eg T Franck, 'Who Killed Article 2(4)? or: Changing Norms Governing the Use of Force by States' (1970) 64 *AJIL* 809–37; A D'Amato, 'Trashing Customary International Law' (1987) 81 *AJIL* 101–05; F Teson, *Humanitarian Intervention: An Inquiry into Law and Morality*, 2nd edn (New York, Transnational Publishers, 1997) 192–93.

[138] ME O'Connel, 'Taking *Opinio Juris* Seriously, A Classical Approach to International Law on the Use of Force', above n 127, 4–16.

[139] ICJ, *Military and Paramilitary Activities in and against Nicaragua*, ICJ Rep (1986) 108, para 207.

The Court's approach then comes down to imposing two conditions on the evolution of the customary rule: first, a State must invoke a new right, in other words claim that a modification of the rule occurred; second, this claim must be accepted by other States.[140] We will outline these two conditions in turn below. From the standpoint of the 'restrictive approach' described above which is sometimes characterised as 'classical', we shall focus here on the evolution of the rule through custom. It is understood that, given the treaty-based character of the prohibition of the use of force, such an evolution presupposes compliance with the interpretative principles set forth in the Vienna Convention on the Law of Treaties. Thus reliance on a novel right (A), supposedly accepted by all other States (B), would be both a customary evolution of the rule and a practice subsequently followed by the parties to the UN Charter and indicative of their agreement on the interpretation of the text.[141]

A. Reliance on a Novel Right

We could imagine, following a military intervention that is controversial from a legal point of view but which is broadly accepted as legitimate, the intervening State or States asking for a formal modification of the UN Charter, whether by way of a revision or an amendment. In this scenario, a possible breach of the rule could lead to its evolution. The hypothesis is, however, theoretical—no precedent to this effect existing today—and would be limited in any case by treaty law. In reality, it is possible only to entertain the theory of an evolution through the informal means of custom. This theory presupposes all the same that the existence of a true legal claim be verified, which implies first, the formulation of a claim; second, the formulation of a claim of a legal nature; and third, the formulation of a claim of a legal nature tending to modify, and not simply to confirm, the rule prohibiting the use of force.

---

[140] This approach appears to privilege *opinio juris*, or a psychological element, over practice, or a material element. In reality, as *opinio juris* can be established only by taking a particular practice into account, the two elements are effectively considered from within a single perspective: see P Weil, 'Le droit international en quête de son identité. Cours général de droit international public' (1992) 237 *RCADI* 170; L Condorelli, 'La coutume' in M Bedjaoui, *Droit international. Bilan et perspectives*, Tome I (Paris, Pedone/UNESCO, 1991), 198–99; L Boisson de Chazournes, 'Qu'est-ce que la pratique en droit international?' in SFDI, *La pratique et le droit international* (Paris, Pedone, 2004), 19–20; PM Dupuy, 'L'unité de l'ordre juridique international. Cours général de droit international public' (2002) 197 *RCADI* 168–69; see also PM Dupuy, *Droit international public*, 7th edn (Paris, Dalloz, 2004), 328–31.

[141] Article 31§3 of the Vienna Convention on the Law of Treaties; see ME O'Connel, 'Taking *Opinio Juris* Seriously, A Classical Approach to International Law on the Use of Force', above n 127, 22; GP Buzzini, 'Les comportements passifs des Etats et leur incidence sur la réglementation de l'emploi de la force en droit international général' in *Customary International Law On the Use of Force. A Methodological Approach* (Leiden, Marinus Nijhoff Publishers/Brill Academic, 2005) 101–02.

The Formulation of a Claim

Often when confronted with an accusation of having breached the rule prohibiting the use of force, a State simply denies the facts. This first scenario
is common enough,[142] and generally covers the case of indirect aggressions
or attacks, or of covert actions, even though it could be extended to other
hypotheses. Thus, State A may dispute having entered the territory of State
B, or having armed or supported irregular forces operating against the government of State B, or even being the author of the bombing of one of State
B's ships. The following examples, all taken from legal practice, illustrate
the point:

—In the case of *Military and Paramilitary Activities in and against Nicaragua*,
  Nicaragua denied having provided military and logistical support to
  Salvadoran rebel forces. This denial, which was accepted by the Court,
  prevented the United States from validly invoking the argument of collective self-defence.[143]
—In the *Oil Platforms* case, Iran denied having led military attacks again
  Kuwaiti ships, attacks to which the United States claimed to have
  responded in collective self-defence.[144]
—In the *Armed Activities on the Territory of the Congo* case, Uganda claimed
  that its intervention in the Congo was justified as an act of defence in
  response to support provided by the Congolese authorities to armed
  groups operating in Ugandan territory. The Democratic Republic of the
  Congo resolutely denied the facts.[145]

Whether Nicaragua, Iran or the Congo, the State accused of having
breached the rule denies the actions attributed to it and so makes no claim
as to the legality of those actions, and even less does it argue that the rule
infringed should be modified. Indeed, in contesting the facts, it focuses the
debate on the enforcement of the existing rule and not on its amendment.
Supposing the breach is proven, it is therefore totally incapable of pro-
mpting any change.[146] This scenario is common enough, and entails the
dismissal of a large part of practice as irrelevant.[147]

---

[142] J Combacau, 'The Exception of Self-Defence in UN Practice' in A Cassese (ed), *The Current Legal Regulation of the Use of Force* (Dordrecht/Boston/Lancaster, Martinus Nijhoff Publishers, 1986) 14; G Cahin, *La coutume internationale et les organisations internationales. L'incidence de la dimension institutionnelle sur le processus coutumier* (Paris, Pedone, 2001) 325.

[143] ICJ, *Military and Paramilitary Activities in and against Nicaragua*, ICJ Rep (1986) 72–73, para 131.

[144] ICJ, *Oil Platforms*, ICJ Rep (2003) 188, paras 54–55.

[145] See: Intervention of the Ugandan delegate to the General Assembly, 23 March 1999, 95th plenary meeting, A/53/PV.95, 14.

[146] TJ Farer, 'The Prospect for International Law and Order in the Wake of Iraq', above n 91, 22.

[147] C Gray, *International Law and the Use of Force*, 3rd edn, above n 2, 11.

The Formulation of a Legal Claim

Even once the intervening State acknowledges the material fact of its intervention, it is not obvious that the State provides a justification for its intervention in legal terms.[148] In practice, many military actions are frequently legitimated by reference to other types of argument, such as politics or morality. For example, certain commentators sometimes evoke the doctrines formulated by several US presidents.[149] Yet, these doctrines generally rely on political arguments pertaining to, say, national security, the struggle against communism (thereafter terrorism) or world peace.[150] They are not generally accompanied by justifications or claims bearing on a potential modification of international law.

This scenario was evoked by the International Court of Justice on two occasions in its judgment in the *Nicaragua* case. The Court observes that:

> The United States authorities have on some occasions clearly stated their grounds for intervening in the affairs of a foreign State for reasons connected with, for example, the domestic policies of that country, its ideology, the level of its armaments, or the direction of its foreign policy. But these were statements in international policy, and not an assertion of rules of existing international law.[151]

The Court notes, moreover, that:

> Nicaragua, for its part, has often expressed its solidarity and sympathy with the opposition in various States, especially in El Salvador. But Nicaragua too has not argued that this was a legal basis for an intervention, let alone an intervention involving the use of force.[152]

The Court clearly distinguishes between legal and extra-legal considerations. Only legal considerations are capable of giving rise to a potential evolution of the rule,[153] which is illustrated in the following famous *dictum*: 'The Court . . . is a court of law, and can take account of moral principles only in so far as these are given a sufficient expression in legal form'.[154]

---

[148] See: G Cahin, 'Le rôle des organes politiques des Nations Unies' in *Customary International Law on the Use of Force. A Methodological Approach* (Leiden, Marinus Nijhoff Publishers/Brill Academic, 2005) 165.

[149] See, eg: M Reisman and A Armstrong, 'The Past and Future of the Claim of Preemptive Self-Defense' (2006) 100 *AJIL* 527–32.

[150] We refer, namely, to the doctrines associated with Presidents Eisenhower, Nixon, Clinton, Bush, etc; see J Heffer, *Les Etats-Unis de Truman à Bush* (Paris, Armand Colin, 1992) 190.

[151] ICJ, *Military and Paramilitary Activities in and against Nicaragua*, ICJ Rep (1986) 108–09, para 207.

[152] ibid, 109, para 208.

[153] G Cahin, *La coutume internationale et les organisations internationales. L'incidence de la dimension institutionnelle sur le processus coutumier*, above n 142, 332–33.

[154] ICJ, *South West Africa*, ICJ Rep (1966) 34, para 49.

In practice, it can at times be difficult to distinguish between the legal character and the political or moral character of a justificatory discourse.[155] This is simple enough if a State claims to be intervening in order to safeguard its security (a political argument) or to put an end to massacres (a moral argument). Unless a reference is also made simultaneously to legal considerations—an explicit reference to international law, a formal source of a legal nature, or a legal institution—,[156] such justifications are hardly determinative of the issue of the evolution of the rule prohibiting the use of force. Difficulties set in once the intervening States develop a discourse coloured by legal considerations, but from which a clear reference to positive international law cannot be deduced.[157] In that case, the justificatory discourse does not seem to refer exclusively to legal concepts or institutions, which alone would allow for a potential evolution of the rule.[158]

Of course, one cannot expect a State to make pronouncements *only* in strictly legal terms. It is perfectly imaginable, even probable, that political or moral arguments will be put forward to justify a military action.[159] The only condition necessary to envisage an evolution of the rule is that a State's arguments be combined or articulated with considerations that enable extrication of 'the considered expression of a legal conception'.[160] Even then, such considerations must allow for interpretation as claims aiming at a modification of the meaning of the rule prohibiting the use of force.

The Formulation of a Claim Bearing on the Evolution of the Legal Rule

Supposing that it properly refers to the positive law rule prohibiting the use of force, an intervening State can either rely on a classical defence to this rule, or claim that its behaviour is based on a new defence or legal justification. A careful examination of practice shows that the first scenario is the more frequent, as shall be shown later in this book.[161] The International Court of Justice has very clearly specified the consequences of this type of

---

[155] See: H Waldock, 'General Course of Public International Law' (1960) 106 *RCADI* 47; VD Degan, *Sources of International Law* (The Hague/Boston/London, Martinus Nijhoff Publishers, 1997) 166.

[156] O Corten and B Delcourt, 'Droit, légitimation et politique extérieure: précisions théoriques et méthodologiques', above n 95, 26–28.

[157] See, eg: European Council Berlin Declaration (26 March 1999) 7433 *Europe Daily Bulletin*, 5–6 and comments by L Weerts, 'Droit, politique et morale dans le discours justificatif de l'Union européenne et de l'OTAN: vers une confusion des registres de légitimité' in O Corten and B Delcourt, *Droit, légitimation et politique extérieure: l'Europe et la guerre du Kosovo* (Bruxelles, Bruylant, 2001) 85 *ff*.

[158] JE Stromseth, 'Rethinking humanitarian intervention: the case for incremental change', above n 45, 234–40; M Kohen, 'La pratique et la théorie des sources du droit international' in SFDI, *La pratique et le droit international* (Paris, Pedone, 2004) 90.

[159] C Gray, *International Law and the Use of Force*, 3rd edn, above n 2, 25.

[160] ICJ, *Fisheries*, ICJ Rep (1951) 136; cp A Carty, 'The Iraq Invasion as a Recent United Kingdom "Contribution to International Law"' (2005) 16 *EJIL* 143–51.

[161] See, eg: the military interventions in Yugoslavia (1999), in Afghanistan (2001) and in Iraq (2003), below.

situation. It has thus noted that 'the United States has, on the legal plane, justified its intervention expressly and solely by reference to the "classic" rules involved, namely, collective self-defense against an armed attack'.[162] As mentioned above, the Court considered that even if a breach of the rule is accompanied by a justification referring to the rule in question, 'the significance of that attitude is to confirm rather than to weaken the rule'.[163] The methodology relies here on a radical separation between fact and law. Practice cannot, as such, modify the law. It is only capable of doing so if it reveals an *opinio juris*, which implies firstly a clear legal position from the intervening State. If this legal position refers to the existing rule, this rule is confirmed in law, even if (maybe because, here again, the question of lawfulness *in casu* of the conduct does not matter) it is breached in fact.[164]

Let us be clear that, in order to be relevant, the legal stance of the intervening State must, as far as possible, be unambiguous, which presupposes a 'constant and uniform practice'.[165] As shall be seen in more detail later, Belgium, for instance, furtively invoked, before the International Court of Justice, a right of humanitarian intervention to justify its military action against Yugoslavia.[166] However, this legal position was not maintained, the Belgian authorities affirming a few months later that the Kosovo war could not be viewed as a precedent giving rise to a right of unilateral military intervention. But 'contradiction in the practice of States or inconsistent conduct, particularly emanating from these very States which are said to be following or establishing the custom, would prevent the emergence of a rule of customary law'.[167] This being the case, it is difficult to conclude in favour of a true claim to change by the intervening State,[168] unless one limits this claim to a very short period, which would imply admitting the possibility of an almost instantaneous custom, a possibility that would in turn presuppose an immediate and massive acceptance on the part of the international community of States as a whole, on terms that will be stipulated below.

---

[162] ICJ, *Military and Paramilitary Activities in and against Nicaragua*, ICJ Rep (1986) 109, para 208.

[163] ibid, 98, para 186.

[164] M Kohen, 'La pratique et la théorie des sources du droit international', above n 158, 90; O Corten and B Delcourt, 'Kosovo: le droit international renforcé?' (2000) 8 *L'Observateur des Nations Unies* 133–47.

[165] ICJ, *Right of Passage over Indian Territory*, ICJ Rep (1960) 40; see also ICJ, *Asylum*, ICJ Rep (1950) 277 ('constant and uniform custom'); Arbitral tribunal, *Interpretation of the Aerial Agreement of 6 February 1948* (United States/Italy), *RIAA* XVI (1965), 100 ('a constant practice, observed in fact and without change'); and ICJ, *Fisheries Jurisdiction*, Judge De Castro, Separate Opinion, ICJ Rep (1974) 89–90; see also V Degan, *Sources of International Law*, above n 155, 150–52.

[166] R Ergec, CR 99/15, Monday, 10 May 1999; see below, ch 8, s II.

[167] ICJ, *Fisheries Jurisdiction*, Judges Forster, Bengzon, Jiménez, de Aréchaga, Nagendra Singh, Ruda, Separate Opinion, ICJ Rep (1974) 50.

[168] See: PM Dupuy, 'L'unité de l'ordre juridique international. Cours général de droit international public', above n 140, 172.

Before that, however, the radical separation between new and existing law, which should guide the interpretation of a State's legal position, must be distinguished. In practice, it is true that intervening powers often tend to rely on classical defence arguments or institutions, such as self-defence, authorisation of the Security Council or State consent.[169] *A contrario*, it is difficult to envisage under customary international law the introduction of other justifications, such as the right of humanitarian intervention, pre-emptive action or *a posteriori* approval by the Security Council.[170] The prudence of intervening States is explained by a fear of frightening other States with new claims, and by the fact that, by definition, they are compelled to justify their conduct with respect to existing law at the time of the acts, hence the classical tenor of their discourse.[171] However, the classical character of the legal discourse can be but a gloss. It is indeed possible for a State to invoke an existing institution while conferring on it a new meaning, which, under the guise of interpretation, amounts to the formulation of a claim for the evolution of the legal rule. The possibility of military intervention on the basis of an implicit Security Council authorisation is a good example; as is reference to pre-emptive self-defence, or even to self-defence targeting a State that allegedly simply tolerated the presence of irregular forces on its territory, without having participated or acquiesced in the organised activities of these groups, nor itself having sent them onto the territory of a third State.[172] In all of these scenarios, it is clear that the intervening State aims to modify the existing law, or at least to interpret it in a very particular way. It could therefore be asked whether or not this rule is capable of evolving in this direction, a question which requires an examination of other States' reactions to this claim.

B. The Acceptance of the Modification of the Legal Rule by the International Community of States as a Whole

In the context of treaty law, an evolution of the rule prohibiting the use of force would require ratification by at least two thirds of the States parties, including all permanent members of the Security Council, pursuant to articles 108 and 109 of the UN Charter. By definition this onerous procedure is not applicable in the realm of custom. However, this does not mean that certain precautions can be dispensed with before concluding that a legal rule actually has evolved. To echo the International Court of Justice, a State's

---

[169] See generally C Gray, *International Law and the Use of Force*, 3rd edn, above n 2, 24.

[170] Above, chs 6–8.

[171] See C Gray, 'From Unity to Polarization: International Law and the Use of Force against Iraq', above n 96, 17.

[172] See generally O Corten and F Dubuisson, 'L'hypothèse d'une règle émergente fondant une intervention militaire sur une 'autorisation implicite' du Conseil de sécurité', above n 83; O Corten and F Dubuisson, 'Opération 'liberté immuable' : une extension abusive du concept de légitime défense', above n 74.

claim to rely on a new right or a new defence could tend to modify international customary law only if 'shared by other States'.[173] More specifically, an effective modification of the legal rule would imply first, an acceptance; second, an acceptance of the modification of the legal rule; and third, an acceptance of the modification of the legal rule by the international community of States as a whole.

An Acceptance

Supposing that we find ourselves in the situation—rare enough in practice, as was shown in the first part of this chapter—where one or more intervening States have justified their actions by invoking an argument tending to modify the legal rule or to interpret it in a new way; it is still not obvious that this claim will be accepted by the other States. A very clear acceptance may well be ascertained, as was the case, for example, at the time of the war fought against Iraq in order to force it to withdraw from Kuwait in 1991; that war was the first in the history of the United Nations to be fought on the basis of a Security Council authorisation.[174] However, it is also possible that an armed action might give rise to substantial opposition, as was the case, for example, during military actions by South Africa in retaliation against its neighbouring States.[175] It is obviously only in the first scenario that an evolution of the rule is imaginable.[176] More specifically, when there is a true acceptance of acts that might constitute a breach of the rule, 'the initial act will begin to appear as a precedent rather than remain stigmatized as delinquency'.[177]

It is not, however, always easy to determine whether, and to what extent, acceptance may be established. Everything will depend in each individual case on how the discourse is interpreted. It will be essential to be able to demonstrate that this discourse reveals an acceptance of the justification of military intervention.

It is important here to mention the hypothesis of silence. Silence is relatively common in practice, many States not officially issuing a legal position after the launch of a military attack. It is quite possible to infer acquiescence from a silence that, in the situation, does indeed convey acceptance,

[173] ICJ, *Military and Paramilitary Activities in and against Nicaragua*, ICJ Rep (1986) 109, para 207.

[174] See: M Weller (ed), *Iraq and Kuwait: The Hostilities and Their Aftermath*, Cambridge International Documents Series, vol 3 (Cambridge, Grotius Publishers Limited, 1993) (notable as a compilation of the panoply of positions adopted by States); see GA Res 45/170 of 18 December 1990 (adopted by 144 in favour, 1 against (Iraq) and 0 abstentions).

[175] See generally examples available on the following website: www.ulb.ac.be/droit/cdi.

[176] One author insists on the necessity of demonstrating an 'absence de protestation' or an 'acquiescement' by the lead State; P Cahier, 'Changements et continuités du droit international. Cours général de droit international public' (1985-VI) 195 *RCADI* 232; see also J Salmon (ed), *Dictionnaire de droit international public* (Brussels, Bruylant-AUF, 2001) 284 (v° 'coutume').

[177] TJ Farer, 'The Prospect for International Law and Order in the Wake of Iraq', above n 91, 623.

whether in the domain of the non-use of force or in some other domain.[178] Again, before reaching such a conclusion, certain precautions must be taken, which can be drawn from a dictum of the Permanent International Court of Justice, which is undoubtedly still valid:[179] 'for only if such abstention were based on their being conscious of having a duty to abstain would it be possible to speak of an international custom'.[180]

First, to be meaningful, the silence must reign in a context where the State concerned is considered to be in a situation in which it is expected to condemn the intervention. If State A attacks State B, the silence of State C is only relevant if, for example, State C is a State close to State B, or had previously expressed its concern about the degradation of relations between A and B. In practice, and even if the rule at stake is legally binding *erga omnes*, it should be stipulated that States may have relatively little concern for a military intervention.[181] This is particularly true in the case of military operations of a regional nature, such as the military actions of African States in Liberia or Sierra Leone, the foreign military interventions in the Democratic Republic of the Congo, the conflict between Ethiopia and Eritrea, between Cameroon and Nigeria or, on another continent, the troubles between India and Pakistan over Kashmir.[182] One may also consider the scenario of a military operation limited in its scope or in its effects, such as that which occurred in Iraqi Kurdistan, in April 1991, or even of the Turkish army's recurrent operations in Iraqi territory[183]. Each of these events has of course prompted reactions from the States more or less directly concerned, but it has not brought about a debate on a universal scale comparable to that which followed the interventions in Yugoslavia (1999), in Afghanistan (2001) or in Iraq (2003). Under the circumstances, it will be particularly difficult to assert that the customary rule has evolved, since the silence of other States may not readily be interpreted as meaningful.

[178] GP Buzzini, 'Les comportements passifs des Etats et leur incidence sur la réglementation de l'emploi de la force en droit international général', above n 141, 84–93; ME O'Connel, 'Taking *Opinio Juris* Seriously, A Classical Approach to International Law on the Use of Force', above n 127, 16; J Salmon (ed), *Dictionnaire de droit international public*, above n 176, 1035 (v° 'silence', definition 'C').

[179] L Condorelli, 'La coutume', above n 140, 197.

[180] PCIJ, *Lotus*, Series A no 10 (1927) 28. The International Court of Justice adopted this test in the case of the North Sea Continental Shelf; ICJ, *North Sea Continental* Shelf, ICJ Rep (1969) 45; see also ME O'Connel, 'Taking *Opinio Juris* Seriously, A Classical Approach to International Law on the Use of Force', above n 127, 13–14.

[181] L Boisson de Chazournes, 'Qu'est-ce que la pratique en droit international?', above n 140, 35.

[182] The United States' military intervention in Liberia in August 1990, which gave rise only to very limited position-taking, is another example; see M Weller (ed), *Regional Peace-Keeping and International Enforcement: The Liberian Crisis*, Cambridge International Documents Series, vol 6 (Cambridge, Cambridge University Press/Grotius Publishers, 1994). This silence is easily explained, particularly in light of the period, the Iraqi invasion of Kuwait monopolising at the time every debate within the United Nations.

[183] See: T Ruys, 'Quo vadit Jus ad bellum? A legal analysis of Turkey's military operations against the PKK in northern Iraq (07-08)' (2008) 10-2 *Melbourne JIL*, 334–64.

Within this perspective, one may recall that, contrary to what a part of a doctrine postulates,[184] the absence of condemnation of a military intervention by the political organs of the United Nations can hardly be considered to be acquiescence. Without denying the importance of the United Nations in the formation of customary law,[185] it must be recalled that this organisation evolves only by the expedient of Member State position-taking, to which UN resolutions give rise, and not through the resolutions adopted by the organs as such.[186] In so far as they are political and not judicial organs, the UN General Assembly and Security Council are not supposed to make systematic pronouncements on the lawfulness of all conduct that is seemingly contrary to the prohibition of the use of force.[187] It is, of course, possible for condemnations to be pronounced, once the political conditions are met.[188] However, it is also common for no resolution to be adopted, or even for a resolution neither to condemn nor condone the intervention.[189] An examination of the resolutions adopted regarding Iraq after the cease-fire in April 1991 illustrates the scenario: the military operations in Kurdistan, and the frequent bombardments by the United States to enforce the no-fly zones, were never mentioned in these resolutions.[190] Similarly, it would be improper to deduce anything from these texts on the potential evolution of the customary rule, simply because the States are not presumed to approve implicitly of interventions by the sole fact that they abstain from condemning them through the United Nations' political organs.[191]

Finally, it must be emphasised that, to be determinative, the silence must convey a true will of acceptance. In practice, the refusal to condemn may

---

[184] See, eg: TM Franck, *Recourse to Force. State Actions Against Threats and Armed Attacks*, above n 2.

[185] See, eg: ICJ, *North Sea Continental Shelf*, Diss Op Tanaka, ICJ Rep (1969) 176; ICJ, *Barcelona Traction Light and Power Co Ltd (Second Phase)*, Judge Ammoun, Separate Opinion, ICJ Rep (1970) 303.

[186] C Gray, *International Law and the Use of Force*, 3rd edn, above n 2, 20. Evoking the Security Council and General Assembly, the author notes that '[b]oth are fora in which states can set out their legal justifications for the use of force and appeal to other states for support'. ibid.

[187] ibid, 18.

[188] With respect to the General Assembly, one may think, for example, of the resolutions condemning the Soviet invasion of Afghanistan (GA Res ES 6/2, adopted 10 January 1980 by 104 in favour, 18 against, with 18 abstentions), or the United States' intervention in Panama. See: Effects on the Situation in Central America of the United States' Military Intervention in Panama, GA Res 44/240, adopted 22 December 1989 by 75 in favour, 20 against, and 40 abstentions.

[189] C Gray, *International Law and the Use of Force*, 3rd edn, above n 2, 21–22.

[190] See: C Denis, 'La résolution 678 (1990) peut-elle légitimer les actions armées menées contre l'Iraq postérieurement à l'adoption de la résolution 687 (1991)?' (1998) 31 *RBDI* 504–18.

[191] M Kohen, 'La pratique et la théorie des sources du droit international', above n 158. In this sense the case of *Military and Paramilitary Activities in and against Nicaragua* may be cited, in which the Court at no point considers the absence of condemnation by the Security Council of the United States' action as relevant.

reveal a simple tolerance which does not necessarily amount to a true acceptance.[192] In this context, it would be excessive to deduce acceptance from an official declaration of a diplomatic nature, in virtue of which one or several States express 'understanding', without clearly approving the military intervention. This kind of formula was regularly used at the onset of certain air strikes against Iraq in the 1990s.[193] Again, the difficulty here lies in revealing an acceptance following this ambiguous conduct and, moreover, an acceptance of the intervening power's claims that is not simply political or diplomatic but legal.

An Acceptance of the Modification of the Legal Rule

Beyond the expression of a simple 'understanding', certain States may more clearly approve, celebrate, or even support a particular military intervention. This approbation of the intervention as a fact will not necessarily be accompanied by an approbation of the legal justification put forward by the intervening State.[194] So some States, while supporting operation *Provide Comfort* in Iraqi Kurdistan, carefully abstained from any pronouncement on the legal validity of the argumentation put forward by the intervening powers.[195] This attitude is perfectly understandable, if one is mindful of the distinction between the legitimacy of the intervention and its legality.[196] Unless confining oneself to a purely legalistic vision of legitimacy, this concept may indeed call forth moral considerations that, under certain circumstances, may justify an action that is otherwise recognised as having been carried out in breach of positive law.[197] It is possible, therefore, for a State to approve

---

[192] See: O Ferrajolo, 'La pratique et la règle de droit. Réflexions à propos de la seconde guerre du Golfe', (February 2004) *Actualité et droit international. Revue d'analyse juridique de l'actualité internationale*, available online at www.ridi.org/adi/articles/2004/200405fer.htm#_ftn15. M Byers, 'The Shifting Foundations of International Law: A Decade of Forceful Measures against Iraq', above n 3, 35. According to M Shaw, 'it is not inconceivable that in some situations the international community might refrain from adopting a condemnatory stand where large numbers of lives have been saved in circumstances of gross oppression by a state of its citizens due to an outside intervention. This does not, of course, mean that it constitutes a legitimate principle of international law'; *International Law*, 3rd edn (Cambridge, Cambridge University Press, 1991) 725; see also G Cahin, *La coutume internationale et les organisations internationales. L'incidence de la dimension institutionnelle sur le processus coutumier*, above n 142, 328 and 345.

[193] See: C Denis, 'La résolution 678 (1990) peut-elle légitimer les actions armées menées contre l'Iraq postérieurement à l'adoption de la résolution 687 (1991)?', above n 190, 489.

[194] C Gray, *International Law and the Use of Force*, 3rd edn, above n 2, 20.

[195] See: 'Note du Département de droit international du Ministre Suisse des affaires étrangères du 20 janvier 1993' (1994) 4 *RSDIE* 626.

[196] O Corten, 'La persistance de l'argument légaliste. Eléments pour une typologie contemporaine des registres de légitimité dans une société libérale' (2002) 50 *Droit et société. Revue internationale de théorie du droit et de sociologie juridique* 185–203.

[197] O Corten and B Delcourt, 'Droit, légitimation et politique extérieure: précisions théoriques et méthodologiques', above n 95, 19–30; see also O Corten, 'Réflexions épistémologiques et méthodologiques sur les spécificités d'une étude politologique de la légitimité' (2000) 1 *Cahiers européens de Bruxelles/Brussels European Papers* 28.

an action in the name of a particular moral or political philosophy, while reserving its position in strictly legal terms.

Such conduct would obviously not suffice to conclude that the customary rule had indeed evolved.[198] In the same way that this presupposes a strictly legal claim on the part of the intervening power, it also presupposes a legal acceptance on the part of other States.[199] This brings us back to the more classical definitions of custom, which do not refer to a simple acceptance of the practice, but to an acceptance of the practice 'as the law',[200] which is incomparably more demanding. According to a classical *dictum* pronounced by the International Court of Justice:

> The States concerned must therefore feel that they are conforming to what amounts to a legal obligation. The frequency, or even habitual character of the acts is not in itself enough. There are many international acts, e.g., in the field of ceremonial and protocol, which are performed almost invariably, but which are motivated only by considerations of courtesy, convenience or tradition, and not by any sense of legal duty.[201]

A contrario, the approval of particular conduct does not necessarily mean that there exists a legal belief (*opinio juris*) that this conduct complies with positive law. This approval can be dictated by courtesy, political alliance, diplomatic concerns, or 'considerations . . . of convenience'.[202]

In some instances, the legal justification of a military intervention is explicitly taken up or accepted. In 1991, a very large number of States thus supported the arguments of collective self-defence and Security Council authorisation advanced by the coalition of States to justify their military attack against Iraq.[203] The same pattern can be observed at the onset of more controversial military operations. In March 2003, the day after the launch of the third Gulf War, otherwise considered by many as contrary to international law, Nicaragua and Micronesia clearly expressed their support for the argument invoked by the intervening States of Security Council authorisation.[204] But, except for these hypotheses, a strictly legal belief is quite difficult to establish in the highly political context of international relations generally, and in the debates surrounding military interventions in particular. Must one then

---

[198] See: BR Roth, 'Bending the law, breaking it, or developing it? The United States and the humanitarian use of force in the post-Cold War era' in M Byers and G Nolte (eds), *United States Hegemony and the Foundations of International Law* (Cambridge, Cambridge University Press, 2003) 252.

[199] M Byers and S Chesterman, 'Changing the rules about rules? Unilateral Intervention and the Future of International Law', above n 67, 180.

[200] ICJ Statute, art 38.

[201] ICJ, *North Sea Continental Shelf*, ICJ Rep (1969) 44, para 77.

[202] ibid.

[203] See: M Weller (ed), *Iraq and Kuwait: The Hostilities and Their Aftermath* (Cambridge, Grotius Publ. Limited, 1993) (positions taken by the above-cited States).

[204] O Corten, 'Opération *Iraqi Freedom*: peut-on admettre l'argument de l' "autorisation implicite" du Conseil de sécurité?', above n 116, 240–41.

conclude that it is impossible to establish a legal belief in cases other than when it is expressed in an explicit manner? Certainly not. Here again the general rules pertaining to the establishment of a customary rule dictate a certain caution, which calls for three qualifications.

In the first place, the State's conduct must express a true belief, which supposes that it is not vitiated by pressure or distorted by excessive emotion.[205] The condition appears to refer to vices of consent such as are found in the law of treaties, even though one may wonder whether it would not be more appropriate to be more rigorous in the case of a customary rule, which requires a belief that an action complies with an already existing rule of law, which is not (necessarily) the case when a treaty is concluded. This condition of sincerity of the State's belief leads one further to consider that the acceptance of the lawfulness of an intervention will be *a priori* more relevant where it does not come from an ally of the intervening power, an ally that can be submitted to strong political, economic or diplomatic constraints.[206] The same logic suggests that a condemnation is much more significant where it comes from an ally of the intervening State.[207] It is also in reference to this condition of sincerity that some commentators have expressed reservations about the possibility of deducing from the fairly broad approval of the military operation against Afghanistan begun in October 2001 that the rule prohibiting the use of force had evolved to include the concept of indirect aggression.[208] The specific context following 11th September, marked at once by compassion for the United States and by concern caused by the at times threatening words of the country's leaders, made any expression of a sincere legal belief a sensitive matter.[209]

These concerns lead us to believe that, to become established, any acceptance of a modification of a rule of law must be deducible from not just one but from multiple precedents.[210] Indeed, the Court insisted that rigour be observed, particularly when claiming to establish a rapid evolution of a customary rule:

> Although the passage of only a short period of time is not necessarily, or in itself, a bar to the formation of a new rule of customary international law on the basis of what was originally a purely conventional rule, an indispensable requirement

---

[205] P Daillier, M Forteau and A Pellet, Nguyen Quoc Dinh, *Droit international public*, 8th edn (Paris, LGDJ, 2009) 361–63.

[206] M Kohen, 'La pratique et la théorie des sources du droit international', above n 158, 91.

[207] C Gray, *International Law and the Use of Force*, 3rd edn, above n 2, 20–21.

[208] M Kohen, 'The Use of Force by the United States after the end of the Cold War, and its impact of International Law', above n 100, 221–26; M Kohen, 'La pratique et la théorie des sources du droit international', above n 158, 92.

[209] A Lagerwall, 'Kosovo, Afghanistan, Irak: le retour des guerres d'agression', above n 88, 93; C Guttierez Espada, 'La 'contaminacion' de Naciones Unidas o las Resoluciones 1483 y 1511 (2003) del Consejo de seguridad' (2003) 19 *Annuario de derecho internacional* 76.

[210] M Kohen, 'The Use of Force by the United States after the end of the Cold War, and its impact on International Law', above n 100, 224.

would be that within the period in question, short though it might be, State practice, including that of States whose interests are specially affected, should have been both extensive and virtually uniform in the sense of the provision invoked; -and should moreover have occurred in such a way as to show a general recognition that that a rule of law or legal obligation is involved.[211]

Thus, independently of knowing beyond what threshold a practice may be termed 'general', the existence of an *opinio juris* cannot reasonably be confirmed by a single case, precisely because that case may be dictated by considerations of courtesy or convenience.[212] To take the example of Afghanistan, a weakening of the concept of armed aggression would presuppose, for it to be recognised, that it is accepted through multiple precedents, in such a way that the strictly legal belief is beyond any doubt.[213] It is in this sense that the possibility for the Security Council to authorise military actions by Member States, which is not provided for in the UN Charter, may be considered to be established custom, since multiple precedents have occurred with the express or tacit approval of the States parties to the UN Charter as a whole.[214]

Finally, we will recall that it is to avoid these difficulties of distinguishing between considerations of convenience and legal belief that case law often tends to rest, not on the reactions caused by this or that specific military operation, but on the positions put forward generally within normative texts. It is increasingly important to take into consideration the attitudes of States towards certain General Assembly resolutions regarding the non-use of force, particularly where they reveal a will to make a specifically legal pronouncement.[215] In the remainder of this book, we shall refer to various resolutions of

---

[211] ICJ, *North Sea Continental Shelf*, ICJ Rep (1969) 43, para 74; see also ICJ, *Fisheries Jurisdiction*, Judge De Castro, Separate Opinion, ICJ Rep (1974) 89–90.

[212] See: P Daillier, M Forteau and A Pellet, Nguyen Quoc Dinh, *Droit international public*, 8th edn, above n 205, 358–59; M Byers, 'The Shifting Foundations of International Law: A Decade of Forceful Measures against Iraq', above n 3, 28 and 35. Consequently, '[t]he shorter the practice the more important is its uniformity and its acceptance by the international community as binding law' (R Bernhardt, 'Customary International Law' in R Bernhardt (ed), *EPIL*, vol I (North Holland, Alphabetical Ed, 1992) 901).

[213] J Verhoeven, 'Les 'étirements' de la légitime défense,' above n 76, 64.

[214] N Blokker, 'Is the Authorization Authorized? Powers and Practice of the United Nations Security Council to Authorize the Use of Force by "Coalitions of the Able and Willing"' (2000) 11 *EJIL* 541–68; C Gray, 'From Unity to Polarization: International Law and the Use of Force against Iraq', above n 96, 3–4; E de Wet, *The Chapter VII Powers of the United Nations Security Council* (Oxford and Portland, Hart Publishing, 2004) 256–310 (ch 7); O Corten and Pierre Klein, 'L'autorisation de recourir à la force à des fins humanitaires: droit d'ingérence ou retour aux sources?' (1993) 4 *EJIL* 506–33.

[215] See: ICJ, *Military and Paramilitary Activities in and against Nicaragua*, ICJ Rep (1986) 107–08, paras 202–03; ICJ, *Legality of the Threat or Use of Nuclear Weapons*, ICJ Rep (1996) 254–55, para 70; see also ME O'Connel, 'Taking *Opinio Juris* Seriously, A Classical Approach to International Law on the Use of Force', above n 127, 17–18; G Cahin, 'Le rôle des organes politiques des Nations Unies', above n 148, 151–54; A Carty, 'The Significance of Legal Declarations on the Non-Use of Force in International Relations' in WE Butler (ed), *The Non-Use of Force in International Law* (Dordrecht, Kluwer, 1989) 53–75; VN Fedorov, 'The United Nations Declaration on the Non-Use of Force', ibid, 77–84.

this type, and especially to three major resolutions, all adopted after several years of debate first in the special committees set up for each of them, then in the General Assembly's Sixth Commission, and finally in plenary session:

—Resolution 2625 (XXV) on friendly relations, adopted without a vote on 24 October 1970, and that expressly purports to be an interpretation of the principles of the UN Charter, including the principle of non-use of force. The International Court of Justice has referred to this declaration on several occasions when interpreting this principle.[216]

—Resolution 3314 (XXIX), adopted without a vote on 14 December 1974, aims to provide criteria for defining aggression. Even if the debates were not unequivocal on this point, many States have underscored the contribution of this resolution to defining armed attack as an essential feature of legitimate defence pursuant to article 51 of the UN Charter.[217] In 1986[218] as in 2005,[219] the International Court of Justice elected to refer to this resolution in this perspective; a move that went largely uncriticised.[220]

—Resolution 42/22 on making the principle of abstention for the use or threat of force in international relations more effective, adopted without a vote by the UN General Assembly on 18 November 1987, contains several parts. The first aims simply to define the various elements of the rule prohibiting the use of force, while subsequent parts propose measures devised to make it more effective. Review of the discussions about its adoption shows that part I of the resolution seems to have been generally considered as a reflection of existing law.[221] Parts II and III prompted certain reservations about their legal value *de lege lata*. We shall make much of this instrument, as other scholarship has already done.[222]

We shall regularly return to these resolutions and the works that preceded their adoption. They contain many positions of principle that are especially interesting in that they are not directly dependent on diplomatic constraints surrounding this or that particular debate about any specific military intervention.

---

[216] ICJ, *Military and Paramilitary Activities*, ICJ Rep (1986) 98–101, paras 187–90; *Legal Consequences of the Construction of a Wall in the Occupied Palestinian Territory*, ICJ Rep (2004) 171, para 87; *Armed Activities on the Territory of the Congo (Democratic Republic of the Congo v Uganda)*, ICJ Rep (2005), para 162; see also ICJ, *Legality of the Threat or Use of Nuclear Weapons*, ICJ Rep (1996) 264, para 102.

[217] See above, ch 7, s I.

[218] ICJ, *Military and Paramilitary Activities*, ICJ Rep (1986) 103, para 195.

[219] ICJ, *Armed Activities on the Territory of the Congo (Democratic Republic of the Congo v Uganda)*, para 146.

[220] See also: ICJ, *Oil Platforms; Counter-Memorial and Counter-Claim Submitted by the USA*, 23 June 1997, 131, para 4.12 (and fn 293).

[221] See, eg: Italy (A/C6/42/SR.16, 7 October 1987, para 3), Greece (A/C6/42/SR.20, 13 October 1987, para 30), Nepal (A/C6/42/SR.21, 13 October 1987, para 21), Panama (A/C6/42/SR.20, 13 October 1987, paras 3 and 4), Turkey (A/C6/42/SR.21, 13 October 1987, para 17).

[222] C Gray, *International Law and the Use of Force*, 3rd edn, above n 2, 9.

Within this perspective, it would make more sense to take into account the positions expressed in general and theoretical terms during the debates raised about the right of humanitarian intervention in October 1999, rather than canvas the reactions of States to the military intervention launched against Yugoslavia in March of the same year.[223] It is obvious in this respect that some States may not wish to condemn a specific operation, while defining their legal position on the same issue in general terms. In the same perspective, we shall rely on the works of the International Law Commission, insofar as these works contain the expression by States of legal positions about the prohibition of the use of force.[224]

Under these circumstances, but only under these circumstances, a breach of the rule prohibiting the use of force may potentially engender an evolution of this rule. It is nevertheless necessary, for it to be so, that the legal acceptance be the act not of a few States but of the international community of States as a whole.

An Acceptance of the Modification of a Legal Rule by the International Community of States as a Whole

In a very large number of cases, the reactions to the launching of a military intervention are diverse and even opposed or polarised. Throughout the Cold War, for example, the military operations of the great powers in their respective 'backyards' provoked a heated debate, during which the weapon of international law was brandished on both sides, even though, in general, it was mostly used by those opposing war.[225] More recently, the military operations against Yugoslavia (1999) and against Iraq (2003) were marked by fierce opposition within the UN and elsewhere between those who considered these operations as lawful and the much larger group who labelled them as a breach of international law and sometimes as acts of aggression.[226]

In such instances, it goes without saying that it would be improper to conclude in favour of an evolution of the rule, and this independently of the issue of lawfulness *in casu* of the intervention.[227] As already mentioned, the International Court of Justice has stated on this subject that the invocation of a new right or a new defence could not purport to modify international customary law unless it was 'shared by other States'.[228] For this modification to

---

[223] Above, ch 8.

[224] P Palchetti, 'Customary Rules on the Use of Force in the Work of Codification of the International Law Commission' in in E Cannizzaro and Paolo Palchetti (eds), *Customary International Law On the Use of Force* (Leiden/Boston, Martinus Nijhoff, 2005) 237–40.

[225] TJ Farer, 'The Prospect for International Law and Order in the Wake of Iraq', above 91, 623.

[226] PM Dupuy, 'L'unité de l'ordre juridique international. Cours général de droit international public,' above n 140, 171–73.

[227] ibid.

[228] ICJ, *Military and Paramilitary Activities in and against Nicaragua*, ICJ Rep (1986) 108, para 206.

be effective, it is without a doubt a very large majority of States that must indicate their approbation.[229] The Court thus notes, in the same judgment, that States frequently mention the prohibition of the use of force 'as being not only a principle of customary international law but also a fundamental or cardinal principle of such law',[230] indeed, as the International Law Commission put it, 'a conspicuous example of a rule in international law having the character of *jus cogens*'.[231] We shall return to this characterisation and the consequences that should be drawn from it.[232] At this point, it can be specified simply that it implies that, in order to evolve, the rule must be able to rest on the acceptance of the 'international community of States as a whole', to recall the words of the Vienna Convention on the Law of Treaties.[233]

This requirement means that it is very difficult to demonstrate that a violation of the rule has brought about a change. That would indeed presuppose, proof not only of an acceptance, but further of an acceptance that signals a specifically legal belief, and finally a quasi-unanimous acceptance.[234] This rigorous condition is not shared by a certain doctrine which, as indicated in the introduction, often tends to value loosely the conditions to which an evolution of the rule would be submitted.[235] Two points are worth noting in this respect.

—First of all, the characterisation of the rule as a rule of *jus cogens* runs clearly against the argument that a privileged status must be reserved to *major* or *leading* States.[236] The fact that these States (which are none other than Western States, even though identification is not always easy) are both democratic (in terms of legitimacy) and more capable than others of enforcing the rule (in terms of effectiveness) is irrelevant.[237] For a rule as fundamental as the prohibition of the use of force to evolve, an acceptance on the part of States as a whole is needed, which entails a criterion that is both quantitative (a very large majority is required)

---

[229] M Byers and S Chesterman, 'Changing the rules about rules? Unilateral Intervention and the Future of International Law', above n 67, 179.

[230] ICJ, *Military and Paramilitary Activities in and against Nicaragua*, ICJ Rep (1986) 100–01, para 190.

[231] ibid.

[232] Below, ch 4.

[233] See arts 53 (on the existence of a *jus cogens* rule) and 64 (on the evolution of a *jus cogens* rule) of the Vienna Convention on the Law of Treaties of 1969.

[234] M Byers and S Chesterman, 'Changing the rules about rules? Unilateral Intervention and the Future of International Law', above n 67, 180.

[235] Above, s I.

[236] Therefore, 'a general custom [. . .] can henceforward no longer be received into international law without taking strict account of the opinion or attitude of the States of the Third World'; ICJ, *Barcelona Traction Light and Power Co Inc (Second Phase)*, Judge Ammoun, Separate Opinion, ICJ Rep (1970) 330.

[237] See: M Byers and S Chesterman, 'Changing the rules about rules? Unilateral Intervention and the Future of International Law', above n 67, 189–94; M Byers, 'The Shifting Foundations of International Law: A Decade of Forceful Measures against Iraq', above n 3, 30 *ff.*

and qualitative (this majority must include States with different political systems and values and belonging to all regions of the world).[238]
—Secondly, the expression 'international community of States as a whole' properly indicates that what is relevant here is a State-centric vision of the international legal system.[239] It is not the commentators (journalists, media or various political actors), nor even international law specialists, who must accept the evolution of the rule, but the States themselves.[240] These States may express themselves by various means, whether through multilateral conferences, the taking of individual positions, or within the organs of international organisations, such as the Security Council. It is, however, indeed the position of the States that matters, and not that of the organs or the conferences. Contrary to what some authors assert,[241] who refer notably to the Security Council, there is no other 'international jury' beyond that of the States as a whole.[242]

It is in this sense that we emphasised earlier the role of the General Assembly in elaborating customary law, especially through the adoption of several resolutions designed to better define the rule banning the use of force. It should be specified here that, contrary to what some scholarship seems to postulate, the Security Council's role is very limited in this respect[243]:

> Generally speaking, the Council's resolutions are not legislative in the sense of applying outside the framework of particular cases of restoration of international peace and security. Moreover, they cannot—by analogy with General Assembly resolutions—be said to reflect either *opinio juris*, nor the generality of the requisite State practice.[244]

Notice that:

1. The Security Council has never been acknowledged to have any role in the codification of international law, and has never set up a subsidiary body specialised in this area, nor any specific legal commission.

---

[238] PM Dupuy, *Droit international public*, above n 140, 324, no 318; G Cahin, *La coutume internationale et les organisations internationales. L'incidence de la dimension institutionnelle sur le processus coutumier*, above n 142, 408 *ff*.

[239] See: V Degan, *Sources of International Law*, above n 155, 148; L Boisson de Chazournes, 'Qu'est-ce que la pratique en droit international?', above n 140, 32 *ff*. Even limiting the determination of *opinio juris* to the position of States, we are still confronted with problems of coherence, a State expressing its position through the intermediaries of various representatives who will not always defend a coherent position; C Gray, *International Law and the Use of Force*, 3rd edn, above n 2, 29.

[240] R Bernhardt, 'Customary International Law', above n 212, 900.

[241] TM Franck, *Recourse to Force. State Actions Against Threats and Armed Attacks*, above n 2, 67.

[242] TM Franck, 'Interpretation and Change in the Law of Humanitarian Intervention', above n 16, 226 *ff*.

[243] O Corten, 'La participation du Conseil de sécurité à l'élaboration, à la cristallisation ou à la consolidation de règles coutumières' (2004) 37 *RBDI* 552–67.

[244] V Gowlland-Debbas, 'The Limits of Unilateral Enforcement of Community Objectives in the Framework of UN Peace Maintenance', above n 80, 377.

2. The Security Council does not adopt resolutions purporting to lay down mandatory general rules of customary international law, but clearly leaves this job to the General Assembly. The Security Council has never adopted anything comparable to resolutions 2625 or 3314. Decision-making within the Security Council is consistent with the particularly politicised character of this body; it is done swiftly, depending on the specific features of a given matter, and not as the outcome of many years of debate on questions of legal principle.

3. The Security Council cannot claim to speak for all UN Member States, even when it speaks unanimously. The difference with the General Assembly, where each State is represented, is particularly telling when dealing with the existence of a general custom.

All of these points should prompt the utmost caution whenever it is asserted that a customary rule is deduced from Security Council resolutions. Admittedly, such an assertion is not necessarily wrong. However, it does assume that the same requirements are demanded of the Security Council as are demanded of the General Assembly. Legal characterisations or interpretations may thus be reiterated by the Security Council and be progressively accepted by States as a whole.[245] The practice of inviting States that are not Security Council members but that sometimes represent a majority of Assembly members (when, say, a State speaks in the name of the non-aligned movement) may favour the development of customary rules.[246] Even so, the legal scope of all the positions of States must be analysed carefully; one cannot merely invoke the terms of the resolution and assume they express a rule that all States accept as law.

In short, it is not impossible for a rule to be characterised as *jus cogens* even though it may require particularly demanding evidence to prove that it has evolved. One may even consider that such a characterisation is easier than for a simple rule *jus dispositivum*. In this latter case, the persistent objector theory—which remains fairly widespread—requires unanimous approval by States, and not just a very large majority.[247] This theory is in any case inapplicable in the context of a peremptory norm, which is so fundamental for international society that it can be accepted as binding *erga omnes*, even against the will of any particular State.[248]

---

[245] G Cahin, *La coutume internationale et les organisations internationales. L'incidence de la dimension institutionnelle sur le processus coutumier*, above n 142, 182–83; 'Le rôle des organes politiques des Nations Unies', above n 148, 154–55.

[246] G Cahin, *La coutume internationale et les organisations internationales. L'incidence de la dimension institutionnelle sur le processus coutumier*, above n 142, 241.

[247] We realise that this theory is far from unanimously shared; see, eg ICJ, *North Sea Continental Shelf*, Judge Ammoun, Separate Opinion, ICJ Rep (1969) 104; ibid, Judge Lachs, Separate Opinion, ICJ Rep (1969) 228 and 231. The characterisation as a norm *jus cogens* allows one, however, to avoid this debate from the outset.

[248] V Degan, *Sources of International Law*, above n 155, 183.

It must not be forgotten either that what is difficult to demonstrate is an evolution of a rule of law. Now, as already indicated, an intervening State will often repudiate the presentation of its justification as supposing an evolution of the rule, and will prefer to assert that it is relying on the existing law alone.[249] Within the framework of the debate on pre-emptive self-defence, for example, the proponents of the idea believe that it has long been a part of customary international law, and it is therefore up to the opponents to demonstrate that this rule has evolved.[250] This attempt to reverse the burden of proof runs aground on the fact that, as the International Court of Justice recognised, the customary rule prohibiting the use of force is supposed—if one excludes the strictly institutional aspects related to the competence of UN organs—to reflect conventional law.[251] The text of the UN Charter, but also General Assembly resolutions having as their purpose its interpretation (such as resolutions 2625 and 3314), must therefore be taken as a starting point from which the *opinio juris* of States is to be determined. Moreover, to the extent that these texts explicitly subordinate a situation of self-defence to the existence of an 'armed attack' (article 51 of the UN Charter), it is up to those who deny this condition to demonstrate that customary law has led to its suppression, or at least to its reformulation.[252]

Conclusion

The non-use of force is perhaps one of the areas where the contrast between the theoretically peremptory character of the rule and a practice of manifest breach of the rule is most patent. Given this contrast, any of several attitudes may be adopted. One attitude, and a perfectly defendable one in theoretical terms, is to assert that there is no such thing as international law since breaches of its most fundamental rule go unpunished. Another is to assert that international law does exist and that it evolves in an extremely flexible manner, with each breach effecting a change in the rule prohibiting the use of force. Between these two positions, I prefer to argue that a breach of international law cannot, as such, bring about a change in the rule against the use of force:

---

[249] C Gray, *International Law and the Use of Force*, 3rd edn, above n 2, 24.

[250] See, eg: D Bowett, *Self-Defence in International Law* (Manchester, Manchester University Press, 1958) 58–60.

[251] ICJ, *Military and Paramilitary Activities in and against Nicaragua*, ICJ Rep (1986) 94–96, paras 176–79.

[252] See generally: T Christakis, 'Vers une reconnaissance de la notion de guerre préventive?' in K Bannelier *et al* (eds), *L'intervention en Irak et le droit international*, above n 67; S Laghmani, 'La doctrine américaine de la "preemptive self-defense": de la guerre par "mesure de prévention" à la guerre par "mesure de précaution" ', above n 71.

As in treaty law, the violation of a norm of customary law does not mean that the norm no longer exists. The disappearance of a customary norm and its replacement by a new norm require again widespread acceptance in the international community.[253]

To conclude otherwise would be to adhere to the maxim *ex injuria jus oritur* and, in the case of custom, to conflate practice and law; this would ultimately be the same as denying the autonomy, and therefore the existence, of a true international legal system. I have opted not to go down that road.

But, while a breach cannot effect a change as such, it can give rise to a situation that makes a change possible: 'violation of law can lead to the formation of a new law'.[254] It has even been held that, especially as regards the non-use of force, 'it appears that significant change through the development of new customary law will usually, if not always, require illegality'.[255] There is nothing absurd about this in theoretical terms. A State acts in breach of a rule of law, adducing a justification that is inconsistent with law. The other States accept that justification. Under the most elementary principles of law from age to age, such acceptance cannot legalise the armed intervention after the fact.[256] The only possible legal effects of their acquiescence could be a situation of debarment for passage of time (with third-party States waiving any claims against the intervening State)[257] or, where applicable, of attenuation of liability.[258] But, while the international responsibility of the intervening State cannot be set aside because of the general acceptance of its action, that acceptance may bring about a change in the legal rule for the future. That change, which to become effective will probably have to be deduced from several precedents, will mean that, should some other intervention of the same type be made subsequently, it will no longer be considered a violation of international law. This does not involve any infringement of the *ex injuria jus non oritur* principle, for the violation does not engender a change in the law as such, but prompts a change of position towards the law: 'in short, acts in opposition to existing

---

[253] R Bernhardt, 'Customary International Law', above n 212, 901.

[254] R Higgins, *Problems and Process. International Law and How We Use It* (Oxford, Clarendon Press, 1994) 19; see also N Blokker, 'Is the Authorization Authorized? . . .' above n 109, 559; P Weil, 'Le droit international en quête de son identité. Cours général de droit international public', above n 140, 168; see also L Boisson de Chazournes, 'Qu'est-ce que la pratique en droit international ?', above n 140, 30–31 and M Kohen, 'La pratique et la théorie des sources du droit international', above n 158, 90.

[255] A Buchanan, 'Reforming the International Law of humanitarian intervention' in *Humanitarian Intervention. Ethical, Legal and Political Dilemmas*, above n 13, 135.

[256] O Corten et F Dubuisson, 'L'hypothèse d'une règle émergente fondant une intervention militaire sur une "autorisation implicite" du Conseil de sécurité', above n 83, 905–07.

[257] See art 45, Responsibility of States for internationally wrongful acts, annexed to GA Res 56/83 of 12 December 2001, adopted by consensus and *Report of the International Law Commission*, 53rd session, 23 April–1 June and 2 July–10 August 2001, GA, 56th session, Supp no 10 (A/56/10).

[258] TM Franck, 'Interpretation and Change in the Law of Humanitarian Intervention', above n 16, 212–15.

rules constitute violations of those rules, whereas statements in opposition do not'.[259]

Finally, in particular instances of the non-use of force, we are effectively led to apply the classical principles governing the establishment or the evolution of customary rules. These principles are, as is well-known, very demanding, particularly in the presence of a peremptory norm. It is surprising, then, that some scholars seem to contemplate the evolution of international law as regards the prohibition of the use of force less rigorously than in other areas, such as the law of the sea or diplomatic law. Such a position is difficult to explain in legal terms, and may convey more of a desire to legitimate certain interventionist policies in moral or political terms.[260] Be that as it may, it must be recognised that a particularly high degree of stringency is required in the case of the prohibition of war, the normal mode of operation remaining a change in treaty-based law, implying the implementation of onerous procedures.[261] It would be improper to insist that such procedures be followed in respect of every development, the customary mode having always been accepted as a more flexible means of adapting law to the shifting pattern of international relations. It would, however, be similarly improper to content oneself with an unlawful practice on the pretext that it was pursued or accepted by several States claiming to be representative of the international community as a whole.[262]

---

[259] M Byers and S Chesterman, 'Changing the rules about rules? Unilateral Intervention and the Future of International Law', above n 67, 188.

[260] Certain authors consider moreover that it would be inadvisable to codify the evolution of the rule on the non-use of force, though they may wish to, admitting that the majority of States are obviously not ready to accept it; JE Stromseth, 'Rethinking humanitarian intervention: the case for incremental change', above n 45, 259.

[261] See above, and the necessity of beginning with the conventional source recalled by Christine Gray. See C Gray, *International Law and the Use of Force*, 3rd edn, above n 2, 6–7.

[262] See: P Klein, 'Les problèmes soulevés par la référence à la "communauté internationale" comme facteur de légitimité' in Corten and Delcourt, *Droit, légitimation et politique extérieure: l'Europe et la guerre du Kosovo*, above n 118, 261–97.

2

What do 'Use of Force' and 'Threat of Force' mean?

ONE OF THE main debates surrounding the interpretation of article 2(4) of the UN Charter is whether the 'force' prohibited is exclusively military force, or whether it can be extended to economic, political or ideological forces. The debate was first engaged during the *travaux préparatoires* on the Charter and continued for many years thereafter, leading even to the development of major normative resolutions of the General Assembly and in particular of resolutions 2625 (XXV)[1], 3314 (XXIX)[2] and 42/22.[3] No opinion shall be given on this specific point in this book. It has been decided to examine and interpret the prohibition of the use of military force, forsaking all others. This deliberately leaves open the question of the field of application of article 2(4) in this respect. Another traditional problem is State consent to military action on its territory: does such consent preclude the characterisation of 'force' under article 2(4)? This question shall be considered in chapter five, and not in this chapter, which covers only cases where no consent is forthcoming from the State whose territory is the theatre of military action.

It remains for us, in this context, to concentrate on the actual concept of military force. Obviously there is no problem of characterisation in the standard case of one State's army entering another State's territory *en masse*. But this is not so for other instances where one may wonder whether we are confronted with a use of 'force' that might be a violation of article 2(4): the arrest of a person by the authorities of one State made in another State's territory without its knowledge; inspection of a foreign vessel by the customs authorities of a coastal State; police measures against a foreign aircraft that has entered a State's airspace without its authorisation. The same question arises in each case: are we dealing with a simple police measure, governed by specific bodies of rules (law of the sea or air law, say) or should it be considered that we are within the field of application of the prohibition of the use of military force under the UN Charter?

---

[1] *UNYB*, 1965, 627; *UNYB*, 1966, 907–08; *UNYB*, 1967, 744; *UNYB*, 1968, 826; *UNYB*, 1969, 760 and 764.
[2] *UNYB*, 1972, 652; *UNYB*, 1974, 841.
[3] *UNYB*, 1976, 107; *UNYB*, 1977, 118; *UNYB*, 1978, 170 and 172; *UNYB*, 1980, 174.

To the best of my knowledge, this question has not been examined in any depth in legal scholarship.[4] And yet there is a good deal at stake: for if such actions are enforcement measures that do not come within the ambit of article 2(4) it shall suffice to implement the specific rules applicable to the case (such as the rules governing the inspection of vessels in the various maritime zones); but otherwise we shall be working within the general legal system of *jus contra bellum* and shall have to ask, for example, whether such an inspection was justified by a situation of self-defence under article 51. Moreover, and as shall be confirmed later,[5] any circumstances precluding wrongfulness (especially distress, state of necessity or counter measures) can be validly relied on exceptionally to justify certain police operations; this is not so for the use of force in international relations.

The examples below will give a better idea of what is at stake. First we address the concept of military force as such (section one). Then we envisage the concept of the 'threat' of use of military force, which is also prohibited by article 2(4) (section two).

I What does 'Force' mean?

'Force' under article 2(4) is a broader concept than 'war', which is an especially serious form of the use of force;[6] war alone was covered by the restrictions set out in the Covenant of the League of Nations[7] or in the Pact of Paris.[8] Before the UN Charter was adopted, it was generally held that certain limited forms of the use of force were not prohibited.[9] Measures 'short of war' (which is what limited and circumscribed military operations, or targeted armed reprisals were considered to be at the time) thus remained authorised, or in any event were not prohibited by international law.[10] Again, according to the doctrine of the time, the implementation of such measures did not bring about a state of war and peacetime rules of law still prevailed.[11] One of the most fundamental aims of the UN Charter is to prohibit much more stringently not just the outbreak of 'war' but, as article 2(4)

---

[4] See: A Randelzhofer, 'Article 2(4)' in B Simma (ed), *The Charter of the United Nations. A Commentary* (Oxford, Oxford University Press, 2002) 118–19.

[5] Below, ch 4.

[6] See: J Salmon (ed), *Dictionnaire de droit international public* (Brussels, Bruylant-AUF, 2001) 595; H Rumpf, 'The Concept of Peace and War in International Law' (1984) 27 *GYIL* 429–43.

[7] See: arts 11 § 1 and 12 § 1 of the Pact.

[8] Art I, *RTSdN*, vol 94, 57.

[9] See: R Kolb, Ius contra bellum. *Le droit international relatif au Maintien de la paix*, 2nd edn (Brussels, Bruylant, Bâle-Genève-Munich, Helbing & Lichtenhahn, 2009) 23*ff*.

[10] CHM Waldock, 'The Regulation of the Use of Force by Individual States in International Law' (1952) 81 *RCADI* 467–68, 471–72 and 475–76.

[11] See: I Brownlie, *International Law and the Use of Force by States* (Oxford, Clarendon Press, 1963) 59–60.

now indicates, any use of 'force'.[12] Article 2(4), especially if read in conjunction with article 2(3) stipulating the peaceful settlement of all disputes in very general terms, clearly purports to make any pre-1945 style measures 'short of war' inadmissible. This broad conception of force has not really been called into question since. On the contrary, it was reaffirmed by several States in the debates preceding the votes on the General Assembly's major resolutions marking out the bounds of the rule prohibiting the use of force.[13] There is no doubt that article 2(4) does not cover just armed attack, a particularly serious form of the use of force, nor just the outbreak of even limited confrontations between the armies of two or more States, but that it is applicable to any military operations conducted by one state against another.

At the same time, it seems difficult to imagine that this provision covers any kind of enforcement measure having cross-border aspects. For example, where police officers of State A improperly enter the territory of State B to make an arrest, can the crossing of the border be characterised as a violation of article 2(4)? The question raises the more general issue of whether there is a threshold for distinguishing military force from a simple police measure. It shall be seen that State practice indicates there is indeed such a boundary (A), and some pointers shall be given as to how to identify the threshold more precisely (B).

A. The Boundary between Military Force and Police Measures

The dividing line between the simple police measure and the use of force against a State prohibited by the Charter can be observed in the various domains where the State exercises its competence: on land, at sea and in the air.

Military Force and Police Measures on Land

Many treaty regimes regulate inter-State coordination of enforcement measures of an extraterritorial scope. Under certain circumstances and on

---

[12] E Giraud, 'L'interdiction du recours à la force. La théorie et la pratique des Nations Unies' (1963) 67 *RGDIP* 511; P Daillier, M Forteau and A Pellet, Nguyen Quoc Dinh, *Droit international public*, 8th edn (Paris, LDGJ, 2009) 1035; A Randelzhofer, 'Use of Force' in R Bernhardt (ed), *EPIL*, vol 4 (Amsterdam, New York, Oxford, North-Holland Publishers, 1982) 267; 'Article 2(4)', above n 4, 117: SD Murphy, 'Terrorism and the Concept of "Armed Attack" in Article 51 of the UN Charter' (2002) 43 *Harvard Int Law Journal* 42.

[13] See, eg: Iran (A/C.6/SR.329, 19 November 1952, para 43), United Kingdom (A/C.6/S.R.805, 5 November 1963, para 4), Ceylan (A/C.6/S.R.805, 5 November 1963, para 21), USA (A/C.6/S.R.808, 11 November 1963, paras 14–15), Madagascar (A/AC.119/SR.9, 3 September 1964), Cyprus (A/C.6/S.R.892, 7 December 1965, para 17), Poland (A/C.6/32/SR.66, 7 December 1977, para 32), Spain (A/C.6/32/SR.67, 8 December 1977, para 113), France (*Report of the Special Committee on Enhancing the Effectiveness of the Principle of Non-Use of Force in International Relations*, A/36/41, 1981, para 145), Gabon (A/C.6/37/SR.38, 5 November 1982, para 61), Chile (A/C.6/42/SR.18, 9 October 1987, para 27).

certain terms and conditions, one State's forces of law and order are thus authorised to enter another State's territory to conduct missions that may have coercive aspects. For example, the Convention implementing the Schengen Agreement provides that police officers may, under certain conditions, carry out surveillance in the territory of another contracting State, and such officers may cross the border in pursuit of an offender, where necessary without any *ad hoc* authorisation.[14] These provisions are part of international criminal law. They plainly come within the scope of a specific treaty and are not conceived of as a derogation from or an adaptation of the rule prohibiting the use of force between States. It is hard to imagine the injured State claiming to be the victim of a violation of article 2(4) of the UN Charter for failure to observe a treaty provision of this type. At any rate, I am unaware of any such precedent. On the contrary, numerous examples attest that States feel that, in such situations, they are acting outside the scope of that provision.

We shall refer first to the precedent of the *Eichmann* case. Adolf Eichmann, one of the principal perpetrators of the 'final solution' under the Nazi regime, was abducted in Argentina on 11 or 12 May 1960 and then taken to Israel where he was tried, sentenced to death, and executed.[15] It transpires from several statements by the Israeli prime minister of the time that the action was carried out by special agents of the State of Israel,[16] even if he first claimed that no officials were involved. Upon learning of the abduction, the Argentine authorities protested to Israel, first bilaterally,[17] then before the UN Security Council. While emphasising that Eichmann had been 'removed to Israel by force'[18] and inveighing against the 'essentially coercive nature of the act',[19] the Argentine delegate to the UN never invoked article 2(4). He referred rather to a violation of his country's sovereignty[20] or an 'interference in its internal affairs'.[21] On the contrary, Argentina was cautious not to evoke any breach of the peace that would have resulted from a violation of article 2(4); it referred to Chapter VI of the Charter rather than to Chapter VII. The issue was to be analysed in those terms by the States that debated it,[22] with the Security Council adopting, upon a proposal from

---

[14] See: Arts 40 and 41 of the Convention.

[15] *Keesing's Contemporary Archives* (1960) 17489–91.

[16] *Keesing's Contemporary Archives*, ibid 17489; see also C Rousseau, 'Chronique des faits internationaux' (1960) 64 *RGDIP* 773; JES Fawcett, 'The *Eichmann* Case' (1962) 38 *BYBIL* 197.

[17] *Letter dated 15 June 1960 from the Permanent Representative of Argentina addressed to the President of the Security Council*, S/4336, 15 June 1960.

[18] S/PV.865, 22 June 1960, 5, para 26.

[19] ibid, 6, para 27.

[20] ibid, 3, para 9; 5, para 26; 7, para 34.

[21] ibid, 6, para 28; see also S/PV.868, 23 June 1960, 8, para 39.

[22] S/PV.865, 22 June 1960, 4, para 18; 9, para 19 (Israel); 13, para 68 (USSR); S/PV.867, 23 June 1960, 3, para 12 (Poland); 6, para 33; 7, para 34 (Italy); 9, para 58 (France); 13, paras 68, 72, 73, 74, and 78 (Tunisia); S/PV.868, 23 June 1960, 1, para 2; 2, para 9; 3, para 12; 6, para 12 (Ceylon); 7, paras 28 and 29 (China); cp Ecuador (S/PV.867, 23 June 1960, 9, para 48).

Argentina, a resolution that actions like Eichmann's abduction 'affect the sovereignty of a Member State'.[23] Doctrine,[24] like Israeli case law,[25] also concentrated on the question of the violation of Argentine sovereignty, seemingly without contemplating that article 2(4) might have been infringed.

More generally, practice confirms that some coercive acts by one State in the territory of another are not deemed to come under article 2(4). Several examples can be given.

—In 1986, when Swiss police pursued offenders into French territory and opened fire on them, France officially asked for explanations and Switzerland expressed its regret.[26] No one, however, thought that this 'right of pursuit', exercised without any legal title, was tantamount to the use of force as meant in the Charter.[27]

—In the *Joint Customs Post Case*, a Dutch citizen was arrested by German customs officers in the territory of the Netherlands.[28] The accused maintained before the German courts that his arrest was illegal. Düsseldorf *Oberlandesgericht* retorted that he could not rely on the circumstances of his arrest as a defence, for its potential unlawful character would follow from a violation of sovereignty of the Netherlands, and the Dutch State alone could raise such a violation.[29] No one characterises an improper arrest made in foreign territory as a use of force within the meaning of the UN Charter.

—In several cases where the accused relied on their unlawful arrest in foreign territory as a defence, the forensic debate concentrated on the question of the violation of extradition treaties between the States concerned, or on the extent of the right to a fair trial under such circumstances.[30] Violation of article 2(4), however, was not invoked.[31]

---

[23] SC Res 138 (1960) of 23 June 1960, para 1; see also *Keesing's Contemporary Archives* (1960) 17654.

[24] C Rousseau, 'Chronique des faits internationaux', above n 16, 772–86; JES Fawcett, 'The *Eichmann* Case', above n 16, 181–215; H Silving, 'In Re Eichmann: A Dilemma of Law and Morality' (1961) 55 *AJIL* 307–58; L Green, 'Aspects juridiques du procès Eichmann' (1986) 32 *AFDI* 7–52.

[25] Israel, *District Court*, 12 December 1961 (1968) 36 *ILR* 57 *ff*; *Supreme Court*, 29 May 1962, ibid, 304–08.

[26] C Rousseau, 'Chronique des faits internationaux' (1986) 90 *RGDIP* 668–70.

[27] See also: 'Canadian Practice in International Law' (1975) 13 *CYIL* 350–52; 'United Kingdom Materials on International Law' (1991) 62 *BYBIL* 553–54; 'Contemporary Practice of the United States' (1969) 63 *AJIL* 122 (cp (1990) 84 *AJIL* 725–29).

[28] (1991) 86 *ILR* 525–32.

[29] 'Such action would be a violation of the duty under international law to respect the territorial sovereignty of the other States at all times', ibid, 529. The judgment refers to a bilateral agreement between FGR and the Netherlands concerning the Merger of Customs Clearance Posts of 30 May 1958, ibid, 528–29.

[30] See: E David, *Éléments de droit pénal international*, 11th edn (Brussels, Presses Universitaires de Bruxelles, 2002–2003) 218 *ff*, paras 4.48 *ff*.

[31] But see: *United States See Toscalino*, Court of Appeals, 15 May 1974 (1981) 61 *ILR* 189 *ff*.

—Doctrine on international abductions, extraterritorial enforcement measures or international police cooperation does not generally refer to the prohibition of the use of force between States, but it too considers the problems in terms of respect of sovereignty or compliance with specific treaty-based provisions.[32]

From all of this evidence, it can be concluded that there is a threshold below which the use of force in international relations, while it may be contrary to certain rules of international law, cannot violate article 2(4). The conclusion holds not just on land but also at sea and in the air.

Military Force and Police Measures at Sea

International law of the sea includes many rules governing the implementation by States of enforcement measures against foreign vessels.[33] To give just one example, article 73(1) of the United Nations Convention on the Law of the Sea (Montego Bay Convention) stipulates that:

> The coastal State may, in the exercise of its sovereign rights to explore, exploit, conserve and manage the living resources in the exclusive economic zone, *take such measures, including boarding, inspection, arrest and judicial proceedings, as may be necessary to ensure compliance with the laws and regulations adopted by it in conformity with this Convention.* (emphasis added)[34]

Provisions of the type are found for stretches of sea other than the exclusive economic zone and extend especially from a 'right of hot pursuit',[35] to 'proportionate' measures to prevent pollution after an accident at sea,[36] or to 'powers of enforcement',[37] that may be exercised by warships or military aircraft.

These provisions, allowing the implementation of 'force' in the ordinary meaning of the term under certain circumstances, are plainly conceived of as covering a different domain of application to that of article 2(4) of the

---

[32] See, eg: FA Mann, 'Reflections on the Prosecution of Persons Abducted in Breach of International Law' in Y Dinstein (ed), *International Law in a Time of Perplexity. Essays in Honour of Shabtai Rosenne* (Dordrecht/Boston/London, Martinus Nijhoff Publishers, 1989) 408–09; V Coussirat-Coustère and PM Eisemann, 'L'enlèvement de personnes privées en droit international' (1972) 76 *RGDIP* 354; P O'Higgins, 'Unlawful Seizure and Irregular Extradition' (1960) 36 *BYBIL* 319; F Morgenstern, 'Jurisdiction in Seizures Effected in Violation of International Law' (1952) 29 *BYBIL*, 1952, 265–80; B Stern, 'Quelques observations sur les règles internationales relatives à l'application extraterritoriale du droit' (1986) 32 *AFDI* 13; 'L'extraterritorialité revisitée' (1992) 38 *AFDI* 263; F Rigaux, 'La compétence extraterritoriale des Etats', Rapport à l'Institut de droit international (1999) 68-I *AIDI* 371 ff.

[33] See: K Skubiszewski, 'Use of Force by States. Collective Security. Law of War and Neutrality' in Max Sorensen (ed), *Manual of Public International Law* (London, Macmillan, 1968) 772–73.

[34] www.un.org/Depts/los/convention_agreements/texts/unclos/closindx.htm.

[35] Art 111 of the Convention.

[36] Art 221 of the Convention.

[37] Art 224 of the Convention.

UN Charter. They seem to cover police measures applied by a State to individuals and not acts of force by one State against another.

The latter possibility is contemplated by other treaty provisions of the international law of the sea. Apart from specific provisions on the right of innocent passage,[38] defined as incompatible with any threat or use of force in violation of the principles embodied in the UN Charter, we can cite above all one of the general provisions of the Montego Bay Convention, article 301 on 'Peaceful uses of the seas':

> In exercising their rights and performing their duties under this Convention, States Parties shall refrain from any threat or use of force against the territorial integrity or political independence of any State, or in any other manner inconsistent with the principles of international law embodied in the Charter of the United Nations.[39]

Article 301 is clearly intended to confirm that article 2(4) of the UN Charter applies to acts carried out in performing the Montego Bay Convention.[40] Implementation of a right of pursuit, of a police measure or of any coercive measure cannot therefore degenerate into the use of force in international relations, at least if such use of force goes against the UN Charter.

In principle, the domains of application are separate. This should lead to an alternative in each individual instance: either we are dealing with a simple police measure and we must consider whether the action is lawful under the articles of the Montego Bay Convention pertaining specifically to it; or we are dealing with the use of force in international relations and article 301 of the Montego Bay Convention, and hence, the UN Charter should be applied.

In the first instance, the lawfulness of the measure is not to be gauged against the Charter. Article 2(4) leaves open the possibility of taking limited police measures, so long as such measures comply with the specific provisions of the aforementioned Convention. Accordingly, the use of the seas for peaceful purposes under article 301 of the Convention 'does not exclude a coastal State's right to take enforcement measures under article 73 with respect to the violation of its laws and regulations applicable in its exclusive economic zone'.[41] A mere 'enforcement measure' cannot be impugned

---

[38] Arts 19§2(a), 39§1 and 54 of the Convention.

[39] See also: Arts 88, 141 and 179 of the Convention.

[40] See: 'Article 301' in MH Nordquist *et al* (eds), Center for Oceans Law and Policy, *United Nations Convention on the Law of the Sea 1982. A Commentary*, vol V (Leiden, Martinus Nijhoff Publishers, 1989) 154–55; see also BR Tuzmukhamedov, 'The Principle of Non-Use of Force and Security at Sea' in WE Butler (ed), *The Non-Use of Force in International Law* (Dordrecht, Kluwer, 1989) 174.

[41] 'Article 88' in MH Nordquist *et al* (eds), *United Nations Convention on the Law of the Sea 1982. A Commentary*, Vol III (Leiden, Martinus Nijhoff Publishers, 1995) 92; see also GA Res 2749 of 17 December 1970.

under article 2(4) provided that it does not degenerate into 'a use of force in international relations', in which case, we would be dealing rather with the second part of the alternative.[42]

When confronted with a genuine use of force in international relations at sea, it should be evaluated in respect of the UN Charter. Use of force consistent with the Charter, in self-defence, say, is not prohibited by article 301. But it also follows from an *a contrario* reading of article 301 that such legitimate use of force cannot be characterised as a violation of the other provisions of the Montego Bay Convention. A military action of self-defence under article 51 of the UN Charter cannot therefore be characterised as contrary to article 73 or to articles 111, 220 and 224 of the Convention, for example, even if the requisite conditions for implementing police powers laid down in those provisions have not been complied with. Again, the essential point is to test whether the threshold between a police measure and the use of force in international relations has or has not been crossed. Only if it has will the UN Charter be enforced rather than the provisions of the Montego Bay Convention on simple police measures of coercion. Practice confirms that some police measures, although sometimes implemented by military means, are not considered a use of force within the meaning of the UN Charter.

The *Saiga* decision by the International Tribunal for the Law of the Sea can be cited as a precedent. On 28 October 1997, the Saiga, a vessel flying the Saint Vincent and the Grenadines flag, was arrested by Guinean patrol boats. During the operation at least two crew members were injured.[43] Saint Vincent and the Grenadines, complaining of being 'attacked',[44] did not invoke article 301 of the Montego Bay Convention or article 2(4) of the UN Charter, or more generally the rule prohibiting the use of force in international relations. The plaintiff State invoked instead a violation of its freedom of navigation (Convention articles 56(2) and 58), of the conditions of the right of pursuit (Convention article 111) and of the rules on prompt release (Convention article 292).[45] In its judgment of 1 July 1999, the Tribunal evoked neither article 301 of the Convention nor the UN Charter in evaluating the lawfulness of the alleged attack. In a part of its decision specifically on the 'Use of force',[46] the Tribunal stated:

---

[42] According to a Report of the Secretary General of the UN, 'a distinction should be made in maritime waters between the use of force in self-defense and the lawful use of force to enforce jurisdiction, which has assumed "particular importance in the law of the sea"'; 'Article 301' in MH Nordquist *et al* (eds), *United Nations Convention on the Law of the Sea 1982. A Commentary*, vol V, above n 40, 155, fn 2.

[43] ITLOS, *The MV Saiga (Saint Vincent and the Grenadines v Guinea)*, Judgment of 4 December 1997, para 30; www.itlos.org.

[44] ITLOS, *The MV Saiga (Saint Vincent and the Grenadines v Guinea)*, Judgment of 1 July 1999, paras 28 and 33; see also the 4 December 1997 Judgment, above n 43, para 35.

[45] ITLOS, *The MV Saiga (Saint Vincent and the Grenadines v Guinea)*, Judgment of 1 July 1999, above n 44, para 28.

[46] ibid, subtitle preceding para 153.

1. In considering the force used by Guinea in the arrest of the Saiga, the Tribunal must take into account the circumstances of the arrest in the context of the applicable rules of international law. Although the Convention does not contain express provisions on the use of force in the arrest of ships, international law, which is applicable by virtue of article 293 of the Convention, requires that the use of force must be avoided as far as possible and, where force is unavoidable, it must not go beyond what is reasonable and necessary in the circumstances. Considerations of humanity must apply in the law of the sea, as they do in other areas of international law. These principles have been followed over the years in law enforcement operations at sea.[47]

Thus, even if it considers that no specific provision of the Montego Bay Convention governs the use of force of the type observed in the case at hand, the Tribunal does not refer to the general prohibition of the use of force in international relations under the Charter, but to a customary rule governing police operations at sea. The Tribunal further specifies that, under this rule, inspectors must avoid the use of force

except when and to the degree necessary to ensure the safety of the inspectors and where the inspectors are obstructed in the execution of their duties. The degree of force used shall not exceed that reasonably required in the circumstances.[48]

It was on this basis that the Tribunal dismissed Guinea's claims[49] and held that 'excessive' force was employed in the circumstances.[50]

This case law is far from isolated. In the *Red Crusader* case, a British vessel was arrested in Danish territorial waters by the Danish authorities in the course of an operation in which shots were fired. The international commission of enquiry set up as a result of the event considered that:

In opening fire at 03.22 hours up to 03.53 hours, the commanding officer of the Niels Ebbesen exceeded legitimate use of armed force on two counts: (a) firing without warning of solid gun-shot; (b) creating danger to human life on board the Red Crusader without proved necessity, by the effective firing at the Red Crusader after 03.40 hours.[51]

When the 'use of armed force' is applied here, there is plainly no question of applying article 2(4) of the UN Charter.

In the *Torrey Canyon* case, facing the threat of an unprecedented oil spillage, the UK authorities decided to bomb the wreck of a Liberian vessel that had run aground outside of British territorial waters in March 1967.[52] The operation, conducted by the RAF, lasted several days with

---

[47] ibid, paras 155–156; see also art 293 of the Convention.
[48] ibid, para 156.
[49] Von Brevern, 16 March 1999, ITLOS, PV.99/15 (www.itlos.org). Guinea did not mention Charter art 2(4).
[50] ITLOS, Judgment of 1 July 1999, above n 44, paras 157, 158 and 159.
[51] Judgment of 23 May 1962 (1967) 35 *ILR* 499.
[52] *Keesing's Contemporary Archives* (1967) 22.002–005.

napalm bombs being dropped on the wreck to release and burn the oil remaining in the ship's tanks.[53] Despite the scale of the military means used by a State to bomb a vessel outside of its territorial waters, significantly no-one claimed the operation was contrary to, or consistent with, article 2(4).[54] Debates turned instead on the lawfulness of police measures on the high seas, whether under a specific rule or because of a potential state of necessity.[55] This precedent largely inspired the development of special treaty rules authorising police measures to prevent pollution risks.[56]

Case law[57] and practice[58] therefore confirm the existence of two separate bodies of rules that can apply to the use of force: one governs police measures, pursuant to certain treaty-based or customary rules of the law of the sea (right of pursuit, reasonable use of force during inspections or operations to prevent serious marine pollution, etc.); the other relates to armed action by one State against another State, a matter covered by the relevant provisions of the UN Charter. One commentator concludes a study on the use of force in the law of the sea:

> With respect to the territorial sea, internal waters, and the EEZ, one must distinguish between use of force in the pursuit of 'police powers' and the 'transborder' use of force under article 2(4) of the Charter. Many of the precedents reviewed indicate that coastal States' action in repelling or arresting foreign intruders represents an exercise of police power which does not constitute prima facie violation of article 2(4) of the Charter. At the same time, the legality of such must be judged in light of the general principles of necessity and proportionality.[59]

Again on this point one may consult certain work by the UN General Assembly on defining aggression, and more specifically its article 3*(d)* of the Definition of Aggression annexed to Resolution 3314 (XXIX). As shall be seen in detail below, several States have been eager to exclude from the

---

[53] ibid, 22003.

[54] C Rousseau, 'Chronique des faits internationaux' (1967) 71 *RGDIP* 1092–99.

[55] See also: M Flory, 'L'incidence de l'affaire du Torrey Canyon sur le droit de la mer' (1968) 14 *AFDI* 701–18.

[56] See: International Convention on the Intervention in the High Seas (970 *UNTS* 211) and United Nations Convention on the Law of the Sea (Article 221).

[57] See also: *I'm Alone* Judgment: '[. . .] the United States might, consistently with the Convention, use necessary and reasonable force for the purpose of effecting the objects of boarding, searching, seizing and bringing into port the suspected vessel; and if sinking should occur incidentally, as a result of necessary and reasonable force for such purpose, the pursuing vessel might be entirely blameless. But the Commissioners think that, on the circumstances [. . .], the admittedly intentional sinking of the suspected vessel was not justified by anything in the Convention' (*RIAA*, vol III, 1617).

[58] See the *Amoco Cadiz* incident (C Rousseau, 'Chronique des faits internationaux' (1978) 82 *RGDIP* 1125–51) and other cases in C Rousseau, 'Chronique des faits internationaux' (1982) 86 *RGDIP* 150–52.

[59] F Francioni, 'Use of Force, Military Activities, and the New Law of the Sea' in A Cassese (ed), *The Current Legal Regulation of the Use of Force* (Dordrecht/Boston/Lancaster, Martinus Nijhoff Publishers, 1986) 377.

definition of aggression the case of police measures by a coastal State to enforce its laws and regulations within its territorial waters.

Similarly, when led to envisage examples of situations of extreme distress, the International Law Commission mentioned a practice by which certain vessels improperly entered another State's territorial waters.[60] This practice was contemplated in the context of specific rules of the law of the sea and not of article 2(4).

Ultimately, there is little doubt that a distinction can be drawn between the case of simple police measures and that of true use of force in international relations. This distinction, already seen on land, can also be found in the air.

Military Force and Police Measures in the Air

Two bodies of rules must be distinguished in international air law: those pertaining to air safety and those referring to the use of force within the meaning of the UN Charter. As in the law of the sea, there are certain treaty-based or customary provisions that specifically set forth the conditions for exercising police measures which, at least if a certain threshold is not crossed, cannot be likened to a use of force in international relations. We are thinking here of rules governing the interception or even neutralising of aircraft entering a State's airspace in violation of its sovereignty.[61]

State sovereignty over its air space[62] first entails a very extensive right for intruding military-type aircraft, a right that may imply opening fire after giving due warning.[63] It is immediately obvious that this is a fundamentally different case from the legal prohibition of the use of force between States. In the latter case, a military aircraft could not be shot down unless one could prove one had Security Council authorisation or was acting in self-defence. Under article 51 of the UN Charter, this would imply prior armed attack, which is difficult to compare with the entry, albeit unlawfully, of a single aircraft into a State's air space.[64] Now, if the measures taken against an intruding aircraft are considered police measures for air security, we are referred on to other conditions of lawfulness: prior warning, unless there is a manifest hostile intent, necessary and proportionate measure, or riposte in self-defence. This, however, is understood here not as the riposte to an armed attack by another State but as a more specific defensive action

---

[60] See, eg: (1979) *YILC* vol II, Part Two, 134–35, paras 6–7, and *Report of the International Law Commission*, 53rd session, 23 April–1st June and 2 July–10 August 2001, GA, 56th session, Supp no 10 (A/56/10), 79, para 3.

[61] See: K Skubiszewski, 'Use of Force by States. Collective Security. Law of War and Neutrality', above n 33, 773–74.

[62] See, eg: Article 1 of the Chicago Convention on International Civil Aviation (www.icao.int/cgi/goto_m.pl?/icaonet/dcs/7300.html) and M de Juglart, *Traité de droit aérien*, 2nd edn (with E du Pontavice, J Dutheil de la Rochère and GM Miller) (Paris, LGDJ, 1989) 585 *ff*.

[63] K-G Park, *La protection de la souveraineté aérienne* (Paris, Pedone, 1991) 315.

[64] Below, ch 7.

by one aircraft that is under attack or threat from another.[65] Likewise, if, in airspace under no one's jurisdiction, an aircraft responds to shots, the lawfulness of the response will not depend on proving a prior armed attack by one State against another under article 51 of the UN Charter. Here we are dealing with a separate body of rules and the 'self-defence' in question must be interpreted specifically in terms of that body of rules.

This also covers rules on intercepting not only military but also civil aircraft. Under article 3bis (a) of the Chicago Convention on International Civil Aviation (Chicago Convention):

> The contracting States recognize that every State must refrain from resorting to the use of weapons against civil aircraft in flight and that, in case of interception, the lives of persons on board and the safety of aircraft must not be endangered. This provision shall not be interpreted as modifying in any way the rights and obligations of States set forth in the Charter of the United Nations.[66]

This final sentence may be construed as confirming that there are two separate domains of application.[67] In the case of a simple police measure, it is possible to intercept a civil aircraft, but in no event to open fire, except, for some scholars, under certain circumstance akin to a state of necessity.[68] If, on the contrary, one is dealing with a genuine use of force in international relations coming within the scope of the UN Charter, the applicable rules are different: *jus contra bellum* and, of course, *jus in bello*, with the latter ruling out civilian targets.

This distinction between two bodies of rules can be illustrated by certain precedents.[69]

Especially emblematic in this respect are the reactions to the tragedy of KAL flight 007 on 1 September 1983. This Korean aircraft had illegally entered Soviet airspace and was shot down by fighters that apparently thought it was a spy plane, resulting in the deaths of the 269 passengers and crew.[70] This serious incident immediately prompted complaints from Korea and other States with citizens on board.[71] It then gave rise to several days of heated debate in the Security Council, debates in which no fewer than 51 Member and invited non-Member States spoke out.[72] Save an

---

[65] See K-G Park, *La protection de la souveraineté aérienne*, above n 63, 316 and 334–38.

[66] www.icao.int/cgi/goto_m.pl?/icaonet/dcs/7300.html.

[67] K-G Park, *La protection de la souveraineté aérienne*, above n 63, 335–38.

[68] ibid, 336–38.

[69] See also: OL Lissitzyn, 'The Treatment of Aerial Intruders in Recent Practice and International Law' (1953) 47 *AJIL* 559–89.

[70] *Keesing's Contemporary Archives* (1983) 32513–17 and C Rousseau, 'Chronique des faits internationaux' (1984) 88 *RGDIP* 435–48.

[71] USA (S/15947, 1 September 1983), South Korea (S/15948, 1 September 1983), Canada (S/15949, 1 September 1983), Japan (S/15950, 2 September 1983) and Australia (S/15951, 2 September 1983); see (1983) 22 *ILM* 1109–13.

[72] S/PV.2470, 2 September 1983; S/PV.2471 and corr 1, 6 September 1983; S/PV.2472, 6 September 1983; S/PV.2473, 7 September 1983; S/PV.2474, 8 September 1983 and S/PV.2476, 12 September 1983.

indirect allusion early on in the discussions,[73] none of the States invoked article 2(4) the UN Charter prohibiting the use of force in international relations. The rules invoked in criticising the Soviet action were essentially either general principles such as considerations of humanity[74] or the principle or proportionality,[75] or the specific rules of the Chicago Convention and more especially its annex 2 that sets out precisely the procedure to take in intercepting a civil aircraft.[76] In the draft resolution presented by 17 States, but that was not passed because of the 'no' vote of the USSR, the Council declared that 'such use of armed force against international civil aviation is incompatible with the norms governing international behaviour and elementary considerations of humanity',[77] without ever referring to article 2(4).[78] Nor was this evoked in the subsequent reports by the ICAO or in the resolutions it passed.[79] This incident was to prompt the drafting of article 3bis of the Chicago Convention, mentioned above, laying down the specific legal rules for intercepting civil aircraft.[80]

The same lessons can be learned from examining the aftermath of the Cuban air forces' destruction of two civil aircraft on 24 February 1996 causing four deaths.[81] This incident was widely condemned but no State seems to have invoked article 2(4) of the UN Charter. Cuba not being party to the Chicago Convention, the States preferred to invoke a customary practice codified by article 3bis of that Convention, as illustrated by the statement made on behalf of the Security Council on 27 February 1996,[82] and then the Security Council resolution that:

---

[73] USA, S/PV.2470, 2 September 1983, para 39; comp S/PV.2471 and corr 1, 6 September 1983, para 18). In its letter addressed to the Security Council, the representative of the USA stated that 'this action by the Soviet Union violates the fundamental legal norms and standards of international civil aviation [. . .] this unprovoked resort to the use of force by the Soviet military authorities in contravention of international civil aviation organization standards and the basic norms of international law must be deplored and condemned [. . .]' (S/15947, 1 September 1983).

[74] USA, S/PV.2470, 2 September 1983, para 38.

[75] Canada, S/PV.2470, 2 September 1983, para 79.

[76] USA, S/PV.2470, 2 September 1983, para 39; Japan, ibid, para 64.

[77] Para 2. In its preamble, the project emphasises 'the rules of international law that prohibit acts of violence which pose a threat to the safety of international civil aviation', S/15966/Rev.1, 12 September 1983.

[78] See: (1983) 22 *ILM* 1148.

[79] See: (1983) 22 *ILM* 1149 *ff* and (1984) 23 *ILM* 864 *ff*. See also 'Canadian Practice in International Law' (1984) 22 *CYIL* 333–36; 'United Kingdom Materials on International Law' (1983) 54 *BYBIL* 534.

[80] See, eg: JC Piris, 'L'interdiction du recours à la force contre les aéronefs civils : l'amendement de 1984 à la Convention de Chicago' (1984) 30 *AFDI* 711–32; GF Fitzgerald, 'The Use of Force against Civil Aircraft: The Aftermath of the KAL Flight 007 Incident' (1984) 22 *CYIL* 296 *ff*; F Hassan, 'The Shooting Down of Korean Airlines Flight 007 by the USSR and the Future of Air Safety for Passengers' (1984) 33 *ICLQ* 712–25; but cp (1984) *UNYB* 1089.

[81] *Keesing's Contemporary Archives* (1996) 40945.

[82] 'The Security Council recalls that according to international law, as reflected in Article 3 bis of the International Convention on Civil Aviation of 7 December 1944 added by the

Notes that the unlawful shooting down by the Cuban Air Force of two civil air-craft on 24 February 1996 *violated the principle that States must refrain from the use of weapons against civil aircraft in flight and that, when intercepting civil aircraft, the lives of persons on board and the safety of the aircraft must not be endangered.* (emphasis added)[83]

The law applicable to this type of use of force relates to specific rules of international air law and not to UN Charter provisions prohibiting the use of force between States.[84] The conclusion is clearer still if we examine the debates that preceded the adoption of this resolution. The States evoke 'international legal standards governing civil aviation',[85] 'ICAO standards',[86] the 'principles and norms of the Chicago Convention',[87] 'established international procedures on interception of such aircraft',[88] 'the standards and recommended practices set down in the Chicago Convention and its annexes',[89] 'the provisions of international law on the non-use of weapons against civil aircraft',[90] 'the principles recognized in customary international law regarding the non-use of weapons against civil aircraft',[91] the rules 'codified in the Protocol adding article 3 *bis* to the Convention on International Civil Aviation',[92] and other similar expressions.[93] As for Cuba, it did not invoke, for example, self-defence within the meaning of article 51 of the UN Charter.[94] In claiming that it merely ensured its security against aircraft that were in fact on military type missions, Cuba plainly admitted that it was the specific rules governing police measures in its airspace that were applicable.

This is far from being an isolated precedent. There are many incidents where civil or sometimes military aircraft have been shot down and sharp protests issued without article 2(4) being evoked. These include:

—The aerial incident of 7 October 1952 in which a Soviet fighter allegedly attacked a US Air Force B-29 gave rise to official protests and an application instituting proceedings before the International Court of Justice. Those documents do not mention article 2(4), but the 'international

---

Montreal Protocol of 10 May 1984, States must refrain from the use of weapons against civil aircraft in flight and must not endanger the lives of persons on board and the safety of aircraft. States are obliged to respect international law and human rights norms in all circumstances' (S/PRST/1996/9, 27 February 1996).

[83] SC Res 1067 (1996) of 26 July 1996, para 2.
[84] See also: Canada, 'Canadian Practice in International Law' (1996) 34 *CYIL* 419.
[85] USA, S/PV.3683, 26 July 1996, 2.
[86] ibid.
[87] Colombia, ibid, 14.
[88] United Kingdom, ibid, 16.
[89] ibid.
[90] China, ibid, 17.
[91] Honduras, ibid, 18.
[92] France, ibid, 25.
[93] See, eg: Germany, ibid, 17.
[94] ibid, 4–13.

obligations relating to the overflight of intruding and intercepting military aircraft'.[95]

—On 10 March 1953, Czechoslovakian military aircraft illegally entered the airspace of the Federal Republic of Germany, over the US zone of occupation; the aircraft allegedly destroyed a US military aircraft. The US made an application to the Court, invoking primarily the 'international obligations relating to the overflight of intruding military aircraft, embodied in part in the Convention of International Civil Aviation'.[96] This wording was used by the US in other similar instances.[97]

—On 1 May 1960, a US military aircraft of the U2 type entered Soviet airspace without authorisation to collect information and was shot down by Red Army units.[98] The USRR raised the matter in the Security Council, qualifying the incident, related to others of the same type observed before and with the general policy of the United States as an 'aggressive act'.[99] This very general expression was not, though, officially associated with a violation of article 2(4);[100] the Soviet Union[101] like Poland[102] preferring, in legal terms, to evoke a violation of the Chicago Convention or of territorial sovereignty. The very large majority of States preferred to emphasise the limited scope of the incident that was likened to a simple spying operation that 'involved no use of force or threat of the use of force against the Soviet Union'.[103]

One final illustration should be given at this point. In its work on certain circumstances precluding wrongfulness such as *force majeure* or extreme distress, the International Law Commission has systematically evoked the case of an aircraft compelled to enter another State's airspace without its

[95] Application instituting proceedings, 26 May 1955; ICJ, *Aerial Incident of October 7th 1952 (USA v USSR), Pleadings, Oral Arguments, Documents*, ICJ Rep (1956) 9.

[96] Application instituting proceedings, 22 March 1955; ICJ, *Aerial Incident of March 7th 1952 (USA v Czechoslovakia), Pleadings, Oral Arguments, Documents*, ICJ Rep (1956) 8.

[97] Application instituting proceedings, 25 July 1958, ICJ, *Aerial Incident of 4 September 1954 (USA v USSR), Pleadings, Oral Arguments, Documents*, 9; Application instituting proceedings, 8 June 1959, ICJ, *Aerial Incident of 7 November 1954 (USA v USSR), Pleadings, Oral Arguments, Documents*, 1959, 9; ICJ, *Aerial Incident of 27 July 1955 (Israel v Bulgaria, USA v Bulgaria, United Kingdom v Bulgaria), Pleadings, Oral Arguments, Documents*, 959, 22; see also applications of Israel (ibid, 5 *ff*) and the United Kingdom (ibid, 34 *ff*) and S/PV.679, 10 September 1954 and S/PV.680, 10 September 1954.

[98] See: Q Wright, 'Legal Aspects of the U-2 Incident' (1960) 54 *AJIL* 836–54; OJ Lissitzyn, 'Some Legal Implications of the U-2 and RB-47 Incidents' (1962) 56 *AJIL* 135–42.

[99] S/PV. 857, 23 May 1960, 4, para 18 and S/4321.

[100] cp *Repertoire of the Practice of the Security Council*, Supp no 3 (1959–1966), vol 1 Article 2(4) (Separate Study), paras 44–52; *Repertoire of the Practice of the Security Council (Supp 1959–1963)*, 281–83.

[101] S/PV. 857, 23 May 1960, para 53, S/PV.860, 26 May 1960, paras 2, 31, and 50.

[102] S/PV.858, 24 May 1960, paras 83 and 85; see also Tunisia (S/PV.859, 25 May 1960, para 4) and Ceylon (ibid, paras 52–53).

[103] United Kingdom (S/PV.858, 24 May 1960, 5, para 25); see also USA (S/PV.857, 23 May 1960, para 106), France (S/PV.858, 24 May 1960, paras 9–11), Argentina (ibid, para 50), or China (ibid, para 64).

authorisation. For the Commission, such entry may be justified either by *force majeure*, if unintentional (in the case of violent winds leaving the pilot no other option), or by extreme distress, if justified by the compelling need to save the lives of those on board. From a reading of the many precedents mentioned, it can be observed that neither article 2(4) nor more generally the prohibition of the use of force between States, is invoked by the States concerned.[104] They rely instead on specific rules for aviation and it is in that context that they contemplate the scope of a possible excuse of *force majeure* or distress, in view of all the circumstance of the case. The States that refuse to accept such excuses in any particular case complain of violations of their sovereignty and not of the use of force or of armed attack. It is plainly along these lines that the Commission has conducted its work.[105] The Commission's reasoning is particularly logical because it has clearly specified that a peremptory rule such as the prohibition of the use of force cannot be avoided by circumstances precluding wrongfulness.[106]

Given all these points, it can be concluded that the exercising of police powers in airspace is governed by special regulations referring to specific conditions such as for interception,[107] approach, identification, communication, ordering to land, escort by military aircraft or for firing, warning, exhaustion of all means, necessity, and so on.[108] These regulations on the use of force are, then, fundamentally different from those on the use of force in international relations within the meaning of the UN Charter. And if it is accepted that article 2(4) sets out a peremptory rule of international law,[109] obviously it cannot be considered that the principles of the Chicago Convention form a sort of *lex specialis* derogating from it. A distinction must be made rather between the two types of rule depending on the type of action in question, whether a simple police measure in the first instance, or an act of force in international relations in the second. Even if State practice[110] and doctrine[111] are not always unambiguous on this point, it can be said generally that this alternative reflects the current state of international law.

---

[104] See, eg: *'Force majeure' and 'fortuitous event' as circumstances precluding wrongfulness: survey of State practice, international judicial decisions and doctrine*, Study prepared by the Secretariat, A/CN.4/315, 27 June 1977, *YILC* (1978) vol II, Part One, 103–04, paras 143–53; *YILC* (1979) vol II, Part Two, 125–26, paras 12–15.

[105] See, eg: ibid, 122–23, para 3, fn 613, 124, para 4, fn 615 and para 7, note 617: *Second report on State responsibility*, James Crawford, 30 April 1999, A/CN.4/498/Add.2, 21, para 252, 21–22, para 266; *Report of the International Law Commission*, A/56/10, 2001, 77, para 5, and 78–79, para 2.

[106] See below, ch 4.

[107] See K-G Park, *La protection de la souveraineté aérienne*, above n 63, 294–96.

[108] ibid, 302–03.

[109] Below, ch 4.

[110] See, eg: S/PV.679, 10 September 1954 and S/PV.680, 10 September 1954.

[111] JC Piris, 'L'interdiction du recours à la force contre les aéronefs civils: l'amendement de 1984 à la Convention de Chicago', above n 80, 712; IL Jahn, 'Applying International Law to the Downing of KAL 007 on September 1, 1983', (1984) 27 *GYIL* 448 and 451–53.

The conclusion just drawn is valid for all the domains where State competence is exercised, whether on land, at sea or in the air.[112] In each domain, there is a threshold below which the use of force cannot be considered to be covered by the rule set out in article 2(4) of the Charter.[113] It remains to be seen, once this has been established, how this threshold is determined.

B. Determining the Threshold: 'Force' within the Meaning of Article 2(4) of the Charter

Setting aside the specific features of the domains covered—whether land, sea or air—all of the examples presented have something in common: they were coercive acts of limited scope. The arrest of a criminal abroad, the inspection of a vessel that had broken the laws of a coastal State, the interception of an aircraft that had unduly entered a State's airspace are all police measures which *a priori* quite understandably are not considered in terms of the prohibition of the use of force between States. However, it cannot be deduced from the foregoing that this rule is inapplicable in *all* situations where such actions are observed. It seems obvious that article 2(4) of the UN Charter is applicable to an arrest made by the army of State A by means of an invasion of State B, to an inspection in the territorial waters of State A by several warships of State B that have opened fire on a massive scale, or the entry into a State's airspace without its consent of not one but fifty or so military aircraft. The threshold above which a situation can be characterised as a use of force plainly does not depend on the action *in abstracto*, but involves other criteria that we shall now examine.

Generally, it can be considered that the applicability of article 2(4) presupposes a use of force by one State against another and not just a simple police operation by one State against individuals who allegedly broke its laws. If an aircraft unduly enters the airspace of a State that decides to shoot it down, the relationship opposes the State whose domestic legal order has been violated and the person or persons responsible for the violation. However, if an entire air force squadron of one State crosses the border of another State, it can be considered that we are now dealing with interstate relations with one State attacking another.

---

[112] See also: 'Canadian Practice in International Law' (1987) 25 *CYIL* 419–20.

[113] Independent International Fact-Finding Mission on the Conflict in Georgia, *Report*, September 2009 (www.ceiig.ch/Report.html), vol II, 242 and fn 49. According to the Commission 'The prohibition of the use of force covers all physical force which surpasses a minimum threshold of intensity'; 'Only very small incidents lie below this threshold, for instance the targeted killing of single individuals, forcible abductions of individual persons, or the interception of a single aircraft'. See also Institut de droit international Resolution on Self-defence, 27 October 2007, Santiago Session (www.idi-iil.org/idiE/navig_chon2003.html), para 5 and my comments in O Corten, 'Les résolutions de l'Institut de droit international sur la légitime défense et sur les actions humanitaires' (2007) 40 *RBDI* 598–613.

To better understand how we move from one situation to the other, two criteria can be combined. The first is objective and pertains to the gravity of the action. The second is more subjective and assumes that a State wishes to compel another State to do or refrain from doing something. These two criteria are set out in detail below. As shall be observed, the one cannot readily be contemplated without the other: the gravity of the action merely reflects the intention of one State to attack another. Thirdly, we shall set out the problematic case of 'targeted' military operations (3), which will allow us to refine the two general criteria of gravity (1) and intent (2).

Gravity of the Coercive Act

The criterion of gravity seems the easiest to grasp at first sight. One need only compare the abduction of Adolf Eichmann in Argentina in 1960 with the abduction of General Noriega in Panama in 1989. The first is a classic example of an improper abduction in breach of the State's sovereignty, without article 2(4) being invoked.[114] The second was carried out subsequent to the invasion of the State of Panama and no one denied that the lawfulness of the action had to be considered in the context of the prohibition of the use of force.[115] An abduction may or may not be covered by the rule, depending on how serious it is.

This criterion of gravity was brought out in the debates preceding the adoption of resolution 3314 (XXIX) defining aggression, and especially those on the wording finally adopted in its article 3(d) which gives as an example of aggression 'an attack by the armed forces of a State on the land, sea or air forces of another State'.

Many States expressed concern about this wording insofar as it could be construed as compromising or diminishing the authority of a coastal State in exercising its rights over the maritime zones under its national jurisdiction.[116] Every State has a sovereign right to ensure its security by taking whatever measures are required to arrest and seize, using armed force if necessary, vessels entering its territorial waters or aircraft entering its airspace.[117] Many States made pronouncements to this effect,[118] some asking

---

[114] Above, s IA.
[115] See, eg: GA Res 44/240 of 29 December 1989.
[116] See, eg: Canada; A/C.6/SR.1473, 10 October 1974, para 12.
[117] Philippines (A/C.6/SR.1482, 22 October 1974, para 17); see also A/C.6/SR.1482, 22 October 1974, para 19) and Mali (A/C.6/SR.1480, 18 October 1974, para 8).
[118] Ecuador (A/C.6/SR.1476, 15 October 1974, para 3), Indonesia (A/C.6/SR.1442, 20 November 1973, para 51), Peru (A/C.6/SR.1474, 11 October 1974, para 8), Chile (A/C.6/SR.1474, 11 October 1974, para 20), Madagascar (A/C.6/SR.1474, 11 October 1974, para 37), Brazil (A/C.6/SR.1474, 11 October 1974, para 50), Colombia (A/C.6/SR.1474, 11 October 1974, para 58), China (A/C.6/SR.1475, 14 October 1974, para 15), New Zealand (A/C.6/SR.1475, 14 October 1974, para 25), Pakistan (A/C.6/SR.1477, 15 October 1974, para 2), Libya (A/C.6/SR.1477, 15 October 1974, para 15), Argentina (A/C.6/SR.1477, 15 October 1974, para 31), Bangladesh (A/C.6/SR.1478, 16 October 1974, para 3), Iraq (A/C.6/SR.1478, 16 October 1974, para 12), Australia (A/C.6/SR.1478, 16 October 1974,

that a motion reflecting their position be added.[119] From reading their declarations, it is clear that police measures by a State in exercising its sovereign rights cannot be likened either to an aggression or more generally to the use of force in international relations within the meaning of article 2(4).[120] It is the criterion of the gravity of the action that is cited foremost as being decisive for distinguishing between police measures and the use of force.[121] It was decided in the end to include an explanatory footnote without altering the wording of the definition.[122] In substance, no one claims that police measures can be characterised as a use of force in international relations, unless such measures are so serious that it must be considered that the threshold has been crossed.[123]

The criterion of the gravity of the action may, however, give rise to certain difficulties, as illustrated by several cases brought before the International Court of Justice or arbitral tribunals.

The first that comes to mind is the *Corfu Channel* case, which some commentators have deemed a relevant precedent for interpreting article 2(4), on the grounds that the Court had adjudicated on the lawfulness of the military operation conducted by the United Kingdom in Albanian territorial waters.[124] Yet the Court never cites this provision, nor generally the prohi-

para 30), India (A/C.6/SR.1478, 16 October 1974, para 47), Sri Lanka (A/C.6/SR.1478, 16 October 1974, para 57), Guatemala (A/C.6/SR.1479, 18 October 1974, para 24), Yemen (A/C.6/SR.1479, 18 October 1974, para 27), Iran (A/C.6/SR.1480, 18 October 1974, para 14), Ghana (A/C.6/SR.1480, 18 October 1974, para 26), Panama (A/C.6/SR.1482, 22 October 1974, para 2), Tunisia (A/C.6/SR.1482, 22 October 1974, para 24), Costa Rica (A/C.6/SR.1482, 22 October 1974, para 30), Dahomey (A/C.6/SR.1482, 22 October 1974, para 41), El Salvador (A/C.6/SR.1483, 23 October 1974, para 1), Cameroon (A/C.6/SR.1483, 23 October 1974, para 13), Sierra Leone (A/C.6/SR.1483, 23 October 1974, para 23), Guinea (A/C.6/SR.1483, 23 October 1974, para 25), and Egypt (A/C.6/SR.1483, 23 October 1974, para 31).

[119] Kenya (A/C.6/SR.1474, 11 October 1974, para 24), Senegal (A/C.6/SR.1480, 18 October 1974, para 17), Venezuela (A/C.6/SR.1483, 23 October 1974, para 18), Peru (A/C.6/SR.1483, 23 October 1974, para 39).

[120] See, however, ambiguous statements by Togo (A/C.6/SR.1480, 18 October 1974, para 31), Uruguay (A/C.6/SR.1482, 22 October 1974, para 13) and Hungary (A/C.6/SR.1478, 16 October 1974, para 39).

[121] See: Ghana (A/C.6/SR.1442, 20 November 1973, para 65), Japan (A/C.6/SR.1443, 20 November 1973, para 23), Syria (A/C.6/SR.1475, 14 October 1974, para 20), United Kingdom (A/C.6/SR.1477, 15 October 1974, para 21).

[122] 'La Sixième Commission est convenue que rien dans la définition de l'agression, et en particulier l'alinéa de l'article 3, ne pourra être interprété comme portant préjudice en aucune manière au pouvoir d'un Etat d'exercer ses droits dans les limites de sa juridiction nationale, à condition que l'exercice de ces droits ne soit pas incompible avec la Charte des Nations Unies' (A/C.6/SR.1502, 20 November 1974, 235, para 10; see also A/C.6/SR.1503, 21 November 1974, 239).

[123] See: Belgium (A/C.6/SR.1475, 14 October 1974, para 25), GDR (A/C.6/SR.1476, 15 October 1974, para 17), Yemen (A/C.6/SR.1482, 22 October 1974, para 38) or Japan (A/PV.2319, 14 December 1974, para 91).

[124] See, eg: B Asrat, *Prohibition of Force under the UN Charter. A Study of Article 2(4)* (Uppsala, Iustus Förlag, 1991) 121–24; CHM Waldock, 'The Regulation of the Use of Force by Individual States in International Law', above n 10, 500–01 and R Jennings, 'International Force and the International Court of Justice' in A Cassese (ed), *The Current Legal Regulation of the Use of Force* (Dordrecht/Boston/Lancaster, Martinus Nijhoff Publishers, 1986) 331–33.

bition of the use of force in international relations.[125] It is true that the second question of the settlement was confined to the issue of possible violation by the UK of 'the sovereignty of the Albanian People's Republic by reason of the acts of the Royal Navy in Albanian waters'.[126] But beyond this circumstance related to the scope of the Court's jurisdiction, it can be asked whether the very targeted character of the Royal Navy's action was not a factor explaining why the Court confined itself to evoking observance of territorial sovereignty and not the principle of the use of force.[127] It can be noted that this rule was never invoked in the Security Council, which dealt with the question in several sessions, whether by Albania or by the other States that spoke on the matter, the general tone being rather to treat the whole series of events as constituting a simple incident.[128] It was only when the matter was before the Court that Albania furtively cited article 2(4) in support of its claim,[129] characterising the UK military operation as an effective invasion followed by a temporary occupation of its territorial waters.[130] The UK for its part rejected the applicability of the rule prohibiting the use of force, emphasising the limited character of its action, which, while coercive, 'did not force on Albania any acceptance of a new state of things',[131] and characterising its operation as the simple 'sweeping of a strait for mines against the will of Albania'.[132] In its judgment, the Court ruled that the mine-sweeping operation had been carried out in violation of Albania's sovereignty, while specifying that it 'does not consider that the action of the British Navy was a demonstration of force for the purpose of exercising political pressure on Albania'.[133] In stating this, the Court suggests that the British operation was not serious enough to come under the prohibition of

---

[125] cp Judge Alvarez, separate opinion, (ICJ Rep (1949) 42 and 47), Judge Krylov, dissenting opinion (ibid, 76–77), Judge Azevedo, dissenting opinion (ibid, 108), Judge Ecer, dissenting opinion (ibid, 130–31). Albany was not party to the UN Charter, as recalled by I Brownlie, *International Law and the Use of Force by States*, above n 11, 288–89; see also RJ Wilhelm, 'La réalisation du droit par la force ou la menace des armes (considérations sur l'arrêt de la Cour internationale de Justice en l'affaire du Détroit de Corfou)' (1958) 15 *ASDI* 105–07 and 128.

[126] ICJ, *Corfu Channel*, ICJ Rep (1949) 6.

[127] G Palmisano, 'Determining the Law on the Use of Force: the ICJ and Customary Rules on the Use of Force' in E Cannizaro and P Palchetti (eds), *Customary International Law On the Use of Force* (Leiden/Boston, Martinus Nijhoff, 2005) 199.

[128] See: SC, 2nd year, no 16, 109th meeting, 19 February 1947; no 18, 111th meeting, 24 February 1947; no 28, 121st meeting, 21 March 1947.

[129] Reply submitted by the Albanian Government according to Order of the Court of 28 March 1948, 20 September 1948, ICJ, *Corfu Channel, Pleadings, Oral Arguments, Documents*, vol 1, 1949, 373, para 154; P Cot, 16 November 1948, *Pleadings, Oral Arguments, Documents*, Oral Proceedings (First Part), vol III, 1950, 408.

[130] Counter-Memorial submitted by the Government of the People's Republic of Albania, 15 June 1948, ICJ, Corfu Channel, *Pleadings, Oral Arguments, Documents*, vol 1, 1949, 143, para 145.

[131] ICJ, *Corfu Channel, Pleadings, Oral Arguments, Documents*, Oral Proceedings (First Part), vol III, 1950, 581 (E Beckett, 18 January 1949).

[132] E Beckett, 18 January 1949, ibid, 595.

[133] ICJ, *Corfu Channel*, ICJ Rep (1949) 35.

the use of force set out in the UN Charter.[134] It should be recalled that the mine-sweeping operation was carried out in a matter of hours, without causing any injury or damage.[135] All told, these factors mean that the *Corfu Channel* precedent can be considered an illustration of the need to cross a certain threshold of gravity before an action can be characterised as a use of force under article 2(4).

The difficulty in determining this threshold precisely arises from an examination of the *Fisheries Jurisdiction* case opposing the United Kingdom and the Federal Republic of Germany to Iceland. The two plaintiff States complained that the Icelandic authorities were engaged in a policy of harassing vessels in the fishing zone, the outer limit of which zone had been unilaterally fixed by Iceland at 50 nautical miles.[136] This harassment was reflected by nearly 200 incidents in which Icelandic coastguards themselves went as far as cutting the nets of recalcitrant vessels, and even firing warning shots, or live rounds in a few rare instances.[137] However, no deaths or injuries were ever caused.[138] The United Kingdom characterised Icelandic practice as 'unlawful', but never cited article 2(4) or evoked the rule of prohibition of the use of force between States.[139] This section of the UK pleadings was withdrawn as a result of a bilateral agreement with Iceland.[140] However, the Federal Republic of Germany maintained its complaint on this point,[141] and, confronted with the same type of incident, explicitly relied on article 2(4), denouncing a violation of the prohibition of the use of force.[142] Iceland chose not to appear before the Court, but it transpires from its correspondence with the two plaintiff States that it considered it was merely

[134] ibid, 36.

[135] ibid, 33.

[136] See: Memorial of the United Kingdom of 31 July 1973, ICJ, *Fisheries Jurisdiction, Pleadings, Oral Arguments, Documents*, vol I (*United Kingdom v Iceland*), 286, para 54 and 375 *ff*; Memory of the FRG, 1st August 1973, ibid, vol II (*FRG v Iceland*) 260 *ff*.

[137] Memorial of the United Kingdom, above n 136, annex 36 ('Major Incidents in the Icelandic Campaign of Harassment of British Vessels') 420 *ff*; Memory of the FRG, above n 136, annex L.

[138] Memorial of the United Kingdom, above n 136, 425 and 426.

[139] United Kingdom, Application instituting proceedings, 14 April 1972, ibid, 10, para 19; see also ibid, 72, para 5, 286, para 54, 377, paras 315 and 427–32.

[140] S Silkin, 25 March 1974, ibid, 446–47.

[141] According to the conclusions of the FRG, 'the acts of interference by Icelandic coastal atrol boats with fishing vessels registered in the FRG or with their fishing operations by the threat or use of force are unlawful under international law, and that Iceland is under an obligation to make compensation therefore to the FRG' (Memory of 1 August 1973, above n 136, 263); see also Jaenike, ICJ, *Fisheries Jurisdiction, Pleadings, Oral Arguments, Documents*, vol II, 349, para 4.

[142] According to the FRG, 'these acts are in conflict with the principle embodied in the UN Charter that disputes between States shall be settled peacefully without use of force' (Memorial, above n 136, 263, para 15); see also *Note verbale* of 20 July 1973, mentioning an 'offence against the prohibition of the use and of the threat of force which, as one of the peremptory rules of general international law, has been embodied in Article 2 (4) of the Charter of the UN [. . .]'; ibid, annex K, 277; see also annexes G and I, 273 and 276.

taking police measures to enforce its fisheries regulations.[143] The Court did not decide this issue in its judgment in the FRG–Iceland case, considering it did not have sufficient evidence about the scope of the incidents.[144] Both these cases show the diversity of the possible interpretations of the criterion of gravity; while the principle is accepted, its scope cannot be determined here precisely because of the diversity of positions defended.

Another dispute provides more specific indications on this point. This is the *Fisheries Jurisdiction* case between Spain and Canada.

On 9 March 1995, a Spanish fishing vessel, the Estai, was arrested on the high seas by Canadian navy vessels acting under a Canadian Act to prohibit the fishing of straddling stocks.[145] The vessel and its crew were arrested and then released a few days later with no deaths or injuries. On the same day, Spain protested officially, claiming a violation of the provisions of the Montego Bay Convention on the freedom of fishing on the high seas and on the exclusive jurisdiction of the flag State in this zone.[146] On 28 March 1995, Spain decided to bring the matter before the Court and invoked for the first time a violation of article 2(4) of the UN Charter.[147] In its memorial, Spain criticised the Canadian Act which, in view of the *travaux préparatoires*, might involve not just the minimum force necessary but also 'greater' force, that is, the force (or threat) expressly prohibited by article 2(4).[148] Spain therefore considers there is a threshold above which the use of force is of such gravity that it is prohibited by article 2(4), a limit that was overstepped in the case at hand. Canada, however, denied it employed anything other than simple conservation and management measures under national regulations laying down stringent criteria for the use of force in the performance of such measures.[149] Canada having excluded from the Court's jurisdiction any examination of disputes to which conservation and management rights adopted by Canada might give rise,[150] the Court had to find it did not have jurisdiction.

The debate over the threshold beyond which a police measure may be characterised as a use of force under the UN Charter was refined before the Court. To accredit its arguments, Spain emphasised the value of the use

[143] See: *Note verbale* addressed to the FRG, 10 January 1973, Memorial of the FRG, above n 136, annex H, 275.

[144] ICJ, *Fisheries Jurisdiction (FRG v Iceland)*, ICJ Rep (1974) 203–05, paras 71–76 and 206, para 77(5); see also Declaration of Judge Dillard (ibid, 207–08), Judge de Castro, separate opinion (ibid, 225–26), Judge Waldock, separate opinion (ibid, 229–33), Judge Gros, dissenting opinion (ibid, 236–37), Judge Petrén, dissenting opinion (ibid, 242–43) and Judge Onyeama, dissenting opinion (ibid, 249–50).

[145] ICJ Rep (1998) 443 *ff*, para 19 *ff*.

[146] Application instituting proceedings, 28 March 1995, Annex, *Note verbale* no 25/95, 9 March 1995.

[147] Application instituting proceedings, 28 March 1995, para 2(h).

[148] Memorial of the Kingdom of Spain, 28 September 1995.

[149] Counter-Memorial of Canada, 29 February 1996, para 31.

[150] ibid, para 4.

of force against the Estai as a precedent, lambasting Canada's 'gunboat diplomacy'[151] a policy reflected not just by this incident but also more fundamentally by the passing of an Act authorising the use of force.[152] It is in this context that Spain defended a broad conception of the field of application of article 2(4) that covered any military coercion by the agents of one State against another.[153] As for Canada, it obviously insisted on the limited character of the measures taken and, while recognising the peremptory character of the rule in article 2(4), it denied that the case in question came within its purview.[154]

The Court, in its judgment finding it had no jurisdiction, refused to follow the line of argument developed by Spain. It found that 'the use of force authorized by the Canadian legislation and regulations falls within the ambit of what is commonly understood as enforcement of conservation and management measures',[155] and so came within the scope of Canada's reservation. The Court added that:

> Boarding, inspection, arrest and minimum use of force for those purposes are all contained within the concept of enforcement of conservation and management measures according to a 'natural and reasonable' interpretation of this concept. (emphasis added)[156]

Without making any explicit pronouncement on this subject, the Court seemed therefore to consider that there is a dividing line between a 'minimum use of force', that can be ascribed to simple police measures, and a more serious use, that might come within the ambit of article 2(4).[157] In the case in point, it can be considered that the limit was not crossed because of the targeted character of the actions in question that only caused very limited damage.[158]

Another interesting precedent is the Guyana/Suriname arbitral award of 17 September 2007. On June 2000, two patrol boats from the Surinamese navy entered a disputed maritime zone and ordered an oil rig and drill ship, operating in the disputed area under licences from Guyana, to withdraw from the area.[159] Guyana qualified this operation as a threat of force pursuant to article 2(4) of the UN Charter, whereas Suriname contended

---

[151] Sanchez Rodriguez, 9 June 1998, CR 98/9, para 20.

[152] Pastor Ridruejo, 15 June 1998, CR 98/13, para 8.

[153] Dupuy, 15 June 1998, CR 98/13, para 22; see also: Pastor Ridruejo, 15 June 1998, CR 98/13, para 10.

[154] Kirsch, 11 June 1998, CR 98/11, para 45; see also: Weil, 12 June 1998, CR 98/12, paras 31 and 32; Hankey, 17 June 1998, CR 98/14, paras 14, 15 and 56.

[155] ICJ Rep (1998) 466, para 84.

[156] ibid.

[157] See also: Judge Torres Bernardez, dissenting opinion, ibid, 599–600 and 722–31.

[158] See also the EU's position in *Second report on State responsibility*, James Crawford, 30 April 1999, A/CN.4/498/Add.2, para 285.

[159] Arbitral Tribunal Constituted Pursuant to Article 287, and in Accordance with Annex VII of the UN Convention on the Law of the Sea (Guyana and Suriname, 17 September 2007, www.pca-cpa.org/showpage.asp?pag_id=1147), para 151 *ff.*

that the measures it undertook were rather of the nature of 'reasonable and proportionate law enforcement measures'.[160] The defendant State relied on the *Fisheries Jurisdiction* case between Spain and Canada to support its argument. Guyana for its part considered that the *Fisheries Jurisdiction* case 'concerned enforcement measures against fishing vessels on the high seas and not the use of force directly arising from a maritime dispute between two sovereign States'.[161] In its award, the tribunal

> accepts the argument that in international law force may be used in law enforcement activities provided that such force is unavoidable, reasonable and necessary. However in the circumstances of the present case, this Tribunal is of the view that the action mounted by Suriname on 3 June 2000 seemed more akin to a threat of military action rather than a mere law enforcement activity.[162]

The existence of a threshold between simple law enforcement measures, on the one hand, and threats or uses of force prohibited by article 2(4), on the other hand, is thus confirmed. In the particular circumstances of the case, especially within the framework of a territorial dispute, the tribunal considered that this threshold was reached. Nevertheless, it remains difficult to determine exactly when the situation becomes serious enough to trigger the application of article 2(4).

It remains therefore to be asked how this criterion of gravity can be interpreted. It seems two lessons can be deduced from an examination of practice.

First, one must consider the *place* where the litigious action took place. If a State took measures in zones under its jurisdiction (whether on land, at sea or in the air), it will be more difficult to show that the stage of simple police measures has been exceeded. This observation stems from examination of the precedents set out above and especially the number of aerial incidents in which a State has merely taken enforcement measures within the bounds of its jurisdiction. It is in this way that one can understand controversies over the exact location of these incidents, with the intercepting State systematically claiming the interception was made within areas under its jurisdiction. The criterion is further confirmed by a review of the works cited earlier on the interpretation of the definition of aggression in article 3*(d)*. Many States have emphasised the territorial character to criticise the wording used as it seems it may limit the police power of each State to its own territory.[163]

Secondly, it should be specified that the seriousness of the action must be appreciated depending on the *context* in which it occurred. Several precedents can be invoked.[164]

---

[160] ibid, paras 443–44.

[161] ibid.

[162] ibid, para 445.

[163] See, eg: Australia, A/C.6/SR.1478, 16 October 1974, para 30.

[164] See also: Gulf of Tunkin incident; *Repertory of Practice of United Nations Organs*, Supp no 3 (1959–66), vol 2, 266, paras 21–23; *Repertory of the Practice of the Security Council (Supp 1964–1965)*, 195–96.

—On 24 April 1980, the United States conducted an airborne operation devised to recover by force their citizens held hostage in Teheran.[165] The operation failed, apparently without a shot being fired.[166] Yet Iran complained of a 'military aggression of the United States'.[167] The US representative at the UN justified his country's action on the grounds of self-defence under article 51 of the UN Charter.[168] What was at first sight a very limited action, involving a few helicopters illegally crossing the border for the sole purpose of saving nationals was considered by both States as coming within the ambit of article 2(4). This characterisation of the situation can probably be explained by the extremely tense context then prevailing between the two States, a context the Security Council had twice underscored.[169] In this highly peculiar context, it is understandable that a few US air force aircraft entering Iran without its consent can be viewed in terms of the prohibition of the use of force between States.

—On 16 April 1988, an Israeli army commando group secretly entered the suburbs of Tunis and executed a leading PLO figure, returning to Israel without engaging combat.[170] This extremely limited operation was denounced as a 'heinous crime'[171] or an 'assassination',[172] but was also characterised as an attack on the sovereignty and territorial integrity of Tunisia in a Security Council resolution making explicit reference to article 2(4).[173] In view of the debates within the Security Council, it is clear that the context in which this action took place was decisive, the targeted assassination[174] having to be considered as one of many displays of the policy of force conducted by Israel, especially against Tunisia, a policy that the Security Council had denounced before.[175]

—On 3 July 1988, the *USS Vincennes* shot down an Iranian civilian airliner killing its 290 passengers and crew.[176] Iran took the matter to the International Court of Justice, arguing that it had jurisdiction under

---

[165] *Keesing's Contemporary Archives* (1980) 30531–34.

[166] ibid, 30531–32.

[167] *Note verbale dated 28 April 1980 from the permanent representative of Iran to the UN addressed to the Secretary-General*, S/13915, 29 April 1980.

[168] *Letter dated 25 April 1980 from the Permanent Representative of the United States of America to the United Nations addressed to the President of the Security Council*, S/13908, 25 April 1980.

[169] SC Res 457 (1979) of 4 December 1979 (preamble); SC Res 461 (1979) of 31 December 1979 (preamble).

[170] *Keesing's Contemporary Archives* (1988) 35874.

[171] Sudan, S/PV. 2810, 25 April 1988, 6.

[172] See, eg: Mauritania, ibid, 8.

[173] SC Res 611 (1988) of 25 April 1988, preamble.

[174] See: N Ronzitti, 'The Legality of Covert Operations Against Terrorism in Foerign Sates' in A Bianchi (ed), *Enforcing International Law Norms Against Terrorism* (Oxford and Portland Oregon, Hart Publishers, 2004) 21–22.

[175] SC Res 573 (1985) of 4 October 1985; see also *Repertory of Practice of United Nations Organs*, Supp no 7 (1 January 1985–31 December 1988), 19–20, paras 26–27 and N Ronzitti, 'The Legality of Covert Operations Against Terrorism in Foerign Sates', above n 174, 22.

[176] *Keesing's Contemporary Archives* (1988) 36064.

article 14 of the Montreal Convention.[177] At the same time, the plaintiff State considered that the US action was a violation of the prohibition of the use of force,[178] particularly in view of all of the 'aggressive actions by the US warships that were themselves operating within the territorial sea'.[179] On the merits, the US defended its action by invoking self-defence, insisting that 'this incident occurred in the midst of an armed engagement between US and Iranian forces in the context of a long series of attacks on US and other vessels in the Gulf'.[180] For the US, the incident should therefore be appraised in the light not of the Montreal Convention—which applies to actions by individuals acting privately—but of the law of armed conflict.[181] The United States claimed, in this context, to have acted in self-defence.[182] Besides the controversy over the Court's jurisdiction, the two States seem, even if examination of their positions reveals some ambiguity on this point, to have agreed to recognise that the rule prohibiting the use of force was applicable to this situation. That agreement is based on the consideration of the context of conflict between the parties against which the gravity of the incident in question had to be gauged.

—On 10 August 1999, a Pakistani air force plane was brought down by air-to-air missiles launched by Indian air force planes. The incident claimed 16 lives. Pakistan applied to the International Court of Justice to have India condemned for 'serious violations of the various provisions of the United Nations Charter, particularly Article 2, paragraph 4' and for violation of the corresponding customary law.[183] India claimed the Court did not have jurisdiction relying on a reservation to its declaration of acceptance covering multilateral treaties, a reservation that was applicable to the matter at hand insofar as it implied the interpretation of article 2(4).[184] Unlike the other precedents evoked above, an aerial incident is

---

[177] Application instituting proceedings, 17 May 1989.

[178] *Letter dated 3 July 1988 from the Acting Permanent Representative of the Islamic Republic of Iran to the United Nations addressed to the Secretary-General*, S/19979, 4 July 1988, 2; see also Memorial of the Islamic Republic of Iran, 24 July 1990, 193, para 3.81, and 238, para 4.46.

[179] ibid, 193, para 3.81.

[180] Preliminary Objections submitted by the United States of America, 4 March 1991, 1; see also 9 and 10. See C Gray, 'The British Position with Regard to the Gulf-Conflict (Iran-Iraq): Part 2' (1991) 40 *ICLQ* 470.

[181] Preliminary Objections submitted by the United States of America, 4 March 1991, 4. According to the USA, 'The incident of Iran Air Flight 655 cannot be separated from the events that preceded it and from the hostile environment that existed on 3 July 1988, due to the actions of Iran's own military and paramilitary forces' (ibid, 9).

[182] *Letter dated 6 July 1988 from the Acting Permanent Representative of the United States of America to the United Nations addressed to the President of the Security Council*, S/19989, 9 July 1988.

[183] Application instituting proceedings, 21 September 1999, II; see also Memorial of the Government of Pakistan on Jurisdiction, 7 January 2000, para 3.

[184] Counter-Memorial of the Government of India—Preliminary Objections to the Jurisdiction of the Court, 28 February 2000, para 80.

here envisaged in terms of the prohibition of the use of force. However, as in the other examples just set out, the context of conflict in which the incident occurred must be emphasised. Pakistan stressed that India had allegedly occupied a part of its territory in the Kashmir region.[185] The aerial incident had to be situated in this context.

A contrario, an isolated incident is not generally considered by States as coming under the prohibition of the use of force under the Charter, even if it implies an act that could, in another context, be characterised otherwise. We have set out several examples to this effect in various land, sea and air domains of the exercise of State jurisdiction.[186]

It is understandable, in view of these precedents, that what matters, besides an abstract evaluation of the gravity of events, is to determine whether there is an intention on the part of a State to use force against another State. Such an intention appears to be an essential characteristic of the use of force under the Charter, and is a second criterion that is really inseparable from that of gravity.

A State's Intention to Resort to Force Against Another State

In the context of debates such as those on the potential existence of a 'right of humanitarian intervention'—a debate we shall return to—some scholars make an *a contrario* reading of article 2(4) to claim that some uses of force in international relations are not prohibited so long as they are not directed against a State's 'territorial integrity' or 'political independence' or against the 'Purposes of the United Nations'.[187] The criterion of intent or willingness might therefore characterise as lawful certain uses of force conducted by one State in another State's territory.

As shall be shown later, I do not think this argument is valid in view of the position taken by the Charter's Member States, whether when the instrument was drawn up or subsequently, especially during the debates that preceded the adoption of the major resolutions of the General Assembly on the use of force.[188] That does not mean that the criterion of intent should be excluded when interpreting article 2(4). To my mind, for the article to apply to a particular situation supposes that a State resorts to force against another, which supposes it intends to force the other State to do or to refrain from doing something. The intention in question does not therefore depend on the more fundamental motives guiding the State's action, whether they are humanitarian, strategic, economic or other. The

---

[185] Munshi, 3 April 2000, CR 2000/1, 6.

[186] See above and R Higgins, *The Development of International Law Through the Political Organs of the United Nations* (London/New York/Toronto, Oxford University Press, 1963) 175–76.

[187] See below, ch 8.

[188] Below, ch 8.

only intention to be considered is that of forcing the will of another State. If there is such an intention, it shall generally be reflected by military action of a certain degree of gravity, and the threshold between a simple police operation and a genuine use of force in interstate relations will be exceeded. The criterion of intention here takes on a quite different meaning from that conferred by the 'interventionist' doctrine just evoked. It cannot, as such, make an act that is contrary to the rule consistent with it. But it can, ahead of that, affect the field of application of the rule. A coercive act of the type set out above (undue arrest in foreign territory, arrest of a vessel, aerial security measure), insofar as it does not reflect the intention of one State to act against another, is generally considered as a police measure that does not come within the ambit of article 2(4). Supposing the action is characterised as unlawful, it will not be so in respect of this provision but rather by application of specific rules (international criminal law, law of the sea, air law) or more generally of the principle of State sovereignty. However, when confronted with an act of a certain degree of gravity by which one State acts against another, the lawfulness of the act will be measured against the rule of the prohibition of the use of force in international relations.

This criterion of intention derives first from the text of article 2(4) and, more fundamentally, from the object and purpose of that provision.[189] By prohibiting the use of force in 'international relations', against the territorial integrity, political independence or sovereignty of a State, the rule seeks to prohibit the use of force by one State against another and not to regulate all cases of enforcement measures that may contain some foreign element.[190]

This at any rate is how we can interpret all of the practice examined above, whether simple matters of police cooperation, mundane sea or air incidents, but also more problematical cases.[191]

—In the *Corfu Channel* case, it can be considered that the mine sweeping by the Royal Navy was not envisaged in terms of article 2(4) because the United Kingdom's intention was not to conduct military actions against Albania.

—In the case of the failed airborne operation to rescue US citizens in Teheran, the reciprocal accusations of violation of the prohibition of the use of force can undoubtedly be explained by both States being convinced that the other had the intention of acting against it.

---

[189] See ICJ, *Threat or Use of Nuclear Weapons*, ICJ Rep (1996) 246–47, para 48.

[190] A Randelzhofer: 'As the prohibition of the threat or use of force is limited to the international relations between States it is the opinion of various authors that this prohibition does not comprise military acts of protection within the State territory against intruding persons or aircraft'; 'Article 2(4)', above n 4, 123.

[191] See references above.

—In the cases of the *USS Vincennes* or of the *Aerial Incident* between India and Pakistan, a similar conclusion may be deduced from an examination of the positions of the parties, which envisaged these air incidents in terms of attacks of one State on another State; these precedents stand apart from the other incidents considered earlier in which the States viewed the problem as one of compliance with the rules of air law.

—In the *Fisheries Jurisdiction* case, it seems plain that the arrest of the Spanish vessel by Canadian coastguards was not deemed a problem of the use of force because the Canadian State had no intention of attacking the Spanish State.

A contrario, when a State takes even limited military measures and admits that such measures are part of a policy conducted against one State, there is no doubt that article 2(4) is applicable. Many examples could be cited in support of this. Here we shall mention just Malaysia's complaint to the Security Council in September 1964 against Indonesia, which had sent several paramilitary units across the border.[192] Although comparatively limited in scope, Malaysia characterised this despatching as a violation of article 2(4) and emphasised certain bellicose declarations by the Indonesian authorities.[193] Indonesia did not deny it had taken measures that might be prohibited by the article, but claimed there was no actual violation because of certain specific circumstances that we shall not comment on here.[194] In any event, this precedent shows that the prohibition of the use of force is applicable whenever it is established that one State intends to defy another.

This criterion of intent may obviously lend itself to different interpretations, but it implies a first observation that is indisputable: one State's use of force against another presupposes, first, that the State in question is *aware* it is undertaking an action against another State. To understand the importance of this observation we can reason by the absurd. Imagine a State A believes it has discovered a remote islet, sends its army there and raises its flag; a few weeks later, a State B, learning of these events, protests to State A and asserts, with supporting title, that the islet is under its sovereignty; and State A then presents its apologies, takes down its flag and removes its troops from the islet. Can it seriously be considered that State B might accuse State A of violating article 2(4)? Would it not be more consistent with the object of the provision to exclude its applicability, it being understood that State A acted without knowledge of and so without intending to infringe State B's sovereign rights? That State B, supposing damage was caused, calls for it to be repaired by relying on the violation of

---

[192] *Repertory of Practice of United Nations Organs*, Supp no 3 (1959–1966), vol 1, Article 2(4) (Separate Study), 158–59, paras 178–85; *Repertoire of the Practice of the Security Council (Supp 1964–1965)*, 202–03.

[193] ibid, 159, para 181; see S/PV.1144, 9 September 1964, paras 31–36 and 60–62.

[194] S/PV.1144, 9 September 1964, paras 65, 68, 102, 104; S/PV.1152, 17 September 1964, para 64.

its sovereignty is one thing. That it should invoke a violation of the prohibition of the use of force between States is another, that seems highly improbable and in truth excessive in view of the actual purpose of the rule.

This requirement of a criterion of awareness, prior to the existence of any intention, arises from an examination of the works preceding the adoption of the General Assembly resolution defining aggression. The hypothetical triggering of the use of force by error was contemplated during those works and the States unanimously excluded the possibility of characterising an act committed by mistake as an aggression.[195] Several examples were put forward and it shall be observed that all relate to acts that were not very serious and in which it is obvious that no State intended to act against another. Instances include a small military unit temporarily crossing the border as a result of its leader's inattention,[196] a bomb that fell accidentally as a result of a technical failure,[197] or an emergency.[198] While they ruled out the characterisation of aggression in such instances, States did not explicitly exclude the applicability of article 2(4) that can also relate to a use of force that does not constitute aggression. Several States more generally asserted that any damage caused by the act committed by error should be compensated for,[199] but they did not make any clear pronouncement on the characterisation of military acts committed by mistake.[200]

However, a review of practice as a whole allows us to affirm that States consider an act, even of a military type, committed by mistake, does not constitute an aggression or even a use of force by one State against another contrary to article 2(4). States do not make accusations of violation of the prohibition of the use of force in international relations in the exceptionally

---

[195] See: Yugoslavia (A/C.6/SR.408, 25 October 1954, para 20), United Kingdom (A/AC.134/SR.32, 10 March 1969 in *Special Committee on the Question of Defining Aggression*, Second Session, A/AC.134/SR.25-51, 38), Cyprus (A/AC.134/SR.56, 17 July 1970 in A/AC.134/SR.52-66), Japan (A/AC.134/SR.57, 20 July 1970 in A/AC.134/SR.52-66 and A/C.6/SR.1206, 26 October 1970, para 43), USA (A/AC.134/SR.68, 31 July 1970 in A/AC.134/SR.67-78), Bulgaria (A/AC.134/SR.57, 20 July 1970 in A/AC.134/SR.52-66 and A/C.6/SR.1206, 26 October 1970, para 25), Syria (A/AC.134/SR.69, 3 August 1970 in A/AC.134/SR.67-78), Ukraine (A/C.6/SR.1207, 27 October 1970, para 44), Zambia (A/C.6/SR.1276, 4 November 1971, para 27; A/C.6/SR.1351, 6 November 1972, para 8), Iraq (A/C.6/SR.1202, 16 October 1970, para 20), USSR (A/AC.134/SR.68, 31 July 1970 in A/AC.134/SR.67-78 and A/AC.134/SR.68, 31 July 1970 in A/AC.134/SR.67-78) and Nicaragua (A/C.6/SR.1480, 18 October 1974, para 47).

[196] United Kingdom; A/C.6/SR.1166, 2 December 1969, para 25.

[197] Italy; A/AC.134/SR.64, 27 July 1970 in A/AC.134/SR.52-66 and A/C.6/SR.1205, 22 October 1970, para 18.

[198] Canada; A/AC.134/SR.68, 31 July 1970 in A/AC.134/SR.67-78.

[199] See: Ecuador (A/AC.134/SR.68, 31 July 1970 in A/AC.134/SR.67-78 and A/AC.134/SR.58, 21 July 1970 in A/AC.134/SR.52-66), Iraq (A/AC.134/SR.59, 22 July 1970 in A/AC.134/SR.52-66, 79), USRR (A/AC.134/SR.68, 31 July 1970 in A/AC.134/SR.67-78, 31).

[200] See: Madagascar (A/C.6/SR.1444, 21 November 1973, para 24), USA (A/AC.134/SR.68, 31 July 1970 in A/AC.134/SR.67-78, 23) and Cyprus (A/AC.124/SR.83, 5 February 1971 in A/AC.134/SR.79-91, 27).

rare cases where military acts are committed in error. First it is to be specified that, in a series of precedents mentioned above, error is invoked to justify unlawful entry into the airspace of one State which, for its part, generally complains of a violation of its sovereignty without evoking either aggression or the use of force against it.[201] The following examples can then be added.

—On 26 August 1961, the South African police entered Basutoland, a British colony at the time, and arrested several persons.[202] South Africa affirmed it had crossed the border 'by mistake' and apologised for the 'violation of British territory'.[203] The United Kingdom accepted the apologies while stating that it took the 'violation of Basutoland territory' very seriously.[204]

—On 15 July 1965, the British Colonial Secretary told the House of Commons that the UAR authorities had assured him they had attacked the Federation of South Arabia as a result of a 'pilot's error'.[205] After careful consideration of the circumstances, the British authorities decided to accept this explanation.

—On 14 October 1968, five shells fired by Swiss artillery during exercises exploded on the territory of the Principality of Liechtenstein.[206] The Liechtenstein government protested at this 'violation of its territorial sovereignty' the very next day;[207] the Swiss government immediately presented its apologies for the 'involuntary violation of the Liechtenstein territory'.[208]

Neither article 2(4), nor more generally the prohibition of the use of force between States was mentioned in situations of this type. Error seems to have the effect of preventing the characterisation of an action as a use of force by one State against another, which does not mean, as the case may be, that the action may not be characterised as unlawful in respect of other legal principles, such as the observance of State sovereignty.

It is true that mistake seems to have been evoked to justify what was also characterised as the use of force in international relations in two cases brought before the International Court of Justice: the *USS Vincennes* case and the *Land and Maritime Boundary between Cameroon and Nigeria* case. Close examination of these two precedents shows, however, that they do not infirm our conclusions.

---

[201] See above.
[202] *'Force majeure' and 'fortuitous event' as circumstances precluding wrongfulness: survey of State practice, international judicial decisions and doctrine*, above n 104, 100, para 127.
[203] ibid.
[204] ibid.
[205] ibid, 104, para 151.
[206] ibid, 100, para 128.
[207] ibid and C Rousseau, 'Chronique des faits internationaux' (1969) 73 *RGDIP* 871.
[208] *'Force majeure' and 'fortuitous event' as circumstances precluding wrongfulness: survey of State practice, international judicial decisions and doctrine*, above n 104, 100, para 128; see also (1969–1970) 26 *ASDI* 158.

Out of concern to justify an action by the USS Vincennes which it characterised as an act of 'self-defence' under article 51 of the UN Charter—which implies we are in the domain of the use of force between States—the United States claimed that the commanding officer had, mistakenly, believed they were facing an imminent attack from an Iranian military aircraft.[209] But this argument must be set in the context of the conflict characterising the relations between Iran and the United States in the Gulf at the time.[210] The United States argued that Iran, in a series of earlier military actions against its vessels, had made an armed attack well before the Airbus A 320 incident.[211] The United States was therefore *already* in a situation of self-defence before that date.[212] The identification error by the commanding officer of the USS Vincennes is not invoked as a basis for the emergence of a situation of self-defence, but rather as one of the factors to consider in evaluating the proportionality of the United States' riposte to hostile Iranian actions.[213] In other words, mistake is not presented here as a factor in the context of *jus contra bellum* but rather in the context of *jus in bello*,[214] the two States concerned being already, at the time of the events, in a situation of international armed conflict.[215]

In the *Land and Maritime Boundary between Cameroon and Nigeria* case, Cameroon claimed that by occupying by force certain pieces of territory belong to Cameroon, Nigeria had violated the prohibition on the use of force.[216] Nigeria replied first that the territories in question were under Nigerian sovereignty, which excluded Cameroon's alleged violation.[217] Secondarily, Nigeria affirmed that its peaceful presence in Cameroon territory could not be deemed to call into question its international responsibility,

---

[209] *Letter dated 6 July 1988 from the Acting Permanent Representative of the United States of America to the United Nations addressed to the President of the Security Council*, S/19989, 9 July 1988, 1 and 2; see also DK Linnan, 'Iran Air Flight 655 and Beyond: Free Passage, Mistaken Self-Defense and State Responsibility' (1991) 16 *YJIL* 245 ff; 'Agora: The Downing of Iran Air Flight 655' (1989) 83 *AJIL* 318–41.

[210] See: M Nash Leich, 'Denial of Liability: *Ex Gratia* Compensation on a Humanitarian Basis' (1989) 83 *AJIL* 319–24.

[211] See: USA, S/PV.2818, 14 July 1988; S/PV.2821, 20 July 1988; *Repertoire of the Practice of the Security Council*, Supp 1985–88, 444–45.

[212] 'The incident of Iran Air Flight 655 cannot be separated from the events that preceded it [. . .]' (Memorial of the USA, 4 March 1991, 9; see also 13.

[213] M Nash Leich, 'Denial of Liability: *Ex Gratia* Compensation on a Humanitarian Basis', above n 210, 321–22.

[214] AF Lowenfeld, 'Looking Back and Looking Ahead' (1991) 85 *AJIL* 341.

[215] 'The actions of the US upon which Iran relies to sustain its claim are governed by the laws of armed conflict [. . .]. Unlike the 1983 incident [KAL 007], the incident of 3 July 1988 involved the rapid approach of an unidentified foreign aircraft to a warship that was itself engaged in armed conflict initiated by the country of the aircraft's registry' (Memorial of the USA, 4 March 1991, 4 and 41).

[216] Additional Application to the Application Instituting Proceedings brought by the Republic of Cameroon, 6 June 1994, paras 4 and 17(c), Memorial of the Republic of Cameroon, 16 March 1995, 670, paras 9(e), (f) and (g), Reply of the Republic of Cameroon, 4 April 2000, 592, para 13.01, paras (e), (f) and (g).

[217] Counter-Memorial of the Federal Republic of Nigeria, 21 May 1999, 638, para 24.33.

since such presence would then have resulted from an 'honest belief and reasonable mistake', with Nigeria mistakenly but sincerely believing it was in its own territory at the time of events.[218] Cameroon claimed, on the contrary, that its territory had been invaded and occupied by force by Nigerian soldiers, who had not hesitated to use their weapons when necessary, the whole incident having prompted many official protests from the Cameroon authorities.[219] In this context, Nigeria could not reasonably claim to have acted by mistake,[220] a mistake that could not in any event exonerate it from responsibility in such a situation.[221] Careful examination of the parties' arguments does not reveal a clear and unequivocal position about the legal status of mistake. It seems, however, that Nigeria conceives of mistake as excluding the characterisation of 'force' within the meaning of article 2(4) of the Charter.[222] As for Cameroon, it does not contest, in principle, that mistake may play a role in the case of acts that are less serious than the use of force.[223] It is simply that, in the case at hand, this is not the position, so mistake cannot play any role.[224] In its judgment, the Court declines to settle the dispute specifically on international responsibility, patently—even if it does not say so—because of the not very serious character of the events in question.[225] On the whole, this case cannot be interpreted as a precedent in which mistake was accepted as a justification for the use of force. It seems rather that mistake can serve only as an element of appreciation of the primary rule when the rule applies to less serious acts.[226]

This precedent could, *a contrario*, accredit the argument that, if a State enters a territory that it is unaware is claimed by another State, its mere presence will not be considered as a use of force, even if that presence is indeed a violation of the territorial sovereignty of the 'invaded' State. In any event, this instance seems purely theoretical. In practice, cases are seen rather of States choosing to send their agents into a piece of territory knowing full well that it is claimed by another State. The State that deems its territory is occupied will then tend to react by invoking a violation of its sovereignty, or even, if the act is more serious and seems to reflect an intention to force it to yield the territory, a violation of article 2(4). Thus, in the

---

[218] ibid, 638–39, para 24.34; see also Rejoinder of the Federal Republic of Nigeria, 4 January 2001, para 15.56.

[219] See: Tomuschat, 11 March 2002, CR 2002/16, 55 *ff*, para 10 *ff*.

[220] Reply of the Republic of Cameroon, 4 April 2000, 466 *ff*, para 10.17 *ff*; Corten, 26 February 2002, CR 2002/07, 43–44, paras 28–29).

[221] Reply of the Republic of Cameroon, 4 April 2000, 470–71, para 10.27, 471–72, para 10.31, and 489–90, para 11.14; Corten, 26 February 2002, CR 2002/07, 44–45, paras 30–33; Tomuschat, 11 March 2002, CR 2002/16, 58, para 16.

[222] Abi Saab, 8 March 2002, CR 2002/14, 22, para 21; Abi Saab, 15 March 2002, CR 2002/20, 21, para 19.

[223] Reply of the Republic of Cameroon, 4 April 2000, 465–66, para 10.16.

[224] Tomuschat, 11 March 2002, CR 2002/16, 57–58, para 15.

[225] ICJ, *Land and Maritime Boundary between Cameroon and Nigeria*, ICJ Rep (2002) 448–53, paras 308–24.

[226] See: Abi Saab, 15 March 2002, CR 2002/20, 20, para 8, and 22–23, para 20.

Temple of Preah Vihear case, Cambodia complained of Thailand sending guardians to the temple site in the late 1940s, and then sending several soldiers in 1954. The mere presence of three Thai guardians in Cambodian territory, while it gave rise to protests, did not give rise to any accusations based on the prohibition of the use of force.[227] However, the despatch of Thai troops in 1954, despite repeated protests, prompted Cambodia to accuse Thailand of 'flagrant violation of Article 2, paragraph 4 of the Charter'.[228] This accusation, which was not reiterated, however,[229] probably reflected Cambodia's belief that Thailand was seeking to force it to yield this part of its territory.

More generally, it will be observed that each border dispute gives rise to claims to sovereignty that are sometimes materialised by the ephemeral despatching of a few troops into the disputed territory, without that implying for the other State an accusation of violation of article 2(4). Once again, everything will depend on the gravity of the act and the way it is seen to materialise one State's intention to use force against another. Should a genuine mistake occur where the State is not even aware of entering territory that is not under its sovereignty, the prohibition of the use of force will not, in principle, be invoked.

To conclude on the question of mistake, one point should be emphasised: that article 2(4) does not apply in such circumstances in no way implies that no other legal provisions are not applicable. Any unlawful incursion by one State, even unwittingly and so unintentionally, may be a violation of sovereignty. It goes without saying in this respect that the State (unintentionally) affected by the act, if it does not rely on a violation of article 2(4) and even less on the existence of an armed attack within the meaning of article 51, retains the right to exercise its police powers within the bounds of its national territory. It may, then, either act against an intruding aircraft, or, in other circumstances, demand that foreign troops that have entered its territory by mistake leave it immediately. In the event of a refusal, the State whose agents have intruded can no longer claim to be mistaken and article 2(4) will indeed apply. An actual aggression may even be evoked with an army stationed in the territory of another State against that State's will, entitling the State to riposte as a right of self-defence. The subtle distinctions affecting the applicability of the system of domestic sovereignty or of prohibition on the use of force in international relations should not make us lose sight of the fact that, in practice, a State that is the victim of a military act may, however serious the act and whatever its author's intent, take appropriate measures to ensure its own security.

---

[227] See: ICJ, *Pleadings, Oral Arguments, Documents*, ICJ Rep (1962) vol 1, annexes XV, XVI, XVII, XVIII, 104, 105–06, 107, 108 and 110.

[228] Application instituting proceedings, 30 September 1959, ibid, 15.

[229] Cambodia did not refer to art 2(4) in its submissions; see ICJ, *Temple of Preah Vihear*, ICJ Rep (1962) 9–14.

Having analysed the hypothesis of mistake—a hypothesis that, it must be recalled, remains exceptional—we can envisage the hypothesis of a conscious and deliberate act, but one that does not for all that reflect the will of one State to attack another. The position seems, at first sight, fundamentally different since this time the agents of a State enter another State's territory no longer by mistake but knowingly. However, it is not sure that one need necessarily deduce that article 2(4) is applicable; everything depends on an attentive examination of the circumstances. To my mind, there are some situations at any rate where it can be thought that the prohibition of the use of force between States is not applicable.

During the discussion before the adoption of General Assembly resolution 3314 (XXIX), Iraq's representative raised the case of a regiment that crosses a State border, knowingly and without authorisation, to go sunbathing on a beach.[230] No State characterised such a hypothesis as a use of force in the debates in the General Assembly, whether in the Sixth Commission or in the special committee on the definition of aggression. I think this omission is significant. Supposing that soldiers cross the border illegally to sunbathe on a beach on another State's territory, and that State learns of this act against its sovereignty; it is hard to imagine that a complaint for aggression or even for violation of article 2(4) would be made to the authorities of the offending troops' State. However, one can examine with interest certain much more frequent precedents where one State deliberately sends agents into another State's territory with the official objective not of acting against the State or its agents, but of carrying out a 'targeted' cross-border police operation or of rescuing people in danger. Both instances are especially emblematic of the difficulty of appreciating the criteria of gravity and of intent that determine whether article 2(4) is applicable. They shall be examined in the third and final part of our reasoning.

The Problem of 'Targeted' Military Operations

In its work on the state of necessity, the International Law Commission evoked the case of violations of territorial sovereignty that could not be put down to a violation of a rule of *jus cogens*. The Commission cites especially 'some incursions into foreign territory to forestall harmful operations by an armed group which was preparing to attack the territory of the State, or in pursuit of an armed band of criminals who had crossed the frontier and perhaps had their base in foreign territory, or to protect the lives of nationals . . . or to eliminate or neutralize a source of troubles which threatened to occur or to spread across the frontier'.[231] We shall return to this case when we consider the possibility of invoking the state of necessity to justify

---

[230] A/C.6/SR.1202, 16 October 1970, para 20.
[231] *YILC* (1980) vol II, Part Two, 44, para 23; see also *Second report on State responsibility*, James Crawford, 30 April 1999, A/CN.4/498/Add.2, 25–26, para 278.

certain uses of force.[232] At this stage, the question is to determine whether the actions contemplated must always be considered as uses of force within the meaning of article 2(4). In the situations we are to examine, one State decides, with full knowledge of what it is doing, to send its agents into another State's territory. Its operation, however, is of very limited scope, both in terms of the objective pursued—which is not to assail the agents of another State or the State itself—and in terms of the means used—only a few lightly armed agents being involved. To my mind, such a violation of sovereignty should not systematically be considered a violation of the prohibition of the use of force between States, but will depend on the circumstances of each case.

Let us envisage a first case. A State A sends an undercover agent into the territory of a State B, without State B's knowledge, with the mission of neutralising a 'terrorist' group composed exclusively of nationals of a State C. The secret agent conducts her operation in a matter of hours; she captures the leader of the private group and in the course of her mission kills two or three other members of the group. State A, however, has been careful not to strike at State B, especially by avoiding any contact with its agents. State B suffers no damage, and only learns of the events once the operation is over. To my mind, this case is very similar to that of the international abductions or more generally of the cross-border police actions examined earlier. State B may protest, invoking a violation of its sovereignty or of more specific treaties on police cooperation. It is doubtful, however, that it can validly accuse State A of violating article 2(4).[233]

It is not uninteresting in this respect to recall the *Rainbow Warrior* case. The vessel was sunk on 10 July 1985 by two French secret service agents, and there was one victim of the operation.[234] The action took place within New Zealand's territorial waters, but did not cause any damage to New Zealand, neither the boat (flying the British flag), nor the victim (a Dutch national of Portuguese origin) having New Zealand nationality. That did not prevent New Zealand from protesting vigorously to the French authorities, reproving an 'attack' that was a 'serious violation of basic norms of international law' and, more especially, of 'New Zealand sovereignty'.[235] After first denying any involvement,[236] France admitted its responsibility while claiming that this 'criminal attack' had been decided by certain DGSE officials without the knowledge of the highest authorities of the State.[237] In

---

[232] Below, ch 4.

[233] cp BL Godfrey, 'Authorization to Kill Terrorist Leaders and Those who Harbor Them: An International Analysis of Defensive Assassination' (2003) 4 *San Diego International Law Journal* 490 ff.

[234] *Keesing's Contemporary Archives* (1985) 33852–55.

[235] *Memorandum of the Government of New Zealand to the Secretary-General of the United Nations, RIAA*, vol XIX, 201.

[236] C Rousseau, 'Chronique des faits internationaux' (1986) 90 *RGDIP* 218–20.

[237] Letter of 8 August 1985, *RIAA*, vol XIX, 205–06 and C Rousseau, 'Chronique des faits internationaux', above n 236, 1094.

a sense, those authorities were assuring New Zealand they had never intended to conduct a military action against it. That probably explains why Charter article 2(4) was not cited by the parties, or by the Secretary-General, who was asked to settle the issue.[238] This precedent does therefore seem to show that, under certain circumstances, sending agents to conduct a military operation in foreign territory is not considered as a use of force between States. This seems, in particular, to be the case when the operation is limited in scope, including insofar as it is purportedly decided by subaltern authorities only and not at the highest echelons of the State.

Another interesting case is that of an operation by a State A that launches a missile against the territory of a State B on which 'terrorist' bases are situated, the missile crossing the airspace of a State C. In such a case, the lawfulness of State A's action against State B is a matter to which article 2(4) applies. That, however, does not necessarily seem to be the case of the settlement of the dispute that may arise between State A and State C. When the United States fired several missiles at Al Qaeda bases in Afghanistan in August 1998, those missiles passed through Pakistan's airspace.[239] Pakistan wrote to the Security Council complaining of a violation of its sovereignty, without claiming, though, that the violation should be characterised as a use of force within the meaning of the Charter, since the United States plainly had no intention of challenging Pakistan.[240] In the same way, when in October 2003 Israeli planes crossed Lebanese airspace to carry out military action against Syria, Lebanon complained of a violation of its sovereignty but only in describing the bombing of Syrian territory did it speak of aggression.[241]

However, what are the circumstances in which the threshold necessary for article 2(4) to be applicable has been crossed?

We might cite, at this juncture, the sending in February 1978 of a commando by the Egyptian authorities to Larnaca airport (Cyprus) to free hostages held by two pro-Palestinian activists who had just killed a former Egyptian minister.[242] Once on the scene, a clash with Cypriot forces resulted in the deaths of 15 members of the commando and in Cairo breaking off diplomatic relations between the two countries a few days later.[243]

---

[238] The Secretary General mentions an 'attack, contrary to international law' (*RIAA*, vol XIX, 213; see also C Rousseau, 'Chronique des faits internationaux', above n 236, 221–25; J Charpentier, 'L'affaire du *Rainbow Warrior*' (1985) 31 *AFDI* 215; M Pugh, 'Legal Aspects of the *Rainbow Warrior* Affair' (1987) 36 *ICLQ* 659.

[239] See: SD Murphy, 'Contemporary Practice of the United States Relating to International Law' (1999) 93 *AJIL* 165.

[240] *Letter dated 22 August from the Permanent Representative of Pakistan to the United Nations addressed to the President of the Security Council*, S/1998/794, 24 August 1998.

[241] S/PV.4836, 5 October 2003.

[242] C Rousseau, 'Chronique des faits internationaux' (1978) 82 *RGDIP* 1096–97.

[243] *Keesing's Contemporary Archives* (1978) 29305; N Ronzitti, *Rescuing Nationals Abroad Through Military Coercion and Intervention on Grounds of Humanity*, (Dordrecht/Boston/Lancaster, Martinus Nijhoff Publshers, 1985) 40–41.

Contrary to what happened in the case of the Rainbow Warrior, the military action resulted in direct combat between forces of the two States. Under the circumstances, it would seem incongruous to deny that the prohibition of the use of force stated in the Charter was applicable, although it has not been established that this rule was actually invoked.[244]

The precedent of the raid on Entebbe, during which there was fighting between Israeli special forces and Ugandan army units, confirms this statement. It will be recalled that an Israeli army commando group engaged in action at Entebbe airport on 4 July 1976 freed the hundred hostages held by a group of the Popular Front for the Liberation of Palestine.[245] Besides damage, 'Operation Thunder' caused some 30 deaths, including 20 Ugandan soldiers on duty at the airport.[246] The matter was raised before the UN Security Council, which was unable to adopt any resolution because of the divergences that arose.[247] The military operation, however, was considered by all States to be a use of force, with Israel invoking article 51 of the UN Charter,[248] and most States condemning the action as an armed attack.[249] It is clear that whenever combat breaks out between the forces of two States as a result of decisions taken by the two governments in question, we are indeed within the ambit of article 2(4), even if the military operation is limited in terms of the forces engaged and the equipment used.

The same conclusions can be deduced from the second instance that is often evoked, that of a military operation to rescue individuals in danger.[250]

Should such an operation result in fighting with the forces of another State, there is no doubt we are dealing with the use of force. The precedent of the Entebbe raid may be seen in this light, as, to some extent, may that of the Larnaca incident. One may cite the Mayaguez incident, from the name of the cargo vessel flying the US flag that was seized by Cambodian authorities in 1975.[251] This capture, judged contrary to international law by the United States, was followed by an armed operation officially to rescue

---

[244] See: R Ago, Addendum to the eighth report on State responsibility, A/CN.4/318/Add. 5-8, *YILC* (1980) vol II, Part One, 43–44, para 65; E Sciso, 'Il raid egiziano a Larnaca' (1978) 61 *Rivista di diritto internazionale* 945–47; C Rousseau, *Droit international public*, vol V (Paris, Sirey, 1983) 96.

[245] C Rousseau (1977) 81 *RGDIP* 286–95.

[246] *Keesing's Contemporary Archives*, 13 August 1976, 27888–91.

[247] S/PV.1943, 14 July 1976.

[248] S/PV.1939, 9 July 1976, para 115; see also USA, 'Contemporary Practice of the United States' (1979) 73 *AJIL* 122–24.

[249] Mauritania, on behalf of the Group of African States (S/PV.1939, 9 July 1976, para 48), Kenya (ibid, para 148), Qatar (ibid, paras 168–74), Cameroon (ibid, paras 209–19), China (ibid, paras 224–25), Libya (ibid, para 244; S/PV. 1940, 12 July 1976, para 7; S/PV.1943, 14 July 1976, para 22), Guinea (S/PV.1940, 12 July 1976, para 29), Mauritius (ibid, para 51), Guyana (ibid, paras 76–81), Benin (S/PV.1940, 12 July 1976, para 9), Somalia (ibid, para 30), Yugoslavia (ibid, para 66–68), Pakistan (S/PV.1941, 12 July 1976, para 134), India (S/PV.1942, 13 July 1976, para 146), Cuba (S/PV.1943, 14 July 1976, paras 81–83); see also the views expressed by the Secretary General (S/PV.1939, 9 July 1976, para 13).

[250] See also below, ch 8.

[251] U Beyerlin, 'Mayaguez Incident' (1997) *EPIL*, vol III, 333–35.

the crew.[252] The operation was carried out by 180 marines and claimed nearly a hundred lives among US and Cambodian soldiers. Under the circumstances, no one denied this was a use of force between States within the meaning of article 2(4) with the United States expressly invoking article 51 to justify its action.[253]

A contrario, if an operation is conducted without causing fighting or any damage to a State, it may be asked whether this still comes within the domain of application of the rule set out in article 2(4). This point can be illustrated by two precedents.

In Liberia in early August 1990 there was fighting between government forces and two rebel forces that were also in conflict with one another. Given the danger to their citizens in this context,[254] the United States decided on a rescue operation conducted by nearly 300 marines who evacuated their nationals from the US Embassy in Monrovia to ships stationed in international waters. It seems that the decision was taken without requesting the prior consent of the Liberian authorities, even if they, and the two rebel groups, had been given prior warning. The highest US authorities, however, took care to specify that 'The Marine Presence does not indicate or constitute any intention on the part of the U.S. Government to intervene militarily in the Liberian conflict'.[255] And on land the marines carefully refrained from engaging in combats that might advantage any of the forces. For that matter, none of the parties seems to have protested at this action that went off without victims or damage.[256] As far as I know, neither the intervening State, nor the other States or parties, under the circumstances, invoked the rules on the prohibition of the use of force. This instance therefore seems to illustrate the possibility of conducting limited military operations that may raise questions about respect of the sovereignty of the State in question, but that are not serious enough to exceed the threshold of use of force between States under article 2(4).

In this respect we can return to one of the aspects of the *Aerial Incident of 10 August 1999 (Pakistan v India)*. In its application to the International Court of Justice, Pakistan complained of a violation of article 2(4) by India

---

[252] N Ronzitti, *Rescuing Nationals Abroad Through Military Coercion and Intervention on Grounds of Humanity*, above n 243, 35–36 and 138–39.

[253] U Beyerlin, 'Mayaguez Incident', above n 251, 333; S/11689, 15 May 1975; *Digest of United States Practice*, Department of State Publication, 1975, 777–83; 'Contemporary Practice of the United States' (1975) 69 *AJIL* 875–77.

[254] See also: 'Report: Delegations Leave for Freetown Peace Talks; Evacuation of Foreigners, 11 June 1990', *BBC Monitoring Report*, 12 June 1990, in M Weller (ed), *Regional Peace-Keeping and International Enforcement: The Liberian Crisis*, Cambridge International Documents Series, vol 6 (Cambridge, Cambridge University Press, 1994) 42; 'US House of Representatives, Subcommittee on Africa of the Committee on Foreign Affairs, 101st Congress, 2nd session, Hearing on US Policy and the Crisis in Liberia, 19 June 1990, *BBC Monitoring Report*, 21 June 1990, in ibid, 43–56.

[255] President Bush, 6 August 1990, *BBC Monitoring Report*, 7 August 1990, in ibid, 65.

[256] 'Report: NPFL to Attend ECOWAS Meeting; Taylor Comments on Hostage-taking, 5 August 1990, *BBC Monitoring Report*, 9 August 1990, in ibid, 65–66.

because of the firing of air-to-air missiles at a Pakistani aircraft that was in Pakistani airspace at the time.[257] It is interesting to point out that Pakistan complained incidentally of an operation by Indian army helicopters that allegedly entered Pakistan to recover certain items of debris from the aircraft that had been shot down. In its application, the plaintiff State considered that in so doing India 'violated Pakistan's air space and territorial sovereignty', but without connecting this particular act with article 2(4).[258] Even if what has been written on this point remained very discrete, it can be considered that this was a significant omission.

Some operations may be devised and carried out in such a limited fashion that they will not be criticised on the basis of the prohibition of the use of force between States, but rather on the basis of other rules of international law, including respect for territorial sovereignty. Instances might include the parachuting of medicines and foodstuffs by the Indian army into Sri Lankan territory in 1987, against the will of the island's government, with Sri Lanka complaining of a violation of its sovereignty without invoking article 2(4).[259]

At this juncture, two points should be emphasised that concern all targeted operations, whether officially directed against 'terrorist' groups or designed to rescue people under threat.

First, the fact that such operations do not necessarily come within the purview of article 2(4) in no way implies that they are consistent with international law. International law protects the territorial sovereignty of each State against any action however serious. *A priori*, any military operation in the territory of another State without its consent violates its sovereignty, unless the intervening State can validly invoke circumstances precluding wrongfulness (distress, state of necessity, counter measures, etc.) on the very stringent terms provided for by international law.[260]

Secondly, there is no question of a State claiming that the military action it is engaged in cannot be faulted under article 2(4) simply because it is not directed against the government of another State, its official goal being to punish 'terrorists' or to save human life. For the prohibition of the use of force to be applicable, it is necessary but sufficient for a State to decide to take action that it knows will involve defying another State, whether its central government, its agents, its population, its territory or its infrastructure. A clear distinction must be drawn, then, between the general motive for an operation—which motive may prove more or less legitimate in the eyes of international law, a point we shall not pronounce on here—and the

---

[257] See also above.

[258] Application instituting proceedings, 21 September 1999.

[259] See: N Chandrahasan, 'Use of Force to Ensure Humanitarian Relief—A South Asian Precedent Examined' (1993) 42 *ICLQ* 666; S Alam, 'Indian Intervention in Sri Lanka and International Law' (1991) 38 *NILR* 346–59.

[260] Below, ch 4.

intention, in achieving that objective, to defy a third State. If such an intention is found, article 2(4) will be applicable, regardless of any more general motive for the intervention. It is worth underscoring this conclusion, since ignorance of it may lead to clearly unreasonable results under article 2(4), as the next two precedents attest.

—When, on 1 October 1985, eight Israeli air force mirage jets bombed the PLO headquarters in Tunis[261], Israel claimed it was targeting the 'terrorist' organisation alone and not Tunisia as such, at least not directly.[262] That did not prevent the States that met in the Security Council from considering that the situation came under article 2(4), most of them condemning the operation on this ground[263]—expressly cited in Security Council resolution 573 (1985)[264]—with the United States not denying its applicability while preferring to see in Israel's action a case of self-defence within the meaning of article 51 of the Charter.[265]

—When, on 22 August 1998, the United States bombed a pharmaceutical plant in Sudan and several Al Qaeda training camps in Afghanistan,[266] it claimed it was targeting the means of action of a terrorist group.[267] The fact that there was no fighting between its forces and those of Sudan or Afghanistan did not prevent States from seeing these events as being covered by the rule prohibiting the use of force between States. The United States thus claimed it acted in self-defence[268] and was criticised on the basis of article 2(4).[269] The article was therefore considered to be fully applicable to what was otherwise presented as a targeted attack.

It is not enough, then, to set aside article 2(4), to claim that an action is not directed against another State's government, or that no fighting took place between the armed forces of the two States. The provision is applicable whenever one State takes action that it perfectly well knows will cause substantial damage to another State. The criterion of gravity will require

---

[261] C Rousseau, 'Chronique des faits internationaux' (1986) 90 *RGDIP* 457.

[262] S/PV.2615, 4 October 1985, paras 193–94; see also *Repertory of Practice of United Nations Organs*, Supp no 7 (1985–1988), vol 1, 19–20, paras 26–28.

[263] S/PV.2615, 4 October 1985; see also M Irish and A de Mestral, 'Canadian Practice in International Law during 1985' (1986) 24 *CYIL* 441 and 'Pratique française du droit international' (1986) 32 *AFDI* 1023.

[264] SC Res 573 of 4 October 1985, preamble; see also Tunisia; S/PV.2615, 4 October 1985, para 183.

[265] S/PV.2615, 4 October 1985, para 252; see also M Nash Leich, 'Contemporary Practice of the United States relating to International Law' (1986) 80 *AJIL* 166–67.

[266] *Keesing's Contemporary Archives* (1998) 42435.

[267] SD Murphy, 'Contemporary Practice of the United States Relating to International Law' (1999) 93 *AJIL* 161–62.

[268] *Letter dated 20 August 1998 from the Permanent Representative of the United States of America to the United Nations addressed to the President of the Security Council*, S/1998/780, 20 August 1998.

[269] *Letter dated 21 August 1998 from the Permanent Representative of the Sudan to the United Nations addressed to the President of the Security Council*, S/1998/786, 21 August 1998.

allowance here for the scale of the effects of the military operation on the State whose territorial sovereignty is infringed.

So, whether we are dealing with a cross-border action aimed at 'terrorist' groups or an operation to rescue people under threat, the problem is the same. If the intervening State's objective is not to challenge another State, and if consequently it uses very limited military means, article 2(4) will not be invoked (as in the Rainbow Warrior or 1990 Liberia precedents). If the military action is against another State that supposedly supports 'terrorists' or threatens nationals of the intervening State, the action will involve the rules on the prohibition of the use of force (as in the *Mayaguez* or Entebbe precedents).

It remains to be asked whether in each particular case the military action meets the criteria of gravity and of intention to act against another State. Practice suggests that six questions can be asked in this respect.

1. Where was the coercive action carried out? If a State acts within its own territorial boundaries, it will be presumed to be implementing police measures as part of the normal exercise of its sovereignty, whether in terms of security on land, at sea or in the air (as in the cases of the aerial incidents set out above). If, however, the coercive action is conducted in another State's territory or in zones that are not subject to any jurisdiction, there will be a greater tendency to characterise the act as serious and to apply article 2(4).

2. In what context does the military action occur? If the two States involved are engaged in armed conflict or if tension is high, the military action will probably be seen in the context of article 2(4), even if the action does not seem serious in absolute terms. The case of the failed US military operation in Iran in 1980, of the Israeli commando in Tunis in 1988 or of certain aerial incidents (*USS Vincennes* or the 1999 incident between India and Pakistan in 1999) illustrate the importance of this question.

3. Who decided on the military operation and who carried it out? If it was the highest authorities of the State that ordered the armed forces to intervene, it will be easier to show that article 2(4) applies than if the operation was decided at a lower level and carried out by persons who are not State officials. In this respect, one need only recall the *Eichmann* or *Rainbow Warrior* cases, in which the governmental authorities of the intervening State tried to minimise the action by attributing responsibility for it to subaltern agents.

4. What is the target of the military operation? If it is the infrastructure, the agents or *a fortiori* the leaders of another State, things will more easily come within the ambit of article 2(4) than for purely private targets (as in the *Rainbow Warrior* case). Of course, as with all the other questions, this one answer alone will not be decisive. As recalled, when Israel carried out an action against a PLO leader in Tunis on 16 April 1988,

criticism related to a violation of the prohibition of the use of force between States.

5. Has the military operation given rise to confrontation between the agents of two States? If so, it seems difficult to set aside article 2(4), even if the fighting remained limited. The Entebbe raid or the *Mayaguez* case, which can be contrasted with the *Rainbow Warrior* and the *Liberia* (1990) cases, are instructive on this point.

6. What is the scope of the means implemented by the intervening State? If confronted with a straightforward abduction or the despatch of a few men who do not open fire (Eichmann affair), there will be less of a tendency to apply article 2(4) than if faced with troop landings, bombardments, or bombings (*Mayaguez* or Entebbe precedents). The greater the means used, the more the State in whose territory the action takes place will be affected, even if the State is not the main target of the operation and there is no fighting between its armed forces and those of the intervening State. This criterion can therefore have decisive effects. It excludes any reasoning that a bombing not directed at or not hitting State agents would elude *ipso facto* the rule prohibiting the use of force between States, as seen in the precedents of the 1985 Israeli bombing of Tunis and the 1998 US bombing of Sudan and Afghanistan.

II What does 'Threat of Force' mean?

The purpose of the rule stated in article 2(4) of the UN Charter is to prohibit not just the use of force but also the *threat* of the use of force. This specific aim of the prohibition is something new for the Charter; the earlier instruments did not refer to it directly.[270] It was introduced in the first stage of the *travaux préparatoires* with the Dumbarton Oaks proposal and thereafter was taken up without any debate or contention.[271] The prohibition of the threat of the use of force was to be reproduced in all the instruments intended to interpret or reaffirm the prohibition set out in article 2(4).[272]

Yet, while it is an essential feature of the provision, the idea of threat has hardly been the subject matter of in-depth scholarly debate.[273] Although

---

[270] K Skubiszewski, 'Use of Force by States. Collective Security. Law of War and Neutrality', above n 33, 741; JL Kunz, 'Bellum justum and Bellum legale' (1951) 45 *AJIL* 533; A Randelzhofer, 'Use of Force' in Bernhardt (ed), *EPIL*, vol 4 (Amsterdam, New York, Oxford, North-Holland Publ, 1982) 267; M Virally, 'Article 2: Paragraphe 4' in A Pellet and J-P Cot (eds), *La Charte des Nations Unies. Commentaire article par article*, 2nd edn (Paris, Economica, 1991) 116.

[271] See *UNCIO*, vol 4, 3; vol 1, 206; vol 6, 102, 339 and 342.

[272] See below.

[273] See: R Sadurska, 'Threats of Force' (1988) 82 *AJIL* 239–67; F Dubuisson and A Lagerwall, 'Que signifie encore l'interdiction de recourir à la menace de la force?' in K Bannelier *et al* (eds), *L'intervention en Iraq et le droit international*, (Paris, Pedone, 2004) 83–104; M Roscini, 'Threats of Armed Force and Contemporary International Law' (2007) 54 NILR 229–77; N Stürchler, *The Threat of Force in International Law* (Cambridge,

there have been many studies of the threat to the peace within the meaning of article 39 of the UN Charter,[274] or to 'threat' as a—highly controversial—feature of 'preventive self-defence',[275] few commentators have set out to interpret the threat of using force in the specific meaning given to it by article 2(4).[276] This observation can probably be explained by the apparent poverty of practice, with States speaking out much more easily about the scope of the prohibition of the use of force, whether generally or in the case of a specific precedent, than about that of an as yet unmaterialised threat.

Several problems that are particularly difficult to interpret arise over the issue of threat.[277] First, the very definition of the idea may be queried: what is the 'threat' covered by article 2(4)? Must it be explicitly stated or can it derive simply from what is perceived as threatening behaviour? Once the notion has been defined, it may be asked to what extent its prohibition corresponds to that of actual use of force. More specifically, can one go along with theories that the paucity of practice is evidence of greater tolerance towards threat than towards an actual use of force? These two questions will be dealt with in turn. We shall begin by showing that 'threat' within the meaning of article 2(4) must be understood in a particularly restrictive sense (A). It will then be seen that, contrary to views held by a minority of scholars, any threat is prohibited on the same basis and to the same extent as the actual use of force (B).

A. The Restrictive Meaning of 'Threat' under Article 2(4) of the Charter

Neither the Charter, nor its *travaux préparatoires*, nor the General Assembly resolutions to interpret the principle of the non-use of force lay down any definition of 'threat'.[278] An examination of doctrine, by contrast, yields a wide variety of definitions, as attested by the following two citations:

—'A threat of force consists in an express or implied promise by a government of a resort to force conditional on non acceptance of certain demands of that government';[279]

—'A threat is an act that is designed to create a psychological condition in the target of apprehension, anxiety and eventually fear, which will erode

Cambridge University Press, 2007); D Kritsiotis, 'Close Encounters of a Sovereign Kind' (2009) 20 *EJIL* 299–330.

[274] Below, ch 6.

[275] See below, ch 7.

[276] A Randelzolfer, 'Article 2(4)' in Bruno Simma (ed), *The Charter of the United Nations. A Commentary*, 2nd edn (Oxford, Oxford University Press, 2002) 124.

[277] See, eg: J-G Castel, *International Law Chiefly as Interpreted and Applied in Canada* (Toronto, Butterworths, 1976) 1220.

[278] See, eg: J Combacau and Serge Sur, *Droit international public*, 5th edn (Paris, Montchrestien, 2001) 629.

[279] I Brownlie, *International Law and the Use of Force by States*, above n 11, 364.

the target's resistance to change or will pressure it toward preserving the status quo';[280]

—'a threat of force under Article 2(4) can be defined as an explicit or implicit promise of a future and unlawful use of armed force against one or more states, the realization of which depends on the threatener's will'.[281]

These definitions are far from unambiguous. It seems, though, that two elements can be identified by comparing and contrasting them with practice. First, the threat covered by article 2(4) is that proferred by one State against another in a specific situation; it does not relate to a general or vague threat resulting from a situation that might degenerate into a breach of the peace. Then, to be covered by the prohibition set out in the Charter, the threat must be clearly established; an uncertain threat does not come within the ambit of this prohibition. In both cases, it is therefore more a restrictive conception of threat that prevails.

An Identified Threat, Not a Vague Risk

If we begin by examining the ordinary meaning of 'threat', it essentially covers two separate meanings.[282] The first refers to behaviour implying a relationship between two persons or groups, the first putting pressure on the second. The second meaning pertains rather to a situation, to a thing, that it is feared may prove dangerous. This double ordinary meaning is reflected in the UN Charter by the distinction between the threat prohibited under article 2(4), governing a specific relation between two States, and a situation of 'threat to the peace' under article 39, allowing the Security Council to take the measures set out in Chapter VII of the Charter.[283] In the second case, we are faced with a situation that does not necessarily result from the threat made by one State to another but one that the Security Council considers might degenerate into an international breach of the peace. As shall be seen,[284] threat takes on here a particularly broad meaning that can cover not just acts of war but also dramatic humanitarian situations, floods

---

[280] R Sadurska, 'Threats of Force', above n 273, 241.

[281] M Roscini, 'Threats of Armed Force and Contemporary International Law', above n 273, 235.

[282] *The Oxford English Reference Dictionary*, 2nd edn, edited by J Pearsall and B Trumble (Oxford, Oxford University Press, 1996) 1502, v° threat; see also J Basdevant (ed), *Dictionnaire de la terminologie du droit international* (Paris, Sirey, 1960) v° 'menace à la paix, contre la paix' and 'menace de guerre' (sens A and B), 386–87; J Salmon (ed), *Dictionnaire de droit international public* (Bruxelles, Bruylant, AUF, 2001) v° 'menaces à la paix ou contre la paix' and 'menace de recours à la force', 693–94; R Savatier (ed), *Nouveau dictionnaire pratique du droit*, tome II (Paris, Dalloz, 1933) 46–47 and EA Martin (ed), *A Dictionary of Law* (Oxford/New York, Oxford University Press, 2002) 498.

[283] M Roscini, 'Threats of Armed Force and Contemporary International Law', above n 273, 231.

[284] Below, ch 6, s 1.

of refugees, the violation of a peace agreement concluded within a State, and so on.[285] The purpose and the aim of introducing this notion of 'threat to the peace' as a situation opening up the path to the use of Chapter VII of the Charter has clearly consisted in conferring extremely broad discretionary power on the Security Council. This is a long way from the idea of threat within the meaning of article 2(4), which is contemplated only as one of the particular manifestations of a policy of force conducted by one State against another.[286] Here we are no longer dealing with a general situation of a vague threat that may be a risk for security. One State directly threatens another with attack. It is only this specific kind of instance that is covered by the wording of article 2.

This restrictive meaning has been shown in the works of the International Law Commission that led to the development of a Draft Code of Crimes Against the Peace and Security of Mankind. Even if not finally materialised in the draft adopted on the second reading because of the excessively subjective character of the notion,[287] the Commission did envisage defining a crime of 'threat of aggression' on the grounds that such a threat was prohibited by article 2(4).[288] In this context the Commission specified:

As to the meaning of the word 'threat', it must be pointed out that generally speaking the term may refer equally well to situations or disputes as to isolated acts. Thus it may be said of a situation that it constitutes a threat to international peace and security. That is so when situations or isolated acts in one region of the world contain germs of conflict liable to have repercussions on peace in that region and even in the rest of the world. It is not, however, in this sense that the word 'threat' is used in article 13 of the draft. Here, the word 'threat' denotes acts undertaken with a view to making a State believe that force will be used against it if certain demands are not met by that State.[289]

---

[285] See also: African Union Non-Aggression and Common Defence Pact, Article Iq.

[286] Above, s 1.

[287] See, eg: Mc Caffrey (1817th meeting, 10 May 1984, *YILC* (1984) vol I, para 38), Njenga (1818th meeting, 11 May 1984, ibid, para 33), Calero Rodriguez (1879th meeting, 9 May 1985, *YILC* (1985) vol I, para 35), Riphagen (1883rd meeting, 17 May 1985, ibid, para 16); see also: Australia (*Draft Code of Crimes against the Peace and Security of Mankind*, A/CN.4/448 and Add 1, Comments and observations received from Governments, *YILC* (1993) vol II, Part One, 14 January 1993, 64, para 22), USA (ibid, 1st February 1993, 103, para 8), Paraguay (ibid, 30 November 1992, 92, para 16), Netherlands (ibid, 18 February 1993, 86, para 53), United Kingdom (ibid, 101, para 21).

[288] See, eg: *Report of the ILC on the work of its 4th session (2 May–21 July 1989)*, *YILC* (1989) vol II, Part Two, 68, para 2; comp *Text of a Draft Code of Offences against the Peace and Security of Mankind suggested as a working paper for the International Law Commission*, *YILC* (1950) vol II, 277–78; *Memorandum prepared by the Secretariat* (A/CN.4/39, 24 November 1950, *YILC* (1950) vol II, 337, para 113); *Second Report of Spiropoulos*, A/CN.4/44, 12 April 1951, *YILC* (1951) vol II, 58.

[289] *YILC* (1989) vol II, Part Two, 68, para 3; see also 1879th meeting, 9 May 1985, *YILC* (1985) vol I, para 18; see also *Third Report on the draft Code of Offences against the Peace and Security of Mankind*, A/CN.4/387, 8 April 1985, *YILC* (1985) vol II, Part One, 73, paras 89–91.

The distinction was again made during debates around the 60th anniversary of the entry into force of the UN Charter. The documents and debates produced at the time plainly show that threat is envisaged both in an extremely broad sense, opening up the path to action by the Security Council or by other UN organs,[290] and in a far narrower sense, in the context of rules about the use of force.[291] In the first case, the threat may possibly be deduced from the outbreak or continuation of non-international armed conflict, deterioration of a humanitarian situation, cross-border movements of population, or even acute health problems. In the second instance, we are confined to the case of a possible outbreak of war by one State against another.

Admittedly some States, like Ghana, formulate an extremely wide definition of threat within the meaning of article 2(4) considering that it covers the mere conclusion of military alliances or the acquisition of weapons.[292] However, it would be excessive to deduce from that fact alone that there had emerged a general agreement on a wide definition of threat covering a vague threat. As concerns the works in the General Assembly, an examination of the position of States as a whole shows that the Ghanaian assertion remained isolated, with most States giving much narrower definitions of threat.[293] As seen, those definitions prevailed in the International Law Commission's works on the Draft Code of Crimes Against the Peace and Security of Mankind. More generally, no precedent is to be found where a State is accused of, and *a fortiori* condemned for, violation of article 2(4) simply for stockpiling weapons or setting up military bases. The International Court of Justice did assert in *Military and Paramilitary Activities* that

> in international law there are no rules, other than such rules as may be accepted by the State concerned, by treaty or otherwise, whereby the level of armaments of a sovereign State can be limited, and this principle is valid for all States without exception.[294]

The mere fact of procuring arms, while it might be a threat to international peace and security, does not constitute a threat against another State under article 2(4).

---

[290] *A more secured world: Our shared responsibility*, Report of the Secretary General's High-Level Panel on Threats, Challenges and Change, UN, 2004, 24–27, paras 44–58, 31–35, paras 74–88, 47–48, paras 145–46, 52–53, paras 165–170, and 63–66, paras 193–203; *In larger freedom: towards development, security and human rights for all: report of the Secretary-General*, A/59/2005, 24 March 2005, paras 77–81, *2005 World Summit Outcome*, GA Res 60/1 of 24 October 2005, paras 69–72 and para 79.

[291] *A more secured world: Our shared responsibility*, above n 290, 63, para 188; *In larger freedom: towards development, security and human rights for all: report of the Secretary-General*, above n 290, para 124; *2005 World Summit Outcome*, above n 290, para 77.

[292] Ghana, A/C.6/S.R.815, 20 November 1963, para 33.

[293] See examples below.

[294] ICJ Rep (1986) 135, para 269.

A debate of this type was started up again in the International Court of Justice in the *Legality of the Threat or Use of Nuclear Weapons* case, with some States considering that the dissuasion policy was, in itself, a threat of the use of force contrary to the Charter.[295] This view, however, is far from shared by States as a whole,[296] including by those which spoke for the argument that the threat or use of nuclear weapons was unlawful. Thus, for the Solomon Islands, a State that is not otherwise particularly sensitive to the arguments of the nuclear powers:

> If States manufacture or possess nuclear weapons it is presumably in the expectation that they could, in certain circumstances, be used. Since the use of nuclear weapons is intended to 'harm' rather than to do some good, it might therefore be said that mere possession constitutes a form of 'threat'. State practice indicates that it is not the case. For half a century a small group of States have possessed nuclear weapons, and such possession has never been considered by the rest of the international community to be a 'threat' which is contrary to international law . . . The use of the term 'threat' by the General Assembly in its request for an Advisory Opinion must therefore be considered to *be limited to the situation where one or more States clearly express an intention to use nuclear weapons against one or more specifically designated States or populations in precise circumstances.* (emphasis added)[297]

The Court, for its part, did not come out plainly on this issue. Emphasising that the dissuasion doctrine might be based on the right of self-defence, it seems to have avoided any pronouncement on the actual definition of threat. But, the Court likens threat to 'a signalled intention to use force if certain events occur',[298] and then relates it to a 'particular use of force envisaged',[299] which explicitly seems to exclude assimilating a vague and unidentified threat to the threat covered by article 2(4).[300]

Along the same lines, we might cite the precedent of the missile crisis between the United States, Cuba and the USSR. In October 1962, on discovering that the Soviet Union had deployed nuclear weapons on Cuban territory, the United States evoked 'a threat to the peace of this hemisphere,

---

[295] Samoa (*Letter dated 11 June 1995 from the Permanent Representative of Samoa to the UN, together with Written Statement of the Government of Samoa*), Nauru (*Letter 15 June 1995 from counsel appointed by Nauru, together with Written Statement of the Government of Nauru*, 1), Malaysia (2 and 25 of the written statement), Indonesia (Berchmans Soedarmanto Kadarisman, 18, para 9) and Qatar (Najeeb Al-Nauimi, CR 95/29, 10 November 1995, 27).

[296] See: United Kingdom (*Letter dated 16 June 1995 from the Legal Adviser to the Foreign and Commonwealth Office of the United Kingdom of Great Britain and Northern Ireland, together with Written Statement of the United Kingdom*, 72–73, para 3.118), France (Perrin de Brichambaut, CR 95/23, 1 November 1995, 64, para 34).

[297] *Letter dated 19 June 1995 from the Permanent Representative of Solomon Islands to the United Nations, together with Written Statement of the Government of Solomon Islands*, 24, paras 3.4. and 3.5.

[298] ICJ, *Legality of the Threat or Use of Nuclear Weapons*, ICJ Rep (1996) 246, para 47.

[299] ibid, 247, para 48.

[300] F Dubuisson and A Lagerwall 'Que signifie encore l'interdiction de recourir à la menace de la force?', above n 273, 88.

and, indeed, to the peace of the world'.[301] On this ground they seized the Organisation of American States and applied for and obtained a resolution recommending the adoption of the necessary measures to prevent Cuba's offensive arms becoming an 'active threat to the peace and security of the Continent'.[302] The texts made no reference to the prohibition of the threat or use of force set out in article 2(4). Save for a declaration made furtively by the US delegate during debates,[303] no representative claimed that Cuba had violated the rule through the simple fact of accepting weapons to be installed on its territory.[304] Several States did assert, though, that the quarantine measures decided by the United States by which any vessel was threatened with coercive action unless it complied with its requirements did constitute a threat of a use of force contrary to the prohibition set out in article 2(4).[305] Others considered that those measures were consistent with Chapter VII of the Charter, without denying that there was a threat to use force.[306] This precedent seems therefore to confirm the distinction between a threat in the broad sense, which may justify the jurisdiction of the organisations competent for maintaining peace and security—such as the UN or the OAS in the case in point—and a threat in the narrow sense of article 2(4), which implies that an intent to use force potentially is clearly identified. The situation resulting from the sending of Soviet arms to Cuba was considered to be a threat of the first type;[307] the quarantine then imposed by the United States, whether considered lawful or unlawful, clearly revealed, in the views of the various States, a threat of the second type.[308]

Another point is worth mentioning to illustrate this distinction. It regularly happens that certain major powers devise political doctrines in the context of which they specify under what circumstances they are ready to use force. One instance is the Brejnev doctrine by which the former Soviet leader asserted that a State could intervene on the territory of the community of socialist States to enforce the values of that community.[309] One also

[301] USA; S/PV.1022, 23 October 1962, para 14; see also paras 74, 79 and 82.
[302] OAS Res of 23 October 1962, S/5193, 3, para 2. See also S/5182, 23 October 1962.
[303] S/PV.1022, 23 October 1962, para 15 and S/PV.1025, 25 October 1962, para 21.
[304] See, eg: Venezuela (S/PV.1023, 24 October 1962, para 7) and France (S/PV.1024, 24 October 1962, para 10).
[305] Cuba (S/PV.1022, 23 October 1962, paras 88, 110, and 122–23), USSR (ibid, paras 157–58, 173 and S/5187), Romania (S/PV.1023, 24 October 1962, para 58), and UAR (S/PV.1024, 24 October 1962, para 67).
[306] France (S/PV.1024, 24 October 1962, para 10), China (ibid, para 18), and USA (S/PV.1025, 25 October 1962, paras 15–16).
[307] B Asrat, *Prohibition of Force under the UN Charter. A Study of Article 2(4)*, above n 124, 140.
[308] Q Wright, 'The Cuban Quarantine' (1963) 57 *AJIL* 557.
[309] See: MM Whiteman (ed), *Digest of International Law*, vol 12 (Washington, Department of State Pub, 1971) 290–94; see also C Zorgbide, 'La doctrine soviétique de la "souveraineté limitée"' (1970) 74 *RGDIP* 872–905; M Bettati, '"Souveraineté limitée" ou "internationalisme prolétarien"? Les liens fondamentaux de la communauté des Etats socialistes' (1972) 8 *RBDI* 455–81; R Charvin, 'Souveraineté et intégration dans la communauté des Etats socialistes' (1973) 9 *RBDI* 411–28; S Schwebel, 'The Brezhnev Doctrine Repealed and Peaceful Co-Existence Enacted' (1972) 66 *AJIL* 816–19.

thinks of several doctrines developed by presidential administrations of the United States affirming that country's right to conduct military actions around the world in the name of the defence of democracy, the free market, or quite simply the national interests of the superpower concerned.[310] While such doctrines were not without their critics, they did not give rise to accusations of violation of article 2(4).[311] Not that they cannot be used to show that a threat to use force was made in some particular case or other. But, in the absence of any more specific element, it seems that speech-making, even with bellicose overtones, so long as it maintains a high level of generality, cannot be assimilated to a threat covered by article 2(4).

At this stage, a final illustration of this problem can be presented. Subsequent to its attack on Iraqi nuclear installations on 7 June 1981, the State of Israel multiplied declarations saying it was ready to destroy other installations of the type in Iraq or in neighbouring countries if and when it deemed it necessary. Those declarations were firmly condemned in several General Assembly resolutions adopted by large majorities.[312] In 1983, the General Assembly reaffirmed article 2(4) and took the view that 'any threat to attack and destroy nuclear facilities in Iraq and in other countries constitutes a violation of the Charter of the United Nations'.[313] In 1985, the same assembly expressed its deep concern further to a declaration by an Israeli cabinet member that 'We are prepared to strike against any nuclear reactor built by Iraq in the future'.[314] This precedent shows that threats may be contemplated under article 2(4) when one can identify the target with some precision, even if the threat does not relate to an attack that has already been decided upon in terms of where and when it will happen. In the current instance, the UN General Assembly's language was prompted by Israel's repeated refusal to give a commitment not to attack its neighbouring States any more.[315] Everything will hang on the circumstances in which the litigious declarations are made.

Finally, to come within the ambit of this provision, a threat must be clearly identifiable in a particular situation: 'only a threat directed towards a specific reaction on the part of the target State is unlawful under the terms

---

[310] See, eg: www.politicalresource.net/truman_doctrine.html; *Message from President Eisenhower to Congress*, January 5, 1957, point VIII, www.us-israel.org/jsource/US-Israel/ike-doc.html; *The National Security Strategy of the United States of America*, September 2002.

[311] See, eg: United Kingdom (A/C.6/35/SR.32, 29 October 1980, para 17).

[312] 'Armed Israeli aggression against the Iraqi nuclear installations and its grave consequences for the established international system concerning the peaceful uses of nuclear energy, the non-proliferation of nuclear weapons and international peace and security'; GA Res 36/27 of 13 November 1981 (109-2-34), preamble and para 2; GA Res 37/18 of 16 November 1982 (119-2-13), preamble and paras 3–4; GA Res 38/9 of 10 November 1983 (123-2-12), preamble and paras 2, 3, 4 and 6; GA Res 39/14 of 8 November 1984 (106-2-33), preamble and paras 2–4; GA Res 40/6 of 1 November 1985 (88-13-39), preamble and paras 2 and 4; GA Res 41/12 of 29 October 1986 (86-5-55), para 2; see also SC Res 487 (1981) of 19 June 1981, para 2.

[313] GA Res 38/9 of 10 November 1983, preamble and para 3.

[314] GA Res 40/6 of 1 November 1985, preamble.

[315] See, eg: GA Res 39/14 of 8 November 1984, para 5.

of Art. 2(4)'.[316] A State that is simply dangerous *in abstracto* does not necessarily violate the UN Charter, which does not mean the Security Council is not competent to manage a situation perceived as a threat to peace and international security. It was observed above that the 'force' prohibited by article 2(4) implied the intention of one State to act against another State.[317] This criterion of intent must be borne in mind when asking whether a threat comes under the prohibition of the use of force. The prohibited threat already reflects the intention to use force. And it shall not be established unless it arises clearly from an examination of the specific situation in question, as shall be seen now.

A Clearly Established Threat, Not an Uncertain Threat

When making pronouncements *in abstracto* on the notion of threat of the use of force, States have generally emphasised the various possible ways for a threat to manifest itself. Two declarations may be cited in illustration:

—'The expression "threat to force" shall refer to any action, direct or indirect, whatever the form it may take, which tends to produce in the other State a justified fear that it or the regional community of which it is a part will be exposed to serious and irreparable harm';[318]
—'the term "threat" referred to an announcement of an act of violence for the purpose of intimidating a State into changing its policies. Such threats could be issued verbally through the Press or by radio, or they could take the form of acts of commission or omission. The fact that a State might concentrate its troops in a border area, for example, might constitute a threat to another country. Acts of omission could also constitute threats, without armed forces necessarily being involved, as for example through the complete or partial interruption of economic relations and of means of communication. While the Charter did not give a precise definition of the term "threat", an analysis of that document showed that threats of the kind he had mentioned lay half-way between threats properly so called and breaches of the peace'.[319]

The threat to use force cannot therefore be reduced to any particular behaviour.[320] Even if it seems complex on some occasions, whether or not

---

[316] A Randelzolfer, 'Article 2(4)', above n 276, 124.
[317] Above, s I.
[318] Chile (A/AC.125/L.23, 24 March 1966, c) and A/AC.125/SR.22, 23 March 1966, para 31).
[319] Madagascar (A/AC.125/SR.19, 21 March 1966, 7, para 9); see also Yugoslavia (A/C.6/S.R.753, 5 November 1962, para 31; A/C.6/S.R.802, 29 October 1963, para 7), Pakistan (A/C.6/S.R.816, 20 November 1963, para 11), Ghana (A/C.6/S.R.815, 20 November 1963, para 33), Sweden (A/AC.125/SR.86, 13 September 1968, 42) and United Kingdom (A/C.6/S.R.805, 5 November 1963, para 10).
[320] See also Mexico: 'such a threat does not necessarily have to be made openly, but that on certain occasions veiled threats could be most effective, yet difficult to prove' (*Note verbale*

article 2(4) has been violated should be determined on a case by case basis in view of the specific circumstances. In any event, 'as for the "threat" of force, it could be direct or indirect'.[321]

Practice, and more especially case law on the subject, shows that this apparent flexibility must not deceive us. While it is true that the threat can be deduced, in principle, from very varied forms of behaviour, it is no less true that it must be clearly established. This requirement arises implicitly from the *Military Activities* case (a), and more directly from the precedents in which the existence of a threat to use force has been recognised (b). It raises the question of determining the circumstances under which it can be concluded that such a threat exists (c).

a) The Dismissal of an Uncertain Threat: the Military Activities *Case Law*

Upon filing its application, Nicaragua asked the Court to condemn the United States for having used force *and* having threatened to use force against it.[322] In its memorial, the plaintiff State emphasised the 'background of a continuous and deliberate campaign of intimidation by regular US land, naval and air forces along the border of Nicaragua and in the sea off its coast'.[323] It denounced several campaigns of military manoeuvres and added that 'The purpose has not been hidden. At the highest levels, the US officials have repeatedly avowed that the object of this activity is to "put pressure on" the Nicaraguan Government'.[324] It was on this basis especially that article 2(4) had allegedly been violated, the infringements of Nicaragua's sovereignty, the support for the *contras* and the laying of mines around its ports being compounded by a threat to use force that is prohibited by the provision.[325]

This part of Nicaragua's application was not accepted by the Court, which said that it had not been 'satisfied that the manoeuvres complained of, in the circumstances in which they were held, constituted on the part of the United States a breach, as against Nicaragua, of the principle forbidding recourse to the threat or use of force'.[326]

As no ground was given in support of this assertion, it is difficult to draw from it any very precise conclusion about the notion of 'threat'. One

---

dated 19 June 1995 *from the Embassy of Mexico, together with Written Statement of the Government of Mexico,* 7, para 36) and GA Res 290 (IV) of 1 December 1949.

[321] Argentina (A/AC.119/SR.3, 31 August 1964, 11).

[322] Application instituting proceedings, 9 April 1984, ICJ, *Military and Paramilitary Activities, Pleadings, Oral Arguments, Documents,* vol I, 9, para 26(c); see also 7, paras 15–16 and 29, para 10; ICJ, *Border and Transborder Armed Actions (Nicaragua v Honduras), Pleadings, Oral Arguments, Documents,* vol I, 5, para 22.

[323] Memorial of Nicaragua, 30 April 1985; ICJ, *Military and Paramilitary Activities, Pleadings, Oral Arguments, Documents,* vol I, 60, para 217.

[324] ibid.

[325] ibid, 117 and 119, para 457, 132, para 507; see also Brownlie, 12 April 1985, ibid, vol V, 226–27.

[326] ICJ, *Military and Paramilitary Activities,* ICJ Rep (1986) 118, para 227.

incontestable point remains. In the case at hand, the Court was in a context where, according to its own pleadings, one State had violated the airspace of another State through several improper intrusions by military aircraft, had resorted to force against it by mining some of its port facilities, had intervened in its internal affairs by giving military support to opposition forces, and had imposed an embargo on it, all without making any bones about its intention to influence Nicaragua in the exercise of its national policy.[327] In this context the Court considered that military manoeuvres, even accompanied by hostile declarations, were not enough to prove the existence of a threat to use force contrary to the UN Charter.

It should be specified, and this may be a decisive point, that Nicaragua did not cite any official declaration before the Court clearly attesting to the United States' intention to carry out acts characterised by the Court as use of force.[328] In its memorial, the plaintiff State evoked a peace proposal made by President Reagan, affirming that this proposal 'was, in reality, an ultimatum announcing recourse to military measures if certain demands are not accepted'.[329] In his speech made on 4 April 1985, the President of the United States asked Congress for $14 million to help the *contras*, and stated that the funds would not be for the purchase of arms and ammunition but only for the purchase of food, clothing and medicine. He added, though, that the use of the funds would only be restricted if the Nicaraguan authorities accepted a ceasefire proposal: 'If the Sandinistas accept this peace offer, I will keep my funding restrictions in effect. But peace negotiations must not become a cover for deception and delay. If there is no agreement after 60 days of negotiations, I will lift these restrictions, unless both sides ask me not to'.[330] The Court did not consider this sufficient evidence to conclude there had been a threat to use force. However, it should be remembered in this respect that the simple sending of funds to the *contras* was characterised by the Court as a violation of the principle of non-intervention, without the prohibition of the threat of the use of force being mentioned.[331] Under the circumstance, the threat that can be deduced from the speech of 4 April 1985 logically falls outside the ambit of the prohibition laid down in article 2(4).[332] There remained the US army manoeuvres that had been cited by Nicaragua as the central manifestation of the threat. But it will be observed that in the same speech of 4 April 1985, the

---

[327] See: *Statement by the Principal Deputy Press Secretary to the President*, May 1, 1985 (1985) 24 *ILM* 810–11; *US Diplomatic Note concerning Economic Sanctions*, no 126, ibid, 811–15; ICJ Rep (1986) 146, para 292.

[328] Memorial of Nicaragua, 30 April 1985, 116–19; Brownlie, 12 April 1985, above n 325, 226–27.

[329] Memorial of 30 April 1985, above n 323, 120, para 457.

[330] *Remarks Announcing a Central AmEan Peace Proposal and a Question-and-Answer Session with Reporters*, April 4, 1985, www.reagan.utexas.edu/archives/speeches/1985/40485e.htm.

[331] ICJ Rep (1986) 118–19, para 228, and 124–25, para 242.

[332] ibid, 123–24, paras 240–41.

President of the United States affirmed that the manoeuvres should not be construed as a threat against anyone.[333]

All told, this affair shows that, to come within the ambit of the rule set out in article 2(4), military manoeuvres should be accompanied by declarations or at any rate evidence of a clear threat of invasion or military incursion, even in a context of extreme tension between the States concerned.

b) The Case of Explicitly Formulated Threats: Declarations of War and Ultimatums

This high standard does not mean that no threat may ever be proved; far from it. A State may very explicitly state its intent to use force against another because it considers that this would be perfectly legitimate and in compliance with international law. In such a case, there is no doubt that we are faced with a threat to use force; what is controversial is not the existence of such a threat but its lawfulness in respect of positive international law.[334] In the debates in the UN General Assembly, the case of the declaration of war was raised, which is supposedly, as such, incompatible with article 2(4).[335] This assertion was not contradicted, perhaps simply because it relates to what has become a hypothetical case in recent decades, the 'declaration of war' seeming to be an outdated institution.[336]

The same is not true of the ultimatum,[337] by which one State explicitly warns another that it will use force if certain demands are not met.[338] A definition of threat that is often cited refers to 'the previous announcement of an act of violence, such as an ultimatum announcing recourse to military measures if certain demands are not accepted'.[339] Many examples illustrate this position.

A precedent traditionally invoked in this respect is the ultimatum issued by France and the United Kingdom during the 1956 Suez crisis.[340] By the terms employed by the British prime minister of the time:

[333] 'If you'll look back through history, you'll find out that we traditionally have used among our neighbors for jungle training exercices of this kind. And they're not—as some loud voices up on the Hill have said—they're not down here as a threat to anyone', above n 330.

[334] See: D Kritsiotis, 'Close Encounters of a Sovereign Kind', above n 273, 308*ff.*

[335] USSR, *Special Committee on Enhancing the Effectiveness of the Principle of Non-use of Force in International Relations. Report, 1979*, GA, 34th session, Supp no 41 (A/34/41), 4 June 1979.

[336] See: K Skubiszewski, 'Use of Force by States. Collective Security. Law of War and Neutrality', above n 33, 779–80.

[337] See, in the ILC, Liang (89th meeting, 25 May 1951, *YILC* (1951) vol I, para 50), and Scelle (ibid, para 56).

[338] K Skubiszewski, 'Use of Force by States. Collective Security. Law of War and Neutrality', above n 33, 780.

[339] E Jiménez de Arechaga, 'General Course of Public International Law' (1978-I) 159 *RCADI* 88.

[340] ND White & R Cryer, 'Unilateral Enforcement of Resolution 687: A Threat too Far?', (1999) 29 *California Western ILJ* 252; B Asrat, *Prohibition of Force under the UN Charter. A Study of Article 2(4)*, above n 124, 140.

[T]he U.K. and French Governments have addressed urgent communications to Egypt and Israel. In these we have called upon both sides to stop all warlike action by land, sea and air forthwith and to withdraw their military forces to a distance of 10 miles from the Canal. Further, in order to separate the belligerents and to guarantee freedom of transit through the Canal by the ships of all nations, we have asked the Egyptian Government to agree that Anglo-French forces should move temporarily—I repeat, temporarily—into key positions at Port Said, Ismailia, and Suez. The Governments of Egypt and Israel have been asked to answer this communication within 12 hours. *It has been made clear to them that if at the expiration of that time one or both have not undertaken to comply with these requirements, British and French forces will intervene in whatever strength may be necessary to secure compliance.* (emphasis added)[341]

The intervening States' position clearly consists in brandishing a threat of the use of force in order to conduct an action that they consider legitimate.[342]

This type of case may be illustrated by examining the behaviour of certain States with regard to Yugoslavia in the Kosovo conflict in the months before the start of the military operation on 23 March 1999.[343] Early in October 1998, the President of the United States declared that NATO was ready to act if President Milosevic did not fulfil his obligations under UN resolutions.[344] On 13 October 1998, the 'ACTORD' activation order was issued by NATO giving the go-ahead for air strikes against the FRY.[345] Refraining from carrying out these threats was plainly conditional upon Belgrade's acceptance of certain demands. It was in this context that agreements were signed between the Yugoslav government and the OSCE on one side and NATO on the other.[346] The leaders of the Member States of these organisations affirmed that the agreements could not have been obtained without credible threats to use force.[347] They continued with this

---

[341] *Keesing's Contemporary Archives* (1956) 15174 and S/PV.949, 30 October 1956, 2–3; see also 'Pratique française du droit international' (1957) 3 *AFDI* 828.

[342] See: G Marchton, 'Armed Intervention in the 1956 Suez Canal Crisis: The Legal Advice tendered to the British Government' (1988) 37 *ICLQ* 773–817.

[343] See: B Simma, 'Nato, the UN and the Use of Force: Legal Aspects' (1999) 10 *EJIL* 1–22; I Brownlie and CJ Apperley, 'Kosovo Crisis Inquiry: Memorandum on the International Law Aspects' (2000) 49 *ICLQ* 897–98; D Kritsiotis, 'Close Encounters of a Sovereign Kind', above n 273, 313–14.

[344] *Le Figaro*, 7 October 1998; see also *Le Monde*, 8 October 1998.

[345] See: *DAI*, 1 December 1998, 889.

[346] Texts in M Weller, *The Crisis in Kosovo 1989–1999*, International Documents and Analysis, vol 1 (Cambridge, Documents & Analysis Pub Limited, 1999) 293 and 281.

[347] According to Madeleine Albright, 'It would not have happened if we had not combined diplomacy with the threat by NATO to use force [. . .] we will continue to pursue diplomacy combined with a credible threat of force. Let me repeat–NATO's threat to use force if necessary remains [. . .]. As a result, we have decided this evening to maintain the Act Ord for limited air operations. Its execution will be subject to a decision and assessment by the North Atlantic Council' (27 October 1998, M Weller, *The Crisis in Kosovo 1989–1999*, above n 346, 284); see also 'Pratique française du droit international' (1999) 45 *AFDI* 883.

policy of pressure.[348] On 30 January 1999, the North Atlantic Council authorised the NATO Secretary-General to launch air strikes against objectives on the territory of the FRY.[349] This was the background to the discussion to adopt the Rambouillet plan in February and then March 1999. On the 23 February, the Secretary-General asserted that 'We remain ready to use whatever means are necessary to bring about a peaceful solution to the crisis in Kosovo and to prevent human suffering. . . . *Our stance in putting the threat of force at the service of diplomacy has helped to create the conditions for the Rambouillet talks to make progress*'. (emphasis added)[350] On 18 March 1999, the US Secretary of State further affirmed: 'I would just like to remind President Milosevic that NATO stands ready to take whatever measures are necessary'.[351] Together the terms of these declarations are unambiguous: the threat is clearly brandished and assumed as an entirely legal and legitimate policy instrument.[352]

The same conclusion may be deduced from examination of the position of the States that envisaged a military intervention against Iraq in the months preceding the outbreak of the war, on 20 March 2003. In February 2002, Vice-President Dick Cheney stated that the US president was determined to put pressure on Iraq and intended to use all the means available, including military means.[353] In October that same year, President Bush and Prime Minister Blair both declared that Iraq had to comply with the UN resolutions, failing which it would be 'forced to do so'[354] or 'confronted with force'.[355] The US authorities, who were beginning massive deployment of military resources in the Gulf region did not conceal the fact that only a credible military threat might get President Saddam Hussein to obey.[356] It was in this context that on 17 March 2003, the US president again declared that 'Saddam Hussein and his sons must leave Iraq within 48 hours. Their refusal to do so will result in military conflict, commenced at a time of our choosing'[357].

[348] According to the Secretary General of NATO, 'We are ready to act, if necessary [. . .]. We will keep them under pressure until they do so' (29 January 1999, M Weller, *The Crisis in Kosovo 1989–1999*, above n 346, 415).

[349] ibid, 416–17.

[350] ibid, 474.

[351] ibid, 493.

[352] M Weller, *The Crisis in Kosovo 1989–1999*, above n 346, 'Chapter 12: The Nato Threat of Force and the Holbrooke Agreement', and comments at 272.

[353] *NYT*, 16 February 2002.

[354] 'Bush Says Confronting Iraq Is Matter of National Security', 15 October 2002; www.uspolicy.be.

[355] 'Prime Minister Statement on Iraq following UN Security Council resolution', 8 November 2002; www.number-10.goSeeuk/output/Page1.asp; see F Dubuisson and A Lagerwall, 'Que signifie encore l'interdiction de recourir à la menace de la force ?', above n 273, 95.

[356] See also: UK and USA (S/PV.4707, 14 February 2003) and 'Netherlands State Practice' (2004) 35 *NYIL* 370–71; 'La pratique belge en matière de droit international' (2005) 38 *RBDI* 259–61.

[357] Remarks by the President in Address to the Nations, 17 March 2003; www.global security.org/wmd/library/news/iraq/2003/iraq-030317-wh-01.htm.

These precedents are particularly emblematic, but they are not isolated[358]. It has already been seen that in October 1962 the United States had threatened to take measures against ships that breached the quarantine on Cuba.[359] It has also been said that Israel, after carrying out its operation against Osirak in 1981, expressly declared that new attacks would be made against any other nuclear facilities.[360] It can also be recalled that in the 1990s the United States and some of its allies defined 'air exclusion zones' over Iraqi territory, warning the authorities that any unauthorised entry into these zones would lead to military strikes.[361] Finally, in the Guyana/ Suriname case cited above, an order to leave an area 'within 12 hours' or 'face the consequences' was considered by the arbitral tribunal as 'an explicit threat that force might be used if the order was not complied with'.[362]

In each of these cases, the threat to resort to force is explicit, as it is assumed as one of the components of the State's foreign policy.[363] The problem is whether this threat is consistent with article 2(4). No one contests, though, that events can be characterised as a 'threat' within the meaning of this provision. The same is not true, however, in a whole series of other examples where no threat is explicitly formulated.

c) The Problematical Case of Implied Threats

As pointed out from the outset, none of the legal definitions of threat requires that it be explicitly stated[364]. It depends on the particular circumstances whether it can be determined that a threat has been made or not.[365]

---

[358] See also the Russian threat vis-a-vis Georgia by mid-2008; Independent International Fact-Finding Mission on the Conflict in Georgia, *Report*, September 2009 (www.ceiig.ch/Report.html), vol II, 234–35.

[359] Above and K Skubiszewski, 'Use of Force by States. Collective Security. Law of War and Neutrality', above n 33, 757 and 780.

[360] Above.

[361] See: *Statement issued by the Members of the Coalition at New York*, 26 August 1992: 'a no-fly zone for all Iraqi fixed and rotary wing aircraft—military and civilian—will be established south of 32 degrees north [. . .]. To be clear:—Iraq may not fly military or civilian aircraft, whether fixed or rotary wing, south of the 32nd parallel. *We will respond appropriately and decisively to any Iraqi failure to comply with this requirement;*—No threat to coalition operations over southern Iraq will be tolerated. *The Iraqi Government should know that coalition aircraft will use appropriate force in response to any indication of hostile intent* [. . .]' (emphasis added); M Weller (ed), *Iraq and Kuwait: The Hostilities and Their Aftermath* (Cambridge, Grotius Pub Limited, 1993) 725); see also ND White and R Cryer, 'Unilateral Enforcement of Resolution 687: A Threat Too Far?', above n 340, 255 *ff*.

[362] Arbitral Tribunal Constituted Pursuant to Article 287, and in Accordance with Annex VII of the UN Convention on the Law of the Sea (Guyana and Suriname, 17 September 2007, www.pca-cpa.org/showpage.asp?pag_id=1147), para 439.

[363] See also: I Brownlie, 'General Course of Public International Law' (1995) *RCADI* 204 and ND White and R Cryer, 'Unilateral Enforcement of Resolution 687: A Threat Too Far?' above n 340, 252.

[364] Independent International Fact-Finding Mission on the Conflict in Georgia, *Report*, September 2009 (www.ceiig.ch/Report.html), vol II, 231.

[365] ND White and R Cryer, 'Unilateral Enforcement of Resolution 687: A Threat Too Far?' above n 340, 253–54.

At this point we can cite article 13 of the Draft Code of Crimes Against the Peace and Security of Mankind, adopted by the International Law Commission at first reading:

Threat of aggression

Threat of aggression consists of declarations, communications, demonstrations of force or any other measures which would give good reason to the Government of a State to believe that aggression is being seriously contemplated against that State.[366]

This text was not included in the code that was finally adopted solely because of circumstances relating to the opportuneness of specifically incriminating threats in criminal law.[367] Even so, the definition of threat contained in it was not fundamentally called into question within the Commission or by the States that made comments. By using the expression 'or any other measures', this definition clearly confirms that the threat is not limited to one or other particular form.[368] On the other hand, it is accepted that a threat is different from simple political pressure, which is a quite common and accepted phenomenon in the international arena.[369]

What then are the criteria that might allow us to conclude that a threat exists in the absence of any explicit statement? Generally, the Commission specifies that 'the word "threat" denotes acts undertaken with a view to making a State believe that force will be used against it if certain demands are not met by that State'.[370] It is indeed, then, the existence of a real ultimatum that is the decisive criterion, even if that ultimatum is not stated in so many words.[371] To establish such existence, certain indications should be taken into account that relate essentially to the behaviour of the intervening State. The threat must be considered as a sign of intent, by one State, to force another State to act in a predetermined manner.[372] As said above, 'threat' must not be understood here by reference to a situation that

---

[366] *Report of the ILC on the works of its 41st session*, YILC (1989) vol II, Part Two, 68; see also Scelle, Cordova and Sandström (89th meeting, 25 May 1951, YILC (1951) vol I, paras 56, 59 and 61).

[367] Above; see also 'La pratique suisse en matière de droit international public' (1990) 47 *ASDI* 181.

[368] *Report of the ILC on the works of its 41st session*, YILC (1989) vol II, Part Two, 68, para 3.

[369] According to the Netherlands, 'it was difficult to prohibit in a general and absolute way the exercise of all forms of pressure. Even in a highly organized national community with a well-developed legal system and a State monopoly of the use of force, individual and collective 'pressure' continued to be an important factor in the actual regulation of society' (A/AC.119/SR.7, 2 September 1964, 9).

[370] *Report of the ILC on the works of its 41st session*, YILC (1989) vol II, Part Two, 68, para 3.

[371] See also: Reuter, 2135th meeting, 12 July 1989, YILC (1989) vol I, para 9; Indonesia, ICJ, *Legality of the Threat or Use of Nuclear Weapons*, Berchmans Soedarmanto Kadarisman, 95/25, 3 November 2005, 32, para 57; Malaysia, Memorial, 19 June 1995, 22–23.

[372] Shi, 2058th meeting, 8 June 1988, YILC (1988) vol I, para 7; see also Thiam, *Third report on the draft Code of Offences against the Peace and Security of Mankind*, A/CN.4/387, 8 April 1985, YILC (1985) vol II, Part One, 73, para 91.

is dangerous for international peace—as is the case under article 39 of the Charter—but must reflect preparation for the use of force contemplated by one State against another.[373] Four clarifications must be made in this respect.

1. A threat within the meaning of article 2(4) presupposes the existence of a national policy, which implies that some acts or declarations have been posited by the highest authorities of the State.[374] *A contrario*, it is hard to imagine that one could conclude there has been a violation of this provision if a simple officer or official becomes carried away and makes bellicose declarations during a meeting of military staff or subaltern officials of two States.[375] As far as I know, no accusation of this order arises in existing practice at any rate.

2. The existence of a threat supposes that things said and done are observed from which demands inherent to the ultimatum can be identified.[376] In theory, such a discourse or manifestation may be understood broadly as not necessarily taking the form of a declaration but as being liable to be inferred from behaviour, provided it is sufficiently eloquent.[377] In practice, accusations of threat invariably refer to things written or spoken publicly[378] by high authorities.[379] It will be recalled on this point that the International Court of Justice likened threat to a '*signalled intention*' to use force or 'the stated readiness to use it'. (emphasis added)[380] Threatening written or spoken words may be expressed directly, by private or official communication between the authorities of the two States or indirectly via interviews, conferences or through the press. The Commission's works specify the need to

---

[373] Above.

[374] See: Central African Republic (A/C.6/S.R.884, 29 November 1965, para 27).

[375] See: Spiropoulos, *Second Report on the draft Code of Offences against the Peace and Security of Mankind*, A/CN.4/44, 12 April 1951, *YILC* (1951) vol II, 58; *Report of the ILC on the work of its 6th session (3 June–28 July 1954)*, GA, 9th session, Supp no 9, A/2693, 11, Article 2.2; see also *YILC* (1984) vol II, Part One, 91, para 16; 4th (11 March 1986, A/CN.4/398, *YILC* (1986) vol II, Part One, 84, art 11 § 2) and 6th report (19 February 1988, A/CN.4/411, *YILC* (1988) vol II, Part One, 202, art 11 § 2); cp Ouchakov, 1965th meeting, 12 June 1986, *YILC* (1986) vol I, para 22).

[376] According to the USA, 'it would seem that the threat must be openly made and communicated by some means to the State threatened' (A/AC.119/SR.3, 31 August 1964, 14); see also France (ICJ, *Legality of the Threat or Use of Nuclear Weapons*, Perrin de Brichambaut, CR 95/23, 1st November 1995, 65, para 34). Comp Independent International Fact-Finding Mission on the Conflict in Georgia, *Report*, September 2009 (www.ceiig.ch/Report.html), vol II, 232–33.

[377] Cyprus (A/C.6/S.R.822, 29 November 1963, para 7).

[378] Liang, 89th meeting, 25 May 1951, *YILC* (1951) vol I, para 51. See M Roscini, 'Threats of Armed Force and Contemporary International Law', above n 273, 238.

[379] Thiam, *Third report on the draft Code of Offences against the Peace and Security of Mankind*, A/CN.4/387, 8 April 1985, *YILC* (1985) vol II, Part One, 73, para 91.

[380] ICJ, *Legality of the Threat or Use of Nuclear Weapons*, ICJ Rep (1996) 246, para 47.

single out, as possible forms of threat of aggression, declarations, in the sense of public messages in verbal or written form; communications, in the sense of expressions of intention, not broadcast publicly but contained in correspondence or orally manifested, even by telephone . . .'.[381]

3. Only a threat with a degree of credibility comes within the scope of article 2(4).[382] In this perspective, article 13 of the International Law Commission's draft requires there to be 'good reason to believe' that an aggression is 'seriously contemplated'.[383] Threat is distinguished from 'mere verbal excesses'[384] that might be heard from certain particularly voluble and perhaps bungling leaders. Words are therefore to be accompanied by concrete measures such as mobilisations, or troop concentrations or movements.[385] To be credible, it seems therefore that the threat must have a certain imminence[386], or immediacy,[387] which is the case when preparations for attack have begun[388] or *a fortiori* if some limited uses of force can already be established.[389] In practice, it is only in such circumstances that accusations of threat have been made.[390]

4. In this respect, the behaviour of the State accused of making threats must be appraised in its political, geographic and historical context.[391]

---

[381] *YILC* (1989) vol I, 2134th meeting, 291, para 57.

[382] Independent International Fact-Finding Mission on the Conflict in Georgia, *Report*, September 2009 (www.ceiig.ch/Report.html), vol II, 232.

[383] Text above n 288; see also Scelle, 89th meeting, 25 May 1951, *YILC* (1950) vol I, paras 43, 46 and 56.

[384] *YILC* (1989) vol I, 2134th meeting, 291, para 56; *Report of the ILC on the work of its 41st session*, *YILC* (1989) vol II, Part Two, 68, para 4 (excluding 'mere passing verbal excesses'); see also Mahiou, 2060th meeting, 10 June 1988, *YILC* (1988) vol I, para 14 and *Report of the ILC on the work of its 40th session (9 May–29 July 1988)*, A/43/10, *YILC* (1988) vol II, Part Two, 58, para 221.

[385] See: Njenga (1885th meeting, 21 May 1985, *YILC* (1985) vol I, para 6); *Report of the ILC on the work of its 40th session (9 May–29 July 1988)* (A/43/10, *YILC* (1988) vol II, Part Two, 58, para 220); Razafindralambo (2135th meeting, 12 July 1989, *YILC* (1989) vol I, para 16).

[386] Barboza, 2135th meeting, 12 July 1989, *YILC* (1989) vol I, para 36; *Report of the ILC on the work of its 41st session*, *YILC* (1989) vol II, Part Two, 68, para 4; see also R Bermejo Garcia, *El marco jurídico internacional en materia de uso de la fuerza: ambigüedades y límites* (Madrid, Editorial civitas, 1993) 252; B Asrat, *Prohibition of Force Under the UN Charter. A Study of Article 2(4)*, above n 124, 140; ND White and R Cryer, 'Unilateral Enforcement of Resolution 687: A Threat Too Far?' above n 340, 253.

[387] See the views expressed by the Netherlands (J Spiropoulos, *Third Report: Draft Code of Offences Against the Peace and Security of Mankind*, A/CN.4/85, 30 April 1954, *YILC* (1954) vol II, 116).

[388] Razafindralambo, 1884th meeting, 20 May 1985, *YILC* (1985) vol I, para 39; see also 2058th meeting, 8 June 1988, *YILC* (1988) vol I, para 18); *Special Rapporteur*, 1889th meeting, 28 May 1985, *YILC* (1985) vol I, para 16.

[389] Independent International Fact-Finding Mission on the Conflict in Georgia, *Report*, September 2009 (www.ceiig.ch/Report.html), vol II, 232.

[390] See, eg: the declaration of the president of the Islamic Republic of Iran in October 2005; SC/8542, 28 October 2005; SG/SM/10188, 27 October 2005.

[391] Independent International Fact-Finding Mission on the Conflict in Georgia, *Report*, September 2009 (www.ceiig.ch/Report.html), vol II, 231–32 and 233 *ff*; M Roscini, 'Threats of Armed Force and Contemporary International Law', above n 273, 241–43; USA

A form of behaviour may more readily be characterised as a threat if it is manifested by a powerful[392] nearby State whose history shows it has not baulked at using force under certain circumstances.[393] A hostile declaration made exceptionally by weak, remote and traditionally peaceful States shall be considered rather as a simple verbal excess.[394]

It is against these criteria that situations liable to give rise to a violation of article 2(4) should be examined on a case by case basis.[395] Noteworthy in this respect is war propaganda, which some States have claimed can be likened to a threat prohibited by the UN Charter.[396] Resolution 2625 (XXV) provides as a consequence of the principle of the prohibition of the threat of or use of force that '[i]n accordance with the purposes and principles of the United Nations, States have the duty to refrain from propaganda for wars of aggression'.[397] In a more nuanced fashion, other States have argued that war propaganda might be characterised, depending on circumstances, either as a threat to peace in the broad sense of article 39 of the Charter or in the narrow sense of article 2(4).[398] The General Assembly has even adopted several resolutions relating war propaganda to the threat to peace within the meaning of article 39 and not within the specific meaning of article 2(4).[399] In practice, it all depends on what is understood by 'propaganda for war'. If a State calls publicly for an attack on another State in circumstances that suggest it may put its threat into action,

(A/C.6/S.R.808, 11 November 1963, 154, para 27); see also Barboza, 2135th meeting, 12 July 1989, *YILC* (1989) vol I, para 34 and Memorial of Malaysia, ICJ, 19 June 1995, 11–13 and 16 (*Legality of the Threat or Use of Nuclear Weapons*).

[392] *Memorandum prepared by the Secretariat* (A/CN.4/39, 24 November 1950, *YILC* (1950) vol II, 337, para 113).

[393] See, eg: 'United Kingdom Materials on International Law' (1994) 65 *BYBIL* 585; USA (A/C.6/S.R.808, 11 November 1963, para 28); Indonesia (ICJ, *Legality of the Threat or Use of Nuclear Weapons*, Berchmans Soedarmanto Kadarisman, 95/25, 3 November 2005, 25–26, para 33; Judge Padilla Nervo, dissenting opinon, ICJ, *Fisheries Jurisdiction (United Kingdom v Iceland)*, *Re 1973*, 47; ICJ, *Fisheries Jurisdiction (FRG v Iceland)*, ICJ Rep (1973) 91.

[394] '[T]he statement of intention to use force must be viewed against the background of the relations between both States with regard to a specific dispute and in the light of the facts surrounding the articulation of the threat' (C Antonopoulos, *The Unilateral Use of Force by States in International Law* (Athens, Sakkoulas, 1997) 100–01, quoted in ND White and R Cryer, 'Unilateral Enforcement of Resolution 687: A Threat too Far?', above n 340, 252). See also Beesley, 2135th meeting, 12 July 1989, *YILC* (1989) vol I, para 11 and SC Res 1172 (1998) of 6 June 1998, para 4.

[395] See also: MM Whiteman (ed), *Digest of International Law*, vol 5 (Washington, Department of State Pub, 1965) 711–14 and R Higgins, 'The Legal Limits to the Use of Force by Sovereign States. United Nations Practice' (1961) 37 *BYBIL* 315–16.

[396] See, eg: Yugoslavia (A/C.6/S.R.753, 5 November 1962, para 31; A/C.6/S.R.802, 29 October 1963, para 7), Poland (A/C.6/S.R.876, 16 November 1965, para 4), Bulgaria (A/C.6/S.R.1181, 25 September 1970, para 3) or Gabon (A/C.6/SR.1443, 20 November 1973, para 12).

[397] GA Res 2625 (XXV) of 24 October 1970, first Principle.

[398] USA (A/C.6/S.R.764, 21 November 1962, para 15).

[399] GA Res 110 (II) of 3 November 1947, para 1; see also GA Res 277 (II) of 13 May 1949; GA Res 381 (V) of 17 November 1950; and GA Res 819 (IX) of 11 December 1954.

it can be considered that article 2(4) has been violated. If it calls generally and vaguely to challenge certain States—characterised as 'rogue States', say—it is doubtful the same conclusion need be drawn. It will all depend, in each individual case, on the consideration given to the four criteria above.

All of these indications relate to as objective an evaluation of the situation as possible. While it is not enough for a State to feel or declare itself threatened for it to be concluded there is a threat within the meaning of article 2(4),[400] neither is it necessary to prove the intervening State's *intention* in order to conclude there is a threat. The characterisation is easily made if the intervening State adopts a policy of force, which it considers legitimate, by stating loudly and clearly that diplomacy must in the case in point be accompanied by a credible threat of the use of force. Such an instance is far from being purely hypothetical. In other cases, the characterisation will presuppose a distinction between a simple threat to international peace and security under article 39 and a real threat by one State against another under article 2(4). To determine whether we are dealing with this second instance, only an evaluation of the entire situation, that can be done using the four criteria set out above, will enable us to conclude whether or not there is a threat. It is only once the existence of a threat has been established that we will ask whether and to what extent such a threat is prohibited under article 2(4), which will raise the question of the scope of the prohibition.

B. The Scope of the Prohibition of Threat: the Absence of any Specific Regime for the Contemplated Use of Force

In a study made specifically of the threat of force, Romana Sadurska develops an argument that can be set out as follows:

> [I]n practice international actors, contrary to the official language of international agreements (which equate in this respect the use and threat of force), recognize a separate set of criteria of lawfulness for the threat of force . . . There is no reason to assume that the threat will always be unlawful if in the same circumstances the resort to force would be illicit . . . The international community seems to approve, or at least tolerate, the actions of a threatener that proceeds with prudence . . .[401]

There would seem to be a disjunction between the use of force as such, which is strictly prohibited by article 2(4), and the threat of such use, which is supposedly prohibited only in a more flexible manner. This difference allegedly derives from practice, which is more tolerant of certain threats pursuing legitimate purposes, provided the authors of those threats proceed in a measured and cautious manner.

---

[400] *Report of the ILC on the work of its 41st session, YILC* (1989) vol II, Part Two, 68, para 4; see also Mahiou (2135th meeting, 12 July 1989, *YILC* (1989) vol I, paras 67–68), Al-Qayzi (ibid, para 4), Bennouna (ibid, para 8), Beesley (ibid, para 12), Jacovides (ibid, para 45); cp Koroma (ibid, para 26) and Calero Rogriguez (ibid, para 53).

[401] R Sadurska, 'Threats of Force', above n 273, 250 and 265.

This argument is reflected in the positions adopted by certain States. In the *Legality of the Threat or Use of Nuclear Weapons* case, France considered that 'the idea of "threat" within the meaning of the principle of non use of force implies the idea of coercion to bring one State to behave or *act in a manner other than it would freely choose to do*'. (emphasis added)[402] By this definition, a threat designed to secure compliance with international law, insofar as it is not designed to compel a State to behave in some way other than it might 'freely choose', does not seem to be prohibited by the Charter. It can be recalled that, in several precedents such as the conflicts in Yugoslavia and Iraq, some States have emphasised the need to enforce the Security Council resolutions by combining diplomacy with a 'credible threat' of the use of force.[403] This is the thrust of Romana Sadurska's argument: where a threat is used by some States in a cautious and legitimate manner, especially to enforce human rights or to maintain international peace and security, it shall not be as strictly prohibited as force engaged under such circumstances.

The asymmetrical view also appears in the Independent International Fact-Finding Mission on the Conflict in Georgia Report, but with a very different meaning. The Commission contends that '[i]n situations of severe crisis between longstanding adversaries, governments must refrain from any kind of military threat, even when their actual use of force might be justified'.[404] Therefore, in some circumstances, a State might violate international law by simply threatening another State, but could actually use force against it in conformity with the UN Charter.

To my mind, the asymmetrical argument is incompatible with international law as it stands. First, because it is contradicted by the positions of principle of States as a whole and the most authoritative case law. Second, because, upon scrutiny, those positions are not contradicted by even the most recent practice.

The Symmetry between the Threat and the Corresponding Use of Force: Positions of Principle

For Romana Sadurska, the asymmetry between the threat of force and the use of force is justified because threats have less harmful effects on the continuation of peace than the actual use of force.[405] A *bona fide* reading of

---

[402] Our translation: *Letter dated 20 June 1995 from the Minister of Foreign Affairs of the French Republic, together with Written Statement of the Government of the French Republic*, 25, para 15; Perrin de Brichambaut, CR 95/23, 1 November 1995, 65, para 34; see also Salomon Islands (Crawford, CR 95/32, 14 November 1995, 64, para 8), McCaffrey (2054th meeting, 1 June 1988, *YILC* (1988) vol I, 71, para 41) and J Salmon (ed), *Dictionnaire de droit international public* (Bruxelles, Bruylant, AUF, 2001) v° 'menace de recours à la force', 694.

[403] See above.

[404] *Report*, September 2009 (www.ceiig.ch/Report.html), vol II, 237.

[405] R Sadurska, 'Threats of Force', above n 273, 249.

article 2(4), however, shows that the prohibition stated relates equally to the threat of the use of force and the actual use of force, the purpose being very broadly to guard against force in international relations. This strict parallelism is found in all texts that are about or that include a statement of the rule, be they conventions,[406] General Assembly resolutions,[407] Security Council resolutions,[408] instruments of regional scope[409] or works of the International Law Commission.[410]

None of those texts distinguishes between the actual use of force and its threatened use.[411] Both are systematically prohibited in the same manner and to the same extent.[412] To the best of my knowledge, during the drafting work on these texts, no State suggested such a parallel should be called into question.

Quite the contrary, several States clearly stated the opposite in the context of the procedure on the opinion on the *Legality of the Threat or Use of Nuclear Weapons* before the International Court of Justice. The following quotations attest to this:

—The United Nations Charter and the treaties and resolutions cited above do not distinguish between the legal status of the threat to use force and that of the use of force itself. Both are equally prohibited. Indeed, *'if the promise is to resort to force in conditions in which no justification for the use*

---

[406] Art I of the Washington Treaty instituting NATO, 4 April 1949; Article I of the Warsaw Pact, 14 May 1955; Article 52 of the Vienna Conventions of 1969 and 1986 on the Law of Treaties; Article 301 of the UN Convention on the Law of the Sea.

[407] GA Res 2625 (XXV) of 24 October 1970; GA Res 42/22 of 18 November 1987; GA Res 37/10 of 15 November 1982; see also: AG Res 34/22 of 14 November 1979; ES-6/12 of 14 January 1980; AG Res 35/37 of 20 November 1980; AG Res 37/9 of 4 November 1982; AG Res 39/6 of 1 November 1984; and AG Res 40/12 of 13 November 1985.

[408] SC Res 186 (1964) of 4 March 1964; SC Res 268 (1969) of 28 July 1969; SC Res 273 (1969) of 9 December 1969; SC Res 294 (1971) of 15 July 1971; SC Res 300 (1971) of 12 October 1971; SC Res 404 (1977) of 8 February 1977; SC Res 461 (1979) of 31 December 1979; SC Res 479 (1980) of 28 September 1980; SC Res 487 (1981) of 19 June 1981; SC Res 496 (1981) of 15 December 1981; SC Res 527 (1982) of 15 December 1982; SC Res 530 (1983) of 19 May 1983; SC Res 552 (1984) of 1 June 1984; SC Res 580 (1985) of 30 December 1985; SC Res 588 (1986) of 8 October 1986; SC Res 611 (1988) of 25 April 1988; SC Res 1234 (1999) of 9 April 1999; Sc Res 1291 (2000) of 24 February 2000; and SC Res 1318 (2000) of 7 September 2000.

[409] Bandoeng Declaration, 24 April 1955 (Afghanistan, China, Egypt, Ethiopia, Gold Coast, Iran, Iraq, Japan, Jordan, Laos, Lebanon, Liberia, Libya, Nepal, Philippines, Saudi Arabia, Sudan, Siam, Vietnam, Yemen), principle 7 (in (1955) 1 *AFDI* 728); Helsinki Final Act, principle II; Charter of Paris (www.osce.org/docs/).

[410] See above and ILC, *Responsibility of States for Internationally Wrongful Acts*, Article 50; annexed to GA Res 56/83 of 12 December 2001.

[411] See: Institut de droit international, Declaration on the use of force, 2 September 2003 (www.idi-iil.org) and J Salmon, 'La déclaration de Bruges sur le recours à la force' (2003) 36 *RBDI* 566–72.

[412] F Dubuisson and A Lagerwall 'Que signifie encore l'interdiction de recourir à la menace de la force?', above n 273, 91–92; ND White and R Cryer, 'Unilateral Enforcement of Resolution 687: A Threat Too Far?', above n 340, 247–48.

of force exists, the threat itself is illegal' . . . Thus, the concepts of *'threat'* and *'use'* in Article 2(4) merge into each other in most circumstances. The threat of use is itself a kind of use;[413]

—The Charter of the United Nations and the aforementioned resolutions make no distinction between the legal status of the threat of use of force and the use of force itself. Both situations are prohibited equally.[414]

It is in relying on the stands of several States that the court, in its opinion, gave an *obiter dictum* that left no room to challenge the symmetry between threat of, and the corresponding use of, force:

> The notions of 'threat' and 'use' of force under Article 2, paragraph 4, of the Charter stand together in the sense that if the use of force itself in a given case is illegal—for whatever reason—the threat to use such force will likewise be illegal. In short, if it is to be lawful, the declared readiness of a State to use force must be a use of force that is in conformity with the Charter.[415]

This position of principle was applied in the specific case of the dissuasion policy, of which the Court declared:

> Whether this is a 'threat' contrary to Article 2, paragraph 4, depends upon whether the particular use of force envisaged would be directed against the territorial integrity or political independence of a State, or against the Purposes of the United Nations or whether, in the event that it were intended as a means of defence, it would necessarily violate the principles of necessity and proportionality. In any of these circumstances the use of force, and the threat to use it, would be unlawful under the law of the Charter.[416]

As far as I know, no State or commentator has challenged the Court's conclusions on this specific point. The symmetrical prohibition of threat and use of force therefore seems to be established both in the minds of States and in case law as in doctrine.[417]

A final point is worth making in this respect. In the debates at the time of the 60th anniversary celebrations of the United Nations, there is no record of any challenge to this symmetry. The use of force is still consid-

---

[413] *Memorial of Malaysia,* 11 and 23 (and Berchmans Soedarmanto Kadarisman, CR 95/25, 3 November 2005, 24, para 29); see also Iran (Javad Zarif, CR 95/26, 6 November 1995, 24, para 32).

[414] *Note verbale dated 19 June 1995 from the Embassy of Mexico, together with Written Statement of the Government of Mexico,* 7, para 34; see also France, Perrin de Brichambaut, CR 95/23, 1st November 1995, 65, para 35; Salomon Islands, Salmon, CR 95/32, 14 November 1995, 40.

[415] ICJ Rep (1996) 246, para 47.

[416] ibid, para 48.

[417] Judge Weeramantry, dissenting opinion, ICJ, *Legality of the Threat or Use of Nuclear Weapons,* ICJ Rep (1996) 525–26; M Roscini, 'Threats of Armed Force and Contemporary International Law', above n 273, 245; F Dubuisson and A Lagerwall, 'Que signifie encore l'interdiction de recourir à la menace de la force ?' above n 273, 92–93; ND White and R Cryer, 'Unilateral Enforcement of Resolution 687: A Threat too Far?', above n 340, 247–48; comp N Stürchler, *The Threat of Force in International Law,* above n 273, 267.

ered in its entirety, as applying both to the actual use of force and to the threat of its use.[418] The idea of threat has even been the subject of certain developments, including as a constituent of the rule set out in article 2(4). It is in this context that the idea of anticipatory self-defence was evoked, that might be implemented in the event of an 'imminent threat' to use force.[419] Far from going in the sense of greater tolerance, this idea supposes that the threat of force is prohibited in an extremely stringent manner,[420] to the extent that it could be likened to an 'armed attack' within the meaning of article 51. If, as shall be detailed later, 'anticipatory self-defence' has come in for criticism, never has that criticism been to claim that a threat, even of imminent use of force, should be tolerated more than a use of force.[421] What was at the heart of the debate was the distinction between the simple violation of article 2(4), whether a threat or a minor use of force, and the existence of an 'armed attack' liable to prompt action in self-defence according to article 51. The debate at no time concerned the breaking of the symmetry set out in the Charter between the threat and the use of force.

In all, it is observed that this symmetry is found in all the texts about the rule prohibiting the use of force, including the most recent ones. It is also found, explicitly or not, in legal scholarship.[422] It is true that the argument that this symmetry has been broken is based more on practice than on texts. It can be replied first that any tendency to make the rule more flexible, while it may perfectly well be inferred from practice, should logically be reflected in the texts, if at least one requires, as I do, the existence of a clear and general *opinio juris* before concluding that such flexibility has been introduced.[423] It will then be noticed, as shall now be seen, that there is nothing in actual practice that allows us to conclude that this symmetry that is so soundly established in the texts has been brought into question.

Symmetry between Threat and the Corresponding Use of Force: Unchanging State Practice

In her reference study, Romana Sadurska bases her argument essentially on practice. She claims that:

> States tend to condemn an illicit threat less explicitly and effectively than an illegal use of force . . . It seems that as long as the threat of force does not

---

[418] *2005 World Summit Outcome*, above n 290, para 77.

[419] *A more secured world: Our shared responsibility*, above n 290, 63, para 188; *In larger freedom: towards development, security and human rights for all: report of the Secretary-General*, above n 290, para 124; see below, ch 7, s 1.

[420] B Asrat, *Prohibition of Force under the UN Charter. A Study of Article 2(4)*, above n 124, 138.

[421] See, eg: J Mrazek, 'Prohibition of the Use and Threat of Force: Self-Defence and Self-Help in International Law' (1989) 27 *CYIL* 81 *ff*.

[422] See authors mentioned above and J Zourek, *L'interdiction de l'emploi de la force en droit international* (Leiden, Sijthoff, Geneva, Institut Henry Dunant, 1974) 72.

[423] See above, ch I, s II.

jeopardize peace or lead to massive violations of human rights, international actors demonstrate varying degrees of approval or more or less reluctant tolerance for unilateral threats.[424]

It should first be pointed out how difficult it is to confirm this assertion. It goes without saying that even a cursory review of international practice shows that condemnations are more or less frequent and more or less insistent depending on situations and above all on the political contexts in which they can be situated. The problem is to determine whether, in law, such practice shows the emergence of an *opinio juris* of which, as just seen, there is no trace in the positions of States.[425]

In my view, nothing allows us to reach such a radical conclusion. Generally, nothing indicates that the ambiguities of practice must be reflected by recognition of the asymmetry argument (a). And the conclusion remains valid, even in regard of certain *a priori* problematical precedents such as those of Yugoslavia or Iraq (b).

a) State Practice does not Support the Asymmetry Argument

There are several precedents where a threat has been condemned as such by the Security Council or by other UN organs.[426] One can cite condemnations of South Africa,[427] Southern Rhodesia,[428] Israel,[429] Iraq[430] or Rwanda.[431] It will be observed more generally that many accusations of violation of the prohibition of the threat of the use of force have been made within the UN, such as by several States against the USSR over the situation in Czechoslovakia in 1948[432] and then Hungary in 1956,[433] of Tunisia against France,[434] of Cyprus against Turkey,[435] of Israel against

---

[424] R Sadurska, 'Threats of force', above n 273, 240 and 250.

[425] See above.

[426] F Dubuisson and A Lagerwall, 'Que signifie encore l'interdiction de recourir à la menace de la force ?', above n 273, 90–91; M Roscini, 'Threats of Armed Force and Contemporary International Law', above n 273, 245 *ff.*

[427] SC Res 326 (1973) of 2 February 1973; GA Res 2383 (XXIII) of 7 November 1968; GA Res 2508 (XXIV) of 21 November 1969.

[428] SC Res 326 (1973) of 2 February 1973; SC Res 411 (1977) of 30 June 1977.

[429] SC Res 347 (1974) of 24 April 1974; GA Res 36/27 of 13 November 1981; GA Res 37/18 of 16 November 1982; GA Res 38/9 of 10 November 1983; GA Res 39/14 of 8 November 1984; GA Res 40/6 of 1 November 1985.

[430] SC Res 949 of 15 October 1994 (and S/PV.3438, 15 October 1994); S/PRST/1994/58, 8 October 1994.

[431] S/PRST/2004/45 of 7 December 1994 (and S/PV.5091, 30 November 1994,). See also *Sixteenth Report of the Secretary-General on the United Nations Organization Mission in the Democratic Republic of the Congo*, 31 December 2004, S/2004/1034, para 21.

[432] *Repertoire of the Practice of the Security Council 1946–1951*, 479.

[433] *Repertory of Practice of United Nations Organs*, Supp no 2 (1955–1959), vol 1, 88, para 68, 89, para 71, 91, para 78.

[434] *Repertory of Practice of United Nations Organs*, Supp no 2 (1955–1959), vol 1, 105, para 127.

[435] *Repertoire of the Practice of the Security Council 1959–1963*, case no 11, 289; *Repertoire of the Practice of the Security Council 1964–1965*, case no 2, 201; *Repertory of Practice of United Nations Organs*, Supp no 3 (1959–1966), vol 1, 153, para 146, 154–55, para 155 and 156, para 158.

Syria,[436] of Nicaragua[437] or of Libya against the United States,[438] of the United Kingdom against Argentina,[439] of Bosnia-Herzegovina against the Federal Republic of Yugoslavia[440] and so on. A first observation is obvious then: the prohibition of the threat to use force can be deduced from legal texts but is also relied on and applied in practice and has been on many occasions.[441] From this point of view, no one seems to consider that the threat of force should be tolerated any more than the actual use of force.

It is true that, on the other side, several precedents can be found where the Security Council has failed to condemn certain actions sometimes characterised as threatening. France and the United Kingdom were not condemned for threatening Egypt in 1956,[442] Egypt was not condemned for threatening Israel in 1967,[443] the USSR was not condemned for threatening Poland in 1981[444] and the United States was not condemned for threatening Nicaragua in the 1980s.[445] It would be misleading, though, to deduce that such threats were, in strictly legal terms, the subject of special tolerance compared with the corresponding use of force. The failure to condemn in these precedents may have arisen from a political choice or context: it is hard to imagine the Security Council condemning one of its permanent members for a threat, just as it is hard to imagine the condemnation might bear on an actual use of force.[446] No asymmetry can be detected at this stage. Nor can any asymmetry be deduced automatically from the consideration of more legal considerations. In *Military and Paramilitary Activities*, the International Court of Justice condemned the United States for an illicit use of force and not for the threat to use force.[447] As already pointed out, this difference in

---

[436] *Repertoire of the Practice of the Security Council (Supp 1981–1984)*, case no 3, 337; *Repertory of Practice of United Nations Organs*, Supp no 3 (1959–1966), vol 1, 148, para 111 and 149, paras 113 and 117.

[437] *Repertoire of the Practice of the Security Council (Supp 1981–1984)*, case no 9, 342; *Repertory of Practice of United Nations Organs*, Supp no 6 (1979–1984), vol 1, 74, para 22.

[438] A/40/224, S/17081, 4 April 1985, 2 and *Repertoire of the Practice of the Security Council (Suppl. 1985–1988)*, case no 5, 444.

[439] *Repertory of Practice of United Nations Organs*, Supp no 6 (1979–1984), vol 1, 86, para 78.

[440] Bosnia and Herzegovina, Application instituting proceedings, 20 March 1993, (f) and (g); ICJ, *Application of the Convention on the Prevention and Punishment of the Crime of Genocide*, ICJ Rep (1996) 601, para 13.

[441] ND White and R Cryer, 'Unilateral Enforcement of Resolution 687: A Threat too Far?' above n 340, 245.

[442] But see: Yugoslavia (S/PV.949, 30 October 1956, para 26), USSR (S/PV.750, 30 October 1956, paras 32 and 52; S/PV.751, 31 October 1956, para 11), Egypt (S/PV.750, 30 October 1956, para 47) and USA (S/PV.949, 30 October 1956, para 22). See also GA Res 997 (ES-I), 2 November 1956, para 3.

[443] See: A/C.6/SR.1076, 21 November 1968.

[444] See below.

[445] See above and *Repertoire of the Practice of the Security Council (Supp 1981–1984)*, 342–343.

[446] ND White and R Cryer, 'Unilateral Enforcement of Resolution 687: A Threat too Far?', above n 340, 246.

[447] ICJ Rep (1986) 53, para 92.

treatment was motivated by a restrictive definition of the idea of 'threat',[448] not by any asymmetry in the scope of the prohibition. More generally, there is nothing to show that States that refuse to condemn a threat would not at the same time refuse to condemn the corresponding use of force, whether their attitude is dictated by political or even legal considerations.

To be confirmed, the asymmetry argument must therefore be based on situations where a threat has been tolerated while the actual use of force has been condemned. Romana Sadurska produces five precedents.

The first is that of the *Corfu Channel*. In this case, the Court refused to consider that the simple passage of British vessels through the channel was contrary to Albanian sovereignty, although such passage was allegedly accompanied by a threat to use arms in the event of an attack against the vessels.[449] Romana Sadurska deduces from this that 'the Court affirmed that the threat of force applied as a measure of enforcement of a right that had been unlawfully denied (in this case, the right of innocent passage through an international waterway in peacetime) was licit'.[450] However, the Court never made any such general and radical pronouncement. On the contrary, it has already been pointed out that the Court never contemplated the question in terms of the prohibition of the threat or of the use of force.[451] In the case in point, it considered simply that the passage of the British vessels remained 'innocent passage' within the specific meaning of the rules of the law of the sea.[452] Besides, it seems immediately obvious that, even if the facts of the matter had been envisaged in terms of article 2(4), the Court would have concluded that there was a threat to exercise a right of self-defence and not a threat to use force offensively.[453] So there is no credible basis for saying this precedent can be ranked as evidence for any asymmetry between the threat of and the use of force.

Romana Sadurska refers besides to the case of Sweden, which in 1983 issued an order officially announcing that any submarines unduly entering its territorial waters would be sunk; this being done to put an end to very frequent violations of its sovereignty.[454] Here again, there is some difficulty in ranking this event as coming within the ambit of article 2(4). To my mind, it should be considered rather as one of the many ways for a State to exercise its coercive competence in a zone within its jurisdiction.[455] As

---

[448] Above.

[449] ICJ, *Corfu Channel*, ICJ Rep (1949) 35.

[450] R Sadurska, 'Threats of force', above n 273, 263.

[451] Above.

[452] F Dubuisson and A Lagerwall, 'Que signifie encore l'interdiction de recourir à la menace de la force?', above n 273, 90, fn 38.

[453] K Skubiszewski, 'Use of Force by States. Collective Security. Law of War and Neutrality', above n 33, 780; see ICJ, *Corfu Channel*, ICJ Rep (1949) 26–32 and 35.

[454] R Sadurska, 'Threats of force', above n 273, 255–56; 'Foreign Submarines in Swedish Waters: The Erosion of an International Norm' (1984) 10 *YJIL* 34 *ff*.

[455] B Asrat, *Prohibition of Force under the UN Charter. A Study of Article 2(4)*, above n 124, 141 ('the Ordinance appears to be no more than an exercice of domestic authority').

shown earlier, simple police measures must be distinguished from actual uses of force by one State against another;[456] the Swedish legislation seems to fall more in the first category than the second. Besides, even if this precedent were envisaged in the context of article 2(4), any asymmetry would still have to be confirmed. That would mean showing that the tolerance manifested in respect of the threat was not manifested in respect of an actual use of force, which, as far as I know, was not done. It may on the contrary be thought that, insofar as States consider it quite legitimate to threaten to take measures to enforce national regulations within their territory, States should logically accept that such a threat should be carried out.

The Cuban missile crisis is the third precedent listed by Romana Sadurska. She claims that the United States, rightly feeling threatened by the deployment of nuclear weapons a hundred or so kilometres from its coasts, itself threatened to use force to ensure compliance with quarantine measures.[457] Insofar as this behaviour was supposedly generally approved, this would be a sign of acknowledgement of the legitimacy of a threat intended to enforce a right or ensure international peace and security. This reasoning raises several problems. First, there is no specific demonstration of any asymmetry. Nothing says the States that supported the quarantine ordered by the United States would not have done so only insofar as that quarantine did not escalate beyond a simple threat. On the contrary, all the signs are that the American States that supported this action in the OAS were equally ready to accept that the threat be implemented as an actual military measure.[458] On principle, it is hard to imagine that a State should support the legitimacy of a threat while adding that the threat can in no event be materialised; logically, the justification of a threat seems to imply the justification of the use of force to which the threat pertains. As seen, the United States justified its action as a whole by implementing regional collective security mechanisms.[459] Last, but not least, it is in any event excessive to assert that the United States' behaviour was 'generally approved'. This crisis, which was especially emblematic of the Cold War, was characterised on the contrary by an opposition between two blocks, with the 'non aligned' countries for their part certainly not having sided with the United States.[460] However it may be viewed, it is difficult then to establish any sufficiently broad *opinio juris* from this precedent.

Romana Sadurska also invokes the introduction of martial law in Poland in 1981.[461] Insofar as the USSR allegedly threatened military intervention

---

[456] Above, s 1.
[457] R Sadurska, 'Threats of force', above n 273, 254–55.
[458] See above.
[459] Above and F Dubuisson and A Lagerwall, 'Que signifie encore l'interdiction de recourir à la menace de la force?' above n 273, 90.
[460] Above.
[461] R Sadurska, 'Threats of force', above n 273, 258–60.

in Poland and most of the allies of the US merely issued meek protests without invoking article 2(4), this is supposedly another precedent as evidence of a degree of tolerance of threatening behaviour. One might even see in it the sign of asymmetry between the threat of and the actual use of force, inasmuch as the Polish precedent supposedly contrasts with the firm condemnation of Soviet military intervention in Czechoslovakia in 1968.[462] Here again, I am not convinced these events support the asymmetry argument. First, it seems excessive to say that the United States' allies tolerated Soviet behaviour in this matter. Quite the contrary, several of them denounced it, invoking the prohibition of the threat to use force.[463] Second, and in any event, there is a radical difference between the case of Czechoslovakia and that of Poland. In the first, Warsaw Pact troops invaded the territory of a sovereign State against the wishes of its government.[464] There was no doubt that this was an instance of the use of force by one State against another within the meaning of article 2(4). In the second case, the Soviet Union showed it was ready to send its troops into another State, but there is nothing to show that such a deployment would have been decided without the consent of the official government, which was very close to Moscow at the time.[465] In other words, the problem was less one of the use of force against another State than of the violation of the Polish people's right to self-determination, the threat being directed much more at the opposition than at the government in place. Under the circumstances, it is difficult to deduce from a comparison of the precedents of Czechoslovakia and Poland that there was a disruption of the symmetry between the threat of and the actual use of force, even if only in the minds of the western States concerned.

The fifth precedent Romana Sadurska discusses is the United Kingdom's setting-up of a 'protection zone' around the Falkland Islands (Malvinas) in July 1982 after the cessation of hostilities.[466] Insofar as the establishment of this zone supposedly raised little protest outside of Latin America,[467] this might be seen as acceptance of a threat implemented with caution and moderation, despite its apparent incompatibility with article 2(4).[468] Here again, the reasoning is hardly convincing. Sadurska herself notes that the UK claimed this measure was taken under article 51 of the Charter.[469] The

---

[462] ibid, 259–60.

[463] See, eg: FRG, Belgium and France (*Report of the Special Committee on Enhancing the Effectiveness of the Principle of Non-use of Force in International Relations*, GA, 37th sess, Supp no 41 (A/37/41), 27 July 1982, para 127).

[464] See below, ch 5.

[465] See *Keesing's Contemporary Archives* (1982) 31453 ff.

[466] R Sadurska, 'Threats of force', above n 273, 260–61 and *Keesing's Contemporary Archives* (1982) 31717–18.

[467] See: *Letter dated 23 September 1982 from the Permanent Representative of Argentina to the United Nations addressed to the President of the Security Council*, S/15427, 23 September 1982.

[468] R Sadurska, 'Threats of force', above n 273, 261.

[469] S/15307, *Letter of 22 July 1982*; ibid, 261, fn 117.

position is hardly compatible with the asymmetry argument in that it shows that the threat of force, like the use of force, was officially justified in the same way as a riposte in self-defence. Had the British authorities claimed that the protection zone was only a moderate threat and not an actual resort to force, and that the threat should be accepted as such, and had the other States as a whole (including the Latin American States) then accepted this reasoning, one might then have concluded that this formed a relevant precedent. However, none of these conditions was fulfilled.[470]

No one thinks to deny that practice is characterised by a wide diversity. Some threats are firmly condemned within the UN, others not. However, this diversity of situations is not specific to threat as an institution; it is typical more widely of all cases of use of force. The extremely sensitive character of these situations explains above all the phenomena of tolerance that can be observed, especially in the minds of the States allied to the intervening State. It seems hazardous indeed to deduce any decisive lessons capable of calling into question all of the official texts which, we have seen, emphasise the well established symmetry between threat of the use of force and actual use of force. This conclusion was not challenged by the events in Yugoslavia in 1998 and 1999, and then in Iraq in 2002 and 2003.

b) The Yugoslav and Iraqi Precedents do not Support the Asymmetry Argument

It has already been pointed out that, in the cases of Yugoslavia and of Iraq, the US and some of its allies officially assumed the threat of force as a legitimate measure designed to enforce international law.[471] Now, it seems, at least at first sight, that this threat was generally tolerated, at least if we compare the lukewarm protests it prompted with the vigorous condemnation that followed the actual outbreak of war against the two countries threatened.[472] In this context, it might be wondered whether a certain practice is not developing in support of the asymmetry argument.[473]

An affirmative answer would first suppose that one could show that this argument was defended by the intervening States themselves, which is far from obvious. In the case of Yugoslavia as in that of Iraq, the United States and its allies emphasised the legitimacy of their objective, which supposedly consisted only in enforcing resolutions adopted by the Security Council and that were seemingly not complied with by the States targeted.[474] Even if certain ambiguities surrounded their position on this point, it may be thought that the intervening States justified their action in law by a sort of

---

[470] See also: S/14944, 1 April 1982.

[471] Above, s 2, A, 2.

[472] Below, ch 6, s 2.

[473] See: F Dubuisson and A Lagerwall, 'Que signifie encore l'interdiction de recourir à la menace de la force?' above n 273, 93.

[474] See below, ch 6.

authorisation, the existence of which could be presumed from the various Security Council resolutions.[475] At any rate, and this is what counts here, nothing allows us to affirm that the official justification of this action should be modulated by distinguishing threat of force from actual use of force. The legitimacy of the objective was officially justified in both cases, with no asymmetry arising in particular from the official discourse. Besides, it is hard to imagine that things could be otherwise. When a State justifies the legitimacy of a threat, it is difficult to see that it does not at the same time justify the legitimacy of its execution. The requirement that the threat be credible makes a fiction of the hypothesis that a State might assert that a threat is admissible whereas the actual use of force is not, or, what amounts to the same thing, that the threat is more admissible than the use of force referred to by the threat; a dissociation that constitutes, though, the condition *sine qua non* for proving the validity of the asymmetry argument. For this reason alone, the argument is difficult to entertain.

This is especially the case since, and this is the second decisive factor, this argument cannot be deduced from an examination of the reactions of States as a whole to the claims of the intervening powers, whether for the Yugoslav or Iraqi precedent.

In the case of Yugoslavia, it is true that the threats brandished by the NATO and US authorities from October 1998 raised only rare protests, if we leave Russia apart.[476] There is no denying it: the military action actually begun in March 1999 was denounced by many States, including western States,[477] whereas the threat that preceded it seems to have met with a degree of tolerance.[478] This contrast can easily be explained on political grounds: States will criticise the taking of action more readily than the mere threat of it, especially if they consider that the threat may have desirable practical effects. Can it be deduced from this legally that the international community of States as a whole thought that a threat to engage in an unlawful use of force was not itself contrary to article 2(4)? There is no ground to assert this, in the absence of an official statement of the positions of States on this point. It can only be recalled in this respect that the intervening

---

[475] O Corten and F Dubuisson, 'L'hypothèse d'une règle émergente fondant une intervention militaire sur une "autorisation implicite" du Conseil de sécurité' (2000) 104 *RGDIP* 885–86; O Corten, 'Opération *Iraqi Freedom*: peut-on admettre l'argument de l'"autorisation implicite" du Conseil de sécurité?' (2003) 36 *RBDI* 205–47.

[476] See the declaration of the Government of Russia, 4 October 1998, (in M Weller, *The Crisis in Kosovo 1989–1999*, above n 346, 277).

[477] Below, ch 6, s 2.

[478] On 1 February 1999, the representative of FRY in UNO requests a meeting of the Security Council 'following the NATO threats to the sovereignty of [his] country [. . .]. The decision by NATO, as a regional agency, to have its Secretary-General authorize air strikes against the FRY territory . . . represents an open and clear threat of aggression against the FRY as a sovereign and and Independent Member State of the UN [. . .]. NATO's threat directly undermines the sovereignty and territorial integrity of the FRY and flagrantly violates the principles enshrined in the Charter of the United Nations, particularly Article 2, paragraph 4' (M Weller, *The Crisis in Kosovo 1989–1999*, above n 346, 418).

States themselves did not defend the asymmetry argument; the threat of force like the actual use of force being equally legitimate in their view. If it were to be concluded that their thesis was accepted, then the threat of force like the use of force would have been justified by the need to enforce the Security Council resolutions: a conclusion that would clash, however, with the many criticisms that were indeed ultimately prompted by the military intervention against Yugoslavia.

The asymmetry argument is not borne out either by the States' positions during the Iraqi crisis.[479] The threat of force, which was clearly made in September 2002, was explicitly characterised as contrary to international law by many States before the outbreak of war. Within the UN, declarations to this effect were forthcoming from States as diverse as Nigeria,[480] Malaysia,[481] Lebanon,[482] Zimbabwe,[483] Nepal,[484] Syria,[485] Belarus,[486] Iraq itself[487] and from organisations like the League of Arab States[488] or the Caribbean Community.[489] Outside of the UN, very strong condemnations came from the majority of States in the Non-Aligned Movement (118 States)[490] and the Organisation of the Islamic Conference (57 States).[491] It is true that other States, including some European States like France, Germany or Belgium, tolerated or even supported the military preparations against Iraq while later condemning the outbreak of war,[492] and admitting the need to put pressure on the Baghdad authorities by making a credible threat of use of force.[493] However, it is not obvious that these States admitted the lawfulness of a unilateral threat of force. To understand their position on this subject, we must place ourselves in the circumstances of the time. In November 2002, the Security Council had adopted resolution 1441 (2002) that made many demands of Iraq and threatened 'serious consequences' if the demands were not met.[494] In this context, the making of

---

[479] F Dubuisson and A Lagerwall, 'Que signifie encore l'interdiction de recourir à la menace de la force?' above n 273, 93–103.

[480] S/PV.4625 (Resumption 1), 16 October 2002, 20–21.

[481] S/PV.4625 (Resumption 2), 17 October 2002, 6–8.

[482] ibid, 8–10.

[483] ibid, 23–24.

[484] ibid, 26–27.

[485] S/PV.4625 (Resumption 3), 17 October 2002, 5–7.

[486] S/PV.4709, 18 February 2003, 34.

[487] S/PV.4707, 14 February 2003, 30–32.

[488] S/PV.4709, 18 February 2003, 25–26.

[489] CARICOM (Antigua and Barbuda, Bahamas, Barbados, Belize, Dominique, Grenada, Guyana, Haiti, Jamaica, Saint Kitts and Nevis, Saint Lucia, Saint Vincent and the Grenadines, Suriname, Trinidad and Tobago); S/PV.4709, 18 February 2003, 33–34.

[490] *Final Document of the XIII Conference of Heads of State or Government of the Non-aligned Movement*, Kuala Lumpur, 24–25 February 2003, www.nam.gov.za.

[491] OIC, Doha, 5 March 2003, www.oic-oci.org.

[492] See: O Corten, 'Quels droits et quels devoirs pour les Etats tiers?' in K Bannelier et al (eds), *L'intervention en Irak et le droit international* (Paris, Pedone, 2004) 105–28.

[493] See, eg: Greece (on behalf of the EU); S/PV.4709, 18 February 2003, 30–31.

[494] See below, ch 6.

preparations for war could be construed in two ways: either as a threat to use force unilaterally, that is without a new Security Council resolution,[495] or as a threat to implement an authorisation that the Security Council might well decide to grant in view of the change in the situation on the ground. In this second instance, the tolerance observed could not be interpreted as acceptance of an unlawful threat, the only threat tolerated being that of carrying out measures decided on under Chapter VII of the Charter. In the absence of any specific stance on this point, it is difficult to decide one way or another.[496] This uncertainty makes it wrong to interpret this precedent as a specific confirmation of the asymmetry argument,[497] even if one claims to limit the assertion to the few States that criticised the war without criticising the threat that preceded it.

Finally, whether for Yugoslavia or for Iraq, the question is asked in the same terms. The intervening States justified their threat then their use of force as a legitimate measure designed to enforce Security Council resolutions in the same way. Either one thinks that their justification was generally and sufficiently accepted, and that tends to accredit the argument of lawful use of force in the case of a presumed authorisation by the Security Council; or one considers on the contrary that such justification, and with it the argument of presumed authorisation, was not accepted. In both cases, the justification, like its possible acceptance, covers the threat of force and the actual use of force in the same way. There is nothing to accredit the asymmetry argument.

Conclusion

The purpose of this chapter has been first to emphasise the problem of the threshold between mere police measures and genuine uses of force. Given the abundant practice, it is undeniable that States make this distinction and do not liken all extraterritorial enforcement measures to a use of force within the meaning of article 2(4). It is true that this threshold is sometimes clouded by certain ambiguous justifications of States that sometimes seem to lie astride the two bodies of rules, as in certain cases where self-defence is invoked. However, it can be considered that the principle of a distinction between police measures and the use of force is accepted by States as a whole. The dividing line is difficult to determine and must be drawn depending on the circumstances specific to each case. Given certain precedents, we have been able to make out two general criteria: the gravity of the coercive act and the intention of a State to use force against another. The

---

[495] See: USA (S/PV.4625, Resumption 3, 17 October 2002, 12; S/PV.4644, 8 November 2002, 3–4; S/PV. 4701, 5 February 2003, 7–8).

[496] F Dubuisson and A Lagerwall, 'Que signifie encore l'interdiction de recourir à la menace de la force?', above n 273, 101.

[497] ibid, 102.

two criteria must be combined; the gravity of the act being just the sign of its author's intent, and vice versa. In each instance, consideration of these criteria raises certain questions: Did the military action take place on the territory of the intervening State? In what context did the military action take place? Who decided on and who carried out the military operation? What was the nature of the target of the operation? Did the operation give rise to confrontation between agents of the two States? What was the scale of resources implemented by the intervening State? It depends on the answers to these questions whether it can be concluded that article 2(4) applies or not. Of course, the conclusion will not entail any consequence for the lawfulness of the action concerned; that lawfulness shall simply be appraised differently depending on the applicable rule (prohibition of the use of force in some instances, observance of sovereignty or of certain specific treaty-based rules in others). The only relevant question at this point is about the domain of application of the rule, a question that covers not just the use of armed force but also the threat of its use, pursuant to article 2(4).

The second part of the chapter tries to give pointers for a definition of the 'threat' to use force by identifying several criteria. The asymmetry argument is dismissed, even if it may find support in a common sense consideration: States will tend more easily to denounce an actual military intervention that is akin in principle to an actual armed attack, than a simple threat of intervention.[498] The schema could be extended to any violation of international law that will prompt so many more protests when it is of a particularly serious character. Yet decisive legal considerations cannot readily be deduced from this. In law, an intervening State will justify a threat in the same way as an actual use of force for the plain and simple reason that such a threat relates to a specific use of force that it is contemplating implementing. Under these circumstances it is worth interpreting the reactions of other States. In many precedents, other States expressly condemn the threat of force by referring to article 2(4), in line with the many positions of principle they have otherwise adopted. More rarely, some States will turn a blind eye to a threat, especially when made by one of their allies. Such tolerance is not enough, though, to establish that there is any *opinio juris* tending to make the prohibition of the threat of the use of force in any way more flexible.

---

[498] ND White and R Cryer, 'Unilateral Enforcement of Resolution 687: A Threat too Far?', above n 340, 246; A Randelzolfer, 'Article 2(4)', above n 276, 124.

3

Do the Prohibition of the Use of Force and Self-defence Apply to Non-State Actors?

T RADITIONALLY THE MAJORITY of scholarship and of case law restricts the scope of the prohibition of the use of force to relations between States. However, there is a trend to challenge this restriction, especially since the events of 11 September 2001.[1] One of the characteristic features of the 'war on terror' rhetoric is to recognise the possibility of acting in 'self-defence' within the meaning of article 51 of the UN Charter against terrorist groups and no longer just against sovereign States.[2] Thus, these private groups acquire a whole new status: once common criminals against whom police measures might be implemented—whether in a strictly national context or through international police or criminal cooperation—, they presumably become genuine entities capable of making an 'armed attack' against a sovereign State; a capacity that implies in return the possibility for the State under attack to start a real 'war' against them in self-defence.[3] This doctrinal position will be contemplated in the context of the possible recognition of the applicability of the prohibition of the use of force to strictly private entities (section two). But first we shall consider some older-standing claims, although they are comparable as they involve extending the scope of the rule not to private but to political non-State entities (section one). Overall, it shall be seen that these various claims have not so far given rise to an *opinio juris* tending to extend the rule in article 2(4) to non-State entities. To my mind, therefore, States still consider this rule as one of the attributes of their sovereignty, a sovereignty allowing them to continue to treat the groups or individuals that challenge them as common criminals.

[1] See: M Reisman, 'International Legal Responses to Terrorism' (1999) *HJIL* 57; R Wedgwood, 'Responding to Terrorism: the Strikes Against bin Laden' (1999) 24 *YJIL*, 1999 564; see also Y Dinstein, *War, Aggression and Self-Defence*, 4th edn, (Cambridge, Cambridge University Press, 2005) 204–08.

[2] See: O Corten, 'La 'guerre antiterroriste', un discours de pouvoir' in *Le discours du droit international, pour un positivisme critique* (Paris, Pedone, 2009).

[3] E Hey, 'International Law in the Aftermath of the War on Iraq' in *International Law. Forum du droit international* (Leiden/Boston, Martinus Nijhoff Publishers, 2003) 236.

I Exclusion of Non-State Political Entities from the Rule's Scope of Application

A 'political entity' shall be understood here as a group of individuals claiming to govern other individuals on a given territory. Political entity is a concept that implies a territorial type of power, which is not the case of strictly private groups such as the mercenaries or 'terrorists' to be considered next. The political entity of reference is the sovereign State, but others can be imagined. There are three cases in which applying the prohibition of the use of force to non-State political entities has been contemplated: (1) relations between a State and a political group that is opposed to it in the context of a straightforward civil war; (2) relations between a State and a national liberation movement; and (3) relations between a State and an entity with a controversial legal status. In my own view, the rule prohibiting the use of force has not clearly been extended to any of these three cases.

A. Inapplicability of the Rule Prohibiting the Use of Force to Civil Wars

The expression 'international relations' used in all the major texts defining the prohibition of the use of force should not be understood as applying to relations between 'nations' in the broad sense. A 'national minority' living in the territory of a State could not therefore rely on the prohibition set out in article 2(4) of the Charter. On the contrary, that article purports only to govern the use of force between States and remains silent about the lawfulness of the use of force within any particular State; attempted secession, for example, being neither authorised nor prohibited by article 2(4).[4] In this sense, it can be said that civil war is fundamentally alien to the regulations on the use of force.[5]

This exclusion of civil war was regularly asserted by the States when working within the UN on the definition of the prohibition of the use of force, as these few statements attest:

[4] See, eg: v° 'sécession' in J Salmon (ed), *Dictionnaire de droit international public* (Brussels, Bruylant, AUF, 2001) 1022; J Salmon, 'Le droit des peuples à disposer d'eux-mêmes. Aspects juridiques et politiques' in *Le nationalisme, facteur belligène. Etudes de sociologie de la guerre* (Brussels, Bruylant, 1972) 364 *ff*; R Higgins, *The Development of International Law Through the Political Organs of the United Nations* (London/New York/Toronto, Oxford University Press, 1963) 125; J Crawford, *The Creation of States in International Law* (Oxford, Clarendon Press, 1979) 266–68.

[5] R Pinto, 'Les règles du droit international concernant la guerre civile' (1965/I) 114 *RCADI* 477; J Salmon, 'Vers l'adoption d'un principe de légitimité démocratique?' in O Corten *et al* (eds), *A la recherche du nouvel ordre mondial. Tome I. Le droit international à l'épreuve* (Brussels, edn complexe, 1993) 63; 'Internal Aspects of the Right to Self-Determination: Towards a Democratic Legitimacy Principle' in C Tomuschat (ed), *Modern Law of Self-Determination* (Dordrecht, Martinus Niihoff Publishers, 1993) 256; see also C Quaye, *Liberation Struggles in International Law* (Philadelphia, Temple Univ Press, 1991) 212–13; JH Leurdijk, 'Civil War and Intervention in International Law' (1977) 24 *NILR* 145.

—[T]he significance of the expression 'in their international relations' in Article 2 (4) of the Charter was that force employed in a civil war fell outside the scope of the provision. Neither international law in general nor the Charter placed any restrictions upon the use of force in the establishment of new internal legal orders. That elaboration of the rule seemed to cover also rebellions which aimed at secession;[6]

—A careful analysis of the first part of the principle showed that the obligation it imposed applied exclusively to States, in other words to entities having legal personality in international law. Thus the prohibition of the threat or use of force did not cover rebellions by groups of individuals against the constituted authorities;[7]

—The view that Article 2, paragraph 4, which prohibited the use of force in international relations, did not in any way affect the use of force within a State, appeared never to have been contested.[8]

It can be readily understood, from reading these statements, that we are confronted with a question of the scope of application of the rule and not of evaluating compliance with it. The fact that article 2(4) does not apply to a civil war does not imply that such a war is lawful or legitimate, nor that it is not. This has led some commentators to speak of 'legally neutral' situations, with international law neither condemning nor justifying as such either insurrection or the repression of insurrection.[9]

'Legally neutral' may appear a misleading expression, if the problem is considered on the scale of general international law.[10] General international law recognises that the State has the right, and even the duty, to maintain or restore order in its territory.[11] Coercive measures to put down rebel movements may therefore be understood as the implementation of a right, which cannot be the case of the rebellious acts.[12] The rebellion may even, in the particular instance of attempted secession, be accused of infringing the State's territorial integrity.[13] In short, it can be considered that contem-

---

[6] Australia (A/AC.119/SR.10, 3 September 1964, 8–9).

[7] Guatemala (A/AC.119/SR.14, 8 September 1964, 7).

[8] Sweden (A/AC.125/SR.25, 25 March 1966, 9, para 13); see also China; A/C.6/SR.875, 15 November 1965, para 5; Central African Republic (A/C.6/SR.884, 29 November 1965, para 27); USA (MM Whiteman, *Digest of International Law*, vol 13 (Washington, Department of State Pub, 1968) 358–59).

[9] J Salmon, 'Vers l'adoption d'un principe de légitimité démocratique?' above n 5, 63.

[10] O Corten, 'Are there gaps in the international law of secession?' in M Kohen (ed), *Secession. International Law Perspectives* (Cambridge, Cambridge University Press, 2006) 231–54; A Cassese, 'La guerre civile et le droit international' (1986) 90 *RGDIP* 556–57.

[11] See: Protocol Additional to the Geneva Conventions of 12 August 1949, and relating to the Protection of Victims of Non-International Armed Conflicts (Protocol II), 8 June 1977, Art 3 § 1; see also CSCE, Code of Conduct on Politico-Military Aspects of Security, 6 December 1994 (www.osce.org).

[12] See also: S/PRST/2001/7, 12 March 2001.

[13] See, eg: SC Res 1065 (1996) of 12 July 1996, para 3; SC Res 1096 (1997) of 30 January 1997, para 3; SC Res 1124 (1997) of 31 July 1997, 3; see also T Christakis, *Le droit à l'autodétermination en dehors des situations de décolonisation* (Paris, La documentation française, 1999) 190–259.

porary international law tends to justify the use of force by the State and to condemn that by rebel groups or at any rate secessionist groups.[14] If there is neutrality, it is undeniably 'benevolent neutrality' towards the State.[15]

That in no way means that the prohibition of the use of force is binding on a rebel group to the benefit of the sovereign State. The right and the duty to maintain order are considered as governing the legal relations between the State and the individuals under its jurisdiction.[16] As for the accusation sometimes made that secessionist entities are challenging the State's territorial integrity, this by no means implies that an entity of this type can be considered as an 'attacker' against which the State can act in 'self-defence'. In respect of the use of violence, civil war is by principle considered as a 'domestic matter', and the State has no need to invoke an exception to the prohibition of the use of force to justify its implementing coercive measures[17] that shall be characterised as simple 'police measures' against criminals or 'terrorists'.[18] Both the State and the rebel entity will have a special legal personality and status in terms of the *jus in bello*.[19] This will not be the case, though, in respect of the *jus contra bellum*, the rebel entity then having no claim to legal personality, even of limited scope.[20]

Of course, this schema presupposes that the conflict remains a domestic one, which leads us to make two clarifications.

First, the prohibition on the use of force continues to govern the relations between the State concerned and other States during the conflict. If some outside State intervenes militarily against the government forces,[21] it is self-evident that an international conflict arises and article 2(4) is then fully applicable.[22] The prohibited use of force extends for that matter not just to direct military action but also to military support for irregular forces

---

[14] O Corten, 'Are there gaps in the international law of secession?' above n 10; see also O Corten, 'Déclarations unilatérales d'indépendance et reconnaissances prématurées: du Kosovo à l'Ossétie du sud et à l'Abkhazie' (2008) 112 *RGDIP*, 721–59. See also Independent International Fact-Finding Mission on the Conflict in Georgia, *Report*, September 2009 (www.ceiig.ch/Report.html), vol II, 279.

[15] T Christakis, *Le droit à l'autodétermination en dehors des situations de décolonisation*, above n 13, 258.

[16] O Corten, 'Are there gaps in the international law of secession?', above n 10.

[17] A Cassese, *International Law*, 2nd edn (Oxford, Oxford University Press, 2005) 56; J Verhoeven, *Droit international public* (Brussels, Larcier, 2000) 673.

[18] C Alibert, *Du droit de se faire justice dans la société internationale depuis 1945* (Paris, LGDJ, 1983) 147–48.

[19] See: Protocol Additional to the Geneva Conventions of 12 August 1949, and relating to the Protection of Victims of Non-International Armed Conflicts (Protocol II), 8 June 1977, Art I § 1.

[20] P Daillier, M Forteau and A Pellet, Nguyen Quoc Dinh, *Droit international public*, 8th edn (Paris, LDGJ, 2009) 585–87.

[21] See also below, ch 5.

[22] A Randelzhofer, 'Article 2(4)' in B Simma (ed), *The Charter of the United Nationmeeting A Commentary*, 2nd edn, (Oxford, Oxford University Press, 2002) 121; C Gray, *International Law and the Use of Force*, 3rd edn (Oxford, Oxford University Press, 2008) 105–07.

engaged in the internal conflict.[23] So, by the terms of the General Assembly's major resolutions on the use of force:

—Every State has the duty to refrain from organizing or encouraging the organization of irregular forces or armed bands, including mercenaries, for incursion into the territory of another State;[24]
—Every State has the duty to refrain from organizing, instigating, assisting or participating in acts of civil strife or terrorist acts in another State or acquiescing in organized activities within its territory directed towards the commission of such acts, when the acts referred to in the present paragraph involve a threat or use of force;[25]
—States shall fulfil their obligations under international law to refrain from organizing, instigating, or assisting or participating in paramilitary, terrorist or subversive acts, including acts of mercenaries, in other States, or acquiescing in organized activities within their territory directed towards the commission of such acts.[26]

These obligations were reasserted by the International Court of Justice in *Military and Paramilitary Activities* as applications of the principle of the non-use of force.[27] The principle that one cannot help rebels in a civil war does not seem to be contested by anyone, and controversies are more about the level above which such aid may be characterised as 'armed attack' opening up the right to self-defence.[28]

Then, the characterisation of the conflict as non-international presupposes, in the case of attempted secession, that the secession is unsuccessful. Otherwise, the former irredentist entity has by definition become a sovereign State, implying, among many other things, the applicability of the prohibition of the use of force as it is stated in the United Nations Charter.[29] The scope of application of the prohibition may therefore depend on the conditions for the existence of a State within the meaning of general international law holding true.[30] Here we shall not go into how such conditions are identified and interpreted. We need only recall that it is not enough for an entity to proclaim its existence as a State for it to be recognised as such in international law and to enjoy the protection of its political independence or territorial integrity against any use of force.[31] Scrutiny of practice seems

---

[23] A Randelzhofer, 'Article 2(4)', above n 22, 121–22; R Pinto, 'Les règles du droit international concernant la guerre civile', above n 5, 478–79.
[24] GA Res 2625 (XXV) of 24 October 1970, first principle.
[25] ibid.
[26] GA Res 42/22 of 18 November 1987, I.6.
[27] ICJ Rep (1986) 91, para 191, 127, para 247.
[28] See below, ch 7, s 1.
[29] See: A Randelzhofer, 'Article 2(4)', above n 22, 121–22.
[30] See: J Crawford, *The Creation of States in International Law*, above n 4; 'The Criteria of Statehood in International Law' (1976–77) 48 *BYBIL* 93–182.
[31] See: A Randelzhofer, 'Article 2(4)', above n 22, 122.

rather to require sufficiently stable effectiveness, effectiveness that can be considered as such when the former central State has abandoned its attempts to prevent the secession from succeeding.[32] Article 2(4) will then be fully applicable between the States in question.

The rules briefly reiterated have been well-established in international law since the adoption of the UN Charter.[33] In the 1990s, some commentators, however, thought they detected a marked change and that there was henceforth a legal rule excluding the right to use force for both secessionist forces and for the government of the State in question.[34] This minority trend in scholarship is essentially based on an analysis of practice that developed in the 1990s; practice that is supposedly evidence of the international community's intention to extend the prohibition of the use of force to its use within States. This practice allegedly began in (former) Yugoslavia, where there were several condemnations of the use of force by the Yugoslav governmental authorities,[35] but also by non-governmental forces, such as the Serb or Croat forces of Bosnia-Herzegovina during the civil war that tore the country apart.[36] The practice was reflected too in the thinking of the Security Council throughout the 1990s, in the course of which resolutions on internal conflicts contained:

—a request to observe a ceasefire,[37] or to refrain from any use of force,[38] in such a situation;

—condemnation of certain violations of the ceasefire by one or other of the parties to the internal conflict;[39]

---

[32] J Crawford, 'State Practice and International Law in Relation to Secession' (1998) 69 *BYBIL* 92 *ff.* Comp Independent International Fact-Finding Mission on the Conflict in Georgia, *Report*, September 2009 (www.ceiig.ch/Report.html), vol II, 127 *ff.*

[33] A Randelzhofer, 'Article 2(4)', above n 22, 121, fn 70.

[34] A Pellet, 'Avis juridique sur certaines questions de droit international soulevées par le renvoi' annexé aux *Rapports d'experts de l'amicus curiae*, Cour suprême du Canada, quoted in T Christakis, *Le droit à l'autodétermination en dehors des situations de décolonisation*, above n 13, 253; see also A Cassese, 'Article 51' in JP Cot and A Pellet (eds), *La Charte des Nations Unies*, 3rd edn (Paris, Economica, 2005) 1333.

[35] See: B Delcourt, *Droit et souveraineté. Analyse critique du discours européen sur la Yougoslavie* (Bruxelles, PIE—Peter Lang, 2003) 125 *ff.*

[36] T Christakis, *L'ONU, le chapitre VII et la crise yougoslave* (Paris, Montchrestien, 1996) 47–50; see, eg GA Res 48/88 of 20 December 1993.

[37] Concerning Georgia: SC Res 849 (1993) of 9 July 1993; SC Res 858 (1993) of 24 August 1993; SC Res 1150 (1998) of 30 January 1998; SC Res 1187 (1998) of 30 July 1998; SC Res 1225 (1999) of 28 January 1999; concerning, Guinea Bissau, see SC Res 1216 (1998) of 21 December 1998; concerning Kosovo (FRY), see SC Res 1199 (1998) of 23 September 1999; concerning Ivory Coast, see SC Res 1584 (2005) of 1 February 2005.

[38] SC Res 876 (1993) of 19 October 1993, para 4; see also SC Res 881 (1993) of 4 November 1993, para 3; SC Res 1225 (1999) of 28 January 1999, para 6; SC Res 1311 (2000) of 28 July 2000), para 5; SC Res 924 (1994) of 1 June 1994, para 3; SC Res 931 (1994) of 29 June 1994, para 6; SC Res 1203 (1998) of 24 October 1998, para 10.

[39] See, eg: SC Res 876 (1993) of 19 October 1993, para 2; SC Res 1096 (1997) of 30 January 1997; SC Res1339 (2001) of 31 January 2001, para 10; SC Res 1364 (2001) of 31 July 2001, para 15; SC Res1427 (2002) of 29 July 2002, para 8; SC Res 1462 (2003) of 30 January 2003, para 10; SC Res1494 (2003) of 30 July 2003, para 19; SC Res 1524 (2004) of

—a proclamation of the principle of the inadmissibility of territorial gains achieved by force by one party to an internal conflict, which principle is traditionally limited to international relations.[40]

None of these points, it seems to me, needs to lead to so radical a change of international law as the extension of the prohibition of the use of force within States.

First of all, when we analyse what States have to say about certain domestic conflicts, it is not always obvious that a specific position can be inferred as to the interpretation of a rule of international law.[41] Emphasis must be placed on the often political or even emotional character of such statements. In the context, the use of the term 'attack' or 'attacker' does not necessarily reflect an *opinio juris* pertaining to the 'armed attack' within the meaning of article 51 but may be much more general.[42] The same goes for condemnation of an act of 'force', a term that is not necessarily used with reference to article 2(4). Even the characterisation of an act as 'unlawful' may cause confusion insofar as, in a domestic context, illegality may relate to national constitutional law rather than to unlawfulness within the meaning of international law.[43] Consideration of such precedents in establishing the customary rules must therefore be given with the utmost circumspection.

Now, from a strictly legal perspective, it will be noted first that the condemnation sometimes made of the use of force within a State is not made by reference to article 2(4) but rather on the basis of observance of the elementary rules of protection of human rights, including in times of non-international armed conflict. In other words, it is not the principle of the use of force that is criticised but the forms it takes. The conclusion is obvious if we examine the positions of third States in the Chechen conflict. Russia's right to restore order in its territory and even to prevent attempted secession by force of arms was never questioned as such.[44] By condemning the use of 'excessive' force—the formula is very common in official discourse—,

30 January 2004, para 22; SC Res 1554 (2004) of 29 July 2004, para 22; SC Res 1582 (2005) of 28 January 2005, para 24; SC Res 1615 (2005) of 29 July 2005, para 25; SC Res 1590 (2005) of 24 March 2005; SC Res 1591 (2005) of 29 March 2005, para 1; SC Res 1089 (1996) of 13 December 1996, para 2.

[40] SC Res 713 (1991) of 25 September 1991; SC Res 752 (1992) of 15 May 1992, para 1; SC Res 757 (1992) of 30 May 1992; SC Res 820 (1993) of 17 April 1993; SC Res 824 (1993) of 6 May 1993, para 2; SC Res 859 (1993) of 25 August 1993, para 6); see TM Franck, 'Postmodern Tribalism and the Right to Secession' in C Brölmann, R Lefever and M Lieck (eds), *Peoples and Minorities in International Law* (Dordrecht/London/Boston, Martinus Nijhoff Publishers, 1993) 26–27; B Delcourt and O Corten, *Ex-Yugoslavie: droit international, politique et idéologies* (Brussels, Bruylant, 1998) 26 *ff*.

[41] See above, ch 1, s II.

[42] T Christakis, *L'ONU, le chapitre VII et la crise yougoslave*, above n 36, 48.

[43] B Delcourt, *Droit et souveraineté. Analyse critique du discours européen sur la Yougoslavie*, above n 35, 236–37.

[44] See, eg: EU's Declarations (Brussels, 17 January 1995, *DAI* (1995) 177; Brussels, 1 April 1995, *DAI* (1995) 318; 18 January 1996, *DAI* (1996) 243).

it is the disproportionate character of the means used that has occasionally been denounced. It is the *jus in bello*, and not the *jus contra bellum* that is the appropriate legal reference framework. Examination of the reactions to the Yugoslav army's repression of secessionist forces of the Kosovo Liberation Army (KLA) leads to the same conclusion.[45] It is the violation of human rights that was denounced and not the actual principle of attempting to restore order. The following excerpt from the Secretary-General's report published in the midst of the civil war summarises the position of most third-party States quite well:

> The authorities of the Federal Republic of Yugoslavia have the inherent right, as well as the duty, to maintain public order and security and to respond to violent acts of provocation. However, this can in no way justify the systematic terror inflicted on civilians . . .[46]

When NATO Member States intervened militarily some months later, they were never to invoke self-defence nor claim that Yugoslavia had previously violated article 2(4).[47] More generally, examination of the States' positions in respect of civil wars that broke out in the 1990s, especially in Eastern Europe, shows that traditional international law is far from having been brought into question.[48] In short, while it is true that some States sometimes developed an ambiguous discourse, especially in the context of the Yugoslav crisis in the early 1990s,[49] a review of the practice that has developed since makes it difficult to challenge the inapplicability of article 2(4) to internal conflicts.

As for the greater role of the Security Council in certain internal conflicts, it would be wrong to infer any extension of the scope of application of the rule prohibiting the use of force. At any rate, the Security Council has never made any claims of the kind, and one will seek in vain for any reference to article 2(4) for governing internal matters.[50] It is true that the Security

---

[45] SC Res 1160 (1998) of 31 March 1998; SC Res 1999 (1998) of 23 September 1998.

[46] *Report of the Secretary-General prepared pursuant to Resolutions 1160 (1998) and 1999 (1999) of the Security Council*, S/1998/912, 3 October 1998, 8, para 29.

[47] KM Meessen, 'Le droit au recours à la force militaire: une esquisse selon les principes fondamentaux' in SFDI, *Les nouvelles menaces contre la paix et la sécurité internationales*, journée franco-allemande (Paris, Pedone, 2004) 113; see F Dubuisson, 'La problématique de la légalité de l'opération "Force alliée" contre la Yugoslavie: enjeux et questionnements' in O Corten and B Delcourt (eds), *Droit, légitimation et politique extérieure: l'Europe et la guerre du Kosovo* (Brussels, Bruylant, 2001) 149–83; see also below, ch 7, s II and ch 8, s II.

[48] T Christakis, *Le droit à l'autodétermination en dehors des situations de décolonisation*, above n 13, 208 *ff*; J Crawford, 'State Practice and International Law in Relation to Secession', above n 32.

[49] B Delcourt, *Droit et souveraineté. Analyse critique du discours européen sur la Yougoslavie*, above n 35, 222–25.

[50] See, eg: SC Res 993 (1995) of 12 May 1995, para 5; SC Res 1494 (2003) of 30 July 2003, para 13; SC Res 1524 (2004) of 30 January 2004, para 13; SC Res1554 (2004) of 29 July 2004, para 8; SC Res 1582 (2005) of 28 January 2005, para 9; SC Res 1615 (2005) of 29 July 2005, para 8.

Council occasionally recalls the 'unacceptability'—and not the illegality, and even less the incompatibly with article 2(4)—of certain territorial gains made by force in civil wars. But it will be observed that, in the same circumstances, the Council has sometimes approved peace plans confirming divisions of territory that result at least in part from territorial conquest. The example of Bosnia-Herzegovina, without being an isolated case, is probably the most instructive.[51] In fact, the Security Council only exercised its discretionary power in the area of maintaining international peace and security.[52] In such or such a case, it characterises an internal conflict as a threat to peace and considers it opportune to decree a ceasefire and discourage violence.[53] Any violation of the ceasefire may lead it to take coercive measures against the offenders, whether State authorities or irregular groups. In other instances, the Security Council might consider it more realistic to support a peace plan including a division of territory. This normative activity is perfectly understandable in view of the Security Council's responsibilities as laid down by the UN Charter and especially its Chapter VII, which refers not only to breaches of the peace but also to internal situations.[54] However, there is no ground for interpreting it as clear evidence of an extension of the principle of the non-use of force to States' internal affairs.

For that matter, this would raise serious problems of principle, even if contemplating things *de lege ferenda*. How can one determine which is the aggressor in a situation where the entities concerned do not have, initially at least, any separate territorial status? Does the irregular group unilaterally asserting that it is removing part of the national territory from the control of the government in place commit an act of aggression? Or is it the State which, by using its military and police forces to restore order—forces that may already be on the ground—itself become an aggressor? It seems very difficult to make any pronouncement on these points in legal terms, the right to use force remaining closely tied up with the notion of territorial integrity and international borders, two concepts that are inoperative in the case of internal conflicts.[55] What is sure, at any rate, is that such situations are not envisaged from this angle by the international community of States as a whole. It does not look to determine which side is the aggressor or which side has the right to self-defence in cases of civil war. Such conflicts

[51] See: SC Res 836 (1993) of 3 June 1993, para 3; cp SC Res 982 (1995) of 31 March 1995, para 7; SC Res 787 (1995) of 19 April 1995, para 4; SC Res 998 of 16 June 1995, para 2; SC Res 1021 (1995) of 22 November 1995; SC Res 1022 (1995) of 22 November 1995.

[52] T Christakis, *Le droit à l'autodétermination en dehors des situations de décolonisation*, above n 13, 253.

[53] SC Res 1114 (1997) of 19 June 1997, para 1; SC Res 1187 (1998) of 30 July 1998, para 11; SC Res 1577 (2004) of 1 December 2004, preamble; SC Res 1234 (1999) of 9 April 1999, para 8; SC Res 1203 (1998) of 24 October 1998, preamble.

[54] See: S/PRST/1997/14, 13 March 1997; SC Res 1101 (1997) of 28 March 1997.

[55] B Delcourt, *Droit et souveraineté. Analyse critique du discours européen sur la Yougoslavie*, above n 35, 233–34, T Christakis, *Le droit à l'autodétermination en dehors des situations de décolonisation*, above n 13, 254.

are still considered in principle as domestic matters, where international law intervenes only to protect human rights or to confer a power on the Security Council in respect of maintaining international peace and security.

Finally, the development of practice since the 1990s certainly testifies to a relatively broad interpretation by the Security Council of its competencies. Contrary to what might have been observed until the end of the Cold War, most Security Council resolutions currently pertain to what are essentially internal conflicts. This point shall be considered later when examining the hypothesis of the authorised intervention.[56] At this stage, it suffices to observe that this hypothesis in no way blurs the traditional dividing line between the use of force in a civil war and the use of force in 'international relations', which alone is covered by article 2(4); a dividing line that, by contrast, has been called into question in the specific instances of national liberation struggles.

B. Inapplicability of the Rule to National Liberation Struggles

Before setting out the legal system of national liberation struggles, it shall first be recalled that this issue is far from outdated.[57] First because it still directly relates to several situations, including what is probably the longest-running, unresolved armed conflict in the international arena, that of Palestine. Then because, as a matter of principle, it is interesting to observe that the community of States as a whole has not made the legal regime of article 2(4) applicable to struggles deriving from a people's right to self-determination, although such struggles were generally held to be legitimate. This observation shall have to be borne in mind when evaluating claims to extend the ambit of the rule to groups with no legitimacy such as 'terrorist' groups.[58]

In the case of a national liberation struggle, a people is recognised as having the right of self-determination including a right to independence in a delimited territory and enjoying a separate territorial status from that of the home country.[59] This law implies a duty for the State authorities concerned: that of not opposing by force a people's exercise of its right to self-determination.[60] Contrary to civil war, where the principle of 'benevolent neutrality' prevails in favour of the State, self-determination is characterised

---

[56] Below, ch 6, s I.

[57] See also: R Kolb, *Ius contra bellum. Le droit international relatif au maintien de la paix*, 2nd edn (Bâle/Genève/Munich, Helbing & Lichtenhahn, Brussels, Bruylant, 2009) 320–22.

[58] See below.

[59] M Shaw, 'Peoples, Territories and Boundaries' (1997) 8 *EJIL* 481; *Title to Territory in Africa. International Legal Issues*, (Oxford, Clarendon Press, 1986) 140–41; T Musgrave, *Self Determination and National Minorities* (Oxford, Clarendon Press, 1997) 150; H Quane, 'The UN and the Evolving Right to Self-Determination' (1998) 47 *ICLQ* 554–56; O Corten, 'Droit des peuples à disposer d'eux-mêmes et *uti possidetis*: deux faces d'une même médaille?' (1998) 31 *RBDI* 166–71.

[60] See, eg: P Rubino, 'Colonialism and the Use of Force by States' in A Cassese (ed), *The Current Legal Regulation of the Use of Force* (Dordrecht, Martinus Nijhoff, 1986) 133.

by legitimacy bestowed on the people struggling for its independence.[61] This legitimacy is reflected by marked internationalisation, with the State no longer validly able to claim that it is acting in its domestic affairs alone.[62] Certain conventional instruments relating to the law of armed conflicts even characterise conflicts between a State and a national liberation movement as an international conflict.[63] The scale of internationalisation of the situation appears as the counterpart of the highly restrictive character of the definition of situations in which a people has the right to create a new State, with only colonial peoples under foreign domination or subjected to a racist regime enjoying this right.[64]

Does this internationalisation make the prohibition of the use of force as set forth in article 2(4) enforceable? This is what some scholars argue. Some consider that a people that is deprived by force of its right to self-determination is a people under attack and which consequently has a right of self-defence.[65] Others consider more generally that a people deprived of the right to independence is entitled to take up arms by application of a sort of exception to the prohibition of the use of force.[66] In both cases, the internationalisation of the situation would be observed therefore not just in the context of the *jus in bello*, but also in that of the *jus contra bellum*.

This doctrinal trend is based on certain excerpts from the General Assembly's major resolutions, including:

—All armed action or repressive measures of all kinds directed against dependent peoples shall cease in order to enable them to exercise peacefully and freely their right to complete independence, and the integrity of their national territory shall be respected;[67]

---

[61] Institut de droit international, 8th commission, *The Principle of Non-Intervention in Civil Wars*, D Schindler, 'Le principe de non-intervention dans les guerres civiles' (1973) 55 *AIDI* 3–4; O Corten, 'Droit des peuples à disposer d'eux-mêmes et *uti possidetis*: deux faces d'une même médaille?' above n 59, note at 173–76.

[62] D Schindler, 'Le principe de non-intervention dans les guerres civiles', above n 61, 4–5.

[63] See: Protocol Additional to the Geneva Conventions of 12 August 1949, and relating to the Protection of Victims of Non-International Armed Conflicts (Protocol II), 8 June 1977, Art I § 4; see HA Wilson, *International Law and the Use of Force by National Liberation Movements* (Oxford, Clarendon Press, 1988) 127–30; LA Sicilianos, *Les réactions décentralisées à l'illicite. Des contre-mesures à la légitime défense* (Paris, LGDJ, 1990) 438.

[64] T Christakis, *Le droit à l'autodétermination en dehors des situations de décolonisation*, above n 13; J Crawford, 'State Practice and International Law in Relation to Secession', above n 32. See also Independent International Fact-Finding Mission on the Conflict in Georgia, *Report*, September 2009 (www.ceiig.ch/Report.html), vol II, 135 *ff*.

[65] See, eg: G Starouchenko, 'La liquidation du colonialisme et le droit international' in G Tounkine (ed), *Droit international contemporain* (Moscou, ed du progrès, 1972) 134–35; see also D Simon and LA Sicilianos, 'La 'contre-violence' unilatérale. Pratiques étatiques et droit international' (1986) 32 *AFDI* 58–59. ICJ, *Legal Consequences for States of the Continued Presence of South Africa in Namibia (South West Africa) notwithstanding Security Council Resolution 276 (1970)*, Judge Ammoun, Separate Opinion, ICJ Rep (1971) 70.

[66] A Cassese, *International Law*, above n 17, 374; 'Article 51', above n 34, 1332–33; see also Verhoeven, *Droit international public*, above n 17, 673; BVA Rölling, 'Aspects of the Ban on Force' (1977) 24 *NILR* 243–44.

[67] GA Res 1514 (XV) of 14 December 1960, para 4.

—Every State has the duty to refrain from any forcible action which deprives peoples referred to above in the elaboration of the present principle of their right to self-determination and freedom and independence. In their actions against, and resistance to, such forcible action in pursuit of the exercise of their right to self-determination, such peoples are entitled to seek and to receive support in accordance with the purposes and principles of the Charter;[68]

—Nothing in this Definition . . . could in any way prejudice the right to self-determination, freedom and independence, as derives from the Charter, of peoples forcibly deprived of that right . . . nor the right of these peoples to struggle to that end and to seek and receive support, in accordance with the principles of the Charter and in conformity with the above-mentioned Declaration.[69]

If it is accepted that these excerpts express positive international law, there is hardly any doubt that a clear distinction is drawn between a people's struggle to achieve its right to self-determination, which is considered lawful, and the forceful deprivation of the exercise of that right by the authorities of a State, which is considered unlawful.

Can this legal regime, that is specific to the realm of the right of peoples to self-determination, be construed for all that as an extension of the scope of application of article 2(4)? For this to be so, one would have to follow the logic through to its conclusion and consider not only that a people deprived by force of its right is the victim of a genuine 'armed attack' within the meaning of article 51 of the Charter but also that, consequently, other States might support this people militarily in exercising its right to collective self-defence. That, basically, is what is behind the *a priori* theoretical question of determining whether the legitimacy of a struggle for self-determination results only from the right of peoples to self-determination or also from an extension of the scope of the principle of the non-use of force.[70] For my own part, I am not convinced that the extension of this logic has been accepted by the international community of States as a whole. On the contrary, it has remained divided over the issue, whether in debates about the principle involved (1), or where precedents have been debated with the UN organs (2). In the absence of any general agreement, it can only be concluded that the interstate character of the rule contained in article 2(4) should be maintained, even if this requirement must be combined with the recognition of a right of peoples to self-determination (3).

---

[68] GA Res 2625 (XXV) of 24 October 1970.

[69] GA Res 3314 (XXIX) of 14 December 1974, art 7; see also GA Res 36/103 of 9 December 1981 (120-22-6).

[70] H Bokor-Szegö, 'The Attitude of Socialist States Towards the International Regulation of the Use of Force' in A Cassese (ed), *The Current Legal Regulation of the Use of Force* (Dordrecht, Martinus Nijhoff, 1986) 468.

The Absence of any Agreement among States in Debates about the Principle Involved

It shall first be noted that no text accepted by all States mentions an 'armed attack' or a right of 'self-defence' to characterise a national liberation struggle between a people and a State government. The excerpts just cited do not go that far, and this omission is certainly not fortuitous. A review of the *travaux préparatoires* of resolutions 2625 (XXV), 3314 (XXIX) and 42/22 shows that the claims made to this effect have always been contested by a large number of States, the wording used being the furthest it was possible to go in the sense of the legitimacy of national liberation struggles.[71]

In the 1960s, attempts were made to redefine the regime of prohibition of the use of force by including the case of the self-determination of peoples. This trend was reflected in the formulation of various arguments that can be summarized thus:

—Some States asserted generally that the prohibition of the use of force was binding on a State in its relations with a national liberation movement.[72] It was argued that the expression 'international relations' in article 2(4) was broad enough to cover such instances.[73]

—Many States then likened wars of liberation to self-defence in response to colonialism as an act of aggression.[74] The conclusion was supposedly justified because article 51 very generally refers to the natural right of self-

---

[71] See: C Gray, *International Law and the Use of Force*, 3rd edn, above n 22, 59*ff*; LA Sicilianos, *Les réactions décentralisées à l'illicite. Des contre-mesures à la légitime défense*, above n 63, 432 *ff*.

[72] Chile (A/C.6/SR.1092, 11 December 1968, para 30), Czechoslovakia (A/C.6/SR.1158, 24 November 1969, paras 27 and 32), UAR (A/C.6/SR.1161, 28 November 1969, para 38), Cyprus (A/C.6/SR.1163, 29 November 1969, para 35), Romania (A/C.6/SR.1161, 28 November 1969, para 7), India (A/C.6/SR.1162, 28 November 1969, para 21), Mexico (A/C.6/SR.1162, 28 November 1969, para 57), Algeria (A/C.6/SR.1163, 29 November 1969, para 4), Iraq (A/C.6/SR.1163, 29 November 1969, para 6), USRR (A/C.6/SR.1163, 29 November 1969, para 9).

[73] Czechoslovakia (A/AC.134/SR.19, 2 July 1968 in A/AC.134/SR.1-24, 201–02).

[74] Algeria (A/C.6/SR.761, 16 November 1962, para 19; see also A/C.6/SR.805, 5 November 1963, para 13; A/AC.125/SR.23, 24 March 1966, para 13; A/AC.125/SR.26, 25 March 1966, para 27; A/C.6/SR.1096, 13 December 1968, para 29), Cuba (A/C.6/SR.820, 27 November 1963, para 23; A/C.6/SR.1091, 10 December 1968, para 41; A/C.6/SR.1162, 28 November 1969, para 35), Tunisia (A/C.6/SR.822, 29 November 1963, para 21), Ukraine (A/C.6/SR.875, 15 November 1965, para 19; A/C.6/SR.999, 16 November 1967, paras 42–43), UAR (A/C.6/SR.875, 15 November 1965, para 38; A/AC.125/SR.19, 21 March 1966, para 8; A/AC.125/SR.25, 25 March 1966, paras 24–25; A/C.6/SR.1091, 10 December 1968, para 16; A/AC.119/SR.8, 2 September 1964; A/AC.119/SR.17, 9 September 1964), USSR (A/C.6/SR.883, 26 November 1965, para 5; A/AC.119/SR.5, 1 September 1964; A/AC.119/SR.14, 8 September 1964; A/AC.119/SR.43, 2 October 1964; A/AC.125/SR.26, 25 March 1966, para 59; A/AC.125/SR.101, 22 August 1969; A/AC.125/SR.106, 4 September 1969), Syria (A/C.6/SR.884, 29 November 1965, para 50; A/AC.125/SR.24, 24 March 1966, para 9; A/AC.125/SR.65, 31 July 1967, 11–12; A/AC.125/SR.96, 30 September 1968, 170;

defence in the event of 'armed attack', without restricting this notion to attacks by States.[75] During the debates preceding the adoption of the definition of attack, many States repeated that the armed struggle for the right of peoples to self-determination may be related to article 51 of the UN Charter.[76]

—Other States evoked the right of peoples to seek and receive support, including military backing, to help them to resist colonialism.[77] Such

A/C.6/SR.1094, 12 December 1968, para 28; A/AC.125/SR.106, 4 September 1969; A/C.6/SR.1160, 26 November 1969, para 47; A/AC.134/SR.73, 6 August 1970 in A/AC.134/SR.67-78), Upper Volta (A/C.6/SR.888, 2 December 1965, para 16), Libya (A/C.6/SR.889, 3 December 1965, para 23; A/C.6/SR.935, 22 November 1966, para 20; A/C.6/SR.1090, 9 December 1968, para 14), Nepal (A/C.6/SR.1092, 11 December 1968, para 6), Bulgaria (A/C.6/SR.891, 6 December 1965, para 7), Mongolia (A/C.6/SR.935, 22 November 1966, para 25), Poland (A/C.6/SR.997, 14 November 1967, para 17; A/C.6/SR.1092, 11 December 1968, para 40; A/AC.125/SR.88, 16 September 1968), Congo-Brazzaville (A/C.6/SR.998, 15 November 1967, para 6), Hungary (A/C.6/SR.999, 16 November 1967, para 8; A/C.6/SR.1158, 24 November 1969, para 15), Somalia (A/C.6/SR.1003, 20 November 1967, para 47), Cameroon (A/C.6/SR.1086, 4 December 1968, paras 19 and 22; A/AC.125/SR.64, 28 July 1967; A/AC.125/SR.106, 4 September 1969; A/C.6/SR.1160, 26 November 1969, paras 16–17), Czechoslovakia (A/C.6/SR.1086, 4 December 1968, para 31; A/AC.119/SR.4, 31 August 1964; A/AC.119/SR.8, 2 September 1964, A/AC.125/SR.18, 21 March 1966, 14, para 40; A/AC.125/SR.26, 25 March 1966, 20, para 50), Ghana (A/C.6/SR.1094, 12 December 1968, para 14; A/AC.119/SR.10, 3 September 1964; A/AC.125/SR.26, 25 March 1966, para 4; A/AC.125/SR.64, 28 July 1967), Kenya (A/C.6/SR.1094, 12 December 1968, para 33; A/AC.125/SR.65, 31 July 1967), Kuwait (A/C.6/SR.1094, 12 December 1968, para 38, A/C.6/SR.1162, 28 November 1969, paras 3–4), Cyprus (A/C.6/SR.1096, 13 December 1968, para 41), Sudan (A/C.6/SR.1162, 28 November 1969, paras 65–66), Iraq (A/C.6/SR.1180, 24 September 1970, para 7), Yugoslavia (A/AC.119/SR.9, 3 September 1964; A/AC.125/SR.22, 23 March 1966, paras 27–29; A/AC.125/SR.26, 25 March 1966, para 38; A/AC.125/SR.65, 31 July 1967), Romania (A/AC.119/SR.16, 9 September 1964; A/AC.125/SR.66, 1 August 1967; A/AC.125/SR.102, 25 August 1969), India (A/AC.125/SR.64, 28 July 1967; A/AC.125/SR.88, 16 September 1968), Madagascar (A/AC.125/SR.106, 4 September 1969).

[75] See, eg: UAR (A/AC.134/SR.22, 5 July 1968 in A/AC.134/SR.1-24) and Romania (A/C.6/SR.1349, 3 November 1972, para 51).

[76] USSR (A/AC.134/SR.39, 21 March 1969 in A/AC.134/SR.25-51), Romania (A/C.6/SR.1164, 1 December 1969, para 11; A/AC.134/SR.59, 22 July 1970 in A/AC.134/SR.52-66), Guyana (A/AC.134/SR.95, 1 March 1972 in A/AC.134/SR.79-91), Syria (A/C.6/SR.1204, 21 October 1970, para 5), Belarus (A/C.6/SR.1206, 26 October 1970, para 16; A/C.6/SR.1441, 19 November 1973, para 6), Afghanistan (A/C.6/SR.1206, 26 October 1970, para 50; A/C.6/SR.1352, 6 November 1972, para 22), Czechoslovakia (A/C.6/SR.1206, 26 October 1970, para 62), Madagascar (A/C.6/SR.1206, 26 October 1970, para 75), Togo (A/C.6/SR.1208, 27 October 1970, para 19), Zambia (A/C.6/SR.1276, 4 November 1971, para 28; A/C.6/SR.1351, 6 November 1972, para 8), Ukraine (A/C.6/SR.1348, 2 November 1972, para 4), Iraq (A/C.6/SR.1348, 2 November 1972, para 12; A/C.6/SR.1440, 16 November 1973, para 55) , Kenya (A/C.6/SR.1350, 3 November 1972, para 33; A/C.6/SR.1442, 20 November 1973, para 24), GDR (A/C.6/SR.1441, 19 November 1973, para 17), China (A/C.6/SR.1442, 20 November 1973, para 75), Haiti (A/C.6/SR.1443, 20 November 1973, para 17); see also Sri Lanka (A/C.6/SR.1349, 3 November 1972, para 76), Senegal (A/C.6/SR.1444, 21 November 1973, para 18), and Sudan (A/C.6/SR.1444, 21 November 1973, para 28).

[77] Zambia (A/C.6/SR.1178, 23 September 1970, para 13) and Kenya (A/C.6/SR.1350, 3 November 1972, para 33).

support could include the despatch of weapons and troop reinforcements.[78] It should logically be authorised in respect of the *jus contra bellum*, which prohibits in principle the provision of military aid to irregular groups but not to peoples whose struggle is recognised to be legitimate.[79]

—In this perspective, some States have defended the theory of the three exceptions to the prohibition of the use of force: self-defence, action authorised by the Security Council, and 'the liberation of an oppressed people in pursuit of the right of self-determination'.[80]

It will be noted that the States that spoke out for an extension of the scope of application of article 2(4) all belong to two groups that regularly joined together on certain common positions on this issue during the Cold War: the Non-Aligned States and the Socialist States.

By contrast, and this is probably no surprise in view of colonial history, the group of 'Western States' invariably refused to support this attempted extension. Various arguments were expressed by those States.

—Some asserted that when article 2(4) was drafted the 'international relations' criterion was intended to restrict the prohibition of the use of force to relations between States.[81] Alongside this, several commentators have also affirmed that the definition of aggression drawn up by the General Assembly was clearly limited to one State against another.[82] A national liberation movement could not fit into this framework.[83]

—It was also emphasised that the rights recognised for national liberation movements were so recognised in the context of the advancement of the right of peoples to self-determination and not in the context of the prohibition of the use of force in international relations.[84] Restricting this

---

[78] Uganda (A/AC.134/SR.73, 6 August 1970 in A/AC.134/SR.67-78), UAR (A/AC.134/SR.58, 21 July 1970 in A/AC.134/SR.52-66; A/AC.124/SR.73, 6 August 1970 in A/AC.134/SR.67-78) Syria (A/AC.134/SR.59, 22 July 1970 in A/AC.134/SR.52-66; A/AC.124/SR.77, 14 August 1970 in A/AC.134/SR.67-78).

[79] Uganda (A/AC.134/SR.45, 26 March 1969 in A/AC.134/SR.25-51), Libya (A/C.6/SR.1477, 15 October 1974, para 15) and Congo (A/C.6/SR.1478, 16 October 1974, para 35).

[80] Syria (A/AC.134/SR.69, 3 August 1970 in A/AC.134/SR.67-78, 42).

[81] *Report of the Special Committee on Enhancing the Effectiveness of the Principle of Non-Use of Force in International Relationmeeting*, GA, 41st session, Supp no 41 (A/41/41), 13 March 1986, para 67.

[82] United Kingdom (A/AC.134/SR.73, 6 August 1970 in A/AC.134/SR.67-78, 93), Italy (A/AC.134/SR.73, 6 August 1970 in A/AC.134/SR.67-78, 94) and Australia (A/AC.134/SR.73, 6 August 1970 in A/AC.134/SR.67-78, 95).

[83] United Kingdom (A/C.6/SR.1163, 29 November 1969, 357, para 25; see also *Report of the Special Committee on Principles of International Law concerning Friendly relations and co-operation among States*, Supp no 18, A/8018, 1970, 112, para 228), Australia (A/AC.119/SR.17, 9 September 1964, 14; see also A/AC.125/SR.19, 21 March 1966, para 5; A/AC.125/SR.26, 25 March 1966, paras 31–32; cp A/C.6/SR.817, 21 November 1963, para 24; see also A/AC.119/SR.10, 3 September 1964; A/AC.125/SR.106, 4 September 1969).

[84] United Kingdom (A/C.6/SR.1092, 11 December 1968, para 10; A/AC.119/SR.16, 9 September 1964; A/AC.125/SR.21, 22 March 1966, para 6; A/AC.125/SR.25, 25 March 1966, paras 41–42; A/AC.125/SR.65, 31 July 1967; A/AC.125/SR.96, 30 September 1968).

latter rule to relations among States therefore did not interfere with the principle of the right of self-determination itself.[85] The Security Council could decide on measures, including coercive measures, if it thought the situation on the ground was a threat to peace.[86]

—In contradistinction, the exercise by a people of its right could in no way infringe the rule prohibiting the use of force between States.[87] Many States thus insisted on the unlawfulness of any outside military intervention in an armed struggle for national liberation.[88] They argued that such an intervention would directly contravene article 2(4). To conclude otherwise would be to reintroduce into international law the concept of 'just war' that the UN Charter had been devised to set aside and replace by objective legal criteria.[89] Such a proposal would be quite unacceptable in view of the dangers of conflict it would engender in international relations, contrary to the object and purpose of the prohibition.[90]

Thus, a probably minority but dogged opposition prevented the proponents of an extension of the scope of application of article 2(4) from securing a general agreement.[91]

This disagreement was maintained until the final stage of adopting each of the resolutions in question.[92] There will be nothing surprising, then, about the ambiguities in the resulting texts, which have also raised certain reservations tending to protect the stringency of the principle of non-use

---

[85] USA (A/AC.134/SR.59, 22 July 1970 in A/AC.134/SR.52-66) and Ecuador (A/C.6/SR.1352, 6 November 1972, para 14).

[86] United Kingdom (A/AC.134/SR.11, 18 June 1968 in A/AC.134/SR.1-24; A/AC.134/SR.55, 16 July 1970 in A/AC.134/SR.52-66, 18; A/AC.134/SR.85, 9 February 1971 in A/AC.134/SR.79-91, 52).

[87] France (*Report of the Special Committee on Principles of International Law concerning Friendly relations and co-operation among States*, Supp no 18, A/8018, 1970, 91, para 151) and USA (*Report of the Special Committee on Principles of International Law concerning Friendly relations and co-operation among States*, Supp no 18, A/8018, 1970, para 269).

[88] USA (A/AC.119/SR.15, 8 September 1964, 19; A/AC.119/SR.17, 9 September 1964, 17), Venezuela (A/AC.119/SR.16, 9 September 1964), Canada (A/AC.125/SR.23, 24 March 1966, para 36; A/AC.125/SR.66, 1 August 1967), Mexico (A/AC.125/SR.66, 1 August 1967), France (*Report of the Special Committee on Principles of International Law concerning Friendly relations and co-operation among States*, Supp no 18, A/8018, 1970, para 149), United Kingdom (A/AC.134/SR.11, 18 June 1968 in A/AC.134/SR.1-24; A/AC.134/SR.55, 16 July 1970 in A/AC.134/SR.52-66; A/AC.134/SR.85, 9 February 1971 in A/AC.134/SR.79-91), Australia (A/AC.134/SR.84, 8 February 1971 in A/AC.134/SR.79-91; A/AC.134/SR.95, 1 March 1972 in A/AC.134/SR.79-91).

[89] Sweden (A/C.6/SR.886, 1 December 1965, para 16; A/AC.125/SR.86, 13 September 1968), Guatemala (A/AC.119/SR.14, 8 September 1964, 7) and Nigeria (A/AC.119/SR.7, 2 September 1964).

[90] Netherlands (A/AC.119/SR.7, 2 September 1964).

[91] See also: 'La pratique belge en matière de droit international' (1972) 8 *RBDI* 340–41; (1975) 11 *RBDI* 355.

[92] Cp eg China, (A/C.6/SR.1475, 14 October 1974, 63, para 13), Cameroon (A/C.6/SR.1483, 23 October 1974, para 14) and FRG (A/C.6/SR.1478, 16 October 1974, para 19), Canada (A/C.6/SR.1473, 10 October 1974, para 15) or Netherlands (A/C.6/SR.1473, 10 October 1974, para 5).

of force, whether it be resolution 2625 (XXV)[93] or resolution 3314 (XXIX).[94]

The Absence of Agreement between States in Debates over Specific Precedents

These ambiguities cannot be completely removed by examining State practices in specific instances. From the beginnings of the decolonisation movement, several precedents gave rise to: opposition between colonial powers, that invoked their right to maintain order in the context of their internal affairs; and other States that denounced aggression and asserted their right to support people fighting for their right to self-determination.[95] Even if there was some shift in the way that positions are expressed on both sides, this disagreement was never fundamentally dissipated. It seems difficult, then, to claim that an interpretative practice of the Charter has led to the *jus contra bellum* being extended to situations of self-determination.

It will be noticed first that virtually no one has followed the logic through to its conclusion by claiming that a third State in a colonial conflict could intervene militarily on the side of a people under attack.[96] Only two precedents are occasionally raised in this perspective, and they are hardly arguments in its favour.

—The first is that of Indian military intervention in the enclave of Goa in 1961, then under Portuguese administration.[97] In its official justifications, India insisted on Portugal's violation of the right of self-determination of peoples as set out in resolution 1514 (XV), deducing from this that its action could not be considered contrary to article 2(4).[98] Notice, however, that according to the Indian position, the military intervention was in a part of Indian territory that was illegally occupied by Portugal.[99] The lawfulness of the intervention therefore derived from the fact that India was only acting within its borders, against a foreign occupying State, a situation subsumed under interstate relations covered by article

[93] See: USA (A/C.6/SR.1180, 24 September 1970, paras 23 and 25) and South Africa (A/C.6/SR.1184, 28 September 1970, 44, para 15).

[94] See: Ecuador (A/C.6/SR.1476, 15 October 1974, para 3), Belgium (A/C.6/SR.1476, 15 October 1974, para 6), USA (A/C.6/SR.1480, 18 October 1974, para 73), Portugal (A/C.6/SR.1478, 16 October 1974, para 22; A/C.6/SR.1207, 27 October 1970, para 51), United Kingdom (A/C.6/SR.1477, 15 October 1974, para 24); see J Stone, 'Hopes and Loopholes in the 1974 Definition of Aggression' (1977) 71 *AJIL* 233–37.

[95] HA Wilson, *International Law and the Use of Force by National Liberation Movements*, above n 63, 103 *ff*.

[96] A Cassese, 'Le droit international et la question de l'assistance aux mouvements de libération nationale' (1986) 19 *RBDI* 313–15.

[97] Q Wright, 'The Goa Incident' (1962) 56 *AJIL* 617–32; M Flory, 'Les implications juridiques de l'affaire de Goa' (1962) 8 *AFDI* 476–91.

[98] S/PV.987, 18 December 1961, para 41 *ff*.

[99] LA Sicilianos, *Les réactions décentralisées à l'illicite. Des contre-mesures à la légitime défense*, above n 63, 446.

2(4).[100] In other words, India did not set itself up as an outside State coming to the assistance of a people under attack in the context of collective self-defence. In any event, and this factor is just as decisive as the first, the Indian argument is far from having convinced States as a whole.[101] The military intervention was not condemned but solely because of the USSR's veto,[102] with the majority of States considering that the intervention was contrary to existing international law.[103]

—The Falklands War has sometimes been presented as a similar precedent insofar as it gave rise to a military intervention that was officially motivated by the liquidation of a colonial situation.[104] Here too, it should be noted, though, that Argentina did not purport to be an outside State acting to help a people aggressed by a colonial power.[105] As in the case of India, the reasoning consisted rather in invoking a right of self-defence in interstate relations against a colonial State that allegedly illegally took over part of another State's territory.[106] This reasoning was no better accepted in the case of the Falklands than in that of Goa, with most States insisting on the need to abide by article 2(4), even in unresolved colonial situations.[107]

These two precedents seem to confirm more than infirm a negative general practice by which third States abstain from using force directly against a colonial State, even when that State manifestly violates a people's right to self-determination.[108] This practice may certainly be thought significant

[100] India (S/PV.987, 18 December 1961, paras 43 and 46).

[101] S/PV.988, 18 December 1961, para 129; see C Gray, *International Law and the Use of Force*, 3rd edn, above n 22, 59–60.

[102] S/PV.987, 18 December 1961, paras 2–4.

[103] See: USA, United Kingdom, France, China, Ecuador, Chile and Turkey (S/PV. 987, 18 December 1961); see P Rubino, 'Colonialism and the Use of Force by States', above n 60, 135–38 and HA Wilson, *International Law and the Use of Force by National Liberation Movements*, above n 63, 131.

[104] P Rubino, 'Colonialism and the Use of Force by States', above n 60, 138–42.

[105] LA Sicilianos, *Les réactions décentralisées à l'illicite. Des contre-mesures à la légitime défense*, above n 63, 448.

[106] Argentina (Report of the Special Committee on Enhancing the Effectiveness of the Principle of Non-Use of Force in International Relations, GA, 37th session, Supp no 41 (A/37/41), 27 July 1982, para 153; S/PV. 2350, 3 April 1952); see also C Alibert, *Du droit de se faire justice dans la société internationale depuis 1945*, above n 18, 128–37.

[107] P Rubino, 'Colonialism and the Use of Force by States', above n 60, 141; see also RJ Dupuy, 'L'impossible agression: les Malouines entre l'ONU et l'OEA' (1982) 28 *AFDI* 337–53; see also France ('Pratique française du droit international' (1982) 28 *AFDI* 1092–93), Belgium ('La pratique belge en matière de droit international' (1984–1985) 18 *RBDI* 438), Netherlands ('Netherlands State Practice' (1983) 14 *NYIL* 330) and United Kingdom ('United Kingdom Materials on International Law' (1982) 53 *BYBIL* 350–54, 503–06 and 519–20; (1983) 54 *BYBIL* 381–82 and 545–49; (1984) 55 *BYBIL* 592–96).

[108] See: A Cassese, 'Le droit international et la question de l'assistance aux mouvements de libération nationale', above n 96, 314; CJR Dugard, 'The Organization of African Unity and colonialism: an Enquiry into the plea of Self-Defense as a justification for the use of force in the eradication of colonialism' (1967) 16 *ICLQ*, 157–90; M Bennouna, *Le consentement à l'ingérence militaire dans les conflits internes* (Paris, LGDJ, 1974) 165.

inasmuch as it reveals an *opinio juris* whereby article 2(4) knows no exception or derogation in this type of situation.[109]

The question, however, remains open as to whether, without going as far as direct military intervention, a third State could militarily support a national liberation movement recognised as such within the UN. At first sight such behaviour seems incompatible with the prohibition of the use of force which, as has been seen, extends to a duty to refrain from supporting 'irregular forces' or 'armed bands' with a view to 'incursions into the territory of another State'.[110] Some commentators consider though that such a conclusion must be dismissed, insofar as the Security Council 'implicitly denied it was unlawful to provide training camps or military bases leading to national liberation wars'.[111] And it is true that, in several precedents, the Security Council has condemned States—like Israel or South Africa—that relied on their right to self-defence to respond to an aggression that allegedly consisted in a third State making its territory available to national liberation movements engaged in an armed struggle.[112] Should it be deduced from this practice that there can be exceptions or derogations from article 2(4) of the UN Charter in the case of national liberation struggles, even if limited to simple military aid? Four factors seem to impose a negative answer.

First, it must be observed that, by characterising their action as unlawful, the Security Council merely denied the intervening States a right of self-defence, which logically supposes that it refused to characterise simple military assistance to national liberation movements as an 'armed attack' within the meaning of article 51.[113] That does not imply that such assistance is perfectly lawful, which at any rate the Security Council did not expressly assert, although the situation could have led to a position of principle being adopted on this point. In some instances, the Security Council has reasserted the right of national liberation movements, recognised in General Assembly resolutions, to receive support from third States, but it has not gone as far as evoking military support.[114] On the contrary, by sometimes characterising military actions as 'reprisals' contrary to international law,[115] the Security Council seems to admit that sometimes such action may

---

[109] A Cassese, *Self-Determination of Peoples. A Legal Reappraisal* (Cambridge, Cambridge University Press, 1995) 199.

[110] GA Res 2625 (XXV) of 24 October 1970.

[111] A Cassese, 'Le droit international et la question de l'assistance aux mouvements de libération nationale', above n 96, 325; *Self-Determination of Peoples. A Legal Reappraisal*, above n 109, 152–55; see also LA Sicilianos, *Les réactions décentralisées à l'illicite. Des contre-mesures à la légitime défense*, above n 63, 444.

[112] SC Res 313 (1972) of 28 February 1972; SC Res 509 (1982) of 6 June 1982; SC Res 573 (1985) of 4 October 1985; SC Res 393 (1976) of 30 July 1976; SC Res 466 (1980) of 11 April 1980; SC Res 527 (1982) of 15 December 1982.

[113] A Cassese, 'Article 51', above n 34, 1344–46; O Corten and F Dubuisson, 'Opération "liberté immuable": une extension abusive du concept de légitime défense' (2002) 106 *RGDIP* 59.

[114] SC Res 465 (1980) of 27 June 1980, preamble.

[115] SC Res 270 (1969) of 26 August 1969, para 4.

follow on from certain unlawful acts. However, the wording of the resolutions adopted usually remains neutral on the specific question of whether limited military assistance to a national liberation movement is contrary to article 2(4) or not. The text implies only that the act, whether consistent with international law or not, is not serious enough to constitute an armed attack that can justify a riposte in self-defence.[116]

Second, examination of the positions of the States that were victims of Israeli or South African actions does not alter this cautious conclusion. It will be observed that those States, far from asserting their right to provide military aid to a national liberation movement, affirmed they were providing only political or humanitarian support and often denied any military implication.[117] In the terms of the Lebanese representative on the Security Council in 1972:

> My Government categorically rejects the Israeli allegation that the incidents which occurred on Israeli-held territory originated from Lebanon . . . Although it does not assume responsibility for the maintenance of order in Israeli-held territories, *Lebanon has done its utmost to control its border.* But experience in other parts of the world has shown that no Government can entirely control its borders. (emphasis added)[118]

In support of this, one might cite the declaration by Tunisia's representative after the 1985 Israeli raid:

> It is true that the Palestinian leadership has been given Tunisian hospitality . . . But I would add that we are speaking here of political leadership, of the legitimate representation of the Palestinian people, of that genuine interlocutor with which discussions must be held if there is a real will to achieve a viable settlement in the Middle East. None the less, *Tunisia has not become a military base, and, a fortiori, has not become a terrorist base. No act of terrorism has been perpetrated from Tunisian territory. No Tunisian has been implicated in any such act.* (emphasis added)[119]

The same position was defended by front-line States further to military action against them by South Africa or Southern Rhodesia. These States consistently insisted on the political or humanitarian character of the assistance provided, without assuming military support. Botswana replied to the arguments of the illegal Southern Rhodesian regime:

> Botswana unequivocally stands by its decision to give political asylum to those who flee from oppression in the minority-ruled States of southern Africa . . . As to charges of freedom fighters operating from Botswana, Botswana has stated unequivocally time and again that there are neither any bases in, nor any operations from, Botswana.[120]

---

[116] See below, ch 7.
[117] C Gray, *International Law and the Use of Force*, 3rd edn, above n 22, 60.
[118] S/PV.1643, 26 February 1972, 3, paras 21 and 24.
[119] S/PV.2615, 4 October 1985, 16, para 184.
[120] *Letter dated 12 January 1977 from the Permanent Representative of Botswana addressed to the President of the Security Council*, S/12275, 12 January 1977.

Here again, the State directly concerned is far from assuming or claiming a right to provide military assistance to a people whose right to self-determination has been recognised. It shall be observed that this view was also aired by the ANC as a national liberation movement:

> Allegations have been made here that the ANC is using Lesotho as a springboard for so-called terrorist activities in South Africa. Nothing could be further from the truth . . . Inspired by and drawing strength from the position of the international community which recognizes the legitimacy of struggle in all forms for the eradication of a system which is universally condemned as a crime against humanity, but also mindful of the vulnerability of countries like Lesotho and mindful of the fascist character of the *apartheid* regime, which will exploit every available pretext in order to commit aggression against those countries, the ANC has deliberately and consistently pursued forms of struggle entailing the infiltration of manpower into South Africa and the establishment of cells inside South Africa.[121]

These assertions, repeated by the States and liberation movements directly concerned, seem to confirm rather than infirm the duty of States to take every measure to prevent their territory being used to conduct military action against another State, even in a situation of violation of the right of peoples to self-determination.[122]

Third, it cannot be asserted either that the other States all accepted, even implicitly, that article 2(4) should know any exceptions or derogations in the case of military aid to a national liberation movement. It is true that some States, especially Third World States, have spoken out in favour of this.[123] But they have been systematically contradicted by Western States which have defended the same position as that found in the *travaux préparatoires* to the adoption of resolutions 2625 (XXV), 3314 (XXIX) and 42/22.[124] These States sometimes condemned Israeli or South African actions as unlawful reprisals or disproportionate self-defence.[125] They also more explicitly affirmed that no support could be given to cross-border armed actions,[126] although the violation of that prohibition could not justify any military riposte. As for the Socialist States, they defended a more ambiguous position, with the USSR declaring itself favourable overall to the Non-Aligned States while incidentally admitting the unlawfulness of sup-

---

[121] S/PV.2409, 16 December 1982, 19, para 183.

[122] See also: 'Pratique française du droit international' (1956) 2 *AFDI* 816–17.

[123] See, eg: China (S/PV.1644, 27/28 February 1972, para 148); see also LA Sicilianos, *Les réactions décentralisées à l'illicite. Des contre-mesures à la légitime défense*, above n 63, 436.

[124] R Higgins, 'The Attitude of Western States Towards Legal Aspects of the Use of Force' in A Cassese (ed), *The Current Legal Regulation of the Use of Force* (Dordrecht, Martinus Nijhoff, 1986) 448–50.

[125] See, eg: France, (S/PV.1643, 26 February 1972, paras 118–19 and 120–21), Italy (ibid, para 142), United Kingdom (ibid, para 134) and Argentina (S/PV.1644, 27/28 February 1972, paras 24–29).

[126] Belgium (S/PV.1643, 26 February 1972, paras 165–166), Argentina (S/PV.1644, 27/28 February 1972, para 23), France (S/PV.1650, 26 June 1972, paras 10–11), USA (ibid, para 127).

port by a State for armed bands formed in its territory and entering another State's territory.[127]

Fourth and last, mention must be made at this stage of the precedent of *Legal Consequences of the Construction of a Wall in the Occupied Palestinian Territory*. In its advisory opinion of 9 July 2004, the International Court of Justice recalled article 2(4) of the UN Charter, relating it to the principle of inadmissibility of the acquisition of territory by force,[128] which might suggest that the prohibition of the use of force is a rule applicable between a State (here Israel) and a people with the right to self-determination (the Palestinian people). Such a conclusion would be excessive, for two reasons. First, the Court clearly considers Israel's crossing of the 'green line' as a violation of the armistice agreement concluded with Jordan in 1948, the relevant terms of that convention being recalled expressly.[129] The *jus contra bellum* still seems to be envisaged in State to State relations. Then and above all because the Court has set aside the Israeli argument of the construction of a wall in self-defence because, to take up the terms of the opinion, 'Article 51 of the Charter thus recognizes the existence of an inherent right of self-defence in the case of armed attack by one State against another State' and consequently 'Article 51 has no relevance in this case'.[130] An assertion that indirectly but clearly excludes the argument of a right to self-defence of a people whose right to self-determination has been violated and which at the same time excludes the applicability of the regime of the prohibition of force in relations other than relations between States.[131]

All told, all of the elements allow us to assert that no agreement has ever been reached to transpose the *jus contra bellum* to situations of self-determination. Practice seems to show rather that, even for States that have supported national liberation movements, it has not officially been claimed that the regime set up by articles 2(4) and 51 could apply as it stands to situations of self-determination. Such situations seem, then, to be governed by a specific *sui generis* legal regime that cannot readily be reduced to the armed attack/self-defence schema that in principle characterises relations among States.[132]

---

[127] S/PV. 1462, 31 December 1968.

[128] ICJ, *Legal Consequences of the Construction of a Wall in the Occupied Palestinian Territory*, ICJ Rep (2004) 171, para 87.

[129] ibid, 166 *ff*, para 72 *ff*.

[130] ibid, 194, para 139.

[131] See also: O Corten and A Lagerwall, 'La violation d'un cessez-le-feu constitue-t-elle nécessairement une violation de l'article 2 § 4 de la Charte des Nations Unies?' (2008) 61 *RHDI* 104–06.

[132] See also: 'La pratique suisse en matière de droit international public' 2000 (10) *RSDIE* 670.

The Linkage Between the Non-Use of Force and the Right of Peoples to Self-Determination

How can one articulate the principles of the non-use of force and the right of peoples to self-determination in this context? To my mind, in the absence of any position of the 'international community of States as a whole' to the contrary, we remain bound by the rules such as set out in the UN Charter and the major resolutions adopted for interpreting their most relevant provisions.[133] The prohibition of the use of force like the right to self-determination both being rules recognised as part of *jus cogens*,[134] it is difficult to imagine that reference to one might allow a derogation from the other. Thus, it can be asserted that the principle of the non-use of force cannot detract from the right of peoples to self-determination. For example, one cannot characterise a people as an aggressor because it challenges the territorial integrity of a State, or more generally deny it a right to insurrection by invoking article 2(4).[135] Nor can one hamper that people's right to ask for and receive support from third States 'in accordance with the principles of the Charter . . .'.[136] Then again, as that expression well indicates, the right of peoples to self-determination cannot be construed in a way that detracts from the principle of the non-use of force. A State that violates the right of a people to self-determination is not, for that alone, an aggressor State against which a riposte, including a collective riposte, in self-defence could be made.[137] Support that may be given to a national liberation movement may be humanitarian, political or economic. No exception or derogation to the principle prohibiting giving military aid to armed bands has, however, been admitted either in the texts, or in practice, or in case law.[138]

Lastly, a national liberation struggle appears to be a special situation in which we are dealing neither with interstate relations nor with purely internal relations, the people concerned being defined in respect of a territory with a separate legal status. Such struggles may admittedly be characterised

---

[133] R Kolb, *Ius contra bellum. Le droit international relatif au maintien de la paix*, 2nd edn, above n 57, 321; see also R Higgins, 'The Attitude of Western States Towards Legal Aspects of the Use of Force', above n 124, 448–50; A Randelzhofer, 'Article 2(4)', above n 22, 128–29; A Cassese, 'Article 51', above n 34, 1356.

[134] Below, ch 4.

[135] K Skubiszewski, 'Use of Force by Statemeeting Collective Security. Law of War and Neutrality' in M Sorensen, *Manual of Public International Law* (London, Macmillan, 1968) 771.

[136] See: GA Res 2625 (XXV) and GA Res 3314 (XXIX), quoted above.

[137] HA Wilson, *International Law and the Use of Force by National Liberation Movements*, above n 63, 135–36; see also A Cassese, *Self-Determination of Peoples. A legal Reappraisal*, above n 109, 197–98.

[138] See: ICJ, Military and Paramilitary Activities, ICJ Rep (1986) 108, para 206; see also LA Sicilianos, *Les réactions décentralisées à l'illicite. Des contre-mesures à la légitime défense*, above n 63, 442–43; W Wengler, 'L'interdiction du recours à la force. Problèmes et tendances' (1971) 7 *RBDI* 432–33 and 438.

as 'international armed conflicts' in respect of the *jus in bello*, but this characterisation cannot be transposed as it stands into the realm of the *jus contra bellum*. In the absence of any general agreement to modify the scope of the prohibition of the use of force, this prohibition has continued to apply to 'international relations' alone, pursuant to article 2(4). This conclusion, however, leaves some questions open, especially those of political entities with controversial legal status.

C. The Case of Territories with Entities of Controversial Legal Status

Under certain assumptions, we are dealing with a use of force involving a political entity whose legal status is controversial. The controversy may relate first to the ownership of a territory claimed by two or more States, the dispute here being about territory or border lines. Another more intricate situation is that of the legal characterisation of the entity as such, when it is wondered whether it is a State, or only a part of a State, or an entity enjoying a status like that of a State. In one (1) or other (2) case, it may be doubted whether the international community of States as a whole has extended the notion of 'international relations' within the meaning of article 2(4) to anything other than interstate relations.

The Case of Territory Claimed by Two or More States

Should a State A intervene militarily in a territory belonging to it but under the *de facto* control of a State B, is the rule prohibiting the use of force applicable? One might *a priori* think not insofar as the military action by State A presumably takes place in its own national territory. However, there is little doubt that the answer is affirmative in light of the relevant texts. These prohibit the use of force in 'international relations' but do not require for all that an international border be crossed. More explicitly, the declaration on friendly relations states that:

> Every State has the duty to refrain from the threat or use of force to violate the existing international boundaries of another State *or as a means of solving international disputes, including territorial disputes and problems concerning frontiers of States.*[139]

The effect of the italicised wording is to provide for the prohibition of the use of force being applicable beyond the classic hypothesis of a cross-border armed action. It shows, more fundamentally, the need to interpret article 2(4) in conjunction with article 2(3) which clearly prescribes the peaceful settlement of any dispute, that is of any 'disagreement on a point of law or fact'.[140]

---

[139] GA Res 2625 (XXV) of 24 October 1970.
[140] PCIJ, *Mavrommatis Palestine Concessions*, Series A no 2, 11.

The applicability of the prohibition of the use of force cannot therefore depend on the prior settlement of a territorial or border dispute.[141] It follows that, even if a State is theoretically within its rights in terms of a territorial dispute, it cannot in principle use force to drive out the troops or authorities of an intruding State, unless it can validly claim to be acting in self-defence (the intruding State being guilty of an occupation akin to an armed attack)[142] or with Security Council authorisation.

Practice confirms this unambiguously. In the Goa affair, there was no general acceptance of India's reasoning that its military intervention, because it took place in its own territory, did not come under article 2(4).[143] In the Falklands case, Argentina did not take up this line of argument but preferred to rely on a right to self-defence, which indeed confirms the applicability of the principle of the non-use of force, when a State claims to be acting only in its own territory.[144] In the conflict between Iraq and Iran, no one made the question of a peaceful settlement of the conflict dependent upon prior determination of the territorial status of the border areas involved.[145] In the *Land and Maritime Boundary between Cameroon and Nigeria*, both Nigeria and Cameroon admitted the applicability of the regime of the non-use of force in territorial disputes, whatever the status of the contested areas of territory.[146] This was confirmed by the Eritrea Ethiopia Claims Commission in a decision about *jus contra bellum*[147] and by an arbitral tribunal judging a maritime territorial dispute between Guyana and Suriname.[148] The prohibition of the use of force applies therefore to all relations among States, even if those relations are deployed only in the territory of one of them.[149] We shall see that this

[141] C Gray, *International Law and the Use of Force*, 3rd edn, above n 22, 65; R Higgins, *The Development of International Law Through the Political Organs of the United Nations*, above n 4, 187.

[142] GA Res 3314 (XXIX) of 14 December 1974.

[143] See: France (S/PV.988, 18 December 1961, para 8), Chile (ibid, para 29), Ecuador (ibid, para 12).

[144] SA Alexandrov, *Self-Defense Against the Use of Force in International Law* (The Hague/London/Boston, Kluwer, 1996) 131–33; R Higgins, *Problems and Processmeeting International Law and How We Use It* (Oxford, Clarendon Press, 1994) 243.

[145] See: SC Res 479 (1980) of 28 September 1980; SC Res 522 (1982) of 4 October 1982; SC Res 540 (1983) of 31 October 1983; SC Res 582 (1986) of 24 February 1986; SC Res 586 (1986) of 8 October 1986; SC Res 598 (1987) of 20 July 1987; SC Res 612 (1988) of 9 May 1988; SC Res 619 (1988) of 9 August 1988; SC Res 620 (1988) of 26 August 1988; SC Res 631 (1989) of 8 February 1989; SC Res 642 (1989) of 29 September 1989; SC Res 651 (1990) of 29 March 1990; SC Res 671 (1990) of 27 September 1990; SC Res 676 (1990) of 28 November 1990; and SC Res 685 (1991) of 31 January 1991.

[146] Counter-Memorial of the Federal Republic of Nigeria, May 1999, 638, para 24.33; Abi Saab, CR 2002/20, 15 March 2002, 21, para 13.

[147] *Partial Award.* Jus contra bellum. *Ethiopia's Claims 1–8*, 19 December 2005, para 10.

[148] Arbitral Tribunal Constituted Pursuant to Art 287, and in Accordance with Annex VII of the UN Convention on the Law of the Sea (Guyana and Suriname, 17 September 2007, www.pca-cpa.org/showpage.asp?pag_id=1147), para 423.

[149] O Schachter, 'General Course in Public International Law' (1982) 178-V *RCADI* 141–43; Independent International Fact-Finding Mission on the Conflict in Georgia, *Report*, September 2009 (www.ceiig.ch/Report.html), vol II, 253 and 264–65.

may entail problems of interpretation in terms of self-defence, inasmuch as some go so far as to consider that any coercive action against foreign citizens might constitute an 'armed attack' within the meaning of article 51 of the Charter.[150] At this stage, we shall simply emphasise that the international character of relations covered by the rule set out in article 2(4) cannot be reduced to a strictly territorial criterion.

Entities whose Statehood is Disputed

In 1968, as part of the UN General Assembly discussions on the definition of aggression, the United States suggested extending this definition to certain political entities that were not recognised as States but upon which certain international obligations were incumbent.[151] In the context of the time, it was clearly the Vietnam War that was at issue, with North and South Vietnam then having contested legal status, with as a consequence some doubt over the applicability of the rule stated in article 2(4) for governing relations between them. A similar problem was raised in the Korean War in the 1950s. One might also evoke the case of China, with two political regimes each with its own territorial base, while claiming in law that their sovereign power extends over all Chinese territory. In the event of an armed attack by one of these entities on the other, would the rule prohibiting the use of force in international relations apply?[152] A similar problem arises concerning Kosovo, Abkhazia and South Ossetia, three entities whose statehood is disputed: are they therefore not protected—and bound—by article 2(4) of the Charter?

An answer to this difficult question might begin with the definition of aggression appended to resolution 3314 (XXIX), which contains an 'Explanatory note' stating that 'In this Definition the term "State": a) Is used without prejudice to questions of recognition or to whether a State is member of the United Nations'. This note pleads for the applicability of the rule in article 2(4) to relations between entities with disputed statehood, provided that there are indeed two States, as required by article 1 of the same definition. The rule applies, then, even if one of the States concerned is not recognised by the other or by certain third States. One cannot, then, by simply asserting that an entity is not officially recognised as a State, set aside application of the prohibition of the use of force.[153] The works that

---

[150] Below, chs 7 and 8.

[151] A/C.6/SR.1080, 25 November 1968, para 76; see also A/C.6/SR.1169, 3 December 1969, para 23.

[152] W Wengler, 'L'interdiction du recours à la force. Problèmes et tendances', above n 138, 426; see also E Lauterpacht, 'Contemporary Practice of the United Kingdom' (1959) 8 *ICLQ* 201–02.

[153] According to Canada, '[t]he explanatory note to Article 1 makes it clear that the concept of statehood, however defined, is not an essential element of the definition of aggression'; HM Kindred *et al* (eds), *International Law Chiefly as Interpreted and Applied in Canada* (Toronto, Emond Montgomery Pub Limited, 1987) 30.

preceded this clarification are clear enough in this respect: the theory of 'constitutive' recognition has been excluded to the benefit of an objective conception of the definition of a State.[154] The peremptory character of the non-use of force would not readily square with a condition for application of the rule of official recognition by each State of an entity that otherwise meets all the conditions for statehood.[155] This point has been emphasised by certain States which, while refusing to recognise Israel officially, do not shy from accusing it of aggression or of violation of article 2(4).[156]

Can one go even further and assert that this explanatory note shows that the object of the aggression may not be solely a Member State or a non-Member State of the United Nations but possibly a political collectivity?[157] The definition says nothing of the sort, but it does not explicitly exclude it. Article 1 of the definition refers to resort to force against the territorial integrity or political independence of another State, 'or in any other manner inconsistent with the Charter of the United Nations', an expression that could be interpreted as being broad enough to leave scope for a case of attack against a non-State political entity. Similarly, the declaration appended to resolution 2625 (XXV) says:

> Every State likewise has the duty to refrain from the threat or use of force to violate international lines of demarcation, such as armistice lines, established by or pursuant to an international agreement to which it is a party or which it is otherwise bound to respect'.[158]

Even if it does not say so in so many words, it leaves open the question whether the use of force violating an international demarcation line delimiting the territory of a non-State political entity is covered by the rule stated in article 2(4) of the Charter.

It would be going too far, to my mind, on the basis of such ambiguous texts alone, to conclude that the scope of application of the rule had been extended. Examination of all the debates that preceded their adoption show that these clauses were the maximum that States favourable to a broad conception of the scope of application of article 2(4) were able to

---

[154] Ecuador (A/AC.134/SR.58, 21 July 1970 in A/AC.134/SR.52-66; A/AC.134/SR.65, 28 July 1970 in A/AC.134/SR.52-66), Bulgaria (A/AC.134/SR.65, 28 July 1970 in A/AC.134/SR.52-66) Guyana (A/AC.134/SR.65, 28 July 1970 in A/AC.134/SR.52-66), Madagascar (A/AC.134/SR.60, 22 July 1970 in A/AC.134/SR.52-66, 88) and USRR (A/AC.134/SR.65, 28 July 1970 in A/AC.134/SR.52-66, 164).

[155] Ghana (A/AC.134/SR.37, 18 March 1969 in A/AC.134/SR.25-51, A/C.6/SR.1169, 3 December 1969, para 49).

[156] According to Iran, the definition 'should be concerned with the use of force in relations between States, although it might, conceivably, take account of political entities which were *de facto* possessed of the characteristics of States and which had received a certain amount of *de jure* recognition by other States' (A/AC.134/SR.41, 24 March 1969 in A/AC.134/SR.25-51, 134; see also A/AC.134/SR.56, 17 July 1970 in A/AC.134/SR.52-66); see also Syria (A/AC.134/SR.65, 28 July 1970 in A/AC.134/SR.52-66).

[157] Guatemala; A/C.6/SR.1479, 18 October 1974, para 19.

[158] GA Res 2625 (XXV) of 24 Octobrer 1970.

secure.[159] It should be recalled that the texts finally adopted do not include the proposals initially defended by several Western States and that tried explicitly to extend applicability of the rule to all 'political entities', including those that could not claim statehood. In a draft presented in 1969, Australia, Canada, Italy, Japan, the UK and the US affirmed that:

Any act which would constitute aggression by or against a State likewise constitutes aggression when committed by a State *or political entity* delimited by international boundaries or internationally agreed lines of demarcation against any State or *other political entity* so delimited and not subject to its authority. (emphasis added)[160]

The US representative explained this text:

An adequate definition should take full account of the existence of political entities whose claims to statehood might not be universally recognized, or which might not even make an unqualified claim to that status, but to which the fundamental obligations of the Charter respecting the use of force nevertheless applied. It should be made clear, for example, that a rebellious dependent Territory might become an aggressor against its neighbours even though its claims to statehood were not universally recognized or were even universally denied. The fact that a political entity consisted of a part of a country divided by international agreement did not absolve it from its fundamental obligations or deprive it of its rights under international law regarding the use of force, and a definition must adequately take that into account.[161]

This position was defended by several other States,[162] but met with firm opposition from many others. For the USSR for example, the Western States' argument

introduced concepts which were not found in contemporary international law or in the United Nations Charter. Any definition of aggression must be based on the

---

[159] See: B Ferencz, 'A Proposed Definition of Aggression: By Compromise and Consensus' (1973) 22 *ICLQ* 422–23; 'Defining Aggression: Where It Stands and Where It's Going' (1972) 66 *AJIL* 498.

[160] A/AC.134/L.17, 25 March 1969, para II.

[161] A/AC.134/SR.19, 2 July 1968 in A/AC.134/SR.1-24, 199; see also (A/AC.134/SR.20, 3 July 1968 in A/AC.134/SR.1-24, 222; A/AC.134/SR.31, 7 March 1969 in *Special Committee on the Question of Defining Aggression*, Second Session, A/AC.134/SR.25-51, 35; A/C.6/SR.808, 11 November 1963, para 18).

[162] See also: Italy (A/AC.134/SR.65, 28 July 1970 in A/AC.134/SR.52-66), Liberia (A/C.6/SR.1203, 20 October 1970, para 40), Japan (A/AC.134/SR.34, 13 March 1969 in A/AC.134/SR.25-51; A/AC.134/SR.57, 20 July 1970 in A/AC.134/SR.52-66), Canada (A/AC.134/SR.11, 18 June 1968 in A/AC.134/SR.1-24; A/C.6/SR.1079, 25 November 1968, para 24; A/AC.134/SR.45, 26 March 1969 in A/AC.134/SR.25-51; A/AC.134/SR.56, 17 July 1970 in A/AC.134/SR.52-66; A/AC.134/SR.11, 18 June 1968 in A/AC.134/SR.1-24; see also A/AC.134/SR.17, 28 June 1968 in A/AC.134/SR.1-24), Australia (A/AC.134/SR.18, 1 July 1968 in A/AC.134/SR.1-24; see also A/AC.134/SR.21, 4 July 1968 in A/AC.134/SR.1-24), Austria (A/C.6/SR.1208, 27 October 1970, para 51), United Kingdom (A/AC.134/SR.18, 1 July 1968 in A/AC.134/SR.1-24), DRC (A/AC.134/SR.65, 28 July 1970 in A/AC.134/SR.52-66) and Uruguay (A/AC.134/SR.19, 2 July 1968 in A/AC.134/SR.1-24).

premise that only full subjects of international law, that was to say States, acted in the international arena.[163]

The Soviet Union then stated clearly that 'a definition which was made to apply to political entities without statehood would be unacceptable to the Soviet Union also, for reasons of principle'.[164] This position was taken up by all Socialist countries,[165] but also by the Non-Aligned States[166] and even certain Western States.[167] It is not surprising, then, that, in the early 1970s, the United States abandoned the idea of introducing the concept of 'political entity' into the definition of aggression,[168] suggesting instead that a clause be added excluding the criterion of recognition, which was quickly accepted.[169] The passage of the declaration on friendly relations relating to demarcation lines must be read in the same way. The *travaux préparatoires* show that what was finally in view were the lines separating the territories of two States and not a territorial boundary of any non-State entity.[170]

[163] A/AC.134/SR.58, 21 July 1970 in A/AC.134/SR.52-66, 50; see also A/C.6/SR.1206, 26 October 1970, para 6.

[164] A/AC.134/SR.65, 28 July 1970 in A/AC.134/SR.52-66, 148; see also A/AC.134/SR.65, 28 July 1970 in A/AC.134/SR.52-66, 148; see also Romania (A/AC.134/SR.65, 28 July 1970 in A/AC.134/SR.52-66).

[165] Ukraine (A/C.6/SR.1207, 27 October 1970, para 42; A/C.6/SR.1274, 3 November 1971, para 26), Belarus (A/C.6/SR.1270, 28 October 1971, para 44), Czechoslovakia (A/C.6/SR.1273, 2 November 1971, para 43), Poland (A/C.6/SR.1275, 3 November 1971, 170, para 7), Romania (A/C.6/SR.1207, 27 October 1970, para 25; A/AC.134/SR.86, 10 February 1971 in A/AC.134/SR.79-91) and Bulgaria (A/AC.134/SR.86, 10 February 1971 in A/AC.134/SR.79-91).

[166] Iraq (A/C.6/SR.1202, 16 October 1970, para 16), Yugoslavia (A/AC.134/SR.58, 21 July 1970 in A/AC.134/SR.52-66), Cyprus (A/AC.134/SR.60, 22 July 1970 in A/AC.134/SR.52-66; A/C.6/SR.1209, 28 October 1970, para 29), Uganda (A/C.6/SR.1203, 20 October 1970, para 10), Mexico (A/C.6/SR.1203, 20 October 1970, para 16), Haiti (A/C.6/SR.1203, 20 October 1970, para 38), Iran (A/C.6/SR.1203, 20 October 1970, para 44), Algeria (A/C.6/SR.1205, 22 October 1970, para 42), Cuba (A/C.6/SR.1206, 26 October 1970, para 68; A/C.6/SR.1167, 3 December 1969, para 45; A/C.6/SR.1273, 2 November 1971, para 31), Central African Republic (A/C.6/SR.1208, 27 October 1970, para 16), Ghana (A/C.6/SR.1269, 27 October 1971, para 5; A/AC.134/SR.65, 28 July 1970 in A/AC.134/SR.52-66), Iraq (A/C.6/SR.1271, 1 November 1971, para 17), Syria (A/C.6/SR.1272, 2 November 1971, para 15 and 17), Zambia (A/C.6/SR.1276, 4 November 1971, para 25), Cameroon (A/C.6/SR.1206, 26 October 1970, para 31), Gabon (A/C.6/SR.1205, 22 October 1970, para 34), Madagascar (A/C.6/SR.1206, 26 October 1970, para 72), Sudan (A/C.6/SR.1272, 2 November 1971, 154, para 52) and Afghanistan (A/C.6/SR.1275, 3 November 1971, para 13).

[167] According to France, 'The provisions of Article 2(4) of the Charter and of Chapter VII governed only the use of force by one State against another [. . .]' (A/AC.134/SR.17, 28 June 1968 in A/AC.134/SR.1-24, 162; see also A/C.6/SR.1441, 19 November 1973, para 46); see also Greece (A/C.6/SR.1270, 28 October 1971, para 19; A/C.6/SR.1348, 2 November 1972, para 27), Chile (A/C.6/SR.1271, 1 November 1971, para 33; see also A/C.6/SR.1167, 3 December 1969, para 9), El Salvador (A/C.6/SR.1272, 2 November 1971, para 28), Costa Rica (A/C.6/SR.1276, 4 November 1971, para 3), Peru (A/C.6/SR.1274, 3 November 1971, para 18), Colombia (A/C.6/SR.1272, 2 November 1971, para 43), Guyana (A/AC.134/SR.33, 12 March 1969 in A/AC.134/SR.25-51; A/AC.134/SR.56, 17 July 1970 in A/AC.134/SR.52-66).

[168] A/AC.134/SR.65, 28 July 1970 in A/AC.134/SR.52-66.

[169] A/AC.134/SR.59, 22 July 1970 in A/AC.134/SR.52-66; A/AC.134/SR.65, 28 July 1970 in A/AC.134/SR.52-66.

[170] See, eg: Iran (A/AC.134/SR.41, 24 March 1969 in A/AC.134/SR.25-51; A/AC.134/SR.56, 17 July 1970 in A/AC.134/SR.52-66).

Discussions related essentially to the legal status of those lines and not to that of the entities in question, which were clearly considered to be States.[171]

All in all, the works conducted within the UN and the texts drafted within it do not speak in favour of the acceptance of a broad definition of 'international relations' as an essential feature of the non-use of force. It remains to be seen whether certain precedents in practice do not reveal an agreement to this effect of the international community of States as a whole.

Upon analysis, it is very difficult to show the existence of such an agreement with regard to the historical precedents of Korea and Vietnam.

—In the first instance, it is true that the Security Council denounced 'the armed attack on the Republic of Korea by forces from North Korea',[172] while the General Assembly spoke of 'an armed attack from North Korea',[173] without for all that considering North Korea as a State. It is also known that the Security Council, 'Having determined that the armed attack upon the Republic of Korea by forces from North Korea constitutes a breach of the peace', recommended that Member States 'furnish such assistance to the Republic of Korea as may be necessary to repel the attack and to restore international peace and security in the area'.[174] This language might suggest that North Korea, although not considered a State, had violated the prohibition of the use of force laid down by article 2(4) and that South Korea thereby had a right to self defence which it supposedly exercised on a collective basis.[175] However, such a conclusion does not clearly arise from examination of States' positions. First, it shall be noticed that the Charter rules on the non-use of force and self-defence were not explicitly relied on by the Republic of Korea,[176] the United States[177] or their allies.[178] The impression is rather that the UN

---

[171] Bolivia (A/C.6/SR.1160, 26 November 1969, para 1), Netherlands (A/AC.125/SR.101, 22 August 1969), India (A/C.6/SR.1183, 28 September 1970, para 8), Syria (A/AC.125/SR.65, 31 July 1967; *Report of the Special Committee on Principles of International Law concerning Friendly relations and co-operation among States*, Supp no 18, A/8018, 1970, para 207; A/AC.125/SR.109, 19 September 1969).

[172] SC Res 82 (1950) of 25 June 1950, preamble; see also SC Res 83 (1950) of 27 June 1950, preamble; SC Res 84 (1950) of 7 July 1950, preamble; SC Res 85 (1950) of 31 July 1950, preamble.

[173] GA Res 376 (V) of 7 October 1950, preamble.

[174] SC Res 83 (1950) of 27 June 1950.

[175] SA Alexandrov, *Self-Defense Against the Use of Force in International Law*, above n 144, 252–63; see also JL Kunz, 'Legality of the Security Council Resolutions of June 25 and 27, 1950' (1951) 45 *AJIL* 139.

[176] S/PV.473, 25 June 1950; S/PV.474, 27 June 1950.

[177] S/PV.473, 25 June 1950; President Truman, *Statement released to the press on June 27, 1950*, XXIII (1950, July 3) 574 *Department of State Bulletin* 5; MM Whiteman (ed), *Digest of International Law*, vol 12 (Washington, Department of State Publ., 1971) 300–03 and C Alibert, *Du droit de se faire justice dans la société internationale depuis 1945*, above n 18, 63–64.

[178] The OAS resolution does not mention self-defence, but refers to art 53 of the UN Charter; *Resolution approved by the Council of the Organization of American States* (OAS, Doc

bodies reacted to an action threatening international peace and security by coming to the aid of what was considered the only legitimate government[179] and that has appealed for aid.[180] The legal basis invoked seems therefore to relate more to the State's consent and to the mechanisms of collective security established in the Charter than to self-defence in riposte to an 'armed attack' within the meaning of article 51 of the Charter, an article that, no more than article 2(4) itself, is cited by the UN bodies.[181] It will be noticed too that the multinational action in Korea gave rise to fierce opposition, with the Socialist bloc characterising it as an intervention in the internal affairs of Korea, which was considered a unitary State.[182] For those States, the military action by the Western States could not be based on self-defence—Korea being a unitary State— nor on a valid resolution adopted by a UN body, as the Security Council had voted in the absence of the USSR.[183] Overall, the Korea precedent gave rise to positions that were too ambiguous and contradictory to estab-

---

C-SA-59-E, 28 June 1950); see also Australia (*Note dated 29 June 1950 from the Acting Head of the Australian mission to the United Nations to the Secretary-General transmitting a communication from the Australian government concerning the Security Council resolution of 27 June 1950*, S/1524), Belgium (*Letter dated 29 June 1950 from the Permanent Representative of Belgium to the United Nations addressed to the Secretary-General, concerning the Security Council Resolution of 27 June 1950*, S/1519), Brazil (*Letter dated 29 June 1950 from the Permanent Representative of Brazil to the United Nations addressed to the Secretary-General, concerning the Security Council Resolution of 27 June 1950*, S/1525), Canada (*Letter dated 30 June 1950 from the Acting Permanent Representative of Canada to the United Nations addressed to the Secretary-General, transmitting the text of a statement made by the Prime Minister of Canada in the House of Commons on 30 June 1950*, S/1538), France (S/PV.474, 27 June 1950, 8 and 9); cp New Zealand (*Cablegram dated 29 June 1950 from the Permanent Representative of New Zealand to the United Nations addressed to the Secretary-General transmitting the text of a statement made by the Prime Minister of New Zealand on 29 June 1950*, S/1522), India (S/PV.475, 30 June 1950, 2 and *Cablegram dated 29 June 1950 from the Prime Minister and Minister of Foreign Affairs of the government of India addressed to the Secretary-General concerning the Security Council Resolution of 27 June 1950*, S/1511), Iceland (S/1567), Norway (S/PV.474, 27 June 1950, 12), United Kingdom (S/PV.474, 27 June 1950, 10 and *Letter dated June 1950 from the Deputy Representative of the United Kingdom of Great Britain and Northern Ireland to the President of the Security Council transmitting the text of a statement by the Prime Minister in the House of Commons on 28 June 1950*, S/1515).

[179] SC Res 82 (1950) of 25 June 1950, preamble; GA Res 376 (V) of 7 October 1950, preamble.

[180] SC Res 83 (1950) of 27 June 1950, preamble; SC Res 84 (1950) of 7 July 1950, para 2.

[181] SC Res 82 (1950) of 25 June 1950, preamble; SC Res 83 (1950) of 27 June 1950, preamble; SC Res 84 (1950) of 7 July 1950, preamble; SC Res 85 (1950) of 31 July 1950; see also 'United Kingdom Materials on International Law' (1993) 64 *BYBIL* 597 and 'La pratique suisse en matière de droit international public' (1983) 39 *ASDI* 250.

[182] USSR (A/C.6/SR.341, 4 December 1952, paras 8–9; S/PV.480, 1 August 1950, 19), China (*Cablegram dated 6 July 1950 from the Minister for Foreign Affairs of the Central People's Government of the People's Republic of China to the Secretary-General concerning the resolution of the Security Council*, S/1583).

[183] Czechoslovakia (*Cablegram dated 29 June 1950 from the Deputy Prime Minister and Minister of Foreign Affairs of Czechoslovakia to the Secretary-General concerning Security Council resolution of 27 June 1950*, S/1523), Ukraine (*Cablegram dated 12 July 1950 from the Minister for Foreign Affairs of the Ukrainian Soviet Socialist Republic to the Secretary-General concerning the Security Council resolutions of 27 June and 7 July 1950*, S/1598).

lish an agreement extending the idea of 'international relations' to non-State political entities.

—A similar conclusion may be inferred from the Vietnam precedent. This time, the United States clearly invoked the right of self-defence to riposte to what was characterised as an armed attack by North Vietnam.[184] In this perspective, South Vietnam was considered as a sovereign State having a right of self-defence, even if this State was not a member of the United Nations.[185] In parallel, even if it was not officially recognised as such for political reasons, it seems that the Democratic Republic of Vietnam was considered to be a State in the context of the principle of the non-use of force.[186] In any event, the vision defended by the Western States is far from having been shared by all UN members. Many States preferred to characterise the United States' military action as an unlawful military intervention in an internal conflict in breach of the right of the Vietnamese people to self-determination.[187] For them, there could be no talk of an attack of the north against the south, as the two territories were part of one and the same State.[188] Whatever the group of States

[184] USA (A/C.6/SR.875, 15 November 1965, para 43; *The Legality of the United States Participation in the Defence of Viet-Nam, dated March 4 1966, Legal Memorandum prepared by Leonard Meeker, Legal Adviser of the Department of State of the United States, submitted to the Senate Committee on Foreign Relations on March 8*, in 'Contemporary Practice of the United States' (1966) 60 *AJIL* 564–85 and R Falk (ed), *The Viet-Nam War and International Law* (New Jersey, Princeton University Press, 1968) 565–85; 'Contemporary Practice of the United States' (1972) 66 *AJIL* 836–40; MM Whiteman (ed), *Digest of International Law*, vol 12, above n 177, 117–34, 303–06; JN Moore, 'The Lawfulness of Military Assistance to the Republic of Viet-Nam' (1967) 61 *AJIL* 1–34; WD Verwey, 'Bombing on the North After Tonkin and Pleiku: Reprisals?' (1969) 5 *RBDI* 460–79.

[185] *Letter dated 6 October 1966 from the Chargé d'affaires a.i. of Thailand addressed to the Secretary-General*, S/7535, 21–23); see also New Zealand (*Letter dated 16 June 1965 from the Permanent Prepresentative of New Zealand addressed to the President of the Security Council*, S/6449), Australia (A/C.6/SR.1081, 26 November 1968, para 61) and Belgium ('La pratique belge en matière de droit international' (1969) 5 *RBDI* 661–62).

[186] USA (A/AC.134/SR.8, 13 June 1968 in A/AC.134/SR.1-24, 85–86), Canada ('Canadian Report signed by Mr J Blair Seaborn, Canadian delegate of the International Control Commission cited in the ICC Reports on U.MEETING Raids-ICC Teams in North Viet-Nam withdrawn to Hanoi', in *Keesing's contemporary archives*, May 29–June 5, 1965, 20761), Australia (*Letter dated 1 June 1965 from the Charge d'affaires a.i. of Australia addressed to the Secretary-General*, S/6399, 213–15); see also W Friedmann, 'United States Policy and the Crisis of International Law' (1965) 59 *AJIL* 865–66 and Q Wright, 'Legal Aspects of the Viet-Nam Situation' (1966) 60 *AJIL* 756 *ff*.

[187] NAM ('17-nation declaration during the Conference of Heads of State or Government of non-aligned countries held in Cairo in October 1964', in *Keesing's Contemporary Archives*, May 29–June 5, 1965, 20769–70), China ('Statement of the Chinese governement on Feb 8 1965', *Keesing's Contemporary Archives*, May 29–June 5, 1965, 20762), Congo Brazzaville (GA, 1443rd plenary session, 14 October 1966), Ivory Coast (GA, 1418th plenary session, 27 September 1966), Cuba (*Yearbook of United Nations*, 1966, 155; GA, 1446th plenary session, 18 October 1966, 11–12), Guinea (GA, 1435th plenary session, 3 October 1966), Indonesia (GA 1424th plenary session, 30 September 1966); see also C Chaumont, 'Analyse critique de l'intervention américaine au Vietnam' (1968) 4 *RBDI* 61–93.

[188] Cambodia (GA, 1444th plenary session, 17 October 1966, 7), Ceylan (GA, 1446th plenary session, 18 October 1966), Belarus (*Letter dated 11 July 1966 from the Permanent*

considered, it is in any instance difficult to show the existence of an *opinio juris* that a non-State entity could be the author or the victim of a use of force in violation of international law.

These two precedents cannot readily be construed in this sense, then. The failure of attempts within the General Assembly to extend the application of the rule set out by article 2(4) has already been underscored. The uncertainties of practice have not been dissipated then by any general acceptance of principle within the forums for specifically dealing with the definition of this rule.

In its 2009 Report, the Independent International Fact-Finding Mission on the Conflict in Georgia proposed a somewhat innovative interpretation.[189] According to the Commission, in so far as the parties to the internal conflict accepted them in particular agreements, articles 2(4) and 51 of the UN Charter did apply to their relations. Therefore, Georgia had violated article 2(4) by using force against South Ossetia on 7 August 2008, South Ossetia being therefore able to invoke self-defence under article 51. Yet, the Commission denied the *collective* self-defence argument was applicable, Russia not being allowed to intervene in favour of the aggressed entity. This line of argument seems rather unpersuasive. None of Georgia, Russia or any third State ever invoked articles 2(4) or 51 of the UN Charter to characterise uses of force in the relations between the Georgian State and non-State entities like South Ossetia and Abkhazia.[190] To argue that Georgia (or South Ossetia, or Abkhazia) has violated particular agreements or relevant Security Council resolutions by using force is one thing; to deduce from it a violation of article 2(4) and the applicability of the classical *jus contra bellum* regime is another. This last step was never taken by the international community of States.[191]

Practice does show, though, a general reluctance to accept the lawfulness of any use of force by a political entity against another political entity,

---

Representative of the Byelorussian Soviet Socialist Republic addressed to the President of the Security Council, S/7402), Poland (Letter dated 12 February 1965 from the Permanent Representative of Poland addressed to the President of the Security Council, S/6190, 62–63), Romania (Letter dated 9 March 1965 from the Permanent Representative of Romania addressed to the President of the Security Council, S/6224), Czechoslovakia (Letter dated 11 February 1965 1965 from the Permanent Representative of Czechoslovakia addressed to the President of the Security Council, S/6187, 59–60), USSR (A/AC.125/SR.65, 31 July 1967) and Yugoslavia (GA, 1432nd plenary session, 7 October 1966, 5).

[189] *Report*, September 2009 (www.ceiig.ch/Report.html), vol II, 239 *ff*.

[190] See, eg: S/PV.5951 and S/PV.5952, 8 August 2008; *Letter dated 11 August 2008 from the Permanent Representative of the Russian Federation to the United Nations addressed to the President of the Security Council, S/2008/545; Letter dated 9 August 2008 from the Permanent Representative of Georgia to the United Nations addressed to the President of the Security Council, S/2008/537;* en.wikipedia.org/wiki/International_reaction_to_the_2008_South_Ossetia_war.

[191] See: O Corten and A Lagerwall, 'La violation d'un cessez-le-feu constitue-t-elle nécessairement une violation de l'article 2 § 4 de la Charte des Nations Unies?' above n 131, 100–103.

provided both can be assimilated to States, with all the controversies and ambiguities this last point may imply. The case of Taiwan is certainly a good example in this respect. If mainland China were to undertake military action against this territory, it would probably claim to be acting in its own territory, in the context of its internal affairs.[192] One might suppose, however, that such action would prompt criticism on the basis of article 2(4), with the criticism probably being backed by military aid from the United States to Taiwan by way of 'self-defence'.[193] In this case, it may be supposed that Taiwan would either be characterised as a State, or at least assimilated to a State, because of its sustained effective government of a given territory. If we confine ourselves to the relevant texts, the answer to the question of the lawfulness of mainland China's military action should in principle depend on the characterisation of Taiwan as a State within the meaning of international law.[194] A similar line of reasoning could be applied to the Kosovo problem. At present, there is nothing to show that any general agreement has been observed in favour of the applicability of article 2(4) to situations that do not pertain to relations among States.

One particularly important point deserves to be recalled at this stage. Under Chapter VII of the Charter, the Security Council remains competent for deciding on any action, including military action, in the case of aggression, breach of the peace or threat to peace. These three situations have been conceived of and interpreted broadly as referring to a discretionary competence of the Security Council.[195] It is by no means necessary, then, to prove the violation of article 2(4) as a basis for a reaction by the UN to uses of force which, in strictly legal and technical terms, do not occur in 'international relations' as meant by that provision. In practice, we have already seen that this discretionary competence has led the Security Council to deal increasingly with the management of non-international conflicts, whether in former Yugoslavia, Georgia, or elsewhere.[196] The limited applicability of the non-use of force to interstate relations should not, therefore, be understood as entailing the absence of applicability of any rule of international law, far from it. It is simply that, in this case, the existing rules prescribe that matters be referred to the Security Council, excluding other mechanisms such as self-defence, which remain limited to relations between States.

---

[192] See: *Letter dated 25 September 2000 from the Permanent Representative of China addressed to to the President of the Security Council*, A/55/420, 26 September 2000; see also Congo-Brazzaville (A/C.6/SR.1169, 3 December 1969, para 85); see JP Jain, 'The Legal Status of Formosa' (1963) 57 *AJIL* 25–45.

[193] See: USA, *Taiwan Relations Act*, April 10, 1979 (1979) 18 *ILM* 873–77.

[194] *cf* J Crawford, *The Creation of States in International Law*, above n 4, 146–52; see also JI Charney and JRV Prescott, 'Resolving Cross-Strait Relations Between China and Taiwan' (2000) 94 *AJIL* 476–77.

[195] See below, ch 6, s 1.

[196] See above.

It regularly happens in the international arena that a political group acquires authority over a given territory and claims statehood on that basis. The conflict that may ensue is not covered, in principle, by the prohibition of the use of force, insofar as that prohibition remains limited to 'international relations' and *a contrario* excludes civil wars. In the case of national liberation movements, the legitimacy of the armed struggle derives from the right of peoples to self-determination, but States have not deduced from this any transposition of the schema of armed attack/self-defence (including collective self-defence) that characterises the inter-State regime of non-use of force. The same goes for the more particular situation of entities whose statehood is contested, even if the debate has developed along different lines. Whereas they seem to have defended the argument of the applicability of article 2(4) to non-state entities in the context of the debate on the right of peoples to self-determination, the Socialist States and Non-Aligned States sided, in the context of controversies over 'political entities' with the classical position of limitation to interstate relations. Conversely, Western States very firmly defended this classical position in opposing the internationalisation of national liberation struggles in respect of the *jus contra bellum*, although some of them seem to have moved stealthily away from it after the Korea and Vietnam conflicts. Ultimately, no group of States has consistently defended an extension of the notion of 'international relations' as an essential element of the prohibition of the use of force. A position confirmed over the question of attacks by private groups that could not even claim any territorial or political standing.

II Exclusion of Private Groups from the Rule's Scope of Application

It has just been observed that, despite the claims made by certain groups of States, no agreement has come about in favour or extending the notion of 'international relations' to non-State political entities. This refusal to extend the scope of application of article 2(4) of the Charter has not only affected groups such as secessionist entities that are not recognised as having any legitimacy in international law; it has also concerned peoples who have otherwise been recognised as having a right to self-determination, by virtue of which right it has been accepted they have a right to fight for their independence. At first sight, it is hard to imagine that something that has been denied to what are recognised as legitimate political entities should be accepted for simple private groups that, unlike political entities, do not exercise or tend to exercise any power over a given territory. Even a broad understanding of the concept of 'international relations' does not seem to cover relations between a State and individuals, whether or not those individuals are brought together under the aegis of a group.

Since 11 September 2001, some scholars have claimed that the scope of application of the prohibition of the use of force has been extended to the activities of private groups characterised as 'terrorists', by considering that article 51 of the Charter could be invoked against them.[197] According to this new doctrine, the Charter provisions on the use of force, that were traditionally applicable only to relations between States, should be extended to terrorist groups that were now capable of using force.[198] This adaptation had supposedly already been made by States, which had purportedly recognised the possibility of invoking and exercising self-defence within the meaning of article 51 in such situations, as shown by the war in 2001 against *Al Qaeda* based in Afghanistan.[199] While private violence was previously understood as a simple breach of the national criminal law of each State concerned,[200] the regulation of the use of force within the meaning of the Charter is supposedly now extended to non-State actors.

It is not always clear whether this doctrine is expressed *de lege lata* or *de lege ferenda*, especially with US scholars.[201] If we confine ourselves to the classical positivist legal method, as specified above,[202] it will be seen that it is premature at least to conclude such a legal revolution has occurred, and there are three major reasons for this.[203] First, extending the rule set forth in article 2(4) to individuals appears to be contrary both to the text and to the object and purpose of the provision, including if it is understood in the current context of the fight against terrorism (A). Next, the way this provision has been interpreted in practice, including in recent practice, does not seem to challenge the modern conception of 'international relations' as conceived of in the UN Charter (B). Lastly, the same conclusion arises from a review of the work of the International Law Commission and the International Court of Justice (C).

---

[197] See, eg: T Franck, 'Terrorism and the Right of Self-Defense' (2001) 95 *AJIL* 840; SD Murphy, 'Terrorism and the Concept of 'Armed Attack' in Article 51 of the UN Charter' (2002) 43 *Harvard IL Journal* 50; CJ Tams, 'Swimming with the Tide or Seeking to Stem It? Recent ICJ Rulings on the Law on Self-Defence' (2005) 18 *RQDI* 275–90; NJ Schrijver, 'The Future of the Charter of the United Nations' (2006) 10 *Max Planck UNYB* 21–22.

[198] cp A Clark Arend and RJ Beck, *International Law and the Use of Force* (London and New York, Routledge, 1993) 146 and M Reisman, 'International Legal Responses to Terrorism', above n 1, 57; R Wedgwood, 'Responding to Terrorism: the Strikes Against bin Laden' (1999) 24 *The Yale Journal of International Law* 564.

[199] E Hey, 'International Law in the Aftermath of the war on Iraq', in *International Law/Forum du droit international*, above n 3, 236; see also F Berman, J Gow, C Greenwood, V Lowe, A Roberts, P Sands, M Shaw, G Simpson, C Warbrick, N Wheeler, E Wilmshurst, M Wood, 'The Chatham House Principles of International Law on the Use of Force on the Use of Self-Defence' (2006) 55 *ICLQ* 969–70.

[200] See: LA Sicilianos, 'L'invocation de la légitime défense face aux activités d'entités non-étatiques', (1989) *Hague YbIL* 147–68.

[201] Above, ch 1, s I.

[202] Above, ch 1, s II.

[203] O Corten, 'L'interdiction du recours à la force dans les relations internationales est-elle opposable aux groupes "terroristes"?' in R Ben Achour and S Laghmani (eds), *Acteurs non étatiques et droit international* (Paris, Pedone, 2007) 129–59.

A. Maintaining 'International Relations' as Relations among States: the Letter and Spirit of the Rule

The line of argument of scholars favourable to application of the *jus contra bellum* to private entities is based mainly on the object and purpose of the rule, which is to prohibit any type of resort to force: an extensive prohibition that is supposedly not contradicted by the relevant texts, which are flexible enough to allow such an interpretation. And yet, both the letter (1) and the spirit (2) of the rule pertain to relations among States, with the repression of acts of violence by individuals acting in a private capacity being excluded in principle from its scope of application.

The Letter of the Rule

Some commentators have noted that article 51 of the UN Charter recognises that States have a right to self-defence in the event of 'armed attack' but 'without saying that this armed attack must come from another State even if this has been the generally accepted interpretation for more than 50 years'.[204] Insofar as it would tend to extend the scope of application of the prohibition of the use of force, such an argument does not seem convincing to me, for several reasons pertaining to the relevant texts. We shall contemplate in turn the text of the Charter itself, including as it was construed on the 60th anniversary of the UN, and the treaty texts applicable in the case of the fight against terrorism. The inter-State character has not been challenged in a regional context, as attested by examination of the African Union's Non-Aggression and Common Defence Pact adopted in January 2005.

The Text of the United Nations Charter

First of all, as an exception to the general rule set out in its article 2(4),[205] self-defence recognised in article 51 of the Charter must *a priori* be understood to refer to the resort to force in 'international relations'. Now,

---

[204] ICJ, *Legal Consequences of the Construction of a Wall in the Occupied Palestinian Territory*, Judge Kooijmans, Separate Opinion, ICJ Rep (2004) 230, para 35; see also Judge Higgins, Separate Opinion, ibid, 215, para 33; Judge Buergenthal, Separate Opinion, 242, para 6; T Franck, 'Terrorism and the Right of Self-Defense', above n 197, 840; SD Murphy, 'Terrorism and the Concept of "Armed Attack" in Article 51 of the Charter', above n 197, 50 and 'Self-Defence and the Israeli *Wall* Advisory Opinion: An *Ipse Dixit* From the ICJ?' (2005) 99 *AJIL* 64; R Wedgwood, 'The ICJ Advisory Opinion on the Israeli Security Fence and the Limits of Self-Defence' (2005) 99 *AJIL* 58; MN Schmitt, *Counter-Terrorism and the Use of Force in International Law*, George C Marshall European Center for Security Studies, The Marshall Center Papers no 5 (2002) 25–26; CJ Tams, 'Swimming with the Tide or Seeking to Stem It? Recent ICJ Rulings on the Law on Self-Defence', above n 197, 278.

[205] See, eg: *Report of the International Law Commission*, 23 April–1 June and 2 July–10 August 2001, GA, Supp no 10 (A/56/10), 74, para 1.

'relations between nations'[206] within the meaning of the Charter are indeed equivalent to interstate relations, the United 'Nations' manifestly being States.[207] Article 2(4) itself confirms this first impression when it says that 'all members'—members which by definition are States[208]—shall refrain from using force. The incumbent of the obligation is thus limited to a State and not to any other subject of international law.[209] As the Ago report underscores:

> First of all, the concept of self-defence should be confined to a defensive reaction against an armed attack by another State, and should exclude an attack by private individuals. Without that restriction, the concept would be far too vague. Self-defence could exist in international law only as an exception to a general prohibition of the use of armed force by a State.[210]

It is difficult therefore to claim that a private group, even if guilty of particularly serious criminal acts, violates the prohibition laid down by article 2(4) and *a fortiori* the prohibition of armed attack that may give rise to self-defence in the meaning of article 51.[211] A reading of the text of the Charter as a whole clearly suggests, then, that the prohibition of the use of force is essentially an inter-State rule,[212] a point that is confirmed for that matter by a reading of the *travaux préparatoires*.[213]

Second, the inter-State character of the rule is reflected too in the major resolutions adopted by the UN General Assembly so as to clarify its outline:

—Resolution 2625 (XXV) contains several passages that impose the prohibition of the use of force on States exclusively and that manifestly confer corresponding rights on other States;[214]

---

[206] A Cassese, *International Law*, above n 17, 56.

[207] See, eg: preamble of the UN Charter, and Art 34; see also J Salmon (ed), *Dictionnaire de droit international public*, above n 4, v° 'nation', 720; see also R Kolb, *Ius contra bellum. Le droit international relatif au maintien de la paix*, 2nd edn, above n 57, 274–77.

[208] Art 4 of the UN Charter; according to A Randelzhofer, 'only States are eligible to become members of the UN. Thus the prohibition of the use of force indisputably only protects and is addressed to States' ('Article 2(4)', above n 22, 121); see also R Kolb, *Ius contra bellum. Le droit international relatif au maintien de la paix*, 2nd edn, above n 57, 239–40; R Higgins, *Problems and Procesmeeting International Law and How We Use It*, above n 144, 243).

[209] *Contra:* J Verhoeven, *Droit international public*, above n 17, 673.

[210] *YILC* (1980) vol I, 16th meeting, 25 June 1980, 184, para 3; see also S Schwebel, *YILC* (1980) vol I, 1621st meeting, 27 June 1980, 192, para 5, and R Ago, *YILC* (1980) vol I, 1629th meeting, 9 July 1980, 238, para 21.

[211] N Schrijver, 'Responding to International Terrorism: Moving the Frontiers of International Law for 'Enduring Freedom', (2001) 48 *NILR* 284. See also A Abbas, *Regional Organisations and the Development of Collective Security. Beyond Chapter VIII of the UN Charter*, (Oxford, Hart Publishing, 2004) 129–30.

[212] A Constantinou, *The Right of Self-Defense under Customary International Law and Article 51 of the UN Charter*, (Athènes/Bruxelles, Ant N Sakkoulas, Bruylant, 2000) 87.

[213] See: Dumbarton Oaks Proposals, *UNCIO*, vol. IV, 3; see also below, ch 8, s I).

[214] See: First principle, paras 4, 8 and 9.

—Resolution 3314 (XXIX) defines aggression as 'the first use of force by a State against . . . another State', and gives as examples only acts of one State against another State.[215] The point that article 51 of the Charter does not explicitly state that self-defence must be against an 'armed attack' by another State seems highly formalistic. The way the expression has been interpreted clearly excludes its extension to private groups. As specified above, this is what the work preceding the adoption of resolution 3314 (XXIX) confirmed, when certain States vainly attempted to extend the concept of aggression to the action of non-State entities, with a view to recognising a right of self-defence either for national liberation movements or for political entities that could not be assimilated to States;[216]

—Resolution 42/22 specifies that the prohibition of the use of force is binding on '[e]very State'[217] or that 'States' have the inherent right of self-defence[218]; here again, it is States that are the subjects of the obligation and the holders of the corresponding right.[219]

In view of all this evidence,[220] there is little doubt that, if we stick to the relevant texts, articles 2(4) and 51 of the Charter refer to instances of armed attack by States.[221]

The United Nations' 60th Anniversary Debates

No intention to change in this respect can be discerned in the UN's sixtieth anniversary debates. And yet these debates were marked by contemplation of the emergence of new threats to international peace and security, threats that arose in particular from the growing activities of terrorist groups. In this context, it might be expected that some would defend the extension of the prohibition of the use of force to relations implicating private groups. This has not been the case, since, on the contrary, it is the existing schema of the UN Charter that was reasserted throughout 2005.

First, one should notice the complete absence of any indication tending to 'privatise' the rule stated in article 2(4) of the discussion held on the subject of the use of force. Quite the contrary, in the *2005 World Summit Outcome*, the heads of State and government 'reiterate[d] the obligation *of*

---

[215] Arts 1 and 3 of the Declaration.

[216] See above.

[217] Principle I,1 of the Declaration.

[218] Principe I.13 of the Declaration.

[219] According to the USA, 'It was plain that the prohibition in Article 2 (4) applied exclusively to disputes between States' (A/AC.119/SR.3, 31 August 1964, 15); see also Hungary (*Letter addressed to the Secretary-General*, 2 June 1977, A/32/108; cp 'United Kingdom Materials on International Law' (1984) 55 *BYBIL* 583.

[220] I Brownlie, *International Law and the Use of Force by States* (Oxford, Oxford University Press, 1963) 278.

[221] See also: SD Murphy, 'Self-Defence and the Israeli *Wall* Advisory Opinion: An *Ipse Dixit* From the ICJ?' above n 204, 70.

all Member States to refrain in their international relations from the threat or use of force in any manner inconsistent with the Charter'. (emphasis added)[222] The italicised wording clearly shows that the prohibition of the use of force is still conceived of as a requirement made of States. In another passage of the document, States affirm explicitly that 'the relevant provisions of the Charter are sufficient to address the full range of threats to international peace and security'.[223] No trace of applicability of article 2(4) to terrorist groups can be found in the preparatory documents either, with the high-level panel report for example recalling the inter-State character of this provision.[224] Discussions within the General Assembly bore especially on the notion of pre-emptive or preventive self-defence, without, to my knowledge, the applicability of this institution to relations between States and private groups ever being raised.[225]

Second, it is interesting to note that the issue of the use of force by private entities was indeed considered during discussion but in a classical perspective of the fight against terrorism through cooperation among States. Especially characteristic in this respect is this passage from the high-level panel report:

> Since 1945, an ever stronger set of norms and laws—including the Charter of the United Nations, the Geneva Conventions and the Rome Statute for the International Criminal Court—has regulated and constrained States' decisions to use force and their conduct in war . . . *The norms governing the use of force by non-State actors have not kept pace with those pertaining to States.* This is not so much a legal question as a political one. Legally, virtually all forms of terrorism are prohibited by one of 12 international counter-terrorism conventions, international customary law, the Geneva Conventions or the Rome Statutes. Legal scholars know this, but there is a clear difference between this scattered list of conventions and little-known provisions of other treaties and the compelling normative framework, understood by all, that should surround the question of terrorism. *The United Nations must achieve the same degree of normative strength concerning non-State use of force as it has concerning State use of force.* Lack of agreement on a clear and well-known definition undermines the normative and moral stance against terrorism and has stained the United Nations image. Achieving a comprehensive convention on terrorism, including a clear definition, is a political imperative. (emphasis added)[226]

Thus the shortcomings of the normative framework must lead, not to an extension of the scope of application of the *jus contra bellum*, but to

---

[222] *2005 World Summit Outcome*, A/RES/60/1, 24 October 2005, para 77.

[223] ibid, para 79.

[224] *A more secure world: Our shared responsibility*, Report of the Secretary-General's High-level Panel on Threats, Challenges and Change, UN, 2004, A/59/565, 58, para 185; see also ibid, 59, para 192).

[225] A/59/PV.85, 5 April 2005; A/59/PV.86, 6 April 2005; A/59/PV.87, 7 April 2005; below, ch 7, s I.

[226] *A more secure world: Our shared responsibility*, A/59/565, above n 224, 47–48, paras 158–59.

reinforced repression of terrorist behaviour in the conventional domain. The Secretary-General too adopted this perspective by noting in passing that 'The use of force by States is already thoroughly regulated under international law', and by going on to recommend the conclusion of a general convention on terrorism.[227] As for the States themselves, they recalled in the final document that 'international cooperation to fight terrorism must be conducted in conformity with international law, including the Charter'.[228]

Reinforcing the Conventional Framework of the Fight against Terrorism

Another point should be mentioned. The reinforcement of the normative framework of the fight against terrorism could have provided an opportunity for any supporters of an extension of self-defence to military ripostes against private groups to recognise this possibility in the relevant treaties. Now, not only did this not happen, but this possibility was clearly ruled out by certain clauses that are found in several relevant instruments:

—The States Parties shall carry out their obligations under this Convention in a manner consistent with the principles of sovereign equality and territorial integrity of States and that of non-intervention in the domestic affairs of other States;
—Nothing in this Convention shall affect other rights, obligations and responsibilities of States and individuals under international law, in particular the purposes of the Charter of the United Nations, international humanitarian law and other relevant conventions.[229]

It is clear from these provisions that no State can claim to carry out a military action in another State's territory on the sole pretext that it is merely riposting in 'self-defence' to terrorist acts conducted from that territory. On the contrary, it is essentially through the classical mechanisms of cooperation that the fight must be conducted. This fight may admittedly exceptionally consist in a military operation conducted pursuant to the Charter, but it must then be shown that the action is based on Security Council authorisation, or a situation of self-defence, that will presuppose the existence of an armed attack by the *State* targeted by the military action and not just by the private group whose activities allegedly unfolded on that State's territory. Of course, the target State may be found responsible for an armed attack if it itself sent a private group to carry out an attack or if it is substantially implicated in such an attack.[230]

---

[227] *In larger freedom: towards development, security and human rights for all: report of the Secretary-General*, A/59/2005, 21 March 2005, 26, para 91.

[228] A/RES/60/1, 24 October 2005, para 85.

[229] 1999 International Convention for the Suppression of the Financing of Terrorism, arts 20 and 22; see also 2005 International Convention for the Suppression of Acts of Nuclear Terrorism, arts 21 and 22 (www.un.org/terrorism/instruments.shtml).

[230] Below, ch 7, s I.

The African Union's Non-Aggression and Common Defence Pact

On 31 January 2005 the African Union adopted a Non-Aggression and Common Defence Pact, some of the provisions of which could be interpreted as extending the prohibition of the use of force to private groups.[231] After insisting in its preamble on the need to 'to put an end to conflicts of any kind within and among States in Africa', the treaty defines aggression in its article 1c as

> the use, intentionally and knowingly, of armed force or any other hostile act by a State, a group of States, an organization of States *or non-State actor(s) or by any foreign or external entity*, against the sovereignty, political independence, territorial integrity and human security of the population of a State Party to this Pact, which are incompatible with the Charter of the United Nations or the Constitutive Act of the African Union. The following shall constitute acts of aggression, regardless of a declaration of war by a State, group of States, organization of States, *or non-State actor(s) or by any foreign entity*. . . . (emphasis added)

A further provision defines 'Threat of Aggression' as

> any harmful conduct or statement by a State, group of States, organization of States, *or non-State actor(s)* which though falling short of a declaration of war, might lead to an act of aggression as defined above. (emphasis added)[232]

At the time of writing, the Pact has not come into force. The italicised terms do seem to attest, though, to an intention of African States to extend the notion of aggression to acts carried out not just by States but also by private groups.

A complete reading of this instrument, however, must lead us to a more precise and nuanced conclusion. 'Aggression' and 'threat of aggression' as defined in its article 1 do not appear to be capable of justifying self-defence within the meaning of article 51 of the UN Charter. As the terms of article 2 of the African Pact indicate, the purpose of these notions is rather 'to define a framework under which the Union may intervene or authorise intervention, in preventing or addressing situations of aggression, in conformity with the Constitutive Act, the Protocol and the Common African Defence and Security Policy'.[233] It is less a matter of making a pronouncement on the conditions governing the prohibition of the use of force in the meaning of articles 2(4) or 51 of the UN Charter than of conferring broader competences on the African Union in view of a collective intervention subject to UN Charter chapters VII and VIII from which the Pact states it does not purport to derogate.[234] This scope of competences is conceived of very

---

[231] www.africa-union.org/root/au/Documents/Treaties/treaties.htm.
[232] Art 1(w).
[233] Art 2(b).
[234] Art 17(a) of the Pact.

broadly as covering not only situations of 'armed force' but also of 'any other hostile act', 'acts of espionage' or 'technological assistance of any kind' to an aggressor State.[235] In all such instances, States 'undertake to provide mutual assistance towards their common defence and security' and especially 'to provide all possible assistance towards the military operations decided by the Peace and Security Council'.[236] Self-defence, however, is never specifically mentioned in the Non-Aggression and Common Defence Pact. It would be misleading, therefore, to claim to extend its scope on the basis of this text, including in the context of the fight against terrorism. On the contrary, that fight is conceived of in the Pact as having to give rise to reinforced mechanisms for legal or police cooperation to combat organised crime.[237]

Object and Purpose of the Rule

One might admittedly retort to all these text-based arguments that article 51 merely recognises an independently-existing, 'inherent' (*naturel*, in the French version) right to self-defence and that this right must be understood to apply more broadly than in 'international relations' within the restrictive meaning of the expression. It is thus in the name of the spirit of the rule that some commentators contemplate its extension to cover the riposte to 'terrorist' attacks.[238] The objection relates more specifically to the hypothesis of a State suffering an attack being deprived of any possibility of riposte because the terrorist group responsible supposedly acted from an area that does not come within any sovereignty or that is within the territory of another State that was unable or unwilling to prevent the attack.[239] In such a situation, the right to survival on which the notion of self-defence is based, a right recognised by the International Court of Justice,[240] allegedly dictates a right to riposte, including in the territory of another State that is not directly guilty of an 'armed attack' by classical standards.[241] It is hard to imagine, in any event, that States would voluntarily have rendered themselves powerless by limiting the notion of self-defence to the hypothesis of purely inter-State uses of force.

---

[235] Arts 1(c) and 1(c) (ix) and (x).

[236] Arts 4(a) and 10(a) of the Pact; see also Arts 3(a), 4(b) and 17(a).

[237] See also: Arts 5(a) and 6.

[238] PM Eisemann, 'Attaques du 11 Septembre et exercice d'un droit naturel de légitime défense' in K Bannelier *et al* (eds), *Le droit international face au terrorisme* (Paris, Pedone, 2002) 241; see also R Wedgwood, 'The ICJ Advisory Opinion on the Israeli Security Fence and the Limits of Self-Defence', above n 204, 61.

[239] PM Eisemann, 'Attaques du 11 Septembre et exercice d'un droit naturel de légitime défense', above n 239, 245.

[240] ICJ, *Legality of the Threat or Use of Nuclear Weapons*, ICJ Rep (1996) 263, para 96.

[241] PM Eisemann, 'Attaques du 11 Septembre et exercice d'un droit naturel de légitime défense', above n 239, 246.

To understand this line of argument, one must begin with the object and purpose of the regime prohibiting the use of force; an object and purpose that plainly refer to the protection of sovereignty. It is in this context that it will be understood that, in fact, States are not rendered powerless in the context of the fight against terrorism and that, ultimately, extending article 2(4) to relations implicating private groups would lead to an obviously absurd and unreasonable result.

The Prohibition of the Use of Force and the Protection of Sovereignty

The essential object of article 2(4) is to protect the sovereignty of States.[242] This observation can hardly be contested, the objective arising clearly from a reading of the text of this provision which prohibits the use of force against the 'territorial integrity' or 'political independence' of States,[243] expressions it is hard to imagine can apply to non-State entities. The *internal* dimension of this sovereignty implies that each State has the possibility of regulating the use of violence in its own territory.[244] In principle, any State may thus sanction violations of its national law by groups or non-State entities, whether through the criminal law or by implementing police measures.[245] In its *external* dimension, sovereignty implies the right of any State not to be subject to coercion by any other sovereign State, whether in general (by application of the principle of non-intervention) or militarily (by application of the prohibition of the use of force).[246] The regime prohibiting the use of force appears, then, as a corollary of sovereignty and consequently as an essentially inter-State regime. Conversely, an individual, group or entity resorting to violence shall be apprehended by law as a delinquent or a criminal that the State may, as necessary, prosecute and punish.[247] An individual or a non-State entity shall therefore not be recognised as having the status of a sovereign subject to which the regime of the non-use of force established by the UN Charter might be applicable.

[242] KM Meessen, 'Le droit au recours à la force militaire: une esquisse selon les principes fondamentaux', above n 47, 110.

[243] See also: GA Res 3314 (XXIX) of 14 December 1974 and O Corten and P Klein, *Droit d'ingérence ou obligation de réaction?* 2nd edn (Brussels, Bruylant, 1996) 172–74.

[244] J Salmon (ed), *Dictionnaire de droit international public*, above n 4, v° 'souveraineté', 1045.

[245] According to B Asrat, 'Force used domestically in cases considered to be within the internal jurisdiction of States will not as a general rule afford ground for the application of the Article [2.4]. Varied grades of internal disturbances, from minor riots to sustained armed conflicts of an advanced nature, against which a State deploys its coercive machinery—be it designated an ordinary police action, or a paramilitary or military operation—belong to this domain'; *Prohibition of Force Under the UN Charter. A Study of Art. 2(4)* (Uppsala, Iustus Förlag, 1991) 69; see also R Bermejo Garcia, *El Marco jurídico internacional en materia de uso de la fuerza: ambigüedades y límites* (Madrid, Editorial Civitas, 1993) 71; C Chaumont, 'Cours général de droit international public' (1970-I) 129 *RCADI* 404.

[246] P Daillier, M Forteau and A Pellet, *Droit international public*, 8th edn, above n 20, 472; see also J Salmon (ed), *Dictionnaire de droit international public*, above n 4, v° 'souveraineté extérieure', 1046.

[247] See, eg: France, A/C.6/35/SR.56, 20 November 1980, para 6.

The Possibilities for Fighting Terrorism Effectively within the Existing Legal Framework

In this context, it seems excessive to me to claim that the existing texts, which we have seen emphasise the interstate character of the rule, render States powerless. Several situations can be distinguished and each time the applicable legal regime considered, to observe that this in no way paralyses the action of a State having suffered an attack, even if the perpetrators are no longer in its territory.

—First, if it is a matter of acting against a private group in the territory under the sovereignty of no State (for example, on the high seas)[248]—or *a fortiori* if the group is in the State's national territory—, the notion of self-defence is not needed. The rules prohibiting the use of force do not in any way oppose any police operation, including, under certain circumstances, of an extraterritorial scope.[249] In such an instance, the State targeting a 'terrorist group' does not act against any other State and so there is no need for it to rely on article 51 of the Charter.[250] Even if, in the ordinary meaning of the word, one might say it is defending itself against an 'attack', that 'defence' shall not be considered an exception to a prohibition of the use of force, since that prohibition has no currency in relations between a State and individuals who have infringed its national legal order. In terms of international law, we are simply in the domain of the exercise of national sovereignty.[251]

—Second, mention must be made of the case of a State in whose territory a 'terrorist group' is situated and that does not have the *capacity* to act against that group. This hypothesis seems purely theoretical, though. Supposing that the State did not have sufficient police or military resources, nothing would prevent it from accepting that an operation be conducted in a part of its territory by another State that was previously the victim of a terrorist action. In other words, a State that is attacked and wishes to bring to book a private group engaging in activities from the territory of another State can always ask that other State either to apprehend and arrest those responsible or at the very least to consent to a cross-border police operation. The existence of failed States does not seem to constitute, as such, an impediment to effective action.[252]

---

[248] See: A Pellet and V Tzankov, 'L'Etat victime d'un acte terroriste peut-il recourir à la force armée?' in SFDI, *Les nouvelles menaces contre la paix et la sécurité internationales*, journée franco-allemande (Paris, Pedone, 2004) 100–01.

[249] See above, ch 2, s I.

[250] Comp Institut de droit international Resolution on Self-defence, 27 October 2007, Santiago Session (www.idi-iil.org/idiE/navig_chon2003.html), para 10.

[251] See: R Ago, *YILC* (1980) vol I, 1629th meeting, 9 July 1980, para 21.

[252] *Contra:* ICJ, *Armed Activities on the Territory of the Congo*, Judge Kooijmans, Separate Opinion, para 30; ibid, Judge Simma, Separate Opinion, para 12; see also CD Classen, '"Failed States" and the Prohibition of the Use of Force' in SFDI, *Les nouvelles menaces*

—It seems then that the only problem liable to arise is that of a riposte that is made difficult not by a lack of capacity but by a lack of *willingness* of a State sheltering a terrorist group responsible for an attack. In such a situation, international law prescribes in principle applying for Security Council authorisation to be able to act, an authorisation that may perfectly well be granted against a State which, by its behaviour, is threatening international peace and security within the meaning of chapter VII of the Charter. If, however, such an authorisation is not granted, the State that is the victim of a terrorist attack will then be reduced to invoking self-defence to justify its military action in the territory of the recalcitrant State. In this case, however, we will be within the context of inter-State relations, with the intervening State reacting both to the attack initially conducted by the terrorist group and to the behaviour of the State, which will at the very least be considered as an accomplice to the attack.[253]

In view of these hypotheses, it does seem we are faced with an alternative: either one can react to a terrorist attack without affecting another State, and self-defence need not be evoked; or the riposte is conducted in the territory of another State and self-defence may come into play, but shall then have to be contemplated from an inter-State perspective, with the State affected by the riposte itself having previously violated international law. In any event, the applicable legal regime in no way renders a State that is the victim of an attack powerless.

Admittedly it should not be denied that, in certain exceptional circumstances, a State that is a victim of a terrorist attack cannot riposte militarily in international relations because of the stringency of the legal regime. This possibility appears to be largely theoretical—I know of no precedent that can be interpreted in this way—, but it can perfectly well be considered. One would have to imagine a particularly serious act of war committed by a terrorist organisation based on the territory of a third State. The injured State, after having called in vain for the cooperation of the third State, would apply for Security Council authorisation, which would be refused despite the seriousness of the situation. Self-defence could not be invoked insofar as the third State, even if it refused to cooperate and as such violated international law would not itself have committed an 'armed attack' against the victim

---

contre la paix et la sécurité internationales, journée franco-allemande (Paris, Pedone, 2004) 133 and 138–139; R Geiss, 'Failed States—Legal Aspects and Security Implications' (2004) 47 *GYIL* 498–500; G Cahin, 'L'Etat défaillant en droit international: quel régime pour quelle notion?' in *Droit du pouvoir, pouvoir du droit. Mélanges offerts à Jean Salmon* (Brussels, Bruylant, 2007) 177–209.

[253] Institut de droit international Resolution on Self-defence, 27 October 2007, Santiago Session (www.idi-iil.org/idiE/navig_chon2003.html), para 10. See below, ch 7, s I and P Lamberti Zanardi, 'Indirect Military Aggression' in A Cassese (ed), *The Current Legal Regulation of the Use of Force* (Dodrecht, Martinus Nijhoff, 1986) 111–19; I Brownlie, *International Law and the Use of Force by States* (Oxford, Clarendon Press, 1963) 370 *ff*; 'International Law and the Activities of Armed Bands' (1958) 7 *ICLQ* 712–85.

State. That State could not then conduct an armed attack against the third State, but could at most contemplate conducting a police operation of such limited scope that it could not be characterised as a use of 'force'.[254] In this quite exceptional situation, it is true that the riposte to a terrorist act could not take the form of an armed attack in international relations. But should consideration of such an exception dictate so revolutionary an interpretation of the rule that it would henceforth justify uses of force against a State that was not guilty of a prior armed attack? To my mind, claims seem to be directed rather at the introduction into international law of a fairly broad notion of indirect aggression.[255] This issue shall not be covered here.[256] But in any event, it should be emphasised that self-defence remains, even in this case, envisaged as an exception to a prohibition of the use of force that is directed only at States and not at private groups.[257]

On this matter, it seems to me somewhat paradoxical to invoke the pacifying objective of the regime established by the Charter to extend it to non-State entities.[258] That the prohibition is reserved to States in no way means that individuals may use violence, this being simply regulated within the national legal context of each State. By contrast, the possible extension of the scope of application of articles 2(4) and 51 of the Charter does risk giving arguments to States wishing to conduct military actions in the territory of other States in circumstances that are incompatible with the regime as it is laid down in the UN Charter.[259] The pacifying objective of the rule pleads therefore in favour of a restrictive interpretation of its scope of application.

The Manifestly Absurd and Unreasonable Character of Recognising Terrorist Groups as Having the Status of Subjects of International Law

Besides, and this is the last point we shall mention on this, extending the prohibition of the use of force to other than State relations would lead to a

---

[254] See above, ch 2, s I.

[255] MN Schmitt, *Counter-Terrorism and the Use of Force in International Law*, above n 204, 41 *ff*; T Ruys and S Verhoeven, 'Attacks by Private Actors and the Right of Self-Defence' (2005) 10 *Journal of Conflict and Security Law* 289–320; TM Franck, *Recourse to Force. State Action Against Threats and Armed Attacks* (Cambridge, Cambridge University Press, 2002) 53 *ff*; SD Murphy, 'Terrorism and the Concept of 'Armed Attack' in Article 51 of the Charter', above n 197, 50–51; ME O'Connel, 'Lawful Self-Defense to Terrorism' (2002) 63 *Univ Of Pittsburgh Law Review* 899–902; C Tams, 'The Use of Force against Terrorists', (2009) 20 *EJIL* 384 *ff*.

[256] Below, ch 7, s I.

[257] E David, 'Sécurité collective et lutte contre le terrorisme: guerre ou légitime défense?' in SFDI, journée franco-tunisienne, *Les métamorphoses de la sécurité collective. Droit, pratique et enjeux stratégiques* (Paris, Pedone, 2005) 144–46; see also M Bothe, 'Terrorism and the Legality of Pre-emptive Force' (2003) 14 *EJIL* 233.

[258] See: R Kolb, Ius contra bellum. *Le droit international relatif au maintien de la paix*, 2nd edn, above n 57, 277.

[259] PM Dupuy, 'State Sponsors of Terrorism: Issues of International Responsibility' in A Bianchi (ed), *Enforcing International Norms Against Terrorism* (Oxford and Portland Oregon, Hart Publishing, 2004) 13.

manifestly absurd and unreasonable result in respect of the rule's purpose, for two reasons.

—First, if we follow the logic through, even a perfectly innocent State could be attacked on the sole ground that a terrorist group supposedly operated from its territory without its knowledge. The State carrying out the military action would just need to claim that it merely acted against a private group and not another State, even though that other State's territory had been the target of bombardments. The State affected by the riposte would then be deprived of the protection granted to it by article 2(4), which does indeed seem a manifestly absurd and unreasonable result in view of the actual object of that provision which is, as seen, to protect State sovereignty.[260]

—Second, the very idea of having to rely on self-defence in respect of a terrorist group supposes, in principle, that it is forbidden for a State to resort to force against individuals. Now, we have seen that one of the implications of a State's national sovereignty is that it alone has the prerogative of the legitimate use of violence against individuals. Moreover, the problem of enforcement of the prohibition of the use of force in this type of relation is that, quite logically, a terrorist group, while being bound by the rule, could also rely on it. The outcome of self-defence being binding against terrorist groups is that it promotes them from the status of common criminals to being subjects of international law with a degree of legal capacity of their own.[261] What has been denied to secessionist movements and even to national liberation movements,[262] would thus have been granted to terrorist groups now holders of a duty not to resort to force but also, logically, of a possible right of self-defence. In theory, still if the scope of application of the Charter regime were extended, a terrorist group that was attacked before it had made an armed attack on a State (but after committing crimes that under this hypothesis were not really serious) would thus be able to argue self-defence.[263] The will to extend the scope of application of a rule devised to govern relations between sovereign States alone plainly leads, then, to manifestly unreasonable results.

---

[260] See above.

[261] See: PM Dupuy, 'State Sponsors of Terrorism: Issues of International Responsibility', above n 260, 7–8; M Bothe, 'The International Community and Terrorism' in SFDI, *Les nouvelles menaces contre la paix et la sécurité internationales*, journée franco-allemande (Paris, Pedone, 2004) 54.

[262] See above.

[263] J Verhoeven, 'Les "étirements" de la légitime défense' (2002) 48 *AFDI* 62. According to the Independent International Fact-Finding Mission on the Conflict in Georgia, 'if the use of force is prohibited in the relations between a State and an entity short of statehood, then self-defence must be available by both sided as well' (*Report*, September 2009 (www.ceiig.ch/Report.html), vol II, 241–42).

In short, even if the idea of territorial sovereignty has come under increasing strain because of the erosion of State power and the growing power of certain private groups, such sovereignty remains an essential legal concept in international law, especially in the context of the prohibition of the use of force. National sovereignty allows each State to exercise its police powers in its own territory without having to resort to any exception or even to any legal title other than that of its responsibility for maintaining law and order within its borders.[264] If criminals operate from abroad, the problem shall in principle have to be solved by police and criminal law cooperation between the States concerned. Should those mechanisms prove inadequate, there is always recourse to the Security Council, or as a last resort, to article 51 of the Charter. This provision cannot however justify the use of force against another State unless that State was guilty of an 'armed attack', an expression that has long covered the hypothesis of State support for an armed attack carried out by a private group, provided, however, that such support fulfils certain conditions.[265] Even in this last instance, the use of force is still envisaged in 'international relations', terrorists being reduced to the status of criminals, who are refused a status equivalent to that of States.

It is in this same optic that one can consider the precedents in which situations have been apprehended involving attacks for which private groups were responsible. The way the rule has been construed in such situations confirms, as shall be seen next, that the question is still considered by reference to relations between States, pursuant to the letter and the spirit of article 2(4) of the UN Charter.

B. Maintaining 'International Relations' as Relations between States: the Interpretation of Texts in Practice

As I see it, there is currently no precedent from which one might deduce that States have agreed to extend the prohibition of the use of force as it is set out in the Charter to relations between States and private groups. We shall envisage below several events when such claims might have been made and then accepted, to observe that this was not so. We shall begin by considering precedents from before the attacks of 11 September 2001 (1) before analysing the consequences of those attacks, which, according to the doctrine favourable to extending the prohibition of the use of force to private groups, supposedly consecrated their arguments (2).

---

[264] P Weckel, 'Coordination entre la prohibition de l'emploi de la force et les exigences de la lutte contre le terrorisme' in E Cannizaro and P Palchetti (eds), *Customary International Law On the Use of Force* (Leiden/Boston, Martinus Nijhoff, 2005) 298 and 299.

[265] See: Art 3(g) of the Definition of Aggression annexed to GA Res 3314 (XXIX) and below, ch 7, s I.

Precedents Prior to 11 September 2001

There are many contemporary precedents in which a State has entered the territory of another State claiming to be acting against a private group that had taken refuge on the other side of the border. I am thinking especially of Israeli military actions in Lebanon, Syria, Jordan and Tunisia, and actions by Portugal, Southern Rhodesia or South Africa in certain States in whose territory national liberation movements were based. As already indicated, such military action was usually expressly characterised as contrary to international law by a great majority of States. At this stage, it shall be observed that these precedents were essentially considered as covering relations between States, even if certain non-State groups were implicated. More often than not, the State taking the military action—Israel, Portugal, South Africa or Southern Rhodesia—claimed to be acting against both a private group, often characterised as terrorists, and the State sheltering it. Other States, for their part, condemned military attacks against sovereign States whose behaviour they often considered as legitimate. In some instances, the action by the State claiming to be acting in self-defence was criticised, explaining that it could not liken an action by a private group to an armed attack conducted by another State.[266] In any event, no new interpretation of the expression of 'international relations' within the meaning of article 2(4) of the Charter can be deduced from these precedents.[267]

Next we concentrate rather on the main precedents traditionally cited as potential evidence of the applicability of the use of force on private groups in the reactions to mercenary attacks in Benin in 1977 and the Seychelles in 1981. In this perspective, military action by the United States against Al Qaeda bases in Sudan and Afghanistan in 1998 is sometimes evoked. Careful examination of these events shows, however, that the prohibition of the use of force was actually considered in relations between States, pursuant to the text and to the object and purpose of the rule.

Mercenary Attacks in Benin (1977) and the Seychelles (1981)

In 1977 the Security Council, after recalling the wording of article 2(4)[268] 'strongly condemn[ed] the act of armed aggression perpetrated against the People's Republic of Benin'.[269] Four years later, the same Security Council again recalled the same wording and then 'condemne[d] the recent mercenary aggression against the Republic of Seychelles and the subsequent hijacking'.[270] In both cases, military action by mercenaries was condemned

---

[266] See, eg: 'Pratique française du droit international' (1969) 15 *AFDI* 892–93.

[267] *Contra:* SD Murphy, 'Self-Defence and the Israeli *Wall* Advisory Opinion: An *Ipse Dixit* From the ICJ?' above n 204, 69.

[268] SC Res 404 (1977) of 8 February 1977, preamble.

[269] SC Res 405 (1977) of 14 April 1977, para 2.

[270] SC Res 496 (1981) of 15 December 1981, preamble and para 2.

as incompatible with article 2(4), which might suggest this article applies to relations between States and certain private groups. Closer scrutiny of the two precedents shows, however, that beyond the mercenary action, it was the States that had instigated each of the operations that was the target. It seems misleading therefore to deduce any radical change to the scope of the prohibition of use force within the meaning of the UN Charter.

As concerns Benin, first it should be clarified that its complaint referred beyond the mercenaries[271] to 'a coalition of reactionary States'.[272] More specifically, accusations were made against Morocco, which allegedly made its territory available for preparing the attack; Gabon, from where the attack was allegedly launched; Togo, which also allegedly lent its territory; and with a lesser degree of involvement, Côte d'Ivoire and Senegal.[273] As for France, it was designated as 'chief instigator of the imperialist armed aggression'.[274] The Security Council did not make any pronouncements on these accusations. After setting up a commission of enquiry, it did though take care to 'condem[n] any State which persists in permitting or tolerating the recruitment of mercenaries and the provision of facilities to them, with the objective of overthrowing the Governments of Member States',[275] while asking States 'to exercise utmost vigilance against the danger posed by international mercenaries and to ensure that their territory and other territories under their control, as well as their nationals, are not used for the planning of subversion'.[276] Under the circumstances, it seems excessive to affirm that this is a precedent in which the prohibition of the use of force was contemplated other than in relations between States. While it is true that the condemnation of an armed attack did not designate any particular State, the declarations of principle by the Security Council clearly show that we are dealing with relations among States, as attested more plainly still in Benin's complaint.

The Seychelles precedent also argues along these lines. From the outset, the representative of the State attacked pointed out that 'mercenaries arrived . . . from South Africa',[277] and returned there after hijacking an aircraft, most of them without being troubled.[278] Several Member States of the Security Council repeated this accusation.[279] A first resolution decided to

---

[271] *Letter dated 26 January 1977 from the Permanent Representative of Benin, addressed to the President of the Security Council*, S/12278, 26 January 1977); see also the NAM's position (S/12283, 7 February 1977).

[272] *Letter dated 4 April 1977 from the Charge d'Affaires a.i. of Benin to the United Nations addressed to the President of the Security Council: addendum, Report on the imperialist armed aggression committed on Sunday, 16 January 1977, against the People's Republic of Benin*, S/12319 and Add.1, 5 April 1977, 52.

[273] ibid, 52–54.

[274] ibid, 61.

[275] SC Res 405 (1977) of 14 April 1977, 1–2, para 3.

[276] ibid, para 4.

[277] S/PV.2314, 15 December 1981, 1–2, para 9.

[278] ibid, 2, para 10 *ff*.

[279] See, eg: USA (ibid, 7, para 83) and Botswana (ibid, 3, para 22).

send a commission to investigate 'the origin, background and financing of the mercenary aggression'.[280] In its report, the commission regretted that it could not establish the facts with any certainty, mainly because of a lack of cooperation from the South African authorities, but it did establish a connection between the attack and South Africa.[281] It was on the basis of this report that the representative of the Seychelles, joined in this by several of his fellows,[282] accused South Africa.[283] The second resolution on this matter adopted by the Security Council referred to an attack 'prepared and executed from South Africa', and then condemned 'any State which persists in permitting or tolerating the recruitment of mercenaries and the provision of facilities to them, with the objective of overthrowing the Governments of Member States' and also condemned 'all forms of external interference in the internal affairs of Member States, including the use of mercenaries to destabilize States and/or to violate the territorial integrity, sovereignty and independence of States'.[284]

Whether in the case of Benin or of the Seychelles, the condemnation of 'aggression' by the Security Council must first be understood as justifying its jurisdiction under Chapter VII of the UN Charter. On the more technical aspect of the rule prohibiting the use of force, it seems hazardous to deduce any will to extend the rule to private groups. A careful reading of all works shows rather that the connection between the mercenary acts and the responsibility of other States has been established each time by the complaining State, with the Security Council reasserting this connection in its principle without explicitly denouncing an unlawful act of the State accused in the absence of proof of the matter. To my mind, nothing more can be deduced from these precedents.

US Military Actions in Sudan and Afghanistan (1998)

In August 1998, the United States conducted targeted military attacks in Sudan and Afghanistan. A letter to the Security Council justifying the attacks stated:

In accordance with Article 51 of the Charter of the United Nations . . . the United States of America has exercised its right of self-defence in responding to a series of armed attacks against United States embassies and United States nationals. My Government has obtained convincing information from a variety of reliable

---

[280] SC Res 496 (1981) of 15 December 1981, para 3.

[281] *Report of the SC Commission of Inquiry established under Resolution 496 (1981)*, S/14905, 15 March 1982, 51–52, paras 278–81.

[282] Jordan (S/PV.2359, 20 May 1982, para 68), Egypt (ibid, para 81), Malta (ibid, para 112), India (ibid, para 120), Benin (ibid, para 143), Angola (ibid, para 199), Czechoslovakia (ibid, para 214), Poland (S/PV.2365, 24 May 1982, para 13), Tanzania (ibid, para 27), Vietnam (ibid, para 62), Bulgaria (ibid, para 80), Yugoslavia (ibid, para 95), Pakistan (ibid, para 119), Mozambique (ibid, paras 191 and 200) and Syria (ibid, para 209).

[283] S/PV.2359, 20 May 1982, 5, paras 47–48.

[284] SC Res 507 (1982) of 28 May 1982, preamble and paras 4–5.

sources that the organization of Usama Bin Ladin is responsible for the devastating bombings on 7 August 1998 of the United States embassies in Nairobi and Dar Es Salaam . . . In response to these terrorist attacks, and to prevent and deter their continuation, United States armed forces today struck at a series of camps and installations used by the Bin Ladin organization to support terrorist actions against the United States and other countries.[285]

The United States seems therefore to have riposted to an armed attack for which a private group, the Al Qaeda organisation, was allegedly responsible.[286] Self-defence, and more generally the regime prohibiting the use of force, seem *a priori* to be envisaged beyond strictly inter-State relations.[287]

A more attentive analysis shows, however, that no general agreement of States can be established on this point. First because the United States itself made the connection between the terrorist groups and the States allegedly harbouring them. Thus, in the terms of the letter to the Security Council in which the United States invoked self-defence:

The Bin Ladin organization maintains an extensive network of camps, arsenals and training and supply facilities in Afghanistan, and support facilities in Sudan, which have been and are being used to mount terrorist attacks against American targets. These facilities include an installation at which chemical weapons have been produced . . . *These attacks were carried out only after repeated efforts to convince the Government of the Sudan and the Taliban regime in Afghanistan to shut these terrorist activities down and to cease their cooperation with the Bin Ladin organization.* (emphasis added)[288]

Upon reading these terms, there is no doubt that article 51 of the Charter is invoked against the States whose territories were targeted by the attacks.[289] Moreover, whatever the justification officially advanced by the

---

[285] *Letter dated 20 August 1998 from the Permanent Representative of the United States of America to the United Nations addressed to the President of the Security Council*, S/1998/780, 20 August 1998.

[286] 'I ordered this action for four reasons: First, because we have convincing evidence these groups played the key role in the Embassy bombings in Kenya and Tanzania; second, because these groups have executed terrorist attacks against Americans in the past; third, because we have compelling information that they were planning additional terrorist attack against our citizens and others with the inevitable collateral casualties we saw so tragically in Africa; and fourth, because they are seeking to acquire chemical weapons and other dangerous weapons' (President William Clinton, quoted in 'Contemporary Practice of the United Sates Relating to International Law' (1999) 93 *AJIL* 161).

[287] SD Murphy, 'Self-Defence and the Israeli *Wall* Advisory Opinion: An *Ipse Dixit* From the ICJ?' above n 204, 69–70.

[288] *Letter dated 20 August 1998 from the Permanent Representative of the United States of America to the United Nations addressed to the President of the Security Council*, S/1998/780, 20 August 1998.

[289] See also this declaration of President Clinton: 'The United States does not take this action lightly. Afghanistan and Sudan have been warned for years to stop harboring and supporting these terrorist groups meeting. But countries that persistently host terrorists have no right to be safe heaven' (quoted in SD Murphy, 'Contemporary Practice of the United States Relating to International Law' (1999) 93 *AJIL* 161; see also 'United Kingdom Materials on International Law' (2001) 72 *BYBIL* 684).

United States, it would certainly be excessive to conclude that it had been accepted by the international community of States as a whole. The League of Arab States denounced the action against Sudan as a 'blatant violation of the sovereignty of a State member of the League of Arab States, and of its territorial integrity, as well as against all international laws and tradition, above all the Charter of the United Nations'.[290] Most States remained silent, probably because of the very limited character of the military actions, without it being possible to deduce a very clear legal position from that.

Finally, it seems that the precedent of the 1998 military actions has to be envisaged in the context of 'indirect aggression'.[291] The question is to determine under what circumstances a State may be held responsible for an act of aggression because of the support it gives to an irregular group that is itself guilty of an attack against another State.[292]

The Consequences of the Attacks of 11 September 2001

The same lessons can be deduced from examining the attacks of 11 September 2001 and their consequences. To my mind, no notable change in international law could be observed on this occasion, with all States continuing to consider the Charter regime regulating the use of force in an essentially inter-State perspective.

The Hardly Innovative Character of Justifications for the War against Afghanistan

The United States with several of its allies decided on a war in Afghanistan which led to the overthrow of the Taliban regime a few weeks after 9/11. Now, that war was justified by self-defence, not only against the Al Qaeda organisation, which was recognised as directly responsible for the attacks, but also against Afghanistan itself.[293] The terms of the letter to the Security Council from the United States on the day operations began leaves little room for doubt in this respect:

> Since 11 September, my Government has obtained clear and compelling information that the Al-Qaeda organization, which is supported by the Taliban regime in Afghanistan, had a central role in these attacks. We may find that our self-defense requires further actions with respect to other organizations and other States. *The attacks of 11 September 2001 and the ongoing threat to the United States and its*

---

[290] *Statement by the Secretariat of the League of Arab States dated 21 August 1998 condemning the American bombing of the pharmaceutal factory in Karthoum*, annexed to *Letter dated 21 August 1998 from the Chargé d'affaires a.i. of the Permanent Mission of Kuwait to the United Nations Addressed to the President of the Security Council*, S/1998/789, 21 August 1998; see also *Letter dated 23 August 1998 addressed to the President of the Security Council*, S/1998/792, 23 August 1998.

[291] See below, ch 7, s I.

[292] J Lobel, 'The Use of Force to Respond to Terrorist Attacks: the Bombing of Sudan and Afghanistan' (1999) 24 *YJIL* 541.

[293] See: C Gray, *International Law and the Use of Force*, 3rd edn, above n 22, 200.

nationals posed by the Al-Qaeda organization have been made possible by the decision of the Taliban regime to allow the parts of Afghanistan that it controls to be used by this organization as a base of operation. Despite every effort by the United States and the international community, the Taliban regime has refused to change its policy. From the territory of Afghanistan, the Al-Qaeda organization continues to train and support agents of terror who attack innocent people throughout the world and target United States nationals and interests in the United States and abroad. In response to these attacks, and in accordance with the inherent right of individual and collective self-defence, United States armed forces have initiated actions designed to prevent and deter further attacks on the United States. *These actions include measures against Al-Qaeda terrorist training camps and military installations of the Taliban Regime in Afghanistan.* (emphasis added)[294]

While it is true that the United States affirms its right to self-defence very generally against 'organisations' and States, it seems clear that a military action affecting a third State is justified here by that State's behaviour.[295] In this sense, the precedent of the war against Afghanistan also raises the question of the degree of implication beyond which it can be considered that a State that tolerates the activity of irregular groups having carried out military attacks against another State is itself guilty of an act of aggression.[296] However, it is not certain that it can be deduced from this that the prohibition of the use of force, and its counter argument of self-defence, must henceforth be envisaged outside of relations between States[297] or more specifically that one can attack a State in self-defence without having shown that the State was guilty of a prior armed attack.[298]

---

[294] *Letter dated 7 October 2001 from the Permanent Representative of the United States of America to the United Nations addressed to the President of the Security Council,* S/2001/946, 7 October 2001; see also 'Contemporary Practice of the United States' (2002) 96 *AJIL* 243–44.

[295] See: United Kingdom, *Letter dated 7 October 2001 from the chargé d'affaires a.i. of the Permanent Mission of the United Kingdom of Great Britain and Northern Ireland to the United Nations addressed to the President of the Security Council,* S/2001/946; 'United Kingdom Materials on International Law' (2002) 73 *BYBIL* 856; see also JA Gonzales Vega, 'Los atentados del 11 de septiembre. La operacion "Libertad duradera" y el derecho de legitima defensa' (2001) 53 *REDI* 253; PM Dupuy, 'State Sponsors of Terrorism: Issues of International Responsibility', above n 260, 9; 'La communauté internationale et le terrorisme' in SFDI, *Les nouvelles menaces contre la paix et la sécurité internationales,* journée franco-allemande (Paris, Pedone, 2004) 38; R Wedgwood, 'Countering Catastrophic Terrorism: An American View' in *Enforcing International Norms Against Terrorism* (Oxford and Portland Oregon, Hart Publishing, 2004) 111–12, nn 27–29.

[296] Below, ch 7, s I and M Kohen, 'The use of force by the United States after the end of the Cold War, and its impact on international law' in M Byers and G Nolte (eds), *United States Hegemony and the Foundations of International Law* (Cambridge, Cambridge University Press, 2003) 204–10; C Stahn, 'Collective Security and Self-Defence After the September 11 Attacks' (2002) 10 *TFLR* 23–34.

[297] *Contra:* C Tams, 'Light Treatment of a Complex Problem: The Law of Self-Defence in the *Wall* Case' (2005) 16 *EJIL* 972–73.

[298] See: A Cassese, 'Terrorism is Also Disrupting Some Crucial Legal Categories of International Law' (2001) 12 *EJIL* 997.

Security Council Resolutions 1368 (2001) and 1373 (2001) and States'
Reactions

Some commentators have claimed that, with resolutions 1368 (2001) and 1373 (2001), a right to self-defence has been recognised as a riposte to terrorist attacks, without the need to establish a connection with Afghanistan or with any other State in particular.[299] Insofar as this legal characterisation supposedly reflects an agreement of the international community of States as a whole,[300] it might henceforth be considered that certain attacks by terrorist groups might engender the right to self-defence.[301]

It may be thought that the reactions to 9/11 showed that, under certain circumstances, a terrorist action could reach the level of gravity of an armed attack, with the resulting possibility of invoking the right to self-defence. However, the essential thing is to determine whether this right could be relied on to justify an attack on the territory of a State without proving that the State was directly or indirectly responsible for the attack. In my view, neither the text of the Security Council resolutions nor more generally the positions taken by various States allow one to assert that this line has been crossed.

As concerns the text of the resolutions, both relating to the fight against terrorism after 9/11, there are two paragraphs in their preambles by which the Security Council 'Recogniz[es] the inherent right of individual or collective self-defence in accordance with the Charter' and then 'Reaffirm[s] the inherent right of individual or collective self-defence as recognized by the Charter of the United Nations'.[302] A first conclusion is manifest: the self-defence referred to is not a challenge or change to existing law, since it is 'as recognized by the Charter'.[303] Now, the Charter, does indeed contemplate in principle the use of force as an essentially inter-State problem, as noted above. No new interpretation seems to arise from the texts of the two resolutions as a whole. On the contrary, in them the Security Council '*Calls* on all States to work together urgently to bring to justice the perpetrators, organizers and sponsors of these terrorist attacks and *stresses* that those responsible for aiding, supporting or harbouring the perpetrators,

---

[299] ICJ, *Legal Consequences of the Construction of a Wall in the Occupied Palestinian Territory*, Judge Buerghental, Separate Opinion, ICJ Rep (2004) 242, para 6; see also A Cassese, 'Article 51', above n 34, 1333; MN Schmitt, *Counter-Terrorism and the Use of Force in International Law*, above n 204, 26–27.

[300] ibid, 27 and 64.

[301] A Cassese, 'Article 51', above n 34, 1352; 'Terrorism is Also Disrupting Some Crucial Legal Categories of International Law', above n 299, 996–97; R Wedgwood, 'The ICJ Advisory Opinion on the Israeli Security Fence and the Limits of Self-Defence', above n 204, 58; SD Murphy, 'Self-Defence and the Israeli *Wall* Advisory Opinion: An *Ipse Dixit* From the ICJ?' above n 204, 67.

[302] SC RES 1368 (2001) of 12 September 2001 and SC Res 1373 (2001) of 28 September 2001, preambles.

[303] See: C Ramon Chornet, 'La lucha contra el terrorismo internacional despues del 11 de septiembre de 2001' (2001) 53 *REDI* 283.

organizers and sponsors of these acts will be held accountable';[304] it then reaffirms that 'every State has the duty to refrain from organizing, instigating, assisting or participating in terrorist acts in another State or acquiescing in organized activities within its territory directed towards the commission of such acts'.[305] If one adheres to the text, there is nothing revolutionary about the two resolutions.[306] A particularly serious act of terrorism, while being characterised as a threat to peace and to international security opening up the way to coercive action under Chapter VII of the UN Charter[307] may be equivalent to an armed attack making the right to self-defence applicable, if all other conditions are satisfied.[308] Insofar as the riposte would be against the territory of another State, all the indications are that the State should be held responsible for supporting the terrorist act, such that it can be characterised as an aggressor State.[309] *A contrario*, there is nothing in these resolutions that opens a general right in the name of self-defence to conduct attacks in the territory of any State, even an innocent one, for the simple reason that a terrorist organisation has set up there.[310] For that matter, it can be seriously questioned whether the Security Council would be competent, in principle, for (re)defining self-defence generally through some sort of authorised interpretation of article 51 of the Charter.[311]

It is in this perspective too that the relative scarcity of condemnations of the war begun on 7 October 2001 on the territory of Afghanistan must be understood.[312] It shall be recalled first on this that the Security Council had, for several years, condemned the Afghan State for the close ties it entertained with the Al Qaeda organisation.[313] This position was reiterated after 9/11, with the Security Council *'Condemning* the Taliban for allowing

---

[304] SC Res 1368 (2001) of 12 September 2001, para 3.

[305] SC Res 1373 (2001) of 28 September 2001, preamble.

[306] A Remiro Brotons, 'Terrorismo, Mantenimiento de la paz y nuevo orden' (2001) 53 *REDI* 156; see also A Pellet and V Tzankov, 'L'Etat victime d'un acte terroriste peut-il recourir à la force armée?', above n 249, 97–98; *contra*: I Scobbie, 'Words My Mother Never Taught Me—In Defense of the International Court' (2005) 99 *AJIL* 81.

[307] Below, ch 6.

[308] ME O'Connel, 'Lawful Self-Defense to Terrorism', above n 256, 892.

[309] M Bothe, 'The International Community and Terrorism', above n 262, 55–56.

[310] G Cahin, 'Le rôle des organes politiques des Nations Unies' in E Cannizzaro and P Palchetti (eds), *Customary International Law on the Use of Force. A Methodological Approach* (Leiden/Boston, Martinus Nijhoff, 2005), 167–68.

[311] See: C Denis, *Le pouvoir normatif du Conseil de sécurité des Nations Unies: portée et limites* (Bruxelles, Bruylant, 2004); M Forteau, *Droit de la sécurité collective et droit de la responsabilité internationale de l'Etat* (Paris, Pedone, 2006) 418; see also above, ch 1, s II.

[312] See: Communique of the ninth extraordinary session of the islamic conference of foreign ministers, Doha, Qatar, 10 October 2001, para 11, www.oic-oci.org and below, ch 7.

[313] SC Res 1214 (1998) of 8 December 1998, 1267 (1999) of 15 October 1999, 1333 (2000) pf 19 December 2000, S/PRSDT/1999/29, 22 October 1999; S/PRSDT/2000/12, 7 April 2000; see O Corten, 'Vers un renforcement des pouvoirs du Conseil de sécurité dans la lutte contre le terrorisme?' in K Bannelier *et al* (eds), *Le droit international face au terrorisme* (Paris, Pedone, 2002) 268–69.

Afghanistan to be used as a base for the export of terrorism by the Al-Qaeda network and other terrorist groups'.[314] In the same way, the NATO Member States did not initially recognise the right of self-defence unless 'it is determined that this attack was directed from abroad against the United States',[315] which was only done when proof of the implication of Al Qaeda, but also of the Taliban regime, was adduced.[316] More generally, the States that supported operation 'Enduring Freedom' usually emphasised Afghanistan's responsibility.[317] Conversely, I know of no declaration clearly asserting the lawfulness of an action in self-defence in the territory of a State with no responsibility in the launch of a terrorist attack that could otherwise be likened to an armed attack.[318]

Precedents Since the Start of the War against Afghanistan

Since 9/11, States intervening militarily in the territory of neighbouring States sometimes do so in the name of the war on terror. But they generally continue to justify their action by a prior violation of international law for which the State whose territory is attacked was responsible, without though convincing the international community of States as a whole.[319]

Israel has regularly accused Lebanon and Syria of supporting organisations like Islamic Jihad, Hamas or Hezbollah, to justify its military operations within those countries.[320] On 5 October 2003, the Israeli army bombarded what it asserted was a Hezbollah camp based in Syrian territory further to the attack on Haifa in which 19 people were killed and more than 60 injured. In the Security Council, Israel's representative argued self-defence within the meaning of article 51 of the Charter,[321] but taking a very clear inter-State stance. Syria in particular, he argued, 'bears direct and criminal responsibility',[322] by making its territory available to terrorist organisations, supporting them and even participating directly in attacks.[323] The argument was far from convincing for the other States that expressed their views in the Security Council.[324] The war against Lebanon in summer 2006, to be examined later, gave rise to the same observation: Israel justified its attack as being

---

[314] SC Res 1378 (2001) of 14 November 2001, preamble.

[315] Statement by the North Atlantic Council, 12 September 2001, www.nato.int.

[316] See: Declaration of Secretary General of NATO, Lord Robertson, 2 October 2001, www.nato.int.

[317] See: www.ulb.ac.be/droit/cdi/fichiers/PEAP1.htm.

[318] See, eg: S/PV.4370, 12 September 2001; see also below, ch 7, s I.

[319] Against: C Tams, 'Light Treatment of a Complex Problem: The Law of Self-Defence in the *Wall* Case', above n 298, 972.

[320] C Gray, *International Law and the Use of Force*, 3rd edn, above n 22, 234–39.

[321] S/PV.4836, 5 October 2003, 7.

[322] ibid.

[323] ibid, 5–6.

[324] ibid: Pakistan, Spain, China, United Kingdom, Russia, Germany, France, Bulgaria, Chile, Mexico, Angola, Guinea, Cameroon, League of Arab States, Lebanon, Algeria, Morocco, Jordan, Egypt, Tunisia, Palestine, Kuwait, Saudi Arabia, Cuba, Iran, Bahrain, Libya, Yemen, Qatar and Sudan.

in riposte to military acts perpetrated by Hezbollah by claiming the Lebanese State was, at least in part, responsible.[325]

Similarly, several months after 9/11, the Russian army entered Georgia officially to combat Chechen terrorists who had taken refuge there.[326] The Russian authorities justified their action on the basis of article 51, asserting that the Georgian authorities were unable to control their territory, but also that they were violating international law, especially Security Council resolution 1373 (2001).[327] Once again, the issue was contemplated from an inter-State standpoint. Once again too, this justification was not universally accepted, with the United States itself being very reserved.[328]

Actually, as far as I know, only two recent cases could be interpreted as a real invocation of self-defence against non-State actors.

The first is the Turkish military intervention against the PKK in northern Iraq in 2007 and 2008.[329] The Turkish authorities contended that its operation 'targeted solely the PKK' and that Turkey remained 'a staunch advocate of the territorial integrity and sovereignty of Iraq'.[330] It seems therefore that Iraq was not accused of complicity with the PKK and consequently of being the author of an indirect aggression against Turkey. Yet it is very difficult to deduce an evolution of the customary international law of self-defence from this precedent. First, the *legal* position of Turkey—which did not invoke self-defence in a letter submitted to the Security Council—remained unclear.[331] Secondly, the reaction of third States was rather ambiguous.[332] Some States appealed to Turkey to exercise self-restraint, insisting on the necessity to use peaceful and diplomatic means to address the issue, but without condemning the military actions. Others remained silent. Against this background, no universal *opinio juris* can be

---

[325] Below, ch 7, s I, and F Dubuisson, 'La guerre du Liban de l'été 2006 et le droit de la légitime défense' (2006) 39 *RBDI* 529–64; E Cannizaro, 'Entités non-étatiques et régime international de l'emploi de la force. Une étude sur le cas de la réaction israélienne au Liban' (2007) 111 *RGDIP* 333–54; A Zimmerman, 'The Second Lebanon War: *Jus ad bellum, jus in bello* and the Issue of Proportionality' (2007) 11 *Max Planck UNYB* 99–126; T Ruys, 'Crossing the Thin Blue Line: An Inquiry into Israel's Recourse to Self-Defence against Hezbollah' (2007) 43 *Stanford JIL* 265 *ff*.

[326] C Gray, *International Law and the Use of Force*, 3rd edn, above n 22, 230–31.

[327] Letter dated 11 September 2002 from the Permanent Representative of the Russian Federation to the United Nations addressed to the Secretary-General (S/2002/1012), 12 September 2002.

[328] Christine Gray concluded about this episode that: 'This reluctance by the USA to acknowledge the right of another State to invoke self-defence against terrorism, even in a neighbouring State, and even where it may legitimately claim to have a strong case, seems to make it more difficult to claim that the events of 9/11 and the response have established a new customary rule' (*International Law and the Use of Force*, 3rd edn, above n 22, 231).

[329] See: T Ruys, '*Quo vadit jus ad bellum?*: A Legal Analysis of Turkey's Military Operations Against the PKK in Northern Iraq' (2008) 9 *Melbourne JIL* 1–30.

[330] Note verbale dated 26 March 2008 from the Permanent Mission of Turkey to the United Nations Office in Geneva Addressed to the Secretariat of the Human Rights Council, UN Doc 1/HRC/7/G/15 (28 March 2008), quoted in ibid at fn 77.

[331] ibid.

[332] ibid, fns 55–75.

established in a favour of any new interpretation of the UN Charter whatsoever.

More conclusive is the precedent of the Colombian military action of 1 March 2008. On that date, Colombia crossed the border with Ecuador to combat FARC 'terrorists', without any invitation or consent of the Ecuadorian authorities.[333] Responding to the Ecuadorian protest against the action, the Colombian authorities issued the following statement:

> The Government of the Republic of Colombia wishes to present to the Illustrious Government of the Republic of Ecuador its apologies for the action which had to be done in the border zone. . . . The Colombian Government has never intended to nor willingly disrespected or injured the sovereignty of the Republic of Ecuador, its people or its authorities for whom it has historically professed affection and admiration.[334]

At this stage, Colombia manifestly did not invoke self-defence against Ecuador, but only against the FARC.[335] Yet this position seemed to shift in the following days with Colombia claiming that Ecuador and Venezuela had supported the FARC.[336] However it might be interpreted, Colombia's legal position was far from accepted by the international community of States as a whole. Conversely, the OAS firmly condemned the Colombian action and 'reaffirmed the principle that the territory of a state is inviolable and may not be the object, even temporarily, of military occupation or of other measures of force taken by another State, *directly or indirectly, on any grounds whatsoever*'. (emphasis added)[337] The Rio Group similarily denounced 'this violation of the territorial integrity of Ecuador' and 'note[d], with satisfaction, the full apology that President Álvaro Uribe offered to the Government and people of Colombia, for the violation on March 1, 2008, of the territory and sovereignty of this sister nation by Colombian security forces'.[338] In sum, the Colombian precedent reveals the reluctance of many States to accept any weakening of the prohibition of the use of force, even under the pretext of a very limited antiterrorist action.

Finally, State practice did not lead to a modification of the *jus contra bellum* regime. Logically, when a State invokes self-defence to justify a military

---

[333] Press Release from the Ministry of Defense, 1 March 2008, web.presidencia.gov.co/sp/2008/marzo/01/08012008.html.

[334] Reply of the Ministry of External Affairs to the Government of Ecuador, 2 March 2008, web.presidencia.gov.co/sp/2008/marzo/02/06022008.html.

[335] See also: Comunicado No 081, Comunicado del Ministerio de Relaciones Exteriores de Colombia, 2 March 2008, web.presidencia.gov.co/comunicados/2008/marzo/81.html.

[336] Press Release, 3 March 2008, web.presidencia.gov.co/sp/2008/marzo/03/14032008.html.

[337] CP/RES 930 (1632/08), 5 March 2008, www.oas.org/consejo/resolutions/res930.asp. See also: Report of the OAS Commission that visited Ecuador and Colombia, OEA/Ser.F/II.25, 16 March 2008 (www.oas.org/CONSEJO/Docs/RC00089E01.doc).

[338] Declaration of the Heads of State and Government of the Rio Group on the recent events between Ecuador and Colombia, 7 March 2008, annex 2 of the Report of the OAS Commission, ibid.

action affecting the territory of another State, the former accuses the latter of an (often indirect) armed attack, consisting of supporting a terrorist group. The rare precedents which could be interpreted in some other way have not led to a change in the *opinio juris* of States, as our examination of the Colombia-Ecuador precedent very clearly shows. This trend is confirmed by an analysis of the work of the ILC and the ICJ, as shall be seen in the final part of this chapter.

C. Maintaining 'International Relations' as Relations between States: The Works of the International Law Commission and of the International Court of Justice

We take up below certain points of the works of the International Law Commission (1) and the International Court of Justice (2), which may be characterised without risk as the most authoritative doctrine and case law. These points are so much more decisive because they are accompanied by very clear State positions, invariably in favour of confining the prohibition of the use of force to relations between States.

Interpretations Defended By and Within the International Law Commission

The works of the International Law Commission confirm that the extension of 'international relations' within the meaning of article 2(4) to relations between States and private groups has not been accepted by the international community of States as a whole; far from it.[339]

Special mention will be made of the work on a Code of Crimes against the Peace and Security of Mankind. This Code has prompted discussions about two types of crime that directly concern the *jus contra bellum*: the threat of the use of force against a State and the crime of aggression. Now, it appears clearly that, while being crimes giving rise to possible individual responsibility in criminal law terms, the two offences have been conceived of as necessarily related to acts perpetrated by one State against another.

As for threat—which concept it has been seen was not in the end adopted in the draft—it had provisionally been defined as the 'recourse *by the authorities of a State* to the threat of aggression against another State'. (emphasis added)[340] To the best of my knowledge, no one claimed that threat, a notion expressly related to article 2(4), was liable to be extended more broadly than in the context of relations among States.[341] And this omission seems significant indeed if set in perspective with debates relating to other

---

[339] SA Alexandrov, *Self-Defense Against the Use of Force in International Law*, above n 144, 182.

[340] *YILC* (1986) vol II, Part One, 84 and above, ch 2, s II.

[341] See also: *YILC* (1989) vol II, Part Two, 68, para 3.

offences such as terrorism, genocide or crimes against humanity, which it has expressly been stated could be committed by individuals, whether acting as agents of a State or acting individually or as members of a group or of a non-State entity.[342]

Similarly, the crime of aggression[343] is defined as an individual's participation in 'the planning, preparation, initiation or waging of aggression committed by a State'.[344] The commentary on this provision confirms unambiguously that:

> Individual responsibility for such a crime is intrinsically and inextricably linked to the commission of aggression by a State. The rule of international law which prohibits aggression applies to the conduct of a State in relation to another State. Therefore, only a State is capable of committing aggression by violating this rule of international law which prohibits such conduct . . . Thus, the violation by a State of the rule of international law prohibiting aggression gives rise to the criminal responsibility of the individuals who played a decisive role in planning, preparing, initiating or waging aggression. The words 'aggression committed by a State' clearly indicate that such a violation of the law by a State is a *sine qua non* condition for the possible attribution to an individual of responsibility for a crime of aggression.[345]

This wording was deliberately chosen to express the position of the vast majority of members of the Commission during the debates preceding the adoption of this Code.[346] Two proposals tending to extend the crime of aggression beyond an act committed by a State were rejected.[347] The State character of the act of aggression has not, to my knowledge, been challenged by States that have given their opinions in the context of the Commission's work.[348] The reference to the definition appended to General Assembly

---

[342] See definitions of these notions in J Salmon (ed), *Dictionnaire de droit international public*, above n 4.

[343] See: *Draft Code of Offences against the Peace and Security of Mankind*, Arts 2 § 2 and 2 § 3, *YILC* (1954) vol II, 116; see also *YILC* (1985) vol II, Part One, 73, para 93.

[344] *YILC* (1996) vol II, Part Two, 42–43; see also *Mémorandum préparé par le Secrétariat*, Doc A/CN.4/39, 24 November 1950, *YILC* (1950) vol II, 331, para 97 and *YILC* (1986) vol II, Part One, 83.

[345] *YILC* (1996) vol II, Part Two, 44, para 4; see also ibid, 40, para 7 ('aggression by a State is a *sine qua non* for individual responsibility for a crime of aggression').

[346] Lacleta Munez (1965st meeting, 12 June 1986, *YILC* (1986) vol I, para 8), Ouchakov (ibid, para 22), Calero Rodriguez (2053st meeting, 31 May 1988, *YILC* (1988) vol I, para 28), Sreenivasa Rao (2061st meeting, 14 June 1988, *YILC* (1988) vol I, para 30), Barboza (2056st meeting, 3 June 1988, *YILC* (1988) vol I, paras 28–29; 2441st meeting, 13 June 1996, *YILC* (1996) vol I, paras 11 and 37), Villagran Kramer (ibid, para 13), Szekely (ibid, para 30), Fomba (ibid, para 34), Tomuschat (2380st meeting, 4 May 1995, *YILC* (1995) vol I, para 19); Rosenstock (2442st meeting, 14 June 1996, *YILC* (1996) vol I, para 7), Lukashuk (ibid, para 14); cp De Saram and Fomba (ibid, paras 15 and 16).

[347] Beesley, 2059st meeting, 9 June 1988, *YILC* (1988) vol I, paras 25–26) and Robinson (2442st meeting, 14 June 1996, *YILC* (1996) vol I, para 20); cp Tomuschat, ibid, para 12, Barboza, ibid, para 8, Bennouna, ibid, para 13).

[348] *Draft Code of Offences against the Peace and Security of Mankind*, Doc A/CN.4/448 and Add.1, *YILC* (1993) vol II, Part One, Comments and observations received from Governments, 59 *ff*.

resolution 3314 (XXIX) has often been criticised but because it is supposedly too imprecise to indict an individual in criminal law, not because it
limits aggression to the use of force of one State against another.[349]

This debate was taken further in the works that led to the setting-up of
an International Criminal Court. A number of controversies arose over the
definition of aggression but, at the time of writing, the definitions proposed
do not call into question the essentially inter-State character of aggression,
including after the events of 11 September 2001.[350]

It shall be pointed out lastly that the inter-State character of the rule prohibiting the use of force is reflected also in the International Law
Commission's works on international responsibility. Self-defence has been
identified as one of the circumstances liable to exclude the unlawfulness of
an act and has been defined as 'recourse *by a State* to the use of armed force
with the specific aim of halting or repelling aggression *by another State*'.
(emphasis added)[351] The commentary of the draft finally adopted specifies
that the provision stating this circumstance has as its effect 'to preclude the
wrongfulness of conduct of a State acting in self-defence vis-à-vis an attacking State'. (emphasis added)[352] This inter-State conception has not, as far
as I know, been challenged by States, which acknowledged the draft by
voting for General Assembly resolution 56/83 of 12 December 2001.

The Case Law of the International Court of Justice

A further illustration may be found in examination of the case law of the
International Court of Justice,[353] with, first, two classical precedents in the
domain of the non-use of force.

—In *Military and Paramilitary Activities*, self-defence was envisaged in a
    strictly interstate perspective, while certain irregular groups implicated—
    such as the Salvadorian rebels or the *contras*—were using armed force.[354]
    The Court specified that a State could be held responsible if providing
    support for subversive activities, without that support alone equating to

---

[349] See, eg: *Report of the ILC on the work of its 47st session (2 May–2 July 1995)*, A/50/10,
YILC (1995) vol II, Part Two, 20, para 61.

[350] *cf* Discussion paper proposed by the Coordinator in *Report of the Preparatory Commission
for the International Criminal Court (continued)*, PCNICC/2002/2/Add, 24 July 2002, 3–5; see
also ICC-ASP/4/SWGCA/INF.1, 18 and *Documents on the Crime of Aggression*, www.un.org
/law/icc and R Kherad, 'La question de la définition du crime d'agression dans le statut de
Rome. Entre pouvoir politique du Conseil de sécurité et compétence judiciaire de la Cour
pénale internationale' (2005) 109 *RGDIP* 344–54.

[351] *Report of the ILC on the work of its 32nd session (5 May–25 July 1980)*, *YILC* (1980) vol
II, Part Two, 52, para 1; see also ibid, paras 3 and 5.

[352] *Report of the ILC, 53st session (23 April–1 June and 2 July–10 August 2001)*, A/56/10,
2001, 75, para 5.

[353] See also: N Schrijver, 'Article 2 § 4' in JP Cot and A Pellet (eds), *La Charte des Nations
Unies Commentaire article par article*, 3rd edn (Paris, Economica, 2005) 461.

[354] ICJ Rep (1986) 98–102, paras 187–92.

armed aggression.[355] It also took up the definition of aggression set out by resolution 3314 (XXIX), and then cited several treaty instruments defining self-defence as a riposte against 'every act of aggression by a State against the territorial integrity or the inviolability of the territory [of another State]'.[356]

—In the opinion on the *Legality of the Threat or Use of Nuclear Weapons*, no State seems to have defended the argument of applicability of the prohibition of the use of force, and of self-defence as an exception, to anyone other than States.[357] The passage by the Court on this issue does not depart any further from this classical conception.[358]

Beyond this general case law, two precedents may be mentioned that more specifically confirm that self-defence within the meaning of article 51 of the Charter is confined to relations between States: *Legal Consequences of the Construction of a Wall in the Occupied Palestinian Territory* (a) and *Armed Activities on the Territory of the Congo* (b).

Legal Consequences of the Construction of a Wall in the Occupied Palestinian Territory

We have already mentioned the case of *Legal Consequences of the Construction of a Wall in the Occupied Palestinian Territory*, where the Court refused to accept the applicability of self-defence in the context of the Palestinian conflict. An important clarification must be made at this stage. In this case, the State of Israel invoked self-defence to riposte to terrorist attacks which, since responsibility was not claimed by the Palestinian authorities, must be considered to be the doings of individuals or private groups. Israel for that matter invoked resolutions 1368 (2001) and 1373 (2001), the contents of which were recalled above.[359] The Israeli argument clearly takes up the positions of certain commentators looking to extend the scope of application of self-defence to relations between States and terrorist groups, especially after the events of 11 September 2001. It is this line of argument that the Court rejected by affirming that article 51 of the Charter 'has no relevance in this case' since that provision recognises

---

[355] ICJ Rep (1986) 103–04, para 195.

[356] ibid, 104, para 196 (Art 27 of the Charter of the OAS).

[357] See, eg: Written Statement of Malaysia, 19 June 1995, 3; Note verbale dated 19 June 1995 from the Embassy of Mexico, together with Written Statement of the Govement of Mexico, 7, para 36; Letter dated 16 June 1995 from the Legal Adviser to the Foreign and Commonwealth Office of the United Kingdom of Great Britain and Northern Ireland, together with Written Statement of the Government of the United Kingdom, 73, para 3.119; see also France (CR 95/23, 1 November 1995, 65, para 34), Indonesia (CR 95/25, 3 November 2005, 18, paras 9–10) and Philippines (CR 95/28, 9 November 1995, 56).

[358] See, eg: ICJ Rep (1996) 246, para 47.

[359] See: Israel, A/ES-10/PV.21, 20 October 2003 and A/ES-10/PV.23, 8 December 2003.

the existence of an inherent right of self-defence in the case of armed attack by one State against another State. However, Israel does not claim that the attacks against it are imputable to a foreign State.[360]

The Court thus remains true to its earlier case law, considering self-defence only as the riposte to a prior action of a State, that State having acted either directly or having supported a group committing violence to such an extent that the violence becomes imputable to it.[361] Likewise, the Court

> also notes that Israel exercises control in the Occupied Palestinian Territory and that, as Israel itself states, the threat which it regards as justifying the construction of the wall originates within, and not outside, that territory. The situation is thus different from that contemplated by Security Council resolutions 1368 (2001) and 1373 (2001), and therefore Israel could not in any event invoke those resolutions in support of its claim to be exercising a right of self-defence.[362]

Even if this wording is not perfectly clear, the Court's position seems to be perfectly consistent with the interpretation of the two Security Council resolutions proposed above.[363] Those resolutions do not claim to modify the Charter but simply state that particularly serious attacks may open up a right to self-defence within the meaning of article 51; this presupposes, however, that those attacks can be connected with a foreign State whose behaviour may be characterised as an 'armed attack', a hypothesis that is to be set aside if the attack originates within a territory controlled by the State that claims to be acting in self-defence, which is indeed the case of Palestinian territory.

This passage of the opinion was criticised by three judges in their separate opinions and declarations.[364] Two of the judges, though, do not deny that the classic schema consisting in verifying the imputation of the acts of violence in question to a State still represents existing law, while regretting that the Court makes no room for 'the completely new element'[365] repre-

---

[360] ICJ, *Legal Consequences of the Construction of a Wall in the Occupied Palestinian Territory*, ICJ Rep (2004) 194, para 139.

[361] C Tams, 'Light Treatment of a Complex Problem: The Law of Self-Defence in the *Wall* Case', above n 298, 976.

[362] ICJ, *Legal Consequences of the Construction of a Wall in the Occupied Palestinian Territory*, ICJ Rep (2004) 194, para 139.

[363] See: CJ Tams, 'Swimming with the Tide or Seeking to Stem It? Recent ICJ Rulings on the Law on Self-Defence', above n 197, 284.

[364] ICJ, *Legal Consequences of the Construction of a Wall in the Occupied Palestinian Territory*, ICJ Rep (2004), Judge Higgins, Separate Opinion, para 33 *ff*; Judge Koojmans, Separate Opinion, para 35 *ff*; Judge Buergenthal, Declaration, para 5 *ff*; see also R Rivier, '*Conséquences juridiques de l'édification d'un mur dans le territoire palestinien occupé*, Cour internationale de Justice, Avis consultatif du 9 juillet 2004' (2004) 50 *AFDI* 334–36; R Wedgwood, 'The ICJ Advisory Opinion on the Israeli Security Fence and the Limits of Self-Defence', above n 204, 57 *ff*; SD Murphy, 'Self-Defence and the Israeli *Wall* Advisory Opinion: An *Ipse Dixit* From the ICJ?' above n 204, 62–76.

[365] ICJ Rep (2004), Judge Koojmans, Separate Opinion, 230, para 35.

sented by the adoption of resolutions 1368 (2001) and 1373 (2001): a somewhat relative new element, in my view, as already expounded when interpreting the very general references to self-defence 'in accordance with the Charter' contained in the preambles to the two resolutions.[366]

Examination of the positions adopted by States in the context of this procedure also confirms the absence of any challenge to the regime established by article 51. It is true that many States underscored the disproportionate character of the measures taken by Israel, which meant nothing further needed to be said about the problems raised by reference to self-defence in justifying the building of a wall.[367] It was observed, however, that article 51 was 'not applicable'[368] and 'irrelevant' because it was more a context of the *jus in bello* than of the *jus contra bellum*;[369] that it 'cannot be triggered by individual criminal acts which call for police and prosecutorial action, and not military action',[370] because 'there has been no "armed attack" against Israel of the kind contemplated in that Article';[371] that the actions the building of the wall was intended to prevent are 'not consonant with the definition of aggression as given in resolution 3314, adopted by the General Assembly on 14 December 1974';[372] that the existence of an armed aggression was supposed to demonstrate, in accordance with the case law in *Military and Paramilitary Activities*, that irregular forces 'must be sent by or act on behalf of a State';[373] that terrorist attacks justify 'security measures' on one's own territory but not 'self-defence'.[374] These are all stances that, even if not very explicit,[375] are far from challenging the inter-State character of the rule.

In a resolution adopted on 2 August 2004, the General Assembly, while recalling its resolution 2625 (XXV) on the Declaration on Principles of International Law concerning Friendly Relations, took note of the opinion entered by the Court and demanded that Israel fulfil its legal obligations as

---

[366] Above and JM Gomez-Robledo, 'L'avis de la ICJ sur les conséquences juridiques de l'édification d'un mur dans le territoire palestinien occupé: timidité ou prudence?' (2005) 109 *RGDIP* 526–33.

[367] See: Written Statements of Saudi Arabia (at paras 32–34), Palestine (at para 533), Jordan (at para 5.275 ff.), Indonesia (at paras 5–7), South Africa (at paras 36–38), Malaysia (at paras 150–51); see also Madlanga (South Africa, CR 2004/2, 23 February 2004, 29, para 62), and Sorel (Belize, CR 2004/3, 24 February 2004, 26, para 43).

[368] Written Statement of Saudi Arabia, para 31; see also Written Statement of South Africa, para 39.

[369] Written Statement of the League of Arab States, para 9.6; see also Written Statement of Palestine, 30 January 2004, para 534 (and Abi Saab, CR 2004/1, 23 February 2004, 44–45).

[370] Written Statement of Palestine, 30 January 2004, para 531.

[371] Written Statement of Jordan, para 5.270.

[372] Written Statement of Lebanon, para 44.

[373] Written Statement of South Africa, para 33.

[374] Written Statement of Malaysia, para 148.

[375] I Scobbie, 'Words My Mother Never Taught Me—"In Defense of the International Court', above n 307, 79.

set out in the advisory opinion.[376] The resolution was carried by an impressive majority of 150 votes to 6, with 10 abstentions.[377] Examination of the General Assembly debates confirms the general acceptance of the Court's position on self-defence.[378] In fact, only the US representative clearly criticised the opinion on this point, arguing that:

> So the Court opinion, which this draft resolution would accept, seems to say that the right of a State to defend itself exists only when it is attacked by another State, and that the right of self-defence does not exist against non-State actors. It does not exist when terrorists hijack planes and fly them into buildings, or bomb train stations or bus stops, or put poison gas into subways. I would suggest that, if this were the meaning of Article 51, then the United Nations Charter could be irrelevant at a time when the major threats to peace are not from States but from terrorists . . . The draft resolution adopts a confusing and troubling interpretation of Article 51. The United States will vote against the draft resolution.[379]

This was an isolated stand that does not seem to have convinced a large number of States,[380] as attested by the very large majority in favour of the resolution.

In any event, it shall be pointed out that the objections raised by the US representative seem to me to be evidence of a certain lack of understanding of the scope of the opinion. The opinion does not deny Israel the right to defend itself against terrorist attacks, with the Court, to the contrary, clearly affirming the legitimacy, in principle, of Israeli security concerns.[381] No State seems for that matter to have contested 'the right of Israel to protect its citizens against attacks'.[382] What is asserted, however, is that the security measures must not be likened to the use of force of one State against another, which explains why self-defence within the meaning of article 51 is inapplicable. Israel, no more than any other State, has no need to invoke this provision to justify measures to combat terrorism, the lawfulness of which must be envisaged relative to human rights and to the *jus in bello*. It is only if certain third States were to be recognised as having a degree of responsibility for attacks by private groups that the question of indirect aggression and consequently of possible self-defence would arise. As such, the Court's opinion remains perfectly consistent with the existing international regime, without however denying the lawfulness of certain measures in combating terrorism.

---

[376] A/RES/ES-10/15, 2 August 2004.

[377] A/ES-10/PV.27, 6.

[378] See, eg: Jordan; A/ES-10/PV.17, 7 May 2002.

[379] A/ES-10/PV.25, 16 July 2004, 2; see also A/ES-10/PV.27, 20 July 2004.

[380] See also: EU (A/ES-10/PV.27, 20 July 2004).

[381] ICJ, *Legal Consequences of the Construction of a Wall in the Occupied Palestinian Territory*, ICJ Rep (2004) 192–94, paras 135–37.

[382] Written Statement of South Africa, para 43.

Armed Activities on the Territory of the Congo

Lastly on this point, we shall mention the decision entered by the Court in the case of *Armed Activities on the Territory of the Congo (DRC v Uganda)*. In this decision, the Court condemned Uganda for having seriously violated article 2(4), while the defendant State affirmed it relied on a right of self-defence to riposte to attacks by Ugandan rebel groups—the 'Allied Democratic Forces' (ADF)—that were operating from the territory of the Democratic Republic of Congo with that State's complicity. In the words of the Court:

> [W]hile Uganda claimed to have acted in self-defence, it did not ever claim that it had been subjected to an armed attack by the armed forces of the DRC. The 'armed attacks' to which reference was made came rather from the ADF. The Court has found above (paragraphs 131–135) that there is no satisfactory proof of the involvement in these attacks, direct or indirect, of the Government of the DRC. The attacks did not emanate from armed bands or irregulars sent by the DRC or on behalf of the DRC, within the sense of Article 3 *(g)* of General Assembly resolution 3314 (XXIX) on the definition of aggression, adopted on 14 December 1974. The Court is of the view that, on the evidence before it, even if this series of deplorable attacks could be regarded as cumulative in character, they still remained non-attributable to the DRC. For all these reasons, the Court finds that the legal and factual circumstances for the exercise of a right of self-defence by Uganda against the DRC were not present.[383]

The Court's approach thus seems to be perfectly consistent with its earlier case law, which comes down to an alternative: either a State has been the victim of an armed attack because of support given by one State to irregular bands that have entered its territory and it may, insofar as the conditions set out in article 3*(g)* of the 1974 definition of aggression are fulfilled, riposte in self-defence in the territory of another State; or the irregular bands acted independently, unknown to any governmental authority, and the victim State cannot act in self-defence by entering the territory of a third State, since that State is not guilty of armed attack. So we are within a strictly inter-State perspective, with self-defence being conceived of as a counter argument to the prohibition of the use of force between sovereign States. As in the *Wall* case, some ambiguity may nonetheless be observed in this precedent insofar as, while explicitly applying the criteria that arise from article 3*(g)* of the definition of aggression and that do indeed refer to the situation of an attack by irregular forces, the Court asserts that it 'has no need to respond to the contentions of the Parties as to whether and under what conditions contemporary international law provides for a right of self-defence against large-scale attacks by irregular forces.'[384] In any event, from

---

[383] ICJ, *Armed Activities on the Territory of the Congo (DRC v Uganda)*, ICJ Rep (2005) at 53, paras 146–47.
[384] ibid, para 147.

a reading of their submissions and the records of what was said in Court, it is clear that the parties never argued about the possibility of extending self-defence to the riposte to attacks by private groups. All told, it transpires that the Court, no more than the parties, did not seemed to admit the possibility that a State might launch an armed action on the territory of another State without having to prove that that State was itself responsible for a prior armed attack.

In his separate opinion, Judge Koojmans criticises this aspect of the decision, pointing out that it is entirely in line with the opinion on the *Wall*[385] and reiterates the argument he had developed in that context.[386] After considering that 'it would be unreasonable to deny the attacked State the right to self-defence merely because there is no attacker State',[387] he adds that 'Whether such reaction by the attacked State should be called self-defence or an act under the state of necessity or be given a separate term, for example "extra-territorial law enforcement" . . . is a matter which is not relevant for the present purpose'.[388] Without taking up all the points that show that it is on the contrary the use of force on the territory of an innocent State that would, to my mind, be manifestly unreasonable, it shall be added at this point that the legal characterisation of riposte is of fundamental importance.[389] If the scope of the riposte is such that self-defence within the meaning of article 51 must be evoked, it will have to be demonstrated that the State suffering the riposte actually intended the armed attack. If, however, the riposte takes such a limited form that it can no longer be likened to a use of 'force' within the meaning of article 2(4),[390] it will be possible to characterise it as a simple extra-territorial coercive measure and in principle nothing will preclude reliance on the state of necessity, provided that all the necessary conditions for this are met.[391]

Judge Simma defends yet another point of view in his separate opinion. He asserts that the Court failed to answer the question of whether Uganda could in principle have acted in self-defence against rebel groups by entering the territory of the Congo, a question the Court should have answered in the affirmative.[392] I have some difficulty in accepting the premise to this argument insofar as the Court clearly affirmed that Uganda had seriously infringed article 2(4), which excludes any legal justification that may be

---

[385] ICJ, *Armed Activities on the Territory of the Congo (DRC v Uganda)*, ICJ Rep (2005), Judge Koojmans, Separate Opinion, para 27.

[386] See above.

[387] Judge Koojmans, Separate Opinion, above n 386, para 30.

[388] ibid, para 31.

[389] See: ME O'Connel, 'Lawful Self-Defense to Terrorism', above n 256, 905–08.

[390] Above, ch 2, s I.

[391] Below, ch 4.

[392] ICJ, *Armed Activities on the Territory of the Congo (DRC v Uganda)*, ICJ Rep (2005), Judge Simma, Separate Opinion, paras 4–15.

raised against this conclusion.[393] If Uganda had any legal entitlement to enter the Congo—in the case in point an entitlement based on 'self-defence' against a non-State actor—, the Court should have examined it. If it did not do so, it was first because neither of the parties contemplated the possibility. Uganda never claimed it was entitled to enter the Congo because its riposte in self-defence was not directed at the State of the DRC but only against irregular forces operating from its territory.[394] The Ugandan party argued instead that the Congo was guilty of armed attack for having tolerated and supported the rebel groups.[395] The defending State itself does not seem to have been convinced of the possibility of invoking self-defence against a non-State entity, at any rate insofar as the riposte was conducted on another State's territory. As for the DRC, it consistently emphasised the need to demonstrate the existence of a prior attack by its forces to be able to establish the existence of an armed attack within the meaning of article 51.[396] A reading of all the items in the case shows, then, that the use of force was consistently debated in an exclusively State perspective. In any event, had Uganda had a right to act in self-defence against irregular groups in the RDC, the Court should have recognised it *ex officio* and admitted the argument of self-defence, even if it were subsequently to characterise it as disproportionate in view of the resources implemented in the field.[397]

Ultimately, the Court's case law is characterised by its great consistency.[398] The prohibition of the use of force is a rule binding States and not non-State actors. The 'indirect aggression' mechanism, under certain circumstances, allows acts akin to an armed attack to be imputed to a State, opening up the way to the exercise of self-defence by the State attacked.

---

[393] According to Judge Koojmans, 'The Court seems to take the view that Uganda would have only been entitled to self-defense *against the DRC* since the right of self-defence is conditional on an attack being attribuable, either directly or indirectly, *to a State*. This would be in line with what the Court said in its Advisory Opinion of 9 July 2004: 'Article 51 of the Charter thus recognizes the existence of an inherent right of self-defence in the case of an armed attack *by one State against another State*' (*Legal Consequences of the Construction of a Wall in the Occupied Palestinian Territory*, ICJ Rep (2004) 194, para 139 (emphasis added)) (Separate Opinion, above n 386, para 27).

[394] Counter-Memorial of Uganda, 21 April 2001, Chapter XVII (at 211–16, paras 360–68), and Rejoinder of Uganda, 6 December 2002 (at 115–26, paras 266–98).

[395] Counter-Memorial of Uganda, 21 April 2001, 181–90, paras 334–40, Rejoinder of Uganda, 6 December 2002, 104–15, paras 239–65; see also Reichler (CR 2005/6, 15 April 2005, 16 *ff*; CR 2005/13, 27 April 2005, 8 *ff*), Brownlie (CR 2005/7, 18 April 2005, 8 *ff*; CR 2005/13, 27 April 2005, 30 *ff*), Mbabazi (CR 2005/7, 18 April 2005, 34 *ff*), and Suy (CR 2005/10, 20 April 2005, 25 *ff*; CR 2005/14, 27 April 2005, 32 *ff*).

[396] Memorial of the DRC, 6 July 2000, 198–203, paras 5.05–17; Reply of the DRC, 29 May 2002, 206–29, paras 3.118–58, Additional Written Observations of the DRC, 28 February 2003, 17–45, paras 1.24–65; see also O Corten (CR 2005/3, 12 April 2005, 28 *ff*; CR 2005/11, 22 April 2005, 19 *ff*; 2005/15, 28 April 2005, 15 *ff*), P Klein (CR 2005/12, 25 April 2005, 23 *ff*) and Tshibangu Kalala (CR 2005/15, 28 April 2005, 11 *ff*).

[397] See: ICJ, *Armed Activities on the Territory of the Congo (DRC v Uganda)*, ICJ Rep (2005), para 147.

[398] Against: CJ Tams, 'Swimming with the Tide or Seeking to Stem It? Recent ICJ Rulings on the Law on Self-Defence', above n 197, 284–90.

Outside of this hypothesis, neither article 2(4) nor article 51 is applicable. To take up a resounding dictum of the Court in *Armed Activities*:

> Article 51 of the Charter may justify a use of force in self-defence only within the strict confines there laid down. It does not allow the use of force by a State to protect perceived security interests beyond these parameters. Other means are available to a concerned State, including, in particular, recourse to the Security Council.[399]

This is a dictum that does indeed seem to exclude any extensive interpretation of this article on the pretext of adapting it to changes in the contemporary world.

Conclusion

The precedent of 9/11 was certainly a turning point in the fight against terrorism insofar as it prompted States to speed up their cooperation in this domain. It is not established, though, that this turning point has led to a radical change in the rules of the *jus contra bellum* that might henceforth be invoked outside of the context of inter-State relations.[400] In reality, examination of all of the positions of States shows, first of all, a desire to bring the perpetrators of terrorist acts to justice, as indicated by the resolutions adopted by the General Assembly after 11 September 2001 that make no reference to self-defence.[401] The Security Council's activity has essentially consisted in furthering cooperation among States, especially through the conclusion or entry into force of international conventions and through the creation of control and sanction mechanisms.[402] In terms of the use of force, the Council has remained very discreet, with just two passages in the preambles to its resolutions generally evoking self-defence.[403] On this basis, there is nothing to lead to the radical conclusion that self-defence, as it must be understood within the meaning of article 51 of the Charter, would henceforth allow military operations to be conducted in the territory of another State that was not guilty, through the scope of its support for a terrorist organisation, of armed attack.[404] Even if the odd general and imprecise

---

[399] ICJ, *Armed Activities on the Territory of the Congo (DRC v Uganda)*, ICJ Rep (2005), para 148.

[400] M Bothe, 'The International Community and Terrorism', above n 262, 56; see also Y Sandoz, 'Lutte contre le terrorisme et droit international: risques et opportunités' (2002) 12 *RSDIE* 336.

[401] A/RES/56/1 of 12 September 2001; see also A/RES/56/88 of 12 December 2001, para 5.

[402] O Corten, 'Vers un renforcement des pouvoirs du Conseil de sécurité dans la lutte contre le terrorisme?' above n 314, 259–77.

[403] Above; cp SC Res 1438 (2002) of 14 October 2002, SC Res 1440 (2002) of 24 October 2002, SC Res (2002) of 13 December 2002, SC Res 1465 (2003) of 13 February 2003; see C Gray, *International Law and the Use of Force*, 3rd edn, above n 22, 199.

[404] E David, 'Sécurité collective et lutte contre le terrorisme: guerre ou légitime défense?', above n 258, 145.

assertion of a right to self-defence against a terrorist group is voiced, the exercise of such a right against a State logically remains subordinate to the implication of its own responsibility. As pointed out, as I see it, any other conclusion would lead to a manifestly absurd and unreasonable outcome, with an innocent State being liable to attack without any violation of article 2(4) of the Charter being imputable to it. It will not be surprising therefore that the inter-State character of that article has been confirmed in practice since 11 September 2001.

4

Can Circumstances Precluding Unlawfulness be Invoked to Justify a Use of Force?

F OR SOME COMMENTATORS, the use of force may sometimes be justified by the theory of countermeasures[1], distress[2] and above all of the state of necessity.[3] In this respect, reference is made essentially[4] to targeted operations strictly confined to the rescue of nationals whose lives and safety are under serious threat,[5] interventions dictated by humanitarian emergencies,[6] or, especially in recent years, actions officially directed against 'terrorist' groups in the territory of States that cannot or will not themselves put a stop to the activities of such groups.[7] In the

[1] Y Dinstein, *War, Aggression and Self-Defence*, 4th edn, (Cambridge, Cambridge University Press, 2005) 221–34.

[2] See: N Melzer, *Targeted Killing in International Law* (Oxford, Oxford University Press, 2008), 54 and 75; O Corten and P Klein, *Droit d'ingérence ou obligation de réaction?* 2nd edn (Bruxelles, Bruylant, 1996) 219–20, 163.

[3] See generally W Wengler, 'L'interdiction du recours à la force. Problèmes et tendances' (1971) 7 *RBDI* 417; P Malanczuk, 'Countermeasures and Self-Defense as Circumstances Precluding Wrongfulness in the International Law Commission's Draft Articles on State Responsibility' (1983) 43 *Zeitschrift für ausländisches öffentliches Recht und Volkerrecht* 783–85; O Corten, 'L'état de nécessité peut-il justifier un recours à la force non constitutif d'agression?' *The Global Community Yearbook of International Law & Jurisprudence*, 2004, vol I, 11–50.

[4] See also: I Brownlie, 'The Use of Force in Self-Defence' (1961) 37 *BYBIL* 262–63.

[5] J Raby, 'The State of Necessity and the Use of Force to Protect Nationals' (1988) 26 *CYIL* 253–72.

[6] WD Verwey, 'Humanitarian Intervention under International Law' (1985) 32 *NILR* 414–18; I Johnstone, 'The Plea of Necessity in International Legal Discourse: Humanitarian Intervention and Counter-Terrorism' (2005) 43 *Columbia Journal of Transnational Law* 337 ff.

[7] T Christakis, 'Unilatéralisme et multilatéralisme dans la lutte contre la terreur: l'exemple du terrorisme biologique et chimique' in K Bannelier *et al* (eds), *Le droit international face au terrorisme* (Paris, Pedone, 2002) 173–76; 'Vers une reconnaissance de la notion de guerre préventive?' in K Bannelier *et al* (eds), *L'intervention en Iraq et le droit international* (Paris, Pedone, 2004) 28–44; M Romano, 'Combatting Terrorism and Weapons of Mass Destruction: Reviving the Doctrine of State of Necessity' (1999) 87 *Georgetown Law Journal* 1023; G Cahin, 'L'Etat défaillant en droit international: quel régime pour quelle notion?' in *Droit du pouvoir, pouvoir du droit. Mélanges offerts à Jean Salmon* (Bruxelles, Bruylant, 2007) 205–07; see also JA Frowein, 'Comments on Chapters 7 and 8' in M Byers and G Nolte (eds), *United States Hegemony and the Foundations of International Law* (Cambridge, Cambridge University Press, 2003) 276; R Wedgwood, 'Responding to Terrorism: the Strikes Against bin Laden' (1999) 24 *YJIL* 568; AD Sofaer, 'On the Necessity of Pre-emption' (2003) 14 *EJIL* 220; N Melzer, *Targeted Killing in International Law*, above n 2, 54.

International Law Commission's Draft Articles on State Responsibility for Internationally Wrongful Acts, a draft the General Assembly took note of on 12 December 2001,[8] countermeasures (article 22), distress (article 24) and necessity (article 25) are recognised as circumstances precluding unlawfulness. We shall see, however, in this chapter, that only justifications admitted by the United Nations Charter, such as self-defence—which shall not be considered a circumstance precluding wrongfulness but a justification inherent to the definition of the primary rule—,[9] may warrant the use of force.[10] The inadmissibility in principle of such circumstances precluding unlawfulness, deriving from examination of existing texts (section one), is confirmed by a review of practice, from which it transpires that such circumstances are only rarely invoked and never accepted by States as a whole (section two).

I Inadmissibility in Principle

The impossibility of admitting causes justifying the use of force is based on two arguments, to be developed in turn. First, under article 26 of the Commission's draft, 'Nothing in this chapter precludes the wrongfulness of any act of a State which is not in conformity with an obligation arising under a peremptory norm of general international law'[11]. The prohibition of the threat or use of force in international relations being a matter of *jus cogens*, none of countermeasures, *force majeure*, distress, or state of necessity

---

[8] Annexed to GA Res 56/83 of 12 December 2001, adopted by consensus.

[9] T Christakis and K Bannelier, 'La légitime défense en tant que circonstance excluant l'illicéité' in R Kherad (ed), *Légitimes défenses* (Paris, LGDJ, 2007) 233–56.

[10] See: K Skubiszewski, 'Use of Force by States, Collective Security, Law of War and Neutrality' in M Sorensen (ed), *Manual of Public International Law* (London, Macmillan, 1968) 764; P Cahier, 'Changements et continuité du droit international' (1985) 195 *RCADI* 74 and 291; J Mrazek, 'Prohibition of the Use and Threat of Force: Self-Defence and Self-Help in International Law' (1989) 27 *CYIL* 106–07; R St John Macdonald, 'L'emploi de la force par les Etats en droit international' in M Bedjaoui (ed), *Droit international. Bilan et perspectives*, tome 1 (Paris, Pedone, Unesco, 1991) 774 and 778; KJ Partsch, 'Self-Preservation' in R Bernhart (ed), *Encyclopedia of Public International Law*, vol IV (Amsterdam/New York, North Holland, 2000) 382; V Gowlland-Debbas, 'The Limits of Unilateral Enforcement of Community Objectives in the Framework of UN Peace Mayntenance' (2000) 11 *EJIL* 363; J Verhoeven, 'Les "étirements" de la légitime défense' (2002) 48 *AFDI* 75; O Corten and P Klein, *Droit d'ingérence ou obligation de réaction?* 2nd edn, above n 2, 215; G Gaja, 'La possibilité d'invoquer l'état de nécessité pour protéger les intérêts de la communauté internationale', *Droit du pouvoir, pouvoir du droit. Mélanges offerts à Jean Salmon*, (Bruxelles, Bruylant, 2007) 423–24. See also A/CN.4/39, Memorandum Concerning a Draft Code of Offences Against the Peace and Security of Mankind, presented by the Secretariat (French only) (1950) *YILC*, vol II, 329–30, para 92 ('si un Etat a pris l'engagement de ne pas recourir à la force des armes, sauf dans le cas de légitime défense ou dans celui d'une de participation à une action commune, cet Etat ne pourra plus invoquer l'état de nécessité pour justifier son agression').

[11] This article is generally recognised as stating existing international law; see *Report of the International Law Commission*, 53rd session, 23 April–1 June and 2 July–10 August 2001, GA, 56th session, Supp no 10 (A/56/10), 84–85.

may be invoked to justify a violation of this rule, even exceptionally (A). Secondly, under article 25(2)(a) of the Commission's draft: 'In any case, necessity may not be invoked by a State as a ground for precluding wrongfulness if: a) The international obligation in question excludes the possibility of invoking necessity'.[12] In the case in point, it can be considered that the UN Charter, which is the 'international obligation in question', excludes the possibility of invoking the state of necessity or again any circumstance alien to the exceptions to the prohibition of the use of force recognised therein (B).

A. The Peremptory Character of the Rule in Article 2(4) of the Charter

The reasoning of the doctrine that claims to justify military intervention on the basis of the state of necessity or of countermeasures relies on a distinction between the prohibition of aggression and the prohibition of the threat or use of force that is not serious enough to be characterised as aggression.[13] Supposedly, it is only in the first situation that we are dealing with a rule of *jus cogens*. It is on this basis that one might admit the arguments of intervening powers referring to the state of necessity or to other circumstances precluding unlawfulness.[14]

The distinction between the prohibition of aggression and the prohibition of other less serious forms of violation of the prohibition, while essential for determining the existence of self-defence within the meaning of the Charter,[15] does not seem to me, however, to have to dictate a difference in status as to the peremptory character of the rule. That status must be established from the definition in article 53 of the 1969 Vienna Convention on the law of treaties, which evokes

> a norm accepted and recognized by the international community of States as a whole as a norm from which no derogation is permitted and which can be modified only by a subsequent norm of general international law having the same character.

The 'derogation' in question here must not be understood as the equivalent to an exception but to the conclusion of treaties purporting to set aside

---

[12] This article is also codifying existing international law; ibid, 80–84.

[13] T Christakis, 'Unilatéralisme et multilatéralisme dans la lutte contre la terreur: l'exemple du terrorisme biologique et chimique', above n 7, 173; G Cahin, 'L'Etat défaillant en droit international: quel régime pour quelle notion?' above n 7, 207. See also M Roscini, 'Threats of Armed Force and Contemporary International Law' (2007) 54 NILR 257 and 276.

[14] T Christakis, 'Vers une reconnaissance de la notion de guerre préventive?' above n 7; 'Existe-t-il un droit de légitime défense en cas de simple 'menace'? Une réponse au "Groupe de personnalités de haut niveau" de l'ONU' in *Les métamorphoses de la sécurité collective. Droit, pratique et enjeux stratégiques* (Paris, Pedone, 2005) 221.

[15] *Below*, ch 7.

enforcement of the rule.[16] Now, by applying these criteria to the use of force, we shall see that (1) it can be concluded that its peremptory character is based on principle; and (2) a claim that cannot be infirmed by examination of conventional practice.

Recognition Based on Principle

The rule prohibiting the use of force has generally been characterised as *jus cogens* both by States (a) and by doctrine and case law (b). Contrary to what some commentators claim, States, judges and mainstream doctrine do not seem to have limited this peremptory status to the prohibition of armed aggression alone.

a) Recognition Duly Made by States

The concept of peremptory law and the prohibition stated in article 2(4) of the Charter have constantly, even systematically, been associated by States.

The affirmation is based first on an analysis of the works that led to the development of article 53 of the 1969 and 1986 Vienna Conventions on the law of treaties. According to the International Law Commission in its Draft Article on the Law of Treaties, 'the law of the Charter concerning the prohibition of the use of force in itself constitutes a conspicuous example of a rule in international law having the character of *jus cogens*'.[17] A reading of all of the works that led to the adoption of articles 53 and 64 of the 1969 Convention confirms that if there is one principle that was admitted as *jus cogens* it was that laid down by article 2(4) of the Charter. There is nothing to indicate that States limited the characterisation of peremptory law to the prohibition of certain particularly serious uses of force, such as acts of aggression. Quite the contrary, the wording used clearly shows that it is the prohibition of the threat or the use of force as a whole that was the target.[18] At the first session of the Vienna Conference in 1968, the United States representative did cite 'wars of aggression' as an example of violation of a rule

---

[16] A Lagerwall, 'Article 64' in O Corten and P Klein (eds), *Les Conventions de Vienne sur le droit des traités. Commentaire article par article* (Bruxelles, Bruylant, 2006) 2317–18.

[17] *Draft Articles on the Law of Treaties with commentaries*, (1966) *YILC* vol II, 247.

[18] Brazil (A/C.6/SR.793, 15 October 1963, para 14), Czechoslovakia (A/C.6/SR.787, 9 October 1963, para 26; A/C.6/SR.906, 10 October 1966, para 16), Cyprus (A/C.6/SR.910, 14 October 1966, para 48 and A/C.6/SR.980, 25 October 1967, para 62), Uruguay (A/C.6/SR.971, 13 October 1967, para 3), Thailand (A/C.6/SR.976, 20 October 1967, para 16), Sweden (A/C.6/SR.980, 25 October 1967, para 15), Netherlands (A/C.6/SR.781, 30 September 1963, para 2; A/C.6/SR.903, 4 October 1966, para 16), USA (in Sir Humphrey Waldock, A/CN.4/183 and Add 1 to 4, 15 November, 4 and 20 December 1965, 3 and 18 January 1966, *YILC*, 1966, II), Ukraine (A/C.6/SR.905, 7 October 1966, para 4), Austria (A/C.6/SR.911, 17 October 1966, para 7), Pakistan, A/C.6/SR.911, para 18), Australia (A/C.6/SR.912, para 23), USRR (A/C.6/SR.910, 14 October 1966, para 23), Bulgaria ((A/C.6/SR.788, 10 October 1963, para 9), Ghana (A/C.6/SR.791, 14 October 1963, para 35), Uruguay (A/C.6/SR.792, 14 October 1963, para 23).

of *jus cogens* without further clarification.[19] However, it would be going too far to deduce from this that other cases of use of force contrary to the Charter are not considered as contrary to peremptory law. Other representatives cite more generally the prohibition of the threat or use of force,[20] or even the principles contained in articles 1 and 2 of the UN Charter as examples of *jus cogens*.[21] Upon reading these declarations as a whole, it is clear that no State claimed to limit the peremptory character of the rule to the specific case of aggression.[22]

This conclusion is confirmed by examination of debates specifically about the rule prohibiting the use of force in the context of the works that led to the major resolutions of the General Assembly on this rule. During discussions of the Committee on friendly relations and of the Sixth Commission of the General Assembly that led to the formulation of resolution 2625 (XXV) in 1970, many States explicitly affirmed that the prohibition of the use of force was a peremptory norm.[23] Others evoked more general formulas such as the assimilation of the rule to an 'absolute rule of international law binding on all States'.[24] To the best of my knowledge, though, no State claimed that only the prohibition of aggression (and not that of the simple

---

[19] UN Conference on the Law of Treaties, 1st session, 52nd meeting, 4 May 1968, para 16; see also Ceylon (55th meeting, 7 May 1968, para 38), Canada (56th meeting, 7 May 1968, para 22).

[20] Greece, 52nd meeting, 4 May 1968, para 18; Kenya, ibid, para 31; Nigeria, ibid, para 48; Uruguay, 53rd meeting, 6 May 1968, 329, para 48; United Kingdom, ibid, para 59; Cyprus, ibid, para 69; FGR, 55th meeting, 7 May 1968, para 31; Ecuador, ibid, para 42; Tanzania, 56th meeting, 7 May 1968, 349, para 2; Ukraine, ibid, para 6; Philippines, ibid, para 20; Switzerland, ibid, para 26; Norway, ibid, para 39; Malaysia, ibid, para 51. See also FGR (UN Conference on the Law of Treaties, 2nd session, 9 April–22 May 1969, para 26); Ecuador, ibid, para 35 and 39; Italy, ibid, para 39; Belarus, ibid, para 48; Nepal, ibid, para 70; Cuba, ibid, para 42.

[21] USSR, ibid, para 3; Cuba, ibid, para 34; Liban, ibid, para 43; Sierra Leone, 53rd meeting, 6 May 1968, para 9; Poland, ibid, para 35; Bulgaria, 54th meeting, 6 May 1968, 340, para 66; Czechoslovakia, 55th meeting, 7 May 1968, para 25.

[22] See also: A Lagerwall, 'Article 53' (Convention of 1986) in O Corten and P Klein (eds), *Les Conventions de Vienne sur le droit des traités. Commentaire article par article* (Bruxelles, Bruylant, 2006) 1921–24.

[23] Ukraine (A/C.6/S.R.757, 12 November 1962, para 13); United Kingdom (A/C.6/S.R.761, 16 November 1962, para 5); Czechoslovakia (A/C.6/S.R.802, 29 October 1963, para 12); Hungary (A/C.6/S.R.806, 6 November 1963, para 4; A/C.6/S.R.999, 16 November 1967, para 6), Mexico (A/C.6/S.R.806, 6 November 1963, para 12), USA (A/C.6/S.R.808, 11 November 1963, para 15), Bolivia (A/C.6/S.R.814, 19 November 1963, para 6), Cyprus (A/C.6/S.R.822, 29 November 1963, para 7; A/C.6/S.R.892, 7 December 1965, para 19), Madagascar (A/AC.119/SR.9, 3 September 1964), Tanzania (A/C.6/S.R.882, 24 November 1965, para 8), Iran (ibid, para 18); Ecuador (A/C.6/S.R.1003, 20 November 1967, para 53), Thailand (A/C.6/S.R.1093, 12 December 1968, para 1), Romania (ibid, para 7), Iraq (A/C.6/S.R.1163, 29 November 1969, para 6), Venezuela (*Report of the Special Committee on Principles of International Law concerning Friendly relations and co-operation among States*, Supp no 18, A/8018, 1970, 77, para 109) and Ethiopia (A/C.6/S.R.1182, 25 September 1970, para 49).

[24] Yugoslavia (A/AC.119/SR.4, 31 August 1964; see also A/C.6/S.R.753, 5 November 1962, para 31; A/AC.125/SR.87, 16 September 1968); Mexico (A/C.6/S.R.886, 1 December 1965, para 36; A/AC.119/SR.9, 3 September 1964); Mali (A/C.6/S.R.882, 24 November 1965, para 25; A/C.6/S.R.997, 14 November 1967, para 1).

threat or again of limited use of force) was a peremptory rule. The same conclusion can be drawn from scrutiny of the discussions that preceded the adoption of the definition of aggression. While this notion was, quite logically, cited as an example of violation of *jus cogens*,[25] States have occasionally cited generally any violation of the rule prohibiting the threat or use of force.[26] Analysis of the works that led to the adoption of resolution 42/22 is yet more instructive insofar as those works were conducted at a time when the very idea of *jus cogens* seemed to be shared by a large number of States, which may explain why they make pronouncements more often on this point. In the matter at hand, back in 1979 the Special Committee reports mention an agreement on the characterisation of article 2(4) as a rule of *jus cogens*.[27] Finally, in the draft Declaration proposed by the Special Committee that was subsequently adopted by the General Assembly as resolution 42/22, point I states that:

2. The principle of refraining from the threat or use of force in international relations is universal in character and is binding regardless of each State's political, economic, social or cultural system or relations of alliance.

3. No consideration of whatever nature may be invoked to warrant resorting to the threat or use of force in violation of the Charter of the United Nations.[28]

No State objected or furnished other clarifications on this point, whether in the Sixth Commission or during the plenary session after the resolution was passed without a vote.[29] In view of the circumstances in which the clauses were passed, there is little doubt that they can be construed in the

---

[25] See, eg: Peru (A/C.6/SR.1349, 3 November 1972, para 45).

[26] Ecuador (A/AC.134/SR.10, 17 June 1968 in A/AC.134/SR.1-24; A/C.6/SR.1078, 22 November 1968, para 36; A/AC.134/SR.35, 14 March 1969 in A/AC.134/SR.25-51; A/AC.134/SR.58, 21 July 1970 in A/AC.134/SR.52-66; A/C.6/SR.1209, 28 October 1970, para 36); DRC (A/AC.134/SR.35, 14 March 1969 in A/AC.134/SR.25-51); Argentina (A/C.6/S.R.888, 2 December 1965, para 37).

[27] *Report of the Special Committee on Enhancing the Effectiveness of the Principle of Non-Use of Force in International Relations*, GA, 34th meeting, Supp no 41 (A/34/41), 4 June 1979, para 31; see also paras 57, 72 and 104. The Committe was composed by representatives of the FRG, Belgium, Benin, Bulgaria, Cyprus, Cuba, Egypt, Ecuador, Spain, USA, Finland, France, Greece, Guinea, Hungary, India, Iraq, Italy, Japan, Morocco, Mexico, Mongolia, Nepal, Nicaragua, Uganda, Panama, Peru, Poland, Romania, United Kingdom, Senegal, Somalia, Togo, Turkey and the USSR. See also *Report of the Special Committee on Enhancing the Effectiveness of the Principle of Non-Use of Force in International Relations*, GA, 38th meeting, Supp no 41 (A/38/41), 1983, paras 20, 46, and 54; *Report of the Special Committee on Enhancing the Effectiveness of the Principle of Non-Use of Force in International Relations*, GA, 39th meeting, Supp no 41 (A/39/41), 4 April 1984, paras 27, 44, and 100; *Report of the Special Committee on Enhancing the Effectiveness of the Principle of Non-Use of Force in International Relations*, GA, 41st meeting, Supp no 41 (A/41/41), 13 March 1986, paras 82, 84, and 89; *Report of the Special Committee on Enhancing the Effectiveness of the Principle of Non-Use of Force in International Relations*, GA, 42nd meeting, Supp no 41 (A/42/41), 20 May 1987, para 26.

[28] *Report of the Special Committee on Enhancing the Effectiveness of the Principle of Non-Use of Force in International Relations*, GA, 42nd meeting, Supp no 41 (A/42/41), 20 May 1987, 21–22, para 56.

[29] A/42/PV.73, 27 November 1987.

sense of qualifying the *jus cogens* rule stated in article 2(4); an interpretation covering the rule as a whole, and not just the prohibition of armed attack.

Were there still any doubt, it would suffice to refer to the declarations made individually by States to appreciate the scale of the *opinio juris* in this respect. In the discussions preceding the adoption of resolution 42/22, all of the States listed below characterised the prohibition of the threat or use of force as a whole as a peremptory rule of law or *jus cogens*. They are listed by chronological order of declaration: USSR,[30] GDR,[31] USA,[32] Ukraine,[33] Italy,[34] Chile,[35] Cuba,[36] Romania,[37] Brazil,[38] Syria,[39] Spain,[40] Senegal,[41] Hungary,[42]

[30] A/C.6/32/SR.64, 6 December 1977, para 3; see also *Report of the Special Committee on Enhancing the Effectiveness of the Principle of Non-Use of Force in International Relations*, GA, 34th meeting, Supp no 41 (A/34/41), 4 June 1979, para 113; A/C.6/31/SR.50, 22 November 1976, para 4; A/32/94, 31 May 1977.

[31] A/C.6/31/SR.50, 22 November 1976, para 57.

[32] A/C.6/31/SR.50, 22 November 1976, para 60; A/C.6/41/SR.14, 10 October 1986, para 39; 'Contemporary Practice of the United States' (1980) 74 *AJIL* 419.

[33] A/C.6/31/SR.51, 23 November 1976, para 4; see also A/C.6/38/SR.16, 17 October 1983, para 72.

[34] A/C.6/31/SR.51, 23 November 1976, para 14; A/AC.6/36/SR.13, 6 October 1981, para 31.

[35] A/C.6/31/SR.51, 23 November 1976, paras 24 and 29; see also *Report of the Special Committee on Enhancing the Effectiveness of the Principle of Non-Use of Force in International Relations*, GA, 37th meeting, Supp no 41 (A/37/41), 27 July 1982, para 165.

[36] *Report of the Special Committee on Enhancing the Effectiveness of the Principle of Non-Use of Force in International Relations*, GA, 37th meeting, Supp no 41 (A/37/41), 27 July 1982, para 216; see also A/C.6/32/SR.64, 6 December 1977, para 16; A/C.6/38/SR.17, 17 October 1983, paras 27 and 32; A/C.6/34/SR.22, 19 October 1979, para 57; A/C.6/31/SR.51, 23 November 1976, para 39.

[37] *Report of the Special Committee on Enhancing the Effectiveness of the Principle of Non-Use of Force in International Relations*, GA, 37th meeting, Supp no 41 (A/37/41), 27 July 1982, para 141; see also A/C.6/33/SR.59, 30 November 1978, para 26; A/C.6/31/SR.52, 23 November 1976, para 2; A/C.6/34/SR.18, 16 October 1979, para 56; *Report of the Special Committee on Enhancing the Effectiveness of the Principle of Non-Use of Force in International Relations*, GA, 35th meeting, Supp no 41 (A/35/41), 23 June 1980, para 56; *Report of the Special Committee on Enhancing the Effectiveness of the Principle of Non-Use of Force in International Relations*, GA, 36th meeting, Supp no 41 (A/36/41), 1981, para 57; A/C.6/36/SR.12, 5 October 1981, para 15; A/C.6/39/SR.15, 10 October 1984, para 5; A/C.6/41/SR.11, 8 October 1986, para 16.

[38] A/C.6/31/SR.53, 24 November 1976, para 2; see also A/36/415, 8 September 1981, para 2.

[39] A/C.6/31/SR.54, 25 November 1976, para 7.

[40] A/C.6/35/SR.29, 24 October 1980, para 26; see also A/C.6/31/SR.54, 25 November 1976, para 17; *Report of the Special Committee on Enhancing the Effectiveness of the Principle of Non-Use of Force in International Relations*, GA, 35th meeting, Supp no 41 (A/35/41), 23 June 1980, para 39; *Report of the Special Committee on Enhancing the Effectiveness of the Principle of Non-Use of Force in International Relations*, GA, 36th meeting, Supp no 41 (A/36/41), 1981, paras 25 and 27; *Report of the Special Committee on Enhancing the Effectiveness of the Principle of Non-Use of Force in International Relations*, GA, 37th meeting, Supp no 41 (A/37/41), 27 July 1982, paras 187 and 189.

[41] A/C.6/38/SR.15, 14 October 1983, para 56; see also A/32/181, 12 September 1977.

[42] 2 June 1977, 35th meeting, Supp no 41 (A/35/41), 23 June 1980, para 37.

Bulgaria,[43] Greece,[44] Belarus,[45] Ethiopia,[46] Cyprus,[47] Egypt,[48] Iran,[49] Mongolia,[50] Argentina,[51] Bangladesh,[52] Ecuador,[53] Tunisia,[54] Pakistan,[55] Honduras,[56] Togo,[57] Somalia,[58] Mauritania,[59] Nigeria,[60] Burundi,[61]

[43] *Report of the Special Committee on Enhancing the Effectiveness of the Principle of Non-Use of Force in International Relations*, GA, 36th meeting, Supp no 41 (A/36/41), 1981, para 70; see also A/C.6/32/SR.65, 7 December 1977, para 24.

[44] A/C.6/34/SR.17, 15 October 1979, para 1; see also A/C.6/35/SR.31, 28 October 1980, para 12; A/C.6/38/SR.14, 13 October 1983, para 1; A/C.6/39/SR.18, 12 October 1984, para 7; A/C.6/40/SR.11, 10 October 1985, para 1; A/C.6/41/SR.13, 9 October 1986, para 1; A/C.6/32/SR.65, 7 December 1977, para 42; A/C.6/35/SR.31, 28 October 1980, para 11; A/C.6/36/SR.14, 6 October 1981, para 18; A/C.6/37/SR.34, 3 November 1982, para 58.

[45] A/C.6/32/SR.67, 8 December 1977, para 25.

[46] A/AC.6/36/SR.10, 2 October 1981, para 62; see also A/C.6/33/SR.53, 21 November 1978, para 43; A/AC.6/37/SR.36, 4 November 1982, para 44; A/C.6/38/SR.15, 14 October 1983, para 32.

[47] A/C.6/33/SR.56, 27 November 1978, para 11; see also A/C.6/36/SR.14, 6 October 1981, para 57; A/C.6/38/SR.14, 13 October 1983, paras 46 and 48; A/C.6/39/SR.17, 11 October 1984, para 33; A/C.6/40/SR.9, 9 October 1985, para 56; A/C.6/41/SR.11, 8 October 1986, para 1; *Report of the Special Committee on Enhancing the Effectiveness of the Principle of Non-Use of Force in International Relations*, GA, 37th meeting, Supp no 41 (A/37/41), 27 July 1982, paras 236 and 238.

[48] *Report of the Special Committee on Enhancing the Effectiveness of the Principle of Non-Use of Force in International Relations*, GA, 36th meeting, Supp no 41 (A/36/41), 1981, para 37; see also *Report of the Secretary General*, A/37/375, 11 August 1982, para 6; A/C.6/33/SR.57, 28 November 1978, para 23; A/C.6/37/SR.35, 3 November 1982, para 17; A/C.6/39/SR.16, 11 October 1984, para 2.

[49] AC.6/34/SR.21, 18 October 1979, para 59; see also A/C.6/33/SR.59, 30 November 1978, para 14.

[50] *Report of the Special Committee on Enhancing the Effectiveness of the Principle of Non-Use of Force in International Relations*, GA, 37th meeting, Supp no 41 (A/37/41), 27 July 1982, para 61; see also A/C.6/34/SR.20, 18 October 1979, para 8; *Report of the Special Committee on Enhancing the Effectiveness of the Principle of Non-Use of Force in International Relations*, GA, 35th meeting, Supp no 41 (A/35/41), 23 June 1980, para 28; *Report of the Special Committee on Enhancing the Effectiveness of the Principle of Non-Use of Force in International Relations*, GA, 36th meeting, Supp no 41 (A/36/41), 1981, para 45; A/C.6/40/SR.9, 9 October 1985, para 37.

[51] A/C.6/34/SR.21, 18 October 1979, para 4; see also *Report of the Special Committee on Enhancing the Effectiveness of the Principle of Non-Use of Force in International Relations*, GA, 35th meeting, Supp no 41 (A/35/41), 23 June 1980, para 26.

[52] A/C.6/41/SR.11, 8 October 1986, para 35; see also A/AC.6/36/SR.13, 6 October 1981, para 21; A/C.6/34/SR.21, 18 October 1979, para 13.

[53] A/C.6/34/SR.21, 18 October 1979, para 49.

[54] A/C.6/34/SR.21, 18 October 1979, para 71; see also A/C.6/40/SR.10, 9 October 1985, para 17.

[55] A/C.6/34/SR.22, 19 October 1979, para 8; see also A/C.6/40/SR.9, 9 October 1985, para 3.

[56] A/C.6/34/SR.23, 22 October 1979, para 17.

[57] A/C.6/34/SR.23, 22 October 1979, para 38.

[58] A/C.6/35/SR.27, 22 October 1980, para 20; see also A/C.6/36/SR.14, 6 October 1981, para 35; A/AC.6/37/SR.36, 4 November 1982, para 53.

[59] A/C.6/35/SR.31, 28 October 1980, para 1.

[60] A/C.6/35/SR.31, 28 October 1980, para 32; see also A/AC.6/36/SR.10, 2 October 1981, para 17; A/C.6/37/SR.40, 9 November 1982, para 82.

[61] A/C.6/35/SR.31, 28 October 1980, para 70.

Japan,[62] Nicaragua,[63] Zaire,[64] Singapore,[65] Poland,[66] Yugoslavia,[67] Iraq,[68] United Kingdom,[69] India,[70] Suriname,[71] Czechoslovakia,[72] Mexico,[73] Cambodia,[74] Australia,[75] Algeria,[76] Venezuela,[77] Congo,[78] Morocco,[79] Trinidad and Tobago,[80] Jordan,[81] Guinea Bissau,[82] FRG,[83] Canada,[84]

---

[62] *Report of the Special Committee on Enhancing the Effectiveness of the Principle of Non-Use of Force in International Relations*, GA, 37th meeting, Supp no 41 (A/37/41), 27 July 1982, para 227; see also A/C.6/35/SR.31, 28 October 1980, para 78; A/C.6/40/SR.11, 10 October 1985, para 13; A/C.6/41/SR.13, 9 October 1986, para 38.

[63] A/C.6/35/SR.32, 29 October 1980, para 10.

[64] A/C.6/35/SR.32, 29 October 1980, para 38; see also A/C.6/37/SR.39, 8 November 1982, para 45.

[65] A/C.6/35/SR.32, 29 October 1980, paras 40 and 43.

[66] *Report of the Special Committee on Enhancing the Effectiveness of the Principle of Non-Use of Force in International Relations*, GA, 36th meeting, Supp no 41 (A/36/41), 1981, paras 128 and 130; *Report of the Special Committee on Enhancing the Effectiveness of the Principle of Non-Use of Force in International Relations*, GA, 37th meeting, Supp no 41 (A/37/41), 27 July 1982, paras 362 and 364; A/C.6/38/SR.13, 13 October 1983, para 6; A/C.6/39/SR.18, 12 October 1984, para 42.

[67] A/C.6/37/SR.36, 4 November 1982, para 49; see also *Report of the Special Committee on Enhancing the Effectiveness of the Principle of Non-Use of Force in International Relations*, GA, 36th meeting, Supp no 41 (A/36/41), 1981, para 191; A/C.6/38/SR.12, 11 October 1983, para 25; A/C.6/39/SR.18, 12 October 1984, para 14.

[68] A/AC.6/36/SR.7, 29 September 1981, para 7; see also *Report of the Special Committee on Enhancing the Effectiveness of the Principle of Non-Use of Force in International Relations*, GA, 37th meeting, Supp no 41 (A/37/41), 27 July 1982, para 234.

[69] A/AC.6/36/SR.7, 29 September 1981, para 7; see also *Report of the Special Committee on Enhancing the Effectiveness of the Principle of Non-Use of Force in International Relations*, GA, 37th meeting, Supp no 41 (A/37/41), 27 July 1982, para 234.

[70] A/C.6/36/SR.15, 7 October 1981, para 22; see also *Report of the Special Committee on Enhancing the Effectiveness of the Principle of Non-Use of Force in International Relations*, GA, 35th meeting, Supp no 41 (A/35/41), 23 June 1980, para 102; A/C.6/37/SR.35, 3 November 1982, para 23; A/C.6/41/SR.12, 9 October 1986, para 9.

[71] A/C.6/36/SR.16, 8 October 1981, para 5.

[72] *Report of the Special Committee on Enhancing the Effectiveness of the Principle of Non-Use of Force in International Relations*, GA, 37th meeting, Supp no 41 (A/37/41), 27 July 1982, para 43; see also A/C.6/38/SR.15, 14 October 1983, para 45.

[73] *Report of the Special Committee on Enhancing the Effectiveness of the Principle of Non-Use of Force in International Relations*, GA, 37th meeting, Supp no 41 (A/37/41), 27 July 1982, para 146; see also A/C.6/38/SR.14, 13 October 1983, para 51; A/C.6/39/SR.15, 10 October 1984, para 55.

[74] A/C.6/37/SR.32, 1 November 1982, para 24.

[75] A/C.6/37/SR.33, 2 November 1982, para 3; see also A/C.6/38/SR.15, 14 October 1983, para 23; A/C.6/40/SR.10, 9 October 1985, para 45; A/C.6/41/SR.14, 10 October 1986, para 54.

[76] A/C.6/37/SR.34, 3 November 1982, para 32.

[77] A/C.6/37/SR.34, 3 November 1982, para 41.

[78] A/C.6/37/SR.35, 3 November 1982, para 1.

[79] A/C.6/37/SR.35, 3 November 1982, para 32; see also A/C.6/38/SR.15, 14 October 1983, para 36.

[80] A/C.6/37/SR.38, 5 November 1982, para 58; see also A/C.6/40/SR.11, 10 October 1985, para 57.

[81] A/C.6/37/SR.39, 8 November 1982, para 71.

[82] A/C.6/37/SR.39, 8 November 1982, para 82.

[83] A/C.6/38/SR.14, 13 October 1983, para 13; see also A/C.6/39/SR.18, 12 October 1984, paras 54 and 60; A/C.6/40/SR.10, 9 October 1985, para 35; A/C.6/41/SR.14, 10 October 1986, para 33.

[84] A/C.6/38/SR.15, 14 October 1983, para 9.

Nepal,[85] Libya,[86] Sudan,[87] Dominican Republic,[88] Sri Lanka[89] and Vietnam.[90] While it may seem somewhat fastidious, this list clearly shows the scale of the agreement within the international community of States as a whole, with the delegations making pronouncements belonging to all the groups of States. It should be mentioned in this respect that these repeated affirmations were not the subject of any objection or denial by any State whatsoever. To my knowledge, no one claimed for example that the prohibition of aggression alone was a matter of peremptory law.

It can be noted, lastly, that the same conclusion arises from an examination of the official positions issued by States before international courts or tribunals in various cases including aspects of the *jus contra bellum*: the decision on *Military and Paramilitary Activities (Nicaragua v USA)*,[91] the opinions on *Legality of the Threat or Use of Nuclear Weapons*,[92] *Land and Maritime Boundary between Cameroon and Nigeria (Cameroon v Nigeria: Equatorial Guinea intervening)*,[93] the decision on *Oil Platforms (Iran v USA)*,[94] the decision on *Armed Activities (DRC v Uganda)*[95] and the *Guyana/Suriname* arbitral award.[96] No State, in the context of these cases, claimed to limit the characterisation of *jus cogens* to the prohibition of aggression alone.

b) Recognition Effected by Doctrine and Case Law

Doctrine has long associated the prohibition of the use of force with the peremptory rule of law.[97] Hans Kelsen pondered whether the idea of an

---

[85] A/C.6/38/SR.16, 17 October 1983, para 41.

[86] A/C.6/38/SR.17, 17 October 1983, para 36.

[87] A/C.6/38/SR.18, 18 October 1983, para 2.

[88] A/C.6/39/SR.18, 12 October 1984, para 66.

[89] A/C.6/40/SR.11, 10 October 1985, para 9.

[90] A/C.6/41/SR.10, 7 October 1986, para 26.

[91] ICJ, *Military and Paramilitary Activities*, ICJ Rep (1986) 101, para 190.

[92] See: Malaysia (Note Verbale of 19 June 1995, 4), India (Letter dated 20 June 1995 from the Ambassador of India, together with written Statement of the Government of India, 1), Indonesia (CR 95/25, 3 November 1995, 19, para 13), New Zealand (CR 95/28, 9 November 1995, 42), Philippines (CR 95/28, 9 November 1995, 56 and 60); *Against*: Qatar (CR 95/29, 10 November 1995, 29).

[93] Reply of Cameroon, 4 April 2000, 469, para 10.24.

[94] *Memorial of the Government Submitted by the Islamic Republic of Iran*, 8 June 1993, 94, paras 4.05–06; see also *Counter-Memorial and Counter-Claim Submitted by the USA*, 23 June 1997, 154–55, paras 4.58–61.

[95] Memory of the DRC July 2000, para 3.08 and paras 3.12–13.

[96] Memorial of the Republic of Guyana, vol I, 22 February 2005 (www.pca-cpa.org/show-page.asp?pag_id=1267), 126, para 10.4 and 128, para 10.10.

[97] See, eg: C Gray, *International Law and the Use of Force*, 3rd edn (Oxford, Oxford University Press, 2008) 30; Y Dinstein, *War, Aggression and Self-Defence*, 4th edn, above n 1, 99 *ff*; B Asrat, *Prohibition of Force Under the UN Charter. A Study of Art. 2(4)* (Uppsala, Iustus Förlag, 1991) 51–52; J Murphy, 'Force and arms' in O Schachter and C Joyner (ed), *United Nations legal order*, Cambridge, Cambridge University Press, 1995, 256; ME O'Connel, 'Taking *Opinio Juris* Seriously, A Classical Approach to International Law on the Use of Force' in E Cannizaro and P Palchetti (eds), *Customary International Law on the Use of Force*

international legal order did not presuppose, at least, that its subjects could not freely resort to force among themselves, failing which it is hard to see what would remain of the other principles of international law.[98] Similarly, upon contemplating recognition of the idea of *jus cogens*, the International Law Commission evoked the prohibition of the threat or use of force, without limitation to the prohibition of aggression alone. It is true that, in his third report, Sir Gerald Fitzmaurice argued that it would be contrary to *jus cogens* for two countries to agree to attack a third 'in circumstances constituting aggression',[99] but there is nothing to show that he did not admit that broader hypotheses such as the threat or the use of armed force were covered too. The subsequent works of the Commission confirm that it is the whole of the rule laid down by article 2(4) of the Charter that was considered peremptory. In its 1966 commentary, the Commission explicitly underlines that 'the law of the Charter concerning the prohibition of the use of force constitutes a conspicuous example of a rule of international law having the character of *jus cogens*'.[100] The concept of *jus cogens* was barely touched upon during debates leading to the drafting of article 53 of the 1986 Vienna Convention on the law of treaties between States and international organisations; however, the Commission incidentally affirmed that 'the most reliable known example of a peremptory norm [is] the prohibition of the use of armed force in violation of principles of international law embodied in the Charter'.[101] Lastly, in the context of its work on responsibility, to which we shall return below, the Commission very generally asserted that

> one obligation whose peremptory norm character is beyond doubt in all events is the obligation of a State to refrain from any forcible violation of the territorial integrity or political independence of another State.[102]

In its 2001 report on State responsibility, the Commission recalls that it gave as an example of treaties contrary to a *jus cogens* obligation 'a treaty contemplating an unlawful use of force contrary to the principles of the

(Leiden/Boston, Martinus Nijhoff, 2005) 19; D Simon and LA Sicilianos, 'La "contre-violence" unilatérale. Pratiques étatiques et droit international' (1986) 32 *AFDI* 72–73; M Forteau, *Droit de la sécurité collective et droit de la responsabilité internationale de l'Etat* (Paris, Pedone, 2006) 222; AA Cançado Trindade, 'The Primacy of International Law Over Force' in M Kohen (ed), *Promoting Justice, Human Rights and Conflict Resolution Through International Law. Liber Amicorum Lucius Caflisch* (Leiden, Martinus Nijhoff, 2007) 1052.

[98] H Kelsen, *General Theory of Law and State* (Cambridge, Harvard University Press, 1946) 328–41.

[99] A/CN.4/115, 18 March 1958 (1958) *YILC*, vol II, 40, para 76; F Dubuisson and A Lagerwall, 'Que signifie encore l'interdiction de recourir à la menace de la force?' in K Bannelier *et al* (eds), *L'intervention en Iraq et le droit international* (Paris, Pedone, 2004) 84.

[100] A/CN.4/L.117 and Add 1, 13 and 14 July 1966 (1966) *YILC*, vol II, Part Two, 247, para 1; see also (1963) *YILC*, vol II, Part Two, 207, para 1; H Waldock, A/CN.4/156 and Adds 1–3, 20 March, 10 April, 30 April and 5 June 1963 (1963) *YILC*, vol II, 54, paras 1 and 4.

[101] A/37/10, 3 May–23 July 1982 (1982) *YILC*, vol II, Part Two, 56, para 2.

[102] (1980) *YILC*, vol II, Part Two, 50, para 37.

Charter'.[103] Further on, while only evoking in the main text the prohibition of aggression,[104] the Commission specifies in a note that 'in the course of the Vienna conference, a number of Governments characterised as peremptory the prohibitions against aggression *and the illegal use of force'*. (emphasis added)[105] The final Special Rapporteur on the question, James Crawford also characterised article 2(4) as a whole as peremptory.[106] Lastly, in the context of work on the responsibility of international organisations, Giorgio Gaja, as Special Rapporteur, came down on the same side.[107] In view of all of this evidence, I find some difficulty in admitting, as some scholars assert,[108] that the ILC has not characterised the prohibition of the threat or use of force as a *jus cogens* rule.

As for international case law, it provides very little insight on this particular point. Neither the International Court of Justice nor any other court has ever been confronted with a question requiring it to make an explicit pronouncement[109] on the peremptory character of the rule laid down in article 2(4). However, in *Military Activities*, the Court did say that:

> A further confirmation of the validity as customary international law of the principle of the prohibition of the use of force expressed in Article 2, paragraph 4, of the Charter of the United Nations may be found in the fact that it is frequently referred to in statements by State representatives as being not only a principle of customary international law but also a fundamental or cardinal principle of such law. The International Law Commission, in the course of its work on the codification of the law of treaties, expressed the view that 'the law of the Charter concerning the prohibition of the use of force in itself constitutes a conspicuous example of a rule in international law having the character of jus cogens'.[110]

According to the president of the time, the ICJ thus recognised that the prohibition of the threat or use of force was a matter of peremptory law.[111] This is a perfectly defendable interpretation, even if, in their literal meaning, the terms of the judgment merely refer to the position of States and of the ILC.[112] In any event, and this is the point that matters here, the Court

---

[103] *Report of the International Law Commission*, 53rd session, 23 April–1 June and 2 July–10 August 2001, GA, 56th session, Supp no 10 (A/56/10), 112, fn 641.

[104] ibid, 112, para 4.

[105] ibid, 283, fn 644.

[106] *Second report on State responsibility*, 30 April 1999, A/CN.4/498/Add.2, 30, para 286; see also ibid, 13–14, para 240(b).

[107] *Fourth report on responsibility of international organizations*, 28 February 2006, 2 A/CN.4/564, 18, para 48.

[108] T Christakis, 'Unilatéralisme et multilatéralisme dans la lutte contre la terreur: l'exemple du terrorisme biologique et chimique', above n 7, 173.

[109] See: ICJ, *Oil Platforms*, ICJ Rep (2003) 181–83, paras 40–42.

[110] ICJ Rep (1986) 100, para 190.

[111] ICJ Rep (1986), Separate Opinion of President Nagendra Singh, 153; see also Separate Opinion of Judge Sette-Camara, 199 and GA Christenson, 'The World Court and *Jus Cogens*' (1987) 81 *AJIL* 93–101.

[112] T Christakis, 'Vers une reconnaissance de la notion de guerre préventive?' above n 7, 33, n 78.

makes no reference to—and *a fortiori* does not embrace—the argument of the distinction between the prohibition of aggression, that supposedly is a matter of *jus cogens* and the more general argument of the prohibition of the threat or use of force, which supposedly is not entirely a matter of *jus cogens*. This is all the more significant as in evaluating the relevance of the argument of self-defence, the Court does indeed draw a distinction between armed aggression and other less serious forms of the use of force.[113] The Court clearly envisages the question of the peremptory character of article 2(4) of the Charter as a whole, without restriction or limitation.[114]

In view of all these points, it is hardly surprising that the vast majority of legal scholars characterise the prohibition of the threat or use of force as a whole as peremptory law.[115] This characterisation has not been called into question by State practice, as shall now be seen.

The Absence of any Challenge in Treaty-Based Practice

For some commentators, the development of a practice of armed intervention in recent years, a practice that is supposedly reflected by reference to new justifications and exceptions, is liable to challenge the peremptory status of the prohibition of the use of force.[116] In terms of method, the assertion can hardly fail to surprise, inasmuch as the only practice that is liable to denote a challenge to the peremptory status of a rule should be reflected by the conclusion of agreements that depart from it. The mere mention of exceptions or of justifications can influence only the interpretation of the rule, not its status as *jus cogens*. It shall therefore be asked whether conventional practice attests to the feeling of States that they could derogate from article 2(4), notwithstanding their affirmations of principle recalled above.

A first point should be specified from the outset. To my knowledge, there is no treaty by which States have claimed to derogate from article 2(4). This is a significant omission. One may well retort that, assuming they wished to escape from the prohibition of the use of force in a particular instance, for example by contemplating attacking another State, it is hardly likely that States would decide to conclude a treaty expressing their intentions. But, this is precisely the point; such refusal to assume an emancipation from the Charter regime governing the use of force is the best evidence that States as a whole have the conviction that the regime is a matter of peremptory law. So, while one can imagine treaties derogating from the general rules on immunities, say, it does seem difficult to imagine a treaty-based derogation from the prohibition of the use of force as it is laid down in the UN Charter.

---

[113] ICJ Rep (1986) 101, para 191.

[114] See also: ICJ, *Legal Consequences of the Construction of a Wall in the Occupied Palestinian Territory*, ICJ Rep (2003) Separate Opinion of Judge Elaraby, para 7.

[115] See authors quoted above.

[116] N Schrijver, 'Article 2 § 4' in JP Cot and A Pellet (eds), *La Charte des Nations Unies. Commentaire article par article*, 3rd edn (Paris, Economica, 2005) 460–61.

The peremptory status of article 2(4) is further confirmed by the various specific treaty provisions that seem indeed to express States' concern to comply with the general regime of the Charter, especially in the area of security.[117] The following examples are illustrative of this point:

—This Treaty does not affect, and shall not be interpreted as affecting in any way the rights and obligations under the Charter of the Parties which are members of the United Nations, or the primary responsibility of the Security Council for the maintenance of international peace and security.[118]

—This Treaty does not affect and shall not be interpreted as affecting in any way the rights and obligations of any of the Parties under the Charter of the United Nations or the responsibility of the United Nations for the maintenance of international peace and security.[119]

—None of the provisions of this Charter shall be construed as impairing the rights and obligations of the Member States under the Charter of the United Nations.[120]

—This Pact shall not derogate from, and shall not be interpreted as derogating in any way from the obligations of Member States contained in the United Nations Charter and the Constitutive Act, including the Protocol, and from the primary responsibility of the United Nations Security Council for the maintenance of international peace and security.[121]

Comparable provisions are found also in the law of the sea[122] or in space law,[123] or again in more specialised treaties, especially in the fight against terrorism.[124] Of course, here again, the mere presence of a clause of this

---

[117] See also the problems relating to the interpretation of Chapter VIII; below, ch 6, s I.

[118] NATO, art 7 of the Washington Treaty (www.nato.int/docu/basictxt/treaty.htm); see also the preamble, commented on by M Sibert, 'L'OTAN: origines, mécanisme, nature' (1956) 60 *RGDIP* 180.

[119] Southeast Asia Collective Defense Treaty, Manilla, 8 September 1954, *UNTS*, vol 209, 32–33 (France, New Zealand, Pakistan, Philippines, Thailand, United Kingdom, USA).

[120] Article 131 of the OAS Charter (www.oas.org/juridico/english/charter.html).

[121] Art 17 of the African Union Non-Aggression and Common Defence Pact (www.africa-union.org/root/au/Documents/Treaties/treaties.htm, still not in force).

[122] According to art 301 of the Montego Bay Convention (*UNTS*, vol 1833, 3), 'In exercising their rights and performing their duties under this Convention, States Parties shall refrain from any threat or use of force against the territorial integrity or political independence of any State, or in any other manner inconsistent with the principles of international law embodied in the Charter of the United Nations'; see above, ch 2, s I.

[123] According to art III of the Treaty on Principles Governing the Activities of States in the Exploration and the Use of Outer Space, including the Moon and Other Celestial Bodies, 'States Parties to the Treaty shal carry on activities in the exploration and use of outer space, including the moon and other celestial bodies, in accordance with international law, including the Charter of the United Nations, in the interest of maintaining international peace and security and promoting international co-operation and understanding' (text annexed to GA Res 2222 (XXI) of 19 December 1966).

[124] According to art 19 § 1 of the 1997 International Convention for the Suppression of Terrorist Bombings, 'Nothing in this Convention shall affect other rights, obligations and responsibilities of States and individuals under international law, in particular the purposes and

type is not enough to characterise the prohibition of the use of force laid down in the Charter as *jus cogens*. However, it must be agreed that the frequency of such provisions is evidence of States' feeling that they cannot derogate from the prohibition.

Besides, no precedent is known by which States have construed a specific treaty provision as a possible derogation from the UN Charter regime prohibiting the use of force.[125] As far as I know, only the Treaty of Guarantee concluded about the status of Cyprus gave rise to discussion of this subject, but without consecrating the argument of a derogation from the Charter, far from it.[126] In criticising Turkey's 1974 military intervention, the Republic of Cyprus specified that, even if such resort to force were to be considered as permissible under the Treaty of Guarantee—which it was not[127]—, it would have to be considered as devoid of legal effect because of its incompatibility with the UN Charter regime.[128] Greece defended a similar position, arguing that the Treaty of Guarantee could not contravene the *jus cogens* rule prohibiting the use of force.[129] As for Turkey, it did not really claim to be able to circumvent the regime set up by the Charter in the name of the Treaty of Guarantee. While its action might, it claimed, indeed be founded on the provisions of that treaty,[130] the treaty in no manner contravened the relevant articles of the UN Charter that expressly provided for the right of self-defence.[131] Turkey's representative considered it had merely riposted to a prior armed attack by Greece,[132] its action being taken in self-defence under article 51 of the Charter and at the same time under the rights conferred by the Treaty of Guarantee.[133] Neither of the parties involved claimed, then, that one could derogate from the UN Charter.

---

principles of the Charter of the United Nations and international humanitarian law'. Similarly, according to art 14 of the International Convention against the taking of hostages, 'Nothing in this Convention shall be construed as justifying the violation of the territorial integrity or political independence of a State in contravention of the Charter of the United Nations' (www.un.org/terrorism/instruments.shtml).

[125] See comments on art 4 of the African Union Pact, below, ch 6, s I.

[126] See also below, ch 5.

[127] A/C.6/SR.1480, 18 October 1974, para 81.

[128] A/C.6/SR.1482, 22 October 1974, paras 67–68; A/C.6/S.R.892, 7 December 1965, para 56. See also A/C.6/SR.1482, 22 October 1974, paras 67–68; A/C.6/33/SR.56, 27 November 1978, para 17.

[129] A/C.6/42/SR.21, 13 October 1987, paras 102 and 103; see also A/C.6/SR.1482, 22 October 1974, para 83; A/C.6/39/SR.19, 12 October 1984, para 125.

[130] See: S/5596, S/5904, S/11356 and C Alibert, *Du droit de se faire justice dans la société internationale depuis 1945* (Paris, LGDJ, 1983) 292–95.

[131] A/C.6/39/SR.19, 12 October 1984, paras 73 and 111; see also A/C.6/39/SR.19, 12 October 1984, para 131; A/C.6/SR.1480, 18 October 1974, paras 76–78; cp S/PV.1780 and S/PV.1781.

[132] A/C.6/42/SR.21, 13 October 1987, para 111; see also A/C.6/34/SR.22, 19 October 1979, para 72.

[133] A/C.6/40/SR.12, 10 October 1985, para 47). See also A/AC.91/SR.19, 13 April 1965; A/C.6/SR.1482, 22 October 1974, paras 70–74; A/C.6/39/SR.19, 12 October 1984, para 131; A/C.6/42/SR.21, 13 October 1987, para 100.

Greece and the Republic of Cyprus considered that the Treaty of Guarantee had to be interpreted in accordance with the Charter and therefore that it could not provide a legal basis for a right of military intervention.[134] Turkey replied that it was in a position of self-defence and that, in that context, it too could invoke the Treaty of Guarantee that was allegedly violated beforehand by Greece. As for third States, they are far from having accepted Turkey's arguments.[135]

Ultimately, States' conventional practice confirms their position of principle: article 2(4) of the Charter must be considered as a matter of peremptory law that allows no derogations. Contrary to what some commentators have claimed, this peremptory character is not limited to the prohibition of armed aggression but extends to the prohibition of any threat or use of force. No treaty-based derogation can justify the use of force, however serious. Yet, in accordance with Article 26 of the ILC Draft Articles quoted above, no circumstance precluding wrongfulness can be invoked to justify a violation of article 2(4) of the UN Charter. Moreover, the Charter itself excludes any justification not enshrined in one of its dispositions, as we shall see in the following point.

B. Inadmissibility of Circumstances Precluding Unlawfulness Not Provided for by the Charter

The UN Charter clearly excludes the lawfulness, even exceptionally, of any use of force that proves contrary to the legal regime provided for by the Charter (1). Examination of the works of the ILC confirms this inadmissibility under the Charter, whether for a state of necessity (2) or other circumstances such as extreme distress or countermeasures (3).

Inadmissibility Deriving from an Interpretation of a Primary Rule:
the Autonomy of the Regime Instituted by the Charter

As already pointed out, article 25(2)(a) of the ILC draft on responsibility excludes the possibility of invoking the state of necessity if 'The international obligation in question excludes the possibility of invoking necessity'. In its work, the ILC emphasised that exclusion could be explicit or implicit, especially in respect of the rule's object and purpose.[136] The Commission cites as an example the rule of military necessities in the law of armed conflict, which strikes a balance between the interest of the

---

[134] A/C.6/40/SR.12, 10 October 1985, para 52; see also A/C.6/42/SR.21, 13 October 1987, para 105.

[135] See, eg: SC Res 353 (1974) of 20 July 1974, 360 (1974) of 16 August 1974, 367 (1975) of 12 March 1975; GA Res 3212 (XIX) of 1 November 1974; see also 'Pratique française du droit international' (1974) 20 *AFDI* 1058 and V Coussirat-Coustère, 'La crise chypriote de l'été 1974 et les Nations Unies' (1974) 20 *AFDI* 441–42.

[136] *YILC*, 1980, vol II, Part Two, 50–51, para 38.

attacking State and humanitarian requirements.[137] In such a case, the *lex specialis* must prevail over the *lex generalis* constituting the state of necessity. This situation also arises with the UN Charter provisions on the use of force, especially insofar as they reserve the case of self-defence.

The relevant provisions of the UN Charter carefully balance the essential and vital interests of States by laying down a strict rule prohibiting the use of force, while providing for certain exceptions, especially Security Council authorisation in the context of measures 'necessary to maintain or restore international peace and security' and the 'inherent right of self-defence'. Self-defence, in particular, is visibly a specific case in which the protection of a State's essential interests justifies force being used, even without the Security Council's authorisation, without jeopardising the purposes of the United Nations. Self-defence supposes compliance with conditions of necessity and proportionality that may be considered equivalent to those surrounding countermeasures of the state of necessity[138] and that were stated in the ILC draft[139] but also recognised in international case law.[140] Thus, just as the *jus in bello* makes allowance for military necessities as justification for behaviour that would otherwise contravene it, the *jus contra bellum* includes the necessity to defend oneself against armed attack and excludes in this instance the wrongfulness of the use of force.[141] In both cases, it is hard to conceive that, being unable to comply with the strictly defined conditions in the *lex specialis* (military necessities in the case of the law of armed conflicts; self-defence in the case of the Charter) a State could validly justify its actions by referring to other conditions under the *lex generalis*. The fine balance struck in the context of the treaty-based regime cannot be threatened by the use of general international law, which has manifestly been excluded by the drafters of the treaty. It is worth noticing in this respect that in *Legality of the Threat or Use of Nuclear Weapons*, the ICJ evoked 'an extreme circumstance of self-defence, in which the very survival of a State would be at stake'.[142] The Court, however, at no time evokes the state of necessity argument, which does seem to confirm the autonomous, or even closed, character of the regime laid down by the Charter.

---

[137] A/35/10, YILC, 1980, vol II, Part Two, 46–47, paras 28 and 50–51, para 38; *Report of the International Law Commission*, 53rd session, 23 April–1 June and 2 July–10 August 2001, GA, 56th session, Supp no 10 (A/56/10), 84, para 19.

[138] O Corten, 'La nécessité et le *jus ad bellum*' in SFDI (ed), *La nécessité en droit international* (Paris, Pedone, 2007) 145–47.

[139] *Report of the International Law Commission*, 53rd session, 23 April–1 June and 2 July–10 August 2001, GA, 56th session, Supp no 10 (A/56/10), 75, para 6.

[140] ICJ, *Military and Paramilitary Activities*, ICJ Rep (1986) 103, para 194; ICJ, *Oil Platforms*, ICJ Rep (2003) 196, para 73; *Armed Activities*, ICJ Rep (2005), para 147; see also below, ch 7, s II.

[141] J Barboza, 'Necessity (revisited) in International Law' in J Makarczyk (ed), *Essays in International Law in honour of Judge Manfred Lachs* (The Hague, Nijhoff, 1984) 34.

[142] ICJ Rep (1996), para 96.

The object and purpose of the Charter are besides to put an end to the possibilities of getting around the prohibition of the use of force that had been denounced by instruments prior to 1945.[143] It has previously been remarked that with the Covenant of the League of Nations and then the Pact of Paris, international law had specifically prohibited 'war' as an instrument of national policy, the Charter having extended the prohibition to any use of 'force', which excluded the lawfulness of measures 'short of war'.[144]

Examination of the *travaux préparatoires* confirms this conclusion. Article 2(4) of the Charter was drafted in such a way as to leave no scope for unilateral armed actions that were not otherwise provided for by the Charter.[145] As such, the drafting Committee insisted on pointing out that 'the unilateral use of force or any other coercive measures of the same kind is *neither authorised nor admitted*'. (emphasis added)[146] The emphasis clearly shows that the drafters of the Charter intended to distinguish between uses of force that are consistent with the UN's purposes and those that are not. In the second instance, visibly no legal reasoning was able to get around a regime that was designed to be free of loopholes. Discussion about the lawfulness or admissibility of the use of force must therefore come down to the question of whether such resort is consistent with the purposes of the UN, either because authorised by the Security Council under Chapter VII of the Charter or because it can be proved that the conditions for self-defence under article 51 are fulfilled. If this is not so, the unilateral use of force is neither 'authorised'—an expression that relates to there being no right—nor 'admitted'—a term generally covering any other situation including a possible state of necessity, extreme distress or 'countermeasure'.

Consideration of the resolutions by which the General Assembly has interpreted the principle of the prohibition of the use of force argues to the same end. In one of its reports, the ILC evokes article 5(1) of the definition of aggression ('No consideration of whatever nature, whether political, economic, military or otherwise, may serve as a justification for aggression') to deduce that it is impossible to invoke the state of necessity in this particular case.[147] Now, other resolutions contain similar expressions covering any form of use of force and not just acts of aggression. This is particularly so[148]

[143] See: I Brownlie, *International Law and the Use of Force by States* (Oxford, Clarendon Press, 1963) 59–60.
[144] Above, ch 2, s I and SD Murphy, 'Terrorism and the Concept of "Armed Attack" in Article 51 of the UN Charter' (2002) 43 *Harvard Int Law Journal* 42; P Daillier, M Forteau, A Pellet, Nguyn Quoc Dinh, *Droit international public*, 8th edn (Paris, LGDJ, 2009) 1036; A Randelzhofer, 'Article 2(4)' in B Simma (ed), *The Charter of the United Nations. A Commentary*, 2nd edn (Oxford, Oxford University Press, 2002) 117; see also J Salmon, 'Les circonstances excluant l'illicéité' in *Responsabilité internationale* (Paris, Pedone, 1987) 155; I Brownlie, *International Law and the Use of Force by States*, above n 143, 298.
[145] See below, ch 8, s I.
[146] *UNCIO*, vol 6, 477 (13 June 1945); see also *UNCIO*, vol 4, 512.
[147] A/35/10 (1980) *YILC*, vol II, Part Two, 43, para 22.
[148] See also: GA Res 2160 (XXI) of 30 November 1966; GA Res 2625 (XXV) of 24 October 1970.

for resolution 42/22, which specifies that any use of force that is incompatible with article 2(4) and

> constitutes a violation of international law and of the Charter of the United Nations and entails international responsibility . . . *No consideration of whatever nature may be invoked to warrant resorting to the threat or use of force in violation of the Charter.* (emphasis added)[149]

Quite clearly the terms emphasised set aside any possibility of justifying the use of force or even of a threat of force that is contrary to the Charter. No circumstance excluding unlawfulness can therefore validly be invoked in cases of this sort. Such clauses, to which one might add others drawn up in a regional framework,[150] attest to the resolve of States to generally set aside reference to any circumstances precluding unlawfulness. To this must be added circumstances that more specifically set aside the possibility of referring to the doctrine of reprisals or countermeasures. Thus, in the terms of several instruments, 'States have a duty to refrain from acts of reprisal involving the use of force'.[151]

In view of all these points, there is scarcely any doubt that the Charter implicitly but clearly rules out the possibility of invoking any circumstance excluding unlawfulness, whether the state of necessity, extreme distress or countermeasures, to justify a use of force in breach of its article 2(4). States have expressed this on several occasions, whether at the time they adopted the Charter or subsequently. The question of whether a limited use of force to rescue nationals or for an 'antiterrorist' action is admissible in international law must therefore be settled in the light of the regime set up by the Charter. No attempt can be made to justify a violation of this instrument by reference to necessity, distress or countermeasures. In other words, either a use of force is necessary to maintaining international peace and security and has been authorised as such by the Security Council or it is necessary to the protection of a State's vital interests and is accepted as such as self-defence—or not so. Under the latter assumption, there is no escaping the Charter requirements by referring more generally to circumstances precluding wrongfulness. It will also have been noted in this respect that no distinction is drawn by States in terms of the gravity of the use of force and its characterisation as aggression: the inadmissibility of circumstances precluding unlawfulness holds, therefore, for all military operations, whatever their objective, provided they are prohibited by the Charter.

---

[149] *Declaration of the Enhancement of the Effectiveness of the Principle of Refraining from the Threat or Use of Force in International Relations*, 18 November 1987, Principles I.1 and I.3.

[150] According to principle II of the Helsinki Final Act of 1 August 1975, referring to non-use of force, 'No consideration may be invoked to serve to warrant resort to the threat or use of force in contravention of this principle'.

[151] GA Res 2625 (XXV), principle I, para 6; see also *Declaration of the Inadmissibility of Intervention and Interference in the Internal Affairs of States*, GA Res 36/103 of 9 December 1981; Helsinki Final Act of 1 August 1975, principle II, para 2.

Examination of the ILC's work confirms this, for whatever the circumstances contemplated.

Inadmissibility Confirmed by the International Law Commission's Works: the Case of Necessity

In his eighth report on State responsibility presented to the ILC in 1980, Roberto Ago, after emphasising the inadmissibility of the state of necessity for justifying an act of aggression, left the question open as regards the use of force of a lesser degree.[152] It is essentially on this basis that some commentators have emphasised the state of necessity as a circumstance that may justify some limited uses of force, especially in the context of the fight against terrorism.[153] And yet, we have seen, with the supporting documents, that it is contradicted both by the texts of the UN Charter and resolutions that interpreted it and by the practice developed within the UN. Moreover, and it is this particular point that shall be developed next, upon scrutiny this argument finds no decisive support in the works of the Commission.

While it may be conceded that, in 1980, the Commission incidentally evoked the possibility of justifying a use of force by the state of necessity, a reading of the whole of the works suggests, however, that this opening was contested from the outset. The Special Rapporteur himself accepted from the beginning that 'it had been agreed that state of necessity could in no event justify recourse to armed force'.[154] A review of the discussions of the UN General Assembly's Sixth Commission shows that several States were insistent about ruling out this possibility.[155] Some States asserted generally that the state of necessity could not justify a use of force contrary to international law. Very clear declarations to this effect were made by Chile,[156] Sri Lanka,[157] the GDR,[158] Czechoslovakia[159] and Italy.[160] In each instance, the State concerned did not restrict its argument to acts of armed attack but extended it ostensibly to any violation of article 2(4).[161] For other States

---

[152] Addendum to the eighth report on State responsibility, A/CN.4/318/Add.5-8 (1980) *YILC*, vol II, Part One, 39, para 56, 40–41, paras 58–59 and 44, para 66; see also *Report of the ILC on the work of its thirty-second session (5 May–25 July 1980)*, A/35/10 (1980) *YILC*, vol II, Part Two, 43–45, paras 23–26); R Ago, 'Le délit international' (1939-II) 68 *RCADI* 540–45; D Anzilotti, *Cours de droit international* (Paris, LGDJ, 1999) 507–15.

[153] T Christakis, 'Unilatéralisme et multilatéralisme dans la lutte contre la terreur: l'exemple du terrorisme biologique et chimique', above n 7, 176.

[154] (1980) *YILC*, vol I, 1618th meeting, 181, para 27.

[155] S Jagota, 'State Responsibility: Circumstances Precluding Wrongfulness' (1985) *NYIL* 270.

[156] A/C.6/35/SR.47, 12 November 1980, para 7.

[157] A/C.6/35/SR.49, 14 November 1980, para 8.

[158] ibid, para 18.

[159] A/C.6/35/SR.54, 19 November 1980, para 16; see also India (ibid, para 29) and Cyprus (A/C.6/35/SR.59, 24 November 1980, para 4).

[160] ibid, 11, paras 33 and 34.

[161] See also: Ethiopia; A/C.6/35/SR.51, 17 November 1980, para 44.

like the Netherlands[162] and Mexico,[163] exclusion of the possibility of invoking the state of necessity under such circumstances was justified because any use of force by definition harmed an essential interest of the State and so was in contradiction with the wording of article 33 of the ILC's draft. Other States like Romania,[164] Tunisia[165] and Egypt[166] considered that the UN Charter implicitly excluded any possibility of invoking the state of necessity. While the arguments advanced are not all identical, they all arise from the same rationale, which is indeed of excluding any possibility of invoking the state of necessity in the event of a use of force that is incompatible with the UN Charter. It should be noticed in this respect that *no* State claimed the contrary, by asserting that the state of necessity could be justified by certain limited forms of armed intervention that were *a priori* contrary to the UN Charter. Besides all of the examples given above, it must be pointed out, on the contrary, that many contributors insisted on the need to interpret the idea of state of necessity restrictively.[167] As for those States favourable to a flexible conception of the prohibition of the use of force, they preferred to formulate certain remarks along these lines on the subject of self-defence.[168] Even in the latter case, discussion was about the interpretation of the relevant provisions of the UN Charter and not about a possible justification of behaviour that would be unlawful in respect of that instrument.

This tendency is further confirmed by the more recent discussion that led to the final adoption of the text noted by the General Assembly in 2001. Those discussions confirmed the intention to exclude necessity as justification for the use of force. In the observations sent to the Commission on the second reading of the draft, the UK considered it 'desirable that an explicit provision be made somewhere in the draft articles for emergency humanitarian action to be taken without risk of international responsibility'.[169] This wish was expressed in the context of the article on extreme distress, with the UK considering conversely that 'A defence of necessity would be open to very serious abuse across the whole range of international relations'.[170] Professor James Crawford, as Special Rapporteur, first observed that this

---

[162] A/C.6/35/SR.44, 11 November 1980, para 29; see also R Boed, 'State of Necessity as a Justification for Internationally Wrongful Conduct' (2000) *Yale Human Rights and Development LJ* 12 *ff*.

[163] A/C.6/35/SR.48, 13 November 1980, para 17.

[164] A/C.6/35/SR.50, 17 November 1980, para 3.

[165] A/C.6/35/SR.52, 18 November 1980, para 45.

[166] A/C.6/35/SR.52, 18 November 1980, para 53.

[167] See, eg: Ukraine (A/C.6/35/SR.56, 20 November 1980, paras 32–34), Thailand (ibid, para 34), Poland (A/C.6/35/SR.58, 21 November 1980, para 16), Indonesia (ibid, para 23), Bulgaria (A/C.6/35/SR.59, 24 November 1980, paras 12–13), Bangladesh (ibid, para 39).

[168] See, eg: Israel, A/C.6/35/SR.50, 5 December 1980, para 15.

[169] *State responsibility. Comments and observations received from Governments*, A/CN.4/488, 25 March 1998, 86.

[170] ibid, 88.

type of situation was 'more a matter of necessity than distress',[171] since humanitarian intervention is not always aimed at protecting people entrusted to the State's care.[172] After recalling the argument that some limited uses of force that did not constitute aggression might prove not to be contrary to *jus cogens* and might be justified by necessity, the Special Rapporteur indicated that:

> This construction raises complex questions about the 'differentiated' character of peremptory norms which go well beyond the scope of the draft articles. For present purposes it seems enough to say that either modern State practice and *opinio juris* license humanitarian action abroad in certain limited circumstances, or they do not. If they do, then such action would appear to be lawful in those circumstances, and cannot be considered as violating the peremptory norm reflected in Article 2(4) of the Charter. If they do not, there is no reason to treat them differently than any other aspect of the rules relating to the use of force. In either case, it seems that the question of humanitarian intervention abroad is not one which is regulated, primarily or at all, by article 33.[173]

He adds in a most interesting footnote that:

> Similar reasoning would apply to the controversy over whether 'anticipatory' self-defence is ever permissible. If it is in specific circumstances, article 33 would appear to be unnecessary. If it is not, then there is no reason why article 33 should be available to preclude responsibility for anticipatory action.[174]

The arguments of the Special Rapporteur are plain as day and were supported by several Commission members.[175] Unlike his predecessor, he visibly sought to clear up any ambiguity by ruling out the possibility of justifying any military action—whether characterised as an act of aggression or not—on the basis of the state of necessity. As he very clearly indicates, the debate presents an alternative: either the use of force can be justified by the Charter and the idea of the state of necessity is pointless, as there is no act the unlawfulness of which is liable to be excluded; or it contravenes the conditions laid down by the Charter and the notion of necessity cannot successfully circumvent such conditions. However, one cannot admit a possibility of 'à la carte' argument authorising the intervening State to circumvent the legal conditions laid down by the UN Charter by referring to circumstances precluding wrongfulness.

Several States spoke in favour of this in the debates within the General Assembly's Sixth Commission. Some supported the position of the Special Rapporteur that the question of humanitarian intervention was settled in

---

[171] *Second report on State responsibility,* above n 106, 23, para 272.
[172] See the text of art 34 of the project adopted by the ILC.
[173] *Second report on State responsibility,* above n 106, 31, para 287.
[174] ibid, 30, n 557.
[175] See: Economides ((1999) *YILC,* vol I, 183–84, 2591st meeting, 173, para 37); Elaraby (ibid, 172, para 26), Kateka (ibid, 171, para 23), He (ibid, 2592nd meeting, 179, para 26).

respect of the primary rules.[176] More specifically, Mexico's representative asserted that 'The provisions on the use of force set out in the Charter were peremptory norms, and necessity could not be invoked to justify their violation',[177] while Cuba's representative repeated that 'a state of necessity must never be invoked as a pretext for the breach of *jus cogens* norms, for example, the provisions of the Charter of the United Nations on the use of force'.[178] No State objected to these assertions.

Such a schema is to be found in the final report enclosed with the draft article of which the General Assembly took note. Far from taking up the argument timidly evoked in 1980 of a use of force that might be justified by necessity, the report specifies that:

> As embodied in article 25, the plea of necessity is not intended to cover conduct which is in principle regulated by the primary obligations. This has a particular importance in relation to the rules relating to the use of force in international relations and to the question of 'military necessity'. It is true that in a few cases, the plea of necessity has been invoked to excuse military actions abroad, in particular in the context of claims of humanitarian intervention. *The question whether measures of forcible humanitarian intervention, not sanctioned pursuant to Chapters VII or VIII of the Charter of the United Nations, may be lawful under modern international law is not covered by article 25.* The same is true of the doctrine of 'military necessity' which is, in the first place, the underlying criterion for a series of substantive rules of the law of war and neutrality, as well as being included in terms in a number of treaty provisions in the field of international humanitarian law. *In both respects, while considerations akin to those underlying article 25 may have a role, they are taken into account in the context of the formulation and interpretation of the primary obligations.* (emphasis added)[179]

It is difficult, in view of these recent elements, to understand how it could be claimed that the Commission leaves open a possibility, even a theoretical and remote possibility, for justifying a use of force that is contrary to the UN Charter on the basis of the state of necessity. What was only hesitantly evoked in 1980 has become decidedly unimaginable if we allow for the latest State of progress of the Commission's work.

Inadmissibility Confirmed by the ILC's Works: Distress and Countermeasures

To the best of my knowledge, scholarship supporting the admissibility of distress or countermeasures for justifying a use of force is not based on the ILC's works on State responsibility. This observation can be readily under-

---

[176] See: Austria (A/C.6/54/SR.22, 1 November 1999, para 16; A/C.6/54/SR.23, 2 November 1999, para 7).

[177] A/C.6/54/SR.23, 2 November 1999, 4, para 20.

[178] A/C.6/54/SR.28, 5 November 1999, 11, para 93.

[179] *Report of the International Law Commission*, 53rd session, 23 April–1 June and 2 July–10 August 2001, GA, 56th session, Supp no 10 (A/56/10), 84, para 21 (fns omitted).

stood if we know that that work plainly rules out that possibility whether for distress (a) or again for countermeasures (b).

a) Distress

Under article 24 of the ILC's draft:

> 1. The wrongfulness of an act of a State not in conformity with an international obligation of that State is precluded if the author of the act in question has no other reasonable way, in a situation of distress, of saving the author's life or the lives of other persons entrusted to the author's care.
> 2. Paragraph 1 does not apply if:
>
> (a) The situation of distress is due, either alone or in combination with other factors, to the conduct of the State invoking it; or
> (b) The act in question is likely to create a comparable or greater peril.

From a reading of this provision and of the discussions during its drafting, it is clear that distress was never contemplated as a circumstance liable to exclude the unlawfulness of the use of force by one State against another. In fact, the hypothesis was first conceived of to cover 'aircraft or ships entering State territory under distress of weather or following mechanical or navigational failure'.[180] The examples mentioned by the Commission, whether specific precedents or treaty provisions,[181] almost all derive from this domain. *A contrario*, the Commission's work does not mention instances of a violation of article 2(4) that might be justified by the existence of 'distress' as meant by the draft.[182]

The situation covered by article 24 therefore seems to be particularly circumscribed both in respect of the objective pursued and the resources used.

—The objective must be to save one's own life or that of people in one's care and no longer generally to save 'lives', or even less to safeguard a vital or an essential interest, as in the state of necessity.[183] It should be made clear on this point that a State could not invoke distress to attack another because of a danger weighing on all of its population, for example further to incursions by terrorist groups based in the territory of the State attacked. The concept of people whose State organ is responsible for protecting them must be understood restrictively as covering the crew or passengers of a ship or aircraft, for example, and not as applying to an undetermined number of people because of a connection of nationality or jurisdiction.[184] It is for this reason too that the hypothesis of an armed humanitarian intervention is in any event incompatible with distress as a

---

[180] ibid, 78, para 2.
[181] ibid, 79, para 5.
[182] See also above, ch 2, s I.
[183] J Salmon, 'Les circonstances excluant l'illicéité', above n 144, 120.
[184] *Report of the International Law Commission*, 53rd session, 23 April–1 June and 2 July–10 August 2001, GA, 56th session, Supp no 10 (A/56/10), 79–80, para 7.

circumstance excluding unlawfulness, the objective then being by definition broader than saving one's own life or the lives of people in one's care.
—As for the means used, they must be strictly necessary for the pursuit of
the objective in question.[185] The act that might be justified must not
create a 'comparable or greater peril', which would certainly be the case
in the event of military action incompatible with article 2(4). The
Commission specified in this context that the State organ invoking distress must not jeopardise 'many of the international obligations of its
State, and particularly the more important of them',[186] an expression that
can perfectly well be interpreted as applying to the prohibition of the use
of force.[187]

The conditions surrounding the idea of distress therefore appear to be
incompatible with a justification relating to the use of force within the meaning of the Charter.[188]

This observation is confirmed by consideration of the opinion of certain
States in the context of the development of the draft. As already stated, in
the final commentary it made on the concept of distress, the UK considered
it desirable to provide expressly in the draft articles for the possibility for a
State to carry out an 'emergency humanitarian action' 'without risk of international responsibility'.[189] From a reading of all of its observations, it is not
clear what is understood by an 'emergency humanitarian action', with the
UK authorities citing the example of people threatened by an imminent and
grave danger (for example the risk of perishing in a fire or flood).[190] In any
event, James Crawford, the last Special Rapporteur on State responsibility
resolutely ruled out this possibility:

> [Article 24] reflects a narrow but historically recognized case of distress involving,
> in particular, ships and aircraft. It should not be extended too far beyond that spe-
> cific context, and certainly not into the general field of humanitarian intervention.
> That is more a matter of necessity than distress, and it will be returned to in the
> context of article [25].[191]

We know, as mentioned above, that the Special Rapporteur also excluded
the possibility of invoking necessity to justify behaviour by a hypothesis
contrary to the primary rule prohibiting the use of force. Neither distress
nor necessity can circumvent or mitigate the conditions laid down by the

---

[185] ibid, 80, para 8.
[186] *Report of the ILC on the work of its 31st session (14 May–3 August 1979)* (1979) *YILC*,
vol II, Part Two, 135, para 9.
[187] See also: ibid, 135, para 11 and O Corten and P Klein, *Droit d'ingérence ou obligation de
réaction?* 2nd edn, above n 2, 218.
[188] J Salmon, 'Les circonstances excluant l'illicéité', above n 144, 120.
[189] *State responsibility. Comments and observations received from Governments*, A/CN.4/488,
25 March 1988, 86.
[190] ibid, 87.
[191] *Second report on State responsibility*, above n 106, 29–30, para 272.

UN Charter for the lawfulness of a use of force, however serious that use.

Admittedly, and as specified in chapter two, some limited coercive operations may simply not be covered by article 2(4). The mere crossing of a border by a ship or an aircraft, even military ones, does not necessarily mean the provision has been violated, even if it implies a violation of the national sovereignty of the State concerned. A use of force in international relations arguably presupposes that such an infringement of territorial sovereignty could be further characterised as an attack by one State against another. Thus the limit above which we enter into the scope of application of the prohibition of the use of force appears particularly important in evaluating the admissibility of an argument based on distress or on some other circumstance excluding unlawfulness.

b) Countermeasures

Under article 50 'Obligations not affected by countermeasures' of the Commission's draft:

1. Countermeasures shall not affect:

   a) The obligation to refrain from the threat or use of force as embodied in the Charter of the United Nations . . .

This clarification was made from the outset of the Commission's work, for which the prohibition of armed reprisals in resolution 2615 (XXV) on friendly relations crystallised the legal conviction of States on this issue.[192] This does not seem to have been challenged, whether in the minds of the Commission's members or by the States led to make their observations.[193] The Commission's reports thus cite in support a constant and concordant practice, doctrine[194] and international case law.[195] To give just one example, in its opinion on *Legality of the Threat or Use of Nuclear Weapons*, the ICJ deemed that it did not even have to examine the 'question of armed

---

[192] *Report of the ILC on the work of its 31st session (14 May–3 August 1979)* (1979) *YILC*, vol II, Part Two, 118, para 10; see also Switzerland ('La pratique suisse en matière de droit international public' (1992) 2 *RSDIE* 737–39) and USA (*Digest of United States Practice*, Department of State Publication, 1979, 1752; 'Contemporary Practice of the United States' (1979) 73 *AJIL* 489–92.

[193] See, eg: Czech Republic (*State responsibility. Comments and observations received from Governments*, A/CN.4/488, 25 March 1998, 128), France (ibid, 129), Ireland (ibid, 128) and J Crawford, *Third Report on State responsibility*, A/CN.4/507/Add.3, 18 July 2000, 13, para 312(a) and 15, para 314.

[194] As stated by the Commission, 'The contemporary doctrine is almost unanimous in characterizing the prohibition of armed reprisals as havong acquired the status of a general or customary rule of international law' (*Report of the ILC on the work of its 47th session (2 May–21 July 1995)* (1995) *YILC*, vol II, Part Two, 67, n 188).

[195] ICJ, *Corfu Channel*, ICJ Rep (1949) 35 (in (1979) *YILC*, vol II, Part Two, fn 590); ICJ, *Military and Paramilitary Activities*, ICJ Rep (1986) 127, para 249 (in *Report of the International Law Commission*, 53rd session, 23 April–1 June and 2 July–10 August 2001, GA, 56th session, Supp no 10 (A/56/10), 132, fn 757).

reprisals in time of peace, which are considered to be unlawful'.[196] More recently, the arbitral tribunal stated in the *Guyana/Suriname* case that 'It is a well established principle of international law that countermeasures may not involve the use of force'.[197]

In one of his reports, James Crawford developed similar reasoning to that held on the issue of state of necessity or distress. The secondary rules of liability cannot circumvent the conditions strictly provided for in the primary rule of the prohibition of the use of force as set out in the UN Charter.[198] In this respect, one cannot fail to mention articles 55 and 59 of the final draft, confirming that the Charter must be conceived of as a *lex specialis* that cannot be avoided by reference to a general circumstance excluding unlawfulness.[199] Thus self-defence is the only 'countermeasure'—in the very general and common meaning of the term—that is admissible in international law.[200]

The Commission also notes, after citing precedents in which armed reprisals were condemned, that 'even those writers who consider the use of force justifiable in the cases in question are none the less inclined to base such justification on notions other than of reprisals'.[201] We touch here on an observation that, as shall be observed, arises also from an examination of the position of States in their practice: often, they prefer to invoke self-defence, interpreting its conditions very loosely, rather than referring to the theory of armed reprisals which it is known no one any longer accepts. The ILC specified that this approach 'aimed at justifying the noted practice of circumventing the prohibition by qualifying resort to armed reprisals as self-defence, does not find any plausible legal justification and is considered unacceptable by the Commission'.[202] The issue turns in fact on an examination of the contours of self-defence and its conditions.[203] Whatever, the refusal to refer to it formally is significant of the manifestly outdated character of the doctrine of armed reprisals. Examination of practice after

---

[196] ICJ Rep (1996) 246, para 46.

[197] Arbitral Tribunal Constituted Pursuant to Article 287, and in Accordance with Annex VII of the UN Convention on the Law of the Sea (Guyana and Suriname, 17 September 2007, www.pca-cpa.org/showpage.asp?pag_id=1147), para 446.

[198] J Crawford, *Third Report on State responsibility*, A/CN.4/507/Add.3, 18 July 2000, para 335.

[199] *Report of the International Law Commission*, 53rd session, 23 April–1 June and 2 July–10 August 2001, GA, 56th session, Supp no 10 (A/56/10), 140 (Article 55. *Lex specialis*) and 143 (Article 59. UN Charter).

[200] *Report of the ILC on the work of its 31st session (14 May–3 August 1979)* (1979) YILC, vol II, Part Two, 118, n 593.

[201] ibid, n 591.

[202] *Report of the ILC on the work of its 47th session (2 May–21 July 1995)* (1995) YILC, vol II, Part Two, 67, para 3.

[203] D Simon and LA Sicilianos, 'La "contre-violence" unilatérale. Pratiques étatiques et droit international' (1986) 32 *AFDI* 62–63; P Klein, 'Vers la reconnaissance progressive d'un droit à des représailles armées?' in K Bannelier *et al* (eds), *Le droit international face au terrorisme* (Paris, Pedone, 2002) 253–57; see also below, ch 7.

adoption of the UN Charter confirms this: barring exceptions, States have systematically preferred to invoke exceptions in the primary rule rather than refer to circumstances precluding wrongfulness as secondary rules of international responsibility.

II Inadmissibility Confirmed in Practice

At first sight, practice is extremely wanting when it comes to causes of exclusion of unlawfulness as justification for a use of force. It is very rare indeed for a State to claim reliance on necessity, distress or countermeasures as a legal basis for military intervention. This observation is significant in itself, insofar as it remains valid even when circumstances could have lent themselves to a reference of this order, which seems to be evidence of serious reluctance by States in this area (A). More significantly still, in some instances, UN bodies have expressly condemned the theory of armed reprisals although it was not formally invoked by the intervening power (B). All told, there are but a few cases in which a circumstance precluding wrongfulness has been invoked, but not accepted by the international community of States as a whole as possible justification for the use of force (C).

A. Precedents Attesting to States' General Reluctance to Invoke Circumstances Precluding Unlawfulness

Obviously here there shall be no question of going over all of the precedents in which States have claimed to justify a military intervention to check whether any circumstances precluding unlawfulness have been invoked. Insofar as the doctrine favourable to admissibility of the state of necessity or of countermeasures emphasises that the argument is limited to circumscribed hypotheses of the use of force that cannot be likened to acts of aggression because of their low level of seriousness, it is not without interest to examine a few precedents of this type, including those that call into question operations for rescuing citizens or actions aimed at 'terrorist' groups on other States' territories. Logically, it might have been expected that, at least in such situations, state of necessity, distress or countermeasures might occasionally have been evoked. However this is not so[204] and this omission may be thought significant in respect of the few examples that follow.

The Israeli Military Operation at Entebbe (1976)

On 4 July 1976, an Israeli army commando unit freed hostages held at Entebbe airport,[205] in an operation that was not condemned by the Security

---

[204] But see below, B and C.

[205] *Keesing's Contemporary Archives*, 13 August 1976, 27888–91; C Alibert, *Du droit de se faire justice dans la société internationale depuis 1945*, above n 130, 270–74; C Rousseau, 'Chronique des faits internationaux' (1977) 81 *RGDIP* 286–95. See also above, ch 2, s I.

Council because of divergences that arose within it.[206] Even if no characterisation was consequently used by any UN body, it may be asked whether, because of its circumscribed and limited character, this use of force might not have been justified by a state of necessity or possibly a state of distress. Notice in this respect that the Ugandan government, truly or falsely, denied any involvement in the hostage-taking.[207] The state of necessity might have made military intervention possible, under the circumstances, in the absence of any prior unlawful act attributable to the State in whose territory the operation was contemplated.[208]

This, however, was not the case if we confine our examination to the position of the State of Israel, which explicitly invoked self-defence, without mentioning the state of necessity or distress.[209] In the same way, all of the discussions in the Security Council invariably concentrated on the interpretation of recognised exceptions in the primary rule and not the possibility of invoking circumstances precluding unlawfulness. In the instance at hand, most States condemned what was characterised as an unlawful operation and even an act of aggression.[210] The condemnation was worded so as to rule out any possible justification, whether the state of necessity or any other argument.[211] Other delegations, while refusing to vote for a resolution condemning Israel for reasons of opportunity, pointed out that the Israeli military action was indeed unlawful,[212] emphasising that the Charter allowed the use of force only in cases of self-defence or measures taken by the Security Council.[213] Some rare delegations preferred not to condemn the Israeli action expressly or even to declare it contrary to international law, but without justifying this in legal terms.[214] The United States alone, as a member of the Security Council, expressly stated that the Israeli action was consistent with international law. However, it was self-defence and not the

---

[206] S/PV.1943, 14 July 1976.

[207] S/PV.1939, 9 July 1976, para 34.

[208] F Boyle, 'The Entebbe Hostage Crisis' (1982) 29 *NILR* 38; C Rousseau, *Droit international public*, vol V (Paris, Sirey, 1983) 96.

[209] S/PV.1939, 9 July 1976, para 115.

[210] Mauritania, on behaf of the Group of African States (S/PV.1939, 9 July 1976, para 48), Kenya (ibid, para 148), Qatar (ibid, paras 168–74), Cameroon (ibid, paras 209–19), China (ibid, paras 224–25), Libya (ibid, para 244; S/PV. 1940, 12 July 1976, para 7; S/PV.1943, 14 July 1976, para 22), Guinea (S/PV. 1940, 12 July 1976, para 29), Mauritius (ibid, para 51), Guyana (ibid, paras 76–81), Benin (S/PV.1940, 12 July 1976, para 9), Somalia (ibid, para 30), Yugoslavia (ibid, paras 66–68), Pakistan (S/PV.1941, 12 July 1976, para 134), India (S/PV.1942, 13 July 1976, para 146), Cuba (S/PV.1943, 14 July 1976, paras 81–83); see also the SG of the UN (S/PV.1939, 9 July 1976, 2, para 13).

[211] See: USSR (S/PV.1941, 12 July 1976, paras 152 and 165; S/PV.1942, 13 July 1976, para 195); Tanzania (S/PV.1941, 12 July 1976, paras 104 and 106; S/PV.1942, 13 July 1976, paras 175–76), Romania (S/PV.1942, 13 July 1976, para 40).

[212] Panama (S/PV.1942, 13 July 1976, paras 27 and 30).

[213] Sweden (S/PV. 1940, 12 July 1976, para 121).

[214] France (S/PV.1939, 9 July 1976, para 202), United Kingdom (S/PV. 1940, 12 July 1976, para 107; S/PV.1943, 14 July 1976, para 170), FRG (S/PV1941, paras 50–61), Japan (S/PV.1942, 13 July 1976, para 58) and Italy (S/PV.1943, 14 July 1976, para 56).

state of necessity that was evoked.[215] By extending the analysis to stances taken outside of the Security Council, emphasis has certainly been placed[216] on a statement made to parliament by the Dutch Minister for Foreign Affairs that 'Israel's decision can only be justified by a state of emergency. There are . . . undoubtedly serious indications that such a state of emergency existed'.[217] However, this declaration remains ambiguous; the expression used may refer to the state of necessity but also to a broader conception of the right of self-defence, or even to the primary rule conferring a real right to conduct an operation to protect its nationals. In any event, this isolated position weighs little in respect of all of the declarations set out above, foremost among them that of the intervening State itself.

Finally, the Israeli raid on Entebbe may, for present purposes, be construed in either of two ways. Either it may be considered that the state of necessity, distress or countermeasures was not truly invoked by the intervening State, while it might have claimed that the conditions necessary for their implementation were satisfied. This omission might then seem significant of a tendency by States (and primarily by States conducting military interventions) to argue in terms of interpretation of the UN Charter, abstaining from resort to the notion of circumstance excluding unlawfulness. Or, in view of the very firm condemnations of the operation, several of which excluded any legal justification whatsoever, it might be considered that we are faced with a precedent attesting the rejection by a large number of States of any justification when confronted with a use of force that is contrary to the Charter. In both instances, the Entebbe precedent is not without interest insofar as it confirms the positions of the States within the UN and in other forums as recalled above.

The Unsuccessful Operation to Rescue Hostages in Iran (1980)

On 24 April 1980, the United States sent a special anti-terrorist unit (the 'Blue Light Squad') to Iran to free 53 of its nationals held hostage in Teheran. The air-borne operation was a resounding failure, especially because of darkness and adverse weather conditions.[218] Although several participants in the operation were victims of flying accidents, no fighting or skirmishing occurred and apparently no substantial injury was caused to the Iranian State. The United States, however, was accused of 'military aggression' by the Iranian authorities,[219] and it might have been expected that,

---

[215] S/PV.1941, 12 July 1976, para 77; S/PV.1943, 14 July 1976, para 76 and 183, see also (1979) 73 *AJIL* 122–23.

[216] J Raby, 'The State of Necessity and the Use of Force to Protect Nationals', above n 5, 270.

[217] 'Netherlands State Practice' (1978) 9 *NYIL* 234.

[218] *Keesing's Contemporary Archives*, 1980, 30531–33. See also above, ch 2, s I.

[219] *Note verbale dated 28 April 1980 from the Permanent Representative of Iran to the UN addressed to the Secretary-General*, S/13915, 29 April 1980, 2.

given the circumstances and in particular the strictly limited character of the operation, the US would invoke the state of necessity, extreme distress or countermeasures. Legally, however, the US did not invoke necessity, distress or countermeasures. The letter sent by the US representative to the president of the Security Council, and to which President Carter's declaration was appended, is clear on this point, since it relies explicitly on self-defence within the meaning of article 51 of the UN Charter.[220] The US argument was therefore to characterise the hostage-taking as an armed attack so opening the way to self-defence pursuant to article 51.[221] Again it was the primary rule that was invoked.

This unsuccessful raid prompted, to the best of my knowledge, only a few States to take positions in terms of international law. When these stances are examined, they do not bear on the relevance of any circumstance precluding wrongfulness. The United States' allies, while sometimes regretting the raid, generally expressed their 'understanding',[222] even if Italy asserted its 'clear opposition to the recourse to action in force in any circumstances for the liberation of the hostages'.[223] By contrast, the USSR,[224] like several Arab States,[225] condemned this armed action. As for the International Court of Justice, it affirmed that the operation was 'of a kind calculated to undermine respect for the judicial process in international relations',[226] without, for want of jurisdiction, making any pronouncement on its conformity with the UN Charter.[227] Lastly, doctrine generally envisaged the problem of lawfulness of the operation by reference to self-defence and not to necessity or to countermeasures.[228]

Finally, it is significant that the concept of self-defence is preferentially construed very broadly rather than having recourse to some other justification which, if admitted, might have proved a more credible legal argument, especially as it was a limited operation that created no Iranian victim and no major damage.[229]

---

[220] *Letter dated 25 April 1980 from the Permanent Representative of the USA to the UN addressed to the President of the Security Council,* S/13908, 25 April 1980, 1.

[221] See also: ICJ, *United States Diplomatic and Consular Staff in Tehran,* ICJ Rep (1980) 17–18, para 32.

[222] *Keesing's Contemporary Archives,* 1980, 30534.

[223] ibid.

[224] ibid.

[225] ibid.

[226] ICJ, *United States Diplomatic and Consular Staff in Tehran,* ICJ Rep (1980) 43, para 93.

[227] ibid, 43–44, para 94; see also Judge Morozov, dissenting opinion, ibid, 56–57; Judge Tarazi, dissenting opinion, ibid, 64–65, and TL Stein, 'Contempt, Crisis and the Court: the Wolrd Court and the Hostage Rescue Attempt' (1982) 76 *AJIL* 499–531.

[228] See, eg: A Jeffery, 'The American Hostages in Tehran: The ICJ and the Legality of Rescue Missions' (1981) 30 *ICLQ* 722–28.

[229] *Keesing's Contemporary Archives,* 1980, 30531–33; see also O Schachter, 'Self-Help and the Iranian Crisis' (1984) *Journal of International Affairs* 213–47.

The Oil Platforms Case (1987–2003)

On 19 October 1987 and then on 18 April 1988, the United States attacked and destroyed three offshore petroleum production installations.[230] There were no victims in these limited armed actions that were officially conducted in riposte to what the US considered to be Iranian attacks against certain neutral vessels moored in the Gulf. It might have been expected, in such a situation, that the US would invoke the theory of countermeasures. However, it preferred to invoke self-defence within the meaning of article 51 of the Charter first in the Security Council,[231] and then in the ICJ which was called on to settle the dispute further to an action filed by Iran.[232] This precedent would probably not have merited any mention had it not given rise to an individual opinion by one of the ICJ judges, who defended the validity of the argument of armed reprisals:

> What we see in such instances is an unlawful use of force short of an armed attack ('agression armée') within the meaning of Article 51, as indeed 'the most grave form of the use of force'. Against such smaller-scale use of force, defensive action—by force also 'short of' Article 51—is to be regarded as lawful.[233]

Judge Simma thus makes his own the minority doctrinal argument which, in the name of the principle of proportionality, defends the possibility of strictly limited armed reprisals in riposte to actions that are not necessarily akin to armed aggression within the meaning of article 51.[234]

This argument does not seem convincing for three reasons.

1. As will have been understood from reading the preceding pages, the argument finds no positive feedback in the opinions of States, which have invariably ruled out any possibility of armed reprisals, without mentioning any exception. The need to balance the interests of the States concerned, but also those of the international community as a whole, has already been taken into account in the definition of the primary rule. This limits the

---

[230] ICJ, *Oil Platforms*, ICJ Rep (2003) 175–76, para 25.

[231] *Letter from the Permanent Representative of the USA to the UN addressed to the President of the Security Council*, S/19219, 19 October 1987 and ICJ, *Oil Platforms*, ICJ Rep (2003) 185, para 48.

[232] ICJ, *Oil Platforms*, ICJ Rep (2003) 181, para 37; *Counter-Memorial and Counter-Claim Submitted by the USA*, 23 June 1997, ch VIII, 150–53; *Rejoinder Submitted by the USA*, 23 March 2001, ch III, 177–79.

[233] Separate Opinion of Judge Simma; ICJ Rep (2003) at 331–32, para 12.

[234] See, eg: D Bowett, 'Reprisals Involving Recourse to Armed Force' (1972) 66 *AJIL* 1–36; see also R Falk, 'The Beirut Raid and the International Law of Retaliation' (1969) 63 *AJIL* 437–43; RW Tucker, 'Reprisals and Self-Defense: The Customary Law' (1972) 66 *AJIL* 586–96; TM Franck, *Recourse to Force. State Action Against Threats and Armed Attacks* (Cambridge, Cambridge University Press, 2002) 91; A Clark Arend and RJ Beck, *International Law and the Use of Force* (London/New York, Routledge, 1993) 186. See also Institut de droit international Resolution on Self-defence, 27 October 2007, Santiago Session (www.idi-iil.org/idiE/navig_chon2003.html), para 5 and my comments in O Corten, 'Les réso-lutions de l'Institut de droit international sur la légitime défense et sur les actions humanitaires' (2007) 40 *RBDI* 698–13.

possibility of a unilateral armed riposte in the case of self-defence, which itself presupposes a prior armed attack.[235] A minor violation of article 2(4), such as a skirmish or a border incident, gives entitlement to the implementation of unarmed countermeasures and, of course, may also give jurisdiction to the Security Council to decide on coercive measures, including in the military domain. To extend this legal regime in the name of a 'an eye for an eye' would be to promote a model that is more a matter of private justice than of collective security.

2. In support of his reasoning, Judge Simma cites an excerpt from *Military Activities*, in which the ICJ sets aside the US argument based on 'counter-intervention':

> While an armed attack would give rise to an entitlement to collective self-defence, a use of force of a lesser degree of gravity cannot as the Court has already observed (paragraph 211 above) produce any entitlement to take collective counter-measures involving the use of force. The acts of which Nicaragua is accused, even assuming them to have been established and imputable to that State, could only have justified proportionate counter-measures on the part of the State which had been the victim of these acts, namely El Salvador, Honduras or Costa Rica. They could not justify counter-measures taken by a third State, the United States, and particularly could not justify intervention involving the use of force.[236]

On reading the terms of the decision, the arguments seem audacious. The Court simply affirms that a possible use of force that does not constitute an aggression does not authorise counter-measures except for the actual victim State and not for a third State. But the Court in no manner asserts that such countermeasures might take the form of armed action,[237] with the end of the paragraph seeming to contradict this possibly rather,[238] as does paragraph 211 of the decision referred to.[239] For want of any more explicit terms, its seems at any rate particularly excessive to claim that the Court has, without any grounds or explanation, departed from the well-established rule of the prohibition of armed reprisals, a rule laid down in resolution 2625 (XXV) and cited for that matter in the decision,[240] and recalled by the Court itself a few years later.[241]

3. Moreover, and here we return to the lesson that arises generally from practice, it should be pointed out that the US itself did *not* claim to be able

---

[235] Below, ch 7.

[236] ICJ Rep (1986) 127, para 249 and comments by JA Green, *The International Court of Justice and Self-Defence in International Law* (Oxford, Hart Publishing, 2009) 54–60.

[237] See: Judge Schwebel, dissenting opinion, ICJ Rep (1986) 349, para 175 and 350, para 177.

[238] See also: ICJ Rep (1986) 134, para 268 and Judge Jennings, dissenting opinion, ICJ Rep (1986) 530.

[239] ICJ Rep (1986) 11011, para 211.

[240] ibid, 99–101, paras 188 and 191.

[241] ICJ, *Legality of the Threat or Use of Nuclear Weapons*, ICJ Rep (1996) 246, para 46.

to implement armed reprisals, regardless of the particular circumstances.[242] The argument of 'defensive reprisals', applicable beyond the strict conditions of self-defence, is an essentially doctrinal argument that does not resonate with the States that would *a priori* be the most ready to take it up.[243]

For all these reasons, it is not surprising that Judge Simma's argument was not followed by the Court which, in its decision on *Oil Platforms*, confined itself to existing international law: outside of the particular instance of Security Council authorisation, the use of force can only be admitted in cases of self-defence as laid down by article 51 of the Charter.[244]

US Military Action Officially Motivated by the Riposte to an Attempted Assassination of Former President Bush (1993)

On 26 June 1993, the United States launched 23 missiles at an Iraqi building allegedly used for preparing an assassination attempt against former President George Bush.[245] In this context, it might have been expected that the US would invoke the theory of countermeasures or of armed reprisals. This was not so since, here again, the letter sent to the Security Council argued on the basis of self-defence recognised by article 51.[246] The line of argument is obviously debatable insofar as it can seriously be questioned whether a simple assassination attempt can as such be characterised as an 'armed attack' within the Charter's meaning.[247] Many States, and not just Non-Aligned States but some Western ones too, criticised the argument.[248] But it is significant that once again, the US preferred to interpret the notion of self-defence broadly rather than rely on arguments like armed reprisals that had little chance of being accepted.[249]

---

[242] ICJ, *Military and Paramilitary Activities*, ICJ Rep (1986) 110–11, para 211.

[243] LA Sicilianos, *Les réactions décentralisées à l'illicite. Des contre-mesures à la légitime défense* (Paris, LGDJ, 1990) 411–13.

[244] ICJ, *Oil Platforms*, ICJ Rep (2003) 183 *ff*, para 43 *ff*.

[245] *Keesing's Contemporary Archives*, 1993, 39531.

[246] *Letter dated 93/06/26 from the Permanent Representative of the United States of America to the United Nations addressed to the President of the Security Council*, S/26003, 26 June 1993; See M Reisman, 'The Raid on Baghdad: Some Reflections on its Lawfulness and Implications' (1994) 5 *EJIL* 120–33. See also 'Pratique française du droit international' (1993) 39 *AFDI* 1018, 'United Kingdom Materials on International Law' (1993) 64 *BYBIL* 731–34; (1994) 65 *BYBIL* 693).

[247] See: P Klein, 'Vers la reconnaissance progressive d'un droit à des représailles armées?' above n 203, 255–56; L Condorelli, 'A propos de l'attaque américaine contre l'Iraq du 26 Juin 1993: Lettre d'un professeur désemparé aux lecteurs du *JEDI*' (1994) 5 *EJIL* 134–44.

[248] 'Netherlands State Practice' (1994) 25 *NYIL* 460. See also D Kritsiotis, 'The Legality of the 1993 US Missile Strike on Iraq and the Right of Self-Defence in International Law' (1993) 42 *ICLQ* 163–64; MG Kohen, 'The use of force by the United States after the end of the Cold War, and its impact on international law' in M Byers and G Nolte (eds), *United States Hegemony and the Foundations of International Law* (Cambridge, Cambridge University Press, 2003) 203; G Cahin, 'Le rôle des organes politiques des Nations Unies' in E Cannizzaro and P Palchetti (eds), *Customary International Law on the Use of Force. A Methodological Approach* (Leiden/Boston, Martinus Nijhoff, 2005) 170.

[249] L Condorelli, 'A propos de l'attaque américaine contre l'Iraq du 26 Juin 1993: Lettre d'un professeur désemparé aux lecteurs du JEDI', above n 247, 136.

US Military Action in Sudan and Afghanistan (1998)

On 20 August 1998, the US Army fired 79 Tomahawk missiles against training camps in Afghanistan and against a pharmaceuticals plant in Sudan that was said to be used for making chemical weapons. President Clinton immediately justified this action by explaining that he was striking at terrorist organisations operating from the territory of the two States, in terms that one could *a priori* relate to the theory of countermeasures.[250] Can this operation be interpreted, though, as a precedent attesting to the legal conviction that a circumstance excluding unlawfulness is liable to justify a use of force? Upon scrutiny, the answer is without doubt no. When it came to advancing a more specifically legal argument, the US once again relied on self-defence, as shown particularly by the letter sent to the Security Council on the very day of the attack.[251] While it was in a situation that lent itself to it, the US did not, then, invoke the state of necessity or countermeasures. All the indications are that, for the US, the only possibility of legally justifying unilateral military action was the institution of self-defence, such as it is provided for in the primary rules laid down by the UN Charter. As mentioned above, reactions to the US operations were mitigated. Many States, especially members of the League of Arab States, condemned the actions against Sudan invoking the principle of the non-use of force.[252] Others remained silent or expressed a degree of understanding, without making any pronouncements in legal terms. Among the few States that expressly supported the US in the legal arena, none thought to raise the argument of state of necessity.[253] On the whole, this episode therefore confirms rather the feeling that the US envisages a use of force only in relation to the rules laid down by the UN Charter, which, when it is a unilateral action, reduces the debate to an interpretation of the institution of self-defence.[254]

---

[250] 'I ordered this action for four reasons: First, because we have convincing evidence these groups played the key role in the Embassy bombings in Kenya and Tanzania; second, because these groups have executed terrorist attacks against Americans in the past; third, because we have compelling information that they were planning additional terrorist attacks against our citizens and others with the inevitable collateral casualties we saw so tragically in Africa; and fourth because they are seeking to acquire chemical weapons and other dangerous weapons' (quoted in SD Murphy, 'Contemporary Practice of the United States relating to International Law' (1999) 93 *AJIL* 161).

[251] *Letter dated 20 August 1998 from the Permanent Representative of the USA addressed to the President of the Security Council*, S/1998/780, 20 August 1998, 1 and 2. See also SD Murphy, 'Contemporary Practice of the United States relating to International Law' (1999) 93 *AJIL* 162.

[252] *Letter dated 21 August 1998 from the Chargé d' affaires a.i. of the Permanent Mission of Kuwait to the United Nations addressed to the President of the Security Council*, S/1998/789.

[253] See, eg: 'Communiqué des Autorités françaises' Paris, 21 August 1998, *DAI*, 1998, 753.

[254] See below, ch 7, s I.

The War Waged Against Iraq by the US and its Allies (2003)

The war against Iraq in 2003 was started on the basis of a complex legal argument that shall be examined later.[255] At this stage it shall simply be noted that it was based on an accusation that Iraq had violated several UN Security Council resolutions. Under the circumstances, it might have been thought that the theory of countermeasures could be invoked, with the US and its allies merely reacting to an initial violation of international law.[256] As shall be specified later, nothing of the sort was done. The US and its allies referred rather to an authorisation that was allegedly given implicitly by the Security Council to engage the operation. The argument did not consist in using any circumstance excluding unlawfulness but rather in making a broad interpretation of a legal justification in the UN Charter.

The precedents just evoked are obviously only examples. There are many other cases in which the intervening States carefully abstained from referring to necessity, distress or countermeasures and preferred to rely on arguments drawn directly from the UN Charter.[257] This attitude is, to my mind, highly significant even if two objections could be made at this stage.

—First, one might claim that States' not referring to a circumstance excluding unlawfulness could be explained by their conviction that the action they are conducting is in fact akin to a real act of aggression. That would not exclude state of necessity, distress or countermeasures being invoked in certain cases of the use of force that are not of such gravity. The problem is that, in the examples just mentioned—and especially the precedent of the US operation in Iran—, the military action was extremely limited in its effects. The objection, that could only apply to precedents where a real war was waged, therefore seems inoperative for our hypothesis unless it is considered that any use of force contrary to the UN Charter is tantamount to an aggression, which would have as its effect, by taking a different slant, the exclusion of the state of necessity in any event.

—According to another objection, intervening States do invoke certain circumstances precluding wrongfulness, but without expressly naming them. For example, in line with what was sometimes said of the *Caroline* case,[258] the appeal to 'self-defence' in this type of precedent should be likened to a reference to the state of necessity.[259] This view, however, does not seem very compatible with the method generally followed for

---

[255] Below, ch 6, s II.

[256] O Corten, 'Opération *Iraqi Freedom*: peut-on admettre l'argument de l'"autorisation implicite" du Conseil de sécurité?' (2003) 36 *RBDI* 226–27.

[257] See: JW Willis, 'Contemporary Practice of the United States' (1979) 73 *AJIL* 491–92.

[258] *Report of the International Law Commission on the work of its 32nd session (5 May–25 July 1980)*, A/35/10, *YILC* (1980) vol II, Part Two, 44, para 24, fn 155. See also J Barboza, 'Necessity (revisited) in International Law', above n 141, 39–40 and 42.

[259] T Christakis, 'Vers une reconnaissance de la notion de guerre préventive?' above n 7, 29.

establishing the existence of a customary rule, a method that requires compliance with the *opinio juris* of the States concerned.[260] If those States invoke self-defence, it is patently because they consider that it is this institution and no other that is applicable.[261] One commentator might, admittedly, consider as an outside observer that the military action in question cannot be justified on the grounds of self-defence, but on some other grounds (such as state of necessity or countermeasures), the existence of which he would then have to prove. But even so he could not claim that his doctrinal reasoning was defended by the intervening State, and even less that the international society of States as a whole had made it their own.[262] So one should adhere to the positions expressed by the States themselves, which finally set aside any circumstance excluding unlawfulness as a basis liable to justify the use of force.

B. Precedents Attesting Unequivocal Condemnation of Armed Reprisals

We saw above that States, the ILC and the ICJ had all explicitly condemned armed reprisals. It is hardly surprising therefore that many *in concreto* condemnations have been pronounced alongside this. To confine ourselves to just two examples, the Security Council 'condemn[ed] reprisals as incompatible with the purposes and principles of the United Nations',[263] and then 'emphasize[d] [. . .] that actions of military reprisals cannot be tolerated'.[264]

It is interesting to observe that some of these condemnations were issued while the intervening State did not evoke countermeasures but self-defence, which clearly shows the Security Council's concern to make no bones about the rejection of armed reprisals. Thus, in condemning British military action in Yemen in 1964, the Security Council condemned 'reprisals' while the UK preferred to refer to self-defence under article 51 of the Charter.[265]

It is true that, on some occasions, Israel developed a line of reasoning based on the idea of countermeasures, claiming that it merely riposted to previous violations of armistice agreements or ceasefires by Syria, Lebanon or some other neighbouring State. However, the Security Council condemned this reasoning. Accordingly, in its resolution 111 (1956), while

---

[260] Above, ch 1, s II.

[261] E Jimenez de Arechaga and A Tanzi, 'La responsabilité internationale des Etats' in M Bedjaoui (ed), *Droit international. Bilan et perspectives*, tome 1 (Paris, Pedone, Unesco, 1991) 376–77.

[262] J Combacau, 'The Exception of Self-Defence in UN Practice' in A Cassese (ed), *The Current Legal Regulation of the Use of Force* (Dordrecht/Boston/Lancaster, Martinus Nijhoff, 1986) 14.

[263] SC Res 188 (1964) of 28 March 1964, para 1.

[264] SC Res 228 (1966) of 25 November 1966, para 3; see also SC Res (270) of 26 August 1969, para 4.

[265] United Kingdom, S/PV.1109, 7 April 1964, para 31 and S/PV.1111, 9 April 1964, para 30.

admitting that 'there has been interference by the Syrian authorities with Israel activities on Lake Tiberias, in contravention of the terms of the General Armistice Agreement between Israel and Syria', the Security Council:

1. Holds that this interference in no way justifies the Israel action.

2. Reminds the Government of Israel that the Council has already condemned military action in breach of the General Armistice Agreements, whether or not undertaken by way of retaliation . . .[266]

From reading these terms, it is clear that the Security Council dismisses any possibility of countermeasures, any dispute relating to the armistice agreement having to be settled by peaceful mechanisms specifically provided for the purpose.[267] It is in application of this reasoning that the Security Council also condemned Israeli military operations in Jordan, as in resolution 248 (1968), by which:

Recalling resolution 236 (1967) by which the Security Council condemned any and all violations of the cease-fire . . .

3. Deplores all violent incidents in violation of the cease-fire and declares that such actions of military reprisal and other grave violations of the cease-fire cannot be tolerated . . .[268]

In the same perspective, the Security Council did not accept the lawfulness of Israeli military actions officially justified by the response to certain incursions from Lebanon. Thus it 'Condemns, while profoundly deploring all acts of violence, the repeated attacks of Israeli forces on Lebanese territory'.[269] In any event, it has been noted that, from the 1960s, even Israel abandoned reference to the theory of reprisals, preferring that of self-defence instead.[270]

Some commentators, however, emphasised the failure to condemn several military operations that could be likened to armed reprisals.[271] This omission could be explained in that, unlike precedents that were formally condemned, these were strictly proportionate actions and, as such, admissible as legitimate countermeasures. One could thus make out the persistence of a customary rule admitting strictly necessary and proportionate

---

[266] SC Res 111 (1956) of 19 January 1956, see also SC Res 171 (1962) of 9 April 1962, para 2.

[267] See also: SC Res 114 (1956) of 4 June 1956, para 2, and 127 (1958) of 22 January 1958, paras 5–6; 'Pratique française du droit international' (1981) 27 *AFDI* 900; HS Levie, 'The Nature and Scope of the Armistice Agreement' (1956) 50 *AJIL* 880–906.

[268] SC Res 248 (1968) of 24 March 1968; see also: SC Res 236 (1967) of 11 June 1967.

[269] SC Res 316 (1972) of 26 June 1972, para 2; see also SC Res 332 (1973) of 21 April 1973.

[270] LA Sicilianos, *Les réactions décentralisées à l'illicite. Des contre-mesures à la légitime défense*, above n 243, 410–11; C Alibert, *Du droit de se faire justice dans la société internationale depuis 1945*, above n 130, 34–35.

[271] D Bowett, 'Reprisals involving recourse to armed force', above n 234, 10 *ff* and 26 *ff*.

reprisals, even if they implied a certain use of force. This reasoning runs up against several objections, though, the first of which it will be recalled is that the unlawfulness of armed reprisals has been reaffirmed on several occasions by States as a whole, whether in resolution 2625 (XXV) or in other instruments, without any justification or attenuation based on a criterion of proportionality.[272] A review of discussions within the Security Council also shows that the absence of condemnation is explained essentially for reasons of alliances or political opportunity.[273] It would be difficult indeed to infer from this an agreement of the international community of States as a whole attesting a return to or rebirth of the institution of armed reprisals.[274]

Finally, an examination of practice shows that the prohibition of armed reprisals remains well anchored in contemporary international law, whatever the shortcomings of the collective security mechanisms.[275] This does not mean that the practice does not pose legal problems.[276] As noted, some States conduct military actions in circumstances that seem to liken them to reprisals, but think they can offset this by characterising such actions as self-defence within the meaning of article 51 of the Charter.[277] This excess has been underscored by doctrine,[278] but must in any event be assessed in terms of the definition of the notion of self-defence, which we shall come to in a later chapter.[279]

C. The Rare Precedents where Circumstances Precluding Unlawfulness have been Invoked to Justify the Use of Force

We have so far mentioned many precedents in which, while the conditions evoked by some scholarship seemed to be fulfilled, no circumstance excluding unlawfulness was invoked. Can it be affirmed, though, that this has never occurred in practice? Leaving aside the rare cases where reprisals were invoked several decades ago by Israel, and were condemned by the Security Council, one might lean towards an affirmative answer. However, doctrine cites a precedent in which the state of necessity was supposedly

---

[272] See above.

[273] LA Sicilianos, *Les réactions décentralisées à l'illicite. Des contre-mesures à la légitime défense*, above n 243, 423–25.

[274] R Barsotti, 'Armed Reprisals' in A Cassese (ed), *The Current Legal Regulation of the Use of Force* (Dordrecht/Boston/Lancaster, Martinus Nijhoff, 1986) 79–110, 97.

[275] LA Sicilianos, *Les réactions décentralisées à l'illicite. Des contre-mesures à la légitime défense*, above n 243, 413–15.

[276] See, eg: O Corten and A Lagerwall, 'La violation d'un cessez-le-feu constitue-t-elle nécessairement une violation de l'article 2 § 4 de la Charte des Nations Unies?' (2008) 61 *RHDI* 110–13.

[277] P Klein, 'Vers la reconnaissance progressive d'un droit à des représailles armées?' above n 203, 253–57.

[278] L Condorelli, 'A propos de l'attaque américaine contre l'Iraq du 26 Juin 1993: Lettre d'un professeur désemparé aux lecteurs du JEDI', above n 247, 136.

[279] Below, ch 7.

invoked to justify a use of force, that of Belgian military intervention in 1960 officially to protect its nationals. Before examining this precedent (2), it will not be without interest to mention other earlier ones, such as the *Corfu Channel* case (1), and later ones such as the case of the Iranian airbus (3), the arrest of a Spanish vessel by Canadian authorities (4), and the military operations of NATO Member States against Yugoslavia (5). In each case, it shall be seen that the reference to the state of necessity was never clearly assumed as a decisive legal basis by the intervening State. It shall also be seen that, in any event, this type of argument is far from having been accepted as reflecting the general state of international law.

1. The Corfu Channel Case (1949)

By the terms of the second special agreement submitted to it, the Court was to determine whether the 'United Kingdom under international law violated the sovereignty of the Albanian People's Republic by reason of the acts of the Royal Navy in Albanian waters . . .'.[280] The question related especially to the sending of ships on 12 and 13 November 1946 to de-mine the channel further to explosions that had earlier caused death, injury and damage.

According to Albania, an affirmative answer to the second question of the special agreement was in no doubt. The activities of the British navy ought to be envisaged in the more general context of an aggressive policy of the UK against it.[281] In this context, the sending of minesweepers to clear the channel without Albania's authorisation was an 'invasion of Albanian territory by the British navy on 12 and 13 November 1946; . . . these foreign armed forces took over by force on the said days a part of Albanian territory, namely a part of the Albanian territorial and interior sea and of the air space above and around it'.[282] Still according to Albania, *Operation Retail* was therefore incompatible with article 2(4),[283] and could be likened to a 'wartime operation', an 'operation of force and prestige designed to show the Albanian populations that they had to kow-tow'.[284] In the terms of an advisor to Albania, 'UN Member States have, even less than others, the right to use force or the threat of force in the conduct of their affairs. They have waived this possibility, this option, this policy in article 2(4) of the Charter'.[285]

In its pleadings, the UK invoked as justification for its action of 12 and 13 November 1946 a 'right of self-help or intervention [which] can only be exercised when there is an immediate necessity'.[286] In the matter at hand,

---

[280] ICJ, *Corfu Channel*, ICJ Rep (1949) 6. See also above, ch 2, s I.

[281] ICJ, *Corfu Channel*, Pleadings, oral arguments, documents, Counter-Memorial of the Albanian Government, 15 June 1948, 107, para 109.

[282] ibid, 138, para 139 and 140, para 143 (see also 106).

[283] ibid, Rejoinder of the Albanian Government, 373, paras 154–55.

[284] ibid, P Cot, 16 November 1948, 419 and 421.

[285] ibid, 408; see also P Cot, 21 January 1949, 675.

[286] Reply of the United Kingdom, 30 July 1948, 284.

necessity arose both from the urgency of collecting evidence to prove Albania's responsibility in the explosion of mines and the delay or even the shortcomings of the UN Security Council. The UK did not deny the importance of the changes made by the UN Charter in the area of the non-use of force, especially because of article 2(4). However, it argued that this provision did not preclude a sort of right of self-preservation in instances of extreme necessity:

> We recognize that the right of self-help has been restricted and controlled by the provisions of the Charter; but we contend that it is precisely in a case of this kind, where there had been a violent attack on our ships in October and there was an urgent necessity to safeguard evidence necessary for the purposes of justice, that a properly limited right of self-help remains in modern international law.[287]

A British lawyer then seemed to place this justification more clearly in the category of circumstances precluding unlawfulness:

> [T]he best analogies will be found in certain rights admitted in municipal laws, rights recognized in special circumstances entitling a person to do something in the nature of self-help or self-redress, whereas in other circumstance, a similar act would be illegal.[288]

The prohibition of the use of force, laid down in the UN Charter, supposedly therefore did not end certain limited possibilities to act in extreme necessity: 'I am asking the Court to do what any Court can do . . . to recognize that international law still permits some rights of self-help'.[289] The limitation of these possibilities to very strict conditions allegedly answered the fears on which Albania heavily insisted of a return to the permissive legal regime of the days before the Charter.

It seems that the reasoning developed by the UK can therefore be considered as an application of the theory of a possible use of the state of necessity under exceptional circumstances of limited and circumscribed use of force. Upon examination, it must, though, be observed that things are more complex and that, if there is a precedent, it runs rather against the admissibility of this theory in contemporary international law.

First, it cannot be deduced from an analysis of the parties' arguments that such a theory was really assumed. If account is taken of its entire line of argument, it is not particularly obvious that the UK truly intended to defend the possibility of invoking the state of necessity as a circumstance precluding wrongfulness of the use of force. Initially, the UK invoked not a circumstance of the type but a real right of intervention, understood quite broadly:

> There is recognized in international law the right of a State, when a state of affairs involving a serious and flagrant breach of the law has been brought about by

---

[287] E Beckett, 11 November 1948, 296.
[288] E Beckett, 18 January 1949, 580.
[289] ibid, 582.

another State or has been permitted to come about to intervene by direct action. The purpose of such intervention may be to prevent the continuance of the situation which is in breach of the law, or, where the intervening State has suffered an injury of a nature capable of being redressed, to further the administration of international justice by preventing the removal of evidence.[290]

This type of intervention, likened to 'certain rights of self-defence and self-redress',[291] might not be incompatible with article 2(4) insofar as it is supposedly not directed against the territorial integrity or the political independence of another State, in the case in point Albania.[292] As such, it is purportedly not a circumstance excluding unlawfulness but a right admitted by the primary rule in question. In the face of virulent criticism by Albania's counsel who inveighed at the excesses of such a theory, UK counsel finally came to argue that *Operation Retail* could be characterised as an 'intervention', denying it was a real use of force. Thus, after having invoked a general right of intervention extending apparently to the use of force, the UK seems to have invoked a limited form of a 'right of self-help', but solely to justify a coercive measure that did not constitute a use of force:

> I am arguing for a limited right of self-help. . . . It is *not*—emphatically *not*—our contention that it is justifiable for State A to invade with armies the territories of B to discover evidence of a trivial suspected offense . . . It was a sweeping of a strait for mines against the will of Albania.[293]

The UK argument seems somewhat ambiguous, but it does seem that it consists in asserting both that a right of intervention is not incompatible with article 2(4), and that some limited forms of action, that are not covered by that provision, could be justified under exceptional circumstances of necessity. In both cases, it is difficult to conclude that the UK assumed a position that the state of necessity was as such a circumstance liable to exclude any use of force that was besides prohibited by the UN Charter.

This reluctance, and here we come to a second interesting lesson, can probably be explained by fear that the Court would not be convinced by the very firm position advanced by the Albanian party on this point. After dismissing the theory of intervention as being 'nothing more than the precept that might is right applied to international affairs'[294] and while re-affirming that *Operation Retail* was tantamount to a use of force,[295] counsel for Albania considered that the UK invoked the state of necessity and specified that this was only admissible inasmuch as it was not confused with self-defence.[296]

---

[290] Reply of the United Kingdom, 30 July 1948, 282, para 82.
[291] E Beckett, 11 November 1948, 296.
[292] ibid.
[293] E Beckett, 18 January 1949, 584 and 595.
[294] P Cot, 16 November 1948, 405; see also Rejoinder of the Albanian Government, 20 September 1948, 370 *ff*.
[295] P Cot, 21 January 1949, 696.
[296] ibid, 689.

It is in this context that one can contemplate the position taken by the Court itself on this particular aspect of the dispute. After having resolutely ruled out any 'alleged right of intervention as a manifestation of a policy of force', the Court observed that:

> The United Kingdom Agent, in his speech in reply, has further classified 'Operation Retail' among methods of self-protection or self-help. The Court cannot accept this defence either. Between independent States, respect for territorial sovereignty is an essential foundation of international relations. The Court recognizes that the Albanian Government's complete failure to carry out its duties after the explosions, and the dilatory nature of its diplomatic notes, are extenuating circumstances for the action of the United Kingdom Government. But to ensure respect for international law, of which it is the organ, the Court must declare that the action of the British Navy constituted a violation of Albanian sovereignty.[297]

The Court therefore does indeed exclude any possibility of invoking any legal justification whatsoever for justifying *Operation Retail*, an operation that it refused besides to consider as a show of force. In view of the arguments presented, it can be considered that the Court rules out the state of necessity for an action it otherwise refrains from characterising as a use of force.[298] *A fortiori*, there is therefore every reason to think that it would have ruled out that justification if it had assimilated the action to a violation of article 2(4).[299]

Finally and more generally, the *Corfu Channel* case is an interesting precedent inasmuch as it marks the willingness to make a transition to the regime of non-intervention and non-use of force laid down by the UN Charter. The Court ostensibly wanted to condemn all of the old doctrines that had justified unilateral actions, especially in the military domain. In this context, the argument of necessity does indeed appear incompatible with the new international law.

2. Belgium's Military Intervention in Congo (1960)

Early in July 1960, after troubles stirred throughout the country by the army mutiny in the wake of the proclamation of independence, the Belgian army intervened in several parts of Congo, officially to protect the foreign population from the doings of certain uncontrolled elements.[300] On 12 and 13 July, the President and Prime Minister of Congo sent telegrams to the UN in which, considering 'the unsolicited Belgian action as [an] act of

---

[297] ICJ Rep (1949) 35.

[298] See: Judge Ecer, dissenting opinion, ICJ Rep (1949) 130.

[299] See: Judge Alvarez, separate opinion, ICJ Rep (1949) 47; cp Judge Azevedo, separate opinion, ibid, 108.

[300] WJ Ganshof van der Meersch, *Fin de la souveraineté belge au Congo*, Documents et réflexions (Bruxelles, Institut Royal des Relations Internationales/La Haye, Martinus Nijhoff, 1963); C Leclercq, *L'ONU et l'affaire du Congo* (Paris, Payot, 1964), 44–65. See also T Franck and J Carey, *The Legal Aspects of the United Nations Action in the Congo* (New York, Oceana Pub, 1963).

aggression'[301] and accusing the Belgian government of having prepared the secession of Katanga, they asked for military aid to 'protect the national territory against the act of aggression by Belgian home troops'.[302] After several sessions of debate, the Security Council adopted a resolution calling on the Belgian government to withdraw its troops and authorised the Secretary-General to take whatever measures necessary to provide the military assistance requested.[303] It was further to this resolution that the ONUC was deployed in Congo and the problem of the attempted secession of Katanga overshadowed that of the initial operation by Belgian troops.[304]

In its 1980 report on international responsibility, the ILC saw in these events the 'only one known case in which a State invoked a state of necessity—and then not exclusively—to justify violation of the territory of a foreign State'.[305] For the ILC, the Security Council debates 'concentrated on determination and evaluation of the facts' without taking 'any position of principle with regard of the possible validity of a "state of necessity"' under such circumstances.[306] The precedent was reportedly not without interest, though, insofar as 'all that can be said is that there was no denial of the principle of a plea of necessity as such'.[307] Even if it was with a great deal of caution, the Commission seems to have considered that the 1960 Belgian intervention could be interpreted as an element consistent with the possible recognition of the state of necessity in the domain of the non-use of force. However, I feel such a conclusion is exaggerated to say the least, for two reasons.

First it should be noted that Belgium stopped well short of clearly invoking the state of necessity as a circumstance excluding the unlawfulness of its behaviour. Some aspects of the Belgian argument could certainly be interpreted in this way.[308] However, Belgium first of all preferred to invoke other arguments to justify its action, relying first on consent from the Congolese authorities,[309] which consent was supposedly granted pursuant to the treaty of friendship just entered into between the two countries.[310] Belgium insisted in this context on 'the complete absence of interference by

---

[301] Our translation; Telegram of 12 July 1960 in J Gerard-Libois and B Verhaegen, *Congo 1960*, tome II (Bruxelles, CRISP, 1961) 544.

[302] ibid, 545.

[303] SC Res 143 (1960) of 14 July 1960.

[304] R Higgins, *United Nations Peacekeeping 1946–1967*, Documents and Commentary, III, Africa (Oxford, Oxford University Press, 1980) and J Gerard-Libois, *Sécession au Katanga* (Bruxelles, CRISP/ Leopoldville, Institut National d'Etudes Politiques, 1963).

[305] *YILC* (1980) vol II, Part Two, 45, para 25.

[306] ibid.

[307] ibid.

[308] Prime Minister, 12 July 1960 in *Chronique de politique étrangère*, vol XIII, nn 4–6, July–October 1969, 'La crise congolaise' 663; see also J Gerard-Libois and B Verhaegen, *Congo 1960*, above n 301, 520 and S/PV.877, 20 July 1960, para 31; S/PV.873, 13 July 1960, para 196; S/PV.879, 21 July 1960, para 151.

[309] See: J Gerard-Libois and B Verhaegen, *Congo 1960*, tome I, above n 301, 446–47.

[310] S/PV.873, 13 July 1960, 34–35, paras 186–191.

the Belgian Government in the internal affairs of the Republic of the Congo'.[311] Belgium plainly thought that its use of force could not be criticised as it was not directed against the territorial integrity or political independence of Congo. Its action could not therefore be considered a violation of international law. In the terms of its Minister for Foreign Affairs, 'I do not have to invoke solemn legal arguments to justify my statement that we had a right to intervene when it was a question of protecting our compatriots, our women, against such excesses. We had the most imperative duty to do so'.[312] Therefore this is supposedly not a circumstance excluding unlawfulness but a genuine right and even a 'sacred duty to protect the lives and honour of our nationals'.[313] Consideration of all of the declarations by Belgian officials casts serious doubt on the resort to a circumstance excluding unlawfulness, whether a state of necessity or not. Plainly Belgium considered it was acting within its rights, rights deriving from a primary rule of international law and not from a circumstance excluding what was *a priori* an unlawful act. It seems very far-fetched at any rate, to interpret this precedent, as did the ILC in 1980,[314] as a genuine appeal to a state of necessity.[315]

Even more misleading still would be the trend to consider this precedent as the sign of a more general acceptance of the state of necessity as an argument liable to justify the use of force.

A first group of States considered this was a real act of aggression.[316] The Belgian action was, in this perspective, condemned on principle.[317] Of course, and this is logical since the argument is not clearly advanced by Belgium itself, the state of necessity is not explicitly excluded by States that criticise the operation. But it is incontestably excluded implicitly, no legal consideration being, in the eyes of these States, acceptable when it comes to conducting a military operation in the territory of a State without its consent.

A second group of States refused to characterise the Belgian action as unlawful, which led to a no vote on a draft amendment sponsored by the Soviet Union and evoking an 'act of aggression'.[318] However, it would be

---

[311] ibid, 35, para 193.

[312] S/PV.877, 20 July 1960, 18, para 91.

[313] ibid, 21–22, para 106. See also *Chronique de politique étrangère*, above n 308, 645 and 715.

[314] See also: *Report of the International Law Commission*, 53rd session, 23 April–1 June and 2 July–10 August 2001, GA, 56th session, Supp no 10 (A/56/10), 84, fn 406.

[315] According to J Raby, 'the Belgian government's statements were not precise, were confused and alluded more to self-standing right approach than to the concept of necessity; the term 'necessity' was used more in its ordinary meaning than as a legal concept'; 'The State of Necessity and the Use of Force to Protect Nationals', above n 5, 269.

[316] Tunisia, S/PV.873, 13 July 1960, para 79.

[317] See: USSR (ibid, para 103), Poland (ibid, para 151 and S/PV.878, 21 July 1960, paras 89–92), Tunisia (ibid, paras 23–24), Ecuador (S/PV.879, 21 July 1960, para 80).

[318] S/4386 and S/PV.873, 13/14 July 1960, para 223.

misleading to conclude that these States admit the state of necessity as a justification of the use of force. Some like the US, the UK and China, preferred to rely on arguments of political opportunity.[319] Others, like France, got into the legal debate but based the lawfulness of Belgium's behaviour on an interpretation of the primary rules, whether this interpretation was based on the consent of the Congo authorities or on the '*intervention d'humanité*'.[320] Only one State made a declaration that could be construed as a recognition of a state of necessity liable to justify the use of force.[321] This isolated stance could obviously not suffice to establish an *opinio juris* for the majority or even for a significant group of States.

On the whole, the Belgian intervention in the Congo in July 1960 did not give rise to the expression of a conviction that certain limited uses of force would be capable of justification by the state of necessity, even among those who thought that the factual circumstances legitimated the Belgian position. It does not seem appropriate therefore to present it as an exceptional or an atypical case in the practice of States relative to the use of force.

3. The Case of the Aerial Incident of 3 July 1988

On 3 July 1988, a US aircraft carrier moored in the Arabian-Persian Gulf, the *USS Vincennes*, launched a missile at a civil aircraft, an Iran Air Airbus that had just taken off.[322] The airliner was shot down and its 290 passengers and crew died in the incident.

Iran immediately referred the matter to the UN Secretary-General and accused the US of an 'act of aggression'.[323] Iran then brought the case to the ICJ on the basis of the Montreal and Chicago Conventions on civil aviation. It specified in its memorial that the US action was incompatible with the principle of the non-use of force and more specifically with article 2(4) of the UN Charter.[324] In its counter-memorial, the US replied that the incident had to be set in the context of a war situation and of military engagements between Iranian and US forces in the Gulf. Having previously been the target of several aggresive actions by Iran, the *USS Vincennes* believed, upon discovering an unidentified aircraft on one of its radars, that an attack on it was imminent:

Consequently, *and as a matter of necessity*, he responded by firing two missiles that downed the aircraft less than eight nautical miles from the US naval vessels . . . The aircraft was perceived as a military aircraft with hostile intentions . . . The

---

[319] USA (S/PV.873, 13 July 1960, para 95), UK (ibid, 25–26) and China (ibid, 29).
[320] S/PV.873, 13 July 1960, para 144.
[321] See: Argentina (S/PV. 879, 21 July 1960, paras 118 and 127).
[322] *Keesing's Contemporary Archives*, 1988, 36064. See also above, ch 2, s I.
[323] *Letter dated 3 July 1988 from the acting Permanent Representative of the Islamic Republic of Iran to the UN addressed to the Secretary-General*, S/19979, 4 July 1988.
[324] Memorial of the Islamic Republic of Iran, 24 July 1980, 193, para 3.81 and 238, para 4.46.

Commanding Officer of the USS Vincennes perceived that his ship was under the threat of an imminent attack. (emphasis added)[325]

As the US counter-memorial contains no other very precise legal argument, it might be thought, from the terms emphasised, that this is a precedent where limited military action was justified by a state of necessity.

An examination of the debates in the UN Security Council can clear up this misunderstanding. From 9 July 1988, the US claimed that its forces had 'In accordance with Article 51 of the Charter of the United Nations . . . exercised their inherent right of self-defence under international law by taking defensive action in response to an attack by the Islamic Republic of Iran'.[326] In the days that followed, States argued in the Security Council over the lawfulness of the US action, but always centred their arguments on self-defence and not on state of necessity or of state of distress.[327]

Upon scrutiny, this affair cannot really then be considered a precedent in which a circumstance excluding unlawfulness has been invoked to justify the use of force. On the contrary, it confirms that States do not envisage this possibility and seem to consider that the only possible legal argument in such a situation is that of self-defence.

4. Fisheries Jurisdiction (1995–1998)

We mentioned earlier this precedent of the *Estai*, a boat flying the Spanish flag, that was stopped and boarded some 245 nautical miles off the Canadian coast by Canadian authorities in the name of a national law prohibiting fishing of certain straddling stocks.[328] Spain took the matter to the ICJ, relying on various legal principles, including that of the peaceful settlement of disputes and the prohibition of the threat or use of armed force in international relations, enacted by article 2(4) of the UN Charter.[329] In its pleadings, Spain specified that it did not claim the Canadian action was an act of aggression, as in the definition appended to General Assembly resolution 3314 (XXIX). This action could, however, be considered a less serious use of force, but one nonetheless prohibited by the Charter.[330]

This case is cited as a precedent in which 'a plea of necessity was apparently in issue'.[331] Confronted with the depletion of certain fish stocks,

---

[325] Preliminary Objections submitted by the United States of America, 4 March 1991, 11 and 40, n 3.

[326] *Letter dated 6 July 1988 from the Acting Permanent Representative of the USA to the UN addressed to the President of the Security Council*, S/19989, 9 July 1989, 1.

[327] S/PV.2818, 14 July 1988; S/PV.2819, 15 July 1988; S/PV.2821, 20 July 1988.

[328] Above, ch 2, s I.

[329] Application instituting proceedings, 28 March 1995; see also Memorial of the Kingdom of Spain, September 1995, para 4.

[330] Dupuy, CR 98/13, 15 June 1998, para 22.

[331] *Report of the International Law Commission*, 53rd session, 23 April–1 June and 2 July–10 August 2001, GA, 56th session, Supp no 10 (A/56/10), 82, para 12.

Canada thought that its legislation should allow it 'to take urgent action necessary to prevent further destruction of those stocks and to permit their rebuilding'.[332] As for the boarding of the Estai, the Canadian authorities thought it was 'necessary in order to put a stop to the overfishing of Greenland halibut by Spanish fishermen'.[333] Perhaps it could then be thought—although the terms are not clear under strictly legal considerations—that a State invoked a state of necessity in the case in point to justify an action that did not constitute an aggression but that was to prove incompatible with article 2(4).

Such a conclusion, though, is difficult to defend if one takes the trouble to analyse the specific features of the Canadian argument more closely. As already pointed out in chapter two,[334] the submission and pleadings presented to the Court show very clearly that Canada never considered that the arrest of the Estai could be considered a use of force within the scope of article 2(4).[335] The Canadian position, then, cannot be interpreted as an attempt to justify a measure that is *a priori* incompatible with article 2(4) by invoking a state of necessity. At best, it could be thought that necessity here seeks to justify coercive measures that are hypothetically contrary to the rules of the international law of the sea prevailing in this instance. Besides, the Court plainly felt that this was the situation that prevailed, and consequently ruled it did not have jurisdiction because of a reservation in the Canadian declaration of acceptance of the Court's jurisdiction.[336]

Once again, the fact that the state of necessity was—although in such an uncertain way here—raised as justification for behaviour provides no support for the claim that this circumstance excluding unlawfulness could be applied in the area of the non-use of force. The value of this case is rather to draw attention to the distinction that should be drawn between certain extraterritorial executive competencies, applicable notably in the law of the sea, and a use of force in international relations that is prohibited by the UN Charter.[337] Plainly no State seems to claim that the state of necessity, that may, as need be, be invoked in the first case, could also be in the second.

5. Military Intervention in Yugoslavia (1999)

On 23 March 1999, several NATO Member States launched a military campaign against Yugoslavia in the context of the Kosovo crisis.[338] The Yugoslav Republic vigorously protested at what it characterised as an aggression

---

[332] ibid.

[333] ICJ Rep (1998) 443, para 20; see also Counter-Memorial of Canada, 29 February 1996, paras 17–35.

[334] Ch 2, s I.

[335] Kirsch, CR 98/11, 11 June 1998, para 45; see also Weil, CR 98/12, 12 June 1998, para 31.

[336] ICJ Rep (1998) 465–66, paras 78–84.

[337] Above, ch 2, s I.

[338] See below, chs 6 and 8.

incompatible with the most elementary principles of international law. On 29 April 1999, Yugoslavia brought the matter before the ICJ, serving notices on ten NATO Member States and applying for the Court to adopt measures to put an end to the war. Called upon to plead as a matter of urgency at this point, most of the defendant States settled to claim that the Court had not even *prima facie* jurisdiction. In his exposition, one of Belgium's counsel expressly invoked, subsidiarily, the state of necessity as a circumstance justifying the military operation conducted against Yugoslavia.[339] Can it be considered that we are this time confronted with a clear precedent where the state of necessity has been invoked to justify a use of force? At first sight, an affirmative answer is not in doubt. To be persuaded of this, one need only compare the terms of the Belgian pleadings with the vague and ambiguous wording found in other precedents set out above. Whatever the case, it would be misleading to deduce from the Kosovo war a precedent attesting to a general acceptance of this type of justification.

First, it should be noticed that the intervening States are far from having taken up the argument of necessity and, in legal terms, preferred to take another line of argument. As shall be set out later, it was essentially on the argument of authorisation deduced from several resolutions adopted earlier by the Security Council that these States—including Belgium itself—justified their action.[340] It is true that, subsequently, several of them asserted that the Kosovo war was an exceptional situation that could not be interpreted as a precedent calling into question the rule prohibiting the unilateral use of force apart from in instances of self-defence,[341] which could be construed as a form of reference to a circumstance excluding unlawfulness. However, such a conclusion would be excessive, especially insofar as it would suppose that, contrary to what was provided for in the ILC's work, the state of necessity might be justified by acts that were *a priori* contrary to a peremptory norm of international law. It is difficult to contest that, assuming it cannot be justified by the Charter, a war like that of 1999 could not be characterised as aggression. The debate, and this is the direction it was taken in not just by States as a whole but by scholarship on the subject, never bore on this point, but concentrated rather on questions such as the possibility of an authorisation that could be deduced from several Security Council resolutions, or again the emergence in international law of a genuine 'right of humanitarian intervention', a right supposedly deduced from an interpretation of the relevant primary rules.[342] In truth, no one picked

---

[339] Ergec, CR 99/15, 10 May 1999, 17–19. See also F Dubuisson, 'La problématique de la légalité de l'opération "Force alliée" contre la Yugoslavie: enjeux et questionnements' in O Corten and B Delcourt (eds), *Droit, légitimation et politique extérieure. L'Europe et la guerre du Kosovo* (Bruxelles, Bruylant, 2001) 170–73.

[340] Below, ch 6, s II.

[341] Below, ch 8, s II.

[342] Below, ch 8.

up on an argument presented stealthily and in urgency by counsel for Belgium.

Secondly, and in any event, it shall be recalled that this argument, that claimed in the case in point to cover an act that was denounced as a true aggression, is however far from having been accepted, with most States having expressed reservations about the lawfulness of this military operation.[343] If there is a precedent, it is against any legal argument that might justify a use of force.

Conclusion

It may well be that, under certain circumstances, a State cannot be held internationally responsible for an 'antiterrorist' military operation or a military action to rescue nationals. This question must, however, be resolved in view of the scope of the rule prohibiting the use of force and in view of its exceptions, whether of self-defence or of a possible UN Security Council authorisation. It is traditionally in this perspective that doctrinal debates have been, and still are, conducted. A minority doctrine, believing it can rely on the ILC's work, has defended the argument that limited military action that does not constitute aggression could, even should it prove incompatible with the UN Charter, be justified by a state of necessity or by countermeasures. Upon analysis, the Commission never really defended this argument. An interpretation of the Charter itself, as it was devised and then construed by several General Assembly resolutions, confirms that the prohibition of the use of force represents a legal regime from which there is no way out. Examination of practice with the UN confirms that States, including those that have conducted military interventions, never envisaged admitting this possibility. As a *jus cogens* rule, the prohibition of the use of force cannot be circumvented, whether by drafting derogatory treaty instruments or by reference to exceptional circumstances other than those envisaged in the primary rule.

It must be remembered, however, that all of the foregoing developments presuppose that we are in the domain of the use of force as regulated by the UN Charter. It may well be, besides, that some coercive acts may be performed by one State outside of its territory, without it being a question of invoking article 2(4), without it being possible to observe any use of force against the territorial integrity, political independence or any other purpose of the United Nations. Thus, the argument that necessity must be accommodated in the domain of the non-use of force because otherwise a State would be prevented from crossing a border to prevent a major fire from crossing it,[344] seems groundless to me. In such a situation, one might

---

[343] Below, ch 8.
[344] See: R Ago in *YILC* (1980) vol I, 1618th meeting, para 46.

seriously doubt whether one is within the scope of application of article 2(4) and that consequently an exclusion of the state of necessity might be deduced from the Charter.[345] In each individual case then, one should question the threshold above which one moves from a simple coercive operation to a real use of force in international relations, the threshold we studied in chapter two.[346]

---

[345] J Salmon, 'Les circonstances excluant l'illicéité' above n 144, 150.
[346] Above, ch 2, s I.

5
Intervention by Invitation

IT IS A FREQUENT occurrence in contemporary international relations for one State to consent to another conducting a military operation in its territory. The operation consented to may range in scope from a simple joint manoeuvres exercise to an all-out military action to repel an aggressor State. This latter case, which is a matter of collective self-defence, shall only be touched on in passing in this chapter, which covers rather the hypotheses where the military intervention consented to does not follow upon an armed attack by a third State. The question we shall ask will be whether, and if so on what conditions, consent can legally justify a military operation which would otherwise have to be considered contrary to article 2(4) of the UN Charter.[1]

Doctrine is comparatively underdeveloped on this topic with only a few books and studies dealing specifically with it.[2] However, all the commentators who have dealt with the question share one point in common: in principle, no one denies that validly given consent can make a military operation lawful.[3] The controversies relate rather to the conditions surrounding the validity of that consent, particularly when we are dealing with civil war or more generally with internal strife. Before addressing this particularly intricate situation (section two) we shall concentrate on the general legal regime of intervention to which consent has been given (section one).

---

[1] See above, ch 2, s I.

[2] See: L Doswald-Beck, 'The Legal Validity of Military Intervention by Invitation of the Government' (1985) 56 *BYBIL*; T Christakis and K Bannelier, '*Volenti non fit injuria?* Les effets du consentement à l'intervention militaire' (2004) 50 *AFDI*; CJ Le Mon, 'Unilateral Intervention by Invitation in Civil Wars: the Effective Control Test Tested' (2003) 35 *International Law and Politics*; M Bennouna, *Le consentement à l'ingérence militaire dans les conflits internes* (Paris, LGDJ, 1974); A Tanca, *Foreign Armed Intervention in Internal Conflict* (Dordrecht, Martinus Nijhoff, 1993); and G Nolte, *Eingreifen auf Einladung* (Berlin/New York, Springer, 1999). See also J Charpentier, 'Les effets du consentement sur l'intervention' in *Mélanges Séfériadès*, vol II (Athènes, Aohnai, 1961) 489–99.

[3] See: R Jennings and A Watts (eds), *Oppenheim's International Law*, 9th edn, vol 1 Peace, (London, Longman, 1996) 435 and L Doswald-Beck, 'The Legal Validity of Military Intervention by Invitation of the Government', above n 2, 189.

I The General Legal Regime of Military Intervention by Invitation

As just emphasised, no one contests that, in principle, consent may justify a military operation by one State in another State's territory.[4] A first clarification to be made on this matter, though, concerns the bounds of peremptory law (*jus cogens*) (A). Within these bounds, it is generally admitted that consent is validly given if it comes from the central authorities of the State in whose territory the operation takes place (B), and if furthermore the consent fulfils several specific conditions, since it must be 'clearly established', 'really expressed', 'anterior to the commmission of the act to which it refers' and 'relevant'. Each of these conditions requires some clarification (C).

A. The Possibility of Consenting to Armed Intervention within the Limits of Peremptory Law (Jus Cogens)

During its work on State responsibility, the International Law Commission envisaged a State's consent as a circumstance precluding wrongfulness, citing by way of example cases of military interventions that had been consented to.[5] By applying this logic to article 2(4) of the Charter, it could be asserted *a priori* that, since this provision is a matter of peremptory law,[6] any violation of it regards not only the State that is materially injured but also the international community of States as a whole. It should therefore be concluded that it is legally impossible for a State to consent to any breach of this norm, even to its detriment. Consent—no more than any other circumstance like necessity, distress or countermeasures—can *never* preclude the wrongfulness of a violation of the prohibition of the use of force.[7]

Closer scrutiny of the relevant texts and practice leads us to a more nuanced conclusion. Although certain limits arise from the existence in international law of norms of *jus cogens* (2), the fact remains that consent may indeed, as a matter of principle, justify a military operation conducted by one State in another State's territory (1).

---

[4] In its Res 387 (1976), the SC recalls 'the inherent and lawful right of every State, in the exercice of its sovereignty, to request assistance from any other State or group of States'.

[5] R Ago, *Eight report on State responsibility*, (1979) *YILC*, vol II (Part One) para 57; (1979) *YILC*, vol II (Part Two), para 21.

[6] See above, ch 4, s I.

[7] See above, ch 4, s II.

The Possibility as a Matter of Principle of Consenting to Military Intervention: the (Conditional) Validity of ad hoc Consent

Some commentators,[8] relying on the ILC's work, have claimed that consent can only justify certain specific small-scale military operations, but not just very limited military actions that could not be characterised as a 'use of force' within the meaning of the provision, such as a simple arrest made in foreign territory, or other coercive measures of extraterritorial scope of the kind.[9] One might classify in this category uses of force falling within the scope of application of article 2(4) of the Charter that are not serious enough to be characterised as aggression. Indeed, according to this branch of scholarship, only the prohibition of aggression—and not that of any use of force, even of a less serious character—can be characterised as a rule of peremptory law.[10] Consequently, a military operation akin to aggression could by no means be justified by the consent of the State in whose territory it occurred, as such consent could only cover some less serious military operation.

While it does have a degree of internal consistency going for it, such reasoning cannot to my mind be accepted for several reasons.

—First and as shown above, States made no distinction according to the gravity of the use of force when they affirmed, on several occasions and in various contexts, that article 2(4) as a whole could be characterised as a *jus cogens* norm.[11] This distinction based on gravity appears to be entirely doctrinal; it is at any rate radically contradicted by the position of States. So no distinction can be relied on when appraising the validity of consent given to a military operation.

—Secondly, the definition of aggression adopted by the General Assembly in 1974 clearly shows that consent may indeed justify a military operation which, without that consent, could be characterised as aggression.[12] Its article 3*(e)* defines as such 'the use of armed forces of one State which are within the territory of another State with the agreement of the receiving State, in contravention of the conditions provided for in the agreement or any extension of their presence in such territory beyond the

---

[8] N Ronzitti, 'Use of Force, *Jus Cogens* and State Consent' in A Cassese (ed), *The Current Legal Regulation of the Use of Force* (Dordrecht, Martinus Nijhoff, 1986) 159; T Christakis, 'Unilatéralisme et multilatéralisme dans la lutte contre la terreur: l'exemple du terrorisme biologique et chimique' in K Bannelier *et al* (eds), *Le droit international face au terrorisme*, (Paris, Pedone, 2002) 173; O Corten and P Klein, *Droit d'ingérence ou obligation de réaction*, 2nd edn (Bruxelles, Bruylant, 1996), 205–11.

[9] See above, ch 2, s I.

[10] See the authors quoted above, ch 4, s I.

[11] See above, ch 4, s I.

[12] C Gray, *International Law and the Use of Force*, 3rd edn (Oxford, Oxford University Press, 2008) 85; L Doswald-Beck, 'The Legal Validity of Military Intervention by Invitation of the Government', above n 2, 189; CJ Le Mon, 'Unilateral Intervention by Invitation in Civil Wars: the Effective Control Test Tested', above n 2, 753–54.

termination of the agreement'. By application of this provision, an act shall or shall not be characterised as aggression—and not as a simple use of force—depending on whether or not consent is forthcoming. Consent therefore seems able to justify *any* military operation, without any limitation in principle.

—Thirdly, close reading of the works of the International Law Commission shows that it never intended to exclude the possibility of a State consenting to another State conducting a military operation, even a large-scale one, in its territory. From the outset, the ILC cites as an example of intervention by invitation the entry of foreign troops into the territory of a State that is 'normally considered as a serious violation of a State's sovereigny, and often even as an act of aggression'.[13] The ILC considers that, in this event 'no State contested the validity *per se* of the principle that consent given by the territorial State excluded, as a general rule, the wrongfulness of sending foreign troops into its territory'.[14]

In other words, and we shall confirm this when further examining the practice of intervention by invitation, consideration of the position adopted by States does not dictate that any distinction be made in terms of the intervention being characterised as aggression, even if that does not mean that consent can cover any military intervention, especially when what is in question is the right of peoples to self-determination—another norm that is generally considered to be a matter of *jus cogens*.[15]

A question arises at this stage: how can one reconcile the theoretically peremptory character of the prohibition of the use of force and the possibility, observed in practice, of derogating from it by consent?[16] This question did not escape Professor James Crawford who, as the ILC's new Special Rapporteur, sought to answer it by purely and simply deleting consent from the list of circumstances excluding wrongfulness. He argued that consent acts in fact as a constituent part of the primary rule and not as a secondary rule of State responsibility. In cases like those of the principle of non-intervention and of the non-use of force between States, validly given consent has as its effect that the rule, whether or not it is considered as one of peremptory law, quite simply cannot have been violated. According to the Special Rapporteur, 'Some peremptory norms contain an "intrinsic" consent element. For example, the rule relating to the non-use of force in international relations embodied in Article 2, paragraph 4, of the Charter of the United Nations does not apply in certain cases where one State has

---

[13] (1979) *YILC*, vol II (Part Two) 110, para 5.

[14] ibid, para 6. See, eg, the views expressed by the Netherlands; A/C.6/54/SR.21, 2 November 1999, para 45.

[15] See below, s II.

[16] According to art 26 of the project: 'Nothing in this chapter precludes the wrongfulness of any act of a State which is not in conformity with an obligation arising under a peremptory norm of general international law'.

consented to the use of force on its territory by another State. But one State cannot by consent *eliminate* the rule relating to the use of force in international relations in its relations with another State. Thus it may be necessary to distinguish between a consent which applies Article 2 (4), which may be valid, and a purported consent which displaces or excludes it entirely, which, if Article 2 (4) is peremptory in character, would be invalid'.[17] It logically follows, then, that it is impossible to evoke a circumstance excluding 'wrongfulness', as no wrongfulness can have been observed, even *a priori*.[18] In its final draft, the ILC chose not to delete consent as a circumstance excluding unlawfulness while recognising the possibility in principle of consenting to a use of force.[19] This somewhat paradoxical attitude can be explained by a concern for pragmatism. To set consent aside would have been to relinquish defining it and laying down strict conditions on its validity, which, for some commentators, would have opened the gates to certain abuses in State practice.[20] Crawford's assertion that consent might, as in article 2(4) of the Charter, sometimes constitute an intrinsic element of the primary rule, has not been called into question, quite the contrary. For example, according to the UK, 'in the case of consent validly given, there is no violation of international law, and therefore no question of wrongfulness should arise'.[21] Besides, the majority of doctrine has come down on this side.[22]

Finally, it may be thought that if a State validly consents to another State using armed force on its own territory it does indeed seem we are not in the presence of a use of force by one State against another.[23] Consent acts neither as a circumstance precluding wrongfulness, nor as an exception to

---

[17] J Crawford, *Second report on State responsibility*, 30 April 1999, A/CN.4/498/Add.2, 12–13, para 240(b).

[18] See: T Christakis and K Bannelier, '*Volenti non fit injuria?* Les effets du consentement à l'intervention militaire', above n 2, 107–08.

[19] According to art 20 of the text adopted by the Commission and annexed to GA Res 56/83 of 12 December 2001, 'Valid consent by a State to the commission of a given act by another State precludes the wrongfulness of that act in relation to the former State to the extent that the act remains within the limits of that consent'.

[20] See the views expressed by Kateka (15 June 1999, 2587th session, (1999) *YILC*, vol I, para 57) and Kamto (ibid, para 61). See also the views expressed by Spain (A/C.6/54/SR.21, 29 October 1999, para 18), Austria (A/C.6/54/SR.22, 1 November 1999, para 12), Slovakia (ibid, para 52), Germany (A/C.6/54/SR.23, 2 November 1999, para 4), Mexico (ibid, para 16), Italy (A/C.6/54/SR.24, 2 November 1999, para 24), Tunisia (A/C.6/54/SR.25, 3 November 1999, para 28).

[21] (A/CN.4/488, 25 March 1998). See also Simma (16 June 1999, 2588th session, (1999) *YILC*, vol I, para 13).

[22] T Christakis, 'Les "circonstances excluant l'illicéité": une illusion optique?' in *Droit du pouvoir, pouvoir du droit. Mélanges offerts à Jean Salmon* (Bruxelles, Bruylant, 2007) 244–51; T Christakis and K Bannelier, '*Volenti non fit injuria?* Les effets du consentement à l'intervention militaire', above n 2, 111; A Tanca, *Foreign Armed Intervention in Internal Conflict*, above n 2, 47.

[23] T Christakis and K Bannelier, '*Volenti non fit injuria?* Les effets du consentement à l'intervention militaire', above n 2, 112; see also above ch 2, s I.

the rule; its effect is rather to preclude concluding that there has been a violation of the rule as such or even that it is applicable.[24] It is in this context that we can specify what the limits are that arise from the allowance for the peremptory character of the prohibition of the use of force.

The Limits Resulting from the Peremptory Character of the Prohibition of the Use of Force: Invalidity of Treaty-Based Consent to a General Right of Military Intervention

When evoking the case of 'intervention by invitation', it should be recalled that consent can take on two forms, one based on treaty, the other non-treaty based or *ad hoc*. In the latter case, we have just seen that no use of force within the meaning of article 2(4) could be observed, which eliminates any problem arising from the peremptory status of the rule. There remains, then, the case of treaty-based consent. It will first be recalled on this subject that, if a State consents to its territory being used by another to attack a third State, that specific agreement is obviously contrary to the *jus cogens* norm of article 2(4). In such a case, we are indeed in the presence of an agreement providing for the use of force against the political independence of a third State. A more intricate matter is the hypothesis of a treaty by which one State consents to the forces of other States entering part of its own territory. In such a situation, it may be asked whether—and to what extent—the treaty concluded is a valid treaty despite the peremptory character of the prohibition of the use of force.

To answer this question, we shall dismiss a radical position straight away.[25] From this standpoint, characterised as the 'freedom to contract model' by some scholars,[26] it is by application of its sovereign rights that each State is supposedly able to conclude a treaty allowing foreign military forces to enter its territory, with no other limit than that laid down by each relevant treaty.[27] From this perspective, consent—given by treaty in the case in point—has the effect of excluding the very idea of the use of force against a State, and so the applicability of article 2(4).[28] In the same way as for *ad hoc* consent, no problem, it is argued, can be deduced from the peremptory character of this provision. However, it seems to me highly artificial to exclude the characterisation of 'force' if, hypothetically, one State

---

[24] See also: G Nolte, *Eingreifen auf Einladung*, above n 2, ch 4, abstract in English, 631.

[25] See also: M Byers and S Chesterman, '"You, the People": pro-democratic intervention in international law' in GH Fox and BR Roth (eds), *Democratic Governance and International Law* (Cambridge, Cambridge University Press, 2000) 312–13.

[26] D Wippman, 'Treaty-Based Intervention: Who Can Say No?' (1995) 62 *University of Chicago Law Review* 616; 'Pro-democratic intervention by invitation' in G Fox and B Roth (eds), *Democratic Governance and International Law* (Cambridge, CUAT, 2000) 312–13.

[27] See: *Wimbledon*, PCIJ, Series A, No 1, 25.

[28] See, eg: A Abass, 'Consent Precluding State Responsibility: A Critical Analysis' (2004) 53 *ICLQ* 223–25.

sends its army into the territory of another against the latter's wishes and if
the armies of the two States engage in fierce fighting. In the absence of any
ad hoc consent, there is cause for evoking the use of 'force' against a State,
even if, as a hypothesis, a treaty concluded beforehand authorised the
contested armed action.

It is therefore by the yardstick not of a position of principle but of the
examination of treaty practice, and also of the allowance for the subject and
the purpose of the peremptory prohibition of the use of force, that this
intricate problem must be settled. The very objective of the rule is to prevent one State from using force against another, with all the risks that this
entails for maintaining international peace and security; it is not to prevent
cooperation in criminal law, police or military matters among States that
may have taken on binding treaty obligations. It is by bearing in mind this
general principle that we can take into account treaty practice (a) and the
few precedents when a problem of this type has arisen (b).

a) The Lessons of Treaty-Based Practice

In the domain of treaties, we can distinguish five situations authorising
armed actions in the territory of a State. As shall be observed, the first four
hypotheses raise no legal problems, unlike the fifth.

A first hypothesis, and the most common in practice, is where one State
accepts the simple stationing of troops in its territory or the simple transit
of another State's troops. In such a case, no problem relating to the peremptory character of the prohibition of the use of force ever seems to
have arisen. Consent here pertains not to a military action but to the
simple presence of foreign troops. It is difficult, under these conditions, to
evoke a use of 'force', unless, of course, the troops whose presence was
accepted intervene in violation of the terms of the treaty concluded. If the
treaty is observed, however, the foreign troops are entitled to station in
foreign territory, even against a possible refusal that the State concerned
might suddenly express at the time of events.

Another category is that of certain treaties by which a State accepts that
another State may conduct a military operation in its territory to maintain
order (military cooperation treaties)[29] or in the context of a peace-keeping
operation. This type of military action shall be analysed in detail below. It
shall just be pointed out at this stage that, by the terms of this type of treaty,
the relevant government gives *ad hoc* consent in such cases by calling on the
State party to the treaty to intervene.[30] The intervening State does not
therefore resort to force against a third State; accordingly, no problem of

---

[29] See, eg: J Basso and J Nechifor, 'Les accords militaires entre la France et l'Afrique sub-
saharienne' in L Balmond (ed), *Les interventions militaires françaises en Afrique* (Paris, Pedone,
1998) 41–67.
[30] See examples in C Pourre, *Les interventions extérieures de l'armée française*, Ph D of
Université de Paris Nord, duplicated nn, 1998, 475 *ff*.

compatibility of the prohibition of the use of force within the meaning of article 2(4) arises.

A third hypothesis is where a State accepts that the agents of another State enter its territory in exercising a 'right of pursuit' delimited by a treaty. As pointed out in chapter two, there are many such treaties that are a matter of police cooperation and not of the use of force within the meaning of article 2(4).[31] What, though, of treaties by which a State accepts that the army of another enter its territory to repress rebel movements that have taken refuge there? Such treaties are difficult to consult, insofar as they are not generally recorded and published with the United Nations.[32] They seem, though, to require a form of *ad hoc* consent that the State must express at the time of the military action, whether the consent is expressed affirmatively (generally further to consultation at the time the action is envisaged) or negatively (by the absence of protest, and probably of denunciation of the relevant treaty at the time of the military action).[33] In such cases, all the indications are that this is the case of military cooperation and not a use of force of one State against another. As shall be detailed below, such cooperation may be understood as the performance of the due diligence principle by which States undertake that their territories should not be used by irregular groups to attack the territories of third States.[34]

Another situation is that where States accept by treaty that an international organisation intervenes, including by military force, in their territory, where need be against the will of their government. It is in this sense that the UN Charter itself can be construed, and in particular its Chapter VII giving the Security Council competence to decide on military action against a Member State. It goes without saying that we are *in the context* here of the rule prohibiting the use of force and not that of any derogation from that rule. The question is more delicate if it pertains to certain regional treaties by which organisations have been recognised as competent to conduct military actions in the territories of their Member States. The problem must not be asked, though, in terms of derogation but rather of interpretation of Chapter VIII of the Charter that accepts in principle the action of regional organisations under the aegis of the Security Council.[35] As already reported, regional security treaties purport to comply with the UN Charter.[36]

Lastly, a fifth and problematic hypothesis must be mentioned; that of a genuine unilateral right of military intervention that a State has recognised

---

[31] See above, ch 2, s I.

[32] See untreaty.un.org.

[33] See examples in C Rousseau, 'Chronique des faits internationaux' (1971) 75 *RGDIP* 219; (1977) 81 *RGDIP* 1182, (1985) 89 *RGDIP* 455, (1987) 91 *RGDIP* 139. See also *Keesing's Contemporary Archives*, 1985, 33497–98 and 'La pratique belge en matière de droit international' (1986) 19 *RBDI* 494.

[34] Below, s II.

[35] Below, ch 6, s I.

[36] Above, ch 4, s I.

to another by treaty. Such treaties were commonplace in the nineteenth century but seem to have progressively disappeared at the same time as the rule stated in article 2(4) was emerging.[37] At any rate I know of no treaty of this type concluded after 1945[38]; this is perfectly understandable in view of the peremptory character of the rule, which precisely precludes admitting that one or more—or even all—States authorise a powerful State to intervene whenever it likes, which appears to be clearly derogatory to the requirements laid down by the UN Charter that reserves such competence to the Security Council.[39]

b) The Lessons of Precedents After 1945

An examination of precedents during which this problem has been addressed confirms that States do not invoke treaties as a legal basis for justifying military intervention conducted against the will of another State expressed at the time of the intervention. If a treaty-basis is sometimes invoked, it is never with a view to setting aside the legal regime instituted by the Charter, as the following few examples attest.

—We shall analyse later the Soviet military interventions in Hungary (1956), Czechoslovakia (1968) and Afghanistan (1979).[40] We shall observe that the USSR invoked the Warsaw Pact (Hungary then Czechoslovakia) or a bilateral treaty (Afghanistan) but to justify the simple *presence* of its troops in the territories in question. *Military action* by those troops was, however, justified by *ad hoc* consent supposedly granted in each instance by the government in power at the time of the events, with a view to riposting to what was otherwise considered to be outside interference.[41] In the case of Afghanistan, it should be pointed out that, while the argument of intervention consented to by treaty was not invoked by the USSR, it was anyway ruled out by the United States in the name of *jus cogens*:

> Nor is it clear that the treaty between the USSR and Afghanistan . . . is valid. If it actually does lend itself to support of Soviet intervention of the type in question in Afghanistan, it would be void under contemporary principles of international law, since it would be in conflict with what the Vienna Convention on the Law of Treaties describes as a 'peremptory norm of general international law' (Article 53), namely, that contained in Article 2, paragraph 4 of the Charter.[42]

---

[37] See examples in N Ronzitti, 'Use of Force, *Jus Cogens* and State Consent', above n 8, 157–59 and I Brownlie, *International Law and the Use of Force by States* (Oxford, Clarendon Press, 1963), 318–20.

[38] See: D Vignes, 'La place des pactes de défense dans la société internationale actuelle' (1959) 5 *AFDI*, 64–65.

[39] Against: D Wippman, 'Treaty-Based Intervention: Who Can Say No?' above n 26, 654.

[40] Below.

[41] See: J Charpentier, 'Les effets du consentement sur l'intervention', above n 2, 494, fn 10.

[42] Secretary of State Warren Christopher, Memorandum dated 29 December 1979, 'Contemporary Practice of the United States' (1980) 74 *AJIL* 419.

—We have already considered the case of the Treaty of Guarantee for the Republic of Cyprus to observe that even Turkey did not claim to be able to rely on such an instrument to benefit from a general right of intervention.[43]

—Likewise, while the US invoked the Panama Canal Treaty to justify its military intervention in that country in December 1989, it did so by combining the argument with one of self-defence within the meaning of article 51 of the Charter.[44] In any event, the General Assembly characterised that intervention as contrary to article 2(4) and by a very large majority, demanding observance of 'the letter and spirit of the Torrijos-Carter Treaties',[45] an expression that seems resolutely to rule out any possible argument based on that treaty to justify the use of force. It was observed that, according to the position the US itself advanced at the time of ratification, that treaty could not be construed as opening up to it a right to intervene in Panama's affairs.[46]

It is probably on the basis of such elements that Professor Crawford, as the ILC Special Rapporteur on State responsibility, was able to affirm without being contradicted that he 'did not think, however, that a State was entitled to waive its right to withdraw its consent to the use of force in its territory by another State'.[47] Professor Giorgio Gaja, ILC Special Rapporteur on the responsibility of international organisations, likewise affirmed:

> While a State may validly consent to a specific intervention by another State, a general consent given to another State that would allow the latter State to intervene militarily on its own initiative would have to be taken as inconsistent with the peremptory norm.[48]

---

[43] Above, ch 4, s I. See also M Byers and S Chesterman, ' "You, the People": pro-democratic intervention in international law', above n 25, 316–18.

[44] See the declarations of the President of the US in VP Nanda, 'The Validity of United States Intervention in Panama under International Law' (1990) 84 *AJIL* 494 *ff* and 'Contemporary Practice of the United States', ibid, 545–49. See also the text of the treaty in 'Contemporary Practice of the United States' (1978) 72 *AJIL* 225–41. See also 'United Kingdom Materials on International Law' (1989) 70 *BYBIL* 692–94; see also (1990) 71 *BYBIL* 632; (1993) 74 *BYBIL* 741. See also S Chesterman, *Just War or Just Peace? Humanitarian Intervention and International Law* (Oxford, Oxford University Press, 2001) 104; A Tanca, *Foreign Armed Intervention in Internal Conflict*, above n 2, 184.

[45] GA Res 44/240, 29 December 1989, para 3; see also 'Pratique française du droit international' (1990) 36 *AFDI* 1055.

[46] VP Nanda, 'The Validity of United States Intervention in Panama under International Law', above n 44, 501.

[47] 16 June 1999, 2588th meeting (1999) *YILC*, vol I, para 40. See also T Christakis and K Bannelier, '*Volenti non fit injuria?* Les effets du consentement à l'intervention militaire', above n 2, 135; Wilhelm Wengler, 'L'interdiction de recourir à la force. Problèmes et tendances' (1971) 7 *RBDI* 441–44.

[48] *Fourth report on responsibility of international organizations*, 28 February 2006, A/CN.4/564, para 48, fn omitted.

These assertions must be properly understood. If consent relates to the mere presence or mere passage of troops, without them conducting any military action, a treaty is perfectly adequate, even if it can be withdrawn so long as the procedures specific to treaty law are observed. If, however, such consent relates to a genuine use of force, it is hard to imagine one can circumvent the requirement for *ad hoc* consent, as only such consent can exclude the characterisation of force and at the same time set aside the principle of observance of the peremptory prohibition stated in article 2(4).

Finally, if a State cannot consent generally and abstractly to another State intervening militarily in its territory via a treaty, there is nothing to prevent it in principle, in any particular instance, from consenting to a military operation conducted by a foreign State.[49] As pointed out, the use of force is not, on this assumption, conducted by a State against the political independence of another State, although it must be asked whether, in certain situations, outside military intervention does not have the effect of keeping a government in place against the will of its people. The political independence of the State would then seem to be in question, as would be its people's right to self-determination. This situation presupposes, however, that we are dealing with an internal conflict, with the government in place being confronted with an organised political opposition challenging its power. This point shall be dealt with below.[50] At this stage, we shall simply affirm that it is possible in principle to consent to a foreign military operation on a case by case basis, provided, however, that such consent is 'validly issued', which leads us to make several clarifications relating first to the author of that consent (B) and then to its intrinsic qualities (C).

B. The Requirement for Consent of the State's Highest Authorities

As emphasised by the Special Rapporteur James Crawford, the question of consent must be treated differently depending on each rule involved.[51] In the case of a military operation, no one contests that only the highest authorities of the State are able to issue such consent validly.[52] It is only on this condition that it can be claimed that a use of force is not directed against the State's independence and so does not violate article 2(4). *A*

---

[49] See: *Planning Staff of the Foreign and Commonwealth Office*, 'Is Intervention ever justified?', 'United Kingdom Materials on International Law' (1986) 57 *BYBIL* 616.

[50] Below, s II.

[51] 'It is one thing to consent to a search of embassy premises, another to the trial of an extraditee on a charge other than that on which the person was extradited and yet another to the establishment of a military base on the territory of a State, or to the conduct of military operations against rebels located on that territory'; *Second report on State responsibility*, 30 April 1999, above n 17, para 235.

[52] A Tanca states that 'the central question becomes whether the government or authority granting the consent of a State to foreign intervention is, at that moment, legally entitled to do so'; *Foreign Armed Intervention in Internal Conflict*, above n 2, 22–23; see also G Nolte, *Eingreifen auf Einladung*, above n 2, 638.

contrario, possible 'consent' from groups opposed to established authority
(1) or from subaltern authorities (2) can never justify a military operation
conducted by a third State.

The Impossibility of Justifying a Use of Force on an Appeal
from the Opposition

We have already cited excerpts from several General Assembly resolutions
emphasising the unlawfulness of military support to an opposition movement, particularly, although not exclusively, in civil war situations.[53] Such
an affirmation, though, has never been made about support for the government in place, support which therefore seems to be admitted in principle.[54]
This distinction was taken up by the ICJ in the case of *Military Activities*
when it affirmed that:

> [I]t is difficult to see what would remain of the principle of non-intervention in
> international law if intervention, which is already allowable at the request of the
> government of a State, were also to be allowed at the request of the opposition.
> This would permit any State to intervene at any moment in the internal affairs
> of another State, whether at the request of the government or at the request of its
> opposition. Such a situation does not in the Court's view correspond to the pre-
> sent state of international law.[55]

This *dictum* was implemented by the Court in the *Armed Activities* case,
with unlawful use of force by Uganda being established from its support for
irregular Congo forces.[56] Contemporary case law thus contradicts the old
doctrine that recognition of belligerence conferred the right on third States
to help either the government forces or the rebel forces.[57] This doctrine,
which has not been applied in practice since the UN Charter was adopted,[58]
is in contradiction with the many texts that not only make no reference to
it but again very clearly state, and without exception, the prohibition on providing military aid to any 'irregular force'.[59]

I know of no precedent where one State has claimed to justify legally its
intervention in another State's territory on the strength of a call by the

---

[53] Above, ch 3, s I.

[54] T Christakis and K Bannelier, '*Volenti non fit injuria?* Les effets du consentement à
l'intervention militaire', above n 2, 115.

[55] ICJ Rep (1986), para 246.

[56] ICJ Rep (2005), paras 162–65 and 345, 1.

[57] CJ Le Mon, 'Unilateral Intervention by Invitation in Civil Wars: the Effective Control
Test Tested', above n 2, 750. See also Independent International Fact-Finding Mission on the
Conflict in Georgia, *Report*, September 2009 (www.ceiig.ch/Report.html), vol II, 279–80.

[58] See: D Schindler, 'Le principe de non-intervention dans les guerres civiles' (1973) 55
AIDI 441–42; M Bennouna, *Le consentement à l'ingérence militaire dans les conflits internes*, above
n 2, 24; CJ Le Mon, 'Unilateral Intervention by Invitation in Civil Wars: the Effective Control
Test Tested', above n 2, 748 *ff* and C Rousseau (1970) 74 *RGDIP* 499.

[59] GA Res 2625 (XXV) and other texts quoted above, ch 3, s I.

opposition alone.[60] It is true that, to justify their 1975 military intervention in East Timor, then under Portuguese administration, the Indonesian authorities claimed that

> various groups of East Timor had asked the Indonesian Government to assist the Timorese people against the terror of a small organization which had usurped political power and declared an independent republic; Indonesia's military presence was required to prevent Timor from sliding into factional bloodshed and anarchy and to restore public order.[61]

It would be overstating things to deduce any new development in international law from this precedent. First because Indonesia seems here to be working on the assumption of a power vacuum where there is no longer any real government in place, which would allow it to rely on an appeal from certain 'sections of the population'[62]—a specific hypothesis that shall be examined below, but which it shall be pointed out at this stage does not correspond exactly to the situation of an appeal by the 'opposition', that term presupposing there is a government in place. Then, and in any event, it shall be noticed that Indonesia's argument is far from having been accepted by the international community of States as a whole, as attested by the resolutions adopted on this subject by the Security Council.[63]

The invasion of Kuwait by Iraq in August 1990 is another relevant precedent. In legal terms, the Iraqi authorities did initially invoke an appeal by certain Kuwaiti authorities.[64] However, it is worth reporting that those authorities were presented as representing a new government that allegedly took power in Kuwait, as attested by this declaration from Iraq's representative on the Security Council, the day after the invasion:

> [T]he Free Provisional Government of Kuwait requested my Government to assist it to establish security and order so that the Kuwaitis would not have to suffer . . . it is the Kuwaitis themselves who in the final analysis will determine their future. The Iraqi forces will withdraw as soon as order has been restored. This was the request made by the Free Provisional Government of Kuwait . . . there are reports that the previous Kuwaiti Government has been overthrown and that there is now a new Government.[65]

---

[60] See: 'Pratique française du droit international' (1979) 25 *AFDI* 908–10 and C Gray, *International Law and the Use of Force*, 3rd edn, above n 12, 105.

[61] *Repertory of Practice of United Nations Organs*, Supp no 5 (1970–1978), vol 1, Article 2 (4) (Separate Study), para 78.

[62] See, eg: AM Weisburd, *Use of Force. The Practice of States Since World War II* (Pennsylvania, The Pennsylvania State University Press, 1997) 247–51.

[63] SC Res 384 (1975) of 22 December 1975, paras 1 and 2 and 389 (1976) of 22 April 1976, paras 1 and 2.

[64] According to AM Weisburd, 'This argument was soon abandoned because of the survival of the Emir of Kuwait and the strong negative reactions to the invasions both from Kuwaitis and from the international community'; *Use of Force. The Practice of States Since World War II*, above n 62, 56.

[65] S/PV.2932, 2 August 1990, 11.

Despite the obvious frailty of the argument in factual terms, the Iraqi authorities therefore preferred to claim they were acting with the consent of governmental forces rather than merely upon an appeal from opposition forces. In any event, the argument convinced no one, with the invasion of Kuwait having been denounced immediately and then having led to unarmed and then armed coercive measures against Iraq.[66]

It will also be noticed that while the consent of opposition forces is never enough to justify an intervention, it is not legally necessary either. In other words, it is quite possible that an intervention against the will of the opposition could nonetheless be consistent with international law, even if, as shall be seen, this will not necessarily be the case in respect of a people's right to self-determination.[67] In any event, one cannot posit a rule that, to be lawful, armed action must have been accepted both by government and by opposition forces[68]—a conclusion that remains valid for 'peacekeeping operations' implemented by the UN even if, for reasons of opportunity relating to the limited means of action of UN forces, the consent of all parties concerned has often been sought.[69] Neither the relevant legal texts,[70] nor practice—as shown by the precedent of the ONUC in the 1960s[71]— can challenge this principle.

In short, to be consistent with international law, an intervention must have been conducted at the 'request of a government', to use the terms of the International Court of Justice in *Military and Paramilitary Activities*.[72] That said, it should still be specified what is meant by 'government', with several problems arising in this respect.

The Impossibility of Justifying a Use of Force by an Appeal to Subaltern Authorities

When authorities take such an important decision as consenting to a foreign military operation, they do so in the name of the State in whose territory the

---

[66] See: SC Res 660 (1990) of 2 August 1990; see also the views expressed by France ('Pratique française du droit international' (1990) 36 *AFDI* 1041–42), United Kingdom ('United Kingdom Materials on International Law' (1990) 61 *BYBIL* 486–91; (1991) 62 *BYBIL* 552–53), Canada ('Canadian Practice in International Law' (1991) 29 *CYIL* 478–79) or Switzerland ('La pratique suisse en matière de droit international public' (1990) *RSDIE* 561–62).

[67] Below, s II.

[68] Against: D Wippman, 'Treaty-Based Intervention: Who Can Say No?' above n 26, 624 *ff*.

[69] O Paye, 'Les opérations de maintien de la paix et les nouveaux désordres locaux' in A Daems *et al*, (eds), *A la recherche du nouvel ordre mondial*, tome II, 'l'ONU: mutations et défis' (Bruxelles, Complexe, 1993) 97–104; T Christakis and K Bannelier, '*Volenti non fit injuria?* Les effets du consentement à l'intervention militaire', above n 2, 118. See also GA, 19th session, plenary, 1289th meeting, 3 December 1964, 3, quoted by MM Whiteman, *Digest of International Law*, vol 13 (Washington, Department of State Publications, 1968) 593.

[70] See, eg: GA Res 49/57, 17 February 1995, para 9.

[71] See below, s II.

[72] *Military and Paramilitary Activities in and against Nicaragua*, ICJ Rep (1986), para 246.

operation is contemplated. It is entirely logical, then, that those authorities should be the highest in the State and not (a) local authorities, (b) dissident authorities or (c) diplomatic authorities. This is confirmed by well-established practice, with attempts to refer to these types of authority never having been admitted by the international community of States as a whole.

a) The Inadequacy of an Appeal from Local Authorities

To justify its military operation in the Congo just after the country had gained its independence, Belgium invoked the consent of the provincial authorities.[73] However, it would be excessive to deduce any legal conclusion whereby a simple appeal from local authorities could suffice to justify an intervention. First because the Belgian authorities also referred to an appeal from the central government of Congo.[74] Then because, in any event, far from being unanimously accepted, this argument was firmly condemned by many States, as pointed out in chapter four. Finally it shall be noted that in 1964 Belgium justified another military operation emphasising that it had been accepted by the government authorities of the Congo.[75] The States that supported the lawfulness of the operation emphasised that circumstance.[76] Beyond any contest, commentators all seem to admit that international law cannot settle for an appeal made by any subaltern or local authority, regardless of whether or not the situation can be characterised as anarchic.[77]

b) The Inadequacy of an Appeal from Dissident Authorities

If, within a given State, certain authorities wish to call on help from a foreign State and others do not wish to do so, only the highest authorities in the State are competent to take the decision.

The precedent of Soviet intervention in Hungary is particularly characteristic in this respect. It will be recalled that when Soviet forces entered Hungarian territory en masse on 1 November 1956, the government presided by Imre Nagy immediately protested to the UN. The USSR then invoked the appeal from a dissident Hungarian government presided by Janos Kadar presented by the USSR as the official government.[78] On principle, the intervening power does not seem then to have challenged the need to secure the consent of the highest authorities of the State, even when those authorities were protesting vigorously to the UN.[79] In the General Assembly

---

[73] S/PV.873, 13/14 July 1960, para 187. See also above, ch 4, s II.
[74] S/PV.873, 13/14 July 1960, para 188.
[75] See below, s II.
[76] See, eg: the views expressed by Brazil, S/PV.1177, 16 December 1964, paras 88–89.
[77] M Bennouna, *Le consentement à l'ingérence militaire dans les conflits internes*, above n 2, 178.
[78] S/PV.746, 28 October 1956, para 156; see also M Bennouna, *Le consentement à l'ingérence militaire dans les conflits internes*, above n 2, 134 and fn 101.
[79] ibid, 133.

most States for that matter condemned the intervention precisely because it was not accepted by the government in place.[80] The Hungarian precedent therefore clearly confirms the necessity to be able to rely on an appeal from the government in office, and not on one from a dissident government, especially one formed for the occasion.[81]

A similar conclusion can be deduced from the precedent of the intervention by the Soviet Union, Poland, Hungary, Bulgaria and the GDR in Czechoslovakia some 12 years later. The USSR based its action on a request from the Czechoslovakian government.[82] From the outset of discussions within the Security Council that justification was vigorously contested by Czechoslovakia's official representative at the UN, who relied on several declarations from the highest authorities of the Czechoslovakian State, all of which had condemned the military intervention: the Presidium of the Central Committee, the Minister for Foreign Affairs, the Presidium of the National Assembly and the President of the Republic.[83] The USSR and Poland then evoked more generally an appeal from Communist Party members.[84] Thus, in the Czechoslovakian case, the intervening States seem indeed to have relied on an appeal from dissident authorities and not on the consent of the central authorities, an argument of which the least that can be said is that it did not achieve broad approval as it was condemned by the United States[85] and other Western[86] and Latin American[87] States, but also by Non-Aligned States,[88] with the intervening States only

[80] See: GA Res 1004 (ES-II), 4 November 1956, GA Res 1005 (ES-II), 9 November 1956; see also L Doswald-Beck, 'The Legal Validity of Military Intervention by Invitation of the Government', above n 2, 224–26; Q Wright, 'Intervention, 1956' (1957) 51 *AJIL* 275.

[81] See: A Tanca, *Foreign Armed Intervention in Internal Conflict*, above n 2, 149–50; R Higgins, *The Development of International Law Through the Political Organs of the United Nations* (London/New York/Toronto, OUAT, 1963) 210–11; C Alibert, *Du droit de se faire justice dans la société internationale depuis 1945* (Paris, LGDJ, 1983) 368–69.

[82] S/8759, 21 August 1968.

[83] S/PV.1441, 21 August 1968, paras 137–42.

[84] S/PV.1441, 21 August 1968, paras 209–10; S/PV.1443, 22 August 1968, para 41.

[85] S/PV.1441, 21 August 1968, paras 40, 162 and 248. See also A/AC.125/SR.84, 12 September 1968 and 'Contemporary Practice of the United States' (1969) 63 *AJIL* 324–29.

[86] See the views expressed by Canada (S/PV.1441, 21 August 1968, paras 52 and 169), United Kingdom (ibid, para 57 and A/C.6/SR.1075, 20 November 1968, para 11), France (S/PV.1441, 21 August 1968, para 175 and 'Pratique française du droit international' (1969) 15 *AFDI* 901–02), Denmark (ibid, paras 185–86), Australia (S/8769, 23 August 1968), Belgium ('La pratique belge en matière de droit international' (1970) 6 *RBDI* 627–30), Switzerland ('La pratique suisse en matière de droit international public' (1969/1970) 26 *ASDI* 174–78), Netherlands (A/C.6/SR.1076, 21 November 1968, para 35), and New Zealand (A/C.6/SR.1080, 25 November 1968, para 24).

[87] Paraguay (S/PV.1441, 21 August 1968, para 107), Brazil (ibid, para 196 and S/PV.1442, 22 August 1968, para 63), Chile (S/8777, 26 August 1968), Jamaica (S/8780, 27 August 1968), Ecuador (S/8784, 27 August 1968; S/8803, 6 September 1968), Haiti (S/8790, 29 August 1968), Panama (S/8800, 4 September 1968), Costa Rica (S/8812, 10 September 1968).

[88] Ethiopia (S/PV.1442, 22 August 1968, para 7), Senegal (S/PV.1443, 22 August 1968, paras 18–19), India (ibid, para 252), Algeria (ibid, para 263), Yugoslavia (S/8765, 22 August 1968; S/PV.1444, 23 August 1968, para 105), Zambia (S/8770, 23 August 1968), Indonesia (S/8798, 3 September 1968), Panama (S/8800, 4 September 1968), Costa Rica (S/8812, 10 September 1968).

escaping Security Council condemnation because of the Soviet Union's veto.[89]

In the light of these precedents, to which one could add others like the dismissal above of Iraq's justification for its invasion of Kuwait,[90] it is clear that military intervention can only be justified by the consent of central government, with that of dissident governmental authorities, whether real or imaginary, not sufficing at all.

c) The Inadequacy of an Appeal from Diplomatic Authorities

It may happen, as in the case of Commonwealth States, that domestic public law designates a diplomatic authority that may formally be considered as representing the head of State. In such cases, to be valid, consent must be given by the government authorities that represent and actually exercise the supreme power within the State in question. *A contrario*, a simple appeal from a diplomatic authority cannot suffice in international law to justify external military intervention.

This condition may be illustrated by the precedent of the 1983 military intervention in Grenada by the US together with Antigua, Barbados, Dominica, Jamaica, Saint Lucia and Saint Vincent and the Grenadines (six Member States of the Organisation of Eastern Caribbean States). Several intervening States, during debates on the subject within the UN, invoked the appeal from the Governor General, the Crown's representative in Grenada, a Commonwealth State.[91] This was the case in particular of Barbados,[92] Saint Lucia[93] and Dominica.[94] But in fact the Governor General's appeal was only invoked incidentally or even marginally by the intervening States. They relied rather on a broad interpretation of Chapter VIII of the UN Charter, referring to a decision of the OECS as a regional collective security organisation.[95] Some of them, like the US, which directed the operation, did not even take up the argument of consent in the UN Security Council,[96] an

---

[89] S/PV.1443, 22 August 1968, para 284); see A Tanca, *Foreign Armed Intervention in Internal Conflict*, above n 2, 160–61.

[90] See above.

[91] See C Walter, 'Security Council Control over Regional Action' (1997) 1 *Max Planck Yb of UN Law* 151; L Doswald-Beck, 'The Legality of the United States Intervention in Grenada', (1984) 31 *NILR* 369–70.

[92] S/PV.2491, 27 October 1983, para 148.

[93] ibid, paras 23–24.

[94] S/PV.2489, 26 October 1983, para 9.

[95] See: ch 6, s I.

[96] S/PV.2487, 25 October 1983, 22, paras 191–93; cp *Digest of United States Practice* (Washington, Department of State Publication, 1981–1988) vol III, 3396–404 and 3403 and 'Contemporary Practice of the United States' (1984) 78 *AJIL* 661–65; see also JN Moore, 'Grenada and the International Double Standard' (1984) 78 *AJIL* 153 and 159–61; JHH Weiler, 'Armed Intervention in a Dichotomized World: The Case of Grenada' in A Cassese (ed), *The Current Legal Regulation of the Use of Force* (Dordrecht, Martinus Nijhoff, 1986) 253; A Tanca, *Foreign Armed Intervention in Internal Conflict*, above n 2, 179; AM Weisburd, *Use of Force. The Practice of States Since World War II*, above n 62, 236.

observation that seems to denote a certain lack of conviction on the part of the intervening States themselves. In any event, and this second remark is obviously decisive, the argument of the Governor General's appeal is very far from having convinced the international community of States as a whole.[97]

Condemnation of this military operation by the Security Council was only avoided by the US using its right of veto.[98] By contrast, the UN General Assembly did condemn the operation by a very large majority including Socialist, Non-Aligned and Western States.[99] Several States specifically denounced the argument of the Governor General's appeal,[100] including the UK whose position is not without interest in the context of the Commonwealth.[101]

In respect of all the precedents just examined, it appears clearly that, to be validly given, consent to external intervention must have been given by the highest authorities of the State such as the Prime Minister, the President or the Government as a whole. *A contrario*, a possible appeal from local, dissident or diplomatic authorities is insufficient, whatever the municipal legal system of the State in question. Beyond conditions relating to the grantor of the consent, further conditions must be met, which refer rather to the intrinsic characteristics of that consent.

C. The Existence of 'Validly Given' Consent

From the beginning of its works on this subject, the ILC specified that, to produce legal effects

> the consent of the State must be *valid in international law, clearly established, really expressed (which precludes merely presumed consent), internationally attributable to the State and anterior to the commission of the act to which it refers.* Moreover, consent can be invoked as precluding the wrongfulness of an act by another State only *within the limits which the State expressing the consent intends with respect to its scope and duration.*[102]

We have already specified the condition that the consent had to be 'internationally attributable to the State'.[103] We now need to examine the other

---

[97] See: L Doswald-Beck, 'The Legal Validity of Military Intervention by Invitation of the Government', above n 2, 237; 'The Legality of the United States Intervention in Grenada', above n 91, 373–77; see also CC Joyner, 'The United States Action in Grenada. Reflections on the Lawfulness of Invasion' (1984) 78 *AJIL* 137–39.

[98] See: S/PV.2491, 27 October 1983, para 431.

[99] AG Res 38/7, 2 November 1983; see also 'La pratique belge en matière de droit international' (1986) 19 *RBDI* 564–65 and the condemnation by the Netherlands; S/PV.2491, 27 October 1983, paras 365–66.

[100] See the views expressed by France (S/PV.2489, 26 October 1983, para 146 and 'Pratique française du droit international' (1984) 30 *AFDI* 1012), Afghanistan (S/PV.2491, 27 October 1983, para 262), and Algeria (S/PV.2489, 26 October 1983, para 99).

[101] See: C Rousseau, 'Chronique des faits internationaux' (1984) 88 *RGDIP* 485 and 'United Kingdom Materials on International Law' (1984) 55 *BYBIL* 581.

[102] (1979) *YILC*, vol II (Part Two), 112.

[103] See above.

conditions of consent, its character of being anterior to the act (1), free and unvitiated (2), certain (3) and relevant (4).

Prior Consent

By application of the general rules of intertemporal law, the lawfulness of an act must be appraised at the time the act occurs.[104] In the case of a military intervention, it is at the time it is conducted that one must ask whether the intervention can be justified by the consent of the State in whose territory it takes place: such consent must logically, then, have been given at the latest by the time the intervention begins.

This condition was set forth by the ILC at the outset of its reflections on consent. Contemplating the possibility of consent after the perpetration of an act, the ILC considered that there was 'a waiver to rely on responsibility and the claims by which it is reflected. But such waiver leaves the wrongfulness of the preceding fact to subsist'.[105] The substance—that is, the unlawfulness of the act, that survives in the event of *ex post* consent—must be distinguished from the procedure, with *ex post* consent possibly being likened to a time-bar precluding the injured State from bringing an action against the intervening State.[106] It is interesting to point out that this distinction was contested in vain by one State in its comments on the ILC's work. For the UK:

> There are emergency situations in which it is appropriate to allow a State to take action to protect persons in another State from imminent and serious danger (for example, from risk of death from fire or flood), but where there may be insufficient time to obtain the consent of that other State. There may be a need to address, in the draft article itself or in the Commentary, the possibility of implied or retrospective consent. The United Kingdom Government hopes that the International Law Commission will consider whether it is possible, either in draft article 29 or elsewhere, to make express provision for a right to take such humanitarian action in emergency situations, with appropriate safeguards to protect the interests of the State in whose territory the action is taken.[107]

---

[104] According to art 13 of the ILC *Draft Articles on Responsibility of States for Internationally Wrongful Acts*, 'An act of a State does not constitute a breach of an international obligation unless the State is bound by the obligation in question at the time the act occurs' (text in (2001) *YILC*, vol II (Part Two)); see also arts 1 and 2(a) of the *Institut de droit international* Resolution adopted in Wiesbaden, 'The Intertemporal Problem in Public International Law', www.idi-iil.org and *Island of Palmas, RSA*, vol II, 845.

[105] (1979) *YILC*, vol II, 2nd part, 125–26, para 16.

[106] See art 45(b) of the ILC *Draft Articles on Responsibility of States for Internationally Wrongful Acts:* 'The responsibility of a State may not be invoked if [. . .]: (b) The injured State is to be considered as having, by reason of its conduct, validly acquiesced in the lapse of the claim' (above n 104), and *Armed Activities on the Territory of the Congo*, ICJ Rep (2005) paras 293–95.

[107] A/CN.4/488, 25 March 1998.

This possibility of retroactive consent in event of emergency, while discussed incidentally afterwards,[108] left no record either in the draft article or its commentary.[109] The ILC's final report repeated that:

> Consent to the commission of otherwise wrongful conduct may be given by a State in advance or even at the time it is occurring. By contrast, cases of consent given after the conduct has occurred are a form of waiver or acquiescence, leading to loss of the right to invoke responsibility. This is dealt with in article 45.[110]

It should be recalled that the General Assembly took note of the ILC's draft in December 2001, with no particular reservation being mentioned in this respect.[111]

This condition of the *ex ante* character of consent may be illustrated by several precedents.

—In the case of Soviet intervention in Hungary in 1956, it was seen that the USSR relied on an appeal by a government directed by Janos Kadar. It seems, though, that this government was formed *after* the beginning of the military operation, which explains why the argument was not accepted in the UN.[112]

—When they contributed to the overthrow of Emperor Bokassa in September 1979 in the Central African Republic, the French authorities invoked an appeal from the new government.[113] However, it seems that this government only came to power after France's intervention.[114] The operation was not formally condemned in the UN, but it certainly cannot be said that the international community of States as a whole admitted it was lawful.[115]

---

[108] (1999) *YILC*, vol I, 2587th meeting, 15 June 1999, paras 66–67 and ibid, 2588th meeting, 16 June 1999, para 34.

[109] According to the Special Rapporteur, 'The commentary limits article 29 to consent given in advance' (J Crawford, *Second report on State responsibility*, 30 April 1999, above n 17, 12, para 237).

[110] *Report of the International Law Commission*, 53rd session, 23 April–1 June and 2 July–10 August 2001, GA, 56th session, Supp no 10 (A/56/10), 73.

[111] GA Res 56/83 of 12 December 2001, adopted by consensus.

[112] M Bennouna, *Le consentement à l'ingérence militaire dans les conflits internes*, above n 2, 134; A Tanca, *Foreign Armed Intervention in Internal Conflict*, above n 2, 43.

[113] 'Pratique française du droit international' (1979) 25 *AFDI* 909; 'Pratique française du droit international' (1980) 26 *AFDI* 878.

[114] P Chapal, 'Les interventions militaires de la France' in JF Guilhaudis and M Torelli (eds), *Force armée et diplomatie*, tome I (Dordrecht, Martinus Nijhoff/Bruxelles, Bruylant, 1985) 85; C Gray, *International Law and the Use of Force*, 3rd edn, above n 12, 85–86; 'Pratique française du droit international public' (1979) 25 *AFDI* 908; *Keesing's Contemporary Archives*, 1979, 29934; see also O Paye, *Sauve qui veut? Le droit international face aux crises humanitaires* (Bruxelles, Bruylant, 1996) 171–72; C Alibert, *Du droit de se faire justice dans la société internationale depuis 1945*, above n 81, 264–67.

[115] According to AM Weisburd, France 'received considerable private criticism from African States with which it was allied'; *Use of Force. The Practice of States Since World War II*, above n 62, 227; see also LA Sicilianos, *Les réactions décentralisées à l'illicite. Des contre-mesures à la légitime défense* (Paris, LGDJ, 1990) 491.

—It will be recalled that on 25 December 1979 Soviet troops entered Afghanistan in number, the government in office being overthrown two days later. It was only on 28 December that the TASS press agency mentioned an appeal from the Afghan government to justify the operation.[116] Some of the many States that criticised the intervention did not fail to emphasise this chronological problem.[117] The USSR replied that the presence of its troops had been consented to much earlier and that the Afghan government had been overthrown without its backing.[118] No one, then, challenged the principle that outside military intervention can only be justified by prior consent.[119]

—In *Armed Activities*, Uganda justified its presence in Congo territory by an agreement concluded at Lusaka on 10 July 1999.[120] The Democratic Republic of Congo criticised this argument, pointing out in particular that the agreement could not retroactively justify the Ugandan military intervention that had begun in August 1998.[121] Uganda did not expressly challenge the principle of the Congo's argument, even if it sometimes seemed to confer a certain retroactive scope on the Lusaka Agreement;[122] scope that at any rate was not upheld by the Court which, in its judgment, approved the DRC's argument on this point.[123]

Practice, then, confirms the requirement of consent being given beforehand, with no precedent having given rise to justification based on an *ex post* appeal accepted by States as a whole,[124] a condition that is related to that of consent not being vitiated, especially by coercion.

Unvitiated Consent

As the expression of a State's will, it goes without saying that consent to the beginning of an outside military operation must have been given freely.[125] In other words, that consent, like any legally binding commitment, must not have been vitiated whether by error, fraud, corruption or coercion of the

[116] A Tanca, *Foreign Armed Intervention in Internal Conflict*, above n 2, 177.

[117] See, eg: Pakistan (S/PV.2185, 5 January 1980, 32); see also below ch 7, s I.

[118] S/PV.2185, 5 January 1980. See also the views expressed by Afghanistan, ibid.

[119] See: CJ Le Mon, 'Unilateral Intervention by Invitation in Civil Wars: the Effective Control Test Tested', above n 2, 778–82.

[120] Ugandan Counter-Memorial, 21 April 2001, 174–77, paras 315–22; Ugandan Rejoinder, 6 December 2002, 129–35, paras 309–20.

[121] Memorial of the Democratic Republic of Congo, July 2000, 225, para 5.78; Rejoinder of the Democratic Republic of Congo, May 2002, 261, para 3.213; M Corten, CR 2005/4, 13 April 2005, 16–17, paras 25–26; M Klein, CR 2005/12, 25 April 2005, para 26.

[122] Ugandan Rejoinder, 129 *ff*; M. Reichler, CR 2005/8, 19 April 2005, 25–26, para 27.

[123] *Armed Activities on the Territory of the Congo*, ICJ Rep (2005), para 96; see also Judge Kateka, dissenting opinion, para 22.

[124] See also: N Ronzitti, 'Use of Force, *Jus Cogens* and State Consent', above n 8, 161–63.

[125] I Brownlie, *International Law and the Use of Force by States*, above n 37, 317; A Abass, 'Consent Precluding State Responsibility: A Critical Analysis', above n 28, 214.

State representative or the State itself. The ILC stated this condition at the outset of its work and it was never contradicted on this point.[126]

The condition has been evoked on certain occasions.

—In the case of military intervention in Czechoslovakia, it has been seen that the Warsaw Pact countries relied on an appeal by certain dissident local authorities, plainly under very intense pressure from Moscow. This point was mentioned to criticise the lawfulness of the operation.[127]
—To justify its military presence in Cambodia from 1979, Vietnam invoked the consent of the Kampuchean United Front for National Salvation, which allegedly brought down the Khmer Rouge regime without outside help.[128] This argument was dismissed by a large majority of States, the General Assembly adopting a resolution demanding in particular the withdrawal of Vietnamese troops.[129] Some more specifically denounced the argument of the appeal from a 'United Front' that was subservient to the Vietnamese government.[130]

These two precedents clearly illustrate cases of coercion, the first under article 51 (coercion of the State representative) and the second under article 52 (coercion of a State) of the Vienna Convention on the law of treaties applied here by analogy with the case of consent to outside military intervention.[131]

The question of determining when there is coercion that vitiates consent—which is the question most often asked in practice—must therefore be evaluated against the Vienna Convention, and it is a question that cannot be dealt with in detail in this book.[132] It will be recalled, however, that only coercion consisting in an unlawful use of force is liable to vitiate consent. *A contrario*, agreements obtained further to a military operation or a threat consistent with the UN Charter must be considered valid.

Can it be considered, on the contrary, that consent obtained after an unlawful use of force must *always* be deemed invalid? The general principle *ex injuria jus non oritur*, and certain precedents such as those of the condemning of the Vietnamese presence in Cambodia recalled above, tend to suggest so. However, other more recent events urge greater caution, as attested by the three precedents below.

---

[126] (1979) *YILC*, vol II, 2nd part, 124–25, paras 12–13.

[127] See the views expressed by the United States; S/PV.1441, 21 August 1968, para 41.

[128] S/PV.2108, 11 January 1979, paras 115–16, 120, 126, 128 and 130 and GA, 35th meeting, Supp no 41 (A/35/41), 23 June 1980, para 140.

[129] GA Res 34/22 of 14 November 1979.

[130] See the views expressed by China, S/PV.2108, 11 January 1979, 2, para 18 and 11, para 100.

[131] M Bennouna, *Le consentement à l'ingérence militaire dans les conflits internes*, above n 2, 64–80.

[132] See: O Corten, 'Article 52' in O Corten and P Klein (eds), *Les Conventions de Vienne sur le droit des traités. Commentaire article par article* (Bruxelles, Bruylant, 2006) 1867–1900.

—After June 1999, troops from several States were sent to Kosovo on the basis of an agreement of the Yugoslav government authorities secured as a direct consequence of the war against that State by NATO Member States.[133] This consent seems to have been considered perfectly valid, even by the States that criticised the lawfulness of the war.[134]

—Likewise, the presence of foreign armed forces in Iraq since the end of the war against that country in March 2003 has been justified by the consent of the new government in Baghdad.[135] The lawfulness of that presence seems generally to have been accepted, including by States that characterised the war as a violation of international law and even as aggression.[136]

—In the *Armed Activities* case, everyone seems to have accepted that the DRC government had, for a time, validly consented to the presence of Rwandan and Ugandan troops in its territory.[137] And yet they were the same troops that had actively contributed to that government taking power by helping to overthrow the previous government, presided over by Field Marshal Mobutu.[138] The argument of coercion was not evoked here to vitiate consent secured after a war that some, however, characterised as unlawful.[139]

Contemporary practice thus shows just how cautious one should be about evaluating the validity of consent given in a context of conflict.[140] That caution must first lead us to check whether the military operation that preceded consent can indeed by characterised as unlawful, failing which it seems no coercion can be established.[141] Then, even supposing an unlawful act did precede the giving of consent, the relation of cause and effect between the two should be examined. It is only if the consent cannot be explained *other than* by the unlawful military intervention that it will have to be considered

---

[133] Text in *ILM*, 1999, 1217–21.

[134] Y Nouvel, 'La position du Conseil de sécurité face à l'action militaire engagée par l'OTAN et ses Etats membres contre la République fédérale de Yougoslavie' (1999) 45 *AFDI* 306–07; see also E Milano, 'Security Council in the Balkans: Reviewing the Legality of Kosovo's Territorial Status' (2003) 14 *EJIL* 999–1022.

[135] See: CS Res 1546 (2004).

[136] A Lagerwall, 'L'administration du territoire irakien: un exemple de reconnaissance et d'aide au maintien d'une occupation résultant d'un acte d'agression?' (2006) 39 *RBDI* 249–73.

[137] *Armed Activities on the Territory of the Congo*, ICJ Rep (2005), paras 45–46.

[138] See, eg: O Lanotte and B Kabamba, *Guerres au Congo-Zaïre (1996–1999): Acteurs et scénarios*, Cahiers Africains nos 39–40 (Paris, L'Harmattan, 1999) 109–10; G Prunier, 'L'Ouganda et les guerres congolaises' (October 1999) 75 *Politique Africaine* 48–50.

[139] See: O Corten, CR 2000/24, 25 June 2000; Memorial of the Democratic Republic of Congo (para 5.83), Rejoinder of the Democratic Republic of Congo (paras 3.213–17); *Armed Activities on the Territory of the Congo*, ICJ Rep (2005), paras 92–105.

[140] G Disteffano, 'Le Conseil de sécurité et la validation des traités conclu par la menace ou l'emploi de la force' in CA Morand (ed), *La crise des Balkans de 1999. Les dimensions historiques, politiques et juridiques du conflit du Kosovo* (Bruxelles, Bruylant/Paris, LGDJ, 2000) 167–92.

[141] O Corten, 'Article 52', above n 132, 1885.

invalid.[142] If, in view of what has been consented to, it can be concluded that the consent reflects the true will of whoever consented, the hypothesis of absence of consent could then be excluded.

These general guidelines will be extremely hard to follow in any particular instance, above all when the situation is managed by the Security Council in a less legal than pragmatic perspective, as was the case in the precedents just mentioned. The fact remains that, on principle, the need to check that consent is not vitiated remains universally admitted and must therefore be applied by the same token as other conditions.

Established Consent

Must consent, to justify an outside military operation, have been expressed in compliance with certain formalities? In debates on the definition of aggression, the representatives of Ceylon[143] and of Panama[144] proposed to characterise as aggression any armed action conducted without the written or express consent of the State concerned. Finally, the definition of aggression mentions the maintenance or use of armed forces contrary to arrangements set out in the agreement concluded with the host State, without setting any conditions as to the form of the agreement.[145] As for the ILC, it very generally evokes 'valid consent by a State', without further clarification. The commentary, though, informs us that 'Consent must be freely given and clearly established. It must be actually expressed by the State rather than merely presumed on the basis that the State would have consented if it had been asked'.[146]

The ILC also insisted on consent being *'clearly established, really expressed (which precludes merely presumed consent)'*,[147] failing which 'cases of abuse would be too common'.[148]

At the same time, international law does not require compliance with any particular formality any more than in the broader domain of any other legal commitment,[149] an absence of formalism that can be very clearly illustrated by the case of *Armed Activities*, when a question of this kind came up before the Court. In the case at hand, the DRC accused Uganda of violating the prohibition of the use of force against it by merely maintaining its troops in DRC territory after 27 July 1998, the date of a declaration by President Kabila allegedly ending all consent to the presence of foreign troops in the

---

[142] ibid, 1886–89 and 1893–1900.
[143] A/C.6/SR.1081, 26 November 1968, para 11.
[144] A/C.6/SR.1482, 22 October 1974, para 4.
[145] See art 3(e) of the definition, cited above.
[146] A/56/10, 73, para 6.
[147] (1979) *YILC*, vol II (Part Two), 112.
[148] ibid, 113, para 14.
[149] J Salmon (ed), *Dictionnaire de droit international public* (Bruxelles, Bruylant/AUF, 2001) 516.

DRC.[150] Uganda considered rather that its troops were in Congolese territory on the basis of a protocol concluded in April 1998 and that, in this context, a simple unilateral declaration that failed to mention Ugandan troops specifically was not enough to constitute a valid withdrawal of the DRC's consent.[151] In its judgment, the Court approved the position of the plaintiff State, drawing a distinction, to relate them, between the questions of prior consent and of its retraction.

—On the first of these points, the Court considered that the DRC had initially consented to the presence of Ugandan troops in its territory, not through the April 1998 protocol, which only enunciated a very general principle of cooperation, but through tolerance or absence of protest. Thus 'The Court believes that both the absence of any objection to the presence of Ugandan troops in the DRC in the preceding months, and the practice subsequent to the signing of the Protocol, support the view that the continued presence as before of Ugandan troops would be permitted by the DRC by virtue of the Protocol'.[152] The Court, however, immediately specified that:

> While the co-operation envisaged in the Protocol may be reasonably understood as having its effect in a continued authorization of Ugandan troops in the border area, it was not the legal basis for such authorization or consent. The source of an authorization or consent to the crossing of the border by these troops antedated the Protocol.[153]

It is very clear, in view of this reasoning, that consent may be given in a completely informal manner; a simple tolerance may suffice to demonstrate its existence in the particular circumstances of the case.

—On the matter of the withdrawal of consent, the Court deduced from the informal character of its existence that 'this prior authorization or consent could thus be withdrawn at any time by the Government of the DRC, without further formalities being necessary'.[154] After noting that the declaration of 27 July 1998 was 'ambiguous',[155] the Court observed that the DRC authorities had from the beginning of August denounced Uganda as an aggressor State in particular at a regional summit. Accordingly, 'it appears evident to the Court that, whatever interpretation may be given to President Kabila's statement of 28 July 1998, any earlier consent by

---

[150] Memorial of the Democratic Republic of Congo, July 2000, 210–11, paras 5.37–40; Rejoinder of the Democratic Republic of Congo, May 2002, 257, para 3.207; M Corten, CR 2005/4, 13 April 2005, paras 14–19.

[151] Ugandan Counter Memorial, 21 April 2001, 161–64, paras 288–98; Ugandan Rejoinder, 6 December 2002, 127–29, paras 302–08; M Brownlie, CR 2005/8, 19 April 2005, 9–15, paras 6–32.

[152] *Armed Activities on the Territory of the Congo*, ICJ Rep (2005), para 46.

[153] ibid, para 47.

[154] ibid.

[155] ibid, para 51.

the DRC to the presence of Ugandan troops on its territory had at the latest been withdrawn by 8 August 1998, ie the closing date of the Victoria Falls Summit'.[156] So, just as it may be given informally, consent may be withdrawn informally too. This 'parallel in the absence of form' goes along with a parallel in the requirement of the established character of (withdrawal of) consent, which must be shown to be beyond doubt.[157]

The *Armed Activities* case shows how the informal and established character of consent must be required and verified in each particular instance. In practice, it must be noted that this consent is usually given expressly, whether through treaty or otherwise.[158]

A final point should be made at this stage: *Armed Activities* confirms that, to be established, consent must always exist at the time the intervention begins, which implies checking that it has not been withdrawn. This right to withdraw consent was highlighted in the ILC's work, where Special Rapporteur Crawford recalled that 'If a State consented in advance to the use of force in its territory and then withdrew its consent, recourse to force became wrongful, even if the State had withdrawn its consent ill-advisedly'.[159] That assertion can rely on established practice, the UN having reaffirmed on several occasions the right of any State to require the withdrawal of foreign troops stationed in its territory.[160] It is not enough, then, to refer to prior consent in order to justify a military intervention. A check must be made that consent was not withdrawn prior to the beginning of the intervention, just as it will be important to ask whether the consent indeed covers all forms of military operation engaged in.

Relevant Consent

The requirement that consent be relevant is explicitly reflected in the applicable texts, such as:

> article 20 of the ILC draft, by which 'Valid consent by a State to the commission of a given act by another State precludes the wrongfulness of that act in relation to the former State *to the extent that the act remains within the limits of that consent*' (emphasis added);[161] and article 3*(e)* of the definition annexed to General Assembly resolution 3314 (XXIX) characterising as aggression 'the use of armed forces of one State which are within the territory of another State with the agreement of the receiving State, *in contravention of the conditions provided for in the agreement* or any extension of their presence in such territory *beyond the termination of the agreement*'. (emphasis added)

---

156 ibid, para 53.
157 See also: Judge Kateka, dissenting opinion, paras 18–19.
158 See, eg, the *Lebanon* case; S/PV.827, 15 July 1958, para 44.
159 16 June 1999, 2588th meeting (1999) *YILC*, vol I, 151, para 40.
160 See: GA res 1622 (S-III).
161 See also: (1979) *YILC*, vol II (2nd Part), 124, para 11.

The requirement is beyond contest in logic: to justify an act, the consent must indeed bear on the act in question. Failing this, the consent invoked is quite simply irrelevant.

This condition can be illustrated by practice. In January 1946, Iran complained to the Security Council of the attitude of Soviet troops that had prevented the Iranian authorities from proceeding to a part of their territory to quell disturbances.[162] The USSR replied that its troops' presence in Iran was based on a treaty instrument that was still in force,[163] but was unable to explain what instruments supposedly authorised its army to interfere in maintaining law and order in Iran.[164] This probably explains why the Soviet argument fell far short of convincing States as a whole.[165]

The need for relevant consent may also be recalled in case law in *Armed Activities* on two counts.

—First, in this matter, the ICJ noted that, assuming it was established, the DRC's consent to the presence of Ugandan troops in the DRC could only have justified limited actions along the border. Such consent could not, however, be invoked to justify all the actions by Uganda, such as the taking of many towns and places sometimes several hundreds of kilometres within the DRC or the active support for rebel forces in the Congo. In the terms of the Court, 'Even had consent to the Ugandan military presence extended much beyond the end of July 1998, the parameters of that consent, in terms of geographic location and objectives, would have remained thus restricted'.[166]

—Next, and still in this matter, the Court took a position on a dispute between the parties over the interpretation of the Lusaka ceasefire agreement of 10 July 1999. For Uganda, this agreement, which provided for the staged withdrawal of its troops, was a legal title justifying the temporary maintenance, until evacuation pursuant to the agreed timetable.[167] For the DRC, however, this agreement was not designed to state a position on the lawfulness of the presence of foreign troops in DRC territory, but was aimed pragmatically at a peaceful settlement of the conflict without prejudice to questions of responsibility.[168] The Court settled the question in these terms:

> The provisions of the Lusaka Agreement thus represented an agreed *modus operandi* for the parties. They stipulated how the parties should move forward.

---

[162] See: AM Weisburd, *Use of Force. The Practice of States Since World War II*, above n 62, 252–54.

[163] Text of the treaty in S/3, SC, PV, 1, 1st ser, Supp no 1, annex 2B, 43–46.

[164] S/W/2, SC, PV, 1, 1st ser, Supp no 1, annex 2A, 18.

[165] See the views expressed by the UK; SC, PV, 1, 1st ser, no 1, 5th meeting, 30 January 1946, 55.

[166] *Armed Activities on the Territory of the Congo*, ICJ Rep (2005), para 52.

[167] M Reichler, CR 2005/8, 19 April 2005, 18 *ff*, para 7 *ff*.

[168] M Corten, CR 2005/4, 13 April 2005, 16 *ff*, para 24 *ff*.

They did not purport to qualify the Ugandan military presence in legal terms. In accepting this *modus operandi* the DRC did not 'consent' to the presence of Ugandan troops. It simply concurred that there should be a process to end that reality in an orderly fashion.[169]

This precedent proves extremely interesting especially in an international context characterised by the conclusion of agreements aimed at resolving armed conflicts comparable to the Lusaka agreements.[170] The Court's reasoning shows that consenting to the presence of foreign troops in one's territory does not imply conferring on them a valid legal title. Everything depends once again on the exact scope of that consent and, in the event of a ceasefire agreement or a peace agreement, the parties may simply come to terms on a way of resolving a situation, without prejudice to the responsibility incurred by the parties for any presence or military operation covered by the agreement.

Finally, it will be understood that, to justify a military intervention, consent will have to comply with very strict conditions. Not only will it have to be granted by the highest authorities of the State, but it will first have to be given prior to the beginning of the intervention; second, not vitiated; third, given clearly and unequivocally (even if informally); and fourth, relevant, in the sense that its purpose is indeed to make the military intervention in question lawful. All of these conditions must be satisfied in a general manner, whatever the situation. But they may also raise particularly thorny questions when dealing with a case of internal conflict, as shall be seen in the second section of this chapter.

II The Legal Regime of Military Intervention by Invitation in an Internal Conflict

This section covers the specific hypothesis of an 'internal conflict', that is, a situation within a State in which particularly serious internal disturbances are observed or there is a genuine 'non-international armed conflict' or even a truly international armed conflict in the case of an outside military intervention.[171] Two problems may complicate the allowance for consent in such situations. The first relates to possible competition between rival authorities all claiming to embody the highest authorities of the State and so to be in a position to validly consent to an outside intervention (A). The second is more fundamental and comes down to the question: even supposing there is validly granted consent from the State's highest authorities,

---

[169] *Armed Activities on the Territory of the Congo*, ICJ Rep (2005), para 99; see also Judge Kateka, dissenting opinion, para 20 *ff*.

[170] See: R Vansteenberghe, 'L'arrêt de la Cour internationale de Justice dans l'affaire des activités armées sur le territoire du Congo et le recours à la force' (2006) 39 *RBDI* 672–701 and C Bell, 'Peace Agreements: Their Nature and Legal Status' (2006) 100 *AJIL* 373–412.

[171] See: D Schindler, 'Le principe de non-intervention dans les guerres civiles', above n 58, 416–17.

can military intervention consist in supporting those authorities against rebel groups in an internal conflict? This is the crux of intervention by invitation, a traditionally highly controversial problem in doctrine (B).

A. The Problem of Concurrent Governments

In an internal conflict it frequently happens that different authorities claim to represent the government of one and the same State. In such a case, how can one determine who will be in a position to validly invite an outside intervention? In international law generally, recognition is an institution that is both declarative of a state of affairs and constitutive of the reality of that state of affairs.[172] So, States will generally deal with another State through the intermediary of a government that they recognise as representative, which will confer on—or reinforce for—that government a degree of effective power . . . which in turn will promote recognition by other governments. The criteria of international recognition (1) and of effectivity (2) must therefore be envisaged as mutually reinforcing, as shall be seen more particularly in the field of the prohibition of the use of force.[173]

The Criterion of International Recognition

It was considered, during the general debates on the prohibition of the use of force, that this rule could not prevent an internationally recognised government from seeking and receiving assistance from an allied State for the purpose of maintaining law and order.[174] Revisiting the precedent of the Korean War illustrates this issue well. It has already been mentioned that, even if it was not without ambiguity, the justification advanced by Western States seemed to be related to consent from the Korean government.[175] Now, from a reading of the relevant documents, emphasis was placed on the international recognition of the government of the Republic of Korea. By way of reminder, on 12 December 1948, the UN General Assembly had recognised the Government of South Korea as the only government entitled to represent the Korean State and had set up in parallel a new commission (the UN Commission on Korea) to facilitate the country's unification.[176] In its first resolution adopted after forces from North Korea had crossed the 38th parallel, the Security Council:

---

[172] See: C de Visscher, *Problèmes d'interprétation judiciaire en droit international public* (Paris, Pedone, 1963) 191.

[173] L Doswald-Beck, 'The Legal Validity of Military Intervention by Invitation of the Government', above n 2, 190–200; see also R Jennings and A Watts, *Oppenheim's International Law*, 9th edn, above n 3, 437–38.

[174] See: A/AC 125/SR 57, 19 July 1967 and M Bennouna, *Le consentement à l'ingérence militaire dans les conflits internes*, above n 2, 93; see also C Rousseau, 'Chronique des faits internationaux' (1979) 83 *RGDIP* 171.

[175] Above, ch 3, s I.

[176] GA Res 195 [III] of 12 December 1948.

Recall[ed] the finding of the General Assembly in its resolution 293 (IV) of 21 October 1949 that the Government of the Republic of Korea is a lawfully established government having effective control and jurisdiction over that part of Korea where the United Nations Temporary Commission on Korea was able to observe and consult and in which the great majority of the people of Korea reside . . .[177]

Two days later, the Security Council:

Having noted the appeal from the Republic of Korea to the United Nations for immediate and effective steps to secure peace and security.

Recommend[ed] that the Members of the United Nations furnish such assistance to the Republic of Korea as may be necessary to repel the attack and to restore international peace and security in the area.[178]

So for a majority of States, it was because the Korean government was internationally recognised that its appeal was legitimate. Admittedly, the lawfulness of the action was questioned by several States that contested the representative character of the South Korean authorities.[179] The dispute did not seem to relate, then, to the criterion of international recognition of the government entitled to give consent, but rather to its evaluation in view of the specific features of the case in point.

In this respect, mention must be made of a certain practice it seems to derive from, under the assumption that several authorities claim in vain to be the recognised government: a duty of abstention upon third States.

Particularly instructive in this respect is the precedent of US military intervention in the Dominican Republic in 1965.[180] It will be recalled that on 24 April 1965 the ruling government was overthrown by the supporters of former president Juan Bosch, who had himself been driven from power in September 1963.[181] A civil war then broke out opposing the revolutionary forces favourable to former president Bosch, who called themselves the 'Constitutional Government' and conservative forces commanded by a few top-ranking Dominican army officers in favour of bringing back the authorities that had been overthrown and united as the 'Government of National Reconstruction'. Both governments claimed to represent the Dominican State. On 5 May 1965 the UN Secretary-General received a letter from the 'Constitutional Government' appointing a representative to the Security

---

[177] SC Res 82 (1950) of 25 June 1950.

[178] SC Res 83 (1950) of 27 June 1950.

[179] Above, ch 3, s I. See the views expressed by the USRR (S/PV.480, 1 August 1950) and Poland (S/1545).

[180] See: W Friedmann, 'United States Policy and the Crisis of International Law' (1965) 59 *AJIL* 867–69.

[181] C Rousseau, 'Chronique des faits internationaux' (1965) 69 *RGDIP* 1117–21 and 1132; *Keesing's Contemporary Archives*, 1965, 20813, 20813–18 and 20855–56; *Yearbook of the United Nations* (1965) 140–45; RJ Dupuy, 'Les Etats-Unis, l'OEA et l'ONU à Saint-Domingue' (1965) 11 *AFDI* 71–110.

Council and on 10 May a letter from the 'Government of National Reconstruction' accrediting another representative.[182] The Secretary-General then considered, 'it is apparent that the situation in that country is far from clear as to which of the contending authorities constitutes the Government of the country'.[183] Some days later, the Security Council heard representatives of each faction without recognising either as the official representative of the Dominican Republic.[184] This situation lasted until September 1965, when the conservative forces had recovered effective power further to the US military intervention.

To justify its military intervention, the US invoked several arguments including the consent of the local authorities, in the case in point the 'Government of National Reconstruction'.[185] The US argued that these authorities alone were able to consent to an outside military operation in a context of instability or even of a power vacuum:

> In the absence of any governmental authority, Dominican law enforcement and military officials informed our Embassy that the situation was completely out of control . . . Faced with that emergency, the threat to the lives of its citizens, and a request for assistance from those Dominican authorities still struggling to maintain order, the United States on 28 April dispatched the first of the security forces that we have sent to the island.[186]

Thus the United States considered that, in the absence of any internationally recognised government, an outside military operation might be based on an appeal from authorities that, in practice, were effectively fighting to maintain law and order and as such could be characterised as 'the only apparent responsible authority in Santo Domingo'.[187]

It cannot be said that this justification was considered consistent with international law by the community of States as a whole; far from it. Several Socialist, Non-Aligned and even Western States voiced serious doubts including on the argument of consent.[188] Some considered that the 'Constitutional Government' alone could have validly consented to an outside military operation, but such consent was not forthcoming since, quite the contrary, that government protested vigorously against the US

---

[182] S/PV.1207, 13 May 1965, 3–4, paras 15–16.
[183] ibid, 4, para 21.
[184] S/PV.1212, 19 May 1965, paras 211–40.
[185] S/6310, 29 April 1965.
[186] S/PV.1196, 3 May 1965, paras 67–68; see also S/PV.1196, 3 May 1965, paras 67–68 and S/PV.1212, 19 May 1965, para 147.
[187] S/PV.1200, 5 May 1965, 5, para 17; see CJ Le Mon, 'Unilateral Intervention by Invitation in Civil Wars: the Effective Control Test Tested', above n 2, 765.
[188] See the views expressed by Cambodia (S/6347, 10 May 1965), China (S/PV.1202, 6 May 1965, paras 19–20), Jordania (S/PV.1200, 5 May 1965, paras 5, 6 and 8 and S/PV.1214, 21 May 1965, para 116), Malaysia (S/PV.1202, 6 May 1965, para 7), Mongolia (S/6341, 5 May 1965), Poland (S/6339, 7 May 1965), USSR (S/6317, 1 May 1965), Uruguay (S/PV.1198, 4 May 1965, para 8), Yugoslavia (S/6330, 4 May 1965) and Ghana (A/C.6/S.R.886, 1 December 1965).

intervention.[189] Other States, like France, disapproved of the intervention, pointing out that the Dominican Republic had been without any central government for several weeks.[190] Similarly, the Côte d'Ivoire representative 'consider[ed] such intervention to be legal only when it is requested by the legally constituted government of the country concerned'.[191] In reality, and even if the military action—which also raised the question of the role of regional organisations, with the OAS then joining in the operation[192]—was not condemned,[193] the fact is that only the UK supported the US argument based on the consent of the military authorities.[194]

Along similar lines, one can recall the precedent of the 1983 military intervention in Grenada.[195] It will be remembered that several intervening States had invoked a call from the island's Governor-General but they also emphasised the anarchy then reigning in the country, which supposedly allowed them to settle for the consent of a diplomatic authority that did not constitute the internationally recognised government of the State in question.[196] The argument was very largely condemned in the UN, including by a resolution of the General Assembly.[197]

Finally, it appears that in the event of doubt as to the identity of the government that legitimately represents a State, international law imposes a duty of abstention.[198] No outside military intervention can be based on internationally contested authorities, the existence of a possible state of anarchy or disorder not justifying settling for an appeal from one of the factions or from some subaltern authority—a duty of abstention that derives both from a problem of international recognition of the government and, it will have been understood, from a problem of effectivity that must now be addressed.

The Effective Power Requirement

Supposing a government is internationally recognised but that it has lost all effective power; can an appeal from it justify outside military intervention? The answer to this question must be modulated by distinguishing three situations: (a) that where no authority exercises power within the State;

---

[189] USSR (S/PV.1222, 9 June 1965, para 72) and Cuba (S/PV.1200, 5 May 1965, para 69).

[190] S/PV.1221, 7 June 1965, paras 60–61 and 'Pratique française du droit international' (1965) 11 *AFDI* 1025–27.

[191] S/PV.1214, 21 May 1965, para 129.

[192] See below, ch 6.

[193] See: S/PV.1216, 22 May 1965, para 47, S/6346/Rev.1, 21 May 1965, S/PV.1216, 22 May 1965, para 69; cp SC Res 203 (1965) of 14 May 1965 and 205 (1965) of 22 May 1965.

[194] S/PV.1198, 4 May 1965, paras 56–57.

[195] See above.

[196] See the views expressed by the USA (S/PV.2491, 27 October 1983, para 68).

[197] See above.

[198] See also: 'Canadian Practice in International Law' (1984) 22 *CYIL* 334 and 'United Kingdom Materials on International Law' (1986) 57 *BYBIL* 616.

(b) that where the authority exercising power is not the internationally recognised government; and (c) that where the internationally recognised government has lost its power as a result of an armed attack by a third country.

a) The Absence of Effective Authority

It may happen that a government that is internationally recognised as the representative of a State no longer has, in fact, effective power within the State, without any other authority being able to claim that it holds effective power either. There is then a political situation of anarchy or of disorder, characterised in practice by a power vacuum even if, in theory, a government continues to represent the State on the international stage. The situation is exceptional, which explains why there is little case law on this subject. What precedents there are suggest, though, that in such cases, the consent of a government, even an internationally recognised one, is not necessarily enough to justify an outside military operation.

One thinks first of Somalia which, in the early 1990s, was plunged into a state of anarchy thereby depriving the then internationally recognised government of effective power. It was in this context that in late 1992 a military operation by several States was conducted to improve the seriously deteriorating humanitarian situation in the country. As shall be detailed elsewhere, this operation was justified by Security Council authorization.[199] However, it seems that Somalia's official government—that no one contested was the only recognised government—had previously called for outside intervention.[200] This suggests that the consent of a recognised government which has no effective power is not sufficient to justify military action. In support of this, it can be noted that the Secretary-General, in the reports that acted as the basis for the Security Council decisions, emphasised the absence of central administration and of public services in Somalia.[201] It is against this background that, on the occasion of the Security Council adopting the resolution authorising the use of force, the Secretary-General considered that:

> At present no Government exists in Somalia that could request and allow such use of force. It would therefore be necessary for the Security Council to make a determination under Article 39 of the Charter that a threat to the peace exists.[202]

To my knowledge, the Secretary-General's position was not contested by any State within the UN. What is more, it is this position that clearly led the Council to adopt a resolution along the lines suggested in the cited

---

[199] Below, ch 6, s I and ch 8, s II.

[200] In its res 794 (1992) of 2 December 1992, the SC 'respond[s] to the urgent calls from Somalia for the international community to take measures to ensure the delivery of humanitarian assistance in Somalia'.

[201] *Report on the situation in Somalia*, 22 July 1992, paras 24, 43 and 55.

[202] S/24868, 29 November 1992, 3.

letter.[203] It may thus be deduced from this that there is a general agreement that, under exceptional circumstances such as those then prevailing in Somalia, no government, even one that is internationally recognised, can give consent justifying an outside military operation.

Such a deduction may also be made from examination of 'Operation Alba' that began on 15 April 1997 in a situation where anarchy had reigned in Albania for several weeks, with the government proving unable to control the disturbances without any authority having managed to replace the government or even attempted to do so.[204] It was in this context that a multinational force of some 7200 men, commanded by Italy and comprising contingents from 11 States,[205] intervened to restore security and supply humanitarian aid. The operation was justified by the prior adoption of a Security Council resolution in which the Council:

> *Taking note* of the letter of 28 March 1997 from the Permanent Representative of Albania to the United Nations to the President of the Security Council (S/1997/259) . . .,
>
> 2. *Welcome[d]* the offer made by certain Member States to establish a temporary and limited multinational protection force to facilitate the safe and prompt delivery of humanitarian assistance, and to help create a secure environment for the missions of international organizations in Albania, including those providing humanitarian assistance . . .;
>
> 4. *Authorize[d]* the Member States participating in the multinational protection force to conduct the operation in a neutral and impartial way to achieve the objectives set out in paragraph 2 above and, acting under Chapter VII of the Charter of the United Nations, further authorize[d] these Member States to ensure the security and freedom of movement of the personnel of the said multinational protection force.[206]

Notice that the Security Council took into account a letter to it from the Albanian representative to the UN. In that letter, the Albanian government mentioned an official request it made to the OSCE and which the permanent council of the OSCE had decided to honour.[207] It then specified that:

> The Albanian Government and the Albanian people highly appreciate this action of OSCE and the readiness of a number of countries to participate in that force. Albania is looking forward to the arrival of such a force. Taking into consideration the situation in Albania, we feel that such a force must also have the necessary support and authorization of the Security Council of the United Nations.[208]

---

[203] SC Res 794 (1992), 2 December 1992.

[204] *Keesing's Contemporary Archives*, 1997, 41596–98.

[205] Austria, Belgium, Denmark, France, Greece, Italy, Portugal, Romania, Slovenia, Spain, Turkey.

[206] SC Res 1101 (1997) of 28 March 1997. See also SC Res 1114 (1997) of 19 June 1997 and S/PRST/1997/14, 13 March 1997.

[207] S/1997/259, 28 March 1997, annex II.

[208] S/1997/259, 28 March 1997, 1.

The official government of Albania itself seems to have considered that its consent would not be enough, insofar as it would have to be supplemented by Security Council authorisation. This was a feeling clearly shared by Italy, which, after relying on an appeal for outside aid from the Albanian government, declared that:

> In this respect, a legal framework for the provision of this assistance should be envisaged. This framework should, in our view, take the form of a resolution by the Security Council authorizing Member States who are willing to participate in such a multinational force to conduct the operation to achieve the above-mentioned objectives.[209]

The consent of the official government was not mentioned, then, when defining the legal framework for intervention.

These precedents seem to lead to the same conclusions that can be summarised in two points. For one thing, an exceptional situation of anarchy or disturbance does not entail the disappearance of the affected State, which continues to exist legally despite its government's loss of effective power. Effective power is a decisive criterion for evaluating the birth of a State but, once it is in being, a State subsists in law without ever returning to a status comparable to that of a *terra nullius*. The only disappearance of a State that can be envisaged is when it follows from a succession mechanism, either by union, absorption or secession.[210] This observation rules out a doctrinal trend that arose in the early 1990s by which a government's loss of effective power supposedly deprived the State of one of its constituent parts, with as a consequence a loss of its capacity as a State and so of its sovereignty.[211] In this context, some commentators have claimed that outside military intervention may be conducted without infringing article 2(4) of the Charter, which is only meaningful for protecting the sovereignty of a State.[212] That claim is in conflict with the precedents of Somalia and Albania, where no intervening State affirmed it could intervene in the territory of those States on the pretext that they had been deprived of their sovereignty because of a loss of effective power by the two respective governments.[213] On the contrary, it has been seen that, in such situations, the internationally recognised government continued to represent the State

---

[209] S/1997/258, 27 March 1997, 2.

[210] See the 1978 Vienna Convention on Succession of States in respect of Treaties, *UNTS*, vol 1946, 3.

[211] J Charpentier, 'Le phénomène étatique à travers les grandes mutations politiques contemporaines' in SFDI, *L'Etat souverain à l'aube du XXIème siècle* (Paris, Pedone, 1994) 24–33; JM Sorel, 'La Somalie et les Nations Unies' (1992) 38 *AFDI* 72, 75 and 77–78.

[212] See: P Weckel, 'Le chapitre VII de la Charte et son application par le Conseil de sécurité' (1991) 37 *AFDI* 193–95; Against: O Paye, *Sauve qui veut? Le droit international face aux crises humanitaires*, above n 114, 176–77.

[213] See also: O Corten and P Klein, 'L'autorisation de recourir à la force à des fins humanitaires: droit d'ingérence ou retour aux sources?' (1993) 4 *EJIL* 517–20; M Byers, 'Terrorism, the Use of Force and International Law After 11 September' (2002) 51 *ICLQ* 403–04.

validly especially within the UN.[214] However, and this is the second lesson
that can be deduced from this, the consent of such a government is not
enough in law to justify an outside military intervention. Such interventions
must be conducted within a multilateral framework after the decision of the
UN Security Council. As such, the State's consent does not seem to suffice
unless given by a government that is both recognised but also able to exercise power with a degree of effectiveness. This combination of recognition
and effective power is found also in another situation, that where the internationally recognised authorities are overthrown.

b) The Overthrowing of Internationally Recognised Authorities

It sometimes happens that a legal government is overthrown as a result of
an internal conflict—revolution, coup d'état, internal disturbances—and
replaced by another government which, while it may have managed to seize
effective power, has not been recognised by third States. It might then be
wondered whether the ousted government can rely on the legitimacy resulting from its international recognition to seek outside military intervention to
restore it to power. This issue involves legal principles such as the right to
self-determination or non-intervention in internal affairs and could therefore be apprehended in the context of the question of the purpose of the
intervention.[215] At this stage, we shall insist, though, from the outset, on the
impossibility for a government deprived of effective power in such circumstances to make a valid call for military intervention by third States.

That this is impossible can be understood logically first of all. Where
effective power changes hands, third States are often divided, some recognising the new government that has come to power (relying on effective
power) while others continue to recognise the ousted government (relying
on their conception of legitimacy). In this context, it is hard to understand
why recognition alone—especially when maintained by some States only—
should confer power on an ousted regime to call for and obtain foreign support to restore its authority.[216] This is then rather a situation of civil war or
internal conflict in which we have seen that the prohibition of the use of
force set out in article 2(4) does not apply and consequently a principle of
'legal neutrality' is evoked.[217] The forcible overthrow of a government by a
rebel or seditious faction cannot readily, in this context, validly give rise to
an appeal by that government to a military riposte by third States.

This logic is borne out in practice insofar as, to the best of my knowledge,
there is no precedent in which the international community as a whole has

---

[214] G Cahin, 'L'Etat défaillant en droit international: quel régime pour quelle notion? in
Droit du pouvoir, pouvoir du droit. Mélanges offerts à Jean Salmon (Bruxelles, Bruylant, 2007)
192.
[215] See below.
[216] D Schindler, 'Le principe de non-intervention dans les guerres civiles', above n 58, 427.
[217] See above, ch 3, s I.

admitted the lawfulness of an outside military intervention conducted on the basis of an appeal from an overthrown government in an internal conflict. Moreover, no claim ever seems to have been made to this end. If situations such as coups d'état or revolutions have sometimes given rise to outside military interventions, these have been based on arguments other than the consent of the ousted regime, as attested by the two precedents below.

In the case of Haiti, it will be remembered that the government presided by Jean-Bertrand Aristide was recognised as the only legitimate one further to the coup that removed him from power in September 1991.[218] After unarmed coercive measures had been decided on and enforced in vain against the putschists,[219] the prospect of a military intervention was evoked. No one, though, seems to have considered that a simple appeal from the legitimate government would have sufficed to overthrow by force a de facto government that had been duly condemned by the General Assembly.[220] States preferred instead the adoption of a resolution by the Security Council on 31 July 1994 authorising military action.[221] As in other instances, whether before (Somalia) or after (Albania), the Security Council did not refrain from referring to an appeal from an internationally recognised government.[222] President Aristide had called on States 'to take prompt and decisive action, under the authority of the United Nations',[223] and it transpires from a reading of the minutes of the discussions that preceded the adoption of the resolution that it was only by dint of an official stance to that end that the Security Council Member States agreed to authorise military measures.[224] It is remarkable that the Security Council insisted on highlighting this circumstance in the wording of its resolution and only began discussion after having heard Haiti's representative call on it to act.[225] The episode shows that the government's appeal was clearly not deemed sufficient to implement outside military action, which explains the Security

---

[218] Y Daudet, 'L'ONU et l'OEA en Haïti et le droit international' (1992) 38 AFDI 89–111.

[219] See: OAS, CP/RES.567 (870/91), 30 September 1991, MRE/RES. 1/91, 3 October 1991, (1992) 86 AJIL 667–69 and SC Res 841 (1993) of 16 June 1993.

[220] GA Res 46/7 of 11 October 1991. See also GA Res 46/138 of 17 December 1991, 47/20 A of 24 November 1992, 47/143 of 18 December 1992 and 47/20 B of 23 April 1993; T Franck, 'The Emerging Right to Democratic Governance' (1992) 86 AJIL 72–75; M Byers and S Chesterman, ' "You, the People": pro-democratic intervention in international law', above n 25, 302.

[221] SC Res 940 (1994) of 31 July 1994, para 4. See O Corten, 'La résolution 940 du Conseil de sécurité autorisant une intervention militaire en Haïti: la consécration d'un principe de légitimité démocratique?' (1995) 6 EJIL 116–33; LA Sicilianos, L'ONU et la démocratisation de l'Etat (Paris, Pedone, 2000) 187–201. See also below, ch 6.

[222] 'Taking note of the letter dated 29 July 1994 from the legitimately elected President of Haiti (S/1994/905, annex) and the letter dated 30 July 1994 from the Permanent Representative of Haiti to the United Nations (S/1994/910)' (SC Res 940 (1994) of 31 July 1994).

[223] S/1994/905, 19 July 1994, 2.

[224] See the views expressed by Spain, New Zealand, Russia and the Czech Republic (S/PV.3413, 31 July 1994).

[225] ibid.

Council's use of the powers it has under Chapter VII of the Charter.[226]

Another interesting precedent is that of events in Sierra Leone in 1998. ECOMOG troops[227] intervened in February 1998 to restore to power an elected government[228] that had been overthrown by a coup in May 1997.[229] This operation seems to have been generally accepted, especially within the UN, even though the Security Council, as in the Haitian case, had not given prior authorisation for it.[230] Should this not be seen as a new development in international law, which seemingly admits the forcible overthrow of authorities that have come to power via a coup on the sole basis of the consent of the regime ousted by the coup?[231] I think not. The legal argument of the intervening States does not seem to have consisted in reference to a rule of this type.[232] When the junta was overthrown by force,[233] ECOMOG more specifically justified the use of armed force by reference to self-defence, envisaged here as a classic feature in the context of peacekeeping operations.[234] It should be recalled that ECOMOG forces were already present in Sierra Leone with the agreement of the effective governmental authorities. ECOMOG's *initial* presence in Sierra Leone must be set in the historical context of the Abidjan Peace Accord between the legitimate government and the rebel forces in late 1996, an agreement guaranteed by the OAU.[235] Acceptance of the deployment of ECOMOG by all parties was formalised after the coup in the Conakry Agreement of October 1997, providing for the restoration of the ousted president within six months.[236] ECOMOG was to supervise enforcement of the agreement, notably as concerned the cessation of hostilities and disarming of combatants. In short, two factors justified the intervention: the *presence* of foreign forces in Sierra Leone had been accepted by the effective government; and the *intervention* of those forces in the conflict can be explained by the implementation of self-defence in riposte to attacks by the government authorities. Under the circumstances, the argument of self-defence was far from sure to win out,

---

[226] D Wippman, 'Pro-democratic intervention by invitation', above n 26, 301–03.

[227] These troops were mainly Nigerian troops (*Keesing's Contemporary Archives*, 1997, 41672).

[228] *Keesing's Contemporary Archives*, 1996, 40982.

[229] *Keesing's Contemporary Archives*, 1997, 41625.

[230] See below, ch 6, s II.

[231] D Wippman, 'Pro-democratic intervention by invitation', above n 26, 293–311; G Nolte, *Eingreifen auf Einladung*, above n 2, 637 (abstract in English).

[232] T Christakis and K Bannelier, '*Volenti non fit injuria?* Les effets du consentement à l'intervention militaire', above n 2, 132, fn 126. See also M Byers and S Chesterman, ' "You, the People": pro-democratic intervention in international law', above n 25, 306–11.

[233] *Keesing's Contemporary Archives*, 1998, 41992 and 42048.

[234] '9ème réunion ministérielle du Comité des Cinq de la CEDEAO sur la Sierra Leone', Final Communiqué (Addis Ababa, 25–27 February 1998), *DAI*, no 8, 1998, 279; see also '7ème réunion ministérielle du Comité des Cinq de la CEDEAO, Final Communiqué (Abuja, 19 December 1997)', *DAI*, 1997, no 5, 187.

[235] S/1996/1034, 11 December 1996.

[236] S/1997/824, 28 October 1997 and *Keesing's Contemporary Archives*, 1997, 41849.

particularly in view of the criterion of proportionality that it implies.[237] One might then have expected the invitation of the 'legitimate' government to be invoked, which was not the case, an omission that might have been thought significant.

Finally, it can be understood that while effective power is not a sufficient criterion for assessing the validity of consent, it is nonetheless a necessary criterion. In view of the legal logic of existing practice, it does not seem that the mere appeal from an internationally recognised government that has lost all effective power is enough to justify outside military intervention. This conclusion supposes, however, that the loss of actual power is not itself the outcome of a prior aggression from outside, as remains to be recalled briefly now.

c) An Authority in Effective Power Further to an Armed Attack

When one State attacks and invades another and manages to overthrow the government in office, that government loses effective power while remaining a legitimate government and being recognised as such by third States. In such circumstances, third States may obviously help the ousted government to recover its authority by intervening to drive the aggressor State from the territory it occupied. This possibility results more, though, from the institution of collective self-defence than from the consent of the government, even if such consent is a necessary condition for the implementation of collective self-defence.[238] The legal basis for a riposte of the kind is to be sought in article 51 of the Charter, while consent is merely an accessory or peripheral feature.[239]

In conclusion, it shall be observed that, apart from the specific case of collective self-defence, the question of concurrent governments in the context of an internal conflict must be handled with great care.[240] In such instances, it seems that an appeal for outside intervention presupposes, for it to be justified, that it comes from a government that is both internationally recognised and that has a certain effective power.[241] In the event of doubt about legitimacy or effective power, practice seems to profess a duty to abstain and refer matters to a Security Council decision. If no doubt remains, an appeal may then be considered admissible. Even so, it must be asked whether the purpose of the intervention consented to does not bar its lawfulness, which shall be dealt with in detail in the final part of this chapter.

---

[237] D Wippman, 'Pro-democratic intervention by invitation', above n 26, 307–08.
[238] ICJ, *Military and Paramilitary Activities*, ICJ Rep (1986), para 199.
[239] Below, ch 7.
[240] C Gray, *International Law and the Use of Force*, 3rd edn, above n 12, 99).
[241] C Walter, 'Security Council Control over Regional Action', above n 91, 150.

B. The Problem of the Purpose of the Intervention by Invitation

Let us now suppose that an internationally recognised government with effective power clearly gives its unvitiated consent without coercion to outside military intervention: will such intervention necessarily be consistent with international law? Should the criterion of the purpose of the intervention consented to be taken into account? More specifically, can the lawfulness of outside military intervention designed to put down a rebel movement in a civil war be admitted?

Scholars have long been divided on these points.[242] For some, validly given consent will invariably make lawful outside military action that, because of that consent, is not directed against the 'political independence' of a State within the meaning of article 2(4) of the Charter. There would seem to be an asymmetry in the case of a civil war, with outside military aid being prohibited for rebels but authorised for government forces.[243] For others, though, the principle of non-intervention must be understood as protecting the State as a whole and not just its government which is only one of its component parts. Outside military action, even if conducted on an appeal from the government, would infringe this principle insofar as it would be designed to influence the outcome of a conflict that is purely internal to the State in question, a State whose political independence would therefore be infringed by that use of force.[244] This second doctrinal trend, which has prevailed especially within the International Law Institute, comes out clearly in favour of a duty of abstention in the event of civil war, which duty is opposed to outside military support, whether in favour of rebels or of government forces.[245]

A first point should be mentioned at the outset. There is no treaty instrument or more generally no text adopted by an international or even regional organisation that makes any direct and explicit pronouncement on this question. Under the circumstances, the debate must be apprehended in terms of the major principles of international law and in particular of the right of peoples to self-determination (1). The importance of this right is reflected in practice, which denotes an admission of outside interventions

---

[242] D Schindler, 'Le principe de non-intervention dans les guerres civiles', above n 58, 428–41; R Kolb, *Ius contra bellum. Le droit international relatif au maintien de la paix*, 2nd edn (Bruxelles, Bruylant/Bâle, Helbing Lichtenhahn, 2009), 326–29; R Randelzhofer, 'Article 2 (4)' in B Simma (ed), *The Charter of the United Nations. A Commentary*, 2nd edn, (Oxford, Oxford University Press, 2002) 122–23.

[243] LC Green, 'Le statut des forces rebelles en droit international' (1962) 66 *RGDIP* 17; JH Leurdijk, 'Civil War and Intervention in International Law' (1977) 24 *NILR* 159.

[244] See, eg: M Bennouna, *Le consentement à l'ingérence militaire dans les conflits internes*, above n 2, 50.

[245] *The Principle of Non-Intervention in Civil Wars*, 15 August 1975, Wiesbaden session, (1975) 56 *AIDI* 544–49. According to 2 § 1 of the resolution, 'Third States shall refrain from giving assistance to parties to a civil war which is being fought in the territory of another State'.

when these are intended to maintain law and order or peace (2) or to riposte to outside interference (3). *A contrario*, it will be observed that it is difficult to demonstrate the existence of a customary rule admitting outside interventions officially aimed at supporting a government in office against rebel forces.

The Unlawfulness in Principle of a Use of Force that is Incompatible with the Right to Self-Determination

It has already been recalled that the right of peoples to self-determination has been progressively recognised as implying a right to accede to independence for colonial peoples and peoples subject to an occupying regime or to a racist regime.[246] It should be added at this point that this legal principle has also been construed as implying the right for a people that already forms a State to maintain its political independence with regard to third States. This is what resolution 2625 (XXV) indicates when it provides that: 'By virtue of the principle of equal rights and self-determination of peoples enshrined in the Charter of the United Nations, all peoples have the right to determine, without external interference, their political status . . .'.[247]

The people and not the government of a State here enjoy a right which can be considered infringed when a foreign State intervenes to favour one or other party in an internal political conflict.[248] There is then outside interference in the determination of an internal political status.[249] In such an event, it can be considered that article 2(4) of the Charter is violated since it opposes any use of force in international relations 'in any other manner inconsistent with the Purposes of the United Nations', and that one of its purposes is without contest the protection of the right of peoples to self-determination.[250]

This interpretation of the Charter is confirmed by consideration of the work that preceded the adoption of resolution 2625 (XXV). The question

[246] Above, ch 3, s I.

[247] GA Res 2625 (XXV) of 24 October 1970, Annex. See also art 1 of the International Covenant on Civil and Political Rights, *UNTS*, no 14668, vol 999 (1976), 171.

[248] L Doswald-Beck, 'The Legal Validity of Military Intervention by Invitation of the Government', above n 2, 242–44; T Christakis and K Bannelier, '*Volenti non fit injuria?* Les effets du consentement à l'intervention militaire', above n 2, 120; R Higgins, 'The Legal Limits to the Use of Force by Sovereign States. United Nations Practice' (1961) 37 *BYBIL* 309; B Asrat, *Prohibition of Force Under the UN Charter. A Study of Art. 2(4)* (Uppsala, Iustus Förlag, 1991) 17.

[249] By virtue of the duty not to intervene in matters within the domestic jurisdiction of any State, 'No State may [. . .] interfere in civil strife of another State' (AG Res 2625 (XXV) of 24 October 1970, Annex); L Doswald-Beck, 'The Legal Validity of Military Intervention by Invitation of the Government', above n 2, 208; T Christakis and K Bannelier, '*Volenti non fit injuria?* Les effets du consentement à l'intervention militaire', above n 2, 116; C Walter, 'Security Council Control over Regional Action', above n 91, 146–47.

[250] See: M Bennouna, *Le consentement à l'ingérence militaire dans les conflits internes*, above n 2, 213; D Schindler, 'Le principe de non-intervention dans les guerres civiles', above n 58, 445–47; see also G Nolte, *Eingreifen auf Einladung*, above n 2, 632 (abstract in English).

of intervention by invitation was briefly evoked during the debates.[251] Now, while recognising a general right to external military assistance,[252] several States have insisted on the unlawfulness of an intervention specifically designed to support a government against rebel forces.[253] No State, to my knowledge, has contradicted this position which fits in perfectly with the text that was finally adopted, particularly in terms of the right to self-determination and the principle of non-intervention[254] and which, as shall be set out below, is confirmed by the development of practice. An examination of military interventions conducted at the request of governments in office shows that such interventions have been justified either by humanitarian objectives, objectives of maintaining law and order or peace, or as a riposte to outside interference. *A contrario*, third States do not claim a right to help a government that makes an appeal for aid to put down a rebel movement in a civil war. So, we can consider consistent with general international law the British position whereby

> any form of interference or assistance is prohibited (except possibly of a humanitarian kind) when a civil war is taking place and control of the State's territory is divided between warring parties. But it is widely accepted that outside interference in favour of one party to the struggle permits counter-intervention on behalf of the other, as happened in the Spanish Civil War and, more recently, in Angola.[255]

Outside Military Interventions Officially for Humanitarian Ends or to Maintain Law and Order or Peace

Very often an intervention by invitation is officially said to be consented to for considerations of maintaining law and order or peace. Several cases can be distinguished: (a) the case of an extraterritorial coercive operation conducted by a third State for its own purposes; (b) that of support by a third State for a government to uphold local law and order; and (c) that of a 'peacekeeping operation'. In each instance, the intervening State denies supporting, or in any event does not claim to support, government forces in the context of an internal conflict.[256]

---

[251] See, eg: India's representative, A/AC.119/SR.3, 31 August 1964.

[252] See the views expressed by the UK; A/AC 125/SR 57, 19 July 1967; and M Bennouna, *Le consentement à l'ingérence militaire dans les conflits internes*, above n 2, 93.

[253] See the views expressed by the UK (A/C.6/S.R.822, 29 November 1963), Indonesia (A/C.6/S.R.935, 22 November 1966), Finland (A/C.6/S.R.1086, 4 December 1968) and the USA (A/C.6/S.R.1180, 24 September 1970, 19, para 23); *Report of the Special Committee on Principles of International Law concerning Friendly relations and co-operation among States*, Supp no 18, A/8018, 1970, 120, para 259.

[254] M Bennouna, *Le consentement à l'ingérence militaire dans les conflits internes*, above n 2, 59; L Doswald-Beck, 'The Legal Validity of Military Intervention by Invitation of the Government', above n 2, 209–12; T Christakis and K Bannelier, '*Volenti non fit injuria?* Les effets du consentement à l'intervention militaire', above n 2, 114.

[255] 'Is Intervention ever justified?' (1986) 57 *BYBIL* 616.

[256] See: M Bennouna, *Le consentement à l'ingérence militaire dans les conflits internes*, above n 2, 41.

a) Extraterritorial Coercive Operations by a Third State for its own Purposes

It sometimes happens that a State A asks the government of a State B for permission to enter its territory for some specific objective such as to defend its security or protect its nationals. In such instances, State A's declared aim is in no way to influence State B's domestic political status by supporting its authorities, State A declaring it is solely pursuing its own interests in a context of international cooperation. It is not surprising therefore that this type of intervention by invitation is not in principle contested whether in terms of the principle of the non-use of force or that of non-intervention and the right to self-determination.

In *Armed Activities*, we have seen that the DRC had accepted that Ugandan troops crossed the border to pursue and punish Ugandan rebels stationed in the Congo.[257] DRC and Ugandan troops had even conducted joint military operations against irregular Ugandan forces again in DRC territory.[258] No one questioned the lawfulness of such action, whether the parties, third States or the ICJ itself.[259] Such practice is far from exceptional. A 'right of pursuit' is sometimes granted by a State that accepts that another State's armed forces or police forces enter its territory while pursuing rebel forces.[260] Such a situation obviously poses no legal problem, quite the contrary.[261] It should be recalled that each State is under an obligation to ensure that its territory is not used by irregular forces to attack other States.[262] This obligation implies that all requisite measures be taken, within the limits of its resources, consistent with the due diligence principle.[263] One way to prevent one's territory from being used for hostile ends is to conduct police or military operations oneself to eradicate the bases from which rebel forces opposed to a foreign government operate. Another method is to cooperate with the government, allowing it to cross the border for a limited and circumscribed purpose.[264] Thus, it can be asserted that the consent so given is not only not prohibited but that it results from the State in question implementing an obligation that itself derives from article 2(4). As for the intervening State, by entering the territory of a consenting State, it does not interfere in its internal affairs or influence the determination of its political status; it merely attacks 'its own' rebels, which, let us

---

[257] See above.

[258] See Rejoinder of the Democratic Republic of Congo, 158–66.

[259] CIJ, Judgment of 19 December 2005, para 45.

[260] Jean Salmon, 'Les circonstances excluant l'illicéité' in K Zemanek and J Salmon, *Responsabilité internationale* (Paris, Pedone, 1987) 97.

[261] See above.

[262] GA Res 2615 (XXV) and above, ch 3, s I; see also below, ch 7, s I.

[263] See above, ch 3, s I and F Dubuisson, 'Vers un renforcement des obligations de diligence en matière de lutte contre le terrorisme?' in K Bannelier *et al* (eds), *Le droit international face au terrorisme* (Paris, Pedone, 2002) 141–58.

[264] See, eg: C Rousseau, 'Chronique des faits internationaux' (1983) 87 *RGDIP* 885.

recall, is not prohibited by contemporary international law.[265] In such a situation, it can be understood that the intervention consented to is perfectly lawful and is recognised as such by the international community of States as a whole.[266]

The same conclusion can be drawn about military operations officially intended to protect the lives of a State's nationals when conducted with the consent of the State in whose territory the operation takes place.[267] One can think, for example,[268] of the action by German security forces in 1978 in Mogadishu when they freed their nationals taken hostage at the city's airport with the cooperation of the local authorities and the Somali government.[269] In such cases, the coercive action does not consist in interfering in an internal conflict and does not seem as such to pose any particular problem.[270] It can even seriously be asked whether we are still within the scope of application of article 2(4), which it has been seen relates only to the use of 'force' by one State against another.[271] It must be considered rather that we are dealing with a simple police operation of extraterritorial scope that is part of international police cooperation.[272]

Certain precedents, though, have raised more controversy when questioning the true motives of States officially conducting operations to protect their nationals. The 1964 rescue operation in Stanleyville by the armed forces of Belgium and the US with the cooperation of the UK is a classic example.[273] While it shows a disagreement between the intervening States and other States about the lawfulness of the action, that disagreement was more specifically about the existence of—and especially the true motives for—an operation that on the ground favoured the action of government forces against Congolese rebels.[274] On the principle of the lawfulness of consented military intervention designed solely to rescue nationals, no disagreement seems to have been shown.

---

[265] Above, ch 3, s 1.

[266] T Christakis and K Bannelier, '*Volenti non fit injuria?* Les effets du consentement à l'intervention militaire', above n 2, 126–27.

[267] See: N Ronzitti, *Rescuing Nationals Abroad Through Military Coercion and Intervention on Grounds of Humanity* (Dordrecht, Martinus Nijhoff, 1985) 77–88 and 'Use of Force, *Jus Cogens* and State Consent', above n 8, 153–54.

[268] See also: T Christakis and K Bannelier, '*Volenti non fit injuria?* Les effets du consentement à l'intervention militaire', above n 2, 124.

[269] ibid, 125.

[270] See: N Ronzitti, *Rescuing Nationals Abroad Through Military Coercion and Intervention on Grounds of Humanity*, above n 268, 81 and 86–88.

[271] ibid, 87–88 and above, ch 2, s I.

[272] See T Christakis and K Bannelier, '*Volenti non fit injuria?* Les effets du consentement à l'intervention militaire', above n 2, 124.

[273] KC Wellens, *Résolutions et déclarations du Conseil de sécurité (1946–1992). Recueil thématique* (Bruxelles, Bruylant, 1993) 81 *ff* and A Gérard, 'L'opération Stanleyville-Paulis devant le parlement belge et les Nations Unies' (1967) 3 *RBDI* 264–69.

[274] *Repertory of Practice of United Nations Organs*, Supp no 3 (1959–1966), vol 1—Art 2 (4) (Separate Study), 160, para 190 and C Gray, *International Law and the Use of Force*, 3rd edn, above n 12, 88.

Thus, from the outset, the Congo government emphasised the strictly humanitarian and neutral character of the military action consented to. The Prime Minister of the time, Moise Tshombe, stated:

> I have authorized the Belgian Government and the United States Government to render my Government the necessary assistance in organizing a humanitarian mission to make it possible for these foreign hostages to be evacuated. I must emphasize that my Government has authorized this intervention solely for the limited period necessary to make possible the evacuation of these persons, whose lives are in grave danger.[275]

The US administration[276] and the Belgian government[277] confirmed this, with the UK providing only logistical support 'in the light of the humanitarian objective of this action'.[278] *A contrario*, neither the intervening States nor the Congo itself, assumed a right to help the government to put down the rebels.[279]

Many States criticised this line of argument, denouncing outside military action as foreign intervention in the Congolese internal conflict,[280] or even an act of aggression.[281] For them, the aim of the intervention was to conquer Stanleyville.[282] The intervention was therefore condemned because the intervening powers failed to comply with a policy of neutrality.[283] In this context, some States considered that Moise Tshombe's government could no longer validly claim to represent the Congolese people,[284] its consent then no longer being able to justify the outside military intervention.

---

[275] S/6060, 24 November 1964. See also S/PV.1173, 11 December 1964.

[276] S/6062, 24 November 1964 and Annex II; see also S/PV.1170, 9 December 1964 and S/PV.1174, 14 December 1964.

[277] S/6062, 24 November 1964, Annex I and S/PV.1173, 11 December 1964.

[278] S/6059, 24 November 1964; see also S/PV.1175, 15 December 1964 and S/6069, 27 November 1964.

[279] See also the views expressed by Bolivia; S/PV.1183, 22 December 1964, 14.

[280] In a letter dated 1 December 1964, 22 States (Afghanistan, Algeria, Burundi, Cambodia, Congo, Dahomey, Ethiopia, Ghana, Guinea, Indonesia, Kenya, Malawi, Mali, Mauritania, Central African Republic, Somalia, Sudan, UAR, Uganda, Tanzania, Yugoslavia and Zambia) stated that 'such actions constitute an intervention in African affairs, a flagrant violation of the Charter of the United Nations and a threat to the peace and security of the African continent' (S/6076 and add.1–5); see also the views expressed by Czechoslovakia (S/PV.1170, 9 December 1964).

[281] USSR (S/PV.1170, 9 December 1964; S/6066, 25 November 1964), Congo (S/PV.1170, 9 December 1964), Ghana (ibid), Guinea (S/PV.1171, 10 December 1964), Mali (S/PV.1171, 10 December 1964), UAR (S/PV.1174, 14 December 1964).

[282] According to Mali, 'the real purpose [. . .] was to facilitate the capture of Stanleyville by the mercenaries' (S/PV.1171, 10 December 1964, 14, para 48). See also the views expressed by the USSR (S/PV.1178, 17 December 1964), Czechoslovakia (S/PV.1181, 21 December 1964), Kenya (S/PV.1175, 15 December 1964) and Tanzania (S/PV.1178, 17 December 1964).

[283] See the views expressed by Burundi (S/PV.1177, 16 December 1964).

[284] Algeria (S/PV.1183, 22 December 1964), USSR (S/PV.1185, 24 December 1964 and S/PV.1170, 9 December 1964), Kenya (S/PV.1175, 15 December 1964). Against: see Ivory Coast (S/PV.1170, 9 December 1964), USA (S/PV.1174, 14 December 1964), Nigeria (S/PV.1176, 15 December 1964), France (ibid), Brazil (S/PV.1177, 16 December 1964) and China (S/PV.1177, 16 December 1964).

The debate focused therefore on the sincerity of the motives officially advanced by the intervening powers. On principle, no one seemed to accept it was lawful for outside military intervention to influence the course of the civil war, whether in favour of the rebels or the authorities. This precedent therefore seems very clearly to make the lawfulness of the intervention consented to dependent upon its purpose, which must remain consistent with a duty of neutrality;[285] a duty of neutrality that does not go so far as to prohibit any military support for a foreign government, provided that such support remains general and logistical, and is not reflected by direct intervention against the rebels. This at any rate is what can be deduced from practice, including in the case of the Stanleyville operation.

b) Support for a Government from a Third State to Maintain Law and Order: Police Operations and Logistical Aid

In the Stanleyville operation, the intervening States did not simply invoke the strictly humanitarian character of their action. Confronted with criticism about the military support they also granted to the government in power, they responded that their support was general and logistical and could not be likened to an intervention in a civil war. The position was very clear for the Belgian representative: 'It is one thing for a foreign Government to take part in the training of the forces of law and order in another country, but quite another for it to take a direct part in systematic repressive operations'.[286]

As for the States that criticised the intervention, it is very significant to observe that they did not contest the possibility in principle of providing outside logistical support to a government.[287] They simply denied that this was what happened in the case in point.

Beyond the differences in the assessment of the events in the Congo, a common legal position arises very clearly from all of the points of view expressed. A government may validly ask for and obtain outside military support from a third State not to take part in military actions in a civil war, but to contribute to maintaining law and order and stability.[288] When law and order are threatened by events such as a mutiny or ordinary crimes, such support may take the form of a limited outside military intervention, which cannot be likened to political intervention that would be contrary to the right of self-determination.[289]

---

[285] See also the military operation in Kolwezi; 'La pratique de l'exécutif en matière de droit international' (1980) 15 *RBDI* 630–49.

[286] S/PV.1173, 11 December 1964, 18, para 86. See also the views expressed by the USA (S/PV.1174, 14 December 1964). Against: Ivory Coast (S/PV.1177, 16 December 1964) and Nigeria (S/PV.1176, 15 December 1964).

[287] See the views expressed by Uganda (S/PV.1177, 16 December 1964), Tanzania (S/PV.1178, 17 December 1964), Kenya (S/PV.1175, 15 December 1964) and Algeria (S/PV.1183, 22 December 1964).

[288] C Gray, *International Law and the Use of Force*, 3rd edn, above n 12, 85.

[289] M Bennouna, *Le consentement à l'ingérence militaire dans les conflits internes*, above n 2, 43; D Schindler, 'Le principe de non-intervention dans les guerres civiles', above n 58, 450–51.

By way of illustration, we can cite the practice of certain States that have often conducted or supported operations at the request of governments in power.

—British military operations in Kenya, Tanzania and Uganda in the 1960s were presented as police measures to put down mutinies and not as interventions in internal conflicts.[290] In parallel, when the UK was criticised for its continued military cooperation with Nigeria during the Biafran war, it replied it had every right to maintain such aid as it was not directly involved in the conflict.[291]

—French military cooperation with many African States can also be understood in this way, as several commentators have emphasised.[292] No cooperation agreement entered into by France provides for granting support to put down a purely internal rebellion. Generally the President of the Republic asserted that France's African policy was based on the refusal to become involved in internal conflicts.[293] Where military aid has been granted, the official motive has not been to help the government in the context of a civil war.[294] In the case of Chad, for example, the French authorities specified in the 1970s that the logistical support to the government in power did not mean that they intended to engage in the fight against the rebels.[295]

—The same reasoning was defended by the US authorities to justify their logistical aid to the Colombian government which was presented as being related to the fight against drugs or against terrorism, not as intervention in a civil war.[296] Similarly, the despatch of US military contingents to the Philippines was presented simply as part of joint military exercises,

---

[290] See also: M Bennouna, *Le consentement à l'ingérence militaire dans les conflits internes*, above n 2, 43; D Schindler, 'Le principe de non-intervention dans les guerres civiles', above n 58, 450–51.

[291] M Bennouna, *Le consentement à l'ingérence militaire dans les conflits internes*, above n 2, 90; C Rousseau, 'Chronique des faits internationaux' (1970) 74 *RGDIP* 497.

[292] L Doswald-Beck, 'The Legal Validity of Military Intervention by Invitation of the Government', above n 2, 218–21; CJ Le Mon, 'Unilateral Intervention by Invitation in Civil Wars: the Effective Control Test Tested', above n 2, 768–72; G Nolte, *Eingreifen auf Einladung*, above n 2, 634–35. See also 'La pratique de l'exécutif en matière de droit international' (1980) 15 *RBDI* 629 and C Rousseau, 'Chronique des faits internationaux' (1979) 83 *RGDIP* 202–08.

[293] 'Pratique française du droit international' (1977) 23 *AFDI* 1012.

[294] cp 'Pratique française du droit international' (1964) 10 *AFDI* 928 and A Tanca, *Foreign Armed Intervention in Internal Conflict*, above n 2, 157; (1969) 73 *RGDIP* 469–71; 'Pratique française du droit international' (1986) 32 *AFDI* 1015–16; M Bennouna, *Le consentement à l'ingérence militaire dans les conflits internes*, above n 2, 44–49; C Gray, *International Law and the Use of Force*, 3rd edn, above n 12, 96–98.

[295] 'Pratique française du droit international' (1970) 16 *AFDI* 989–91; L Doswald-Beck, 'The Legal Validity of Military Intervention by Invitation of the Government', above n 2, 219; A Tanca, *Foreign Armed Intervention in Internal Conflict*, above n 2, 162; see also P Chapal, 'Les interventions militaires de la France', above n 114, 83–84; 'Pratique française du droit international' (1980) 26 *AFDI* 879 and 880–81.

[296] C Gray, *International Law and the Use of Force*, 3rd edn, above n 12, 87.

consisting in training in counter-insurgency methods.[297] By the terms of the cooperation agreement between the two countries, US armed forces are not authorised to engage in military operations against rebel forces active on several islands of the Philippines.[298]

—Finally, we can mention the appeal by the government of East Timor to the forces of Portugal, Australia and New Zealand in May 2006. This invitation was officially made not to intervene in an internal conflict but 'in order to establish measures of security and confidence among the populations so as to restore tranquillity throughout the national territory . . . .'[299]

Thus, and though it does not necessarily correspond to reality,[300] a State that provides military aid to a foreign government invariably claims to be doing so while maintaining a strictly neutral attitude in the event of internal strife. This often leads it to minimise the scale of the conflict and to present it as a simple internal disturbance.[301] *A contrario*, it does seem that a legal conviction of a general order can be made out, prohibiting direct military intervention in favour of government forces in the context of a conflict against opposition forces—direct military intervention to which one cannot, however, assimilate the simple provision of arms and equipment, even in times of civil war. Government and rebels, then, are by no means on an equal footing in the context of contemporary international law. If compliance with the right of self-determination implies not directly supporting one or other side, it is no impediment to continuing normal interstate relations, including in the domain of military cooperation with the authorities in power.[302] Similarly, international law is not opposed to the deployment of 'peacekeeping operations', whatever the scale of the conflict.

c) The Deployment of 'Peacekeeping Operations'

Since the 1990s especially, there have been many precedents attesting to the validity of outside military operations officially for peacekeeping purposes with the consent of the local authorities. The situation is very similar to the foregoing, expect that the outside military action is conducted at the initiative of or under the aegis of the international collective security organisa-

---

[297] *Kessing's Contemporary Archives*, 2002, 44622.

[298] C Gray, *International Law and the Use of Force*, 3rd edn, above n 12, 229–30.

[299] S/2006/319, 25 May 2006; see also S/PRST/2006/25.

[300] See A Peyro Llopis, 'Le système de sécurité collective entre anarchie et fiction. Observations sur la pratique récente' in N Angelet, O Corten, E David and P Klein (eds) *Droit du pouvoir, pouvoir du droit. Mélanges offerts à Jean Salmon* (Bruxelles, Bruylant, 2007) 1402–05.

[301] See C Gray, *International Law and the Use of Force*, 3rd edn, above n 12, 87–88; D Schindler, 'Le principe de non-intervention dans les guerres civiles', above n 58, 427–28; R Jennings and A Watts (eds), *Oppenheim's International Law*, 9th edn, above n 3, 438.

[302] M Bennouna, *Le consentement à l'ingérence militaire dans les conflits internes*, above n 2, 81.

tions, whether the UN or regional bodies. The common point of these precedents is that the operation is once again not officially intended to support the government against rebel movements. The objective is rather to ensure security or peace, without siding with any internal actor, the principle of neutrality being proclaimed instead.

Peacekeeping operations within the UN since the 1950s have been the subject of much scholarship.[303] It shall be recalled here simply that, initially, these operations were devised as non-coercive actions that, as such, depended on the consent of the local authorities.[304] So it was on the legal basis constituted by State consent that operations were conducted either to supervise precarious situations between States (FUNU, FINUL, UNFICYP, etc) or, and more frequently, to stabilise the situation within a given State.[305] In the latter case, it is interesting to note that these operations have always been conducted on the basis of compliance with a principle of neutrality: the objectives have always consisted in maintaining peace or internal security, but without claiming to impose any particular solution.[306] *A fortiori*, no precedent is known where UN forces had the official mission of supporting a government to put down a purely internal rebellion.[307]

Since the early 1990s the very concept of 'peacekeeping operation' has changed, sometimes taking on a more resolutely coercive aspect, with the Security Council authorising UN forces to employ force as in Bosnia-Herzegovina.[308] We shall return to the practice later.[309] At this stage, we shall observe only that, while military actions of this new type may legally be based on a Security Council resolution adopted in application of Chapter VII of the Charter—and so no longer depending on the consent of a State—, compliance with the principle of neutrality has remained applicable.[310] In other

---

[303] See, eg: R Ben Achour, 'Les opérations de maintien de la paix' in JP Cot and A Pellet (eds), *La Charte des Nations Unies. Commentaire article par article*, 3rd edn (Paris, Economica, 2005) 265–86 and G Fermann, *Bibliography on International Peacekeeping* (Dordrecht, Martinus Nijhoff, 1992).

[304] Above and PA Fernandez Sanchez, *Operaciones de las Naciones Unidas para el Mantenimiento de la Paz. Analisis juridico de las Operaciones de las Naciones Unidas para el Mantenimiento de la Paz*, vol I (Madrid, Universidad de Huelva Pub, 1998) 109–17; E Suy, 'Peace-Keeping Operations' in *Manuel sur les organisations internationales*, Académie de droit international de La Haye (Dordrecht, Martinus Nijhoff, 1988) 379–96; JW Halderman, 'Legal Basis for United Nations Armed Forces' (1962) 56 *AJIL* 989; JI Garvey, 'United Nations Peacekeeping and Host State Consent' (1970) 64 *AJIL* 241–69.

[305] See: *The Blue Helmets. A review of United Nations Peace-keeping Forces*, 3rd edn, (New York, United Nations, 1996).

[306] PA Fernandez Sanchez, *Operaciones de las Naciones Unidas para el Mantenimiento de la Paz. Analisis juridico de las Operaciones de las Naciones Unidas para el Mantenimiento de la Paz*, vol I, above n 305, 124–33.

[307] See also the ONUC case, detailed below.

[308] SC Res 836 (1993) of 4 June 1993, para 9; see also SC Res 871 (1993) of 4 October 1993, para 9 and 958 (1994) of 19 November 1994.

[309] Below, ch 6, s I.

[310] See, eg, the UNPROFOR mandate; SC Res 743 (1992) of 21 February 1992; SC Res 776 (1992) of 13 August 1992, para 2; SC Res 836 (1993) of 4 June 1993; SC Res 998 (1995) of 16 June 1995.

words, 'blue helmets' have not openly claimed to impose a political solution
nor to support one side, whether the government or not, in an internal
conflict.[311] The official objective has remained to maintain peace, and it soon
came to be duplicated by more limited purposes such as the supply of
humanitarian aid or the protection of human rights.[312] In short, whether non-
coercive (and as such still based on the consent of the government in power)
or coercive, whether designed to maintain, restore or enforce peace, contemporary operations by UN forces are characterised by their signalled political
neutrality.

The same reading can be made of the examination of operations by
regional organisations, on the basis of the consent of local authorities,
officially to maintain or to restore peace.

In the case of the Commonwealth of Independent States (CIS), two
examples may be mentioned.[313]

—In the civil war in Georgia, from 1993 Russian troops were operating
  within Georgian-Abkhaz-Russian 'tripartite control groups' to monitor the
  ceasefire with the agreement of all sides.[314] A UN Observer Mission in
  Georgia (ANOMIC) was then set up and despatched[315] with Security
  Council approval.[316] This operation was formally designed to adhere
  strictly to the principle of neutrality,[317] even if in practice that neutrality
  might be seriously challenged. This became particularly obvious during the
  war of August 2008, which will not be commented upon at this point.[318]
—On 24 September 1993, Russia, Kazakhstan, Kyrgyzstan and Uzbekistan
  decided with the agreement of the Tajik government to set up a CIS
  peacekeeping force in Tajikistan.[319] On 17 September 1994, a ceasefire
  was concluded between government and opposition forces under UN
  auspices.[320] It stated that:

---

[311] See: *Report of the Secretary-General pursuant to Security Council resolution 815 (1993)*, 15
May 1993, S/25777, para 20.

[312] O Corten and P Klein, 'Action humanitaire et Chapitre VII. La redéfinition du mandat
et des moyens d'action des Forces des Nations Unies' (1993) 39 *AFDI* 105–30.

[313] See also: G Nolte, *Eingreifen auf Einladung*, above n 2, 636.

[314] *Agreement on a Cease-Fire in Abkhazia and Arrangements to Monitor its Observance*,
S/26250, 6 August 1993, Annex I.

[315] SC Res 858 (1993) of 14 August 1993.

[316] SC Res 934 (1994) of 30 June 1994, 937 (1994) of 21 July 1994, 971 (1995) of 12
January 1995, 993 (1995) of 11 May 1995, 1036 (1996) of 12 January 1996, 1069 (1997) of
12 July 1996, 1150 (1998) of 30 January 1998.

[317] SC Res 858 (1993) of 24 August 1993, para 2; 881 (1993) of 4 November 1993, para
4; 892 (1993) of 22 December 1993, para 2; 937 (1994) of 21 July 1994, para 6; see also
*Letter dated 94/06/21 from the Permanent Representative of the Russian Federation to the United
Nations addressed to the Secretary-General*, S/1994/732, 21 June 1994.

[318] See below, ch 7.

[319] *The United Nations and the situation in Tadjikistan*, United Nations, Reference Paper,
March 1995, 4.

[320] Text in *Report of the Secretary-General on the situation in Tajikistan*, S/1994/1102, 27
September 1994, Annex I.

The Collective Peace-keeping Forces of the Commonwealth of Independent States and the Russian troops in Tajikistan shall carry out their duties in keeping with the principle of neutrality, which is part of their mandate, and shall cooperate with United Nations military observers.[321]

This principle of neutrality was recalled by several States within the Security Council,[322] and guided the setting up of a UN Mission of Observers in Tajikistan (UNIMOT).[323]

The Economic Community of West African States (ECOWAS) has also developed operations of this type, as instanced by three precedents.

—ECOWAS intervention in Liberia could be justified by the invitation given by the Liberian President.[324] ECOWAS forces, and after them the forces of the UN Observer Mission in Liberia (UNOMIL), never had as their official assignment to support government forces in the civil war that was then tearing the country apart.[325] Here again, it was formally without taking sides that the so-called peacekeeping forces were deployed on the ground.

—Mention has already been made of the operation in Sierra Leone at the behest of the government in office.[326] As in the case of Liberia, this action was likened to a peacekeeping operation with a reference to the principle of neutrality as its tenet.[327]

—On 8 June 1998, Senegal and Guinea supported the government troops of Guinea-Bissau in their fight against seditious forces.[328] After several months of fighting, a peace agreement was reached on 1 November 1998 by which foreign troops were to be withdrawn and replaced by ECOWAS troops that would guarantee security along the border with Senegal.[329] The Security Council welcomed this operation, emphasising its impartiality and neutrality.[330]

---

[321] ibid, article 2(a).

[322] See: S/PV.3482, 16 December 1994: declarations of Tajikistan, Czech Republic, France, United Kingdom, USA and Argentina.

[323] SC Res 968 (1994) of 16 December 1994; 999 (1995) of 16 June 1995; 1030 (1995) of 14 December 1995; 1061 (1996) of 14 June 1996; 1089 (1996) of 13 December 1996.

[324] Georg Nolte, 'Restoring Peace by Regional Action: International Legal Aspects of the Liberian Conflict' (1993) 53 *Zaörv* 621–26. In a letter dated 14 July 1990 addressed to the ECOWAS, the President of Liberia stated that 'it would seem most expedient at this time to introduce an ECOWAS Peace-keeping Force into Liberia to forestall increasing terror and tension and to assure a peaceful transitional environment' (*Letter addressed by President Samuel K Doe to the Chairman and Members of the Ministerial Meeting of ECOWAS Standing Mediation Committee*, 14 July 1990, Document 39 in M WELLER (ed), *Regional Peace-keeping and International Enforcement: The Liberian Crisis* (Cambridge, Cambridge University Press, 1994) 61. See also *Keesing's Contemporary Archives*, 1990, 37602 and below, ch 6, s II.

[325] According to the Minister of External Affairs of Nigeria, 'ECOWAS intervention is in no way designed to save one part or punish another' (S/21485, 10 August 1990, Annex, 3).

[326] See above.

[327] SC Res 1162 (1198) of 17 April 1998 and 1171 (1998) of 5 June 1998.

[328] *Keesing's Contemporary Archives*, 1998, 42323.

[329] *Keesing's Contemporary Archives*, 1998, 42601.

[330] SC Res 1216 (1998) of 21 December 1998, para 4; see also SC Res 1233 (1999) of 6 April 1999.

Lastly, some States, acting outside the framework of any regional organisation or of the UN, have participated in operations to maintain peace at the request of government authorities.[331] In 1997 the Inter-African Mission to Monitor the Bangui Accords (MISAB) was formed in the Central African Republic, comprising contingents from France and six African States (Burkina Faso, Chad, Gabon, Mali, Senegal and Togo).[332] On 6 August 1997, the Security Council adopted resolution 1125 (1997), by which it 'Approve[d] the continued conduct by Member States participating in MISAB of the operation *in a neutral and impartial way* to achieve its objective to facilitate the return to peace and security by monitoring the implementation of the Bangui Agreements'. (emphasis added)[333] The characteristics of neutrality and impartiality were recalled by several States within the Council,[334] leading to the creation of a UN Mission in the Central African Republic (MINURCA).[335] Several States underscored that it was merely an action to restore security and not an intervention in favour of any particular side in a civil war.[336]

Abundant and varied practice attests to the reluctance of States to claim the right to carry out military intervention in favour of a government in office confronted with internal opposition, and even if a request in due form has been made to that effect. The intervening State will prefer rather to invoke either its own motives (extraterritorial police action, protection of its nationals) or simple logistical aid or help in maintaining law and order without any direct engagement in an armed conflict, or again an operation to maintain or restore peace conducted in a neutral and impartial manner. Of course, it happens that in practice, beyond the official discourse, the government is indeed supported by allied States in its fight against rebel forces. The fact that such aid is denied only makes the non-interventionist legal discourse that much more significant: patently, the inviting States and the intervening States alike are not ready to assume military action to quell a rebellion. Unless, and it is on this final point that we now lay emphasis, that rebellion is itself supported by one or more foreign States.

---

[331] See also the Indian intervention in Sri Lanka, presented as a sending of 'Indian Peace-Keeping Forces'; C Gray, *International Law and the Use of Force*, 3rd edn, above n 12, 86–87; CJ Le Mon, 'Unilateral Intervention by Invitation in Civil Wars: the Effective Control Test Tested', above n 2, 782–85 and S Alam, 'Indian Intervention in Sri Lanka and International Law', *NILR*, 1991, 349–59.

[332] S/1997/561, 22 July 1997, app I.

[333] SC Res 1125 (997), para 2; see also SC Res 1136 (1997) of 6 November 1997, para 3, 1152 (1998) of 5 February 1998, paras 4–5; 1155 (1998) of 16 March 1998, paras 3–4; 1159 (1998) of 27 March 1998, paras 5–6.

[334] See: Letter dated 4 July 1997 from Mr Ange-Félix Patasse, President of the Central African Republic, addressed to the Secretary-General, S/1997/561, 22 July 1997, Annex.

[335] SC Res 1159 (1998) of 27 March 1998.

[336] S/PV.3808, 6 August 1997 (Guinea-Bissau and Portugal); see also S/1997/543, 14 July 1997 (Gabon).

Military Interventions Officially Motivated by Riposte to Outside Interference

So far we have consistently assumed conflicts were strictly domestic, imply-ing that the opposition forces or rebels were acting autonomously, with no outside support. It may be, though—and the hypothesis is far from theo-retical—that the rebels are on the contrary actively supported by a foreign State in violation of the rules of international law recalled above. If the out-side intervention is so intense that it can be characterised as an armed attack within the meaning of article 51 of the Charter, then we are dealing with a situation of self-defence, authorising the government of the attacked State to seek and obtain backing from third States. However, the case of legiti-mate collective defence shall not be contemplated at this point.[337] However, it may also be that the initial outside interference is not tantamount to an armed attack, because it is not of a very serious character. In this event, can the government of the aggressed State call on help from a foreign State to end such interference? It seems self-evident that the answer is yes, in view of the text of article 2(4) of the Charter. As seen, that article prohibits any use of force against the independence of a State or any purpose of the UN, including the protection of the right to self-determination. This is what jus-tifies not taking sides either for rebels or for the government in the event of civil war. In the event of initial outside interference, however, the inter-vention of a third State in support of the government does not pose any problem, since, far from infringing it, it seeks to uphold the political inde-pendence and the right to self-determination of the State and the people concerned. So, for a government to accept that another State send its army into its territory to end an armed action by rebels supported by another State appears to be fully consistent with the UN Charter and the resolutions interpreting it.[338]

Examination of practice illustrates this conclusion. It also confirms *a contrario* the refusal of States to assume a right to intervene in purely domes-tic conflicts. In practice, true military intervention against rebels is almost systematically motivated by the fact that the rebels are merely the agents of some foreign power.[339] This trend appeared hesitantly at first, after the

---

[337] See below, ch 7.

[338] According to art 5 of the Institute of International Law resolution quoted above n 246, 'Whenever it appears that intervention has taken place during a civil war in violation of the preceding provisions, third States may give assistance to the other party only in compliance with the Charter and any other relevant rule of international law, subject to any such measures as are prescribed, authorized or recommended by the United Nations', *The Principle of Non-Intervention in Civil Wars*; see also M Bennouna, *Le consentement à l'ingérence militaire dans les conflits internes*, above n 2, 158; R Higgins, *The Development of International Law Through the Political Organs of the United Nations*, above n 81, 211.

[339] L Doswald-Beck, 'The Legal Validity of Military Intervention by Invitation of the Government', above n 2, 213; C Gray, *International Law and the Use of Force*, 3rd edn, above n 12, 92 *ff*.

entry into force of the UN Charter, and then more markedly from the late 1950s. To illustrate this change, some significant precedents are discussed in what follows.

a) The Greek Civil War in the Aftermath of the Second World War

At the end of the Second World War, Greece was prey to a murderous civil war that lasted several years. The Greek government immediately asked for support from the British forces already on the ground as part of the common combat against the Axis forces. The USSR criticised this British involvement in January 1946 and filed a complaint with the UN over such meddling in Greek internal affairs.[340] Greece immediately answered that its government was entitled to ask for support to maintain law and order, seeming to extend that right to backing in the fight against rebels.[341] Similarly, the British representative asserted very generally the lawfulness of his government's action based on the Greek government's consent, with no particular limit;[342] a position that was supported by other States.[343] The Security Council, having abandoned examination of the matter,[344] the General Assembly then took up a position criticising the support given to the rebels by neighbouring States such as Albania, Yugoslavia and Bulgaria.[345] British intervention was not condemned, however, and it seems that it was motivated by such a general objective of maintaining law and order that it might imply direct support against rebel forces, even before outside help in their favour was denounced.[346]

b) The Immediate Post-War Indonesian Crisis

Consideration of another contemporary precedent suggests that the *opinio juris* of States at the time was already taking account of a duty of neutrality inspired by the right of self-determination. In its first sessions, the Security Council examined, alongside the Greek affair, the situation in Indonesia where British armed forces allegedly intervened against rebel forces at the request of the Dutch authorities. The action brought criticism from Ukraine[347] and the USSR,[348] who considered that there had been a violation of the right of self-determination.

---

[340] SC PV, 1st year, Ser no 1, Supp no 1, annex 3, 21 January 1946, 73–74; see also SC PV, 1st year, Ser no 1, no 1, 6th s, 1 February 1946, 78; ibid, 7th meeting, 4 February 1946, 99.

[341] SC PV, 1st year, Ser no 1, no 1, 6th s, 1st February 1946, 89; ibid, 7th, 4 February 1946, 110.

[342] SC PV, 1st year, Ser no 1, no 1, 6th s, 1 February 1946, 85 and 88.

[343] See, eg: ibid, 7th, 4 February 1946, 117 (Poland).

[344] SC Res 34 (1947) of 15 September 1947.

[345] GA Res 193 (III) of 27 November 1948 and 288 (IV) A and B of 18 November 1949; see also *Yearbook of the United Nations*, 1948–49, 238–56.

[346] cp I Brownlie, *International Law and the Use of Force by States*, above n 37, 325.

[347] SC PV, 1st year, Ser no 1, no 1, 12th mt, 7 February 1946, 177; ibid, 13th mt, 9 February 1946, 189.

[348] SC PV, 1st year, Ser no 1, no 1, 13th mt, 9 February 1946, 200.

It is most interesting to observe that this argument was not challenged in law. The Dutch and UK defence was rather that the British action was not aimed at the Indonesian rebel movement, but that force was used in self-defence in exceptional circumstances.[349] It is true that this precedent is specific in that it involves decolonisation and as such is governed by specific rules.[350] However, it is significant in that it is, to my knowledge, the first case where the right to self-determination is invoked to criticise military action by a third State in favour of a government implicated in what was still considered at the time to be an internal conflict,[351] a case that was to be followed by others, especially from the late 1950s onwards.

c) Events in Lebanon and Jordan (1958)

Further to the overthrow of King Faisal of Iraq on 14 July 1958, US and UK troops were deployed in Lebanon and Jordan respectively at the request of the governments of the two States.[352] This double intervention prompted debate in the UN where the question was directly posed of the effect of consent on the lawfulness of a use of force.[353] The USSR immediately claimed that US forces were directly interfering in the internal affairs of the Lebanese people.[354] The Soviet representative was far from questioning the principle of intervention consented to in the context of an internal conflict, but considered that this principle could not be implemented unless the conflict had already given rise to outside interference,[355] which was allegedly not the case in the matter at hand.[356] A similar argument was defended over the sending of British troops to Jordan.[357]

The position of the USSR failed to convince a sufficient number of States within the UN.[358] The controversy was, though, clearly less about law than about fact, with many States considering that Lebanon and Jordan had been victims of outside interference, justifying an appeal to the allied governments.[359] *A contrario*, no one evoked a right to intervene for a government in a purely internal conflict.[360] This is attested, for example, by the words of the US representative, for whom 'our forces are not there to engage in

---

[349] SC PV, 1st year, Ser no 1, no 1, 15th mt, 10 February 1946, 218 (Netherlands); SC PV, 1st year, Ser no 1, no 1, 12th mt, 7 February 1946, 179 and 180.

[350] Above, ch 3, s I.

[351] See also above, ch 3, s I.

[352] *Keesing's Contemporary Archives*, 1957–1958, 16293–97 and 16307–09.

[353] See, eg: RJ Dupuy, 'Agression indirecte et intervention sollicitée. A propos de l'affaire libanaise' (1959) 5 *AFDI* 431–67.

[354] S/PV.835, 21 July 1958.

[355] S/PV.838, 7 August 1958.

[356] S/PV.827, 15 July 1958.

[357] S/PV.831, 17 July 1958.

[358] See SC Res 129 (1958) of 7 August 1958.

[359] S/PV.828, 15 July 1958; S/PV.831, 17 July 1958; S/PV.832, 17 July 1958.

[360] G Nolte, *Eingreifen auf Einladung*, above n 2, 630 (ch 2).

hostilities of any kind, much less to fight a war'.[361] Likewise, the British representative was particularly explicit:

> There is nothing either in the Charter or in the established rules in international law to inhibit a Government from asking a friendly Government for military assistance as a defensive measure when it considers itself to be in danger. Nor is there anything to inhibit the Government thus appealed to from responding.[362]

The US and UK argument seems to attest to reluctance to accept that simple government consent—although well established in the case in point—could provide a basis for outside military intervention of any kind. The two States insisted on the existence of foreign interference allegedly from the United Arab Republic, itself manipulated by the Soviet Union,[363] while in fact such interference was sharply contested.[364] Mention was even made of actual indirect attack (of somewhat nebulous character, extending from hostile propaganda to the sending of Syrian agents, via a threatened coup), and so of self-defence within the meaning of article 51 of the Charter.[365] All of these arguments would have been quite useless had it been enough to invoke the consent from a government in order to be authorised to support it against rebel forces.[366]

d) Other Precedents Characteristic of the Cold War

The *opinio juris* of States as a whole seems therefore to have been well established by the end of the 1950s, confirming the consideration of a number of precedents typical of the Cold War. The following examples are purely illustrative.[367]

—In 1958, the UK intervened militarily to support the Sultan of Muscat and Oman at his request. The British authorities claimed they were

---

[361] S/PV.827, 15 July 1958, 6–7, para 35; see also S/PV.824, 10 June 1958 and MM Whiteman (ed), *Digest of International Law*, vol 12 (Department of State Publ, 1971), 137 and 221–25.

[362] S/PV.831, 17 July 1958, 6, para 29; see also S/PV.827, 15 July 1958; S/PV.834, 18 July 1958, 13–14. According to the Prime Minister 'a legitimate Government has, it seems to me, the right to ask for help in its difficulties from another friendly Government. Whether that help should be forthcoming or not is, of course, a matter of judgment, but *I do not think that there is anything legally improper for a nation faced with aggression from outside, or with international disturbances supported from outside, to ask for help*' (emphasis added); House of Commons, 16 July 1958, quoted in E Lauterpacht, 'Contemporary Practice of the United Kingdom' (1959) 8 *ICLQ* 149.

[363] See also: *Letter dated 58/05/22 from the Representative of Lebanon addressed to the President of the Security Council*, S/4007, 23 May 1958 and S/PV.831, 17 July 1958 (Jordan).

[364] See: S/PV.823, 6 June 1958; S/PV.824, 10 June 1958; S/PV.828, 15 July 1958; S/PV.830, 16 July 1958; S/PV.831, 17 July 1958.

[365] See below: ch 7 and L Henkin, 'The Reports of the Death of Article 2 (4) Are Greatly Exaggerated' (1971) 65 *AJIL* 545.

[366] See, eg: Q Wright, 'United States Intervention in the Lebanon' (1959) 53 *AJIL* 124–25.

[367] See also: MM Whiteman (ed), *Digest of International Law*, vol 12, above n 362, 141–42 or art I of the Treaty between the USA and Japan, 8 September 1951, *UNTS*, vol 136, 1952, no 1835, 217–18.

merely responding to a prior outside intervention in the conflict which was

> at the request of a friendly ruler who has always relied on us to help him *resist aggression or subversion . . . The reasons for this action are that the dissidents have clearly received assistance from outside the territory of the Sultan'.* (emphasis added)[368]

The States that criticised British action considered that 'the rules of international law did not permit foreign intervention in order to assist a Government to repress an internal rebellion. Aggression was never justified, even by the request of a Government or by obligations flowing from a treaty'.[369]

—In the events in Congo, it will be recalled that the initial appeal in 1960 by the government to the UN was in response to outside interference from Belgium, which allegedly supported the attempted secession.[370] It was in this context that the ONUC was created, with the mission not of supporting any particular side in an internal conflict but of restoring security in the country,[371] incidents between UN forces and mercenaries being justified rather as self-defence.[372] Until the crisis was over, the UN authorities insisted on compliance with the principle of neutrality.[373]

—In the case of the intervention of Belgium and the US at Stanleyville in 1964, already examined above, one of the arguments of the two powers, and of their Congo governmental ally, was that the Congolese rebels were supported from abroad.[374] It was this that supposedly justified their backing for the established government.

—When in the 1970s the Chadian government called on French troops for support in its fight against rebels, it justified its demand by the links the

---

[368] Foreign Secretary in E Lauterpacht, 'Contemporary Practice of the United Kingdom' (1958) 7 *ICLQ* 100–01.

[369] *Repertory of Practice of United Nations Organs*, Supp no 3 (1959–1966), vol 1—Art 2 (4) (Separate Study), 164, para 215; C Gray, *International Law and the Use of Force*, 3rd edn, above n 12, 95–96; A Tanca, *Foreign Armed Intervention in Internal Conflict*, above n 2, 150–51.

[370] See above, ch 4, s II and SC Res 143 (1960) of 14 July 1960, para 1; 145 (1960) of 22 July 1960, para 1; 146 (1960) of 9 August 1960, para 2; 161 (1961) of 21 February 1961, para 2; 169 (1961) of 24 November 1961, para 1.

[371] SC Res 146 (1960) of 9 August 1960, para 4.

[372] See: M Bennouna, *Le consentement à l'ingérence militaire dans les conflits internes*, above n 2, 210–11.

[373] ibid, 108–22; C Walter, 'Security Council Control over Regional Action', above n 91, 147; L Doswald-Beck, 'The Legal Validity of Military Intervention by Invitation of the Government', above n 2, 240–41. According to the SG, 'the UN operation in the Congo at all times has scrupulously avoided intervention in internal affairs of that country; it has not taken sides in political or constitutional differences' (S/5784, 29 June 1964); see other declarations quoted in JJA Salmon, *La reconnaissance d'Etat. Quatre cas: Mandchoukouo, Katanga, Biafra, Rhodésie du sud* (Paris, Armand Colin, 1971) 126–29.

[374] S/PV.1173, 11 December 1964; S/PV.1174, 14 December 1964; S/PV.1184, 23 December 1964; S/PV.1189, 30 December 1964.

rebels allegedly had with Libya. Initially France declared it was not convinced that there were such connections, leading it not to intervene. It was only once it was established that Libyan soldiers were directly involved in military actions by Chadian rebels that the French army engaged in the conflict.[375]

—Whether in Hungary, Czechoslovakia or Afghanistan for the USSR or in Vietnam, the Dominican Republic or Grenada for the US, the two superpowers always claimed to be intervening to end outside interference.[376] *A contrario*, they never, any more than the governments of those States did when making their appeals, assumed a right to intervene in any purely internal conflict.

This final conclusion can thus be generalised from the many precedents stretching from the 1950s to the late 1980s.

e) Precedents after 1989

The end of the Cold War does not seem to have had any influence on the *opinio juris* of States in this respect. France's position towards African States was very clearly reaffirmed in a speech at La Baule in June 1990.[377]

Intervention, even when consented to, would be confined to riposting to outside interference or to protecting nationals, without extending to the settlement of internal strife.

Moreover, it shall be recalled that the surge in UN activity led to a multiplication of peacekeeping operations or military actions by third States in internal conflicts. It will be observed at this stage that those operations, conducted with the consent of the local authorities, were sometimes justified as being reactions to outside interference.

---

[375] 'Pratique française du droit international' (1983) 29 *AFDI* 915–16; (1984) 30 *AFDI* 1023–24; (1985) 31 *AFDI* 1014; (1986) 32 *AFDI* 1028–29; (1987) 33 *AFDI* 991–94 (see also (1978) 24 *AFDI* 1092; (1980) 26 *AFDI*, 875–77); see L Doswald-Beck, 'The Legal Validity of Military Intervention by Invitation of the Government', above n 2, 218–21; CJ Le Mon, 'Unilateral Intervention by Invitation in Civil Wars: the Effective Control Test Tested', above n 2, 768–77 and 775; A Alibert, 'L'affaire du Tchad' (1986) 90 *RGDIP* 374–98 and *Du droit de se faire justice dans la société internationale depuis 1945*, above n 81, 433–49. According to the French Minister of Foreign Affairs, 'si la France a été amenée à intervenir sur le continent africain, elle l'a toujours fait à la demande du gouvernement reconnu du pays intéressé, et en limitant le volume et la durée de son assistance aux nécessités de la situation. *Dans chaque cas, il s'est agi de répondre à l'appel d'Etats victimes d'une agression extérieure*' (emphasis added); C Rousseau, 'Chronique des faits internationaux' (1979) 83 *RGDIP* 171; see also 'Pratique française du droit international' (1978) 24 *AFDI* 1083–84, (1980) 26 *AFDI* 875.

[376] See above and L Doswald-Beck, 'The Legal Validity of Military Intervention by Invitation of the Government', above n 2, 224 and 230–33; C Gray, *International Law and the Use of Force*, 3rd edn, above n 12, 92–96.

[377] '[. . .] notre rôle à nous, pays étranger, fut-il ami, n'est pas d'intervenir dans les conflits intérieurs. Dans ce cas là, la France, en accord avec les dirigeants, veillera à protéger ses concitoyens, ses ressortissants; mais elle n'entend pas arbitrer les conflits' (Declaration of the President of France on the occasion of the sixteenth conference of Heads of States of France and Africa, La Baule, 19–21 June 1990, www.diplomatie.gouv.fr).

—In the case of Tajikistan, for example, CIS and then UN forces were assigned to secure the southern border with Afghanistan, a State with which rebels allegedly had certain ties.[378] It is with this perspective that the Security Council asserted its attachment to the sovereignty and territorial integrity of the Tajikistan Republic and to the inviolability of its borders.[379] The international aspect of the conflict and more especially its connections with the situation in Afghanistan was emphasised by the representatives of several States.[380]

—The precedent of Côte d'Ivoire is also significant in this respect. In September 2002, the country's government appealed to France for support in its fight against rebels. The French authorities declined, arguing that there was insufficient evidence of outside aggression and that it should abide by the principle of non-interference in Côte d'Ivoire's internal affairs.[381] French troops only accepted being deployed in the field in the context of a peacekeeping operation undertaken by ECOWAS, on which the Security Council subsequently congratulated itself,[382] before creating a UN Mission in Côte d'Ivoire (MINUCI)[383] and then a UN Operation in Côte d'Ivoire (ONUCI).[384] Here too, government consent does not seem to justify outside intervention in a civil war but just a peacekeeping operation, one aspect of which is to oppose or end any outside interference.[385]

—On 2 September 2004, the Security Council 'Call[ed] upon all remaining foreign forces to withdraw from Lebanon'.[386] This decision was aimed especially at Syrian forces, although they were present with the consent of the Lebanese government. The government for that matter immediately protested, pointing out that the Syrian army was in Lebanon to riposte to Israeli actions.[387] The US and their allies saw the Syrian presence more as interference in Lebanese domestic policies, which justified

---

[378] *Report of the Secretary-General on the situation in Tajikistan*, S/26311, 16 August 1993, para 4.

[379] SC Res 999 (1995) of 16 June 1995; 1030 (1995) of 14 December 1995; 1061 (1996) of 14 June 1996; 1089 (1996) of 13 December 1996; 1099 (1997) of 14 March 1997; 1113 (1997) of 12 June 1997; 1128 (1997) of 11 September 1997; 1138 (1997) of 14 November 1997; 1167 (1998) of 14 May 1998; 1206 (1998) of 12 November 1998; 1240 (1999) of 15 May 1999; 1274 (1999) of 12 November 1999.

[380] See: S/PV.3482, 16 December 1994; S/PV.3724, 13 December 1996. See also CJ Le Mon, 'Unilateral Intervention by Invitation in Civil Wars: the Effective Control Test Tested', above n 2, 789.

[381] See the declarations quoted in T Christakis and K Bannelier, '*Volenti non fit injuria?* Les effets du consentement à l'intervention militaire', above n 2, 129, fn 112.

[382] SC Res1464 (2003) of 4 February 2003.

[383] SC Res 1479 (2003) of 13 May 2003.

[384] SC Res 1528 (2004) of 27 February 2004.

[385] See: SC Res 1479 (2003) of 13 May 2003, para 13; 1572 (2004) of 15 November 2004, para 1; 1633 (2005) of 21 October 2005, para 19.

[386] SC Res 1559 (2004) of 2 September 2004, para 2.

[387] S/PV.5028, 2 September 2004.

the passing of the resolution.[388] Here again, the debate was more about fact (What was the true objective of the intervention consented to? Was there really outside interference?) than about law: it seems clear in this respect that there is a consensus whereby outside intervention cannot be admitted, even if consented to, in a purely internal conflict, whether this can be characterised as armed conflict or not.[389]

—Finally, mention can be made of Ethiopia's intervention in Somalia in December 2006, which was officially justified by the fight against Somali rebels of the Islamic Courts, rebels that were allegedly supported by foreign elements.[390] As in other precedents just mentioned, the use of force in favour of the government was justified by outside backing for the rebel forces. In this particular instance, though, the intervention was criticised notably on the basis of several Security Council resolutions that seemed incompatible with the deployment of Ethiopian troops in Somalia.[391] Just as the law of self-defence cannot be exercised without compliance with Security Council resolutions,[392] so interventions that are consented to can only be conducted pursuant to those same resolutions.[393]

Lastly, there is a practice whose teaching can be resumed as follows: either we are in the case of a purely internal conflict and outside intervention, even with the established and valid consent of the authorities in office, cannot consist in a fight against rebel or irregular forces—the official objective will then be rather to maintain law and order or peace, while stringently abiding by the principles of impartiality and neutrality; or, in a second situation, one or more foreign powers are militarily supporting rebel forces. The government of the State in question may then validly call for foreign intervention which may then, as need be, go beyond a simple peacekeeping operation, by directly combating rebel forces. In any event, consent of the government alone never seems to have been considered enough to justify any form of outside intervention, its lawfulness depending on its objective, pursuant to the alternative we have just presented.

Some commentators have thought they detected an exception to this pattern emerging from practice for wars of secession in which outside

---

[388] ibid.

[389] T Christakis and K Bannelier, '*Volenti non fit injuria?* Les effets du consentement à l'intervention militaire', above n 2, 131.

[390] S/PV.5614, 26 December 2006, 3; see also *Report of the Secretary General on the situation on Somalia*, S/2007/115, 28 February 2007, para 5.

[391] SC Res 1725 (2006), 6 December 2006, para 4; see also SC Res 1704 (2006), 29 November 2006; see O Corten, 'La licéité douteuse de l'action militaire de l'Ethiopie en Somalie et ses implications sur l'argument de l'intervention consentie' (2007) 111 RGDIP 533–35.

[392] See below, ch 7, s II.

[393] O Corten, 'La licéité douteuse de l'action militaire de l'Ethiopie en Somalie et ses implications sur l'argument de l'intervention consentie', above n 392 and below, ch 6, s I.

intervention in favour of government forces was accepted by principle.[394] Yet, to me, practice does not seem to point clearly in this direction.[395] As seen, the ONUC intervention in the early 1960s was presented as consistent with the principle of neutrality and at the same time as a reaction to outside support by Belgium for the Katanga secessionists.[396] Remember too that Indian intervention in Sri Lanka was presented as a simple peacekeeping action, as was the NATO operation in Macedonia in 2001.[397] A contrario, third States have not settled for the appeal from the government in office to claim to be able to contribute to the fight against secessionists. The same conclusion can be drawn from the intervention against the Serb party of Bosnia-Herzegovina in 1995 which was justified by the implementation of Security Council resolutions that took account of outside support for the Serb secessionists.[398]

Conclusion

No State has ever contested that, in principle, a State's consent to outside military intervention makes such intervention lawful, the use of force not then being of one State against another, as required by article 2(4) of the Charter. The lawfulness of such interventions is often challenged in practice, as will have been seen from the many precedents set out in this chapter. Generally, a first problem relates to the validity of consent: it must have been given by the very highest authorities of the State (and not seditious or subordinate authorities), without being vitiated (especially by coercion), prior to the intervention (and not *ex post facto*), and must be established (and not ambiguous or presumed) and relevant (in that it must relate to the outside action in all its aspects). In the event of internal strife, the problem is complicated first in that there may be competition between two or more authorities claiming to exercise power and so apt to consent to outside intervention. In such cases, practice proves to be very cautious, the only valid consent being that from the internationally recognised government that is in a position to exercise effective power in the territory of the State in question. In any case, and this point is certainly not the least important one, the intervention consented to, even by an uncontested government, cannot be to settle the internal conflict in favour of the authorities. The practice that has developed from the 1950s attests to the will of States to limit any outside intervention by invitation to other objectives, ranging from the

---

[394] T Christakis and K Bannelier, 'Volenti non fit injuria? Les effets du consentement à l'intervention militaire', above n 2, 133–35; G Nolte, *Eingreifen auf Einladung*, above n 2, 637.

[395] Independent International Fact-Finding Mission on the Conflict in Georgia, Report, September 2009 (www.ceiig.ch/Report.html), vol II, 277.

[396] Above.

[397] Above.

[398] See below, ch 6.

protection of its nationals to peacekeeping, all in compliance with the right to self-determination with no outside interference.

It should be recalled on this point that the official justification of the intervening State (which systematically denies it is supporting the government against rebel forces) does not always correspond to reality (in which 'humanitarian' or 'peacekeeping' interventions often have the effect if not the purpose of supporting the authorities in office). This mismatch must be clearly understood. In terms of method, it reinforces the principle of non-intervention in civil wars, with States not daring to assume their interventionist practice in law.[399] In substance, though, it may well be that any particular operation, if proved to have had as its aim to settle an internal conflict in favour of one side or another, including the government side, is contrary to existing international law. Remember, however, that our purpose here is not to make pronouncements on the lawfulness of this or that operation; it is rather to determine, generally, the overall sense of the treaty-based and customary law of the prohibition of the use of force in international relations.[400]

---

[399] C Gray, *International Law and the Use of Force*, 3rd edn, above n 12, 68.
[400] See above, ch 1, s II.

6
Intervention Authorised by the UN Security Council

U NDER THE SYSTEM laid down in Chapter VII of the UN Charter, it is the Security Council that is tasked with undertaking any action, including military action, in the event of a threat to peace, breach of the peace or act of aggression. Theoretically such military action is to be carried out by armed forces made available to the Security Council by the Member States pursuant to articles 43–46 of the Charter, under the strategic leadership of the Military Staff Committee provided for by article 47.[1] By the letter of the Charter, collective security is thus highly institutionalised, the United Nations being, as such, in charge of the military operations necessary to maintain or restore peace.[2] In practice, however, no military action has been conducted by strict application of the scheme set out in the Charter.[3] The Security Council has instead exercised it responsibilities under Chapter VII through the authorisation or delegation mechanism, especially since the early 1990s.[4] Is 'authorised intervention' consistent with the UN Charter and, if so, under what conditions and within what limits? These are the questions that shall be answered initially, by outlining the general legal regime of authorised intervention (section one). Then we shall turn to the particularly controversial question of 'presumed authorisation', whether authorisation as such or a sort of *a posteriori* approval of armed intervention (section two).

[1] JA Frowein and N Krisch, 'Article 42' in B Simma (ed), *The Charter of the United Nations. A Commentary*, 2nd edn (Oxford, Oxford University Press, 2002) 755; H Kelsen, 'The Old and the New League: The Covenant and the Dumbarton Oaks Proposals' (1945) 39 *AJIL* 76–78.

[2] P Lagrange, 'Sécurité collective et exercice par le Conseil de sécurité du système d'autorisation de la coercition' in SFDI, *Les métamorphoses de la sécurité collective. Droit, pratique et enjeux stratégiques* (Paris, Pedone, 2005) 56; R Kolb, *Ius contra bellum. Le droit international relatif au maintien de la paix*, 2nd edn (Bâle, Genève, Munich, Helbing & Lichtehahn/Bruxelles, Bruylant, 2009) 73ff.

[3] D Sarooshi, *The United Nations and the Development of Collective Security. The Delegation by the United Nations Security Council of its Chapter VII Powers* (Oxford, Clarendon Press, 1999) 4; L Delbez, 'La collaboration militaire entre Etats' (1962) 66 *RGDIP* 746–47.

[4] E de Wet, *The Chapter VII Powers of the United Nations Security Council* (Oxford & Portland Oregon, Hart Publishing, 2004) 256–57; C Dominicé, 'La sécurité collective et la crise du Golfe' (1991) 2 *EJIL* 9 and 98–105; see also R Higgins, 'Peace and Security. Achievements and Failures' (1995) 6 *EJIL* 445–60.

I The General Legal Regime of Authorised Military Intervention

Even if it is not covered by explicit regulations in the UN Charter, no one contests the lawfulness of the principle of military intervention authorised by the Security Council (A). The lawfulness of such intervention presupposes, however, that it is indeed the Security Council that grants authorisation and not some other UN organ or *a fortiori* some other subject of international law (B).

A. The Lawfulness of Military Intervention Authorised by the Security Council

There is now plentiful practice by which the Security Council has resorted to the mechanism of authorised military operation.[5] Except in the very special instances of the Korean War[6] and the implementation of an embargo against the illegal authorities of Southern Rhodesia,[7] no precedent is observed before 1990. Since then, the Security Council has very frequently given authorisation, including in:

—the Gulf War (1991), with Security Council resolution 678 (1990) authorising States to use 'all necessary means' to free Kuwait and restore peace and security in the region;[8]
—the Yugoslav conflict, where the Security Council authorised States on several occasions to use all necessary means to achieve certain objectives, including the supply of humanitarian aid or the protection of security zones;[9]
—the cases of Somalia (1992),[10] Rwanda (1994),[11] Zaire (1996),[12] Albania

---

[5] LA Sicilianos, 'L'autorisation par le Conseil de sécurité de recourir à la force: une tentative d'évaluation' (2002) 106 *RGDIP* 6; P Lagrange, 'Le Conseil de sécurité et l'autorisation de prendre toutes les mesures nécessaires' (2007) 1 *Les annales de droit* 206 *ff*.

[6] SC Res 83 (1950) of 27 June 1950. See also above (chs 3 and 4) and below (B).

[7] SC Res 221 (1966) of 9 April 1966; see CG Fenwick, 'When is There a Threat to the Peace? Rhodesia' (1967) 61 *AJIL* 753–55; J Combacau, *Le pouvoir de sanction de l'ONU: étude théorique de la coercition non militaire* (Paris, Pedone, 1974) 27; T Christakis and K Bannelier, 'Acteur vigilant ou spectateur impuissant? Le contrôle exercé par le Conseil de sécurité sur les Etats autorisés à recourir à la force' (2004) 37 *RBDI* 500, n 19; see also 'United Kingdom Materials on International Law' (1979) 50 *BYBIL* 385–91 and Planning Staff of the Foreign and Commonwealth Office, 'Is Intervention ever justified?', 'United Kingdom Materials on International Law' (1986) 57 *BYBIL* 616–17.

[8] SC Res 678 (1990) of 29 November 1990, para 2.

[9] See: SC Res 816 (1993) of 31 March 1993, para 4; 836 (1993) of 4 June 1993, para 10; see also SC Res 770 (1992) of 13 August 1992, para 2.

[10] SC Res 794 (1992) of 3 December 1992, para 10 and JM Sorel, 'La Somalie et les Nations Unies' (1992) 38 *AFDI* 74–78.

[11] SC Res 929 (1994) of 22 June 1994, para 3 and JD Mouton, 'La crise rwandaise de 1994 et les Nations Unies' (1994) 40 *AFDI* 220–24.

[12] SC Res 1080 (1996) of 15 November 1996, para 5 and 'Canadian Practice in International Law' (1997) 35 *CYIL* 387–90.

(1997)[13] and East Timor (1999),[14] where the Security Council authorised States to conduct military actions in pursuit of humanitarian objectives;

—the case of Haiti (1994),[15] where the Security Council authorised States to take all necessary measures to ensure the performance of the peace agreements providing for the return of the lawfully elected president toppled by a military junta;

—the cases of the aftermath of the wars in Bosnia-Herzegovina (1995),[16] Kosovo (1999),[17] Afghanistan (2001)[18] and Iraq (2003),[19] where the Security Council authorised multinational forces to conduct military operations designed to consolidate peace;

—the cases of the Central African Republic,[20] Congo (2003)[21] and Côte d'Ivoire (2003),[22] where the Security Council authorised States to carry out actions to enforce peace agreements.

To all of these precedents,[23] we can add those in which UN forces were authorised to use all 'necessary means' to achieve all or part of their mandates,[24] whether in Somalia,[25] or in the former Yugoslavia,[26] initially, and then in other States.[27]

[13] SC Res 1114 (1997) of 19 June 1997, para 4 and M Castillo, 'L'opération Alba: une réussite pour l'ONU, un bilan mitigé pour l'Union européenne et l'UEO' (1998) 44 *AFDI* 246–52.

[14] SC Res 1264 (1999) of 15 September 1999, para 3 and G Cahin, 'L'action internationale au Timor oriental' (2000) 46 *AFDI* 148–51; J-M Sorel, 'Timor oriental: un résumé de l'histoire du droit international' (2000) 104 *RGDIP* 52–55.

[15] SC Res 940 (1994) of 31 July 1994, para 4, and SC Res 1529 (2004) of 29 February 2004, para 6. See MJ Glennon, 'Sovereignty and Community after Haiti: Rethinking the Collective Use of Force' (1995) 89 *AJIL* 72; O Corten, 'La resolution 940 du Conseil de sécurité autorisant une intervention militaire en Haïti. L'émergence d'un principe de légitimité démocratique en droit international?' (1995) 6 *EJIL* 116–33.

[16] SC Res 1031 (1995) of 15 December 1995, paras 15–17; 1088 (1996) of 12 December 1996, paras 18–21.

[17] SC Res 1244 (1999) of 10 June 1999, para 7.

[18] SC Res 1386 (2001) of 20 December 2001, para 1.

[19] SC Res 1511 (2003) of 16 October 2003, para 13.

[20] SC Res 1125 (1997) of 6 August 1997, para 3; 1136 (1997) of 6 November 1997, para 4; 1152 (1998) of 5 February 1998, para 5; 1155 (1998) of 16 March 1998, paras 4 and 5.

[21] SC Res 1484 (2003) of 30 May 2003, paras 1 and 4.

[22] SC Res 1464 (2003) of 4 February 2003, para 9; see also SC Res 1527 (2004) of 4 February 2004, para 2; 1528 (2004) of 27 February 2004, para 16.

[23] See: H Freudenschub, 'Between Unilateralism and Collective Security: Authorizations of the Use of Force by the UN Security Council' (1994) 5 *EJIL* 493–522.

[24] R Ben Achour, 'Les opérations de maintien de la paix' in JP Cot and A Pellet (eds), *La Charte des Nations Unies. Commentaire article par article*, 3rd edn (Paris, Economica, 2005) 273–83; P Lagrange, 'Sécurité collective et exercice par le Conseil de sécurité du système d'autorisation de la coercition', above n 2, 86–92; E Lagrange, *Les opérations de maintien de la paix et le Chapitre VII de la Charte des Nations Unies* (Paris, Montchrestien, 1999).

[25] SC Res 814 (1993) of 26 March 1993, para 4.

[26] SC Res 836 (1993) of 4 June 1993, para 9; 871 (1993) of 4 October 1993, para 9.

[27] See the UNAMSIL in Sierra Leone (SC Res 1270 (1999) of 22 October 1999, para 14; 1289 (2000) of 7 February 2000, para 10), MONUC in the DRC (SC Res 1493 (2000) of 28 July 2003, para 25) or UNOCI in Ivory Coast (SC Res 1528 (2004) of 27 February 2004, para 8).

The situations covered are extremely varied. Except for the precedents of Iraq (1990) and Haiti (1994), all of the resolutions authorising the use of force were adopted with the consent of, or even at the request of, the State in whose territory the military operation was to take place.[28] By using authorisation under Chapter VII, the Security Council tends, though, to make military action independently of the existence, and also of the scope, of the State's consent.[29] The very purpose of this type of resolution is to confer extended and autonomous power on the intervening force that is dependent solely on the will of the Security Council itself.

The scale and diversity of this practice does seem to indicate that, in principle, authorised intervention has a legal basis in the UN Charter. At the same time, analysis of these precedents shows that only under certain conditions can a military operation be based on a Security Council authorisation under the Charter.

The Legal Basis for the Authorisation to Use Force: the Lawfulness in Principle of Authorised Intervention

As recalled in the introduction to this chapter, the drafters of the UN Charter conceived of Security Council action as highly institutionalised, pursuant to article 43 and following articles of that instrument.[30] Now, the very principle of 'authorising' States to use force seems to depart from this pattern and to be tantamount rather to a delegation of competencies by the Security Council rather than the exercise thereof.[31] No commentator seems, however, to have questioned the conformity of this process with the UN Charter for reasons pertaining both to the wording and to the way the Charter has been construed in practice.

Purely in terms of wording, it can be observed first of all that the authorisation mechanism is found explicitly in article 53(1) of the Charter which provides that:

> The Security Council shall, where appropriate, utilize such regional arrangements or agencies for enforcement action under its authority. But no enforcement action shall be taken under regional arrangements or by regional agencies without the authorization of the Security Council . . .

This provision lays down an explicit legal basis for all authorisation pertaining to enforcement action undertaken 'under regional arrangements or by regional agencies'.[32] For all other cases, the very general character of article 42 shall be emphasised whereby:

---

[28] C Gray, *International Law and the Use of Force*, 3rd edn (Oxford, Oxford University Press, 2008) 328.

[29] See above, ch 5.

[30] See: B Simma (ed), *The Charter of the United Nations. A Commentary*, 2nd edn (Oxford, Oxford University Press, 2002).

[31] D Sarooshi, *The United Nations and the Development of Collective Security. The Delegation by the United Nations Security Council of its Chapter VII Powers*, above n 3, 3 ff.

[32] See below, B, and s II.

Should the Security Council consider that measures provided for in Article 41 would be inadequate or have proved to be inadequate, it may take such action by air, sea, or land forces as may be necessary to maintain or restore international peace and security.

Such action may include military actions carried out by forces of 'Members of the United Nations'. As such, article 48(1) allows the Security Council very generally to turn to States or to some of them to perform the measures necessary for the enforcement of its decisions.[33] Even if the authorisation given to States to use force is not explicitly taken up in these provisions, it seems difficult to contest that such a mechanism is consistent with both their spirit and their letter.[34]

In any event, the abundant practice that has developed since the 1990s leaves little doubt about the lawfulness of the process.[35] It has not, as such, been challenged by the UN Member States, the criticism sometimes made relating rather to the observance of certain conditions surrounding the authorisation mechanism. Before examining those conditions, two clarifications must be made that stem from consideration of the practice. —First, it seems that the distinction between Chapters VII (articles 42 and 48) and VIII (article 53) of the Charter is largely theoretical. To avoid any controversy over the scope of Chapter VIII—and especially over the notion of agreement or of regional organisation within the meaning of that chapter[36]—

[33] BO Bryde and A Reinich, 'Article 48' in B Simma (ed), *The Charter of the United Nations. A Commentary*, 2nd edn (Oxford, Oxford University Press, 2002) 777; O Corten, 'Article 48' in JP Cot and A Pellet (eds), *La Charte des Nations Unies. Commentaire article par article*, 3rd edn (Paris, Economica, 2005) 1301–02.

[34] TD Gill, 'Legal and Some Political Limitations on the Power of the United Nations Security Council to Exercise its Enforcement Powers under Chapter VII of the Charter' (1995) 26 *NYIL* 57; ND White and O Ülgen, 'The Security Council and the Decentralized Military Option: Constitutionality and Function' (1997) 44 *NILR* 385–87; B Conforti, *The Law and Practice of the United Nations* (The Hague, Kluwer, 1996) 203–04; JA Frowein and N Krisch, 'Article 42', above n 1, 751–53; E de Wet, *The Chapter VII Powers of the United Nations Security Council*, above n 4, 260–61; LA Sicilianos, 'Entre multilatéralisme et unilatéralisme: l'autorisation par le Conseil de sécurité de recourir à la force' (2008) 339 *RCADI*, 110 *ff*.

[35] ibid, 169 *ff*; E de Wet, *The Chapter VII Powers of the United Nations Security Council*, above n 4, 308; R Kolb, *Ius contra bellum. Le droit international relatif au maintien de la paix*, 2nd edn, above n 2, 218 *ff*; P Lagrange, 'Sécurité collective et exercice par le Conseil de sécurité du système d'autorisation de la coercition', above n 2, 68; JA Frowein and N Krisch, 'Article 39' in B Simma (ed), *The Charter of the United Nations. A Commentary*, 2nd edn (Oxford, Oxford University Press, 2002) 728–29; N Blokker, 'Is the Authorization Authorized? Powers and Practice of the United Nations Security Council to Authorize the Use of Force by "Coalitions of the Able and Willing"' (2000) 11 *EJIL* 547; D Dormoy, 'Réflexions à propos de l'autorisation implicite de recourir à la force' in SFDI, *Les métamorphoses de la sécurité collective* (Paris, Pedone, 2005) 223–24; G Cahin, 'Le rôle des organes politiques de l'ONU' in E Cannizzaro and P Palchetti (eds), *Customary International Law on the Use of Force. A Methodological Approach*, (Leiden/Boston, Martinus Nijhoff, 2005) 156.

[36] See: U Villani, 'Les rapports entre l'ONU et les organizations régionales dans le domaine du maintien de la paix' (2001) 190 *RCADI* 271–77; D Momtaz, 'La délégation par le Conseil de sécurité de l'exécution de ses actions coercitives aux organizations régionales' (1997) 43 *AFDI* 107–11; M Zwanenburg, 'NATO, its Members States, and the Security Council' in N Blokker and N Schrijver (eds), *The Security Council and the Use of Force. Theory and*

the Security Council prefers to address States, specifying as need be that they may act either nationally or as regional agencies.[37] The process does not pose any problem as no provision of the Charter compels the Security Council to address regional agencies as such.[38]

—Similarly, while it may have been criticised politically, the authorisation to use force sometimes given to UN forces is clearly consistent with the Charter.[39] Traditionally, peace-keeping operations appear to be non-coercive measures, taken in principle under Chapter VI of the Charter.[40] Since the early 1990s, the UN forces have on several occasions been given mandates with a coercive aspect under Chapter VII. The lawfulness of such practice is not in any doubt, with the 'blue helmets' conducting military operations as need be under UN authority pursuant to the rationale underpinning Chapter VII of the Charter.[41]

Finally, the expression 'action' ('toute action', in French) in article 42 is broad enough to cover the practice that has developed over several years, without being contested as such. The legal basis of the authorisation mechanism is not seriously contended, unlike the existence and interpretation of certain conditions that it is important to examine now.

The Conditions of Lawfulness of Authorised Intervention

The question of the conditions of lawfulness of a military operation authorised by the Security Council may be envisaged from two standpoints. First, it may be asked whether the resolution on which the operation is based is consistent with the Charter (a). Then, it can be appraised whether the military action undertaken is consistent with the resolution validly adopted by the Security Council (b).

a) The Conformity of the Resolution Adopted with the UN Charter

Logically, for a resolution to validly constitute a legal basis justifying military action, the resolution must be valid; that is, consistent with the UN Charter.[42] That first presupposes that the voting conditions laid down in

---

Reality—A Need for Change? (Leiden/Boston, Martinus Nijhoff, 2005) 194 *ff*; H Kelsen, 'Is the North Atlantic Treaty a Regional Arrangement?' (1951) 45 *AJIL* 162–66.

[37] A Geslin, 'Le pouvoir d'habilitation du Conseil de sécurité. La délégation des pouvoirs du Conseil aux organizations internationales' (2004) 37 *RBDI* 485–87; F Capotorti, 'Cours général de droit international public' (1994) 248 *RCADI* 319–21.

[38] LA Sicilianos, 'L'autorisation par le Conseil de sécurité de recourir à la force: une tentative d'évaluation', above n 5, 27–28; E de Wet, *The Chapter VII Powers of the United Nations Security Council*, above n 4, 294.

[39] P Lagrange, 'Sécurité collective et exercice par le Conseil de sécurité du système d'autorisation de la coercition', above n 2, 86–94.

[40] See above, ch 5.

[41] O Corten and P Klein, 'Action humanitaire et Chapitre VII: la redéfinition du mandat et des moyens d'action des Forces des Nations Unies' (1993) 39 *AFDI* 129.

[42] See more generally M Bedjaoui, 'Un contrôle de la légalité des actes du Conseil de sécurité est-il possible?' in SFDI, *Le Chapitre VII de la Charte des Nations Unies*, Colloque de

article 27 are met: a majority of nine votes and no negative votes by any of the five permanent members.[43] Beyond this procedural condition that is particularly easy to evaluate, there are also basic conditions that are specific to Chapter VII of the Charter and that form the appropriate legal framework for military action.

The Existence of a Threat to International Peace

First, by the wording of article 39 and pursuant to the very title of Chapter VII, the Security Council observes 'the existence of any threat to the peace, breach of the peace, or act of aggression'. The expression is to be compared with that in article 33 covering, within the framework of Chapter VI, 'any dispute, the continuance of which is likely to endanger the maintenance of international peace and security'.[44] Thus the adoption of enforcement measures by the Security Council presupposes that a situation has deteriorated to the point of being a threat to, or even an actual breach of the peace, or an act of aggression.[45] *A contrario*, if the situation is merely 'likely to' threaten the peace, the Security Council may only investigate (article 34) or recommend suitable adjustment procedures or methods (article 36) or even, if the parties so ask, make recommendations for a peaceful settlement of the dispute (article 38).[46] At the same time, the idea of 'threat to the peace' presupposes by definition that there has necessarily so far been no breach of the peace nor, *a fortiori*, any aggression.[47] Again if we stick to the wording of the Charter, nothing precludes the Security Council from adopting enforcement measures to react to a domestic situation within a State provided that the situation constitutes a threat to *international* peace and not just a risk of internal disorder.[48] This will obviously be the case if one State has threatened another State with the use of force in violation of article 2(4) of the Charter. But beyond this case which has been seen to be very limited, the idea of 'threat' within the meaning of article 39 takes on a broader

Rennes (Paris, Pedone, 1995) 264–66; N Angelet, 'International Law Limits to the Security Council' in V Gowlland-Debbas (ed), *United Sanctions and International Law* (The Hague, London, Boston, Kluwer, 2001) 71–82.

[43] See: *Namibie*, ICJ Rep (1971), 22, para 22.

[44] See: Q Wright, 'The Prevention of Aggression' (1956) 50 *AJIL* 526; H Ascencio, 'Article 33' in JP Cot and A Pellet (eds), *La Charte des Nations Unies. Commentaire article par article*, 3rd edn (Paris, Economica, 2005) 1051.

[45] See: ND White, *The United Nations and the maintenance of international peace and security* (Manchester and New York, Manchester University Press, 1990) 36–41.

[46] R Kolb, *Ius contra bellum. Le droit international relatif au maintien de la paix*, 2nd edn, above n 2, 92–93; P d'Argent, J d'Aspremont Lynden, F Dopagne, R van Steenberghe, 'Article 39' in JP Cot and A Pellet (eds), *La Charte des Nations Unies. Commentaire article par article*, 3rd edn (Paris, Economica, 2005) 1154.

[47] ibid, 1145–53; see also ND White, *The United Nations and the maintenance of international peace and security*, above n 45, 41–49.

[48] So, 'peace' is characterised by the absence of armed conflict between States'; E de Wet, *The Chapter VII Powers of the United Nations Security Council*, above n 4, 138; see also 171, and JA Frowein and N Krisch, 'Article 39', above n 35, 720.

sense,[49] relating to a risk whose evaluation is left to the Security Council under article 39. Notice again on this point that the situation observed has an objective character that does not depend on whether or not there has been a violation of international law.[50] As its name indicates, the Security Council is not tasked with enforcing the law but with maintaining or restoring peace.[51]

Beyond the wording of the Charter, the way the idea of threat to the peace has been interpreted confirms the particularly flexible or even fleeting character of the idea of a threat to the peace.[52] In the 1950s the UN established a general tie between maintaining peace and observance of human rights, as illustrated by this excerpt from a General Assembly resolution on the situation in South Africa:

> [E]nduring peace will not be secured solely by collective security arrangements against breaches of international peace and acts of aggression, but . . . a genuine and lasting peace depends also upon the observance of all the Principles and Purposes established in the Charter of the United Nations . . . and especially upon respect for an observance of human rights and fundamental freedoms for all and the establishment and maintenance of conditions of economic and social well-being in all countries.[53]

Such a connection was to be reasserted several times after the end of the Cold War, as shown by the declaration of the Security Council president on 31 January 1992 after a meeting of the heads of State and government of its fifteen members: 'The absence of war and military conflicts amongst States does not in itself ensure international peace and security. The non-military sources of instability in the economic, social, humanitarian and ecological fields have become threats to peace and security'.[54]

---

[49] See above, ch 2, s II.

[50] H Kelsen, 'Collective Security and Collective Self-Defense under the Charter of the United Nations' (1948) 42 *AJIL* 788; R Higgins, *The Development of International Law Through the Political Organs of the United* Nations (London/New York/Toronto, Oxford University Press, 1963) 174; E Lagrange, 'Le Conseil de sécurité peut-il violer le droit international?' (2004) 37 *RBDI* 578–79; P Weckel, 'Le Chapter VII de la Charte et son application par le Conseil de sécurité' (1991) 37 *AFDI* 171.

[51] JA Frowein and N Krisch, 'Introduction to Chapter VII' in B Simma (ed), *The Charter of the United Nations. A Commentary*, 2nd edn (Oxford, Oxford University Press, 2002) 705; V Gowlland-Debbas, 'Security Enforcement Action and Issues of State Responsibility' (1994) 43 *ICLQ* 61; M Forteau, *Droit de la sécurité collective et droit de la responsabilité internationale de l'Etat* (Paris, Pedone, 2006) *ia* at 68–69, 107 and 489; see also H Kelsen, *The Law of the United Nations. A Critical Analysis of Its Fundamental Problems* (London, Stevens & Sons Limited, 1951) 732–37.

[52] See: LA Sicilianos, 'Entre multilatéralisme et unilatéralisme: l'autorisation par le Conseil de sécurité de recourir à la force', above n 34, 45–53; JM Sorel, 'L'élargissement de la notion de menace contre la paix' in SFDI, *Le Chapitre VII de la Charte des Nations Unies*, Colloque de Rennes (Paris, Pedone, 1995) 3–57.

[53] GA Res 721 (VIII) of 8 December 1953, referring to GA Res 103 (I) of 19 November 1946, 377 (A), s E of 3 November 1950 and 616 B (VII) of 5 December 1952.

[54] S/23500, 11 February 1992, *La responsabilité du Conseil de sécurité en ce qui concerne le maintien de la paix et de la sécurité internationales*, 3.

Again it was with this perspective that the General Assembly Member States spoke out in the 2005 World Summit Outcome:

We acknowledge that peace and security, development and human rights are the pillars of the United Nations system and the foundations for collective security and well-being. We recognize that development, peace and security and human rights are interlinked and mutually reinforcing . . . We acknowledge that we are living in an interdependent and global world and that many of today's threats recognize no national boundaries, are interlinked and must be tackled at the global, regional and national levels in accordance with the Charter and international law.[55]

Such terminology, that is found in other UN instruments, does indeed seem to lead to a watering down of the idea of threat, which is no longer fundamentally distinct from international concerns such as development, human rights or even crime, poverty or epidemics.[56]

Can it be inferred for all that that the characterisation of threat to peace within the specific meaning of article 39 of the Charter has become entirely meaningless? I do not think so. If, beyond the texts of a general scope,[57] we analyse the precedents in which the Security Council has concretely authorised the use of force, it can be seen that it has invariably endeavoured to state grounds for its competence by characterising the situation in question as a threat against international peace. That characterisation has indeed been made on the strength of variable criteria.[58] In the cases of Bosnia-Herzegovina,[59] Somalia[60] and Rwanda,[61] the resolutions refer to risks engendered by humanitarian dramas.[62] In the case of Albania,[63] the

---

[55] *2005 World Summit Outcome*, A/RES/60/1, 24 October 2005, paras 9 and 71.

[56] See: *In larger freedom: towards development, security and human rights for all. Report of the Secretary-General*, A/59/2005, 21 March 2005, 29, para 78 and *A more secure world: Our shared responsibility*, UN, 2004, 21 *ff* and 65, para 200.

[57] The Security Council stated for example that 'international terrorism' or 'terrorism' was a threat to the peace; see SC Res 1373 (2001) of 28 September 2001; 1438 (2002) of 14 October 2002, para 1; 1440 (2002) of 24 October 2002, para 1; 1450 (2002) of 13 December 2002, para 1; 1455 (2003) of 17 January 2003; 1456 (2003) of 20 January 2003; 1465 (2003) of 13 February 2003, para 1; 1516 (2003) of 20 November 2003, para 1; 1530 (2004) of 11 March 2004, para 1; 1535 (2004) of 26 March 2004; 1566 (2004) of 8 October 2004; 1611 (2005) of 7 July 2005, para 1; 1617 (2005) of 29 July 2005; 1618 (2005) of 4 August 2005, para 1; 1624 (2005) of 14 September 2005. See also SC Res 1673 (2006) of 27 April 2006.

[58] See: R Kolb, *Ius contra bellum. Le droit international relatif au maintien de la paix*, 2nd edn, above n 2, 101–06.

[59] SC Res 770 (1992) of 13 August 1992 and *Letter dated 92/08/10 from the Permanent Representative of Bosnia and Herzegovina to the United Nations addressed to the President of the Security Council*, S/24401, 10 August 1992.

[60] SC Res 794 (1992) of 4 December 1992.

[61] SC Res 929 (1994) of 22 June 1994.

[62] SC Res 1080 (1996) of 15 November 1996 and *Letter dated 96/11/14 from the Secretary-General addressed to the President of the Security Council*, S/1996/941, 14 November 1996.

[63] SC Res 1101 (1997) of 28 March 1997 and *Letter dated 97/03/28 from the Permanent Representative of Albania to the United Nations addressed to the President of the Security Council*, S/1997/259, 28 March 1997.

relevant documents emphasise rather the harmful repercussions of the breakdown of State structures. In the cases of Haiti,[64] the Central African Republic,[65] Congo (2003),[66] and the Côte d'Ivoire (2003),[67] the Security Council seems to consider that the violations of agreements to end an internal conflict threaten peace in the regions. In the cases of Bosnia-Herzegovina (1995),[68] Kosovo,[69] Afghanistan,[70] and Iraq,[71] the threat to peace arises from the risks engendered by a precarious post-war situation. When it takes such a radical measure as an authorisation to resort to force, the Security Council therefore justifies its action by the existence of a situation that is a concrete threat to international peace. A threat that, in each given case, could be observed with some credibility since, apart from the specific case of Haiti,[72] all of the precedents are characterised by serious crises or disorder, or even actual, domestic or international, armed conflict.[73] Humanitarian, economic or social problems, as such, do not appear sufficient to warrant adopting enforcement measures. In all, analysis of Security Council practice reveals what has been designated as a 'double strategy': emphasis is placed on the possibility of acting on the basis of Chapter VII in internal situations but at the same time a connection is made between the situation in question and international peace and security.[74] A contrario, the Security Council does not consider it is freed from the obligation to demonstrate that its competence is justified by referring to the legal categories set out in article 39 of the Charter. So we cannot, then, subscribe to the idea that the only valid definition of the threat to peace would refer to what has been so characterised by the Security Council.[75] Apart from the fact that it would not sit well with the useful effect of the relevant provisions of the Charter—which does indeed lay down a limit on competence by requiring a particular degree of gravity for the measures provided

---

[64] See SC 940 (1994) and SC Res 873 (1993) of 13 October 1993.

[65] SC Res 1125 (1997) of 6 August 1997.

[66] SC Res 1484 (2003) of 30 May 2003.

[67] SC Res 1464 (2003) of 4 February 2003.

[68] SC Res 1031 (1995) of 15 December 1995.

[69] Sc Res 1244 (1999) of 10 June 1999.

[70] SC Res 1386 (2001) of 20 December 2001.

[71] SC Res 1511 (2003) of 16 October 2003.

[72] MJ Glennon, 'Sovereignty and Community after Haiti: Rethinking the Collective Use of Force', above n 15, 72–73; O Corten, 'La resolution 940 du Conseil de sécurité autorisant une intervention militaire en Haïti. L'émergence d'un principe de légitimité démocratique en droit international?' above n 15, 126–28; R Kolb, *Ius contra bellum. Le droit international relatif au maintien de la paix*, 2nd edn, above n 2, 104; C Gray, *International Law and the Use of Force*, 3rd edn, above n 28, 328–31.

[73] E de Wet, *The Chapter VII Powers of the United Nations Security Council*, above n 4, 175.

[74] ibid, 154.

[75] J Combacau, *Le pouvoir de sanction de l'ONU*, above n 7, 99–100; JM Sorel, 'Le caractère discrétionnaire des pouvoirs du Conseil de sécurité: remarques sur quelques incertitudes partielles' (2004) 37 *RBDI* 467.

for by Chapter VII to be adopted[76]—, such a nominalist conception is contradicted by the Security Council's actual practice, from which there arises the reference to a notion of threat as a condition legally limiting its competence.

Examination of the minutes of certain meetings preceding the adoption of resolutions under Chapter VII confirms this. In some cases, the characterisation of threat is the subject of contestation and debate that would be pointless if States thought they were not limited by any concept of threat.[77] Thus, in 1975 the US vetoed a draft resolution referring to Chapter VII to characterise the occupation of Namibia, affirming that the situation could not be considered a threat to peace.[78] Later, this type of qualification was debated in the context of the Haitian precedent[79] and questioned in the Somali case.[80] Lastly we can mention the interesting precedent of Myanmar, about which a draft resolution evoking simply 'risks for peace and security in the region', with no mention of Chapter VII,[81] was vetoed by China and Russia which, like other States, considered there was no threat for international peace in Myanmar to warrant Security Council action.[82]

Finally the Security Council's competence in its qualification of situations set out in article 39 appears particularly broad. The threat may arise not just from an international conflict, whether actually ongoing or at flashpoint, but also from an internal situation of conflict.[83] In this context, it appears difficult indeed to show the abusive character of a qualification of threat to peace. In the discussions around the sixty years of the UN, most Member States within the Non-Aligned Movement expressed their concern 'over the increasing resort by the Security Council to Chapter VII of the Charter as an umbrella for addressing issues that do not necessarily pose a threat to international peace and security'.[84] At the same time, no strict definition of threat was developed and even less adopted in the final document of the

---

[76] JA Frowein and N Krisch, 'Article 39', above n 35, 719–20; E de Wet, *The Chapter VII Powers of the United Nations Security Council*, above n 4, 136–37; M Forteau, *Droit de la sécurité collective et droit de la responsabilité internationale de l'Etat*, above n 51, 88–92.

[77] JA Frowein and N Krisch, 'Article 39', above n 35, 720.

[78] 'Contemporary Practice of the United States' (1975) 69 *AJIL* 880–82.

[79] See: S/PV.3413, 31 July 1994.

[80] 'La pratique suisse en matière de droit international public' (1994) 4 *RSDIE* 626–27.

[81] S/2007/14, 12 January 2007.

[82] S/PV.5619, 12 January 2007.

[83] See also: ICTY, *Tadić*, IT-94-I-AR72, 2 October 1995, para 29.

[84] Special Meeting of the Ministers of Foreign Affairs of the Non-Aligned Movement, Doha, Qatar, 13 June 2005, NAM/2005/SFMM/05, 13 June 2005, para 13; www.un.int/malaysia. See also Statement by HE Ambassador Rastam Mohd Isa, Permanent Representative of Malaysia to the UN, in his capacity as Chairman of the Coordinating Bureau of the NAM, on behalf of the NAM, at the Informal Thematic Consultations of the GA on the report of the SG entitled 'In larger freedom: towards development, security and human rights for all' (a/59/2005) on Cluster II: Freedom from fear, New York, 21 April 2005, www.un.int/malaysia, and Ministerial Meeting of the Coordinating Bureau of the NAM, Putrajaya, Malaysia, Final Document, 30 May 2006, para 19.2, ibid.

2005 World Summit. However, we can set aside the hypothesis that the Security Council would authorise military action within a State where the situation is perfectly calm to the point that the very affirmation of the existence of a threat of international war would appear manifestly arbitrary.[85] In such an instance, it would be difficult to conclude that the UN Charter had not been violated and so that the resolution was invalid as consequently would be any military action based thereon.

'Such action . . . as may be necessary'

Whenever there is a situation that can reasonably be characterised as a 'threat to the peace', the Security Council can choose among the set of measures provided for in Chapter VII of the Charter. For armed action, we have seen that it is essentially article 42 that is liable to form the legal basis for its action. Now, that provision very generally allows the Security Council to take 'such action by air, sea, or land forces as may be necessary to maintain or restore international peace and security'. The text theoretically states a condition relating to the objective behind the measure, which must aim either to maintain peace and so to remove a threat or to restore peace in the event of a breach of the peace or an act of aggression.[86] *A contrario*, the Security Council could not claim to be acting on the basis of article 42 to secure compliance with international law, restore democracy or defend moral values . . . unless such objectives were related to a broader objective of collective security.

However, it is hard to imagine the Security Council being criticised for adopting—or failing to adopt—any particular collective security measure. Since article 42 relates to an action that 'may be necessary' rather than one that 'is' necessary, the choice of a military option could not readily be contested, as such. The only condition laid down by the Charter is that 'the Security Council consider' that non-military measures 'would be inadequate or have proved to be inadequate'. The wording indicates just how very flexible the meaning of necessity is here.[87] *A priori* criticising the Security Council because it might have taken other measures than military ones, or because it might not have exhausted peaceful means entirely before taking

---

[85] See: JA Frowein and N Krisch, 'Article 39', above n 35, 726; E de Wet, *The Chapter VII Powers of the United Nations Security Council*, above n 4, 176.

[86] ND White and O Ülgen, 'The Security Council and the Decentralized Military Option: Constitutionality and Function', above n 34, 401; JA Frowein and N Krisch, 'Introduction to Chapter VII', above n 51, 710.

[87] R Kolb, *Ius contra bellum. Le droit international relatif au maintien de la paix*, 2nd edn, above n 2, 121–23; JA Frowein and N Krisch, 'Introduction to Chapter VII', above n 51, 712; but see ME O'Connel, 'The United Nations Security Council and the Authorization of Force: Renewing the Council through Law Reform' in N Blokker and N Schrijver (eds), *The Security Council and the Use of Force. Theory and Reality—A Need for Change?* (Leiden/Boston, Martinus Nijhoff, 2005) 48 and 58; M Forteau, *Droit de la sécurité collective et droit de la responsabilité internationale de l'Etat*, above n 51, 233.

steps to use force, seems improbable.[88] Likewise, article 51 of the Charter reserves the right for the Security Council '*to take at any time such action as it deems necessary* in order to maintain or restore international peace and security'. (emphasis added)[89] The Charter terms are clear enough: it is the Security Council that judges whether the measures to be taken are opportune and that consequently decides which measures are 'necessary'. Consideration of practice largely confirms this conclusion, the Security Council having very broadly interpreted the competencies the Charter recognises it to have.[90]

In the report intended to serve as a basis for discussion of UN reform sixty years after its inception, the Secretary-General recommended that the Security Council adopt a resolution setting out the principles it relied on in authorising the use of force.[91] The proposal prompted various reactions. Some States came out in favour of it, while specifying that this could not legally restrict the Security Council's room for manoeuvre;[92] others thought it was more for the General Assembly to adopt a resolution of the sort;[93] yet others thought the undertaking was pointless or even dangerous and so objected to it.[94] However, the Secretary-General's concern was shared by most States, with the Non-Aligned Movement considering that the Security Council should avoid overuse of Chapter VII and proposing that the final document simply affirm that it was to act pursuant to the Charter's provisions.[95] The Movement had already expressed that position in the weeks preceding the war against Iraq, early in 2003, with its representative affirming that:

> It would therefore be inconsistent with the spirit and letter of the United Nations Charter if the Security Council were to authorise the use of military force against Iraq at a time when Iraq has indicated its willingness to abide by the Security Council's resolutions'.[96]

With a similar perspective, the 46 French-speaking States considered that the authorisation to use force granted by the Security Council should, as a

---

[88] JA Frowein and N Krisch, 'Article 42', above n 1, 753.

[89] See also below, ch 7, s II.

[90] See: O Corten and B Delcourt, 'La face cachée du nouvel ordre mondial: l'application discriminatoire du droit international' in *A la recherche du 'nouvel ordre mondial'*, tome I, 'Le droit international en question', Association droit des gens (Brussels, Complexe ed, 1993) 21–57.

[91] *In larger freedom: towards development, security and human rights for all. Report of the Secretary-General*, A/59/2005, 24 March 2005, 39, para 126.

[92] Russia; A/59/PV.87, 7 April 2005, 6.

[93] Algeria; A/59/PV.86, 6 April 2005, 10.

[94] Uruguay; A/59/PV.87, 7 April 2005, 12.

[95] *Special Meeting of the Ministers of Foreign Affairs of the Non-Aligned Movement*, Doha, Qatar, 13 June 2005, NAM/2005/SFMM/05, 13 June 2005, paras 13 and 14; see text at www.un.int/malaysia; *Proposed Amendments by the NAM to the Draft Outcome Document of the High-Level Plenary Meeting of the GA* (A/59/HLPM/CRP.1/Resee2), paras 55 and 134; www.reformtheun.org.

[96] South Africa (on behalf on NAM); S/PV.4625, 16 October 2002, 5.

matter of principle, 'remain a last solution'.[97] Ultimately, the affirmation of the existence of a limit on the Security Council's discretionary powers was not reflected very specifically in the final document of the 2005 Summit, which very generally underscores 'the importance of acting in accordance with the purposes and principles of the Charter',[98] without further clarification of the limits which that may imply in legal terms.[99]

In view of these factors, the only legal limit bounding the Security Council's action is its obligation under the Charter to assume the main responsibility for maintaining international peace and security.[100] In military matters, then, it is the Security Council itself that must 'take' ('entre-prendre', in the French text) action,[101] and not any other UN body or, *a fortiori*, any other subject of international law.[102] Such requirements do not prevent the Security Council from using States or other third organisations to enforce its decisions. Delegation can only extend, though, to limited aspects of the exercise of certain competencies. Thus, it is hard to imagine that the Security Council should authorise such or such a State or organisation to determine whether there is a threat to peace and to use force if that State or organisation considers necessary.[103] It is the Security Council which, on a case by case basis, must characterise the situation and take the ensuing decision. Similarly, once an action has been taken, it is the Security Council that must continue to oversee it.[104] Article 53 of the Charter, which we have seen is the only one relevant for expressly providing for the authorisation technique, specifies that the enforcement measures authorised by the Security Council shall be taken 'under its authority'[105]—a requirement that is perfectly transposable to cases where the Security Council chooses

---

[97] *Déclaration de Ouagadougou du XXème sommet de la Francophonie*, 27 November 2004; www.diplomatie.gouseefr/fr/article-imprim.php3?id_article=6144.

[98] *2005 World Summit Outcome*, A/RES/60/1, 24 October 2005, para 79.

[99] ibid, paras 152–54.

[100] Art 24(1) of the UN Charter; D Sarooshi, *The United Nations and the Development of Collective Security. The Delegation by the United Nations Security Council of its Chapter VII Powers*, above n 3, 163; V Gowlland-Debbas, 'The Limits of Unilateral Enforcement of Community Objectives in the Framework of United Nations Maintenance' (2000) 11 *EJIL* 369; N Blokker, 'Is the Authorization Authorized? Powers and Practice of the United Nations Security Council to Authorize the Use of Force by "Coalitions of the Able and Willing"', above n 35, 552–54.

[101] Art 42 of the UN Charter.

[102] See below.

[103] LA Sicilianos, 'L'autorisation par le Conseil de sécurité de recourir à la force: une tentative d'évaluation', above n 5, 89; JA Frowein and N Krisch, 'Introduction to Chapter VII', above n 51, 713; E de Wet, *The Chapter VII Powers of the United Nations Security Council*, above n 4, 295; D Sarooshi, *The United Nations and the Development of Collective Security. The Delegation by the United Nations Security Council of its Chapter VII Powers*, above n 3, 33–42.

[104] ibid, 35 and 146; JA Frowein and N Krisch, 'Introduction to Chapter VII', above n 51, 713.

[105] U Villani, 'Les rapports entre l'ONU et les organizations régionales dans le domaine du maintien de la paix', above n 36, 349.

to authorise States to use force.[106] In such cases, the Security Council must not only frame its delegation of power by setting out precise objectives related to maintaining or restoring the peace but also institute the mechanisms for supervision and control that will allow it to check that the operation is indeed conducted under its aegis.[107] This is how practice can be interpreted, the Security Council having effectively coupled its authorisations with guarantees to prevent excessive decentralisation of the use of force.[108] A change has been noted in this respect.[109] Although the authorisation given to use force on the basis of which the war against Iraq was conducted in 1991 was made in a very broad fashion,[110] subsequent resolutions showed evidence of States' concern to ring-fence the authorised use of force more closely.[111] As a minimum, the States concerned are required to present periodic reports informing the Security Council of their actions and of their conformity with the stated objectives.[112] In other cases, cooperation is

[106] LA Sicilianos, 'L'autorisation par le Conseil de sécurité de recourir à la force: une tentative d'évaluation', above n 5, 12; D Sarooshi, *The United Nations and the Development of Collective Security. The Delegation by the United Nations Security Council of its Chapter VII Powers*, above n 3, 148.

[107] O Corten and P Klein, 'L'autorisation de recours à la force à des fins humanitaires: droit d'ingérence ou retour aux sources?' (1993) 4 *EJIL* 527–31; D Sarooshi, *The United Nations and the Development of Collective Security. The Delegation by the United Nations Security Council of its Chapter VII Powers*, above n 3, 155; E de Wet, *The Chapter VII Powers of the United Nations Security Council*, above n 4, 265 ff; LA Sicilianos, 'L'autorisation par le Conseil de sécurité de recourir à la force: une tentative d'évaluation', above n 5, 12–13; T Christakis and K Bannelier, 'Acteur vigilant ou spectateur impuissant? Le contrôle exercé par le Conseil de sécurité sur les Etats autorisés à recourir à la force', above n 7, 498–527; G Tunkin, 'Politics, Law and Force in the Interstate System' (1989) 219 *RCADI* 350; P Picone, 'L'évolution du droit international coutumier sur l'emploi de la force entre obligations "*erga omnes*" et autorisations du Conseil de sécurité' in E Cannizaro and P Palchetti (eds), *Customary International Law On the Use of Force* (Leiden/Boston, Martinus Nijhoff, 2005) 306; P Picone; 'Le autorizzazioni al-l'uso della forza tra sistema delle Nazioni Unite e dirritto internazionale generale' (2005) *RIDI* 5–75; P Lagrange, 'Le Conseil de sécurité et l'autorisation de prendre toutes les mesures nécessaires', above n 5, 228 ff.

[108] D Sarooshi, *The United Nations and the Development of Collective Security. The Delegation by the United Nations Security Council of its Chapter VII Powers*, above n 3, 168 ff; LA Sicilianos, 'Entre multilatéralisme et unilatéralisme: l'autorisation par le Conseil de sécurité de recourir à la force', above n 34, at 65–88.

[109] N Blokker, 'The Security Council and the Use of Force: on Recent Practice' in N Blokker and N Schrijver (eds), *The Security Council and the Use of Force. Theory and Reality—A Need for Change?* (Leiden/Boston, Martinus Nijhoff, 2005) 23 and N Blokker, 'Is the Authorization Authorized? Powers and Practice of the United Nations Security Council to Authorize the Use of Force by 'Coalitions of the Able and Willing'', above n 35, 560–66.

[110] SC Res 678 (1990) and S/PV.2963, 29 November 1990, 33/35 (Yemen) and 76 (Malaysia); see also BH Weston, 'Security Council Resolution 678 and Persian Gulf Decision Making: Precarious Legitimacy' (1991) 85 *AJIL* 526; Y Le Bouthillier and M Morin, 'Réflexions sur la validité des opérations entreprises contre l'Iraq en regard de la Charte des Nations Unies et du droit canadien' (1991) 29 *CYIL* 155–64.

[111] SC Res 770 (1992) of 13 August 1992 (paras 2 and 4) and 794 (1992) of 3 December 1992 (paras 10, 12, 13, 14, 15 and 18); S/PV.3106, 13 August 1992, 12 (India); S/PV.3145, 3 December 1992 (China); see O Corten and P Klein, 'L'autorisation de recours à la force à des fins humanitaires: droit d'ingérence ou retour aux sources?' above n 107, 530.

[112] D Sarooshi, *The United Nations and the Development of Collective Security. The Delegation by the United Nations Security Council of its Chapter VII Powers*, above n 3, 160–62; E de Wet,

more institutionalised, with the UN administration giving its consent expressly on a case by case basis for triggering a military operation by States.[113] Conversely, I know of no precedent where the Security Council has considered it is authorised to delegate a purely unilateral right to use force with no mandate or limit.[114] In this sense, emphasis has also been placed on the time limits that an authorisation must necessarily have,[115] whether such limits are expressly stated in the resolution,[116] or arise from the statement of objectives which, once achieved, void the authorisation.[117]

Ultimately, emphasis is on the discretionary but not absolute character of the Security Council's competence.[118] It is true that the legal limits of its competence may appear largely theoretical. At bottom, it is hard to imagine the Security Council actually being sanctioned for overstepping its powers. One might imagine a resolution in which the Security Council declares there is no threat to peace and where, nonetheless, it deems it necessary to decide on military measures, or again a resolution by which the Security Council adopts such measures by declaring they are not motivated by maintaining the peace but, say, by the mere overthrow of the government of a State, or again a resolution conferring on some State or organisation an unlimited right to use force. All of these hypotheses seem largely theoretical, precisely because the Security Council is fully aware of the limits of its power.[119] In

The Chapter VII Powers of the United Nations Security Council, above n 4, 272; LA Sicilianos, 'L'autorisation par le Conseil de sécurité de recourir à la force: une tentative d'évaluation', above n 5, 21; T Christakis and K Bannelier, 'Acteur vigilant ou spectateur impuissant? Le contrôle exercé par le Conseil de sécurité sur les Etats autorisés à recourir à la force', above n 7, 516; D Dormoy, 'Réflexions à propos de l'autorisation implicite de recourir à la force', above n 35, 228.

[113] SC Res 836 (1993), para 10; see D Sarooshi, The United Nations and the Development of Collective Security. The Delegation by the United Nations Security Council of its Chapter VII Powers, above n 3, 259.

[114] See: T Christakis and K Bannelier, 'Acteur vigilant ou spectateur impuissant? Le contrôle exercé par le Conseil de sécurité sur les Etats autorisés à recourir à la force', above n 7, 506–09.

[115] T Christakis and K Bannelier, 'Acteur vigilant ou spectateur impuissant? Le contrôle exercé par le Conseil de sécurité sur les Etats autorisés à recourir à la force', above n 7, 521–26; N Blokker, 'Is the Authorization Authorized? Powers and Practice of the United Nations Security Council to Authorize the Use of Force by "Coalitions of the Able and Willing"', above n 35, 562–63. According to D Sarooshi, 'it is not for the delegate to decide when the objective which the Council has stated has been fulfilled and therefore when the delegation of powers ceases to exist'; The United Nations and the Development of Collective Security. The Delegation by the United Nations Security Council of its Chapter VII Powers, above n 3, 157.

[116] SC Res 929 (1994) of 22 June 1994, para 4; SC Res 1484 (2003) of 30 May 2003, para 1.

[117] SC Res 678 (1990); see above, s 2. See also SC Res 940 (1994) of 31 July 1994, para 8 and E de Wet, The Chapter VII Powers of the United Nations Security Council, above n 4, 270 ff; LA Sicilianos, 'L'autorisation par le Conseil de sécurité de recourir à la force: une tentative d'évaluation', above n 5, 17; LA Sicilianos, 'Entre multilatéralisme et unilatéralisme: l'autorisation par le Conseil de sécurité de recourir à la force', above n 34, 88–104.

[118] ibid, 208–11.

[119] JM Sorel, 'Le caractère discrétionnaire des pouvoirs du Conseil de sécurité: remarques sur quelques incertitudes partielles', above n 75, 479–80.

procedural terms, we know that Security Council control is far from being systematically ensured by a legal organ, with the International Court of Justice only incidentally making pronouncements.[120] The sanction for abuse of power remains limited therefore to a possible refusal by States—or some of them—to enforce the measures decided on.[121] That is how broad the Security Council's margin for determining what is necessary is; even more so in practice than in law—a conclusion that can be transposed to States when they apply the Security Council's resolutions, albeit, as we shall see, to a lesser extent.

b) The Conformity of the Military Action Carried Out with the Resolution Adopted

For military action to rely validly on an authorisation, that action must obviously remain within the framework set out by that authorisation. This question refers back to the case by case interpretation of the resolution adopted by the Security Council. In practice, the Security Council often chooses to refer to a criterion of necessity.[122] More specifically, the Security Council very often adopts the 'necessary means' wording, an expression that confers on States great leeway for appreciation, if that scope is probably less extensive than that of the Security Council, which under the Charter is competent to take whatever measures 'may be necessary'.[123] Here we must return to the ordinary meaning of 'necessary' which was recalled by the International Court of Justice: '[W]hether a measure is necessary [is not] purely a question for the subjective judgment of the party; the text does not refer to what the party "considers necessary"'.[124]

Generally, it will be suitable to transpose the criteria and methods of necessity which, as will be seen, are applicable to the area of self-defence: relations between the military measure and a legitimate goal—as set out in the relevant Security Council resolution—, effectiveness of the measure and proportionality, including allowance for any alternative to the use of force.[125]

More specifically, the first thing to do, when confronted with a resolution containing the expression 'necessary means', is to check whether the

---

[120] G Guillaume, 'Quel contrôle sur les mesures de sécurité collective?' in SFDI, Les métamorphoses de la sécurité collective. Droit, pratique et enjeux stratégiques (Paris, Pedone, 2005) 241–52.

[121] T Kalala, 'La décision de l'OUA de ne plus respecter les sanctions décrétées par l'ONU contre la Libye: désobéissance civile des Etats africains à l'égard de l'ONU' (1999) 33 RBDI 545–76 and JM Sorel, 'Le caractère discrétionnaire des pouvoirs du Conseil de sécurité: remarques à propos de quelques incertitudes partielles', above n 75, 479–81.

[122] O Corten, 'La nécessité et le jus ad bellum' in SFDI, La nécessité et le droit international, Actes du colloque de Grenoble (Paris, Pedone, 2007) 127–50.

[123] Art 42 of the UN Charter and our comments above.

[124] ICJ, Military and Paramilitary Activities in and against Nicaragua, ICJ Rep (1986), para 282.

[125] Below, ch 7, s II.

wording does indeed extend to a possible use of force. The clarification may have been made explicitly by the Security Council,[126] but that is seldom the case. The wording 'all' necessary means or measures, which is very commonplace in practice, seems clearly though to indicate that the use of force is possible in principle, although that hypothesis will have to be confirmed by reading the discussions that preceded the adoption of the relevant resolution.[127]

Another question to ask is whether, supposing the use of force is potentially covered by the formula used by the Security Council, such resort is indeed 'necessary' under given circumstances. The conclusion is far from self-evident, with States very clearly admitting that force can only be made use of under certain circumstances. This conviction transpires first from the declarations made before the adoption of a resolution invoking the criterion of necessity. Thus, on the use of force to secure the embargo against Iraq in August 1990, the French government specified that 'it goes without saying that the resolution must not be understood as a blanket authorisation for the indiscriminate use of force . . . this naturally must take place only as a last resort and be limited to what is strictly necessary'.[128] This is a restrictive conception of necessity that may also be observed in the period following the adoption of a resolution of this kind. For example, in April 1991, several States declared they did not intend to interfere in the internal conflict between Kurdish rebels and the Iraqi government and so manifestly, it seems, considered that such intervention was not 'necessary' within the meaning of resolution 678 (1990).[129] It seems besides that, for other States, some of the military actions by the allies exceeded the mandate in the resolution,[130] which confirms that no one considered that the wording by 'all necessary means' gave an unconditional and unlimited right to resort to force.[131]

As pointed out, it was out of fear that this wording might be taken as a 'blank cheque' or blanket authorisation by intervening States that the Security Council itself developed control mechanisms to objectivise the interpretation of what constitutes 'necessary means' within the meaning of its own resolutions.[132] Such mechanisms, which we have seen were justified

---

[126] See, eg: SC Res 836 (1993) of 4 June 1993, para 10.

[127] S/PV.2963, 29 November 1990, 62 (China), 71 (Canada), 73 (Malaysia) and 103 (USA); see also 'Netherlands State Practice' (1992) 23 *NYIL* 365; 'United Kingdom Materials on International Law' (1990) 61 *BYBIL* 631.

[128] S/PV.2938, 25 August 1990, 32.

[129] See the USA (*Keesing's Contemporary Archives*, 1991, 38081 and 38127), France ('Pratique française du droit international' (1991) 37 *AFDI* 1012), United Kingdom ('United Kingdom Materials on International Law' (2003) 74 *BYBIL* 786). See also JF Murphy, *The United States and the Rule of Law in International Affairs* (Cambridge, Cambridge University Press, 2004) 150.

[130] *Keesing's Contemporary Archives*, 1991, 37989 and *DAI*, 1991, 103.

[131] K Boustany, 'La guerre du Golfe et le système d'intervention armée de l'ONU' (1990) 28 *CYIL* 392–93.

[132] See above.

by the necessity to maintain the Security Council's authority pursuant to the Charter, are plainly meaningless unless the right to use force attributed by the wording 'necessary means' is not absolute. However, there is no known precedent where a State has been condemned for exceeding an authorisation granted by the Security Council to use 'necessary means'. Practice is extremely varied. In some cases, States have used force further to such a resolution;[133] in others, they have though it necessary not to go down the military path;[134] in yet others, this path has only been taken late on and partially.[135] This variability complicates any attempt at legal systematisation, even if the criteria we have set out above can theoretically be used to evaluate the lawfulness of any military action in a concrete instance.

In the end, the question of the lawfulness of military action authorised by the Security Council shall have to be examined on a case by case basis, taking account of both the legal validity of the relevant resolution and the conformity of this action with the text of the resolution. In any event, we have seen that there was nothing, in principle, to stop the Security Council authorising States to use force which affirmation is valid, though, only for the Security Council itself and not for other UN bodies or *a fortiori* other subjects of international law.

B. The Unlawfulness of Military Intervention 'Authorised' by Another UN Body or by Another Subject of International Law

The 'primary responsibility' of the Security Council in the area of maintaining international peace and security as recognised in article 24 of the Charter does not exclude possible action by other organs or organisations, such as the General Assembly or regional bodies. However, it may be thought that the 'primary' character of the Security Council's responsibility implies exclusive competence to undertake or authorise enforcement measures implying the use of force. Neither the General Assembly nor the regional arrangements or agencies can stand in for the Security Council in taking as essential a decision as triggering the use of force in international relations.

The Absence of Validity of Any Authorisation to Use Force Granted by the General Assembly

On 3 November 1950, the General Assembly adopted a resolution entitled 'Uniting for Peace' by which it:

> *Resolves* that if the Security Council, because of lack of unanimity of the permanent members, fails to exercise its primary responsibility for the maintenance of

---

[133] Like against Iraq in 1991 (SC Res 678 (1990), in Somalia in 1992 (SC Res 794 (1992)).
[134] Like in Haiti (SC Res 940 (1994)) or in Zaire (SC Res 1080 (1996)).
[135] Like in Bosnia (SC Res 836 (1993)).

international peace and security in any case where there appears to be a threat to the peace, breach of the peace, or act of aggression, the General Assembly shall consider the matter immediately with a view to making appropriate recommendations to Members for collective measures, *including in the case of a breach of the peace or act of aggression the use of armed force when necessary, to maintain or restore international peace and security.* (emphasis added)[136]

In view of this resolution, it might be wondered whether the General Assembly could authorise a use of force by being substituted for the Security Council in the context of the competencies exercised under Chapter VII of the Charter.[137] To my mind, an affirmative response would be excessive; first because, in view of practice, it is not obvious that the General Assembly has ever itself made such a claim; then because, in any event, it cannot reasonably be asserted that such an extension of competencies has been accepted by all UN Member States.

For the first of these points, one needs to begin with the text of the main resolution on 'Uniting for Peace'. This text does not confer on the General Assembly any general competence to decide on or authorise military action.[138] First, it is aimed only at the specific case of a 'breach of the peace' or an 'act of aggression'. *A contrario*, a simple threat to peace does not seem, according to the resolution, to confer any power whatsoever on the General Assembly in the military domain.[139] Next, even in the event of a breach of the peace, the General Assembly only has a power to make recommendations, not decisions. The text seems to stand apart from article 42 of the Charter, which bestows on the Security Council the power to take and conduct military action and not just to make recommendations, the power to do which is granted to it rather under Chapter VI of the Charter. So, and still adhering to the wording of the resolution, the General Assembly could perfectly well recommend to States to exercise a legitimate right to collective self-defence at the request of another State that had been the victim of a prior aggression.[140] However, there is nothing to show that the General Assembly can authorise States to conduct military action in the territory of

---

[136] GA Res 377 (V) of 3 November 1950, A 1 (52-5-2) and LH Woolsey, 'The 'Uniting for Peace' Resolution of the United Nations' (1951) 45 *AJIL* 129–37.

[137] R Kolb, *Ius contra bellum. Le droit international relatif au maintien de la paix*, 2nd edn, above n 2, 159–66; see also ND White, *The United Nations and the maintenance of international peace and security*, above n 45, 130. See also *4th Report of the House of Commons Foreign Affairs Committee*, HC28-I, para 128, quoted in (2000) 49 *ICLQ* 877 and Declaration on the Use of Force, 2 September 2003, Institut de droit international, www.idi-iil.org/index.html.

[138] F Vallat, 'The Competence of the United Nations General Assembly' (1959) 97 *RCADI* 261–67.

[139] Y Dinstein, *War, Aggression and Self-Defence*, 4th edn (Cambridge, Cambridge University Press, 2005) 317; see also P Brugière, 'Les résolutions amendant les pouvoirs de l'Assemblée des Nations Unies pour la sécurité collective' (1953) 57 *RGDIP* 468.

[140] K Skubiszewski, 'The Problem of the Application of Military Measures by the General Assembly of the United Nations' in *Mélanges Andrassy* (La Haye, Martinus Nijhoff, 1968) 258; J Andrassy, 'Uniting for Peace' (1956) 50 *AJIL* 574.

another State without that action being otherwise based on an autonomous legal title.[141] Here we touch on the very essence of an authorisation, which is to transfer to someone a right he does not have or that he has but cannot exercise unilaterally.[142] The Security Council, possessing the right to use force, may delegate that right to Member States under certain circumstances.[143] The General Assembly, which does not hold the right, may only recommend to Member States to exercise a right they already have: *nemo dat quod non habet*.[144] The beneficial effect of the 'Uniting for Peace' resolution is to allow the General Assembly to centralise the exercising of military action by Member States, which is consistent with international law.[145] It does not consist in conferring a right on the General Assembly that the Charter clearly reserves for the Security Council.[146]

Such a schema is entirely consistent with the precedent of the Korean War, in the context of which the 'Uniting for Peace' resolution was adopted. As already pointed out, it is difficult to interpret this precedent as a classical case of a collective security measure insofar as Korea was not then a UN Member State.[147] In this context, both the Security Council and the General Assembly merely recommended that, to end the breach of peace by North Korean forces, Member States respond to the appeal from only those Korean authorities that were considered legitimate. The legal basis for the military action by the US and its allies is therefore to be sought in the Korean government's consent, or if one thinks that North Korea should be characterised as a State at the time, in the institution of collective

---

[141] As Y Dinstein states, 'In any event, when the General Assembly adopts a recommandation for action by States in the realm of international peace and security, such a resolution—while not bereft of political significance—does not alter the legal rights and duties of those States'; *War, Aggression and Self-Defence*, 4th edn, above n 139, 317.

[142] According to N Sarooshi, 'an authorization, thus, may represent the conferring of an entity to a very limited right to exercice a power or part thereof; or the conferring on an entity of a right to exercise a power it already possesses but the exercise of which is conditional on an authorization that triggers the competence of the entity to use the power'; *The United Nations and the Development of Collective Security. The Delegation by the United Nations Security Council of its Chapter VII Powers*, above n 3, 13; see also M Forteau, *Droit de la sécurité collective et droit de la responsabilité internationale de l'Etat*, above n 51, 436; J Verhoeven, 'Etats alliés ou Nations Unies? L'ONU face au conflit entre l'Iraq et le Koweït' (1990) 36 *AFDI* 178. But see Lauterpacht, separate opinion, *Voting Procedure on Questions relating to Reports and Petitions concerning the Territory of South West Africa*, ICJ Rep (1955) 115.

[143] See above.

[144] N Sarooshi, *The United Nations and the Development of Collective Security. The Delegation by the United Nations Security Council of its Chapter VII Powers*, above n 3, 20; see also C Leben, 'Les contre-mesures inter-étatiques et les réactions à l'illicite dans la société internationale' (1982) 28 *AFDI* 33.

[145] K Skubiszewski, 'The Problem of the Application of Military Measures by the General Assembly of the United Nations', above n 140, 259; see also M Virally, 'La valeur juridique des recommandations des organizations internationales' (1956) 2 *AFDI* 90.

[146] K Skubiszewski, 'The Problem of the Application of Military Measures by the General Assembly of the United Nations', above n 140, 257 and 'La pratique suisse en matière de droit international public' (1983) 39 *ASDI* 250.

[147] Above, ch 3, s I and ch 5.

self-defence. Assuming that the action finds no ground in these legal bases, it is conversely more doubtful that it can be justified on the sole basis of rec-ommendations governing a situation in a UN non-Member State.[148] In my view, in the particular context of its adoption, the 'Uniting for Peace' reso-lution should not be interpreted as bestowing the right on the General Assembly to carry out itself or to authorise military action against a State, without some other legal title validating such action too.[149]

Moreover, and this is certainly a decisive factor, no precedent is known where the General Assembly has claimed to authorise a use of force, as the Security Council has done on many occasions. In some instances, the General Assembly has overseen peace-keeping operations but with the agreement of the States concerned.[150] Apart from this situation, that is not one of 'use of force' within the meaning of article 2(4) of the Charter,[151] practice may be expounded by taking up the following examples that arise from extraordinary sessions of the General Assembly.[152]

—In 1951 the General Assembly 'call[ed] upon all States and authorities to refrain from giving any assistance to the aggressors in Korea', aimed at the government of the People's Republic of China.[153]
—In 1956 the General Assembly asked for a ceasefire between Israel and Egypt to be observed and for troops of both States to be moved back behind the demarcation lines drawn by the armistice.[154]
—In 1960, the General Assembly 'request[ed]' all States

> to refrain from any action which might tend to impede the restoration of law and order and the exercise by the Government of the Republic of the Congo of its authority and also to refrain from any action which might undermine the unity, territorial integrity and the political independence of the Republic of the Congo.[155]

—In 1980 the General Assembly 'strongly deplore[d]' the armed interven-tion in Afghanistan, and 'appeal[ed]' to all States to respect the sover-eignty, territorial integrity, political independence and non-aligned character of Afghanistan'.[156]

[148] K Skubiszewski, 'The Problem of the Application of Military Measures by the General Assembly of the United Nations', above n 140, 262; E de Wet, *The Chapter VII Powers of the United Nations Security Council*, above n 4, 277.
[149] ibid, 279; J Combacau and S Sur, *Droit international public*, 8th edn (Paris, Mont-chrestien, 2004) 643; Y Dinstein, *War, Aggression and Self-Defence*, 4th edn, above n 139, 317.
[150] K Skubiszewski, 'The Problem of the Application of Military Measures by the General Assembly of the United Nations', above n 140, 262–66.
[151] Above, ch 5.
[152] JF Guilhaudis, 'Considérations sur la pratique de l'"union pour le maintien de la paix"', (1981) 27 *AFDI* 382–98; J Leprette, 'Le Conseil de sécurité et la résolution 377/A (1950), (1988) 34 *AFDI* 424–35.
[153] GA Res 498 (V) of 1 February 1951, para 5.
[154] GA Res 997 (ES-I) of 2 November 1956, paras 1 and 2.
[155] GA Res 1474 (ES-IV), para 5a.
[156] Res ES-6/2, 14 January 1980, paras 2 and 3.

—In 1981 the General Assembly asked for aid to be provided to States that were victims of acts of aggression by South Africa.[157]

In the military realm, then, the General Assembly refrains from authorising States to carry out acts that, without that authorisation, would be contrary to international law.[158] Either it recalls obligations under the UN Charter, or it recommends States to use a right they hold under the Charter, such as the right to collective self-defence. Even so it should be noticed that the practice referred to is quite long-established, the General Assembly hardly being active in this domain since the end of the Cold War.[159] Patently, while it considers it is authorised to meet and make pronouncements in parallel to the Security Council, the General Assembly makes no claim to act as a substitute for the Security Council in the exercise of its responsibilities in terms of maintaining international peace and security.[160] Beyond these particular cases, it can be pointed out that the possibility of an authorisation to use force granted by the General Assembly has never been accepted by Member States as a whole in the texts laying down principles. It is instructive to revisit the debates that preceded the major resolutions of the General Assembly dealing with the use of force. In the 1960s, several States defended the claim that 'the use of force is lawful when undertaken by or under the authority of a competent United Nation's organ, including in appropriate cases the General Assembly'.[161] Such a proposal was vehemently rejected by the USSR,[162] the entire Socialist Bloc,[163]

---

[157] Res ES-8/2, 14 September 1981, para 7.

[158] N Schrijver, 'Challenges to the Prohibition to Use Force: Does the Straitjacket of Article 2 (4) United Nations Charter Begin to Gall too Much?' in N Blokker and N Schrijver (eds), *The Security Council and the Use of Force. Theory and Reality—A Need for Change?* (Leiden/Boston, Martinus Nijhoff, 2005) 37.

[159] R Kolb, *Ius contra bellum. Le droit international relatif au maintien de la paix*, 2nd edn, above n 2, 166; S Marchisio, 'Le rôle de l'Assemblée générale dans le maintien de la paix et de la sécurité internationales' in SFDI, *Les métamorphoses de la sécurité collective. Droit, pratique et enjeux stratégiques* (Paris, Pedone, 2005) 103–04.

[160] K Hailbronner and E Klein, 'Article 10' in B Simma (ed), *The Charter of the United Nations. A Commentary*, 2nd edn (Oxford, Oxford University Press, 2002) 264–67; E Stein and R Morrissey, 'Uniting for Peace Resolution' in *EPIL*, vol 4, 1234–35; L Cavaré, 'Les sanctions dans le cadre de l'ONU' (1952) 80 *RCADI* 282; P Daillier, M Forteau and A Pellet, Nguyen Quoc Dinh, *Droit international public*, 8th edn (Paris, LGDJ, 2009) 1109. See also GA Res 47/121 of 18 December 1992, para 7.

[161] UK; A/AC.119/L.8, 31 August 1964, para 5; USA, UK, Canada and Australia (action 'under the authority of a competent United Nations organ or by regional agency acting in accordance with the Charter' (A/AC.125/L.22, 23 March 1966, para 3). See also other States' views in A/AC.119/SR.8, 2 September 1964, 8; A/C.6/S.R.891, 6 December 1965, 331, para 18; A/AC.125/SR.19, 21 March 1966, 6, para 4; A/AC.125/SR.64, 28 July 1967, 16; A/AC.134/SR.85, 9 February 1971 in A/AC.134/SR.79-91, 44.

[162] According to this State, 'the Charter clearly laid down that the application of enforcement measures or the use of force could be decided on and undertaken solely by the Security Council' (A/AC.119/SR.14, 8 September 1964, 12; see also A/AC.125/SR.96, 30 September 1968, 179–80; A/AC.134/SR.58, 21 July 1970 in A/AC.134/SR.52-66, 51).

[163] Romania (A/AC.119/SR.16, 9 September 1964, 6), Bulgaria (A/AC.134/SR.67, 30 July 1970 in A/AC.134/SR.67-78; A/AC.134/SR.86, 10 February 1971 in A/AC.134/SR.79-91),

but also by France.[164] It was not taken up in the texts of the resolutions that were finally adopted. Resolution 2625 (XXV) specifies that no provision shall be construed as affecting 'the powers of the Security Council under the Charter', without mentioning the General Assembly. Resolution 3314 (XXIX) recalls that the Security Council shall 'decide what measures shall be taken in accordance with Articles 41 and 42, to maintain or restore international peace and security',[165] without mentioning the General Assembly. Resolution 42/22 pinpoints 'the special responsibility of the Security Council' and the obligation for States to 'accept and carry out the decisions of the Council in accordance with the Charter',[166] and more generally evokes 'the important role conferred by the Charter on the General Assembly in the area of the peaceful settlement of disputes and the maintenance of international peace and security'.[167] Lastly, the same trend is reflected in all of the debates at the time of the sixty years of the UN: the Security Council's role was debated at length, especially in the domain of the use of force; never, though, did States assert that the General Assembly might be a substitute for the Security Council in such an important decision as the use of force.[168] To the best of my knowledge, no State has recently defended a position of the kind either.[169]

Finally, the developments incidentally devoted to this subject by the ICJ in 1962 seem to be fully relevant still. Under article 11 of the Charter, the General Assembly may discuss any question as to maintaining international peace and security and make recommendations in this context. However, by its paragraph 2 'Any such question on which action is necessary shall be

Czechoslovakia (A/AC.125/SR.18, 21 March 1966, para 38), Ukraine (A/C.6/S.R.889, 3 December 1965, 316, para 10; A/C.6/SR.1274, 3 November 1971, para 27) and Cuba (A/C.6/S.R.893, 8 December 1965, para 39; A/C.6/SR.1167, 3 December 1969, para 39).

[164] A/C.6/SR.1166, 2 December 1969, para 4; see also A/AC.134/SR.68, 31 July 1970 in A/AC.134/SR.67-78, 19.

[165] Preamble of the declaration.

[166] Point III, para 27 of the declaration.

[167] Point III, para 30.

[168] *2005 World Summit Outcome*, A/RES/60/1, 24 October 2005, paras 79 and 80; *In larger freedom: towards development, security and human rights for all. Report of the Secretary-General*, A/59/2005, 21 March 2005, 39, paras 125–26; *A more secure world: Our shared responsibility*, Report of the High-level Panel on Threats, Challenges and Change, UN, 2004, para 194 *ff*; see also International Commission on Intervention and State Sovereignty, *The Responsibility to protect* (December 2001), paras 6.29–30 and 6.7 (www.iciss-ciise.gc.ca/menu-en.asp).

[169] According to the United Kingdom, 'the only other, and much more uncertain, form of intervention provided for in the UN system is that under the 'Uniting for Peace' Resolution of 1950. The Charter gives the Security Council responsibility for maintaining or restoring 'international peace and security', if necessary by desatching military forces (Chapter VII). If, however, the Security Council could not agree, the General Assembly was designed by its American sponsors to give the Assembly powers to deal with these issues, for example, holding an emergency special session of the Assembly to discuss the matter. It is generally accepted today that the Assembly can meet to discuss threats to 'international peace and security' if the Council cannot agree (for example, on Afghanistan in 1980). *But it is not now considered to have the power to disatch military forces to deal with such disputes'* (emphasis added); 'Is intervention ever justified?' (1986) 57 *BYBIL* 616–17.

referred to the Security Council by the General Assembly either before or after discussion'. In the case of *Certain Expenses of the United Nations*, the Court specified that 'the kind of action referred to in Article 11, paragraph 2, is coercive or enforcement action'.[170] It does not therefore prevent the General Assembly from organising operations aimed at maintaining peace with the consent of the interested States.[171] However

> the 'action' which is solely within the province of the Security Council is that which is indicated by the title of Chapter VII of the Charter, namely 'Action with respect to threats to the peace, breaches of the peace and acts of aggression'.[172]

The terms are plain, and they clearly go against the argument that the General Assembly could authorise States to use force against another State.[173] Such authorisation, whether explicitly expressed or whether expressed by the terms 'recommends', 'asks' or 'requests' would incontestably be akin to enforcement action directed against the State in question.[174] It is understandable then that, in practice, the General Assembly merely recommends that States use a right they already have, in particular in terms of collective self-defence or consent of the State in whose territory a peace-keeping operation is contemplated.[175]

To conclude on this point, we shall not make any pronouncement on the influence that the 'Uniting for Peace' resolution may have had on the interpretation of certain rules of the Charter, and in particular on the possibility for the General Assembly to hold extraordinary sessions or meet in parallel to Security Council meetings.[176] It would be clearly excessive, on the other hand, to infer from this resolution and its consequences, such a radical amendment to the Charter as that which would open the way to the General Assembly having the possibility of authorising military action in the context

---

[170] ICJ Rep (1962) 164.

[171] ibid.

[172] ibid, 165. See also FA Vallat, 'The General Assembly and the Security Council of the United Nations' (1952) 28 *BYBIL* 97–100.

[173] See: ND White, *The United Nations and the maintenance of international peace and security*, above n 45, 102; see also 'Written Statement submitted by the Government of the United States of America', February 1962; ICJ, *Certain Expenses of the UN*, Pleadings, oral arguments, Documents, ICJ Rep (1962) 206; and ibid, 419 and 423; MM Whiteman, *Digest of International Law*, vol 13 (Washington, Department of State Publ, 1968) 563–70.

[174] As C Schreuer states, 'needless to say, the coercive element is relevant primarily in relation to the State which is the object of the sanctions and not in relation to States participating in them'; 'Regionalism see Universalism' (1995) 6 *EJIL* 492; see also C Walter, 'Security Control over Regional Action' (1997) *Max Planck Yearbook of UN Law*, 136; U Villani, 'Les rapports entre l'ONU et les organizations régionales dans le domaine du maintien de la paix', above n 36, 370.

[175] According to P Sands and P Klein, 'the resolution [United for Peace] may now be treated as justifiable, at least to the extent that it envisages a 'peace-keeping' operation as opposed to 'enforcement action' on the basis of the purposes and principles of the organization'; *Bowett's Law of International Institutions* (London, Sweet & Maxwell, 6th edn, 2009) 32–33.

[176] ibid, 34; see also J Andrassy, 'Uniting for Peace', above n 140, 571–74.

of Chapter VII of the Charter. It would also be misleading to claim that a regional organisation might, as such, confer a valid legal title by authorising a use of force.

The Absence of Validity of an Authorisation to Use Force Granted by a Regional Organisation

As already pointed out, article 53(1) of the UN Charter states that 'no enforcement action shall be taken under regional arrangements or by regional agencies without the authorization of the Security Council . . .'. Whether taken directly by a regional organisation or whether that organisation delegated its exercise to its Member States, any military action carried out under the collective security mechanisms must therefore be authorised by the Security Council itself.[177] Initially, some States wanted to preserve greater autonomy for regional agencies, allowing them to take enforcement action without prior UN authorisation.[178] However, such a position did not prevail in the debates preceding the drawing up of the Charter, a review of which shows that article 53(1) was deliberately drafted in such plain terms.[179] By way of a compromise, the States in favour of maintaining a form of decentralisation of the use of force secured both the preservation of a right to self-defence set out in article 51—which right could be exercised collectively under regional arrangements—and the inclusion of article 107 to which article 53 expressly refers.[180] Article 107 justified possible military action against enemy States during the Second World War, without prior Security Council authorisation. *A contrario*, the need for such authorisation for regional agencies is beyond contest.[181] Has subsequent practice revealed an agreement to make article 53 less stringent? I do not think so, whether

---

[177] R Kolb, 'Article 53' in JP Cot and A Pellet (eds), *La Charte des Nations Unies. Commentaire article par article*, 3rd edn (Paris, Economica, 2005) 1412–13; ND White and O Ülgen, 'The Security Council and the Decentralized Military Option: Constitutionality and Function', above n 34, 388; see also H Kelsen, 'Collective Security and Collective Self-Defense under the Charter of the United Nations', above n 50, 786.

[178] Dumbarton Oaks, ch VIII, s C, para 2; *UNCIO*, vol 4, 17–18; see also ibid, 782–83 and 885; ibid, 764–84.

[179] T Franck, 'Who Killed Article 2 (4)?' (1970) 64 *AJIL* 822–35; U Villani, 'Les rapports entre l'ONU et les organizations régionales dans le domaine du maintien de la paix', above n 36, 239–57; see also M Khadduri, 'The Arab League as Regional Arrangement' (1946) 40 *AJIL* 770–75.

[180] JL Kunz, 'Individual and Collective Self-Defense in Article 51 of the Charter of the United Nations' (1947) 41 *AJIL* 872–74; G Bebr, 'Regional Organizations: A UN Problem' (1955) 49 *AJIL* 169–73; G Res and J Bröhmer, 'Article 53' in B Simma (ed), *The Charter of the United Nations. A Commentary*, 2nd edn (Oxford, Oxford University Press, 2002) 1404.

[181] R Kolb, *Ius contra bellum. Le droit international relatif au maintien de la paix*, 2nd edn, above n 2, 144 ff; E de Wet, *The Chapter VII Powers of the United Nations Security Council*, above n 4, 295; D Sarooshi, *The United Nations and the Development of Collective Security. The Delegation by the United Nations Security Council of its Chapter VII Powers*, above n 3, 248–49; H Kelsen, 'The Old and the New League: The Covenant and the Dumbarton Oaks Proposals', above n 1, 79.

this practice is examined from particular precedents (a) or through texts of principle drawn up in the context of regional agencies (b).

a) The Absence of Precedents Forming an Established Challenge to Article 53(1) of the Charter

As a general rule, when regional agencies have intervened militarily in the territory of States, they have not done so claiming a right to conduct or authorise a military action without the Security Council's authorisation. For example, the 'Brejnev doctrine' of limited sovereignty was not reflected in legal terms by a challenge to Chapter VIII of the Charter.[182] When Warsaw Pact troops intervened in Hungary and then in Czechoslovakia, they did so invoking the legal argument of consent of the local authorities and not that of some 'authorisation' supposedly granted by that organisation.[183] More recently, ECOWAS has intervened in several West African States but without claiming to derogate from Chapter VIII of the Charter either, as shall be seen later.[184] As for NATO, when it intervened in Bosnia-Herzegovina (1994–95) then in Yugoslavia (1999), it did so invoking an authorisation from the Security Council itself. In the context of the inter-American system, two precedents have sometimes been invoked in favour of relaxing the stringent terms of article 53(1): the intervention in the Dominican Republic (1965) under the aegis of the Organisation of American States (OAS) and the intervention in Grenada (1983) under the aegis of the Organisation of Eastern Caribbean States (OECS). However, examination of the position of States on these occasions shows that what happened was more a formal reaffirmation of the stringency of Chapter VIII of the Charter.

In the case of the Dominican Republic first, while the initial sending of US troops was officially justified by the consent of the local authorities,[185] the deployment of contingents in the country's capital was then justified by an OAS decision to send in a peace-keeping force. In the Security Council discussions, the US did not, however, invoke a specific right of that regional organisation to authorise a military intervention. For the US representative:

> [E]nforcement action, within the meaning of Chapter VII of the Charter, remains the prerogative of the United Nations and of the Security Council but . . . the action being taken by the OAS in the Dominican Republic is most certainly not enforcement action, any more than the action taken by the UN in Cyprus, the Congo or the Middle East was enforcement action.[186]

By this logic, the deployment of OAS forces in the Dominican Republic should be likened to a peace-keeping operation and not to 'enforcement

---

[182] See above, ch 2, s II.
[183] Above, ch 5, s I.
[184] Below, s 2.
[185] Above, ch 5.
[186] S/PV.1222, 9 June 1965, 5, para 21; see also S/PV.1217, 22 May 1965, para 28.

action' within the meaning of article 53.[187] *A contrario*, the US made no claim to be released from the requirements of Chapter VIII of the UN Charter on military enforcement action.[188] This precedent could not therefore be construed in this sense, particularly as, as pointed out earlier, the arguments advanced by the intervening powers far from convinced all of the UN Member States, with most of them considering that this was indeed enforcement action and so a violation of the UN Charter.[189]

The case of the 1983 intervention in Grenada is very different, even if it has to lead us to the same conclusions. The US justified its intervention in the country by referring to various arguments, the legal scope of which cannot always be readily perceived.[190] Among these arguments, it seems however that that the decision of the OECS[191] (the OAS and CARICOM having declined to intervene[192]) to trigger military action occupied a certain place, as attested by the declaration of the US representative on the Security Council: 'Such action fully accorded with relevant provisions of the Charter of the United Nations, which accorded regional agencies the authority to undertake collective action'.[193]

The Grenada affair is, to my knowledge, the only precedent in which it has been so clearly possible to invoke the right for regional agencies to conduct military action with no form of Security Council authorisation.[194] However, most of the UN Member States rejected this line of argument.[195] France, for example, declared it had 'never accepted certain interpretations

---

[187] S/PV.1200, 5 May 1965, para 163. See also Malaysia (S/PV.1222, 9 June 1965, para 104; S/PV.1222, 9 June 1965, paras 106–07 and paras 109–11) and United Kingdom (S/PV.1198, 4 May 1965, para 60).

[188] S/PV.1220, 3 June 1965, paras 79–81).

[189] See above, ch 5, s I. See France (S/PV.1221, 7 June 1965, paras 60–61), Jordan (S/PV. 1221, 7 June 1965, para 22). See also Bulgaria (A/C.6/S.R.891, 6 December 1965, para 7).

[190] See above, ch 5, s I.

[191] OECS, Statement on the Grenada situation of 25 October 1983; text in WC Gilmore, *The Grenada Intervention: Analysis and Documentation* (New York, Mansell Publishing Limited, 1984) 97–98.

[192] S/PV.2491, 27 October 1983, paras 279 and 281.

[193] S/PV.2491, 27 October 1983, 8, para 71; see also S/PV.2487, 25 October 1983, 22, paras 191–93; *Digest of United States Practice* (Washington, Department of State Publication, 1981–1988) vol III, 3396–404). See also Antigua and Barbuda (S/PV.2489, 26 October 1983, para 157), Barbados (S/PV.2491, 27 October 1983, paras 144 and 146), Dominica (S/PV.2489, 26 October 1983, para 10), Jamaica (ibid, paras 53, 55 and 56), Saint Lucia (S/PV.2491, 27 October 1983, para 28) Saint Vincent and the Grenadines (ibid, para 331), and L Doswald-Beck, 'The Legality of the United States Intervention in Grenada' (1984) 31 *NILR* 362–78.

[194] See: JN Moore, 'Grenada and the International Double Standard' (1984) 78 *AJIL* 153–59.

[195] See: Grenada (S/PV.2487, 25 October 1983, para 96), Afghanistan (S/PV.2491, 27 October 1983, para 262), Algeria (S/PV.2489, 26 October 1983, para 99), Ethiopia (S/PV.2489, 26 October 1983, para 87), Mexico (S/PV.2487, 25 October 1983, para 14), Mongolia (S/PV.2491, 27 October 1983, 35, para 338). See also CC Joyner, 'The United States Action in Grenada. Reflections on the Lawfulness of Invasion' (1984) 78 *AJIL* 136–37; FA Boyle, A Chayes, I Dore, R Falk, M Feinrider, CC Ferguson Jr, JD Fine, KN, B Weston, 'International Lawlessness in Grenada' (1984) 78 *AJIL* 173.

of the Charter whereby other organs could authorise armed intervention without the approval of the Security Council'.[196] As pointed out previously, the only reason this military operation was not condemned by the Security Council is because of the US veto,[197] the General Assembly having characterised it by a very large majority as a violation of international law.[198] In short, allowance for this precedent plainly pleads against any challenge to the rule stated in article 53(1).

b) The Absence of Positions of Principle Having Formed an Established Challenge to Article 53(1) of the Charter

This provision has not been challenged for that matter by treaty-based practice, particularly in the context of existing regional agencies. Mention has already been made of the provisions of several constituent instruments of organisations such as NATO and the OAS that insist on the primary responsibility of the Security Council pursuant to the Charter.[199] While some treaties remain silent on this particular point,[200] it would obviously be going too far to deduce a challenge to the primary responsibility of the Security Council. A new interpretation of Chapter VIII of the Charter might only be envisaged if, first, a regional organisation clearly claimed to be released from it and, secondly, if that claim were accepted by UN Member States as a whole. Neither of these two conditions has been met to date, as shall be seen by successively analysing the positions of NATO and then of the African Union before returning to the positions expressed by States within the UN.[201]

Changes in NATO's Strategic Concept

For the first of these, it will be noted that NATO, even if it manifested a certain hankering for autonomy in the war against Yugoslavia, did not challenge Chapter VIII of the UN Charter on a legal basis.[202] First, this was because the 1999 war was not justified on the basis of a right of the regional organisation to resort to force, the intervening States relying generally on

---

[196] S/PV.2489, 26 October 1983, 15, para 146.

[197] S/PV.2491, 27 October 1983, para 431.

[198] GA Res 38/7 of 2 November 1983, para 1.

[199] Above, ch 4, s I.

[200] See: A Peyro Llopis, *Les relations entre l'Organisation des Nations Unies et les organisations régionales en matière coercitive* (Bruxelles, Bruylant, forthcoming).

[201] For the EU, see art J.1 of the Treaty of Amsterdam and art I-3 para 4 of the Constitutional Treaty. For OAS, see *Declaration on Security in the Americas*, 28 October 2003, OEA/Ser.K/XXXVIII, CES/DEC.1/03resee1, point II, 4z), www.oas.org.

[202] See: L Weerts, 'Droit, morale et politique dans le discours justificatif de l'Union européenne et de l'OTAN: vers une confusion des registres de légitimité' in O Corten and B Delcourt (eds), *Droit, légitimation et politique extérieure. L'Europe et la guerre du Kosovo* (Bruxelles, Bruylant, 2001) 103–07 and 112–18. More generally, see R Higgins, 'Some Thoughts on the Evolving Relationship between the Security Council and NATO' in *Mélanges Boutros-Ghali* (Bruxelles, Bruylant, 1998) 511–30.

authorisation supposedly given by the Security Council,[203] whose
supremacy was thus indirectly recognised.[204] Then this was because, in
the document made public at the summit marking NATO's Fiftieth
Anniversary, in April 1999 (that is while the war against Yugoslavia was in
progress) there is no sign of any new legal concept challenging Chapter VIII
of the UN Charter.[205] On the contrary, the NATO Member States reaffirm
in it that 'As stated in the Washington Treaty, we recognise the primary
responsibility of the United Nations Security Council for the maintenance
of international peace and security'[206], wording which, far from challenging
the UN Charter system, refers back to it,[207] and even takes up its terms
word for word.[208] The German Constitutional Court came out clearly on
this side when, after examining the document stating NATO's strategic
concept, it concluded:

> This means that the following is not called into question: the obligatory prohibi-
> tion on the threat or use of force (Article 2, N°4 of the Charter of the United
> Nations); the accepted prerequisites for the use of military force, which include the
> grant of a UN mandate to States (Article 42 in conjunction with Article 48 of the
> Charter of the United Nations) or to regional agencies (Article 53 of the Charter
> of the United Nations) by the United Nations; collective defence also of third
> States; and intervention by request, and the proportionality of such action.[209]

Still in the same sense, in November 1999, the OSCE States, that include
all NATO Member States, adopted a 'Charter for European Security' containing the following excerpt:

> We recognize the primary responsibility of the United Nations Security Council
> for the maintenance of international peace and security and its crucial role in con-
> tributing to security and stability in our region. We reaffirm our rights and oblig-
> ations under the Charter of the United Nations, including our commitment on the
> issue of the non-use of force or the threat of force. In this connection, we also

---

[203] See below, s II and ch 8, s II.

[204] See: 'Pratique française du droit international' (1998) 44 *AFDI* 737 and 738; 'La pratique belge en matière de droit international' (2002) 35 *RBDI* 252.

[205] B Delcourt and F Dubuisson, 'Contribution au débat juridique sur les missions 'non-
article 5' de l'OTAN' (2002) 35 *RBDI* 458–65; *DAI*, 1999, 307 (France); 'Netherlands state
practice' (2000) 31 *NYIL* 194.

[206] An Alliance for the 21st Century, Washington Summit Communiqué, 24 April 1999,
para 38; www.nato.int/docu/pr/1999/p99-064e.htm. See also The Alliance's Strategic Concept
Approved by the Heads of State and Government participating in the meeting of the North
Atlantic Council in Washington DC on 23rd and 24th April 1999, para 15; www.nato.int/
docu/pr/1999/p99-065e.htm

[207] According to art 7 of the Washington Treaty, 'This Treaty does not affect, and shall not
be interpreted as affecting in any way the rights and obligations under the Charter of the
Parties which are members of the United Nations, or the primary responsibility of the Security
Council for the maintenance of international peace and security'.

[208] See art 24 of the UN Charter.

[209] Federal Constitutional Court, 22 November 2001, BverfG, 2 BvE 6/99, para 33, quoted
in B Delcourt and F Dubuisson, 'Contribution au débat juridique sur les missions 'non-article
5' de l'OTAN', above n 205, 460.

reaffirm our commitment to seek the peaceful resolution of disputes as set out in the Charter of the United Nations.[210]

Given all of these factors, there is hardly any doubt that the official legal position of the NATO Member States confirms much more than it invalidates the hierarchical system provided for in Chapter VIII of the UN Charter.[211]

The Ambiguous Position of the African Union States

It has also been thought that the conclusion of the Constitutive Act of the African Union (AU) on 11 July 2000 might be considered a challenge to Chapter VIII of the Charter.[212] Article 4(h) of the treaty evokes 'the right of the Union to intervene in a Member State pursuant to a decision of the Assembly in respect of grave circumstances, namely: war crimes, genocide and crimes against humanity'.[213] Moreover, an amendment to this provision was signed in July 2003 (without having come into force at the time of writing), aimed at completing the current text by adding the expression '. . . as well as a serious threat to legitimate order to restore peace and stability to the Member State of the Union upon the recommendation of the Peace and Security Council'.[214] Lastly, in July 2005, the AU States adopted a common position on UN reform, stating:

> With regard to the use of force, it is important to comply scrupulously with the provisions of Article 51 of the UN Charter, which authorize the use of force only in cases of legitimate self-defence. In addition, the Constitutive Act of the African Union, in its Article 4 (h), authorizes intervention in grave circumstances such as genocide, war crimes and crimes against humanity. Consequently, any recourse to force outside the framework of Article 51 of the UN Charter and Article 4 (h) of the AU Constitutive Act, should be prohibited.[215]

[210] Istanbul, 18–19 November 1999, para 11; www.osce.org/mc/documents.html.

[211] See also the Prague Summit Declaration: '[w]e are steadfast in our commitment to the transatlantic link; to NATO's fundamental security tasks including collective defence; to our shared democratic values; and to the United Nations Charter' (21 November 2002, para 1; www.nato.int/docu/pr/2002/p02-127e.htm). See also F Dubuisson, 'La problématique de la légalité de l'opération "Force alliée" contre la Yougoslavie: enjeux et questionnements' in O Corten and B Delcourt (eds), *Droit, légitimation et politique extérieure. L'Europe et la guerre du Kosovo* (Bruxelles, Bruylant, 2001) 190–91; M Zwanenburg, 'NATO, its Members States, and the Security Council', above n 36, 201–03.

[212] See: B Kioko, 'The Right of Intervention Under the African Union's Constitutive Act: From Non-Interference to Non-Intervention' (2003) 852 *IRRC* 821; AA Yusuf, 'The Right of Intervention by the African Union: A New Paradigm in Regional Enforcement Action?' (2003) 11 *African Yearbook of International Law* 3 *ff*.

[213] www.africa-union.org.

[214] Art 4, Protocol on Amendments to the Constitutive Act of the African Union, 11 July 2003; www.africa-union.org. See E Baimu and K Sturman, 'Amendment of the African Union's Right to Intervene. A shift from human security to regime security?' (2003) 12 *African Security Review*.

[215] The Common African Position on the Proposed Reform of the United Nations. 'The Ezulwini Consensus', Ext./EX.CL/2(VII), 7, Executive Council, 7th Extraordinary Session, 7–8 March 2005, Addis Ababa, Ext/Ext.CL/2 (VII). See also the Sirte Declaration on the Reform of the United Nations (Assembly/AU/Decl.2(V), 5 July 2005, www.africa-union.org).

None of these excerpts mentions the need for prior authorisation from the Security Council. *A priori*, they could therefore be construed as challenging that provision.[216]

This interpretation falls foul from the outset of the observation that, while the excerpts just cited do not mention the need to obtain Security Council authorisation, they do not exclude it either. Article 4(h) of the Constitutive Act of the AU bestows on the organisation a right of intervention within its Member States,[217] a right which its forerunner the OAU did not have in its articles.[218] The primary effect of this provision is therefore to attribute expressly to the AU a legally required competence in terms of its articles for the law of international organisations.[219] Without such competence, the Union could not as such act militarily under its own legal order even if so authorised by the Security Council. The legal effects of article 4(h) are therefore above all internal to the organisation and do not tend to modify general international law. In this context, the argument of a challenge to Chapter VIII of the Charter runs into serious obstacles, as the following points illustrate.

First, it is true that a textual interpretation can lead to two contradictory positions, the first presuming that the AU has intended to abide by the UN Charter, the second that it has sought to derogate from it. Now, the second part of this alternative raises serious issues of general international law, since it would imply a possible nullity of the AU's Constitutive Act, as it derogates from a norm of peremptory law.[220] There is good cause therefore to favour *a priori* a principle of restrictive interpretation, tending to reconcile rather than oppose the various legal texts applicable.[221] This reconciliation may

---

[216] JI Levitt, 'The Peace and Security Council of the African Union and the Security Council: The Case of Darfur, Sudan' in N Blokker and N Schrijver (eds), *The Security Council and the Use of Force. Theory and Reality—A Need for Change?* (Leiden/Boston, Martinus Nijhoff, 2005) 229–36; JI Levitt, 'The Evolving Intervention Regime in Africa: From Basket Case to Market Place?' *ASIL Proceedings*, 2002, 142; see also KD Magliveras and GJ Neldi, 'The African Union—A New Dawn for Africa?' (2002) 51 *ICLQ* 418.

[217] CA Packer and D Rukare, 'The New African Union and Its Constitutive Act' (2002) 96 *AJIL* 372–73.

[218] Art III of the OAU; A Abass and M Baderin, 'Towards Effective Collective Security and Human Rights Protection in Africa: an Assesment of the Constitutive Act of the New African Union' (2002) 49 *NILR* 8–13 and 16; see also TO Elias, 'The Charter of the Organization of African Unity' (1965) 59 *AJIL* 247–48; JA De Yturriaga, 'L'Organisation de l'unité africaine et les Nations Unies' (1965) 69 *RGDIP* 375–79; JI Levitt, 'The Peace and Security Council of the African Union and the Security Council: The Case of Darfur, Sudan', above n 216, 217; B Kioko, 'The Right of Intervention Under the African Union's Constitutive Act: From Non-Interference to Non-Intervention', above n 212, 812–13; GJ Naldi, 'Peace-Keeping Attempts by the Organization of African Unity' (1985) 34 *ICLQ* 593–601.

[219] R Kolb, 'Article 53', above n 177, 1422.

[220] Above, ch 4, s I; see also A Abass and M Baderin, 'Towards Effective Collective Security and Human Rights Protection in Africa: an Assesment of the Constitutive Act of the New African Union', above n 218, 18; C Gray, *International Law and the Use of Force*, 3rd edn, above n 28, 53.

[221] R Kolb, 'Article 53', above n 177, 1423; see also R Kolb, *Ius contra bellum. Le droit international relatif au maintien de la paix*, 2nd edn, above n 2, 146–48.

come about in two ways. First, it could be envisaged that UN members have accepted to revise article 53(1) in an informal way, by allowing the AU to intervene militarily without Security Council authorisation.[222] This general agreement would, however, have to be the subject of a demonstration which, as shall be seen, runs up against the constant reminders of Chapter VIII of the Charter in recent UN texts that make no mention of any revision or new interpretation of this Chapter.[223] It seems preferable then to favour a second way of reconciling the different legal instruments applicable, by considering that the AU texts must be consistent with the Charter rather than the other way round. In this perspective, it is logical to consider that, even in the absence of any express mention, the AU's right of intervention is subordinate to compliance with article 53(1) and so, if this right implies implementation of enforcement action, with Security Council authorisation.

This latter interpretation is justified in regard of other provisions of the institutional system laid down in the context of the African Union. Article 4 of the Constitutive Act cited contains only general principles for the organisation's operation, which have then been specified through various instruments. Among these, the Protocol relating to the establishment of the Peace and Security Council of the African Union is of particular interest since it institutes the organ tasked with implementing article 4(h) of the Constitutive Act of the Union.[224] Now, this protocol explicitly provides that the Peace and Security Council is guided by the principles set out in the UN Charter.[225] More specifically, article 17 of the instrument provides that:

> In the fulfillment of its mandate in the promotion and maintenance of peace, security and stability in Africa, *the Peace and Security Council shall cooperate and work closely with the United Nations Security Council, which has the primary responsibility for the maintenance of international peace and security* . . . Where necessary, recourse will be made to the United Nations to provide the necessary financial, logistical and military support for the African Union's activities in the promotion and maintenance of peace, security and stability in Africa, *in keeping with the provisions of Chapter VIII of the UN Charter on the role of Regional Organizations in the maintenance of international peace and security.* (emphasis added)[226]

From a reading of these terms, it appears that the African Union does not intend to derogate from or duck out of the requirements of the UN Charter,

---

[222] See: A Abass and M Baderin, 'Towards Effective Collective Security and Human Rights Protection in Africa: an Assessment of the Constitutive Act of the New African Union', above n 218, 20–24. See below, s II.

[223] See below.

[224] According to 7 § 1e) of the Protocol, the Peace and Security Council shall 'recommend to the Assembly, pursuant to Article 4(h) of the Constitutive Act, intervention, on behalf of the Union, in a Member State in respect of grave circumstances, namely war crimes, genocide and crimes against humanity, as defined in relevant international conventions and instruments'; see also art 13 § 1 and 3 of the Protocol (www.africa-union.org).

[225] Art 4 of the Protocol.

[226] Art 17, paras 1 and 2. See also Article 13 § 5 of the Protocol.

in particular its Chapter VIII.[227] This conclusion is confirmed by the reading of the text adopted in January 2005 of the African Union Non-Aggression and Common Defence Pact (which has not yet come into force), expressly providing for compliance with the Charter and the primary responsibility of the Security Council.[228]

Thirdly, it shall be emphasised that these texts have never, so far, been construed as conferring on the African Union a right of intervention that might be exercised outside of Chapter VIII of the UN Charter, notably in the case of the Darfour crisis.[229] Article 4(h) was indeed cited by the Conference when it noted that 'according to the terms of Articles 3 (h), 4 (h) and 4 (o) of the Constitutive Act of the African Union, the crimes of which Hissène Habré is accused fall within the competence of the African Union', before mandating Senegal to judge the former Chadian President in the name of the AU.[230] This precedent confirms that this provision must be interpreted as conferring a particular competence on the organisation, but not necessarily as granting it a right of military intervention without the Security Council's authorisation.

Finally, it should be observed that even after the 'Ezulwini consensus' was adopted, no African State ever made a claim to revise or reinterpret article 53(1) within the UN. No right of intervention by the AU, without Security Council authorisation, has ever been claimed in the General Assembly, including at the time of discussions on 'responsibility to protect'.[231] Some days after the adoption of the *2005 World Summit Outcomes*, which it shall be seen merely reaffirm the requirements of Chapter VIII of the Charter, the Security Council adopted a 'Declaration on strengthening the effectiveness of the Security Council's role in conflict prevention, particularly in Africa'. After reaffirming 'its commitment to the Purposes and Principles of the Charter of the United Nations' and '*Bearing* in mind its primary responsibility for the maintenance of international peace and security', the Security Council recalled the AU Constitutive Act and the Protocol on the setting up of the AU Peace and Security Council and then:

> Call[ed] for the strengthening of cooperation and communication between Nations and regional or subregional agencies or arrangements, in accordance

---

[227] P Sands and P Klein, *Bowett's Law of International Institutions*, 6th edn, above n 175, 250–51.

[228] According to Art 17 a) of the Pact '[t]his Pact shall not derogate from, and shall not be interpreted as derogating in any way from the obligations of Member States contained in the United Nations Charter and the Constitutive Act, including the Protocol, and from the primary responsibility of the United Nations Security Council for the maintenance of international peace and security'. See also Arts 1 and 3 of the Charter, www.africa-union.org.

[229] JI Levitt, 'The Peace and Security Council of the African Union and the Security Council: The Case of Darfur, Sudan', above n 216, 213–51; C Gray, *International Law and the Use of Force*, 3rd edn, above n 28, 53–55.

[230] Assembly of the African Union, 7th ordinary session, Banjul, 2 July 2006, 'Décision sur le procès d'Hissène Habré et l'UA', Doc Assembly/AU/3 (VII), www.africa-union.org.

[231] See below, ch 8, s I.

with Chapter VIII of the Charter, particularly with respect to mediation initiatives.[232]

This text was filed by the three African States that were then Security Council members.[233] It shows that the AU States are far from claiming power to revise Chapter VIII of the Charter.[234] Such a claim does not seem to have been advanced at the high-level meeting between the UN and regional and intergovernmental organisations held at the UN headquarters on 25 and 26 July 2005.[235]

All of these factors clearly show that no right to derogation from article 53(1) and no will to revise or reinterpret this provision in a fundamentally new way have been advanced by AU States.[236] A change to existing law is far from being established on this point, especially as, if one looks at the universal texts, it will be observed that this right is constantly reaffirmed by UN Member States as a whole.

The Reaffirmation of the System Laid Down by Article 53 of the UN Charter
The problem of the autonomy of regional agencies has long been posed within the UN. In the 1960s, as part of the debates preceding the adoption of the major resolution on the use of force, certain texts filed by the US and some of their allies in the General Assembly suggested that regional agencies could decide on the use of force without necessarily obtaining the prior authorisation of the Security Council.[237] These texts were forcefully criticised by a vast majority of States, whether Socialist,[238] Non-Aligned[239] or

---

[232] SC Res 1625 (2005) of 14 September 2005, preamble and para 7.

[233] S/2005/578; Algeria, Benin and Tanzania (with USA).

[234] S/PV.5261, 14 September 2005, 4.

[235] See: S/PV.5282, 17 October 2005; see also S/PV.5649, 28 March 2007, 3.

[236] *Contra:* G Gaya, *Fourth report on responsibility of international organizations*, 28 February 2006, 2 A/CN.4/564, 18, para 47 and fn 72.

[237] See the six Powers' proposition of definition, Article III: 'The use of force in the exercice of the inherent right of individual or collective self-defence, or pursuant to decisions by competent United Nations organs or regional agencies consistent with the Charter of the United Nations, does not constitute aggression' (A/AC.134/L.17 and Add.1).

[238] USSR (A/AC.134/SR.58, 21 July 1970 in A/AC.134/SR.52-66; A/C.6/SR.1206, 26 October 1970; A/AC.134/SR.84, 8 February 1971 in A/AC.134/SR.79-91), Bulgaria (A/C.6/SR.1206, 26 October 1970), Czechoslovakia (A/C.6/SR.1206, 26 October 1970), Belarus (A/C.6/SR.1165, 2 December 1969), Romania (A/AC.134/SR.59, 22 July 1970 in A/AC.134/SR.52-66).

[239] Iraq (A/AC.134/SR.47, 27 March 1969 in A/AC.134/SR.25-51; A/AC.134/SR.67, 30 July 1970 in A/AC.134/SR.67-78; A/C.6/SR.1167, 3 December 1969; A/AC.134/SR.59, 22 July 1970 in A/AC.134/SR.52-66; A/C.6/SR.1202, 16 October 1970), Sudan (A/AC. 134/SR.65, 28 July 1970 in A/AC.134/SR.52-66), Afghanistan (A/C.6/SR.1206, 26 October 1970; A/C.6/SR.1352, 6 November 1972), Yugoslavia (A/C.6/SR.1167, 3 December 1969; A/AC.134/SR.58, 21 July 1970 in A/AC.134/SR.52-66), Syria (A/AC.134/SR.59, 22 July 1970 in A/AC.134/SR.52-66), Indonesia (A/AC.134/SR.60, 22 July 1970 in A/AC.134/SR.52-66), Cuba (A/C.6/SR.1273, 2 November 1971; A/C.6/SR.1349, 3 November 1972; A/C.6/SR.1441, 19 November 1973; A/C.6/SR.1479, 18 October 1974; A/C.6/SR.1206, 26 October 1970), Colombia (A/C.6/SR.1474, 11 October 1974; A/C.6/SR.1271, 1 November 1971), Uruguay (A/C.6/SR.57, 20 July 1970 in A/AC.134/SR.52-66), Ecuador

Western,[240] that insisted on stringent compliance with article 53. The US itself reacted to this criticism by denying it wished to challenge the provisions of Chapter VIII of the Charter.[241] The episode explains why there is no trace of a more relaxed interpretation of article 53 in resolutions 2625 (XXV), 3314 (XXIX) and 42/22, which, as has been seen, on the contrary recalled the responsibility of the Security Council under the Charter.[242]

This position has been reasserted on many occasions, as the following examples show.[243]

—In 1995, in its Declaration on the Enhancement of Cooperation between the United Nations and Regional Arrangements or Agencies in the Maintenance of International Peace and Security, the General Assembly recalled that regional organisations may use force 'in coordination with the United Nations and, when necessary, under the authority or with the authorization of the Security Council, in accordance with the Charter'.[244]

—In 1998, the Security Council, speaking through its president, 'reaffirm[ed] that all such activity taken under regional arrangements or by regional agencies, including enforcement action, *shall be carried out in accordance with Articles 52, 53 and 54 of Chapter VIII of the Charter of the United Nations*'.[245]

—In the *Millennium Declaration*, the heads of State and government of the UN member nations decided 'To strengthen cooperation between the United Nations and regional agencies, in accordance with the provisions of Chapter VIII of the Charter'.[246]

—By the terms of the *2005 World Summit Outcome* adopted by States on the sixtieth anniversary of the UN:

(A/C.6/SR.1352, 6 November 1972; A/AC.134/SR.58, 21 July 1970 in A/AC.134/SR.52-66), Chile (A/C.6/SR.1167, 3 December 1969), Guyana (A/AC.134/SR.65, 28 July 1970 in A/AC.134/SR.52-66).

[240] France (A/C.6/SR.1166, 2 December 1969; A/AC.134/SR.68, 31 July 1970 in A/AC.134/SR.67-78), Sweden (A/C.6/SR.1079, 25 November 1968), Italy (A/AC.134/SR.18, 1 July 1968 in A/AC.134/SR.1-24), Cyprus (A/AC.134/SR.21, 4 July 1968 in A/AC.134/SR.1-24); see also Japan (A/AC.134/SR.67, 30 July 1970 in A/AC.134/SR.67-78).

[241] A/AC.134/SR.59, 22 July 1970 in A/AC.134/SR.52-66; A/AC.134/SR.59, 22 July 1970 in A/AC.134/SR.52-66; A/C.6/SR.1273, 2 November 1971; A/AC.134/SR.67, 30 July 1970 in A/AC.134/SR.67-78; A/C.6/SR.1480, 18 October 1974, 98. See also United Kingdom; A/AC.119/SR.16, 9 September 1964.

[242] See: Czechoslovakia (A/C.6/S.R.871, 8 November 1965), Argentina, Chile, Guatemala, Mexico and Venezuela (A/AC.125/SR.66, 1 August 1967; A/AC.125/L.49, III; A/C.6/S.R.1002, 20 November 1967), Cuba (A/C.6/S.R.893, 8 December 1965), Sweden (A/AC.125/SR.86, 13 September 1968, 44), Trinidad and Tobago (A/C.6/S.R.1183, 28 September 1970); see also Iran (A/C.6/32/SR.67, 8 December 1977).

[243] See also: 'La pratique suisse en matière de droit international public' (1992) *RSDIE* 742–45; (1994) 4 *RSDIE* 626.

[244] GA Res 49/57 of 17 February 1995, para 10.

[245] S/PRST/1998/35 of 30 November 1998, 'the situation in Africa'.

[246] GA Res 55/2 of 8 September 2000, para 9.

Recognizing the important contribution to peace and security by regional agencies *as provided for under Chapter VIII* of the Charter and the importance of forging predictable partnerships and arrangements between the United Nations and regional agencies, and noting in particular, given the special needs of Africa, the importance of a strong African Union: (*a*) We support the efforts of the European Union and other regional entities to develop capacities such as for rapid deployment, standby and bridging arrangements . . . The international community, through the United Nations, also has the responsibility to use appropriate diplomatic, humanitarian and other peaceful means, *in accordance with Chapters VI and VIII of the Charter*, to help to protect populations from genocide, war crimes, ethnic cleansing and crimes against humanity. In this context, we are prepared to take collective action, in a timely and decisive manner, through the Security Council, *in accordance with the Charter*, including Chapter VII, on a case-by-case basis and in cooperation with relevant regional agencies as appropriate . . . (emphasis added)[247]

—On 17 October 2005, the Security Council adopted resolution 1631 (2005):

Emphasizing that the growing contribution made by regional agencies in cooperation with the United Nations can usefully complement the work of the organization in maintaining international peace and security, and *stressing* in this regard that *such contribution must be made in accordance with Chapter VIII of the United Nations Charter.* (emphasis added)[248]

No States seem to have seen any point, at these times, and in particular when considering a reform of the UN Charter, in proposing to modify or relax article 53(1), the text of which continues therefore to apply with its full stringency.[249] By way of illustration, the Non-Aligned Movement of 115 States adopted this declaration in April 2000:

We reiterate that the maintenance of international peace and security is a primary responsibility of the United Nations and that the role of regional arrangements in that regard, should be in accordance with Chapter VIII of the United Nations Charter, and should not in any way substitute the role of the United Nations.[250]

In conclusion, all of these points show that it would be exaggerated to question the need in principle to obtain Security Council authorisation.

[247] GA Res 60/1, 24 October 2005, paras 93 and 139. See also below, ch 8, s I.

[248] 'Cooperation between the United Nations and regional agencies in maintaining international peace and security'; see also declarations of 20 September 2006 (S/PRST/2006/39) and of 28 March 2007 (S/PRST/2007/7).

[249] See, eg: China: 'The Security Council is the only body that can decide the use of force. Regional arrangements or organizations must obtain Security Council authorization prior to any enforcement action' (*Position paper of the People's Republic of China on the UN Reform*, 7 June 1965, point 7; www.reformtheun.org). See also Indonesia (on behalf on ANASE, A/C.4/54/SR.10, 18 October 1999), Malaysia (A/C.4/54/SR.11, 26 October 1999), Belarus (A/C.4/54/SR.12, 26 October 1999), Mexico (ibid), Russia (ibid) and Pakistan (ibid).

[250] Final Document, Ministerial Conference, Cartagena (Columbia) 8–9 April 2000, para 11; www.nam.goseeza/xiiiminconf.

However, it might be claimed that some texts and practice since the 1990s attest to a move towards a more flexible interpretation of article 53, especially as concerns the possibility of presumed authorisation, deduced if need be from *ex post* approbation. This is the point that shall be addressed next.

II The Problem of Presumed Authorisation

As has just been seen, the Charter allows the Security Council to authorise States, regional agencies and UN troops to use force to maintain or restore international peace and security. At first sight nothing in the Charter limits the Security Council's competence as regards the form of authorisation. It may therefore be explicit—a resolution containing specific terms authorising States 'to use force'[251]—or the authorisation may be implicit, when the Security Council authorises States to use 'all necessary means' to achieve some particular objective.[252] In practice, it may even be asserted that the technique of implicit authorisation is the one more frequently used by the Security Council.[253]

In recent years, however, some commentators have tended to relax further the legal regime of authorisation by accepting to presume an authorisation has been given from a range of indications which, as we shall see, may be inferred from the behaviour of the Security Council before, or even after, military action has been taken. In such instances, no Security Council decision to use force can be directly established whether from an examination of the terms of the resolution—which contains neither an explicit mention of the use of force nor an expression such as 'all necessary means'—or from the discussions preceding its adoption during which the use of force was not contemplated. In this context, the authorisation is neither explicit nor even implicit, but might even so be presumed from the Security Council's behaviour. The purpose of this section is to demonstrate that, in positive international law, the hypothesis of 'presumed authorisation' has so far not been consecrated. This conclusion is obvious if we confine ourselves to the texts of the various instruments about the use of force, which have never evoked this possibility. It shall be shown, however, that even recent practice has not revealed the emergence of an agreement by UN Member States about a presumed authorisation of the Security Council (A). Such an absence of agreement is hardly surprising, if one sizes up all the legal obstacles of principle that the introduction of such a rule into international law would come up against, as shall be shown second (B).

---

[251] See: SC Res 836 (1993) of 4 June 1993, para 10.
[252] See: E Robert, 'La licéité des sanctions des Nations Unies contre l'Irak' in Centre de droit international de l'ULB, *Entre les lignes. La guerre du golfe et le droit international,* (Bruxelles, Créadif, 1991) 51.
[253] See above, s I.

A. The Absence of Recognition of Presumed Authorisation in Practice

Traditionally, the issue of a presumed authorisation was based on two precedents both dating from the 1960s and that it seems can be usefully invoked today.[254]

—The first concerns the diplomatic and economic measures adopted by the OAS against the Dominican Republic in 1960 without the prior authorisation of the Security Council. The matter was, though, brought before the Security Council by the USSR, which asked that the enforcement action be approved; the Security Council finally settling for taking note of the measures.[255] Some commentators saw in this a precedent attesting to the possibility of implicit *ex post* authorisation.[256] To my mind there seem to be two radical objections to this argument. First, this precedent relates only to unarmed measures and not to any military action, and even supposing that any lessons could be inferred from it, there is nothing to say that they could be transposed to such a specific domain as that of the use of force.[257] Besides, the discussions bore mainly on the possibility for a regional organisation to take *economic* measures in the absence of the authorisation required by article 53.[258] Secondly, the Security Council only 'takes note' of the measures adopted, which appears insufficient to liken this precedent to that of an authorisation or even an approbation.[259]

—A second classical precedent is that of the Cuban missile crisis of 1962.[260] It will be recalled that on 23 October of that year, the OAS had adopted

---

[254] See also the Suez crisis; S/PV.749, 30 October 1956, paras 5, 7, 8, 10, 11, 12, 140, 143 and 182; S/PV.751, 31 October 1956, paras 11, 25, 45, 50, 63 and 69; GA Res 997 (ES-I) of 2 November 1956, para 3. See also E Lauterpacht, 'Contemporary Practice of the United Kingdom' (1956) 5 *ICLQ* 435; (1957) 6 *ICLQ* 325–33; G Marchton, 'Armed Intervention in the 1956 Suez Canal Crisis: The Legal Advice tendered to the British Government' (1988) 37 *ICLQ* 773–817; Q Wright, 'Intervention, 1956' (1957) 51 *AJIL* 272–74; C Alibert, *Du droit de se faire justice dans la société internationale depuis 1945* (Paris, LGDJ, 1983) 69–90; LA Sicilianos, 'Entre multilatéralisme et unilatéralisme: l'autorisation par le Conseil de sécurité de recourir à la force', above n 34, 212–18; A Abbas, *Regional Organisations and the Development of Collective Security. Beyond Chapter VIII of the UN Charter*, (Oxford, Hart Publishing, 2004) 43–44.

[255] cp USSR's Resolution draft (S/4481/Res 1) and text of SC Res 156 (1960) of 9 September 1960.

[256] LC Meeker, 'Defensive Quarantine and the Law' (1963) 57 *AJIL* 520.

[257] U Villani, 'Les rapports entre l'ONU et les organizations régionales dans le domaine du maintien de la paix', above n 36, 385; C Walter, 'Security Control over Regional Action', above n 174, 178.

[258] See: USSR (S/PV.893, 8 September 1960, paras 22–23); cp Argentina (ibid, para 32); USA (ibid, para 50); Ecuador (ibid, para 65); Venezuela (ibid, paras 76–77), United Kingdom (ibid, para 96); China (ibid, para 102); Italy (S/PV.894, 9 September 1960, para 47). According to France, '[. . .] to attempt to apply Article 53 to this case would be self-contradictory, since the provision invoked involves the authorization of the Security Council *and it is clear that this authorization must be given in advance*' (emphasis added; S/PV.893, 8 September 1960, para 90).

[259] U Villani, 'Les rapports entre l'ONU et les organizations régionales dans le domaine du maintien de la paix', above n 36, 373.

[260] See above, ch 2, s II.

a resolution by which the US had deemed itself authorised to inspect vessels bound for Cuba.[261] Now, it was only subsequently that the US brought the matter before the Security Council, which did not approve, but neither did it condemn, the coercive US action.[262] Some might construe this as a precedent in favour of the possibility of *ex post* authorisation based on an approbatory silence.[263] The argument seems difficult to make insofar as the US action was criticised by many States as being contrary to international law, a sufficient factor to show that no *opinio juris* of the international community of States as a whole can be established on the basis of this precedent.[264]

The currency of these precedents is that much more doubtful because those who invoked them relied largely on the circumstance, specific to the Cold War years, of Security Council paralysis, which supposedly justified greater autonomy for regional agencies. As seen in the previous section, the Gulf War was to be a turning point, with the Security Council thereafter being presented as an effective player, able to circumscribe the use of force in the name of the international community. Many precedents from the 1990s (Somalia, Bosnia-Herzegovina, Rwanda etc.) may be interpreted in this way, and none of them illustrates the case of a presumed authorisation, the Security Council having made very clear pronouncements to the contrary.[265]

Beyond this practice, doctrine favourable to the hypothesis of presumed authorisation is based on precedents from the 1990s and 2000s that can be classified into two categories depending on whether the authorisation is deduced from Security Council behaviour before or after the military action taken.

---

[261] OAS Res of 23 October 1962 (S/5193).

[262] See: S/PV.1022–1025, 23 to 25 October 1965.

[263] LC Meeker, 'Defensive Quarantine and the Law', above n 256, 522; A Chayes, 'Law and the Quarantine of Cuba', *Foreign Affairs*, 1962, 556 *ff*; see also CQ Christol, 'Maritime Quarantine: The Naval Interdiction of Offensive Weapons and Associated Matériel to Cuba, 1962' (1963) 57 *AJIL* 537–39 and 543. See also Q Wright, 'The Cuban Quarantine', (1963) 57 *AJIL* 9–10.

[264] See above and C Walter, 'Security Control over Regional Action', above n 174, 183–84; RSJ MacDonald, 'L'emploi de la force par les Etats en droit international' in M Bedjaoui (ed), *Droit international. Bilan et perspectives* (Paris, Pedone/UNESCO, 1991) 782 and 'The Developing Relationship between Superior and Subordinate Political Bodies at the International Level: A Note on the Experience of the UN and the OAS' (1964) 2 *CYIL* 48–49; M Akehurst, 'Enforcement Action by Regional Agencies with Special Reference to the Organization of American States' (1967) 42 *BYBIL* 216–19; Q Wright, 'The Cuban Quarantine' (1963) 57 *AJIL* 559; FX De Lima, *Intervention in International Law* (Den Haag, Uitgeverij Pax Nederland, 1971) 101; C Alibert, *Du droit de se faire justice dans la société internationale depuis 1945*, above n 254, 96–97.

[265] See above, s I and Canadian Practice in International Law' (1993) 31 *CYIL* 369; (1994) 32 *CYIL* 330; (1996) 34 *CYIL* 389; 'Pratique française du droit international' (1993) 39 *AFDI* 1023; 'La pratique suisse en matière de droit international public' (1994) 4 *RSDIE* 626–27.

Presumed Authorisation Before Military Action?

Under this first hypothesis, we are in a situation where military action is justified by resolutions adopted previously by the Security Council, although those resolutions do not contain any clear authorisation to use force. In this context, the presumption is aimed at both the very existence of an authorisation (a) and its maintenance, as shall be seen in the case of the 2003 war against Iraq (b).

a) The Presumption of the Existence of an Authorisation

This particular hypothesis has been evoked in several precedents that shall be expounded successively: Operation Provide Comfort in Iraqi Kurdistan in 1991; Operation Allied Force against Yugoslavia in 1999; and Operation Enduring Freedom against Afghanistan in 2001.

Operation Provide Comfort

Operation Provide Comfort was launched in April 1991 by French, British, US, Dutch, Italian, Spanish and Australian troops officially to set up secure areas in Iraqi Kurdistan so as to favour the return of people trapped in the mountains forming the borders with Turkey and fleeing repression by Saddam Hussein's regime.[266] The intervening parties relied above all on moral considerations, evoking the humanitarian drama afflicting the Iraqi Kurds, but this ethical register was combined with a legal argument based on the existence of Security Council authorisation.[267] On 5 April 1991, the UN Security Council adopted resolution 688 (1991), by which it condemned 'the repression of the Iraqi civilian population in many parts of Iraq', 'the consequences of which threaten international peace and security in the region'.[268] Several States justified their military intervention by referring to this resolution. For the Dutch authorities 'an adequate judicial basis for this action is provided by Security Council Resolution 688 . . . Both the Twelve and the United States Government also take this position'.[269]

Before evaluating its scope, it should first be noticed that such an argument undeniably comes down to presuming the existence of an authorisation. Nothing at all in the text of resolution 688 (1991) suggests that the Security Council might, for the first time in its history, have authorised a military intervention in the territory of a State that was not guilty of a prior

---

[266] *Keesing's Contemporary Archives*, 1991, 38126 and C Rousseau, 'Chronique des faits internationaux' (1991) 95 *RGDIP* 738–40.

[267] E Spiry, 'Interventions humanitaires et interventions d'humanité: la pratique française face au droit international' (1998) 102 *RGDIP* 424.

[268] SC Res 688 of 5 April 1991, para 1.

[269] 'Netherlands State Practice' (1992) 23 *NYIL* 362; see also 'United Kingdom Materials on International Law' (1992) 63 *BYBIL* 825–27 and 'Pratique française du droit international' (1991) 37 *AFDI* 941; M Bettati, 'Un droit d'ingérence?' (1991) 95 *RGDIP* 644, fn 5.

aggression.[270] The Security Council simply condemns the repression of civilian populations and calls on Iraq to end its repression, but without stating what the consequences of such violation would be, and it has been pointed out in this respect that it even abstained from referring explicitly to Chapter VII of the Charter.[271] Not only is there not the formula authorising the use of any 'necessary means', but the only part of the text that addresses third States is a call for them to 'contribute to these humanitarian relief efforts',[272] which cannot readily be construed as an authorisation to use armed force.[273] The final paragraph of the resolution states that it is the Security Council and not the Member States that remains tasked with the matter.[274] The discussions that preceded that adoption of the resolution confirm that the possibility of military action was at no time discussed, contemplated or even evoked indirectly.[275] One observes rather a challenge, by some States—including one permanent member—to the principle that the Security Council can *deal with* this type of question.[276] In short, there is no credible argument attesting that the Security Council wished to authorise a military intervention.

So it is indeed, then, a 'presumed authorisation' that was invoked to justify Operation Provide Comfort. However, it seems to me misleading to say the least to infer from this any change in international law. First because, even among the States that supported the intervention, no corresponding *opinio juris* can readily be established. Next, because it is even more problematical to conclude there has been any general approbation of this supposed new rule.

Upon analysis, one can but note the great ambiguity of the legal argument of those States that supported the intervention. In any event, it is hard to deduce from it any *opinio juris* clearly claiming that military action can be justified by a presumed authorisation of the Security Council. On the contrary, it shall be observed that some States, while very generally evoking resolution 688 (1991) have expressly rejected the 'presumed authorisation'

---

[270] PM Dupuy, 'Après la guerre du Golfe . . .' (1991) 95 *RGDIP* 629; O Schachter, 'United Nations Law in the Gulf Conflict' (1991) 85 *AJIL* 469; P Malanczuk, 'The Kurdish Crisis and Allied Intervention in the Aftermath of the Second Gulf War' (1991) 2 *EJIL* 129; JF Murphy, 'Force and Arms' in O Schachter and C Joyner (eds), *United Nations Legal Order*, vol I (Cambridge, Cambridge University Press, Grotius Pub, 1995) 290; S Chesterman, *Just War or Just Peace? Humanitarian Intervention and International Law* (Oxford, Oxford Univerity Press, 2001) 201; JF Murphy, *The United States and the Rule of Law in International Affairs*, above n 129, 151. Against: F Teson, *Humanitarian Intervention: An Inquiry into Law and Morality*, 2nd edn (New York, Transnational Publ, 1997) 239–41.

[271] R Zacklin, 'Le droit applicable aux forces d'intervention sous les auspices de l'ONU' in SFDI, *Le Chapitre VII de la Charte des Nations Unies*, Colloque de Rennes (Paris, Pedone, 1995) 195; JF Murphy, 'Force and Arms', above n 270, 290.

[272] SC Res 688 of 5 April 1991, para 6.

[273] See: Military and Paramilitary Activities, ICJ Rep (1986) paras 243 and 268.

[274] SC Res 688 of 5 April 1991, para 8.

[275] S/PV.2982, 5 April 1991.

[276] Yemen, Zimbabwe and China; ibid.

argument. This is the case of the UK which, when questioned about the legal basis of the operation, asserted through its Foreign Secretary that:

> [T]he intervention in northern Iraq 'Provide Comfort' was in fact, *not specifically mandated by the United Nations*, but the States taking action in northern Iraq did so in exercise of the customary international law principle of humanitarian intervention . . . As I said, *Resolution 688 did not actually authorize it* . . . (emphasis added)[277]

For the case in point, the Foreign Secretary quite clearly contradicts the argument developed by other intervening States. But, and this is no less important, for the future, the Foreign Secretary seems to think that the only feasible authorisation must not be presumed nor even implicit but 'specific'. Other States have advanced highly ambiguous arguments from which it is difficult to make out a well-defined legal position. This is true of France, for which, it has been seen that this resolution '*prefigures* the right of humanitarian intervention',[278] wording that seems to mark out a *future*—and a far from certain—change in existing law, and that cannot readily be construed as expressing an opinion that resolution 688 (1991) authorised the operation *in casu*.[279] It seems more generally that the States that supported the intervention were faced with a dilemma: either to invoke a 'right of intervention' regardless of any authorisation—an option most States, including European ones, rejected—or to evoke the hypothesis—which was not very credible in the case in point—of a Security Council authorisation. Lastly, when despite everything the argument was brandished, it was done so in a way that was very difficult to interpret. One cannot readily understand, on the basis of the scant declaration that might be construed along those lines, what the factors are that would henceforth suffice for one to be confronted with a 'presumed authorisation'. Is it sufficient that the Security Council characterises, even implicitly, the situation as a threat to peace (without even referring explicitly to Chapter VII)?[280] Will the resolution contain a condemnation,[281] or some requirement[282] of the State in question? In justifying the intervention, the Belgian authorities went so far as to evoke the paragraph of the resolution asking the Secretary-General 'to use all the resources at his disposal' to address urgently the critical needs of the refugees and displaced Iraqi population.[283] Should it

---

[277] A Aust, Legal Counsellor, FCO, 'United Kingdom Materials on International Law' (1992) 63 *BYBIL* 827–28; see also C Gray, 'From Unity to Polarization: International Law and the Use of Force against Iraq' (2002) 13 *EJIL* 9–10 and S Chesterman, *Just War or Just Peace? Humanitarian Intervention and International Law*, above n 270, 204–05.

[278] Our translation; 'Pratique française du droit international' (1991) 37 *AFDI* 941.

[279] See also: 'Netherlands State Practice' (1997) 28 *NYIL* 261.

[280] 'Netherlands State Practice' (1992) 23 *NYIL* 362.

[281] 'Netherlands State Practice' (1994) 25 *NYIL* 445.

[282] 'United Kingdom Materials on International Law' (1992) 63 *BYBIL* 822–23.

[283] SC Res 688 of 5 April 1991, para 4; A Daems, 'L'absence de base juridique de l'opération *Provide Comfort* et la pratique belge en matière d'intervention armée à but humanitaire' (1992) 25 *RBDI* 266.

be concluded that the simple reproduction of this type of wording in a resolution will authorise any States to take military action, without otherwise having obtained any authorisation from the Secretary-General himself?[284] In
truth, it seems obvious that while the position of the intervening powers is difficult to define, this is because the legal argument has only been an instrument
that, depending on circumstances, has been used to justify things that could
not readily be justified. This instrumental character was well expressed by the
Belgian Foreign Minister of the time who, when asked about the lawfulness of
the operation, began by conceding that 'a legal basis must be found' and that
'if it does not exist it must be created', and went on to clarify that, since no
agreement was reached within the Security Council, 'we find it more appropriate to give an extensive interpretation to an existing text'.[285] Decidedly, it
is a haphazard thing to conclude there is any *opinio juris* in favour of the
existence of a rule accepting military intervention conducted on the basis of a
'presumed authorisation'. It is all the more so as what is true for the States
that supported the operation is true also for other States. While Operation
Provide Comfort was seldom condemned (without, though, having been
approved by a substantial number of States),[286] it seems hazardous, to say the
least, to deduce from this that there is an *opinio juris* in favour of the emergence of a new rule of international law. It should be recalled that, especially
where there is strictly limited humanitarian intervention, silence may be a sign
of tacit acceptance on political or moral grounds and not motivated by legal
considerations.[287]

It is probably all of these factors that can explain the considerable reluctance of doctrine to entertain the 'presumed authorisation' argument in the
case of Operation Provide Comfort.[288]

Operation Allied Force
The 'Kosovo War', triggered by NATO Member States against Yugoslavia
in March 1999 provided another opportunity to wield the 'presumed authorisation' argument, based this time on the three resolutions adopted on the

---

[284] See: R Zacklin, 'Le droit applicable aux forces d'intervention sous les auspices de
l'ONU', above n 271, 1995, 195.
[285] Our translation; quoted in A Daems, 'L'absence de base juridique de l'opération *Provide
Comfort* et la pratique belge en matière d'intervention armée à but humanitaire', above n 283,
266.
[286] E de Wet, *The Chapter VII Powers of the United Nations Security Council*, above n 4, 285.
[287] See above, ch 1, s II, and 'La pratique suisse en matière de droit international public'
(1994) *RSDIE* 626.
[288] See: P Malanczuk, 'The Kurdish Crisis and Allied Intervention in the Aftermath of the
Second Gulf War', above n 270, 129; O Schachter, 'United Nations Law in the Gulf Conflict'
(1991) 85 *AJIL* 469; T Franck, 'The Security Council and "Threats to the Peace": Some
Remarks on Recent Developments' in Académie de droit international de la Haye (ed),
Le développement du rôle du Conseil de sécurité (Dordrecht, Martinus Nijhoff, 1993) 102–03;
LA Sicilianos, 'Entre multilatéralisme et unilatéralisme: l'autorisation par le Conseil de sécu-
rité de recourir à la force', above n 34, 219 *ff*.

subject by the Security Council in 1998.[289] While these resolutions were usually evoked in a general way,[290] the reasoning was occasionally expounded more precisely, especially in the context of parliamentary debates in some intervening States.[291]

Before evaluating it any further, it shall be noted that this argument is indeed based on a presumed authorisation: nothing in the texts of the resolutions cited above suggests that the Security Council adopts such an exceptional measure as the authorisation to use force for the benefit of States acting individually or in the context of regional agencies or arrangements.[292] While Chapter VII is explicitly invoked three times and Yugoslavia nominally condemned, the only coercive measure adopted is an arms embargo, which it is hard to construe as authorising or justifying a massive bombing campaign.[293] Third States were invited besides to comply with and enforce compliance with the embargo,[294] to provide resources to bring humanitarian assistance to the region[295] and to make personnel available to the OSCE verification mission.[296] Those are the only provisions that refer to third States and it will be noticed that it is the Security Council itself that reserved the right, should the measures required in resolutions 1160 (1998) and 1199 (1998) not be taken 'to consider further action and additional measures to maintain or restore peace and stability in the region'.[297] The absence of any, even remote, reference to the possibility of

---

[289] SC Res 1160 (1998) of 31 March 1998, 1199 (1998) of 23 September 1998 and 1203 (1998) of 24 October 1998.

[290] See, eg: 'Contemporary Practice of the United States' (1999) 93 *AJIL* 631–32.

[291] 'Pratique française du droit international' (1999) 32 *AFDI* 885; 'Netherlands State Practice' (2000) 31 *NYIL* 192 and 194; (2001) 32 *NYIL* 194; 'United Kingdom Materials on International Law' (1998) 69 *BYBIL* 593; (1999) 70 *BYBIL* 569 and 571–76; see also I Brownlie and CJ Apperley, 'Kosovo Crisis Inquiry: Memorandum on the International Law Aspects' (2000) 49 *ICLQ* 879, para 8.

[292] M Spinedi, 'Uso della forza da parte della NATO in Jugoslavia e diritto internazionale', *Quaderni Forum*, 1998, XII, 27–28; M Kohen, 'L'emploi de la force et la crise du Kosovo: vers un nouveau désordre juridique international' (1999) 32 *RBDI* 133; N Valticos, 'Les droits de l'homme, le droit international et l'intervention militaire en Yougoslavie' (2000) 104 *RGDIP* 8–9; P Weckel, 'L'emploi de la force contre la Yougoslavie ou la Charte fissurée' (2000) 104 *RGDIP* 30 and 33; F Dubuisson, 'La problématique de la légalité de l'opération "Force alliée" contre la Yougoslavie: enjeux et questionnements', above n 211, 154–58; Y Nouvel, 'La position du Conseil de sécurité face à l'action militaire engagée par l'OTAN et ses Etats membres contre la République fédérale de Yougoslavie' (1999) 32 *AFDI* 295–98; I Brownlie and CJ Apperley, 'Kosovo Crisis Inquiry: Memorandum on the International Law Aspects', above n 291, 895; C Chinkin, 'The Legality of NATO's Action in the Former Republic of Yugoslavia (FRY) under International Law' (2000) 49 *ICLQ* 911–12; C Greenwood, 'International Law and the NATO Intervention in Kosovo' (2000) 49 *ICLQ* 927; V Lowe, 'International Legal Issues Arising in the Kosovo Crisis' (2000) 49 *ICLQ* 936. Against: R Wedgwood, 'Unilateral Action in the United Nations System' (2000) 11 *EJIL* 358 and n 38; Tribunal permanent des peuples, 'Le droit international et les nouvelles guerres', session de Rome, December 2002 (2003) 36 *RBDI* 257.

[293] SC Res 1160 (1998) of 31 March 1998 and SC Res 1199 (1998).

[294] SC Res 1199 (1998) of 23 September 1998, paras 7 and 11.

[295] Res 1199 (1998) of 23 September 1998, para 12 and SC Res 1203 (1998), para 13.

[296] Res 1203 (1998) of 24 October 1998, para 7.

[297] Res 1199 (1998) of 23 September 1998, para 16.

unilateral military intervention is all the more significant as resolutions 1199 (1998) and 1203 (1998) were adopted at a time when the use of force had been clearly contemplated by NATO members and when those States had plainly tried in vain to obtain authorisation to that effect.[298]

Under the circumstances, it would be excessive, to say the least, to claim that the use of the 'presumed authorisation' argument brought about a change in the *opinio juris* of States. First because the justifications of the intervening powers themselves appear equivocal. On some occasions, it is a right of intervention *outside of* any authorisation that was evoked.[299] The US seems to have essentially come out in favour of this, affirming either implicitly or explicitly that it could forego Security Council authorisation.[300] This position of principle, intended to influence other NATO Member States with a view to its consecration in the document that was to be adopted for NATO's fiftieth anniversary,[301] did not prevail in the end.[302] Evidence of it can be found, though, in certain stands in favour of a 'right of humanitarian intervention' invoked generally by the UK, Germany, Belgium and the Netherlands.[303] Whatever the intrinsic value of this line of argument, it can be seen to be highly ambiguous, for either military intervention is justified by an authorisation—presumed authorisation in the case in point—from the Security Council (which makes the reference to the 'right of humanitarian intervention' pointless) or it is justified by an existing right, as the aforementioned declarations mention, in the absence of an authorisation. It would probably be possible to hitch together the two registers of argument, one as the main claim, the other as a subsidiary claim. In the absence of any clarification on this issue, we are confronted with some highly confused rhetoric, with the intervention being justified sometimes without, and sometimes with, Security Council authorisation. In any event, it is difficult indeed to discern any clear legal conviction that the action supposedly took place on the basis of a presumed authorisation.[304]

---

[298] S/PV.3930, 23 September 1998; S/PV.3937, 24 October 1998, 14 (Russia) and 15 (China). See also SC Declarations of 19 January 1999 (S/PRST/1999/2) and 29 January 1999 (S/PRST/1999/5) and P van Walsum, 'The Security Council and the Use of Force: the cases of Kosovo, East Timor and Iraq' in N Blokker and N Schrijver (eds), *The Security Council and the Use of Force. Theory and Reality—A Need for Change?* (Leiden/Boston, Martinus Nijhoff, 2005) 67.

[299] M Forteau, *Droit de la sécurité collective et droit de la responsabilité internationale de l'Etat*, above n 51, 424.

[300] J Fitchett, 'Use of Force in Kosovo Splits NATO' *IHT*, 8 February 1999 and *Le Monde*, 9 December 1998.

[301] See: Javier Solana in *Le Monde*, 8 October 1998.

[302] The Alliance's Strategic Concept approved by the Heads of State and Government participating in the meeting of the North Atlantic Council in Washington DC, 24 April 1999, www.nato.int/docu/comm/1999/comm99.htm. See above, s I.

[303] See below, ch 8, s II.

[304] G Cahin, 'Le rôle des organes politiques des Nations Unies' in E Cannizzaro and P Palchetti (eds), *Customary International Law on the Use of Force. A Methodological Approach* (Leiden/Boston, Martinus Nijhoff, 2005) 170–71; S Sur, 'L'affaire du Kosovo et le droit international: points et contrepoints' (1999) 32 *AFDI* 286.

The uncertain character of the conviction of the intervening States in legal terms is confirmed by an examination of how their position varied over time. By October 1998, while the threat of military intervention was growing, the Italian premier Romano Prodi affirmed that any military action would have to be legitimated by the UN.[305] He was supported by several European States.[306] Similarly, when questioned on 5 November 1998 about the Iraq and Kosovo crises, that is *after* the adoption of the three resolutions referred to, the German Foreign Minister declared that 'the use of force, if it becomes the extreme resort, requires a mandate from the UN and from international law'.[307] At the same time, the Belgian Foreign Minister revealed, in the context of the preparatory debates for NATO's fiftieth anniversary meeting, that 'a series of European countries are adamant that NATO should not intervene outside the territory of its members unless it has a *clear mandate* from the UN Security Council'.[308] Belgium's position, stated when the situation in Kosovo was seriously deteriorating, is very remote from the hypothesis of a 'presumed authorisation'.[309] This also seems to be the case of the French position, which, if not wholly unambiguous,[310] consisted in a staunch attempt to maintain the effective authority of the Security Council over the situation. Thus, after resolution 1203 (1998) was adopted, the French Foreign Minister again asserted that acting without a Security Council mandate would be 'contrary to the UN Charter and to the Treaty of Washington'.[311] Lastly, it shall be noted that, some weeks after the end of the war, several European States insisted on asserting very clearly that in legal terms Kosovo could not be considered a precedent, which excludes it being used to establish a rule admitting a presumed authorisation of the Security Council.[312]

In any event, it shall be noted again that, as for Operation Provide Comfort, it would be extremely difficult to determine under what circumstances one could henceforth consider that there is a 'presumed authorisation' from the Security Council. The mere mention of Chapter VII,[313] together with a condemnation of the State concerned, does not seem sufficient, insofar as those factors were already in resolution 1160 (1998) and were apparently deemed inadequate. Besides, it is hard to understand what resolutions 1199 (1998) and 1203 (1998) add in the way of decisive

---

[305] *Le Soir*, 9 October 1998 and *La Libre Belgique*, 29 September 1998.

[306] *Le Soir*, 9 October 1998, and 'Time to Act on Kosovo', *IHT*, 3 October 1998; 'Pratique française du droit international' (1998) 31 *AFDI* 736.

[307] Our translation; AFP, 5 November 1999.

[308] Our translation; 'Washington présente sa vision de l'OTAN du 21ème siècle', Belga, 8 December 1998.

[309] See also: 'La pratique belge en matière de droit international' (2002) 35 *RBDI* 254–55.

[310] 'Pratique française du droit international' (1998) 31 *AFDI* 737.

[311] 'Pratique française du droit international' (1998) 31 *AFDI* 738.

[312] See below, ch 8, s II.

[313] 'Pratique française du droit international' (1998) 31 *AFDI* 737.

elements that might provide relevant legal criteria. Fundamentally, no definition of what constitutes a 'presumed authorisation' can be deduced from the Kosovo case.[314] In actual fact, it must be considered that, in the views of the intervening powers, reference to the Security Council resolutions cannot readily be taken seriously in legal terms. Some within NATO do not rule out reforming existing law in the more or less near future,[315] but it would be misleading to deduce from this any *opinio juris* attesting to the existence or even to the emergence of a rule authorising a use of force on the basis of a presumed authorisation of the Security Council.

A fortiori the same goes for States that did not support the intervention in Kosovo. First, it will be noted that some States clearly asserted the need for a resolution explicitly authorising any military action. This was the case of Russia, which condemned the strikes as they had not been authorised by the Security Council.[316] Other States condemned the intervention, invoking the classical legal rules. This was the case during the debates in the Security Council of China,[317] India,[318] Namibia,[319] Gabon,[320] and to a lesser extent of Argentina,[321] and Brazil,[322] to which may be added Belarus,[323] Ukraine,[324] Cuba[325] and, of course, Yugoslavia itself.[326] In another context, most Latin American States (Argentina, Brazil, Chile, Peru, Venezuela, Bolivia, Colombia, Paraguay, Ecuador, Uruguay, Panama, Costa Rica and Mexico), within the 'Rio Group', adopted a press release on 25 March 1999 by which:

> The countries members of the Rio Group express their anxiety about the commencement of air strikes by the North Atlantic Treaty Organization against Serbian military targets and, in particular, their concern that no peaceful means of solving, in conformity with international law, the existing dispute among the various parties to the conflict in Kosovo has been found . . . The Rio Group also regrets the recourse to the use of force in the Balkan region in contravention of the provisions of Article 53, paragraph 1, and Article 54 of the Charter of the United Nations . . .[327]

---

[314] See also the ambiguous declaration of the President of the USA; A/54/PV.6, 21 September 1999.

[315] See: NATO-PA, 1999 Annual Session, Plenary Resolution: NATO and Humanitarian Intervention adopted by the NATO Parliamentary Assembly, Amsterdam, 15 November 1999 (Unofficial Text).

[316] S/PV.3988, 24 March 1999, 2–4 and S/PV.3989, 26 March 1999.

[317] S/PV.3988, 24 March 1999, 12–13; S/PV.3989, 26 March 1999, 9; see also A/54/PV.8, 22 September 1999.

[318] S/PV.3988, 24 March 1999, 15–16; S/PV.3989, 26 March 1999, 15–16.

[319] S/PV.3988, 24 March 1999, 10.

[320] ibid.

[321] ibid, 10–11.

[322] ibid, 8.

[323] S/PV.3988, 24 March 1999, 15; S/PV.3989, 26 March 1999, 12.

[324] S/PV.3989, 26 March 1999, 9–10.

[325] S/PV.3989, 26 March 1999, 12–14.

[326] S/PV.3988, 24 March 1999, 13–15; S/PV.3989, 26 March 1999, 11–12.

[327] GRIO/SPT-99/10; A/53/884-S/1999/347, 26 March 1999.

Similarly, on 9 April 1999, in the midst of the bombing campaign, the Non-Aligned Movement adopted a declaration that:

The Non-Aligned Movement reaffirms that the primary responsibility for the maintenance of international peace and security rests with the United Nations Security Council . . .

The Non-Aligned Movement calls for an immediate cessation of all hostilities, and the swift and safe return of all refugees and displaced persons.

The Non-Aligned Movement firmly believes that the urgent resumption of diplomatic efforts, under the auspices of the United Nations and the relevant Security Council resolutions 1199 and 1203, constitutes the only basis for a peaceful, just and equitable solution to the conflict.[328]

While the text is probably less explicit than that adopted by the Rio Group, probably because of the large number of signatory States (116), it testifies again to a reluctance of States to caution the war triggered by the NATO States and to the legal arguments they advanced. The press reported objections from several other States such as South Africa, Libya, Iran and Iraq, with criticism based in particular on the observance of international law.[329] Criticism was again made along these lines several months later in the General Assembly.[330] In short, all the indications are that a significant number of States dismissed the possibility of basing a military action on a presumed authorisation.[331]

Operation Enduring Freedom

On 7 October 2001, the US began Operation Enduring Freedom against Afghanistan, invoking the existence of close connections between the Taliban regime and *Al Qaeda*.[332] This operation followed upon the murderous attacks of 9/11 and marked the beginning of what the Bush administration called the 'War on Terror'. In this context, it shall be recalled

---

[328] *Statement by the NAM on the situation in Kosovo*, Federal Republic of Yugoslavia, 9 April 1999; www.nam.goseeza/media/990409kos.htm.

[329] *Le Monde*, 3 April 1999.

[330] See: Colombia (A/54/PV.35, 20 October 1999), China (ibid), Ivory Coast (ibid and A/54/PV.5, 20 September 1999), Senegal (A/54/PV.36, 20 October 1999), Malaysia (ibid and A/55/PV.16, 15 September 2000), Brazil (A/54/PV.4, 20 September 1999), Georgia (A/54/PV.4, 20 September 1999), Chile (A/54/PV.14, 25 September 1999), Vietnam (A/54/PV.15, 25 September 1999) and Pakistan (A/54/PV.32, 8 October 1999).

[331] LA Sicilianos, 'Entre multilatéralisme et unilatéralisme: l'autorisation par le Conseil de sécurité de recourir à la force', above n 34, 245–49. Moreover, the ICJ stated that the military intervention 'raises very serious issues of international law' (*Legality of Use of Force*, orders of 2 June 1999, (Serbia and Montenegro v Belgium), para 17; (Serbia and Montenegro v Canada), para 16; (Serbia and Montenegro v France), para 16; (Serbia and Montenegro v Germany), para 16; (Serbia and Montenegro v Italy), para 16; (Serbia and Montenegro v Netherlands), para 17; (Serbia and Montenegro v Portugal), para 16; (Serbia and Montenegro v United Kingdom), para 16; (Serbia and Montenegro v Spain), para 16; (Yugoslavia v USA), para 16).

[332] See below, ch 7, s I.

that on 12 September 2001 the Security Council adopted resolution 1368 (2001) condemning the attacks. This resolution was invoked by some States to justify the war in Afghanistan. On 21 September, an extraordinary European Council meeting adopted a declaration that 'On the basis of Security Council Resolution 1368, a riposte by the US is legitimate. The Member States of the Union are prepared to undertake such actions, each according to its means'.[333]

In the same perspective, a few days after the start of the war, 'The European Council confirm[ed] its staunchest support for the military operations which began on 7 October and which are legitimate under the terms of the United Nations Charter and of Resolution 1368 of the United Nations Security Council'.[334]

Other similar statements to the same effect by leading figures in European States might be cited.[335]

However, that resolution contains no authorisation to use force against Afghanistan.[336] That State is not named in the resolution any more than it is in the discussions that preceded its adoption, which can be perfectly well explained if it is recalled that the resolution was adopted at a time when no aggressor State could be identified for want of any evidence from the investigation.[337] Admittedly, as already pointed out,[338] the Security Council recalls in its preamble the right to self-defence, pursuant to the Charter. That reference may not readily be interpreted as an authorisation to use force, such authorisation not having been sought by the US.[339] Unless, of course, one considers that such vague terms might suffice to *presume* there is a Security Council authorisation . . .

To my mind, there is no need for long developments to show that the Afghanistan precedent does not argue in this direction. The discourse of

---

[333] europa.eu/european-council/index_en.htm.

[334] Declaration by the Heads of State or Government of the European Union and the President of the Commission, Brussels, 19 October 2001, www.consilium.europa.eu/cms3_ applications/Applications/newsRoom/loadBook.asp?target=2001&infoTarget=before&bid=76 &lang=1&cmsId=347.

[335] France, 7 October 2001 (www.elysee.fr); Belgium ('La pratique belge en matière de droit international' (2005) 38 *RBDI* 256–57).

[336] LA Sicilianos, 'Entre multilatéralisme et unilatéralisme: l'autorisation par le Conseil de sécurité de recourir à la force', above n 34, 229–31; LA Sicilianos, 'L'autorisation par le Conseil de sécurité de recourir à la force: une tentative d'évaluation', above n 5, 46–47; G Cahin, 'Le rôle des organes politiques des Nations Unies', above n 304, 167; Tribunal permanent des peuples, 'Le droit international et les nouvelles guerres', Rome session, December 2002, (2003) 36 *RBDI* 257; see also S/PV.4370, 12 September 2001.

[337] JA Fernandez, 'La 'guerra contra el terrorismo': una 'OPA hostil' al derecho de la comunidad internacional' (2001) 53 *REDI* 299.

[338] Above, ch 3, s I; see also below, ch 7.

[339] M Kohen, 'The Use of Force by the United States after the end of the Cold War, and its impact on international law' in M Byers and G Nolte (eds), *United States Hegemony and the Foundation of International Law* (Cambridge, Cambridge University Press, 2003) 209; J Verhoeven, 'Les étirements de la légitime défense' (2002) 35 *AFDI* 76–77; see also above, ch 3, s I.

European States is far too ambiguous to embody a stand in favour of presumed authorisation. Plainly, it attests to the political will of its authors to place the war under the aegis of the Security Council. Legally, it should be noted that it is self-defence and self-defence alone that was invoked by the US and then relayed within organisations such as the OAS or NATO.[340] If one takes the position of the intervening States and of their allies as a whole, it is therefore self-defence and not Security Council authorisation that is the decisive argument.[341] This argument shall be examined in the chapter on self-defence.[342] In any event, Operation Enduring Freedom can certainly not be invoked as evidence of a general acceptance of an argument of presumed authorisation. It would be more misleading still to claim that, on the basis of resolutions adopted by the Security Council after 11 September 2001, one might presume an authorisation to conduct a 'war on terror' more generally with undefined contours.[343]

Ultimately, one might conclude that while with Operation Provide Comfort the gates were opened slightly to a possible relaxation of the classical rule requiring clear prior authorisation from the Security Council (although, as observed, that is already a very extensive interpretation), they have been progressively closed with the military intervention in Yugoslavia. That intervention gave rise to very clear positioning which, as observed, was not only by a large number of States but also concerned the intervening powers themselves. As for the Afghanistan precedent, it did not give rise either to the emergence of a general feeling that one could resort to force on the basis of a simple presumption of authorisation.[344]

b) The Presumed Maintenance of an Authorisation

There are, however, certain precedents where the 'presumed authorisation' argument has taken a more subtle form. In the cases we are to look at, all of which relate to the situation in Iraq, it is no longer the actual existence but the maintenance of an authorisation that has been presumed so as to justify uses of force; first limited force, in the 1990s essentially, and then massive force, with the outbreak of the war in March 2003.[345]

---

[340] See below, ch 7, s I.

[341] M Byers, 'Terrorism, the Use of Force and International Law after 11 September' (2002) 51 *ICLQ* 402–03.

[342] Below, ch 7, s I.

[343] O Corten and F Dubuisson, 'La guerre 'antiterroriste' engagée par les États-Unis a-t-elle été autorisée par le Conseil de sécurité?' *Journal des Tribunaux* (Bruxelles), 15 December 2001.

[344] LA Sicilianos, 'Entre multilatéralisme et unilatéralisme: l'autorisation par le Conseil de sécurité de recourir à la force', above n 34, 237–45.

[345] O Corten, 'Opération *Iraqi Freedom:* peut-on admettre l'argument de l'"autorisation implicite" du Conseil de sécurité?' (2003) 36 *RBDI* 205–47.

Targeted Military Operations against Iraq after the Adoption of Resolution 687 (1991)

Several States and foremost among them the US and the UK regularly conducted targeted military actions against Iraq between 1991 and the invasion of Iraq in March 2003.[346] Here again the argument of 'presumed authorisation' was evoked by reference either to resolution 688 (1991) mentioned before (in the case where the stated objectives of the intervention referred back to the protection of civilian populations)[347] or to Security Council resolutions 678 (1990) and 687 (1991). The first aspect relating to debates subsequent to Operation Provide Comfort shall not be taken up again here. The second aspect is based on a premise: the existence of an authorisation for States to use 'all necessary means' to enforce international peace and security in the region contained in resolution 678 (1990), which we have already examined.[348] The effects of this resolution were suspended after the end of the Gulf War further to resolution 687 (1991) of 3 April 1991 by which the Security Council adopted a resolution establishing obligations for Iraq to prevent it from threatening or breaking the international peace again. By the argument defended by several intervening States, any violation of resolution 687 (1991) by Iraq, however, opened up the possibility of referring again to the authorisation in resolution 678 (1990).[349]

The presumption specifically relates here to the maintenance (or 'renewal') of an authorisation clearly granted by the Security Council in November 1990, but which could still be invoked several years later, even after the end of the liberation of Kuwait, which was the only military action that was specifically covered by debates at the time.[350] That presumption was supposedly based on the circumstance that resolution 678 (1990) did not expressly set any time limit to the authorisation and that, besides, resolution 687 (1991), in stating several obligations incumbent upon Iraq, only suspended that authorisation conditionally. As several commentators have remarked[351] we are indeed here in the realms of presumption. Nothing in

---

[346] C Denis, 'La résolution 678 (1990) peut-elle légitimer les actions armées menées contre l'Iraq postérieurement à l'adoption de la résolution 687 (1991)?' (1998) 31 *RBDI* 485–89; S Spiliopoulou Akermark, 'Storms, Foxes and Nebulous Legal Arguments: Twelve Years of Force against Iraq, 1991–2003' (2005) 54 *ICLQ* 231–32.

[347] 'United Kingdom Materials on International Law' (1992) 63 *BYBIL* 824 and 827; (1993) 64 *BYBIL* 737–38 and 739–40; (1994) 65 *BYBIL* 683; (1998) 69 *BYBIL* 592; 'Netherlands State Practice' (1994) 25 *NYIL* 444–45; (1997) 28 *NYIL* 261.

[348] Above, s I.

[349] 'United Kingdom Materials on International Law' (2002) 73 *BYBIL* 871–72.

[350] See: S/PV.2963, 29 November 1990 and 'Pratique française du droit international' (1991) 24 *AFDI* 1012–13.

[351] C Denis, 'La résolution 678 (1990) peut-elle légitimer les actions armées menées contre l'Iraq postérieurement à l'adoption de la résolution 687 (1991)?' above n 346, 485–537; see also J Lobel and M Ratner, 'Bypassing the Security Council: Ambiguous Authorizations to Use Force, Cease Fires and the Iraqi Regime' (1999) 93 *AJIL* 124–54; O Corten and F Dubuisson, 'L'hypothèse d'une règle émergente fondant une intervention militaire sur une "autorisation implicite" du Conseil de sécurité' (2000) 104 *RGDIP* 878–84; LA Sicilianos,

these resolutions, nor for that matter in those that were subsequently adopted about Iraq, allows one to assert that the Security Council intended to authorise Member States to use force to react to any violation of obligations under resolution 687 (1991). None of the many texts adopted contains the wording of an authorisation to use all 'necessary means' to achieve the defined ends, nor *a fortiori* mentions any 'use of force'. The debates preceding the adoption of these resolutions do not attest either to any will of the Security Council to authorise the use of force.[352] Yet military operations were indeed carried out on several occasions on the basis of reasoning about the survival or renewal of the authorisation in resolution 678 (1990).

Can one then consider that this is a precedent attesting to acceptance of the argument of presumed authorisation? I do not think so; first because the argument of the intervening States themselves was not always unequivocal. Apart from the fact that they did not always set out their argument in a very coherent way,[353] it shall be noticed that some of them occasionally spoke out against the idea of a presumed authorisation. It is particularly characteristic in this respect to note the negative answer from the British government to a question about the existence of a possible authorisation supposedly contained in Security Council resolution 949 (1994).[354] In that resolution, adopted further to the massive deployment of Iraqi troops near its border with Kuwait, the Security Council, reaffirming some of its resolutions 'and in particular paragraph 2 of resolution 678 (1990)', condemned the deployment and demanded the withdrawal of the military units in question.[355] If such a forceful text, that reasserts a paragraph containing a clear authorisation to use force, is not considered sufficient by the UK,[356] it is very difficult to ascertain what requirement would then determine the existence of a 'presumed authorisation'. We shall also mention the position of France, which progressively marked its distance with the 'presumed authorisation' argument. When resolution 1154 (1998) was adopted by which the Security Council emphasised that any violation of resolution 687 (1991) 'would have severest consequences for Iraq',[357] the French delegate specified that the intent was

'L'autorisation par le Conseil de sécurité de recourir à la force: une tentative d'évaluation', above n 5, 13, fn 28 and 16–17.

[352] See: H Freudenschub, 'Between Unilateralism and Collective Security: Authorizations of the Use of Force by the Security Council' (1994) 5 *EJIL* 499.

[353] cp 'United Kingdom Materials on International Law' (1992) 63 *BYBIL* 825; (1993) 64 *BYBIL* 736 *ff*; (1999) 70 *BYBIL* 568, 569 and 578–79; (2000) 71 *BYBIL* 650; (2001) 72 *BYBIL* 692–94; (2002) 73 *BYBIL* 861–67, 869 and 882; 'Contemporary Practice of the United States' (1999) 93 *AJIL* 471–79; 'Netherlands State Practice' (1994) 25 *NYIL* 444; 'La pratique belge en matière de droit international' (1995) 28 *RBDI* 649.

[354] 'United Kingdom Materials on International Law' (1995) 66 *BYBIL* 727; see also (2005) 76 *BYBIL* 915.

[355] CS Res 949 (1994) of 15 October 1994, preamble and paras 1 and 2.

[356] See: S/PV.3438, 15 October 1994 and C Denis, 'La résolution 678 (1990) peut-elle légitimer les actions armées . . .' above n 346, 509.

[357] SC Res 1154 (1998) of 2 March 1998, para 3; see also para 5.

to underscore the prerogatives of the Security Council in a way that excludes any question of automaticity . . . It is the Security Council that must evaluate the behaviour of a country, if necessary to determine any possible violations, and to take the appropriate decisions.[358]

France's position clearly excludes the existence of a presumed authorisation, despite an expression that might prove equivocal.[359] In fact, the ambiguities of the legal position of Western States can be explained by political considerations, making it delicate in the least to establish an *opinio juris* modifying existing law. The intervening powers consider it preferable to have a clear authorisation[360] but, if they fail to obtain one, they resort to extensive interpretations, first of texts containing a genuine authorisation (which was the case of resolution 678 (1990)) and then of texts not containing any.

In any event, the 'presumed authorisation' argument does not stand up to examination of the positions of many States that expressly condemned the military operations conducted in Iraq after the adoption of resolution 687 (1991).[361] Several States clearly dismissed the argument of authorisation that could be presumed on the basis of wording in the afore-cited Security Council resolutions. This was the case, for example, of Russia, which specified, before its adoption, that resolution 949 (1994) 'does not contain any provisions that could have served as justification for the use of strikes or force'[362] or of China which made a similar remark before the vote on resolution 1154 (1998).[363] Many States, outside the UN framework, condemned the military actions against Iraq, sometimes characterising them as contrary to the UN Charter.[364] At the end of 1998, when the military attacks against Iraq were of a scale unprecedented since the 1991 Gulf War, the Non-Aligned Movement, composed of 116 States, adopted a declaration whereby it 'deplores the ongoing military actions against Iraq by individual countries *without any authorization from the Security Council* in flagrant disregard of the United Nations Charter'. (emphasis added)[365]

---

[358] S/PV.3858, 2 March 1998, 15; see also S/PV.3939, 5 November 1998 and JM Thouvenin, 'Le jour le plus triste pour les Nations Unies. Les frappes anglo-américaines de Decembre sur l'Iraq' (1998) 31 *AFDI* 214.

[359] See also: 'Pratique française du droit international' (1998) 31 *AFDI* 743; (1999) 32 *AFDI* 888–89; (2000) 33 *AFDI* 764 and 804–05; 'La pratique belge en matière de droit international' (2002) 35 *RBDI* 256–58; (2005) 38 *RBDI* 266–67.

[360] 'United Kingdom Materials on International Law' (1998) 69 *BYBIL* 588.

[361] C Gray, 'From Unity to Polarization: International Law and the Use of Force against Iraq', above n 277, 12.

[362] S/PV.3438, 15 October 1994, 4.

[363] S/PV.3858, 2 March 1998, 14. In a similar way, Kenya's representative stated that: 'We should like to place on record our conviction, based on assurances we have been given by the sponsors, that the draft resolution contains nothing that could open the door, in any eventuality, for any kind of action without the clear authority of the Security Council' (ibid, 10); see also Brazil (ibid, 6–7), Costa Rica (ibid, 5) and Japan (ibid, 10–11).

[364] *Keesing's Contemporary Archives*, 1996, 41297, and C Denis, 'La résolution 678 (1990) peut-elle légitimer les actions armées . . .' above n 346, 489.

[365] *Statement on Situation in Iraq*, New York, 17 December 1998, www.nam.goseeza/media/981217ira.htm, consulted in December 2000.

This position was reiterated in September 1999,[366] February 2001[367] and February 2003.[368] The Islamic Conference Organization (of 57 States) and the League of Arab States (22 States) adopted declarations with similar contents.[369] To take just one example, in June 2001, the ICO 'demanded that illegitimate actions taken against Iraq *outside the framework of the relevant Security Council resolutions* be brought to an end'. (emphasis added)[370]

All in all, we are faced with a situation where only a few rare States (two to my knowledge) defended an argument that they never managed to sell to the Security Council and that was expressly rejected by the very large majority of UN Member States. The argument of 'presumed authorisation' was therefore clearly rejected, just as it was with the 2003 invasion of Iraq.

The 2003 War against Iraq

It was in March 2003 that Operation Iraqi Freedom was launched, with the massive bombing and then invasion of Iraq and the overthrow of its government.[371] On 20 March 2003, the US Permanent Representative at the UN sent a letter to the Security Council president setting out what he considered was the legal basis for military action. Here are the main excerpts:

> The actions being taken are authorized under existing Council resolutions, including its resolutions 678 (1990) and 687 (1991). Resolution 687 (1991) imposed a series of obligations on Iraq, including, most importantly, extensive disarmament obligations, that were conditions of the ceasefire established under it. It has been long recognized and understood that a material breach of these obligations removes the basis of the ceasefire and revives the authority to use force under resolution 678 (1990) . . .

[366] *Final Communique of the Meeting of Ministers for Foreign Affairs and Heads of Delegation of the Non-Aligned Movement*, held in New York on 23 September 1999, para 92 (www.nam.gov.za/).

[367] 'The Movement wishes to reiterate that it deplores the imposition and continued military enforcement of "No Fly Zones" on Iraq by individual countries, and reiterates that this imposition is without any authorization from the United Nations Security Council or General Assembly'; *Statement by the Chair of the Non-Aligned Movement (NAM) on the bombing of Iraq*, 19 February 2001, (www.nam.gov.za/).

[368] 'The Heads of State or Government deplored the imposition and continued military enforcement of "No-Fly Zones" on Iraq by individual countries without any authorization from the United Nations Security Council or General Assembly. In this respect, they recalled the statement on the situation in Iraq issued by the Movement of the Non-Aligned Countries on 17 December 1998, which was issued as a document of United Nations General Assembly (A/53/762)'; *Final Document of the XIII Conference of Heads of State or Government of the NAM*, Kuala Lumpur, 24–25 February 2003, para 193 (www.nam.gov.za/).

[369] www.arableagueonline.org; see also C Rousseau, 'Chronique des faits internationaux' (1996) 100 *RGDIP* 1053 and 'Netherlands State Practice' (1994) 25 *NYIL* 443.

[370] ICFM/28-2001/FC/FINAL, *Final Communiqué of the 28th session of the Islamic Conference of Foreign Ministers*, Bamako, 25–27 June 2001 (www.oic-oci.org/oicnew/); see also *Final Communiqué of the 8th session of the Islamic Conference*, Teheran, 9–11 December 1997; *Final Communiqué of the 25th session of the Islamic Conference of Foreign Ministers*, Doha, 15–17 March 1998; *Final Communiqué of the 26th session of the Islamic Conference of Foreign Ministers*, Ouagadougou, 28 June to 1 July 1999.

[371] *Keesing's Contemporary Archives*, 2003, 45313–20 and 45370–76.

Iraq continues to be in material breach of its disarmament obligations under resolution 687 (1991), as the Council affirmed in its resolution 1441 (2002). Acting under the authority of Chapter VII of the Charter of the United Nations, the Council unanimously decided that Iraq has been and remained in material breach of its obligations and recalled its repeated warnings to Iraq that it will face serious consequences as a result of its continued violations of its obligations. The resolution then provided Iraq a 'final opportunity' to comply, but stated specifically that violations by Iraq of its obligations under resolution 1441 (2002) to present a currently accurate, full and complete declaration of all aspects of its weapons of mass destruction programmes and to comply with and cooperate fully in the implementation of the resolution would constitute a further material breach.

The Government of Iraq decided not to avail itself of its final opportunity under 1441 (2002) and has clearly committed additional violations. In view of Iraq's material breaches, the basis for the ceasefire has been removed and use of force is authorized under resolution 678 (1990) . . .[372]

This reasoning was taken up in letters sent to the Security Council and dated the same day by the UK[373] and Australia.[374] It is, as will have been noticed, very similar to that used to justify the more limited military action taken previously against Iraq. The only difference is in the reference to resolution 1441 (2002) which, still according to the argument of the intervening States, supposedly constituted a factor confirming the 'presumed authorisation' argument.

There is no doubt that it was a presumption and not an established authorisation.[375] The terms of resolution 1441 (2002), adopted on 8 November 2002, indicate as much: in the event of Iraq violating its obligations, it is the Security Council itself that shall hear the matter 'for assessment',[376] and 'in order to consider the situation and the need for full compliance with all of the relevant Council resolutions'.[377] Moreover, it is the Security Council that decided to this effect 'to remain seized of the matter'.[378] It is therefore through a multilateral procedure that the use of force may, as need be, be

---

[372] Letter of 20 March 2003, S/2003/351; see also 'Contemporary Practice of the United States' (2003) 97 *AJIL* 419–32; (2005) 99 *AJIL* 269–70.

[373] Letter of 20 March 2003, S/2003/350. See also Attorney General, Lord Goldsmith, *Legal basis for use of force against Iraq*, Attorney General Lord Goldsmith, 17 March 2003, www.number10.gov.uk and 'United Kingdom Materials on International Law' (2003) 74 *BYBIL* 779–812; (2004) 75 *BYBIL* 829–45; (2005) 76 *BYBIL* 907–13 and 919–20; (2003) 52 *ICLQ* 811–14; (2005) 54 *ICLQ* 767–78 (Attorney General, Lord Goldsmith, 'Iraq: Resolution 1441').

[374] Letter of 20 March 2003, S/2003/352.

[375] V Lowe, 'The Iraq Crisis: What Now?' (2003) 52 *ICLQ* 865–66; U Bernitz, N Espejo-Yaksic, A Hurwitz, V Lowe, B Saul, K Ziegler, J Crawford, S Marks, R O'Keefe, C Chinkin, G Simpson, D Cass, M Craven, P Sands, R Wilde and PM Dupuy, 'War would be illegal', *The Guardian*, 7 March 2003 (and (2003) 36 *RBDI* 291–92); 'Statement by Japanese International Law Scholars on the Iraqi Issue' (2003) 36 *RBDI* 293–96.

[376] SC Res 1441 (2002) of 8 November 2002, para 4.

[377] ibid, para 12.

[378] ibid, para 14.

decided[379]—a procedure that was certainly incompatible with a unilateral evaluation of the situation, and in any event with unilateral implementation of military measures by any State whatsoever.[380] Attempts have sometimes been made to escape from the clarity of these terms by citing certain excerpts of the resolution that, taken out of context, might suggest a form of indirect authorisation.[381] This is essentially so with the remainder of resolutions 678 (1990) and 687 (1991), in the preamble, and the assertion that 'Iraq has been and remains in material breach of its obligations under relevant resolutions, including resolution 687 (1991)', further to which the Security Council decided 'to afford Iraq, by this resolution, a final opportunity to comply with its disarmament obligations . . .'.[382] The simple observation of the violation of international law by Iraq does not allow States to conduct a military operation. It must be considered rather that the Security Council clearly threatened Iraq with military action, which explains that it reminded it of the precedent of resolution 678 (1990). However, this reminder cannot be likened to a form of authorisation to resort unilaterally to force, which, for the first time in the Security Council's history, was purportedly accorded incidentally in the preamble to a resolution. The 'final opportunity' afforded to Iraq cannot be interpreted as opening the way to unilateral action, since it refers to the reinforced inspection regime instituted by the Security Council itself and consequently to its competence to examine the situation, including the choice of inflicting 'serious consequences' on Iraq to ensure compliance with 'all of the relevant Council resolutions'.[383] It is the Security Council that is tasked with sanctioning failure to abide by 'all' of its resolutions, including resolutions 678 (1990) and 687 (1991). The Security Council does not therefore abdicate its main responsibility in the realm of peace-keeping and, it is to that end that it decided 'to remain seized of the matter'.[384] Such a textual interpretation is confirmed besides by allowance for the debates that preceded the adoption of that resolution. Not only is it in vain that the US attempted to introduce in the resolution an expression clearly authorising the use of force,[385] but it was the US and the UK that managed to have resolution 1441 (2002) passed only by expressly affirming that 'as we have said on numerous occasions to Council members, this resolution contains no "hidden triggers" and no "automaticity" with respect to

---

[379] S Sur, 'La résolution 1441 du Conseil de sécurité et l'affaire iraquienne: un destin manqué', *Dalloz*, 2003, 836.

[380] ME O'Connel, 'Addendum to Armed Force in Iraq: Issues of Legality', April 2003, *ASIL Insight*, www.asil.org.

[381] WH Taft IV and TF Buchwald, 'Preemption, Iraq and International Law' (2003) 97 *AJIL* 560–63; R Wedgwood, 'The Fall of Saddam Hussein: Security Council Mandates and Preemptive Self-Defense' (2003) 97 *AJIL* 580–81.

[382] SC Res 1441 (2002) of 8 November 2002, preamble and paras 1 and 2.

[383] ibid, paras 12 and 13.

[384] ibid, para 14. See S Laghmani, 'Du droit international au droit impérial? Réflexions sur la guerre contre l'Irak', *Actualité et droit international*, April 2003, 2–3.

[385] *Le Monde*, 29–30 September, 9 October and 19 October 2002.

the use of force'.[386] This clarification was emphasised by many Security Council Member States, including the other three permanent members.[387] When, some weeks later, the States and their allies invoked resolution 1441 (2002) to justify the invasion of Iraq, they were indeed compelled to fall back on a 'presumption of authorisation'.[388]

Now, and this is one of the central legal lessons of the war against Iraq, it cannot be said, and this is an understatement, that the idea of a presumed authorisation was accepted by the community of States as a whole. Well before the beginning of Operation Iraqi Freedom, many States asserted the unlawfulness of any military action, despite the existence of resolutions 678 (1990), 687 (1991) and 1441 (2002).[389] As these few examples show, many Member States insisted on the principle of a clear and well-established authorisation. Thus, by the terms used within the Security Council itself:

—The Council *should be explicit* and clearly define the objectives of its resolutions and set clear, implementable benchmarks for compliance; (emphasis added)[390]
—[A]ny decision involving the use of collective force to secure implementation of Security Council decisions has such grave and serious implications that there must remain no doubt in anyone's mind that it has been *clearly and expressly authorised* by the Security Council. Article 42 does not provide the authority to one or more Member States to resort to force unilaterally and on their own judgement, independently of the Security Council or without its *explicit approval*; (emphasis added)[391]
—Only the Security Council—when the facts and circumstances so require—will thus be able to determine whether or not there are grounds to use force *through an explicit resolution* that would set forth the conditions for the use of force, if appropriate. (emphasis added)[392]

---

[386] S/PV.4644, 8 November 2002, 3. See also the views expressed by the United Kingdom: 'Let me be equally clear in response, as a co-sponsor with the United States of the text we have just adopted. There is no "automaticity" in this resolution. If there is a further Iraqi breach of its disarmament obligations, the matter will return to the Council for discussion as required in paragraph 12. We would expect the Security Council then to meet its responsibilities' (ibid, 5).

[387] Joint Declaration of France, Russia and China of 8 November 2002, www.diplomatie.fr/actu/. See also 'La pratique belge en matière de droit international' (2005) 38 *RBDI* 262–65.

[388] M Forteau, *Droit de la sécurité collective et droit de la responsabilité internationale de l'Etat*, above n 51, 423–24.

[389] S Spiliopoulou Akermark, 'Storms, Foxes and Nebulous Legal Arguments: Twelve Years of Force against Iraq, 1991–2003', above n 346, 224–26.

[390] South Africa, S/PV.4625, 16 October 2002, 6.

[391] Pakistan, ibid, 18.

[392] Ecuador, S/PV.4709 (Resumption 1), 19 February 2003, 15. See also Chile and New Zealand (S/PV.4625 (Resumption 1), 16 October 2002, 12 and 17–18), Nepal (S/PV.4625 (Resumption 2), 17 October 2002, 27). See also Belgium ('La pratique belge en matière de droit international' (2005) 38 *RBDI* 263).

The idea of a presumed authorisation was also clearly rejected by the many condemnations that followed the outbreak of war. Several States characterised the war as an aggression,[393] and many of them noted that it had not been authorised by the Security Council.[394] The Malaysian representative, in his capacity as President of the Coordination Bureau of the Non-Aligned Movement asserted that 'the war against Iraq has been carried out without the authorization of the Security Council . . . We view unilateral military action as an illegitimate act of aggression'.[395] The Arab League representative repeated with many other States[396] that the war was conducted unilaterally and 'without the Council's authorization'.[397] Similar criticisms were made by the heads of very different States, including France, Russia, China and Liechtenstein.[398]

In all, by my calculations, in the Security Council debates on 26 and 27 March 2003—that is in the days that directly followed the outbreak, 37 States clearly condemned the military intervention while 23 supported it, 21 having preferred to abstain from any formal condemnation or approval. However, such summary accounts must not deceive. For one thing, because the 37 opponents can legitimately claim to represent a larger number of States insofar as some of them spoke in the name of larger groups (and especially the Non-Aligned Movement of 116 member States). For another thing, because the States that supported the war are, unlike its opponents, far from having justified their views by reference to international law.[399] Upon examination, it can be seen that only the British,[400] Australian,[401] Spanish,[402] Nicaraguan,[403] Micronesian[404] and, of course, US[405] delegates, that is six States out of some 80 that spoke in the debate, developed legal arguments based on an authorisation allegedly indirectly given by the Security Council.[406] The least that can

---

[393] League of Arab States, Res of 24 March 2003; The American/British aggression against fraternal Iraq and its implications for the security and safety of neighbouring Arab States and Arab national security, S/2003/365, 26 March 2003.

[394] See also: March 20, 2003 Press Release, Secretary General of the Organization of the Islamic Conference Declares the Organization's rejection of Military Attack against Iraq.

[395] S/PV.4726, 26 March 2003, 7. See also NAM, A/58/68-S/2003/357.

[396] See, eg: Iran, Algeria, Yemen, Libya, Indonesia, South Africa, India, Brazil, Morocco, Laos, Switzerland; S/PV.4726, 26 March 2003 (and 'La pratique suisse en matière de droit international public' (2004) *RSDIE* 712). See also Tanzania, Palestine, Timor Leste, Kyrghyzstan, Mexico, Syria, Pakistan, Syria; S/PV.4726 (Resumption 1), 26 March 2003.

[397] S/PV.4726, 26 March 2003, 8.

[398] S/PV.4726 (Resumption 1), 26 March 2003; see also S/2003/347 and S/2003/348.

[399] See: www.whitehouse.gov/infocus/iraq/news/20030326-7.html.

[400] S/PV.4726, Resumption 1, 27 March 2003, 22–24.

[401] S/PV.4726, 26 March 2003, 26–27.

[402] S/PV.4726, Resumption 1, 27 March 2003, 29–30.

[403] S/PV.4726, 26 March 2003, 42–43.

[404] S/PV.4726, Resumption 1, 27 March 2003, 8–9.

[405] ibid, 25–26.

[406] See also: Uganda, Letter dated 2003/03/24 from the *Chargé d'affaires* ai of the Permanent Mission of Uganda to the United Nations addressed to the President of the Security Council, S/2003/373, 26 March 2003.

be said is that this position is far from having met with approval, particularly as the same States carefully abstained from defending it *in tempore non suspecto*, that is, before the official outbreak of war, an attitude that can legitimately cast doubt on the sincerity of their *opinio juris*.[407] Lastly, it shall be observed that, among the 23 States that abstained from formally condemning the military operation in the Security Council on 26 and 27 March 2003, several did so manifestly for purely diplomatic reasons and so they can certainly not be ranked among the supporters of the 'presumed authorisation' argument.

Ultimately, beyond the diversity of factual circumstances surrounding the precedents examined, there arises a common position for a very large majority of States: the argument of Security Council authorisation cannot be admitted unless that authorisation is clearly established. Conversely, one cannot settle for a presumption inferred from a few expressions in the texts of resolutions adopted prior to the outbreak of armed action. In the same perspective, it shall now be seen that authorisation cannot be presumed either on the basis of the Security Council's behaviour after the triggering of a military operation.

Presumed Authorisation Deduced from Approval of a Military Action already Engaged?

The 'presumed authorisation' argument has not only been evoked by reference to resolutions actually adopted at the time a military intervention was triggered. In some cases, reliance has been placed on the behaviour adopted by the Security Council *after* the intervention was triggered. In precedents as different as those of Liberia, Sierra Leone and Kosovo, the 'presumed authorisation' was deduced from an approbation given after the event by the Security Council.[408] This approval has supposedly itself been revealed explicitly—when the approval appears directly in the text of the relevant resolutions—, or implicitly—insofar as it is supposedly deduced from a simple absence of condemnation of the military action contemplated. These two hypotheses are covered in succession.

a) Precedents Where There Would Seem to be Explicit Approval of a Military Intervention

On several occasions in the 1990s armed operations were carried out by regional collective security organisations, whether ECOWAS in Liberia and Sierra Leone or the CIS in Georgia. While conducted in the absence of

---

[407] 'Netherlands State Practice' (2004) 25 *NYIL* 369–78 and O Corten, 'Opération *Iraqi Freedom*: peut-on admettre l'argument de l'"autorisation implicite" du Conseil de sécurité?' above n 345, 222–23.

[408] See: International Commission on Intervention and State Sovereignty, *The Responsibility to Protect* (December 2001), para 6.5 (www.iciss-ciise.gc.ca/menu-en.asp).

prior authorisation, these operations subsequently seem to have been the subject of approval by the Security Council. For all that, it is difficult to see in them precedents establishing the emergence of a rule consecrating the possibility of an armed intervention on the basis of a presumed authorisation from the Security Council.

ECOWAS Action in Liberia

On 24 August 1990, the Economic Community Of West African States (ECOWAS) sent a 4000-strong military observer group, ECOMOG, to Liberia to supervise a ceasefire intended to end the civil war between the regime of President Doe and rebel movements.[409] This force remained on the ground for several years and intervened on many occasions in fighting between the parties in this internal conflict.[410] Now, the ECOWAS operation did not have prior authorisation from the Security Council, no resolution having been adopted at the time the operation began. However, the Security Council seemed to approve of the ECOWAS operation long after it had been launched.[411] In several resolutions adopted from 1992 onwards, the Security Council 'commend[ed] ECOWAS for its efforts to restore peace, security and stability in Liberia',[412] urged 'all Member States to provide financial, logistical and other assistance in support of ECOMOG to enable it to carry out its mandate',[413] while thanking 'those African States that have contributed troops to ECOWAS's Cease-fire Monitoring Group (ECOMOG)',[414] and condemning 'the continuing armed attacks against the peace-keeping forces of ECOWAS in Liberia by one party of the conflict'.[415] Similarly, it was in full cooperation with that organisation that the Security Council decided to send a UN Force (MONUL) to maintain peace in the region.[416] It is on the basis of this evidence that several commentators consider that the Liberian precedent illustrates the

---

[409] *Keesing's Contemporay Archives*, 1990, 37644; N Tabiou, 'L'intervention de l'ECOMOG au Libéria et en Sierra Leone' in M Benchikh (ed), *Les Organisations Internationales et les conflits armés* (Paris, L'Harmattan, 2001) 265 *ff*.

[410] *Keesing's Contemporary Archives*, 1990, 37699 and 37766; *Keesing's Contemporary Archives*, 1992, 39131.

[411] G Cahin, 'Les Nations Unies et la construction de la paix en Afrique: entre désengagement et expérimentation' (2000) 104 *RGDIP* 100.

[412] SC Res 856 (1993) of 9 August 1993, para 6; see also SC Res 866 (1993) of 21 September 1993, 950 (1994) of 21 October 1994, 1001 (1995) of 30 June 1995, 1014 (1995) of 15 September 1995; 1020 (1995) of 10 November 1995, 1041 (1996) of 29 January 1996, 1059 (1996) of 30 May 1996, 1071 (1996) of 30 August 1996.

[413] SC Res 1014 (1995) of 15 September 1995, para 6; see also SC Res 1059 (1996) of 30 May 1996, 1071 (1996) of 30 August 1996.

[414] SC Res 950 (1994) of 21 October 1994, preamble; see also SC Res 1014 (1995) of 15 September 1995, 1041 (1996) of 29 January 1996.

[415] SC Res 788 (1992) of 19 November 1992, 4; see also SC Res 1041 (1996) of 29 January 1996, 1071 (1996) of 30 August 1996.

[416] SC Res 866 (1993) of 21 September 1993.

possibility of approving a military intervention *ex post* and authorising it retroactively.[417]

Such an interpretation is highly debatable.[418] Careful examination of the chronology of events shows that the Security Council never purported to approve, or *a fortiori* to authorise retroactively, any *enforcement* action by ECOWAS. The terminology used in the resolutions and in the debates that preceded them accredits rather the image of a peace-keeping operation conducted in the absence of opposition from the authorities of the State in question, with as a consequence the inapplicability of article 53(1) of the Charter that requires prior authorisation from the Security Council for enforcement measures only.[419]

Let us first contemplate the question of the time the operation was triggered. In July 1990 and unlike some rebel factions the Liberian President had spoken in favour of the arrival of an ECOWAS 'peace-keeping force'[420] and then accepted a ceasefire at the request of that organisation.[421] In this context, on 9 August 1990, Nigeria sent a declaration to the Security Council in ECOWAS' name, stating its intention of 'carrying out a *peace-keeping role* and monitoring the peace process in Liberia', with the strictest compliance to the principle of neutrality. (emphasis added)[422] At that stage, there was no question of an authorisation to use force, but of requesting 'considerable moral support'.[423] The government authorities in place and ECOWAS were agreed therefore from the outset on the non-coercive character of the operation.

The lesson is all the more significant as another option was available legally. It should be noted that, in the ECOWAS case, a *Protocol on Mutual*

---

[417] C Walter, 'Security Control over Regional Action', above n 174, 181; D Momtaz, 'L'intervention d'humanité de l'OTAN au Kosovo et la règle du non-recours à la force', (2000) 837 *IRRC* 95; J Lobel and M Ratner, 'Bypassing the Security Council: Ambiguous Authorizations to Use Force, Cease Fires and the Iraqi Regime', above n 351, 132; R Kolb, 'Article 53', above n 177, 1429; R Wedgwood, 'Unilateral Action in the United Nations System', above n 292, 357; D Wippman, 'Pro-Democratic Intervention in Africa', *ASIL Proceedings*, 2002, 144; see also S Chesterman, *Just War or Just Peace? Humanitarian Intervention and International Law*, above n 270, 137.

[418] See: LA Sicilianos, 'Entre multilatéralisme et unilatéralisme: l'autorisation par le Conseil de sécurité de recourir à la force', above n 34, 190–92.

[419] I Brownlie and CJ Apperley, 'Kosovo Crisis Inquiry: Further Memorandum on the International Law Aspects', above n 291, 907–08; C Gray in Hazel Fox (ed), *The Changing Constitution of the United Nations*, BIICL, 1997, 107–08.

[420] *Letter addressed by President Samuel K Doe to the Chairman and Membres of the Ministerial Meeting of ECOWAS Standing Mediation Committee*, 14 July 1990, Doc 39 in M Weller (ed), *Regional Peace-keeping and International Enforcement: The Liberian Crisis* (Cambridge, Cambridge University Press, 1994) 61. See G Nolte, 'Restoring Peace by Regional Action: International Legal Aspects of the Liberian Conflict', (1993) *ZaöRV* 621–26.

[421] *Keesing's Contemporary Archives*, 1990, 37602.

[422] *Letter dated 9 August 1990 from the Permanent Representative of Nigeria to the UN addressed to the Secretary-General*, S/21485, 10 August 1990, 3; 'ECOWAS intervention is in no way designed to save one part or punish another'.

[423] ibid.

Assistance on Defense, adopted at Freetown on 29 May 1981, provided that 'any armed threat or aggression directed against fellow members shall constitute a threat or aggression against the entire Community', mentioning specifically the case of 'internal armed conflict within any member State engineered and supported from the outside . . . likely to endanger the peace and security in the region'.[424] The press at the time reported a degree of support allegedly provided to the Liberian rebels by the Côte d'Ivoire, Burkina Faso and Libya.[425] One might therefore have imagined that the intervening States invoke government consent to repel irregular forces with foreign support, as in numerous other precedents.[426] But nothing of the sort was done, probably because such an argument would not have squared with the image of neutrality that ECOWAS wished to portray, which was better served by presenting the military action as a peace-keeping operation.

In this context, it is not surprising that the Security Council did not, at the time of events, adopt any resolution authorising or approving the deployment of ECOWAS forces that entered Monrovia in late August. As Georg Nolte states:

> [W]hen ECOMOG entered Liberia in August 1990 there was no immediate official reaction from the Security Council. Indeed, the issue was not even put on its agenda. This fact is a clear indication that the Council did not consider its authorisation under Art. 53 of the UN Charter necessary for ECOMOG to proceed.[427]

The non-coercive character of the operation may then rely on the agreement of all of the parties to the internal conflict, and no longer just that of the government. In October 1991, after several months of disorder and of short-lived ceasefires[428] during which rebel forces had several run-ins with ECOWAS forces,[429] the Yamoussoukro IV peace accords were concluded and accepted by all parties.[430] Under these agreements, ECOWAS forces were deployed in the border area with Sierra Leone, initially controlled by the National Patriotic Front of Liberia (NPFL).[431] It was further to renewed conflict with this rebel force[432] that ECOWAS decided to set up an arms embargo and asked the Security Council to make it binding on all UN members.

---

[424] www.cedeao.org.

[425] *Keesing's Contemporary Archives,* 1990, 37174 and 37601; see also E Kannyo, 'Civil Strife and Humanitarian Intervention in Africa: A Preliminary Assesment' (1996) 4 *African Yearbook of International Law* 61; F Meledje Djedjro, 'La guerre civile au Libéria et la question de l'ingérence dans les affaires intérieures des Etats' (1993) 26 *RBDI* 401.

[426] See above, ch 5, s II.

[427] G Nolte, 'Restoring Peace by Regional Action: International Legal Aspects of the Liberian Conflict', above n 420, 631–32.

[428] *Keesing's Contemporary Archives,* 1990, 37700 and 37908.

[429] *Keesing's Contemporary Archives,* 1990, 3770; *Keesing's,* 1992, 38951.

[430] *Keesing's Contemporary Archives,* 1991, 38518.

[431] *Keesing's Contemporary Archives,* 1992, 38853.

[432] *Keesing's Contemporary Archives,* 1992, 39084, 39131 and 39180–81.

On 19 November 1992 the Security Council adopted its first resolution on Liberia,[433] in which, having welcomed 'the continued commitment of the ECOWAS to and the efforts towards a peaceful resolution of the Liberian conflict', it 'reaffirm[ed] its belief that the Yamoussoukro IV Accord offers the best possible framework for *a peaceful resolution* of the Liberian conflict' and called upon ECOWAS 'to continue its efforts to assist in the *peaceful implementation* of this Accord'. (emphasis added)[434] Further on, the Council 'condemn[ed] the continuing armed attacks against *the peace-keeping forces of ECOWAS* in Liberia by one of the parties of the conflict' and decided, under Chapter VII of the Charter, to establish a full arms embargo, while specifying that the embargo 'shall not apply to weapons and military equipment destined for the sole use of *the peace-keeping force of ECOWAS* in Liberia'. (emphasis added)[435] Thus, the only enforcement measures decided by the Security Council do not constitute, *a contrario*, an approval or *ex tunc* authorisation of a military intervention, but the establishment of an *ex nunc* arms embargo, pursuant to article 41 of the Charter. In this context, it is clear that the ECOWAS action was considered a peace-keeping operation that was by its essence peaceful and non-coercive.[436]

At the time it addressed the Security Council in November 1992, ECOWAS did not ask for any authorisation, whether retroactive or not,[437] to use force for the simple reason that it had always presented its action as non-coercive.[438] Through Benin's representative to the Security Council, ECOWAS requested 'the assistance and support of the Security Council' for the measures taken to restore peace to Liberia and not an authorisation to use force.[439] Liberia's representative commended the Council for its earlier support given 'to the peace initiatives of the ECOWAS', referring to the organisation's 'peace-keepers'.[440] More specifically, the Côte d'Ivoire representative recalled the chronology of events and concluded that they

---

[433] See also: *Note by the President of the Security Council*, S/22133, 22 January 1991 (and S/PV.2974); *Note by the President of the Security Council*, S/23886, 7 May 1992 (and S/PV.3071), and G Nolte, 'Restoring Peace by Regional Action: International Legal Aspects of the Liberian Conflict', above n 420, 632–34.

[434] SC Res 788 (1992) of 19 November 1992, preamble and para 2.

[435] ibid, paras 4 and 8; see also SC Res 985 (1995) of 13 April 1995.

[436] See also: GA Res 47/154 of 18 December 1992 and E de Wet, *The Chapter VII Powers of the United Nations Security Council*, above n 4, 301; AD Mindua, 'Intervention armée de la CEDEAO au Libéria: illégalité ou avancée juridique?' (1995) 7 *RADIC* 275; D Wippman, 'Enforcing the Peace: ECOWAS and the Liberian Civil War' in L Fisler Damrosch (ed), *Enforcing Restraint. Collective Intervention in Internal Conflicts* (New York, Council on Foreign Relations Press, 1993) 178; A Peyro Llopis, 'Le système de sécurité collective entre anarchie et fiction. Observations sur la pratique récente' in *Droit du pouvoir, pouvoir du droit. Mélanges offerts à J Salmon* (Bruxelles, Bruylant, 2007) 1408–09.

[437] C Gray, *International Law and the Use of Force*, 3rd edn, above n 28, 417–18.

[438] G Nolte, 'Restoring Peace by Regional Action: International Legal Aspects of the Liberian Conflict', above n 420, 626–28.

[439] S/PV.3138, 19 November 1992, 7.

[440] ibid, 12 and 17.

'show that, *in accordance with the provisions of Article 52 of the United Nations Charter*, ECOWAS has spared no effort to bring about a peaceful settlement of this conflict'. (emphasis added)[441]

No State contradicted that assertion. The legal basis for the ECOWAS action is still therefore, if one keeps to the official statements, to be sought in article 52 of the Charter on the peaceful means for regional conflict settlement. *A contrario*, article 53, on enforcement measures, is not cited as a relevant provision.[442] Similarly, it is interesting to report how the military actions against Liberian rebels were presented to the Security Council by Nigeria's representative:

> It has become well accepted over the years that a peace-keeping force can in the performance of its duties resort to the use of force to defend itself when it is a victim of unprovoked armed attack, to avert tragic incidents that constitute crimes against humanity, and to implement essential details of a peace plan over which parties to the conflict have agreed, as in the case of Liberia'.[443]

The statement from the country directing ECOWAS forces, just like those of the other that spoke on the subject,[444] clearly placed them in the legal context of peace-keeping operations. It is in this context that the use of force was justified as a measure of self-defence, not as an enforcement action consisting in a use of force according to article 53 of the Charter. In the light of this evidence, it is difficult to contest that what the Security Council approved in November 1992 was support for a peace process that was reflected by accords accepted by all parties, and not a military enforcement intervention.[445]

On analysis, it will besides have been noted that the Security Council's approval relates only to the operation as it was conducted from the time of the Yamoussoukro IV accords, that is, after consent was obtained from all parties to the conflict. *A contrario*, the Council did not specifically approve, no more than it specifically condemned, the initial action by ECOWAS in August 1990 with the agreement of the president in office but against the wishes of one of the parties to the conflict.

Some scholars have presented another interpretation of this precedent, relying mainly on the terms of resolution 866 (1993), which defines the MONUL mandate in these terms: 'Without participation in *enforcement operations*, to coordinate with ECOMOG in the discharge of ECOMOG's

---

[441] ibid, 32.

[442] C Gray, *International Law and the Use of Force*, 3rd edn, above n 28, 400.

[443] S/PV.3138, 19 November 1992, 47; see also Ivory Coast, ibid, 31.

[444] See: Burkina Faso, Sierra Leone, Togo, China, USA, UK, Mauritius; ibid.

[445] According to D Wippman, the Council 'appears to accept, or at least fails to question, the Community's position that its military actions constitute either peacekeeping or self-defense'; therefore, the Council 'never explicitly authorized enforcement action, although it ultimately approved, at least implicitly, the deployment of ECOMOG'; 'Enforcing the Peace: ECOWAS and the Liberian Civil War', above n 436, 186.

separate responsibilities'. (emphasis added)[446] This terminology is supposedly evidence, *a contrario*, of the coercive character of the ECOMOG action.[447] Besides, it has been revealed that in several resolutions the Security Council congratulated ECOWAS 'for its efforts to restore [and not 'to maintain'] peace, security and stability in Liberia';[448] similar wording to that used for an authorisation to use force pursuant to chapter VII, in the case in point in resolution 678 (1990), on the situation between Iraq and Kuwait.[449] So, for some scholars, the Security Council approved the use of force in terms equivalent to the authorisation provided for by article 53.[450]

We must first recall the exact terms used by the Security Council in its resolution 678 (1990) to rule out any possible comparison. In that resolution, the Security Council, *'Acting under Chapter VII of the Charter'*, 'authorize[d] Member States co-operating with the Government of Kuwait . . . to use all necessary means . . . to restore international peace and security in the area'. (emphasis added)[451] The wording used in the case of Liberia is very different. For one thing, no reference is made to chapter VII of the Charter, a significant omission when one thinks that, in practice, the Council explicitly mentions this chapter when it wishes to resort to enforcement measures.[452] For another thing, 'to restore peace, security and stability in Liberia' is quite different from 'to restore international peace and security in the area'. In the latter case, we are manifestly dealing with a breach of international peace, which observation is made in resolution 678 (1990).[453] In the first, by contrast, 'peace', 'security' and 'stability' are terms that must be understood in another sense, equivalent to that used in evoking a 'peace agreement' that is supposed to end an *internal* conflict. The Security Council terminology must therefore be understood, as a whole, as relating to a peace-keeping mission carried out with the agreement of the parties to an internal conflict.

---

[446] SC Res 866 (1993) of 22 September 1993, para 3(h).

[447] C Walter, 'Security Control over Regional Action', above n 174, 185–86.

[448] SC Res 788 (1992) of 19 November 1992, para 1; see also SC Res 813 (1993) of 26 March 1993, para 2; 856 (1993) of 10 August 1993, para 6; 866 (1993) of 22 September 1993, preamble; 911 (1994) of 21 April 1994, preamble; 950 (1994) of 21 October 1994, preamble, 1001 (1995) of 30 June 1995, preamble, 1014 (1995) of 15 September 1995, preamble, 1020 (1995) of 10 November 1995, preamble, 1041 (1996) of 29 January 1996, preamble, 1059 (1996) of 31 May 1996, preamble, 1071 (1996) of 30 August 1996, preamble, 1083 (1996) of 27 November 1996, preamble, 1100 (1997) of 27 March 1997, preamble, 1116 (1997) of 27 June 1997, preamble. See also S/PV.3281, 22 September 1993.

[449] C Walter, 'Security Control over Regional Action', above n 174, 181–82; see also A Peyro Llopis, 'Le système de sécurité collective entre anarchie et fiction. Observations sur la pratique récente', above n 436, 1409.

[450] U Villani, 'Les rapports entre l'ONU et les organizations régionales dans le domaine du maintien de la paix', above n 36, 373.

[451] SC Res 678 (1990) of 29 November 1990, para 2.

[452] JA Frowein and N Krisch, 'Article 39', above n 35, 727.

[453] SC 678 (1990) of 20 November 1990, referring to SC Res 660 (1990) of 2 August 1990.

The same is true, to my mind, when the Security Council incidentally used the expression of *'enforcement operations'* in its resolution 866 (1993). At first sight, the terminology seems to relate to an 'enforcement measure' which, unlike a peace-keeping measure, would not require the consent of the interested parties.[454] Closer scrutiny of the Council's resolutions confirms, however, that this expression—which it shall be noted in passing was used once only by the Council[455]—cannot be interpreted in that way. In its resolution 866 (1993), the Security Council insists on the existence of the Cotonou Peace Agreement accepted by all the parties to the conflict and which asks the UN and ECOWAS to support its enforcement.[456] The Council then emphasises that 'the Peace Agreement assigns ECOMOG the primary responsibility of supervising the implementation of the military provisions of the Agreement and envisages that the United Nations' role shall be to monitor and verify this process'.[457] It is in this context that it notes that 'this would be the first *peace-keeping mission* undertaken by the United Nations in cooperation with a *peace-keeping mission* already set up by another organisation, in this case ECOWAS'. (emphasis added)[458]

The reading of the entire text of the resolution clearly shows that, in the case in point, the ECOWAS action is indeed presented as relying on the parties' consent, and therefore as by definition a non-coercive 'peace-keeping mission'. This too is how the mission was presented by the Secretary-General, in the report on the basis of which the resolution was adopted,[459] and by the States in the debates that preceded its adoption.[460] The 'enforcement operations' are therefore, in the case in point, based on consent, which is further confirmed by examination of the Cotonou Agreements, expressly permitting ECOWAS to take 'peace enforcement' measures.[461] There is no cause to infer from the use of this latest expression that we are faced with enforcement measures taken by virtue of Chapter VII or article 53(1) of the Charter, which are besides never cited in the texts or debates. It is simply that, in the consensus framework of the

---

[454] *Supplement to an Agenda for Peace*, A/50/60, S/1995/1, 25 January 1995, 7, para 23.

[455] cp SC Res 788 (1992) of 19 November 1992, 813 (1993) of 26 March 1993, 856 (1993) of 10 August 1993, 911 (1994) of 21 April 1994, 950 (1994) of 21 October 1994, 972 (1995) of 13 January 1995, 985 (1995) of 13 April 1995, 1001 (1995) of 30 June 1995, 1116 (1997) of 27 June 1997.

[456] SC Res 866 (1993) of 22 September 1993, preamble.

[457] ibid; see also SC Res 911 (1994) of 21 April 1994, preamble.

[458] SC Res 866 (1993) of 22 September 1993, preamble.

[459] According to the Secretary-General, 'the peace process in Liberia poses a special opportunity to the United Nations in that ONUMIL would be *the first peace-keeping operation undertaken by the United Nations in co-operation with a peace-keeping mission already set up by another organization*, in this case a sub-regional organization' (emphasis added; Report of 9 September 1993, S/26422, 9 September 1993, para 36).

[460] See: USA, France and Japan; S/PV.3281, 22 September 1993, 13.

[461] Text in *Letter from the Chargé d'affaires ai of the Permanent Mission of Benin to the United Nations addressed to the Secretary-General, 6 August 1993* (S/26272, 9 August 1993, s G, art 8 ('Peace Enforcement Powers'), and art 3 § 2).

various agreements, ECOWAS had more lax rules of engagement than MONUL, which remained confined to a peace-keeping mission in the more traditional sense. It would be going too far to liken the Liberian precedent to that of Somalia or Bosnia-Herzegovina in which the Security Council, acting expressly under Chapter VII, authorised UN forces to use all 'necessary means' to attain certain objectives, an expression that clearly aims to make the mission independent of the consent of any particular party to the conflict.[462] All told, the ECOWAS mission in Liberia is properly presented as a non-coercive peace-keeping operation.[463]

One might admittedly contest this characterisation in view of the facts by noting that the operation could not, at least initially, be based on the consent of all the parties to the conflict as the rebels were initially opposed to an outside intervention that in practice deprived them of conquest of the capital.[464] It has also been emphasised that, again initially, ECOWAS did not base its action explicitly on the consent of the government in place,[465] probably to avoid being associated with one of the parties to the conflict. Likewise, doubts have been expressed about the strict neutrality of ECOWAS forces that were called on for help by the presidential authorities at the time when they were on the brink of succumbing to rebel attacks.[466] It has also been pointed out that, on several occasions, foreign forces, mostly Nigerian ones, actually took part in fighting.[467] That most States were eager to consider, despite this evidence, that the ECOWAS action was non-coercive, only makes even more significant the choice made in favour of a version of events that does not challenge existing law. By characterising this action as non-coercive, especially in the UN, it is set within the framework of article 52 and we avoid, at the same time, the requirement of an authorisation as contained in article 53(1).[468] The Liberian precedent is thus

---

[462] See above, s I.

[463] See also: *Final communiqué of the summit of the ECOWAS, held at Abuja on 28 and 29 August 1997*, annex I of the Letter dated 97/09/08 from the Permanent Representative of Nigeria to the United Nations addressed to the President of the Security Council, 8 September 1997, para 21.

[464] *Keesing's Contemporary Archives*, 1990, 37644; C Walter, 'Security Control over Regional Action', above n 174, 134; see also D Wippman, 'Enforcing the Peace: ECOWAS and the Liberian Civil War', above n 436, 178.

[465] C Walter, 'Security Control over Regional Action', above n 174, 152–53; see *ECOWAS Standing Mediation Committee, Decision A/DEC.1/8/90 on the Cease-fire and Establishment of an ECOWAS Cease-fire Monitoring Group for Liberia*, Banjul, Republic of Gambia, 7 August 1990, in *Regional Peace-keeping and International Enforcement. The Liberian Crisis*, above n 420, 67–69.

[466] D Momtaz, 'La délégation par le Conseil de sécurité de l'exécution de ses actions coercitives aux organizations régionales', above n 36, 112 and 'Pratique française du droit international' (1993) 26 *AFDI* 1020.

[467] C Walter, 'Security Control over Regional Action', above n 174, 181; AD Mindua, 'Intervention armée de la CEDEAO au Libéria: illégalité ou avancée juridique?', above n 436, 277; D Wippman, 'Enforcing the Peace: ECOWAS and the Liberian Civil War', above n 436, 165 *ff*.

[468] See: A Abbas, *Regional Organisations and the Development of Collective Security. Beyond Chapter VIII of the UN Charter*, above n 254, 45.

evidence of a will to interpret the scope of this last disposition restrictively, with it not applying whenever an agreement underlies the action of a regional organisation. Conversely, it cannot accredit the argument of an *a posteriori* authorisation being admissible within the meaning of that same article 53.

Ultimately, it will be observed that the '*a posteriori* authorisation' argument is essentially a scholarly one. No State and no international organisation, whether ECOWAS or the UN, claimed that the operation in Liberia was an enforcement measure retroactively authorised by the Security Council under article 53(1). Accordingly no *opinio juris* is to be found there attesting to the emergence of a rule admitting military interventions based on a presumed authorisation.[469] As such, the Liberian precedent seems very similar to that of Sierra Leone, which also gave rise to certain doctrinal controversies.

The ECOWAS Operation in Sierra Leone

In the case of Sierra Leone, Nigerian troops mostly, of ECOWAS,[470] intervened militarily in February 1998 in an internal conflict, officially to restore to power the elected government[471] overthrown by a coup in May 1997.[472] The Security Council not only refrained from condemning the operation but apparently approved it through several resolutions adopted after it had been launched,[473] resolutions which provided notably for the setting up of a UN Force (MONUSIL) to act in 'full cooperation' and 'close coordination' with ECOMOG.[474] It is on this basis that some commentators evoked an *ex post* authorisation by the Security Council.[475]

As in the case of Liberia, the action of this regional organisation was, however, presented as a non-coercive operation and not as a military intervention that should have been authorised under article 53(1) of the Charter. It should be recalled in this respect that ECOWAS itself was careful not to refer to this provision, but on the contrary preferred, when it fought the military junta in February 1998, to invoke the right of its forces to defend themselves pursuant to the international rules of engagement applicable to 'peace-keeping operations'.[476] In this context, there was no need, in that

---

[469] E de Wet, *The Chapter VII Powers of the United Nations Security Council*, above n 4, 299.
[470] *Keesing's Contemporary Archives*, 1997, 41672.
[471] *Keesing's Contemporary Archives*, 1996, 40982.
[472] *Keesing's Contemporary Archives*, 1997, 41625.
[473] See: SC Res 1156 (1998) of 16 March 1998, 1162 (1998) of 17 April 1998, 1171 (1998) of 5 June 1998, 1181 (1998) of 13 July 1998, 1220 (1999) of 12 January 1999 and 1231 (1999) of 11 March 1999.
[474] SC Res 1181 (1998) of 13 July 1998, para 11.
[475] BD Lepard, *Rethinking Humanitarian Intervention* (Pennsylvania, Pennsylvania University Press, 2002) 337.
[476] *9ème réunion ministérielle du Comité des Cinq de la CEDEAO sur la Sierra Leone, Communiqué final* (Addis Ababa, 25–27 February 1998), *DAI*, n° 8, 1998, 279. See also above, ch 5, s II.

organisation's view, to seek Security Council authorisation. It should further be specified in this respect that ECOMOG's presence on the ground had been accepted earlier by the local authorities in October 1997[477] further to an embargo specifically authorised by the Security Council under Chapter VII of the Charter.[478] *A contrario*, the Council never authorised, nor approved *a posteriori*, any military enforcement action against the Sierra Leone authorities, which were besides considered to be unlawful.[479] A few days after the overthrow of the authorities, the Security Council President adopted a declaration in which the Council 'welcome[d] the fact that the rule of the military junta has been brought to an end' and 'commend[ed] the important role that the Economic Community of West African States (ECOWAS) has continued to play towards the *peaceful resolution* of this crisis'. (emphasis added)[480] In another declaration, on 20 May the President evoked that organisation's 'peace-keeping role'.[481] Similarly, in its resolution 1181 (1998) of 13 July 1998, the Council 'Commend[ed] the positive role of ECOWAS and ECOMOG in their efforts to restore peace, security and stability throughout the country *at the request of the Government of Sierra Leone . . .*'. (emphasis added)[482] The debates having taken place within the UN confirm an intent of States as a whole to present the ECOWAS action as non-coercive.[483]

It is true that a communiqué of 26 June 1997 revealed that the ECOWAS foreign ministries emphasised the need 'to work towards the reinstatement of the legitimate government by a combination of three measures, namely, dialogue, imposition of sanctions and enforcement of an embargo *and the use of force*', and immediately called 'on the international community to support the ECOWAS initiative on Sierra Leone'.[484] Insofar as that support was immediately forthcoming, including after the overthrow of the regime, it might be thought there genuinely was an approval of the use of force. Closer scrutiny of the existing texts and the context in which they were adopted shows otherwise, though. On 6 August 1997, the President of the Security Council

> expresse[d] its appreciation to the Committee of Four Foreign Ministers of the Economic Community of West African States (ECOWAS) for their efforts to

---

[477] See the Conakry Agreement of 23 October 1997, S/1997/824, 28 October 1997). On 17 June 1997, the junta accepted 'the deployment of ECOMOG and UN peacekeeping forces under a 10-point proposal' (*Keesing's Contemporary Archives*, 1997, 41672).

[478] SC Res 1332 (1997) of 8 October 1997.

[479] E de Wet, *The Chapter VII Powers of the United Nations Security Council*, above n 4, 302–03.

[480] S/PRST/1998/5, 26 February 1998.

[481] S/PRST/1998/13, 20 May 1998.

[482] SC Res 1181 (1998), para 5.

[483] S/PV.3902, 13 July 1998; see also S/PV.3857, 26 February 1998; S/PV.3872, 17 April 1998; S/PV.3882, 20 May 1998; S/PV.3889, 5 June 1998.

[484] *Communiqué* in S/1997/499, 27 June 1997, paras 9 and 14.

negotiate with representatives of the military junta from 17 to 18 July and 29 to 30 July 1997 in Abidjan on a *peaceful resolution of the crisis*, and reiterate[d] its full support for the objectives of *this mediation*' (emphasis added)[485]

which terminology is hardly compatible with endorsement of a decision to use force.[486] In actual fact, such use of force was never evoked again, with ECOWAS asking for and then obtaining rather an authorisation to set up and enforce an embargo.[487] This authorisation, *a contrario*, was never aimed at the overthrow of the military junta.[488]

On the matter of the embargo measures, one commentator noted that on 29 August 1997, that is, before the Security Council adopted its first resolution on the issue, ECOWAS had decided to adopt sanctions against the military junta, specifying that:

> The sub-regional forces shall employ all necessary means to impose the implementation of this decision. They shall monitor closely the coastal areas, land borders and airspace of the Republic of Sierra Leone, and shall inspect, guard and seize any ship, vehicle or aircraft violating the embargo imposed by this decision.[489]

Insofar as it was only on 8 October that the Security Council authorised ECOWAS to enforce the embargo, it might be thought that it thereby retroactively authorised the use of force decided by the organisation.[490] However, there is no ground for this interpretation either of the text of resolution 1332 (1997) or of the stances taken by States at the time it was adopted.[491] No one asked for a retroactive authorisation, the authorisation having then been given *ex nunc* if the text is given its plain meaning.[492] In fact, it can be considered that the police measures to enforce the embargo, that were adopted before the Security Council resolution, could not be and never could have been based on an authorisation within the meaning of article 53 of the Charter. At most, the ECOWAS Member States could have agreed to give the organisation the competence to take police measures aimed at vessels flying their flags. It was to broaden the scope of action, by extending it to all States, that ECOWAS asked for and obtained authorisation in due form from the Security Council.

---

[485] S/PRST/1997/42, 6 August 1997 and S/PV.3809, 6 August 1997.

[486] See also: Final Communiqué of the ECOWAS summit meeting, Abuja, 28–29 August 1997, S/1997/695, 8 September 1997, Annex I, paras 24 and 25.

[487] SC Res 1132 (1997) of 8 October 1997 and S/PV.3822, 8 October 1997.

[488] See also declarations of 27 May 1997, S/PRST/1997/29; 11 July 1997, S/PRST/1997/36; 6 August 1997, S/PRST/1997/42; SC Res 1332 (1997) of 8 October 1997.

[489] ECOWAS, *Decision on sanctions against the Junta in Sierra Leone*, S/1997/695, 8 September 1997, Annex II, art 7.

[490] U Villani, 'Les rapports entre l'ONU et les organizations régionales dans le domaine du maintien de la paix', above n 36, 386–97.

[491] S/PV.3822, 8 October 1997.

[492] SC Res 1332 (1997) of 8 October 1997, para 8. See LA Sicilianos, 'Entre multilatéralisme et unilatéralisme: l'autorisation par le Conseil de sécurité de recourir à la force', above n 34, 202–03.

Admittedly, as in the case of Liberia, one may have certain reservations about this presentation of the ECOWAS action as being a simple 'peace-keeping mission'. On the ground, it was indeed by force and against the will of the military junta actually in power that the legitimately elected president was restored to office,[493] and it was only after the first signs of this intervention that a new agreement (for it should be remembered that the initial presence of the regional forces had been accepted before the junta came to power) could be wrought among all the parties concerned authorising the presence of ECOWAS troops.[494] Once again, this criticism only makes more significant the Security Council's choice and that of the States within it in favour of characterising the operation as a peace-keeping and so as non-coercive action not requiring in principle its authorisation. Finally, and this is certainly a decisive factor, it will be observed that the question of the lawfulness of the use of force by ECOMOG against the junta forces was never raised in the Security Council. More generally, no State invoked the argument of an *ex post facto* authorisation, which was only used by scholars. It seems excessive in the least, therefore, to infer from this precedent any authorisation to use force,[495] just as it would be misleading to do so from the case of the intervention of CIS forces in Georgia.

The CIS Operation in Georgia

Even if it is under different factual circumstances again, we can discern in the case of Georgia, which has sometimes been evoked as evidence of an incipient rule consecrating the possibility of *ex post* authorisation,[496] the same sequence of events as observed in Liberia and Sierra Leone. In 1993, certain Russian units deployed in Georgia to supervise a ceasefire between the government authorities and Abkhaz independentist forces,[497] and it was only then that the Security Council decided to create an observation mission, UNOMIG, tasked with overseeing the application of the ceasefire.[498] The reluctance of the Security Council to send in UN forces, despite the request from the parties and the support of the Secretary-General,[499] led the Commonwealth of Independent States (CIS) to set up what was designated as a 'peace-keeping operation'.[500] That mission, composed essentially

[493] *Keesing's Contemporary Archives*, 1997, 41672; *Keesing's Contemporary Archives*, 1998, 42048.

[494] *Keesing's Contemporary Archives*, 1997, 41672.

[495] E de Wet, *The Chapter VII Powers of the United Nations Security Council*, above n 4, 304.

[496] U Villani, 'Les rapports entre l'ONU et les organizations régionales dans le domaine du maintien de la paix', above n 36, 413–14.

[497] See: JM Ballencie and A de la Grange (eds), *Mondes Rebelles. Guerres civiles et violences politiques* (Paris, Michalon, 1999) 1342.

[498] SC Res 858 (1993) of 24 August 1993.

[499] *Report of the Secretary-General concerning the situation in Abkhazia, Georgia*, 25 January 1994, S/1994/80.

[500] See: *Statement by the Council of Heads of State of the Commonwealth of Independent States concerning a peace-keeping operation in the Georgian-Abkhaz conflict zone*, 25 April 1994, S/1994/476.

of Russian troops, was subsequently approved by the Security Council in the context of various resolutions consecrating the deployment of the MONUG, in close collaboration with the CIS troops.[501]

As in the case of ECOMOG operations in Liberia and Sierra Leone, a reading of the relevant documents shows that Security Council approbation related only to the peace-keeping operations that are non-coercive in their essence. The 1993 operation by Russian troops within 'tripartite control groups' (Georgian–Abkhaz–Russian) was then approved by the Security Council in its resolution 858 (1993) of 24 August 1993, by which it 'welcome[d] the planned deployment of mixed temporary control groups composed of Georgian, Abkhaz and Russian units whose task was to consolidate the ceasefire'.[502] In the discussions surrounding the voting of this resolution, several States emphasised that the deployment of the tripartite control groups was done under the Sotchi Agreement among all the parties to the conflict.[503] As for the 1994 CIS operation it was approved by the Security Council in several resolutions by which it 'Commend[ed] the efforts of the members of the CIS directed towards the maintenance of a cease-fire in Abkhazia', while speaking of a 'peace-keeping force'.[504] The Council reaffirmed several times that the operation was being carried out in its view with the agreement of the parties to the conflict.[505] The debates that surrounded the adoption of these resolutions further confirm that it was as a non-coercive peace-keeping operation not requiring its authorisation that the UN Security Council intended to approve of the operation. Most States highlighted the point that the CIS intervened at the request of both the Georgian authorities and Abkhaz separatists.[506]

It is true that before the beginning of these 'peace-keeping operations', Georgia had complained of support from Russian units stationed in Abkhazia for independentist forces.[507] However, it cannot be considered that those interventions against Georgia's will, if they did happen, would have been the subject of approval by the Security Council for the peace-keeping operations by Russia. As seen, the operations that were approved by the Council were precisely defined, precluding any extension of the scope of that approval to other interventions, even if they too were by Russian troops. On the contrary, the interventions of the type Georgia complained of were condemned by the Security Council in its resolution 876

---

[501] See below.

[502] SC Res 858 (1993) of 24 August 1993, para 6.

[503] France and United Kingdom; S/PV.3268, 24 August 1993.

[504] SC Res 937(1994) of 21 July 1994, paras 3 and 4; see also SC Res 971 (1995) of 12 January 1995, 993 (1995) of 11 May 1995, 1036 (1996) of 12 January 1996, 1069 (1997) of 12 July 1996, 1150 (1998) of 30 January 1998.

[505] SC Res 934 (1994) of 30 June 1994 and 937 (1994) of 21 July 1994.

[506] France and Russia (S/PV.3398, 30 June 1994, 2–3); Germany, USA, France, Argentina, New Zealand, Brazil, Spain and Nigeria (S/PV.3407, 21 July 1994).

[507] *Report of the Secretary-General on the situation in Abkhazia, Republic of Georgia*, S/25188, 28 January 1993, 3.

(1993) by which it 'Call[ed] on all States to prevent the provision from their territories or by persons under their jurisdiction of all assistance, other than humanitarian assistance, to the Abkhaz side and in particular to prevent the supply of any weapons and munitions'.[508]

Under these circumstances, the case of Georgia can be understood by using the same reasoning as for Liberia and then Sierra Leone. Even if one may contest their viewpoint in the light of the facts, the intervening States themselves relied on the assent of the parties[509] and considered they were acting in a non-coercive framework that consequently did not require Security Council authorisation. When the mandate of the collective forces for restoring peace in Georgia was extended by the CIS, it was specifically underscored that the presence of those forces in Abkhazia was based on the consent of the Georgian and Abkhaz parties.[510] Third States too seem to have interpreted the events in this way; at any rate, one cannot deduce from their silence any *opinio juris* attesting to the emergence of a rule admitting armed interventions on the basis of a retroactive authorisation from the Security Council.

Finally, these three precedents are certainly significant. By characterising armed operations by States or regional agencies in a context of incomplete consensus (especially insofar as one of the parties to the conflict at some time at least opposed the operation) as non-coercive measures, they convey a relatively loose interpretation of article 53 of the UN Charter. It will be recalled on this issue that in 1965 the US had developed the same type of argument to justify its intervention in the Dominican Republic under the aegis of the OAS, an intervention which it characterised as a non-coercive peace-keeping operation.[511] The argument did not at the time convince all of the UN Member States. Things seem to have been different in the cases of Liberia, Sierra Leone and Georgia, perhaps because the consent of the State in question could be more clearly established. In any event, it seems clear that the scope of article 53 does not apply to actions conducted with the consent of the State concerned. In such cases, one cannot therefore presume the existence of an 'authorisation' within the meaning of that provision.

b) Precedents Where There is Supposedly Implicit Approval of Military Intervention

Several commentators have defended the idea that an armed intervention undertaken without the prior authorisation of the Security Council could be

---

[508] SC Res 876 (1993) of 19 October 1993, para 8.

[509] See the agreements in *Report of the Secretary-General in pursuance of Security Council Resolution 849 (1993)*, S/26250, 5 August 1993.

[510] *Cease-fire Agreement*, Moscow, 14 May 1994, S/1994/583; *Decision concerning an extension of and an addition to the mandate of the Collective Peacekeeping Forces in the conflict zone in Abkhazia*, Georgia, 17 October 1996, S/1996/874.

[511] Above, s I.

legitimised not only *ex post*, but also implicitly. In some instances, it has been considered that the simple absence of condemnation by the Security Council was equivalent to an authorisation;[512] in others, such *a posteriori* authorisation was deduced from resolutions that, unlike the precedents of Liberia, Sierra Leone and Georgia, did not explicitly approve an intervention but consecrated its effects on the ground.[513] This type of argument was defended especially to justify the 1999 military intervention against Yugoslavia where, in addition to the 1998 resolutions, the behaviour of the Security Council after the outbreak of war was invoked. And yet, upon examination, it turns out that there is no precedent establishing a legal intent to approve armed interventions undertaken without prior authorisation.

The War Against Yugoslavia (1999)

The argument that the absence of condemnation by the Security Council of an armed intervention is tantamount to tacit approval of it was raised as a legal basis for NATO's intervention in Kosovo.[514]

First, emphasis was laid on a Russian draft resolution condemning the action by the Atlantic Alliance and that was rejected by 12 votes to three.[515] The reasoning is no more convincing in the case of Kosovo than in that of many other precedents where military interventions were conducted without Security Council approval or condemnation.[516] This situation simply reflects the differences in points of view that may prevail among the permanent members of the Security Council. To consider otherwise would be to make lawful all the armed interventions during the Cold War by the major powers, whether in Afghanistan, Hungary or Czechoslovakia on one side or the Dominican Republic, Grenada or Panama on the other.[517] Patently, this is not what the permanent members of the Security Council themselves thought, since they did not fail to accuse each other of blatant violations of the UN Charter. Moreover, that the Security Council's silence cannot have the effect of making lawful an armed operation carried out

---

[512] D Momtaz, 'La délégation par le Conseil de sécurité de l'exécution de ses actions coercitives aux organizations régionales', above n 36, 113.

[513] B Simma, 'NATO, the UN and the Use of Force: Legal aspects' (1999) 10 *EJIL* 4 and 10.

[514] M Bettati, 'Les premières leçons du Kosovo', *Le Courrier de l'UNESCO*, July/August 1999, 60; see also Y Nouvel, 'La position du Conseil de sécurité face à l'action militaire engagée par l'OTAN et ses membres contre la RFY' (1999) 32 *AFDI* 297.

[515] S/PV.3989, 26 March 1999, 6.

[516] P van Walsum, 'The Security Council and the Use of Force: the cases of Kosovo, East Timor and Iraq', above n 298, 68.

[517] M Kohen, 'L'emploi de la force et la crise du Kosovo: vers un nouveau désordre juridique international', above n 292, 123; F Dubuisson, 'La problématique de la légalité de l'opération "Force alliée" contre la Yougoslavie: enjeux et questionnements', above n 211, 158–59; A Pellet, 'La guerre du Kosovo—Le fait rattrapé par le droit', *Forum du droit international*, 1999/1, 163–64; P Pirrone, 'The use of force in the framework of the Organization of American States' in A Cassese (ed), *The Current Legal Regulation of the Use of Force* (Dordrecht/Boston/Lancaster, Martinus Nijhof, 1986) 228.

without authorisation is also confirmed by the case law of the International Court of Justice. In *Military and Paramilitary Activities*, the fact that the armed intervention in question was not condemned by the Security Council did not prevent the Court from declaring the intervention unlawful.[518] It was to deal with this type of legal hairsplitting that the Court had, in its first decision on the merits, recalled that the principle of non-intervention still held 'whatever be the present defects in international organization'.[519] There is, then, no reason, in cases where the Security Council has not condemned armed action undertaken without its authorisation, to see precedents capable of relaxing the terms of the UN Charter.[520]

By a second argument, Security Council authorisation might be presumed from the adoption of a resolution consecrating the effects of Operation Allied Force against Yugoslavia: resolution 1244 (1999), by which the Security Council approved the agreement between the belligerents, without condemning in any way the military intervention that led to it. For some commentators, by endorsing the position of the G8 of 6 May 1999 which itself legitimised the 'war goals' of the NATO member countries, the Security Council allegedly approved the military intervention against Yugoslavia.[521] And yet, no evidence for this can be extracted from an objective examination of the text of resolution 1244 (1999) and of the discussions over its adoption.[522] The actual text remains silent on the issue of the lawfulness or even the legitimacy of NATO's action: the Security Council merely authorises the deployment of security forces, with a substantial participation by NATO, in the context of the agreement between the Alliance, Russia and the FRY.[523] The text also provides for the deploy-

---

[518] ICJ Rep (1986).

[519] ICJ, *Corfu Channel*, ICJ Rep (1949) 35. See also: GA Res 377(V) ('Uniting for Peace') of 3 November 1950: 'failure of the Security Council to discharge its responsibilities on behalf of all Member States [. . .] does not relieve Member States of their obligations [. . .]'.

[520] E Jimenez de Arechaga, 'International Law in the Past Third of a Century', *RCADI* (1978) I, vol 159, 142; FX de Lima, *Intervention in International Law* (Den Haag, Uitgevrij Pax Nederland, 1971) 102; J Lobel and M Ratner, 'Bypassing the Security Council: Ambiguous Authorizations to Use Force, Cease Fires and the Iraqi Regime', above n 351, 130; U Villani, 'Les rapports entre l'ONU et les organizations régionales dans le domaine du maintien de la paix', above n 36, 377–79; Y Nouvel, 'La position du Conseil de sécurité face à l'action militaire engagée par l'OTAN et ses Etats membres contre la République fédérale de Yougoslavie', above n 292, 299–300; JF Murphy, *The United States and the Rule of Law in International Affairs*, above n 129, 158.

[521] A Pellet, 'La guerre du Kosovo—Le fait rattrapé par le droit', above n 517, 164.

[522] E de Wet, *The Chapter VII Powers of the United Nations Security Council*, above n 4, 307; LA Sicilianos, 'Entre multilatéralisme et unilatéralisme: l'autorisation par le Conseil de sécurité de recourir à la force', above n 34, 206–08; LA Sicilianos, 'L'autorisation par le Conseil de sécurité de recourir à la force: une tentative d'évaluation', above n 5, 46; F Dubuisson, 'La problématique de la légalité de l'opération "Force alliée" contre la Yougoslavie: enjeux et questionnements', above n 211, 160–61; M Kohen, 'L'emploi de la force et la crise du Kosovo: vers un nouveau désordre juridique international', above n 292, 128–29; G Cahin, 'Le rôle des organes politiques des Nations Unies', above n 304, 172–73.

[523] SC Res 1244 (1999) of 10 June 1999, para 5; see also C Rousseau, 'Chronique des faits internationaux' (1999) 103 *RGDIP* 739–41.

ment in Kosovo of international civil and security presences for an initial period of 12 months and the appointment by the Secretary-General of a special representative tasked with directing Kosovo's civil administration that should allow the population to enjoy substantial autonomy within the FRY.[524] However, one will seek in vain any form of legalisation—or conversely of condemnation—of the military operation that preceded the conclusion of these agreements.[525] This is a long way from the terms used for example in the resolutions on Liberia, Sierra Leone and Georgia, by which the Security Council had provided its clear and explicit support for the operations conducted there.[526] Consideration of the circumstances under which this text was adopted confirms this observation. In the debates that preceded its adoption, no State claimed that resolution 1244 (1999) should be construed as a legalisation of NATO's armed action. Conversely, several States on this occasion reiterated their condemnation of the military operation.[527] In this context, it seems awkward to say the least to see in resolution 1244 (1999) more than a simple political ratification of the *fait accompli* among the FRY, Russia and NATO and the establishment for the future of an interim administrative regime for Kosovo.[528] Had the resolution contained a specific approbation of the operation, it would in all likelihood not have been adopted, just as the draft resolution concerning the intervention by NATO Member States was not adopted.[529] In both instances, only the deep divide among Member States (especially permanent members) of the Security Council is an established fact.

Lastly, let us note that, no more outside the Security Council than in it, did States claim that resolution 1244 (1999) legalised NATO's military intervention *a posteriori*. For the intervening powers, it should be observed that several of them were eager to affirm that the intervention in Kosovo should not be considered a legal precedent.[530] Those declarations, made well after resolution 1244 (1999) was adopted, are generally valid and opposed then to any hypothesis that the existing rule is relaxed, whether through presumed prior authorisation or any hypothetical *ex post* approval. As for the many States that condemned the intervention,[531] they obviously did not backtrack after the adoption of resolution 1244 (1999). Once again,

---

[524] SC Res 1244 (1999) of 10 June 1999, paras 5, 6 and 10.

[525] The intervention was condemned by the UN Sub-Commission on the Promotion and Protection of Human Rights, Res 1999/2, August 1999, E/CN.4/2000/2; see M Dennis, 'The 55th session of the UN Commission of the Human Rights' (2000) 94 *AJIL* 191.

[526] C Chinkin, 'The Legality of NATO's Action in the Former Republic of Yugoslavia (FRY) under International Law', above n 292, 915.

[527] See, eg: Russia, China and Brazil; S/PV.4011, 10 June 1999.

[528] M Kohen, 'L'emploi de la force et la crise du Kosovo: vers un nouveau désordre juridique international', above n 292, 128–29.

[529] P Weckel, 'L'emploi de la force contre la Yougoslavie ou la Charte fissurée' (2000) 104 *RGDIP* 30.

[530] See above and below, ch 8, s II.

[531] See below.

there is no evidence for the emergence of a new rule of international law, the Kosovo precedent paradoxically showing States' (including the intervening States') concern for maintaining the existing legal regime.[532]

The Wars Against Afghanistan (2001) and Iraq (2003)

As already indicated, it is difficult to consider the Afghanistan and Iraq precedents as pleading in favour of an authorisation that might be presumed from the Security Council's behaviour before the outbreak of those wars.[533] It should, however, be noted that in both instances the Security Council not only never condemned the military interventions when they were launched but furthermore later authorised the intervening powers to deploy on the ground with a view to normalising the situation. Might one deduce from this some sort of approval, and therefore *a posteriori* authorisation of the military actions previously engaged upon? I do not think so, for either of these precedents.

As concerns Afghanistan, in resolution 1378 (2001) of 14 November 2001, adopted when there were prospects of a rapid success of the Afghan opposition forces of the Northern Alliance against the Taliban, the Security Council 'Supporting international efforts to root out terrorism', 'Expresse[d] its strong support for the efforts of the Afghan people to establish a new and transitional administration leading to the formation of a government' and affirmed that the UN had 'a central role' to play in the crisis.[534] That resolution did not contain, though, any reference to the ongoing military operation under US command. Under the circumstances, it seems to attest rather to the Security Council's will not to make any explicit pronouncement on the scope of Operation Enduring Freedom. In any event, it cannot be considered an approval of it.[535] On 20 December 2001, the Security Council adopted resolution 1386 (2001), by which it noted the agreement of the new Afghan authorities, and then 'Authorize[d] the Member States participating in the International Security Assistance Force to take all necessary measures to fulfil its mandate'.[536] Nothing at all in the text or in the debates that preceded its adoption indicates that the authorisation could have a retroactive character.[537] In short, the Afghan precedent confirms that the Security Council tends to substitute for inter-

---

[532] O Corten and B Delcourt, 'Kosovo: le droit international renforcé?' (2000) 8 *L'Observateur des Nations Unies* (Aix-en-Provence) 133–47; see also X Pacreau, *De l'intervention au Kosovo en 1999 à l'intervention en Irak de 2003* (Paris, LGDJ, 2006) 149–52; A Peyro Llopis, 'Le système de sécurité collective entre anarchie et fiction. Observations sur la pratique récente', above n 436, 1411–13.

[533] See above.

[534] SC Res 1378 (2001) of 14 November 2001, preamble and paras 1 and 3.

[535] cp Liberia and Sierra Leone; O Corten and F Dubuisson, 'L'hypothèse d'une règle émergente fondant une intervention militaire sur une "autorisation implicite" du Conseil de sécurité', above n 351, 893–97.

[536] SC Res 1386 (2001) of 20 December 2001, para 3.

[537] S/PV.4443, 20 December 2001.

vening powers to manage a post-conflict situation, as part of its mission to maintain international peace and security.[538] This pragmatic behaviour cannot, though, readily be construed as some form of *ex post* authorisation.

In the case of Iraq, the Security Council adopted several resolutions in the weeks and months following the outbreak of conflict.[539] None of those resolutions purports to legalise or declare lawful or to authorise retroactively the war that was begun on 23 March 2003.[540] In the debates that preceded their adoption, some States wished 'to caution the Security Council from being drawn into drafting a resolution that would provide tacit or implied approval of the military operations that are under way in Iraq at this time'.[541] Russia stipulated that the adoption of resolution 1483 (2003) 'of course, in no way signifies any type of legitimization of the military action being carried out by the coalition in violation of the Charter of the United Nations'.[542] In short, here too, while the Council's pragmatism led it to consecrate, in fact, the effect of the military intervention, that intervention was never, in law, authorised or legalised *a posteriori*.[543]

All told, no precedent attests to a general agreement of States to admit, in positive international law, a merely presumed authorisation of the Security Council. While some arguments to this effect might have been advanced by certain States when they relied on existing resolutions to justify a military intervention, they are far from having convinced the community of States as a whole, whether in the case of Iraq or of Kosovo. As for the possibility of authorisation after the beginning of an operation, it has only been evoked in doctrine, with the precedents sometimes cited (Liberia, Sierra Leone and Kosovo) not revealing any *opinio juris*, even of the intervening States.[544] This observation drawn from practice alone should not come as a surprise. Allowance must also be made for refusals and objections on principle to the evolution of international law in this direction.

---

[538] O Corten, 'Vers un renforcement des pouvoirs du Conseil de sécurité dans la lutte contre le terrorisme?' in K Bannelier *et al* (eds), *Le droit international face au terrorisme* (Paris, Pedone, 2002) 259–78.

[539] SC Res 1472 (2003) of 28 March 2003; SC Res 1476 (2003) of 24 April 2003; SC Res 1483 (2003) of 23 May 2003, para 1; SC Res 1511 (2003) of 16 October 2003.

[540] E de Wet, *The Chapter VII Powers of the United Nations Security Council*, above n 4, 289–90; but see L Condorelli, 'Le Conseil de sécurité entre autorisation de la légitime défense et substitution de la sécurité collective: remarques au sujet de la résolution 1546 (2004)' in SFDI, *Les métamorphoses de la sécurité collective* (Paris, Pedone, 2005) 239.

[541] South Africa, S/PV.4726, 26 March 2003, 21; see also Cuba (ibid, 23), Brazil (ibid, 28) and A Lagerwall, 'L'administration du territoire irakien: un exemple de reconnaissance et d'aide au maintien d'une occation résultant d'un acte d'agression?' (2006) 39 *RBDI* 265.

[542] S/PV.4732, 28 March 2003, 3.

[543] G Cahin, 'Le rôle des organes politiques des Nations Unies', above n 304, 172–74; JM Sorel, 'L'ONU et l'Irak: le vil plomb ne s'est pas transformé en or pur' (2004) 108 *RGDIP* 849–54.

[544] See also: 'United Kingdom Materials on International Law' (1994) 65 *BYBIL* 695.

B. Refusals and Obstacles of Principle to Recognition of a Presumed Authorisation

Beyond the debates about any particular event, mention must also be made of the refusal upon principle of the argument of presumed authorisation, which refusal was manifested by many States, and that can probably be explained by obstacles of principle with regard to the UN Charter.

States' Reluctance to Admit, on Principle, the Possibility of 'Presumed Authorisation'

The possibility of a presumed authorisation was raised during debates about the prohibition of the use of force, first in the context of the development of General Assembly resolutions 2625 (XXV) and 3314 (XXIX), and then in that about the documents produced for the sixtieth anniversary of the UN. In view of the stances taken on these occasions it can certainly not be asserted that the argument of presumed authorisation was accepted by all UN Member States, far from it.

a) The Discussions Preceding the Adoption of General Assembly Resolutions 2625 (XXV) and 3314 (XXIX)

In the 1960s, probably in the face of fears raised by certain enforcement measures taken under the cover of regional agencies,[545] many States made pronouncements on the notion of authorisation in article 53 of the Charter. Those States emphasised the need to obtain what they called 'express' authorisation, while specifying sometimes that such authorisation had to be 'prior'. The following two affirmations may be mentioned along these lines:

—The use of force by regional agencies, except in the case of self-defence, requires the *express authorisation* of the Security Council in accordance with Article 53 of the United Nations Charter; (emphasis added)[546]
—[F]orce could lawfully be used when it was decided upon by a regional agency with the *express authorisation of the Security Council*. It would be very serious if the formulation of the principle under consideration did not reflect the Charter's severe restrictions on the right of regional agencies to use force. Any relaxation of those restrictions would jeopardize the right of States to territorial integrity and political independence, which was upheld in the Charter, and would undermine the role of the Organization. The Charter principles, includ-

---

[545] See above; Dominican Republic (1960) and Cuba (1962).
[546] Para II of the project presented by Argentina, Chile, Guatemala, Mexico and Venezuela A/AC.125/L.49, III, quoted by Mexico; A/AC.125/SR.66, 1 August 1967, 7; see also A/C.6/ S.R.886, 1 December 1965, 293, para 34 and the views expressed by Chile (A/AC.125/L.23, 24 March 1966, para h) and A/AC.125/SR.22, 23 March 1966, para 31) and Venezuela (A/C.6/S.R.1002, 20 November 1967, para 14).

ing the one on non-use of force, applied fully as between all States, whether or not they were members of regional agencies. (emphasis added)[547]

As far as I know, no challenge was raised whether in the Friendly Relations Committee or in the Sixth Commission of the UN General Assembly.

However, a contrary opinion in the early 1970s can be pointed out in the debates about the definition of aggression. US representative M Schwebel considered a presumed authorisation could be justified for regional organisations since 'Article 53 of the Charter referred, not to a decision, but to an authorisation by the Security Council and it did not specify whether such authorisation should be anterior or posterior, expressed or implied'.[548]

To the best of my knowledge, only Italy officially declared as much.[549] Many other States, on the contrary, vigorously opposed that claim. In the terms of the Cypriot representative:

> It had been argued that the Council's authorization might be implicit or given after the event . . . There was no question, either in Chapter VI or in Article 53, of implicit authorization. Under Article 53, 'the Security Council shall, where appropriate', utilize the regional agencies. To do that, it must decide, in each case, whether regional agencies ought to be utilized. The possibility of implicit authorization was therefore excluded. Article 53 further stipulated that no enforcement action was to be taken by regional agencies without the authorization of the Security Council. It was therefore clear that authorization must precede action. Actually, it did happen that action was taken illegally as a result of exceptional emergency situations, and that authorization was given only after the event. However, the exception must not be confused with the well-established rule.[550]

Examples as varied as those of Ecuador,[551] Gabon,[552] Lebanon,[553] Yugoslavia[554] and Cuba[555] may be cited, to which one might add Chile[556] and Uruguay.[557] In view of these stances, to which one might add those set

---

[547] Representative of Sweden; A/AC.125/SR.86, 13 September 1968, 44; see also Czechoslovakia (A/C.6/S.R.871, 8 November 1965 and A/AC.125/SR.18, 21 March 1966) and Cuba (A/C.6/S.R.893, 8 December 1965).

[548] A/AC.134/SR.67, 30 July 1970 in A/AC.134/SR.67-78, 11.

[549] According to the representative of this State, 'while Article 53 of the Charter made enforcement action by regional agencies contingent upon the authorization of the Security Council, it was arguable that in certain cases such authorization might follow the enforcement action or be given implicitly' (A/AC.134/SR.85, 9 February 1971 in A/AC.134/SR.79-91, 44).

[550] A/AC.134/SR.68, 31 July 1970 in A/AC.134/SR.67-78, 18.

[551] A/AC.134/SR.67, 30 July 1970 in A/AC.134/SR.67-78, 13–14.

[552] A/C.6/SR.1205, 22 October 1970.

[553] A/C.6/SR.1212, 30 October 1970.

[554] *Rapport du Comité spécial pour la question de la définition de l'agression*, 11 March–12 April 1974, AG, *doc off*, 29th sess, Supp no 19 (A/9619), 28; A/C.6/SR.1478, 16 October 1974.

[555] A/C.6/SR.1479, 18 October 1974.

[556] A/C.6/SR.1167, 3 December 1969.

[557] M Gros Espiell, representing Uruguay, stated that 'the right to use force under regional arrangements or through regional agencies must be vested only in the legally organized international community as a whole, i.e. with *the express authorization of the Security Council in accordance with Article 53 of the Charter*' (emphasis added; A/AC.134/SR.57, 20 July 1970 in A/AC.134/SR.52-66, 33).

out above in the context of discussion on friendly relations, it cannot be denied that the presumed authorisation argument did not meet with general or even significant approval among UN Member States, far from it. The balance of power has not changed since if one examines the debates for the sixty years of the UN.

b) The UN Discussions Preceding the Adoption of the World Summit Outcome

The presumed authorisation question was not directly addressed in the debates held for the UN's sixtieth anniversary.[558] Nonetheless, the published documents do contain a record of the possibility of *ex post* authorisation. Two excerpts should attract our attention in this respect. First the High-Level Panel Report of December 2004 that formed a basis for discussion states that 'Authorization from the Security Council should in all cases be sought for regional peace operations, recognizing that in some urgent situations that authorization may be sought after such operations have commenced'.[559] A few weeks later, the African Union States adopted a common position whereby 'The African Union agrees with the Panel that the intervention of Regional Organisations should be with the approval of the Security Council; although in certain situations, such approval could be granted "after the fact" in circumstances requiring urgent action'.[560] From the highlighted expressions one might think that article 53 of the Charter is henceforth to be interpreted as admitting some retroactive authorisations, despite all the problems that such an interpretation raises.

To my mind, for such a conclusion to be taken into account it should be based on clearer legal positions. If we turn back to the High-Level Panel Report, it will be observed that its emphasis, in the part on the lawfulness of the use of force, is on the Security Council's responsibility and on the broader opportunities to authorise the use of force which that body may rely on.[561] No possibility for unilateral military intervention by States or other organisations, even provisionally, is envisaged, at least outside of the specific hypothesis of self-defence. In fact, the excerpt from the 'High-Level Panel' report taken up by the AU must be understood politically: it is intended to encourage closer and more integrated cooperation between the UN and regional agencies, especially in the case of peace-keeping operations. It is in that framework alone that the group considers that 'the intervention of Regional Organisations *should be* with the approval of the Security Council', without for all that claiming it is a legal obligation arising from article 53. (emphasis added)[562] It can be understood that

---

[558] But see the views expressed by Russia, reaffirming the necessity to respect Chapter VIII of the Charter; A/55/PV.29, 27 September 2000.

[559] *A More Secure World. Our shared Responsibility*, A/59/565, 78, para 272(a).

[560] Ezulwini consensus, Ext/EX.CL/2 (VII); www.africa-union.org; see also above.

[561] *A more secure world: Our shared responsibility*, Report of the Secretary-General's High-level Panel on Threats, Challenges and Change, UN (2004) at 62 *ff*, para 185 *ff*.

[562] ibid, para 272(a).

authorisation and overseeing of regional peace-keeping actions by the Security Council will provide better coordination and confer a clearer and more forceful mandate on the relevant forces. It is in this context that the emphasis on the possibility of seeking authorisation 'after the fact', which the African Union underscores, must be understood. The schema defended corresponds then to what was observed in Liberia and then in Sierra Leone: a regional organisation intervenes initially at the request of the local author-ities and so presents its action as a peace-keeping operation; thereafter, the UN is called on to oversee and bolster the operation, including financially; that collaboration is reflected by a clear mandate given both to the UN forces and to the relevant regional organisation. In this schema, there is nothing to assert that a regional organisation can intervene militarily against a State—so without its consent—and then to ask for the retroactive autho-risation of the Security Council. It will be noticed besides that mention of 'after the fact' authorisation is not to be found in the part of the document specifically about 'the question of legality'.

It will further be observed that absolutely no excerpt from the 2005 World Summit Outcome, which is the only text finally accepted by all the States, can plead for a revision or new interpretation of article 53. On the contrary, in the part of this text on the use of force, States reassert that 'the relevant provisions of the Charter are sufficient to address the full range of threats to international peace and security. We further reaffirm the authority of the Security Council to mandate enforcement action to main-tain and restore international peace and security'.[563] In the part on peace-keeping, States emphasise the need for better cooperation between the UN and regional agencies,[564] but without making pronouncements on the pos-sibility of 'after the fact' authorisation. This possibility was not evoked either by the Secretary-General in his report,[565] nor by States when they discussed these texts in the UN General Assembly. Some States besides asserted on this occasion that no new interpretation of the Charter was needed to face the new challenges[566] and more specifically that Security Council authori-sation had to be, under the Charter, both prior[567] and explicit.[568] In short, no agreement by the international community of States as a whole can be made out seeking a change or relaxation of article 53 of the UN Charter.

[563] *2005 World Summit Outcome*, A/RES/60/1, 24 October 2005, para 79.
[564] ibid, para 93.
[565] *In larger freedom: towards development, security and human rights for all*, A/59/2005, 21 March 2005, paras 213–15.
[566] Russia; A/59/PV.87, 7 April 2005.
[567] According to China, 'the Security Council is the only body that can decide the use of force. Regional arrangements or organizations must obtain Security Council authorization prior to any enforcement action'; *Position paper of the People's Republic of China on the UN Reform*, 7 June 1965, point 7; www.reformtheun.org.
[568] Azerbaijan demands an 'explicit mandate of the Security Council'; *Statement by the Delegation of Azerbaijan at the Informal Meeting of the Plenary on the High-Level Plenary Meeting of the GA of September 2005*, 1 July 2005, para 10; www.reformtheun.org.

One final point should be made along these lines. In late 2004, the 46 French-speaking States (la Francophonie) from all regions of the world made a statement on the concept of the responsibility to protect, to which we shall return later.[569] On this occasion, the States affirmed that the international community is responsible for reacting to protect populations that are victims of human rights abuses 'under a *precise and explicit* Security Council mandate'. (emphasis added)[570] That declaration seems decidedly to reflect the *opinio juris* of the vast majority of States that is plainly against the idea of presumed authorisation, probably because of the problems of principle that should now be touched upon.

Incompatiblity of the Presumed Authorisation with the Legal Regime of the UN Charter

As already pointed out, the UN Charter does not require that to be valid, a Security Council authorisation need comply with any special forms.[571] Article 53 simply requires an authorisation, and the practice that has developed since the 1990s has led to a broad interpretation of article 42 by virtue of which the technique of authorisation allows the Council, provided certain conditions are met, to delegate the exercise of its police power.[572] The rationale behind the legal regime of collective security appears to me, however, to be radically incompatible with the very idea of a presumed authorisation, *a fortiori*, if one claims it is based on an *a posteriori* approval.[573] Five factors can be evoked from the outset.

First, it will be recalled[574] that, in the part of its draft on State responsibility given over to consent as a circumstance precluding unlawfulness, the International Law Commission, which notably envisaged cases of the use of force, had always insisted on '*clearly established, really expressed (which precludes merely presumed consent)*' consent, failing which cases of abuse would be too common. (emphasis added)[575] Likewise, the International Court of Justice insisted on the consent being clearly established, especially in the domain of the non-use of force.[576] The *ratio legis* underpinning this reasoning is entirely transposable to the hypothesis of Security Council authorisation. In the case where we are faced *a priori* with a violation of article 2(4), the purpose and goal of the rule, as well as its peremptory

---

[569] Above, ch 8, s I.

[570] Our translation; *Déclaration de Ouagadougou du XXème sommet de la Francophonie*, 27 November 2004; www.diplomatie.gouv.fr.

[571] Above.

[572] Above, s I.

[573] LA Sicilianos, 'Entre multilatéralisme et unilatéralisme: l'autorisation par le Conseil de sécurité de recourir à la force', above n 34, 251–55.

[574] Above, ch 5, s I.

[575] (1979) *YILC*, vol II (Part Two), 112.

[576] See: ICJ, *Armed Activities (DRC v Uganda)*; above, ch 5, s I.

character,[577] require a restrictive interpretation.[578] This general principle excludes any idea of presumption from a circumstance that would have the effect of validating a use of force, whether consent of the relevant State or a Security Council authorisation.[579]

Secondly, the idea of a presumption is incompatible with the institutional logic behind the Security Council's powers. Under article 27 of the Charter, a Security Council decision requires a positive vote of nine of its members *and no negative vote* from any of its permanent members. This condition presupposes that, at the time of voting, each State knows exactly what the object of the Security Council decision is, especially in the case of so serious a matter as the use of force.[580] So, the scholarly assertions that such or such a resolution contains an authorisation to use force cannot be admitted unless this authorisation, short of appearing clearly in the text, was explicitly contemplated and accepted at the time of the debates.[581] There can be no question, then, of claiming that such an authorisation exists because, *after* the resolution was adopted, some States claimed as much, although they had not done so at the time of voting.[582] One cannot circumvent the existence of a right of veto—and more generally voting conditions—in that way: it is *at the time* the resolution is adopted that the authorisation must be established.[583]

Thirdly, it is important once again to take into account the limits on the power of delegation the Security Council can employ. As seen, there is nothing to stop the Council taking armed action by entrusting such a mission to Member States acting on a national basis or within the framework of regional agencies. The collective security requirement surrounding the

---

[577] Above, ch 4, s I.

[578] AA Cançado Trindade, 'The Primacy of International Law Over Force' in M Kohen (ed), *Promoting Justice, Human Rights and Conflict Resolution Through International Law. Liber Amicorum Lucius Caflisch* (Leiden, Martinus Nijhoff, 2007) 1053; D Dormoy, 'Réflexions à propos de l'autorisation implicite de recourir à la force', above n 35, 224; U Villani, 'Les rapports entre l'ONU et les organizations régionales dans le domaine du maintien de la paix', above n 36, 371; LA Sicilianos, 'L'autorisation par le Conseil de sécurité de recourir à la force: une tentative d'évaluation', above n 5, 47; D Sarooshi, *The United Nations and the Development of Collective Security. The Delegation by the United Nations Security Council of its Chapter VII Powers*, above n 3, 44.

[579] See also: *La politique étrangère de la France*, September–October 1983, 109 in 'La pratique suisse en matière de droit international public' (2002) *RSDIE*, n° 9.1.

[580] As M Wood states: 'it is not helpful to suggest that authorization may be express or implied: what is needed is simply that the force has been authorized', 'Towards New Circumstances in Which the Use of Force May Be Authorized? The Cases of Humanitarian Intervention, Counter-Terrorism, and Weapons of Mass Destruction' in N Blokker and N Schrijver (eds), *The Security Council and the Use of Force. Theory and Reality—A Need for Change?* (Leiden/Boston, Martinus Nijhoff, 2005) 79.

[581] O Corten and F Dubuisson, 'L'hypothèse d'une règle émergente fondant une intervention militaire sur une 'autorisation implicite' du Conseil de sécurité', above n 351, 907.

[582] LA Sicilianos, 'L'autorisation par le Conseil de sécurité de recourir à la force: une tentative d'évaluation', above n 5, 45.

[583] ibid; see also C Schreuer, 'Regionalism v Universalism' (1995) 6 *EJIL* 492.

Charter implies, however, that the Council keep control of the military operation so delegated at all times, which implies the existence of certain guarantee mechanisms, consisting particularly in the filing of reports by the delegate States.[584] As several commentators have pointed out, such mechanisms are only meaningful if objectives and limits have been clearly drawn up by the Security Council. By definition, that is not the case if the authorisation itself cannot be clearly established.[585] Under such a hypothesis, States intervene militarily without limitation or constraint, which is plainly incompatible with the Charter requirements that confer on the Security Council itself the main responsibility for maintaining international peace and security.[586]

Fourthly, it will be observed that while the three problems just mentioned generally oppose any presumed authorisation, they more radically still exclude the idea of retroactive authorisation as evoked until now by doctrine. This is particularly true of the need to comply with article 27(3) of the Charter. In the examples evoked, whether Liberia, Sierra Leone or Georgia, the Council merely approved or welcomed some military operation or other.[587] Never was a vote held on any genuine 'authorisation' or even on a 'validation' which, in a strictly legal sense, would have had as its purpose to legalise the military action taken.[588] To be admissible, the authorisation argument should be based on a vote relating clearly to this point, and not on any general considerations that seem above all to be political in scope. *A fortiori* an *ex post* authorisation cannot be deduced from a mere silence.[589]

Fifth and finally, the question can be seriously raised of the effects of a possible first precedent where the Security Council would claim, clearly this time, to 'authorise' a military action already underway. This hypothesis of *a posteriori* validation would go against the whole logic of the intertemporal law of international responsibility.[590] An act is characterised as unlawful if, *at the time it is done*, it proves contrary to a rule of international law.[591] A

---

[584] Above, s I.

[585] E de Wet, *The Chapter VII Powers of the United Nations Security Council*, above n 4, 268–70; D Sarooshi, *The United Nations and the Development of Collective Security. The Delegation by the United Nations Security Council of its Chapter VII Powers*, above n 3, 155; J Wolf, 'Regional Arrangements and the United Nations Charter', *EPIL*, vol 4, 95.

[586] J Lobel and M Ratner, 'Bypassing the Security Council: Ambiguous Authorizations to Use Force, Cease Fires and the Iraqi Regime', above n 351, 135.

[587] See above.

[588] U Villani, 'Les rapports entre l'ONU et les organizations régionales dans le domaine du maintien de la paix', above n 36, 379; D Dormoy, 'Réflexions à propos de l'autorisation implicite de recourir à la force', above n 35, 224; see also LA Sicilianos, 'L'autorisation par le Conseil de sécurité de recourir à la force: une tentative d'évaluation', above n 5, 39–40.

[589] C Walter, 'Security Control over Regional Action', above n 174, 183–84.

[590] M Forteau, *Droit de la sécurité collective et droit de la responsabilité internationale de l'Etat*, above n 51, 427.

[591] Article 18 § 1 of the ILC Articles on State Responsibility; GA Res 56/83 of 12 December 2001; see also *Island of Palmas, RSA*, vol II, 845.

military action begun without prior authorisation must therefore be considered contrary to article 2(4) of the Charter and might even be characterised as an armed attack within the meaning of its article 51, with consequently a right of self-defence for the State attacked.[592] If the Security Council came to authorise a military action *ex post*, the situation of the parties to the conflict would be suddenly reversed, with the State that until then had been acting in self-defence becoming *a posteriori* an aggressor State and the State initially considered the aggressor possibly suddenly—and after the event—being able to rely on a law of self-defence. Such a system would generate extreme legal insecurity, with neither the States involved, nor third States—which also have obligations in this respect[593]—being able to determine who is the aggressor and who is aggressed at the critical time.[594] In this context, some States might count on a future Council resolution—that they might consider they are entitled to secure in view of the political context—and think themselves authorised to take *a priori* military action contrary to the Charter.[595] It is pointless insisting on the radical incompatibility of this schema with the very purpose of the rule prohibiting the use of force, which is to discourage military interventions as far as possible.[596] The Security Council's competence to legalise armed attacks *ex post* can also be seriously doubted, as the Charter only gives it competence to 'take' (article 42) or to 'authorise' them (article 53). It will come as no surprise therefore that in practice the Security Council has never claimed to act in this way.

In an attempt to escape from these objections some scholars have tried to justify certain limited forms of *ex post* authorisation. One commentator drew a distinction between authorisation for an armed action already carried out at the time of the resolution and an armed action underway at the time of the authorisation.[597] While the first hypothesis would prove incompatible with the UN Charter, not so the second. In such a case, the Security Council would assume its supervisory function by overseeing and directing the military action undertaken without its approval.[598] Apart from the fact that it cannot, to my mind, rely on any precedent,[599] such a line of

---

[592] Below, ch 7.

[593] Above, ch 3, s II.

[594] F Dubuisson, 'La problématique de la légalité de l'opération "Force alliée" contre la Yougoslavie: enjeux et questionnements', above n 211, 161–62; O Corten and F Dubuisson, 'L'hypothèse d'une règle émergente fondant une intervention militaire sur une 'autorisation implicite' du Conseil de sécurité', above n 351, 906.

[595] D Dormoy, 'Réflexions à propos de l'autorisation implicite de recourir à la force', above n 35, 224; U Villani, 'Les rapports entre l'ONU et les organizations régionales dans le domaine du maintien de la paix', above n 36, 380.

[596] See: L Henkin, 'International Law and the Behaviour of Nations', *RCADI*, t 114, 261; M Akehurst, 'Enforcement Action by Regional Agencies with Special Reference to the Organization of American States', above n 264, 214.

[597] U Villani, 'Les rapports entre l'ONU et les organizations régionales dans le domaine du maintien de la paix', above n 36, 381–89.

[598] ibid, 381.

[599] See above.

argument does not seem convincing to me. First because it seems sometimes difficult to distinguish a military action 'already carried out' from a
military action 'being carried out'. One need only look as far as the war in
Afghanistan, where the US and its allies continue to consider, several years
after it was begun, that certain military actions in that country are still part
of Operation Enduring Freedom launched on 7 October 2001.[600] Should
it be deduced from this that the Security Council might validate an action
several years after it was begun? More fundamentally, it seems to me that
the problems of intertemporal law just evoked are not settled in any way by
this proposal; it is at the time an armed action is *triggered* that the question
of determining the aggressor is posed and so of the State that is acting in
self-defence. In this context, all the fears of excesses in the sense of a
policy of force and of *fait accompli* remain perfectly valid.

Another commentator has sought to answer these objections by invoking
an institution of French administrative law based on the urgency of the situation and the temporary impossibility for the public authorities to remedy
it. By this rationale, 'the subsequent intervention of the Security Council
will not strictly validate the operation after the fact but only note *a posteriori* the existence of exceptional circumstances justifying the enforcement
intervention', with the acting having to be considered as legal *ab initio*.[601]
This claim raises several difficulties, foremost of which is the absence of any
basis in positive international law.[602] Once again, the Charter does not
provide the possibility of exceptional circumstances justifying the taking of
unilateral military action in the expectation or hope that such action will
subsequently be characterised as lawful by the Security Council. The only
notion of urgency written into it relates to the right of self-defence, which
may be exercised even before the Security Council takes a decision.[603] In
the case of a simple threat to peace, however, it follows from the Charter
that there is still time for the Council to meet and to decide whether
enforcement action is opportune. In practice a 'threat' always takes some
time to clarify, which tends to make the idea of urgency inoperative. It is
hard to imagine a situation in which the Security Council would not have
time to convene and rule on a threatening situation. Whether in the case of
Liberia, Sierra Leone or other precedents about which the particular role of
regional organisation has been evoked, there was nothing to prevent the
Security Council from examining the situation and making a ruling.[604] In

---

[600] See www.army.mil/operations.

[601] Our translation; A Geslin, 'Le pouvoir d'habilitation du Conseil de sécurité: la délégation des pouvoirs du Conseil aux organizations internationales' (2004) 37 *RBDI* 493–94.

[602] As M Kohen states, The Security Council is not competent 'to preclude the wrongfulness of a previous State action'; 'The Use of Force by the United States after the end of the
Cold War, and its impact on international law', above n 339, 217.

[603] Below, ch 7, s II.

[604] Above.

short, even when contemplated *de lege ferenda*, legalisation *ab initio* obeys a logic that is very far removed from that of the UN Charter.

It remains for us to envisage a situation that has not arisen in practice, where the Security Council unanimously authorises an armed action that began a few hours or minutes earlier. In this exceptional case, perhaps the intervening State knew that the agreement of the Council members had already been secured, even if it had not yet been reflected by the formal vote of a resolution? Might one not in this case admit the legal mechanism of *ex post* validation? I do not think so, for the reasons of intertemporal law already evoked. It is simply that in such an instance, military action would become lawful *ex nunc*, with as a consequence that it would only have been unlawful for a few hours or minutes. In practice, the unlawful act—which, in view of the circumstances, would be a use of force that was not serious enough to be characterised as an aggression—would never be sanctioned, as the UN Member States would waive implementing the international responsibility of the intervening State.[605] Here again, one must return to the institution of consent, which the ILC insisted must be prior to the act, while specifying that *ex post* consent might be tantamount to a waiver of responsibility.[606] That mechanism could probably be transposed in the case—which one can only repeat remains exceptional and even purely hypothetical—of an action being authorised a few minutes after it has begun. This would have the advantage of letting the unlawfulness of the proximate cause subsist—and so keeping the stringency of the prohibition of the use of force intact—and of managing an exceptional situation in a pragmatic manner.

All in all, the technique of presumed authorisation seems to be incompatible with the existing legal regime, *de lege lata*. *De lege ferenda*, this argument raises problems of principle that relate to the legal logic of collective security as a whole, and even of the general law of international responsibility. At most, this might open up a certain leeway in terms of the implementation of the responsibility of an intervening State. The unlawfulness of an armed action conducted at the time it was begun without Security Council authorisation cannot be contested without prejudice to self-defence or to possible consent of the State.

Conclusion

In conclusion, emphasis shall be placed on the importance of the specific circumstances of authorised intervention which, since the early 1990s, has seen many practical applications. In legal terms, we have underscored the breadth of the Security Council's competencies in this domain. The line of

---

[605] C Walter, 'Security Control over Regional Action', above n 174, 179.
[606] Above, ch 5, s I.

argument that, throughout the Cold War, consisted in opposing the Security Council's action in internal conflicts on the pretext that they were 'internal affairs' is hardly tenable today. So long as the situation may reasonably be characterised as a threat to international peace, and this characterisation has actually been made by the Council, the Council may take all measures it deems necessary, including a possible use of force. No other body, whether the General Assembly or a regional organisation, has competence of this order, collective security remaining the prerogative of the UN and more especially of the Security Council which exercises its main responsibility in this domain. The scope of the Security Council's competencies has a counterpart, though; when it authorises the use of force, it must do so clearly, which excludes any presumed authorisation, whether on the basis of resolutions adopted before military action begins or on the basis of resolutions adopted after the triggering of such action. Academic claims about indirect authorisation have never been admitted by the international community of States as a whole, as shown in particular by the Iraq precedent. Likewise, the possibilities of *a posteriori* authorisation have only been evoked by scholars and not by States. Whether in the cases of Liberia or of Sierra Leone, that are often evoked by doctrine, States have preferred to characterise operations as peace-keeping actions because they were conducted with the agreement of the authorities and so as 'non-coercive', with the consequence that no authorisation was required under article 53(1) of the Charter. Such an interpretation is to be related to the role of consent, which we saw in chapter five had the effect of setting aside the coercive character of a military action that was then characterised rather as a police operation.[607]

---

[607] See also above, ch 2, s I.

7

Self-Defence

ARTICLE 51 OF THE UN Charter states:

> Nothing in the present Charter shall impair the inherent right of individual or collective self-defence if an armed attack occurs against a Member of the United Nations, until the Security Council has taken the measures necessary to maintain international peace and security. Measures taken by Members in the exercise of this right of self-defence shall be immediately reported to the Security Council and shall not in any way affect the authority and responsibility of the Security Council under the present Charter to take at any time such action as it deems necessary in order to maintain or restore international peace and security.

This provision expresses the ordinary law of self-defence.[1] It is binding on all States[2] as a constituent part of the peremptory rule of the prohibition of the use of force,[3] both by treaty and, except for its purely procedural aspects, by custom.[4] Its purpose is to govern relations among States,[5] with relations among individuals bringing into play self-defence on another basis, to be determined by the applicable substantive law.[6]

Before addressing all of the hard questions that article 51 of the Charter raises, a clarification about method is required: self-defence shall be contemplated as an exceptional right; a right, first of all, and not just a situation or circumstance that might exclude wrongful behaviour.[7] An action

---

[1] ICJ, *Legality of the Threat or Use of Nuclear Weapons*, ICJ Rep (1996), paras 38–41; R Ago, *8th report on State responsibility: the internationally wrongful act of the State, source of international responsibility (continued)*, A/CN.4/318/Add.5–7; Institut de droit international Resolution on Self-defence, 27 October 2007, Santiago Session (www.idi-iil.org/idiE/navig_chon2003.html), para 1.

[2] See: O Schachter, 'Self-Defense and the Rule of Law' (1989) 83 *AJIL* 259–66.

[3] Above, ch 4, s I.

[4] ICJ, *Military and Paramilitary Activities*, ICJ Rep (1986), para 193.

[5] Above, ch 3, s I.

[6] Above, ch 2, s I.

[7] ICJ, *Military and Paramilitary Activities*, ICJ Rep (1986), para 176; see also JL Kunz, 'Individual and Collective Self-Defense in Article 51 of the Charter of the United Nations' (1947) 41 *AJIL* 876; Y Dinstein, *War, Aggression and Self-Defence*, 4th edn (Cambridge, Cambridge University Press, 2005) 178–79; A Constantinou, *The Right of Self-Defense under Customary International Law and Article 51 of the UN Charter* (Athènes, Ant N Sakkoulas/ Bruxelles, Bruylant, 2000) 51; Nguyen Quoc Dinh, 'La légitime défense d'après la Charte des Nations Unies' (1948) 52 *RGDIP* 227; T Christakis and K Bannelier, 'La légitime défense en tant que circonstance excluant l'illicéité' in R Kherad (ed), *Légitimes défenses* (Paris, LGDJ, 2007).

in self-defence is therefore quite lawful since it may rely on a feature of the primary rule, in the case in point as expressed in article 51.[8] At the same time self-defence is conceived of as an exception to the general principle of the prohibition of the use of force.[9] It is therefore for the State relying on self-defence to prove it in the circumstances in question.[10] More generally, a principle of restrictive interpretation holds,[11] and it is that principle that will be our guide in this chapter.

While no one contests the principle of self-defence, substantial divergences emerge when it comes to clarifying the exact scope of this institution.[12] Two main types of discussion can be identified in this respect. The first relates to the condition for there being a prior armed attack, the outline of which shall be covered first (section one). A second problem relates to the conditions, which are very closely related as shall be seen, of necessity and proportionality. The conditions also pertain to the relationship between self-defence and Security Council action (section two).

I 'Armed Attack' According to Article 51 of the Charter

Before addressing the controversies to which it gives rise, we shall first note a number of hardly contestable points about the conditions for the existence of an armed attack.

—First, the attack, to give rise to a right of self-defence, must be an armed attack. It is true, especially in debates over the notion of coercion as a cause of invalidity of treaties, that some States have supported the idea of economic or even ideological aggression or constraint.[13] Yet this was generally without prejudice to the restriction of self-defence to a riposte to an 'armed attack', by the very terms of article 51.[14] Some commentators may therefore claim that an 'economic aggression' breaches the principles of non-intervention, or even that of the non-use of force.[15] However, it cannot be claimed that such an 'aggression' would entitle the victim State to riposte using force.[16]

---

[8] J Zourek, 'La notion de légitime défense en droit international' (1975) 56 *AIDI* 46.

[9] ICJ, *Military and Paramilitary Activities*, ICJ Rep (1986), para 193.

[10] ICJ, *Oil Platforms*, ICJ Rep (2003), paras 57 and 61; *Armed Activities on the Territory of the Congo*, ICJ Rep (2005), paras 106–47.

[11] A Constantinou, *The Right of Self-Defense under Customary International Law and Article 51 of the UN Charter*, above n 7, 30.

[12] A Cassese, 'Article 51' in JP Cot and A Pellet (eds), *La Charte des Nations Unies*, 3rd edn (Paris, Economica, 2005) 1334–35; C Gray, *International Law and the Use of Force*, 3rd edn (Oxford, Oxford University Press, 2008) 114.

[13] O Corten, 'Article 52' in O Corten and P Klein (eds), *Les Conventions de Vienne sur le droit des traités. Commentaire article par article* (Bruxelles, Bruylant, 2006) 1873–85.

[14] SA Alexandrov, *Self-Defense Against the Use of Force in International Law* (The Hague/London/Boston, Kluwer, 1996) 112.

[15] A Constantinou, *The Right of Self-Defense under Customary International Law and Article 51 of the UN Charter*, above n 7, 36.

[16] A Cassese, 'Article 51', above n 12, 1357.

—Secondly, to give rise to a right of self-defence, an armed action must present a certain degree of gravity.[17] In other words, not just any violation of article 2(4) necessarily gives entitlement to a right of self-defence.[18] A minor use of force, such as a border incident, entails its author's international responsibility. It does not, however, allow its victim to riposte by military action unless, of course, the Security Council has adopted a resolution authorising it to do so.[19] The 'gravity' of any action must be appraised depending on circumstances.[20]

—Thirdly, an armed aggression may take various forms, whether classical, such as the invasion or bombing of a State's territory, or other forms such as an attack against a State's shipping or aircraft, or again, as shall be seen, support for irregular forces operating in the territory of another State.[21] An armed attack consists in a use of force of a certain gravity by one State against another, the attack being aimed at the territory or the agents or even the nationals of the target State.[22] This last possibility has sometimes been challenged by denouncing military operations that abusively combine self-defence and the rescue of nationals.[23] Without getting into this debate at this point,[24] we shall merely refer to the criterion of

[17] See: Art 2 of the definition of aggression, annexed to GA Res (XXIX), 14 December 1974. According to the ICJ, 'it [is] necessary to distinguish the most grave forms of the use of force (those constituting an armed attack) from other less grave forms' (*Military and Paramilitary Activities*, 101, para 191; *Oil Platforms*, ICJ Rep (2003), paras 51 and 64). See also Institut de droit international Resolution on Self-defence, 27 October 2007, Santiago Session (www.idi-iil.org/idiE/navig_chon2003.html), para 5 and Independent International Fact-Finding Mission on the Conflict in Georgia, *Report*, September 2009 (www.ceiig.ch/Report.html), vol II, 242 and 245.

[18] cp Art 2(4) ('threat', 'use of force') and art 51 ('armed attack') of the Charter; A Randelzhofer, 'Article 51' in B Simma (ed), *The Charter of the United Nations. A Commentary*, 2nd edn (New York, Oxford University Press, 2002) 790.

[19] I Brownlie, 'General Course of Public International Law' (1995) 255 *RCADI* 204. See also Eritrea-Ethiopia Claims Commission: 'Localized border encounters between small infantry units, even those involving loss of life, do not constitute an armed attack for purposes of the Charter [. . .]. The Commission is satisfied that these relatively minor incidents were not of a magnitude to constitute an armed attack by either State against the other within the meaning of Article 51 of the Charter'; *Partial Award. Jus ad Bellum. Ethiopia's Claims 1–8*, 19 December 2005, paras 11–12 (www.pca-cpa.org/).

[20] For example, the ICJ 'does not exclude the possibility that the mining of a single military vessel might be sufficient to bring into play the "inherent right of self-defence"' (*Oil Platforms*, ICJ Rep (2003) 195, para 72). See also F Berman, J Gow, C Greenwood, V Lowe, A Roberts, P Sands, M Shaw, G Simpson, C Warbrick, N Wheeler, E Wilmshurst, M Wood, 'The Chatham House Principles of International Law on the Use of Force on the Use of Self-Defence' (2006) 55 *ICLQ* 966 and 'Contemporary Practice of the United States' (2004) 98 *AJIL* 598–99.

[21] See examples in art 3 of the definition of aggression, quoted above.

[22] F Berman, J Gow, C Greenwood, V Lowe, A Roberts, P Sands, M Shaw, G Simpson, C Warbrick, N Wheeler, E Wilmshurst, M Wood, 'The Chatham House Principles of International Law on the Use of Force on the Use of Self-Defence', above n 20, 965; R Higgins, 'The Legal Limits to the Use of Force by Sovereign States. United Nations Practice' (1961) 37 *BYBIL* 316. See also art 3d) of the definition of aggression; A Randelzhofer, 'Article 51', above n 18, 797.

[23] See: A Cassese, 'Article 51', above n 12, 1347–50.

[24] See below, ch 8.

gravity which can invariably be used to evaluate whether or not there is a situation of self-defence, including in such instances.[25] As a matter of principle, there is nothing to my mind to permit the assertion that only attacks against a State's territory and not those against its agents or nationals are covered by article 51.[26] It is true that, in practice, there is no precedent where an attack on nationals alone has been recognised by the international community of States as a whole as an armed attack within the meaning of article 51 of the Charter.[27]

—Fourthly, self-defence may be individual but it may be collective too with one or more third States helping the State under attack with its riposte to the attacking State. In this case, self-defence may only be exercised provided that the existence of a prior armed attack is followed by the State under attack formulating a request.[28]

—Fifthly, and in more methodological terms, we shall rely more specifically in this section on the definition of aggression appended to resolution 3314 (XIX) adopted by consensus by the UN General Assembly in 1974. Admittedly, this instrument was initially conceived of as being about not an 'armed attack'—'agression armée', in the French version—provided for by article 51 but 'aggression'—'agression', in the French version—as set out in article 39 and in the very title of Chapter VII. The distinction is an essential one. The second notion is much broader than the first: the Security Council may perfectly well characterise a situation as an 'aggression' in a broad sense as a basis for its competence to take measures provided for in Chapter VII without there necessarily being an 'armed attack' within the meaning of article 51.[29] In the debates that surrounded the elaboration and then the adoption of this text, many States, though, thought of aggression as a constituent part of self-defence.[30] In practice, the Security Council has never used this definition to guide it in charac-

---

[25] R Kolb, *Ius contra bellum. Le droit international relatif au maintien de la paix*, 2nd edn (Bâle, Helbing and Lichtenhahn/ Bruxelles, Bruylant, 2009) 291–92. See also above, ch 2, s I.

[26] T Franck, *Recourse to Force. State Action Against Threats and Armed Attacks* (Cambridge, Cambridge University Press, 2002) 77–96; Y Dinstein, *War, Aggression and Self-Defence*, 4th edn, above n 7, 200–01. See also Independent International Fact-Finding Mission on the Conflict in Georgia, *Report*, September 2009 (www.ceiig.ch/Report.html), vol II, 253.

[27] See, eg: the Entebe incident, above, ch 2, s I.

[28] ICJ, *Military and Paramilitary Activities*, ICJ Rep (1986), paras 196–99; *Oil Platforms*, ICJ Rep (2003), para 51; Institut de droit international Resolution on Self-defence, 27 October 2007, Santiago Session (www.idi-iil.org/idiE/navig_chon2003.html), para 8; see also DB Bowett, 'Collective Self-Defence under the Charter of the United Nations' (1955–1956) 32 *BYBIL* 130–61.

[29] See: SA Alexandrov, *Self-Defense Against the Use of Force in International Law*, above n 14, 113.

[30] See, eg: France (A/AC.134/SR.30, 6 March 1969 in *Special Committee on the Question of Defining Aggression*, Second Session, A/AC.134/SR.25-51, 28; A/C.6/SR.1474, 11 October 1974), Romania (A/C.6/SR.1475, 14 October 1974), GDR (A/C.6/SR.1476, 15 October 1974), FRG (A/C.6/SR.1478, 16 October 1974), Greece (A/C.6/SR.1482, 22 October 1974).

terising situations of aggression within the sense of article 39.[31] However, the International Court of Justice, without being contradicted by the States that were parties to the disputes in question, has held that resolution 3314 (XXIX) expressed a definition that was applicable for evaluating the existence of an armed attack as a condition for implementing self-defence.[32] This resolution, of which certain marks are found in a number of treaties,[33] shall therefore be used in this perspective, as is the case in a great deal of scholarship.[34]

—Lastly, it shall be recalled at this point that the absence of a right of self-defence does not render powerless a State that has been the victim of a violation of international law.[35] First because, as underscored in chapter two, the State has sovereign rights over its territory, authorising it to deploy military forces there without having to appeal to any rule creating an exception whatsoever, whether self-defence or not.[36] Then because, if the situation is, without being serious enough to evoke the occurrence of an armed attack, tantamount to a threat to international peace, the State in question may always bring the matter before the Security Council.[37] As set out above, the Council is competent, including for taking military measures, in the event of a simple threat, which is a highly flexible notion as we have emphasised.[38]

Alongside these points that are little contested if at all, there are lively debates about the conditions of the occurrence of an armed attack. First, while it is explicitly stated in article 51, this condition has been contested by theories of 'preventive self-defence'. These theories shall be addressed first (A). We shall then look into another contemporary debate, about a State's responsibility for acts of force perpetrated by private individuals or entities. As shown in chapter three, a private group cannot, as such, invoke or be bound by the prohibition of the use of force.[39] However, in some situations

[31] P d'Argent, J d'Aspremont Lynden, F Dopagne, R van Steenberghe, 'Article 39' in JP Cot and A Pellet (eds), *La Charte des Nations Unies*, 3rd edn (Paris, Economica, 2005) 1149–50.

[32] ICJ, *Military and Paramilitary Activities*, ICJ Rep (1986), para 195 (and Schwebel dissenting opinion, 338 ff); *Armed Activities on the Territory of the Congo*, ICJ Rep (2005), para 146.

[33] See: Art I of the 26 July 1975 Protocol, amending the Rio Treaty; www.oas.org.

[34] C Gray, *International Law and the Use of Force*, 3rd edn, above n 12, 130; T Franck, *Recourse to Force. State Action Against Threats and Armed Attacks*, above n 26, 53; J Verhoeven, 'Les 'étirements' de la légitime défense' (2002) 48 *AFDI* 56; *contra:* A Randelzhofer, 'Article 51', above n 18, 795.

[35] See, eg: Institut de droit international Resolution on Self-defence, 27 October 2007, Santiago Session (www.idi-iil.org/idiE/navig_chon2003.html), para 5.

[36] Above, ch 2, s I.

[37] A Randelzhofer, 'Article 51', above n 18, 790; R Kolb, *Ius contra bellum. Le droit international relatif au maintien de la paix*, 2nd edn, above n 25, 291; J Zourek, *L'interdiction de l'emploi de la force en droit international* (Leiden, Sijthoff, 1974) 113.

[38] Above, ch 6, s I.

[39] Above, ch 3, s I.

that does not preclude the use of force by a private group generating a right of self-defence for a State that has allegedly been attacked. This is what we shall call the problem of 'indirect aggression' that shall be dealt with secondly (B).

A. 'Preventive Self-Defence' Theories

For some scholars a right of self-defence arises not just in the event of an actual armed attack but also if there is a threat of a use of force.[40] This is what we call the doctrine of 'preventive self-defence', a notion that requires two clarifications from the outset.

—First, some academics are at loggerheads over the question of the intensity of the threat. For some, the threat needs to be 'imminent'; that is, on the verge of materialising.[41] For others, self-defence could also be admitted in the case of a more hazy threat, sometimes characterised as a latent threat.[42] In the first instance, one sometimes speaks of 'pre-emptive' self-defence, in the second 'preventive' self-defence, and the term 'anticipatory self-defence' is occasionally used besides.[43] These distinctions, which it shall be seen are found neither in the Charter nor in the major texts governing the use of force accepted by States, are essentially doctrinal.[44]

---

[40] T Franck, *Recourse to Force. State Action Against Threats and Armed Attacks*, above n 26, 97–107; J Brumée and SJ Toope, 'Slouching Towards New "Just" Wars: International Law and the Use of Force After September 11th' (2004) 51 *NILR* 373–76; see also JN Maogoto, 'New Frontiers, Old Problems: The War on Terror and the Notion of Anticipating the Enemy' (2004) 51 *NILR* 16–17.

[41] R Higgins, *The Development of International Law Through the Political Organs of the United Nations* (London/New York/Toronto, Oxford University Press, 1963), 199; R Hofmann, 'International Law and the Use of Military Force Against Iraq' (2002) 45 *GYIL* 31; J Brumée, 'The Security and Self-Defence: Which Way to Global Security?' in N Blokker and N Schrijver (ed), *The Security Council and the Use of Force. A Need for Change?* (Leiden/Boston, Martinus Nijhoff, 2005) 118–19; J Brumée and SJ Toope, 'The Use of Force: International Law After Iraq', (2004) 53 *ICLQ* 792; NJ Schrijver, 'The Future of the Charter of the United Nations' (2006) 10 *Max Planck UNYB* 21–22; J Verhoeven, 'Les 'étirements' de la légitime défense', above n 34, 70; JG Castel, 'The Legality and Legitimacy of Unilateral Armed Intervention in an Age of Terror, Neo-Imperialism, and Massive Violations of Human Rights: Is International Law Evolving in the Right Direction?' (2004) 42 *CYIL* 10–14; N Maogoto, 'New Frontiers, Old Problems: The War on Terror and the Notion of Anticipating the Enemy', above n 40, 39.

[42] M Reisman, 'International Legal Responses to Terrorism' (1999) 22 *Houston Journal of IL* 17–19; AD Sofaer, 'On the Necessity of Pre-emption' (2003) 14 *EJIL* 209–26; R Wedgwood, 'Unilateral Action in the UN System' (2000) 11 *EJIL* 355; *contra*: PB Potter, 'Preventive War Critically Considered' (1951) 45 *AJIL* 142–45.

[43] S Laghmani, 'La doctrine américaine de la *preemptive self-defense*' in R Ben Achour and S Laghmani (eds), *Le droit international à la croisée des chemins. Force du droit et droit de la force* (Paris, Pedone, 2004) 137–40.

[44] See also the ambiguous notion of 'actual or manifestly imminent armed attack' in the Institut de droit international Resolution on Self-defence, 27 October 2007, Santiago Session (www.idi-iil.org/idiE/navig_chon2003.html), para 3 (cp paras 6 and 7) and O Corten, 'Les résolutions de l'Institut de droit international sur la légitime défense et sur les actions humanitaires' (2007) 40 *RBDI* 601–08.

They shall not be dealt with further in what follows. All those doctrines by which self-defence is said to be lawful in the event of any threat regardless of its intensity shall be referred to here as theories of 'preventive self-defence'.

—Next, to properly grasp the specific character of these theories, it must be understood that self-defence invariably includes a preventive dimension, insofar as it must be aimed at ending an ongoing attack whether resulting from an invasion, a bombing campaign or from action by armed bands sent by a third State.[45] It is not, then, because a State asserts it is acting to prevent fresh attacks that it avails itself of a doctrine of 'preventive self-defence'; this doctrine presupposes also that no armed attack has yet been launched.

To my mind, contemporary international law does not enshrine any such doctrine. 'Preventive self-defence' does not seem readily compatible with article 51, nor can it be deduced from observation of actual practice, whether in the major debates on the use of force within the UN or in the few precedents where 'preventive self-defence' has been evoked.

The Exclusion of 'Preventive Self-Defence' by Article 51 of the Charter

By applying the principles of interpretation codified in the Vienna Conventions on treaty law, we shall begin with the actual text of article 51, viewed in the context of the UN Charter (a), before examining the provision's object and purpose (b) and then, subordinately, mentioning its *travaux préparatoires* (c).

a) The Text of Article 51 in the Context of the UN Charter: 'if an armed attack occurs'

Under article 31 of the 1969 Vienna Convention any expression is presumed to have its ordinary meaning; no special or out-of-the-ordinary meaning can be admitted unless it can be shown that such was the parties' intent.[46] Now, and this observation is the starting point for any contemplation of the matter, article 51 explicitly reserves the right of self-defence for 'if an armed attack occurs against a Member of the United Nations'. The terms are plain: the Charter does not speak of an 'aggression' or an 'attack', which are comparatively vague, but of an 'armed attack'.[47] Either it is a case

---

[45] See the condition of necessity, below, s II.

[46] JM Sorel, 'Article 31' in O Corten and P Klein (eds), *Les Conventions de Vienne sur le droit des traités. Commentaire article par article* (Bruxelles, Bruylant, 2006) 1289–34.

[47] H Kelsen, 'Collective Security and Collective Self-Defense under the Charter of the United Nations' (1948) 42 *AJIL* 791, and *The Law of the United Nations* (London, Stevens and Son, 1951) 797; therefore, 'a merely "imminent" attack or any act of aggression which has not the character of an attack involving the use of armed force does not justify resort to force as an exercice of the right established by Article 51'; ibid, 797–98. I Brownlie, *International Law and the Use of Force by States* (Oxford, Clarendon Press, 1966) 275; 'The Use of Force in Self-Defence' (1961) 37 *BYBIL* 242.

of an armed attack and the victim State has a right to defend itself, or it is some other case, no matter which, and that right cannot be exercised. The existence of a simple threat, whether imminent or not, is undeniably in the second category. Theories of preventive self-defence therefore immediately run into a fundamental obstacle, since they directly contradict article 51 of the Charter.[48]

A reading of the Charter as a whole confirms this, insofar as the hypothesis of a threat is specifically provided for therein and gives rise to specific regulation. Aticle 2(4) prohibits not just the use but also the threat of the use of force. In this context, it seems logical to consider that mention of the threat of use of force was intentionally omitted from article 51, self-defence being reserved to the most serious cases of the use of force.[49] For all other cases, the Charter leaves it for the Security Council to decide on the measures to be taken, whether a breach of the peace—by hypothesis one that does not follow from the launch of an attack—or more generally a simple threat to international peace. The occurrence of this notion in article 39 is a decisive factor since it clearly shows that, in the event of a mere threat, it is the pathway of collective security that is to be followed. *A contrario*, it is understood that article 51 allows a unilateral armed riposte only 'if an armed attack occurs against a Member of the United Nations'.

What do commentators favourable to preventive self-defence theories answer to these text-based arguments? For some, article 51 does not include the expression 'if, *and only if,* an armed attack occurs against a Member of the United Nations', an omission that allegedly justifies not excluding threats.[50] The argument does not merit any lengthy refutation inasmuch as it undeniably clashes with the ordinary meaning of the provision at issue, which is to provide for self-defence in a certain instance, which clearly means excluding it in others.[51] In actual fact, the argument, which is not

---

[48] Nguyen Quoc Dinh, 'La légitime défense d'après la Charte des Nations Unies' (1948) 52 *RGDIP* 240–41; JL Kunz, 'Individual and Collective Self-Defense in Article 51 of the Charter of the United Nations', above n 7, 878; M Bothe, 'Terrorism and the Legality of Pre-emptive force' (2003) 14 *EJIL* 229; A Randelzhofer, 'Article 51', above n 18, 803; T Christakis, 'Existe-t-il un droit de légitime défense en cas de simple "menace"'? Une réponse au "groupe de personnalités de haut niveau" de l'ONU' in SFDI, *Les métamorphoses de la sécurité collective* (Paris, Pedone, 2005) 208; 'Vers une reconnaissance de la notion de guerre préventive?' in K Bannelier *et al* (eds), *L'intervention en Irak et le droit international* (Paris, Pedone, 2004) 19; DN Kolesnik, 'The Development of the Right to Self-Defence' in WE Butler (ed), *The Non-Use of Force in International Law* (Dordrecht, Kluwer, 1989) 153–55.

[49] M Bothe, 'Terrorism and the Legality of Pre-emptive force' (2003) 14 *EJIL* 229.

[50] MS McDougal, 'The Soviet-Cuban Quarantine and Self-Defense' (1963) 57 *AJIL* 600; Schwebel, dissenting opinion, ICJ, *Military and Paramilitary Activities*, ICJ Rep (1986) 347–48; see also H Waldock, 'General Course of Public International Law' (1962-II) 106 *RCADI* 234–36 and J Stone, 'Hopes and Loopholes in the 1974 Definition of Aggression' (1977) 71 *AJIL* 244; P Weckel, 'Coordination entre la prohibition de l'emploi de la force et les exigences de la lutte contre le terrorisme' in E Cannizaro and P Palchetti (eds), *Customary International Law On the Use of Force* (Leiden/Boston, Martinus Nijhoff, 2005) 301.

[51] Y Dinstein, *War, Aggression and Self-Defence*, 4th edn, above n 7, 183–84; R Kolb, *Ius contra bellum. Le droit international relatif au maintien de la paix*, 2nd edn, above n 25, 278, n 417.

often raised, comes down either to purely and simply ignoring the litigious expression, or presuming that it would be preceded by the adverb 'notably', which, however regrettable the proponents of the preventive self-defence argument may find it, is not the case.[52]

Another text-based argument is then put forward, this time much more widely. Many commentators underscore the first words of article 51: 'Nothing in the present Charter shall impair the inherent right of individual or collective self-defence . . .'. This expression is supposedly to be interpreted as a form of reference to the customary, natural and inherent law of self-defence.[53] Now, customary law purportedly traditionally accepts armed riposte in the event of an imminent threat to use force, not just in the event of an armed attack that has actually been launched.[54] This line of argument raises many problems that have already been emphasised several times by doctrine.

First, the 'inherent right' argument relies on an assertion that is far from proven: the existence, at the time the Charter was drawn up, of a customary right of preventive self-defence that supposedly then subsisted without ever being fundamentally called into question. The existence of this customary right is generally based on the citation of a diplomatic exchange between the USA and Great Britain in the 1830s in the context of what is often called the *Caroline* case.[55] At that time, the two States involved seem to have agreed on a possibility of self-defence when 'the necessity of that self-defence is instant, overwhelming and leaving no choice of means, and no moment for deliberation'.[56] As will have been noted, this excerpt from a diplomatic exchange does not specifically mention, without excluding it either, the hypothesis of preventive self-defence.[57] It was inferred from the aforecited doctrine that, under the circumstances of the case, this hypothesis had been enshrined in international law.[58] And yet, if we wish to understand them using current day legal categories, the circumstances of the case seem to refer rather to the hypothesis of 'indirect aggression' that we shall consider later. The rebels who were operating from the US had already, at the time of the British operation against the *Caroline*, conducted several military actions in Canadian territory, rendering the purely 'preventive' character of this operation problematic. In any event, there is nothing to

---

[52] T Christakis, 'Existe-t-il un droit de légitime défense en cas de simple "menace"? Une réponse au "groupe de personnalités de haut niveau" de l'ONU', above n 48, 208–09.

[53] H Waldock, 'General Course of Public International Law', above n 50, 234–35.

[54] DW Bowett, *Self-Defence in International Law* (Manchester, MUP, 1958) 187–92.

[55] See, eg: MN Schmitt, *Counter-Terrorism and the Use of Force in International Law* (Garmisch-Partenkirchen, The Marshall Center Papers, No 5, 2002), 22–23.

[56] Text in JB Moore, *Digest of International Law*, 1906, 412.

[57] See: WR Manning, *Diplomatic correspondance of the United States. Canadian Relations: 1784–1860*, vol III (Washington, Carnegie Endowment for International Peace, 1943).

[58] V PW Shortridge, 'The Canadian-American frontier during the rebellion of 1837–1838', *The Canadian Historical Review*, 1926.

prove that this interpretation was shared by all the States of the planet more than a century later, at a time when the rules on the use of force had undergone radical change, since there had been a shift from authorisation with relatively wide bounds—or even, for some commentators, an unlimited competence to use force—to a stringent principle of prohibition.[59] The transposition of self-defence as it was supposedly conceived of at the time of the *Caroline* can be criticised *per se*, especially as, under the circumstances of the case as it unwound in the 1830s, the institution of self-defence was conceived of as applying in relations between individuals much more than in relations between States, the US and Great Britain never having thought of themselves as being at war.[60] Of course, these criticisms could be answered if it could be shown that there was, in the inter-war years, some custom admitting preventive self-defence. That task is an exacting one because the period is one of progressive codification of an increasingly stringent prohibition that ended with the drafting of the UN Charter.[61] In this context, all the evidence seems to show that, by providing for self-defence in the event of 'armed attack', the drafters of the Charter intended to state the law as it then stood.[62]

Secondly, and in any event, supposing that it could be shown there was a custom in 1945, in order to be able to invoke it subsequently, it would still not have to be contrary to treaty law as set out in article 51. Now, as recalled, there is no removing from the Charter that part of it requiring there be a case of armed attack. Invoking customary law to circumvent or challenge the plain terms of article 51 is a method that is difficult to defend.[63] One fails to see in the name of what principle a custom should be declared superior to a treaty, especially when the treaty contains a provision affirm-

---

[59] A Constantinou, *The Right of Self-Defense under Customary International Law and Article 51 of the UN Charter*, above n 7, 113–14; I Brownlie, 'General Course of Public International Law', above n 19, 203 and, from the same author, 'The UN Charter and the Use of Force, 1945–1985' in A Cassese (ed), *The Current Legal Regulation of the Use of Force* (Dordrecht, Martinus Nijhoff, 1986) 497; 'The Principle of Non-Use of Force in Contemporary International Law' in WE Butler (ed), *The Non-Use of Force in International Law* (Dordrecht, Kluwer, 1989) 19; RA Müllerson, 'The Principle of Non-Threat and Non-Use of Force in The Modern World', ibid, 32; J Zourek, 'La notion de légitime défense en droit international', above n 8, 63.

[60] T Christakis, 'Existe-t-il un droit de légitime défense en cas de simple "menace"? Une réponse au "groupe de personnalités de haut niveau" de l'ONU', above n 48, 204–05; R Ago, *YILC*, 1980, vol I, 1619th session, 25 June 1980, para 19; see also M Francis, *YILC*, 1980, vol I, 1621st session, 27 June 1980, para 11.

[61] R Ago *YILC*, 1080, I, 1619th session, 25 June 1980, para 21; T Christakis, 'Existe-t-il un droit de légitime défense en cas de simple "menace"? Une réponse au "groupe de personnalités de haut niveau" de l'ONU', above n 48, 205–06; LA Sicilianos, *Les réactions décentralisées à l'illicite. Des contre-mesures à la légitime défense* (Paris, LGDJ, 1990) 297–99; I Brownlie, *International Law and the Use of Force by States*, above n 47, 274–75.

[62] I Brownlie, 'The Use of Force in Self-Defence', above n 47, 238–39.

[63] ibid, 239–41; A Constantinou, *The Right of Self-Defense under Customary International Law and Article 51 of the UN Charter*, above n 7, 114; A Cassese, 'Article 51', above n 12, 1336; T Christakis, 'Vers une reconnaissance de la notion de guerre préventive?', above n 48, 17.

ing its superiority over other instruments, as is the case of article 103 of the Charter.[64] Besides, the International Court of Justice has refused to accept that customary rules can be opposed to treaty rules set out in the Charter, especially in the domain of the use of force.[65] It is a recognised principle that, of two interpretations, one must choose the one that reconciles rather than the one that brings into contention the different terms of a statement. So then it must be presumed that, for UN member States, the 'inherent right' of self-defence can only be exercised 'if an armed attack occurs' regardless of the content of earlier law.[66]

The text of article 51 must always act as the starting point and benchmark for any discussion of preventive self-defence. This text could only be circumvented if it were to be shown, as stated in article 32 of the 1969 Vienna Convention, that its meaning is 'ambiguous or obscure'—and we have just seen that this is not so—or that it 'leads to a result which is manifestly absurd or unreasonable', which requires consideration of the object and purpose of the provision construed.[67]

b) Object and Purpose of Article 51 of the Charter

A reading of article 51 shows that its object is to reserve on an exceptional ('if an armed attack occurs') and provisional ('until the Security Council has taken measures necessary to maintain international peace and security') basis a right of armed riposte that might be conducted without Security Council authorisation.[68] The overall logic of the Charter may therefore be resumed in this way: the decision to use force is reserved in principle to the Security Council so as to avoid the unilateralism that prevailed in earlier times.[69] But in emergency situations and provisionally, a unilateral right of armed riposte is still recognised. The object and purpose of self-defence must therefore be included within the broader context of the legal regime prohibiting the use of force as it has been set up under the UN Charter. In this perspective it is entirely logical—and at any rate it is not 'manifestly absurd or unreasonable'—that the multilateral pathway be resolutely

---

[64] T Christakis, 'Existe-t-il un droit de légitime défense en cas de simple "menace"? Une réponse au "groupe de personnalités de haut niveau" de l'ONU', above n 48, 207–08.

[65] ICJ, *Military and Paramilitary Activities*, ICJ Rep (1986), paras 176 and 181.

[66] According to H Kelsen, 'the effect of Article 51 would not change if the term "inherent" were dropped. In declaring that nothing in the Charter shall impair the inherent right of self-defence, the Charter confers such right upon the Members, whether positive general international law or natural law establishes it or not'; *The Law of the United Nations*, above n 47, 792; see also R Kolb, 'Self-Defence and Preventive War at the Beginning of the Millenium' (2004) 59 *Zaitschrift für öffentliches Recht* 115.

[67] O Corten, *L'utilisation du 'raisonnable' par le juge international. Discours juridique, raison et contradictions* (Bruxelles, Bruylant, 1997) 53–55.

[68] A Randelzhofer, 'Article 51', above n 18, 792 and 803.

[69] I Brownlie, *International Law and the Use of Force by States*, above n 47, 275; see also O Corten, *Le retour des guerres préventives: le droit international menacé* (Bruxelles, Labor, 2003) 11–27.

favoured, which explains why article 51 is restricted to particularly serious cases of the triggering of an armed attack.[70]

An argument that is very commonly raised in favour of the preventive self-defence thesis is that, in the event of an imminent threat, a State could not passively wait to suffer the effects of an attack before reacting.[71] In particular, since the advent of the nuclear age and even more since new forms of terrorism that appeared with the 11 September 2001,[72] such an attitude would be incompatible with the very object of self-defence which, as the ICJ recalls, is to ensure the State's very survival.[73] Under these circumstances there is cause to presume that States have implicitly reserved the hypothesis of preventive self-defence, despite the terms of article 51 that theoretically require the occurrence of an armed attack. Otherwise we would be in the patently absurd and unreasonable situation of States that have themselves organised their own demise by concluding a form of 'Suicide Pact'.[74]

The first problem raised by such an argument is that, by accepting it, we would open up the floodgates to precisely those risks of abuse that the Charter set out to eradicate.[75] There are many examples in history where States have claimed there was a threat in order to justify an attack on another State. During the Second World War—which it should be remembered was the backdrop against which the new legal regime of prohibition of the use of force was devised—Germany claimed it was invading Belgium and the Netherlands to forestall an 'imminent attack against the Ruhr district through Holland and Belgium' by France and Great Britain,[76] while

---

[70] T Christakis, 'Existe-t-il un droit de légitime défense en cas de simple "menace"? Une réponse au "groupe de personnalités de haut niveau" de l'ONU', above n 48, 209–10; AA Cançado Trindade, 'The Primacy of International Law Over Force' in M Kohen (ed), *Promoting Justice, Human Rights and Conflict Resolution Through International Law. Liber Amicorum Lucius Caflisch* (Leiden, Martinus Nijhoff, 2007) 1045–46; R Kolb, 'Self-Defence and Preventive War at the Beginning of the Millennium', above n 66, 119.

[71] R Higgins, *Probems and Process. International Law and How We Use It* (Oxford, Clarendon Press, 1994) 242; W Wengler, 'L'interdiction de recourir à la force. Problèmes et tendances' (1971) 7 *RBDI* 404–05; J Nyamuya Maogoto, 'New Frontiers, Old Problems: The War on Terror and the Notion of Anticipating the Ennemy', above n 40, 30.

[72] R Wedgwood, 'The Fall of Saddam Hussein: Security Council Mandates and Preemptive Self-Defense' (2003) 97 *AJIL* 584; RN Gardner, 'Neither Bush nor the "Jurisprudes"' (2003) 97 *AJIL* 586; T Franck, 'What Happens Now? The UN After Iraq' (2003) 97 *AJIL* 619; JE Stromseth, 'Law and Force After Iraq: A Transitional Moment' (2003) 97 *AJIL* 634.

[73] ICJ, *Legality of the Threat or Use of Nuclear Weapons*, ICJ Rep (1996) 266; see T Franck, *Recourse to Force. State Action Against Threats and Armed Attacks*, above n 26, 98.

[74] ibid; MS McDougal, 'The Soviet-Cuban Quarantine and Self-Defense', above n 50, 597; R Jennings and A Watts, *Oppenheim's International Law*, vol 1 (London and New York, Longman, 1996) 422; M Koskenniemi, 'Irak and the "Bush Doctrine" of Pre-Emptive Self-Defense', *Crimes of War Project*, expert analysis, August 20, 2002; see also F Berman, J Gow, C Greenwood, V Lowe, A Roberts, P Sands, M Shaw, G Simpson, C Warbrick, N Wheeler, E Wilmshurst, M Wood, 'The Chatham House Principles of International Law on the Use of Force on the Use of Self-Defence', above n 20, 964.

[75] A Randelzhofer, 'Article 51', above n 18, 803; R Kolb, *Ius contra bellum. Le droit international relatif au maintien de la paix*, 2nd edn, above n 25, 280–82; T Christakis, 'Vers une reconnaissance de la notion de guerre préventive?', above n 48, 20.

[76] *Keesing's Contemporary Archives*, 1937–1940, 4043.

Japan justified its attack on Pearl Harbour as a preventive measure to remove a threat of attack by the USA.[77] However, there is no known precedent where compliance with article 51 has rendered a State powerless and *a fortiori* led to its annihilation. In this context, it should be observed that the requirement for an armed attack to have actually occurred, while it does not eliminate it, does reduce the risk of any abusive use of self-defence.[78] To add the case of imminent threat, a notion that eludes any attempt at definition much more than that of actual attack does, comes down to heading back down the road to unilateralism as concerns the use of force, which certainly does not seem consistent with the object and purpose of the UN Charter.[79] This fear seems that much more grounded in view of the ever wider interpretations of the concept of threat that have been defended since 11 September 2001.[80] Since that date a discourse has developed justifying preventive war by supposed connections among 'terrorist groups', 'rogue States' and 'weapons of mass destruction'.[81] That discourse has tended progressively to blur the boundaries between the ideas of imminent threats, latent threats or more generally of a state of peace and a state of war.[82] In short, we are faced with a question of balance: between the risk of abuse if the notion of threat is introduced—a risk that is very real and illustrated by history—and the risk that a State anxious to comply to the letter with article 51 be threatened with annihilation—a risk that seems rather theoretical—we should give precedence to the solution that is most in keeping with the object and purpose of the prohibition of the use of force.

Another point should be made at this stage. The situation has sometimes been evoked of a nuclear missile which, having been launched, has not yet entered the territory of its target State.[83] Would it not be absurd to condemn that State to waiting for its sovereignty to be actually infringed before reacting? Most certainly. But preventive self-defence should not be confused with what has been termed 'interceptive' self-defence.[84] If a State destroys a missile heading for its territory—but that has not yet reached it—

[77] 'Our Empire, for its existence and self-defence, has no other recourse but to appeal to arms and to crush every obstacle in its path'; *Keesing's Contemporary Archives*, 1940–1943, 4923.

[78] T Christakis, 'Existe-t-il un droit de légitime défense en cas de simple "menace"? Une réponse au "groupe de personnalités de haut niveau" de l'ONU', above n 48, 221–22.

[79] A Constantinou, *The Right of Self-Defense under Customary International Law and Article 51 of the UN Charter*, above n 7, 119; T Christakis, 'Vers une reconnaissance de la notion de guerre préventive?', above n 48, 20–21; I Brownlie, *International Law and the Use of Force by States*, above n 47, 259.

[80] M Sapiro, 'Iraq: The Shifting Sands of Preemptive Self-Defense' (2003) 97 *AJIL* 599.

[81] *The National Security Strategy of the United States of America*, September 2002, n 6; www.whitehouse.gov.

[82] O Corten, 'La 'guerre antiterroriste', un discours de pouvoir' (2004) 105 *Contradictions*, Les guerres antiterroristes 3–13.

[83] MS McDougal, 'The Soviet-Cuban Quarantine and Self-Defense', above n 50.

[84] Y Dinstein, *War, Aggression and Self-Defence*, 4th edn, above n 7, 187–92.

it ripostes to an armed attack that has indeed materially begun.[85] The question is not, then, one of defining the threat but of determining when the armed attack began.[86] It is difficult to make any judgement because, here again, it should be recalled that this situation is to date a purely theoretical one. The question was evoked, but not settled, in the discussions that preceded the adoption of the definition of aggression.[87] One can still, though, lay down the principle that, as regards its object and purpose, self-defence can only be implemented once the armed attack has materially begun.[88] *A contrario*, an armed riposte could not be accepted in the event of simple preparations for a future action, whether an invasion plan or even an order transmitted to troops or military commanders.[89] It is the beginning of performance that is the critical instant from when one can assert that one is faced with a situation of armed attack.[90] And it is, of course, for the State claiming to be acting in self-defence to prove that an armed attack has actually been initiated.[91]

c) The Travaux Préparatoires of the UN Charter

Some proponents of the preventive self-defence thesis believe they can successfully rely on the *travaux préparatoires* of the UN Charter by noting that States never manifested their intention to modify the definition of the right of self-defence which, as we have seen, then extended to a riposte in the event of an imminent threat.[92]

However, the question is poorly framed to my mind. The question is not whether, abstractly, the drafters of the Charter intended to change existing law but what the scope of that law was in their view. There is nothing to show that States were convinced at the time that preventive self-defence should be considered as consistent with the Charter. In this respect, it can be pointed out that the text of what was to become article 51 included from

---

[85] ibid, 189–90; LA Sicilianos, *Les réactions décentralisées à l'illicite. Des contre-mesures à la légitime défense*, above n 61, 403–05; T Christakis, 'Vers une reconnaissance de la notion de guerre préventive?', above n 48, 21. See also USRR, A/C.6/SR.288, 16 January 1952, para 21.

[86] I Brownlie, *International Law and the Use of Force by States*, above n 47, 367.

[87] India; A/C.6/SR.1274, 3 November 1971, para 4.

[88] R Kolb, *Ius contra bellum. Le droit international relatif au maintien de la paix*, 2nd edn, above n 25, 266.

[89] Mary Ellen O'Connel considers that 'there must be a plan for the attack, and the plan must be in the course of implementation' ('Lawful Self-Defense to Terrorism' 63 (2002) *Univ of Pittsburgh Law Review* 894).

[90] According to Y Dinstein, 'The crux of the issue . . . is who embarks upon an apparently irreversible course of action, thereby crossing the legal Rubicon'; *War, Aggression and Self-Defence*, 4th edn, above n 7, 191; see also A Constantinou, *The Right of Self-Defense under Customary International Law and Article 51 of the UN Charter*, above n 7, 125 *ff*.

[91] See also: Y Dinstein, *War, Aggression and Self-Defence*, 4th edn, above n 7, 191–92.

[92] H Waldock, 'The Regulation of the Use of Force by Individual States in International Law', *RCADI*, 1952-II, tome 81, 497–98; MC Wood, 'Towards New Circumstances in Which the Use of Force May Be Authorized? The cases of Humanitarian Intervention, Counter-Terrorism, and WMD' in N Blokker and N Schrijver (ed), *The Security Council and the Use of Force. A Need for Change?* (Leiden/Boston, Martinus Nijhoff, 2005) 80.

the outset the requirement of an armed attack, without reserving the case of an imminent threat.[93] Now, this text has never been fundamentally challenged by any State, nor has any State considered that it should be broadly construed as implicitly including the notion of imminent threat.[94] On the contrary, several indications suggest that this notion of threat has been intentionally excluded by the drafters of the text. In presenting the draft Charter to his colleagues, the representative of France clearly distinguished between prevention and repression of aggression, specifically restricting self-defence to the latter.[95] Similarly, to a legal advisor who pointed out that the draft of what was to become article 51 was limited to the case of an armed attack alone, the head of the US delegation in San Francisco replied: 'this was intentional and sound. We did not want exercised the right of self-defense before an armed attack occurred'.[96] In this same discussion, it was asked what was 'our freedom under this provision in case a fleet had started from abroad against an American republic, but had not yet attacked', to which it was replied that 'we could not under this provision attack the fleet, but we could send a fleet of our own and be ready in case an attack came'.[97] Lastly, it will be observed that a British proposal to extend the scope of self-defence to any situation entailing a breach of the peace was dropped.[98] It will be agreed that none of that argues for interpreting article 51 as covering the notion of preventive self-defence.[99]

In any event, it shall be recalled that *travaux préparatoires* are insufficient to set aside the terms of a provision when these are precise and do not seem manifestly absurd or unreasonable,[100] which are conditions that article 51 satisfies, as seen. The text of the latter must therefore prevail unless, of course, it has been recognised as having a different meaning by all of the States *after* the Charter was adopted. There is nothing to preclude that some informal modification of the article might result from subsequent practice revealing an agreement of the parties, as provided for by article 31(3) of the 1969 Vienna Convention. However, the existence of such an agreement

---

[93] See: *UNCIO*, vol IV, 3 *ff*; *UNCIO*, vol 4, 532 and 902; *UNCIO*, vol 12, 853 and 727; *UNCIO*, vol 20, 40, 277, 371 and 532.

[94] See: *UNCIO*, vol 4, 675; *UNCIO*, vol 12, 691 ff; *UNCIO*, vol 11, 66.

[95] *UNCIO*, vol 11, 72–73.

[96] *Foreign relations of the United States: Diplomatic Papers—1945*, 1967, 818.

[97] ibid, 709; see also *Charter of the UN, Report to the President on the Results of the San Francisco Conference by the Chairman of the US Delegation, the Secretary of State, June 26, 1945*, Department of State publication 2349, Conference series 71, 1945, 41 in MM Whiteman, *Digest of International Law*, vol 13 (Washington, Department of State Publ, 1968) 357.

[98] T Christakis, 'Existe-t-il un droit de légitime défense en cas de simple "menace"? Une réponse au "groupe de personnalités de haut niveau" de l'ONU', above n 48, 210; LA Sicilianos, *Les réactions décentralisées à l'illicite. Des contre-mesures à la légitime défense*, above n 61, 299.

[99] Y Dinstein, *War, Aggression and Self-Defence*, 4th edn, above n 7, 184.

[100] Art 32 of the Vienna Convention on the Law of Treaties; see Y Le Bouthillier, 'Article 32' in O Corten and P Klein (eds), *Les Conventions de Vienne sur le droit des traités. Commentaire article par article* (Bruxelles, Bruylant, 2006) 1350–53.

must be proved, which appears somewhat difficult, whether one takes account of the positions of principle reiterated by States or precedents over which the notion of preventive self-defence might have been evoked.

The Persistent Refusal of the International Community of States as a Whole to Admit the Principle of Preventive Self-Defence

Practice since the Charter was drawn up seems to confirm the interpretation based on the ordinary meaning of its article 51. Several collective security treaties drawn up at regional level have been concluded and drafted adopting the formulation of the Charter and in particular the restriction of self-defence to the case of armed attack. Such treaties include those of the OAS,[101] WEU,[102] NATO,[103] the Warsaw Pact[104] or more recently the European Union.[105] The same trend is reflected in the conclusion of bilateral treaties on security.[106] *A contrario*, I know of no treaty instrument that defines self-defence as the riposte to a mere threat. In view of this treaty practice, it does not seem that States have tried in any way to challenge the clear terms of article 51.

Beyond the texts of existing treaties, several scholars have argued the cause of preventive self-defence by invoking the stances taken by States in less formal contexts. This is why, after briefly evoking the immediate post-war years (a), we shall look at the many discussions and the positioning that marked out the Cold War (b) before envisaging the debates on the reform of the UN sixty years after it was set up (c).

a) The Immediate Post-War Years

Scholarship in favour of preventive self-defence sometimes invokes two series of events that directly followed the adoption of the Charter: the Nuremberg case law and the early work of the International Atomic Energy Agency.[107] Upon examination, it would seem excessive to see in them precedents challenging the letter of article 51.

In particular, the case law of the Nuremberg tribunal contains the assertion that

> preventive action in foreign territory is justified only in case of an 'instant and overwhelming necessity for self-defense, leaving no choice of means, and no

---

[101] Art 3 § 1 of the Inter-American Treaty of reciprocal assistance, 2 September 1947; www.oas.org.

[102] Art V of the Brussels Treaty; www.weu.int.

[103] Arts 5 and 6 of the Washington Treaty; www.nato.int.

[104] Art 4 of the Pact; avalon.law.yale.edu.

[105] See, eg: Art I-41§7 of the Treaty establishing a Constitution for Europe; eur-lex. europa.eu.

[106] See, eg: Art 8 of the 16 March 1984 Agreement between Mozambique and South Africa; *UNTS*, vol 1352, 28–31.

[107] DW Bowett, *Self-Defence in International Law*, above n 54, 138.

moment for deliberation (The Caroline Case, Moore's *Digest of International Law*, II, 412)'.[108]

This *dictum* calls for several remarks, all of which restrict its scope somewhat. First, the tribunal does not make any claim to interpret article 51 of the UN Charter, for obvious reasons of intertemporal law, especially in criminal matters. At most, this precedent might be invoked to interpret the law that existed before the UN Charter was adopted. Even then, allowance would have to be made for the circumstance that, upon analysis, the tribunal does not claim explicitly to specify the meaning or limits of the institution of self-defence, but more generally refutes the much broader argument of 'preventive action'.[109] It is not easy, then, to determine whether legally it is referring here to self-defence, to the state of necessity or to ancient doctrines of self-protection.[110] It should be added in this respect that the tribunal was made up of specialist criminal judges—and not of recognised international lawyers—who were adjudicating on individual responsibilities and not State-type responsibilities, which obey quite different rationales.[111] In this context, the passing reference to the *Caroline* case, which is not accompanied by any proof or grounds, can certainly not be considered to be an authorised interpretation of the contemporary prohibition of the use of force among States.

On the other hand, one may wonder about the scope of the UN General Assembly's adoption of resolution 95 (I), 'Affirmation of the Principles of International Law recognized by the Charter of the Nürnberg Tribunal'. In this resolution, the Assembly 'affirms the principles of international law recognized by the Charter of the Nürnberg Tribunal and the judgment of the Tribunal' and then invites the International Law Commission to make a draft for the formulation 'in the context of a general codification of offences against the peace and security of mankind, or of an International Criminal Code, of the principles recognized in the Charter of the Nürnberg Tribunal and in the judgment of the Tribunal'.[112] This text has sometimes been invoked to claim that the UN Member States indirectly but clearly accepted the idea of preventive self-defence as it was set out in the case law cited.[113] A straightforward reading of the terms of the resolution shows,

---

[108] *Trial of the major war criminals before the international military Tribunal*, Nuremberg, 14 November 1945–1 October 1946, Nuremberg, 1948, vol XXII, 448 (www.loc.gov/rr/frd/Military_Law/NT_major-war-criminals.html).

[109] ibid.

[110] J Zourek, 'La notion de légitime défense en droit international', above n 8, 63; LA Sicilianos, *Les réactions décentralisées à l'illicite. Des contre-mesures à la légitime défense*, above n 61, 396.

[111] *Trial of the major war criminals before the international military Tribunal*, above n 108, vol I, 1 ff.

[112] GA Res 95 (I), 11 December 1946.

[113] See: O Schachter, 'In Defense of International Rules on the Use of Force' (1986) *The Univ Of Chicago LR* 113–14 and 133–36.

however, that this would be very largely to exaggerate its scope. Clearly its purpose is to confirm the existence in international law of notions that were embryonic—or even non-existent—until then such as crimes against peace, the crime of genocide or crimes against humanity which, unlike preventive self-defence, are recognised in the Nuremberg statute. The way the ILC interpreted its mandate confirms this. In the context of the work that followed the adoption of this resolution, it at any rate never claimed to introduce or recognise preventive self-defence in international law.[114] It seems particularly hazardous, therefore, to use the Nuremberg case law and its consequences to claim that this notion has been recognised by UN Member States as a whole.

Another event of the immediate post-war years that is sometimes invoked[115] in favour of the argument of preventive self-defence is the activity of the Atomic Energy Commission which, in its first report on the establishment by treaty of a system of control of atomic weapons declared in the part on recommendations that:

> In consideration of the problem of violation of the terms of the treaty or convention [on atomic energy matters], it should also be borne in mind that a violation might be so of so grave character as to give rise to the inherent right of self-defence recognized in Article 51 of the Charter of the United Nations.[116]

This report was evoked by the General Assembly which, in its resolution 191 (III)

> approve[d] the general findings (part II C) and recommendations (part III) of the first report and the specific proposals of part II of the second report of the Commission as constituting the necessary basis for establishing an effective system of international control of atomic energy to ensure its use only for peaceful purposes and for the elimination from national armaments of atomic weapons in accordance with the terms of reference of the Atomic Energy Commission.[117]

Upon reading the actual terms of the resolution it seems exaggerated to say the least to claim that the UN Member States accepted the argument of preventive self-defence, even supposing such an acceptance were considered legally possible at the time on the basis of a General Assembly

---

[114] See above, ch 2, s II.

[115] H Waldock, 'The Regulation of the Use of Force by Individual States in International Law', above n 92, 498; R Higgins, *The Development of International Law Through the Political Organs of the United Nations*, above n 41, 203; SM Schwebel, 'Aggression, Intervention and Self-Defence', *RCADI*, 1972-II, tome 136, 481; see also Netherlands; A/C.6/SR.410, 28 October 1954, 40 and 42; *contra*, Mexico; A/C.6/SR.415, 4 November 1954, paras 39–42.

[116] *Official Records of the Atomic Energy Commission, 1946, Special Supp, Report to the Security Council*, 3rd part, recommendations, 17–19, cited in *Report of the Special Committee of 1956 on the Question of Defining Agression*, 8 October–9 November 1956, GA, Off Doc: 12th sess, Supp no 16 (A/3574), New York, 1957, 8, para 56 (see also *Repertory of Practice of the Un Organs*, 1945–1954, vol II, 435; www.un.org/law/repertory).

[117] GA Res 191 (III) of 4 November 1948.

resolution alone.[118] While the Assembly approves certain features, it is only as a 'necessary basis' to be taken into consideration for drawing up a treaty system to be developed subsequently. It was on the basis of this resolution that work was begun that was subsequently to lead to the creation of the International Atomic Energy Agency and to the development of treaty-based and institutional mechanisms governing atomic weapons. Now, there is nothing in these mechanisms to suggest that States would have accepted that a breach of a treaty would have been enough as such to justify the unilateral exercise of a right of self-defence.[119] Quite the contrary, and as practice has confirmed, it is the Security Council that is in charge of reacting to any threats following from violations of the treaty arrangements in question.[120]

As can be seen, there is nothing to establish that, in the aftermath of its drafting, article 51 was interpreted by States as a whole, despite its actual wording, as not including the condition of an armed attack. In actual fact, it was only in the 1950s that some Member States began to call clearly for the suppression of this condition by pleading for self-defence in the event of a simple imminent threat.[121] Such positions have never, though, secured the agreement of the international community of States as a whole, whether during the Cold War (b) or more recently at the time of the debates on the sixty years of the UN (c).

b) The Cold War Period

Preventive self-defence has been evoked in the context of several debates within the UN over many years. Notable are discussions that preceded the adoption of the major resolutions on the prohibition of the use of force such as resolutions 2625 (XXV), 3314 (XXIX) and 42/22, and those on self-defence as a circumstance precluding wrongfulness, in the context of the ILC draft on international responsibility. We shall not detail here the many stances taken during those discussions, however great their interest. More generally we shall show that the claims in favour of preventive self-defence not only have never convinced a large majority of States but have become scarcer over time. That probably explains, as shall be observed below, why no trace of them is found in the main texts finally adopted.

The proposal to accept preventive self-defence in international law was first made in the context of work on a definition of aggression in the early

---

[118] See also: Q Wright, 'The Cuban Quarantine' (1963) 57 *AJIL* 561; G Bebr, 'Regional Organizations: A UN Problem' (1955) 49 *AJIL* 177, fn 42.

[119] I Brownlie, *International Law and the Use of Force by States*, above n 47, 276–77; 'The Use of Force in Self-Defence', above n 47, 243.

[120] LA Sicilianos, *Les réactions décentralisées à l'illicite. Des contre-mesures à la légitime défense*, above n 61, 397; see also SC Res 255 (1968) of 19 June 1968, paras 1 and 3.

[121] See also: *ILCY*, 1949, 108 *ff*; art 11 of the Declaration on rights and duties of States; GA Res 375 (IV) of 6 December 1949 ('Every State has the right of individual or collective self-defence against armed attack').

1950s. That proposal was defended by the Netherlands[122], Greece,[123] Belgium,[124] China,[125] Panama,[126] Peru[127] and Colombia.[128] The following arguments were set out:

—preventive self-defence was allegedly enshrined in the Nuremberg case law;[129]
—preventive self-defence could be considered as a general principle of law insofar as the notion occurs in many national legal systems;[130]
—preventive self-defence is required especially in the atomic age, as a State threatened with destruction must not be rendered powerless,[131] which the General Assembly supposedly acknowledged when it enshrined the IAEA's conclusions in 1948;[132]
—'armed attack' within the meaning of article 51 supposedly refers to any violation of article 2(4).[133]

These arguments, though, are far from having convinced all the States that were then UN members, with Socialist (USSR,[134] Ukraine,[135] Belarus,[136] Poland,[137] Romania,[138] Czechoslovakia[139]), African or Asian (Egypt,[140] Iran,[141] Syria[142]), Latin-American (Chile,[143] Mexico,[144]

---

[122] A/C.6/SR.337, 28 November 1952, para 6; A/C.6/SR.410, 28 October 1954, paras 40–42 and 46; A/C.6/SR.417, 8 November 1954, para 19.

[123] A/C.6/SR.279, 7 January 1952, para 10.

[124] A/C.6/SR.287, 15 January 1952, paras 27, 28 and 29; A/C.6/SR.290, 16 January 1952, paras 60–61 and 65; but see A/C.6/SR.409, 28 October 1954, para 15.

[125] A/C.6/SR.329, 19 November 1952, para 6; A/C.6/SR.417, 8 November 1954, para 31; A/C.6/SR.337, 28 November 1952, paras 42–43; A/C.6/SR.1168, 3 December 1969, 387, para 24.

[126] A/C.6/SR.403, 14 October 1954, para 25.

[127] A/C.6/SR.528, 4 November 1957.

[128] A/C.6/SR.532, 13 November 1957.

[129] Netherlands; A/C.6/SR.410, 28 October 1954, para 42; A/C.6/SR.417, 8 November 1954, para 17.

[130] Belgium; A/C.6/SR.287, 15 January 1952, para 27.

[131] China (A/C.6/SR.337, 28 November 1952, para 43) and Netherlands (A/C.6/SR.417, 8 November 1954, para 5).

[132] Netherlands; A/C.6/SR.527, 1 November 1957.

[133] China; A/C.6/SR.337, 28 November 1952, paras 42–43.

[134] A/C.6/SR.288, 16 January 1952, paras 21 and 34; A/C.6/SR.341, 4 December 1952, para 14; A/C.6/SR.414, 3 November 1954, paras 33 and 37.

[135] A/C.6/SR.290, 18 January 1952, para 3.

[136] A/C.6/SR.411, 29 October 1954, para 15; A/C.6/SR.528, 4 November 1957.

[137] A/C.6/SR.292, 19 January 1952, para 24; A/C.6/SR.406, 20 October 1954, para 39; A/C.6/SR.415, 4 November 1954, paras 22 and 24.

[138] A/C.6/SR.520, 22 October 1957, para 11; A/C.6/SR.1349, 3 November 1972, para 50.

[139] A/C.6/SR.413, 3 November 1954, paras 10–11; A/C.6/SR.418, 9 November 1954, para 46; A/C.6/SR.524, 29 October 1957; see also A/AC.134/SR.19, 2 July 1968 in A/AC.134/SR.1-24.

[140] A/C.6/SR.291, 19 January 1952, paras 10–11; A/C.6/SR.414, 3 November 1954, para 2.

[141] A/C.6/SR.405, 18 October 1954, paras 3 and 5; A/C.6/SR.416, 5 November 1954, para 32.

[142] A/C.6/SR.517, 14 October 1957.

[143] A/C.6/SR.281, 9 January 1952, para 28; see also A/C.6/SR.290, 18 January 1952, paras 56–57.

[144] A/C.6/SR.408, 25 October 1954, para 32.

Paraguay[145]), or Western countries (Norway,[146] or even France[147] and the UK[148]) opposing the idea of preventive self-defence, with emphasis on the arguments that:

—the text of the Charter clearly shows that the Security Council alone is competent for answering simple threats, the plain meaning of article 51 limiting self-defence to the case of armed attacks;[149]

—the State that is the victim of a threat of the use of force is not without means of defence; it can take any military measure without crossing the border and submit the dispute to the mechanisms for peaceful settlement or collective security;[150]

—acceptance of preventive self-defence would consecrate the return to the 'law of necessity' that the Charter was devised to stamp out; the risk of abuse is greater when preventive self-defence makes the proportionality criterion inoperative;[151]

—the analogy with criminal law is irrelevant for governing relations among States[152] and in any event some national legal systems do not admit of any preventive self-defence.[153]

It is clear therefore that in the 1950s there was no general agreement for recognising the notion of preventive self-defence.

The controversy continued into the 1960s with a similar balance of power setting a minority of States favourable to preventive self-defence against a majority that were highly critical of it. In the main, the first group comprised Western States[154] and the second Socialist,[155] Third

[145] A/C.6/SR.419, 10 November 1954, para 15.

[146] A/C.6/SR.413, 3 November 1954, para 30.

[147] AC Kiss, *Répertoire de la Pratique française en matière de droit international public*, tome VI (Paris, edn CNRS, 1969) 63, no 84; see also ibid, 72, nos 100 and 101.

[148] A/C.6/SR.412, 1 November 1954, para 10; A/C.6/SR.416, 5 November 1954, paras 18–28; but the British position changed later; see below and 'United Kingdom Materials on International Law' (1984) 60 *BYBIL* 583 and 591 and (1986) 62 *BYBIL* 642.

[149] Iran (A/C.6/SR.405, 18 October 1954, para 5), Czechoslovakia (A/C.6/SR.413, 3 November 1954, para 11), Mexico (A/C.6/SR.415, 4 November 1954, paras 39–42).

[150] Norway (A/C.6/SR.413, 3 November 1954, para 30), USSR (A/C.6/SR.419, 10 November 1954, para 2; A/AC.77/L.4 (art 7) and A/C.1/603, 4 November 1950).

[151] Czechoslovakia; A/C.6/SR.413, 3 November 1954, para 11.

[152] Ukraine (A/C.6/SR.290, 18 January 1952, para 3).

[153] Chile (A/C.6/SR.281, 9 January 1952, para 28).

[154] United Kingdom (A/C.6/S.R.805, 5 November 1963, para 7; A/AC.125/SR.65, 31 July 1967; A/AC.134/SR.85, 9 February 1971 in A/AC.134/SR.79-91, 50; but see also; A/C.6/S.R.761, 16 November 1962, 147, para 13), Australia (A/C.6/S.R.817, 21 November 1963, para 23; but see A/AC.119/SR.10, 3 September 1964, 11), Norway (A/AC.134/SR.67, 30 July 1970 in A/AC.134/SR.67-78; but see A/C.6/SR.1208, 27 October 1970, para 43), Greece (A/C.6/SR.1208, 27 October 1970, para 6), Belgium (A/C.6/SR.1351, 6 November 1972, para 1).

[155] Czechoslovakia (A/C.6/S.R.871, 8 November 1965, para 35; A/AC.125/SR.62, 26 July 1967; A/C.6/S.R.1086, 4 December 1968, para 30), USSR (A/AC.134/SR.67, 30 July 1970 in A/AC.134/SR.67-78; A/C.6/SR.1272, 2 November 1971, para 8; A/C.6/SR.1351, 6 November 1972, para 33), Romania (A/C.6/SR.1164, 1 December 1969, para 9), Yugoslavia

World[156] and Latin American[157] States. The distinction, though, was not a radical one, with several Western States also criticising the notion, as illustrated notably[158] by this declaration by Spain: '[it] was clear that only when a country has first been attacked could it exercise its legitimate right of self-defence under Article 51. Any possibility of legalizing preventive war was out of the question'.[159]

(A/C.6/SR.1167, 3 December 1969, para 25; A/AC.134/SR.87, 11 February 1971 in A/AC.134/SR.79-91), Bulgaria (A/AC.134/SR.33, 12 March 1969 in A/AC.134/SR.25-51; A/AC.134/SR.57, 20 July 1970 in A/AC.134/SR.52-66, 46).

[156] Ceylon (A/C.6/S.R.805, 5 November 1963, para 21; Sri Lanka; A/C.6/SR.1478, 16 October 1974, para 56), Indonesia (A/C.6/S.R.809, 12 November 1963, para 8), Philippines (A/C.6/S.R.823, 2 December 1963, para 4), Mongolia (A/C.6/S.R.935, 22 November 1966, para 24; A/C.6/SR.1274, 3 November 1971, para 37; A/C.6/SR.1169, 3 December 1969, para 4; A/C.6/SR.1474, 11 October 1974, para 12), Ethiopia (A/C.6/S.R.936, 22 November 1966, para 40), Syria (A/AC.125/SR.88, 16 September 1968; *Report of the Special Committee on Principles of International Law concerning Friendly relations and co-operation among States*, Supp no 18, A/8018, 1970, para 207; A/AC.134/SR.70, 4 August 1970 in A/AC.134/SR.67-78), Jordan (A/C.6/SR.1271, 1 November 1971, para 14), Dahomey (A/C.6/SR.1075, 20 November 1968, para 33), Sudan (A/C.6/SR.1078, 22 November 1968, para 2; A/AC.134/SR.47, 27 March 1969 in A/AC.134/SR.25-51), Iraq (A/C.6/SR.1167, 3 December 1969, para 16; A/C.6/SR.1202, 16 October 1970, para 19; A/C.6/SR.1348, 2 November 1972, para 12; A/AC.134/SR.39, 21 March 1969 in A/AC.134/SR.25-51; A/AC.134/SR.47, 27 March 1969 in A/AC.134/SR.25-51; A/AC.134/SR.67, 30 July 1970 in A/AC.134/SR.67-78; A/C.6/SR.1271, 1 November 1971, para 22), Congo-Brazzaville (A/C.6/SR.1169, 3 December 1969, para 84), Gabon (A/C.6/SR.1205, 22 October 1970, para 36), UAR (A/AC.134/SR.22, 5 July 1968 in A/AC.134/SR.1-24; A/AC.134/SR.64, 27 July 1970 in A/AC.134/SR.52-66), Algeria (A/AC.134/SR.86, 10 February 1971 in A/AC.134/SR.79-91), Iran (A/AC.134/SR.41, 24 March 1969 in A/AC.134/SR.25-51), Pakistan (A/C.6/SR.1207, 27 October 1970, para 20; A/C.6/SR.1347, 1 November 1972, para 6), Lebanon (A/C.6/SR.1212, 30 October 1970, para 28), Egypt (A/C.6/SR.1269, 27 October 1971, para 17; A/C.6/SR.1483, 23 October 1974, para 28), Kenya (A/C.6/SR.1350, 3 November 1972, 231, para 32), Nigeria (A/C.6/SR.1351, 6 November 1972, para 20).

[157] Peru (A/C.6/S.R.765, 23 November 1962, para 22), Cuba (A/C.6/S.R.820, 27 November 1963, para 22; A/C.6/S.R.893, 8 December 1965, para 36; A/C.6/S.R.1091, 10 December 1968, para 41; A/C.6/SR.1479, 18 October 1974, para 41; see also A/C.6/SR.1076, 21 November 1968, para 8; A/C.6/SR.1206, 26 October 1970, para 70; A/C.6/SR.1273, 2 November 1971, para 32; A/C.6/SR.1349, 3 November 1972, para 28; A/C.6/SR.1441, 19 November 1973, para 30), Panama (A/C.6/S.R.824, 2 December 1963, para 8), Uruguay (A/C.6/S.R.997, 14 November 1967, para 25; A/AC.124/SR.74, 7 August 1970 in A/AC.134/SR.67-78), Mexico (A/C.6/SR.119/SR.9, 3 September 1964; A/C.6/S.R.1095, 13 December 1968, para 36; A/AC.125/SR.22, 23 March 1966, para 20; A/AC.134/SR.6, 11 June 1968 in A/AC.134/SR.1-24; A/C.6/SR.1165, 2 December 1969, para 35; A/C.6/SR.1074, 19 November 1968, para 22; A/C.6/SR.1075, 20 November 1968, para 24), Chile (A/AC.125/L.23, 24 March 1966, g); A/AC.125/SR.22, 23 March 1966, para 31; A/AC.125/SR.66, 1 August 1967; A/C.6/SR.1167, 3 December 1969, para 11; A/AC.134/SR.15, 26 June 1968 in A/AC.134/SR.1-24; A/C.6/SR.1276, 4 November 1971, para 34), Jamaica (A/C.6/SR.1077, 22 November 1968, para 24), Ecuador (A/C.6/SR.1078, 22 November 1968, para 36; A/AC.134/SR.10, 17 June 1968 in A/AC.134/SR.1-24; A/AC.134/SR.58, 21 July 1970 in A/AC.134/SR.52-66; A/C.6/SR.1273, 2 November 1971, para 22), Guyana (A/AC.134/SR.33, 12 March 1969 in A/AC.134/SR.25-51, 54; A/AC.134/SR.95, 1 March 1972 in A/AC.134/SR.79-91, 37).

[158] See also: France (A/C.6/SR.1166, 2 December 1969, para 3), Sweden (A/C.6/SR.1079, 25 November 1968, para 6), and Italy (A/AC.134/SR.47, 27 March 1969 in A/AC.134/SR.25-51, 203; see also A/AC.134/SR.70, 4 August 1970 in A/AC.134/SR.67-78, 54–61).

[159] Representative of Spain; A/AC.134/SR.9, 14 June 1968 in A/AC.134/SR.1-24, 101.

Moreover, it is observed that some States have not always defended coherent positions.[160] Thus, some delegations that are traditionally amenable to the idea of preventive self-defence have seemed to dismiss it on some occasions. The US has criticised the tendencies to define aggression too widely: 'With regard to the scope of the definition, this delegation agreed that acts not involving the use of force within the meaning of the Charter should not be described as aggression; *that excluded, for example, mere threats of the use of force*, as also economic, political or ideological activities'. (emphasis added)[161]

It seems besides that the proponents of preventive self-defence have progressively given up wanting to have their view prevail within the General Assembly. In the second part of the 1970s and at any rate in the 1980s, the debates preceding the adoption of resolution 42/22 contrast with those of the 1950s. In the 1984 working document presented by five Western European countries—Belgium, France, Italy, West Germany and the UK—, self-defence is very classically defined with no mention of preventive self-defence,[162] the recognition of which no longer seems to be called for in the texts.[163] Several States, however, emphasise that the notion is not consistent with the UN Charter.[164] A 1985 report by the Special Committee specifies that several delegations asserted that the preventive use of force was contrary to article 51 while others preferred to place the debate not on the legal ground but on that of political necessity to ensure that no State should find itself with no option but to use force preventively to ensure its survival.[165] Plainly, if doubts still arise and if questions are still asked, the dominant reference remains the text of article 51, and therefore the refusal in principle of preventive self-defence. This seems to be reduced from being no longer a legal but a political notion, with States reserving the possibility of ensuring their survival whatever the state of positive international law.[166]

---

[160] See, eg: Cyprus; cp A/C.6/S.R.822, 29 November 1963, para 7; and A/AC.134/SR.89, 22 February 1971 in A/AC.134/SR.79-91.

[161] USA; A/AC.134/SR.10, 17 June 1968 in A/AC.134/SR.1-24; see also A/AC.134/SR.31, 7 March 1969 in *Special Committee on the Question of Defining Aggression*, Second Session, A/AC.134/SR.25-51.

[162] *Report of the Special Committee on Enhancing the Effectiveness of the Principle of Non-Use of Force in International Relations*, Supp no 41 (A/39/41), 4 April 1984; see also *Report of the Special Committee on Enhancing the Effectiveness of the Principle of Non-Use of Force in International Relations*, Supp no 41, A/34/41.

[163] See, eg: Australia (A/C.6/31/SR.50, 22 November 1976, para 44) or Greece (A/C.6/40/SR.11, 10 October 1985, para 2).

[164] Cuba (A/C.6/31/SR.51, 23 November 1976, para 41), USSR (*Report of the Special Committee on Enhancing the Effectiveness of the Principle of Non-Use of Force in International Relations*, Supp no 41, A/34/41, 4 June 1979, 106), Trinidad and Tobago (A/C.6/40/SR.11, 10 October 1985, para 59), Mexico (A/C.6/42/SR.17, 8 October 1987, para 11). See also 'La pratique belge en matière de droit international' (1987) 20 *RBDI* 470.

[165] *Report of the Special Committee on Enhancing the Effectiveness of the Principle of Non-Use of Force in International Relations*, Supp no 41 (A/40/41), 10 June 1985, para 89.

[166] But see: 'United Kingdom Materials on International Law' (1986) 62 *BYBIL* 617; 'Canadian Practice in International Law' (1982) 20 *CYIL* 303–04; (1989) 27 *CYIL* 373–74.

In view of this development it is hardly surprising that preventive self-defence does not appear in any of the texts finally adopted. Resolution 2625 (XXV) does not deal explicitly with the question of self-defence but recalls that 'States have a duty to refrain from acts of reprisal involving the use of force',[167] confirming that a simple violation of international law—which a threat to use force may constitute—does not of itself justify an armed riposte. The annex to resolution 3314 (XXIX) defines aggression as '*the use of armed* force by a State against the sovereignty, territorial integrity or political independence of another State, or in any other manner inconsistent with the Charter of the United Nations . . .'. (emphasis added)[168] Given the debates that preceded the adoption of this provision, it is difficult not to deduce that threat was knowingly excluded. Similarly, in reading this excerpt from the declaration appended to resolution 42/22, one can but see in it confirmation of the text of article 51, requiring there to be an actual armed attack: 'States have the inherent right of individual or collective self-defence *if an armed attack occurs, as set forth in the Charter*'. (emphasis added)[169] Article 2 of the definition of aggression has sometimes been invoked as an argument in favour of preventive self-defence since this article recognises the Security Council's right not to characterise a use of force in breach of the Charter as an aggression.[170] Such provision, however, merely recalls the discretionary power of characterising or not characterising a situation as an aggression, which article 39 does already and which has been abundantly confirmed in practice.[171] This clearly shows, besides, that the absence of characterisation as aggression by the Council under article 39 does not mean that, in law, no armed attack within the meaning of article 51 has been committed.

To close the examination of this period, we shall mention the debates in the context of the International Law Commission's work on State responsibility and more specifically on self-defence as a circumstance precluding wrongfulness. While asserting that the ILC had to abstain from deciding on legal controversies about the scope of article 51,[172] Rapporteur Ago affirmed that 'The State finds itself in a position of self-defence when it is confronted by an armed attack against itself in violation of international

---

[167] GA Res 2625 (XXV) of 24 October 1970, first principle.

[168] Art 1, GA Res 3314 (XXIX) of 14 December 1974; see also art 5 of the definition, according to which 'No consideration of whatever nature, whether political, economic, military or otherwise, may serve as a justification for aggression'.

[169] Art I.13, GA Res 42/22 of 18 November 1987.

[170] See: P Malanczuk, 'Countermeasures and Self-Defense as Circumstances Precluding Wrongfulness in the International Law Commission's Draft Articles on State Responsibility' (1983) 43 *Zaörv* 762.

[171] T Christakis, 'Vers une reconnaissance de la notion de guerre préventive?', above n 48, 22–23.

[172] *YILC*, 1980, II, part One, 67, para 116.

law'.[173] Its relevant draft article evokes an action 'to defend itself or another State against armed attack as provided for in Article 51 of the Charter of the United Nations'.[174] Several ILC members thought, though, that the rapporteur had gone too far in his interpretation of self-defence and that a more cautious approach should be taken,[175] differing opinions being incidentally voiced on the subject of preventive self-defence.[176] The 1980 draft therefore refers more generally to a 'lawful measure of self-defence taken in conformity with the Charter of the United Nations'.[177] It shall be observed though that in its commentary the ILC specifies that in the case of self-defence, the dangers must be represented by 'the particularly serious offence of wrongful recourse to armed force',[178] an expression that does seem to exclude the hypothesis of a simple threat. Examination of debates within the General Assembly's Sixth Commission confirms this trend. Several States call for a very stringent interpretation of self-defence that would consist in taking up the terms of article 51 of the Charter.[179] In this context no fewer than nine States seem to dismiss the notion of preventive self-defence: Brazil,[180] GDR,[181] Romania,[182] Iraq,[183] Mongolia,[184] Trinidad and Tobago,[185] Libya,[186] Pakistan[187] and Yugoslavia.[188] Conversely only Israel declares itself explicitly for the notion,[189] with other States adopting more ambiguous positions.[190]

---

[173] ibid, 51–52, para 87; see also ibid, 62–64, paras 111–13; *YILC*, 1980, I, 1619th session, 25 June 1980, para 3; ibid, para 19; the rapporteur 'd[oes] not think the authors of Article 51 of the Charter could have any intention of departing from the concept of self-defence recognized by general international law, namely, self-defence allowed only as a response to aggression and not as a reaction to other unlawful acts'; ibid, para 21).

[174] *YILC*, 1980, II, part One, 70 (art 34).

[175] Riphagen (*YILC*, 1980, I, 1620th session, 26 June 1980, para 8), Ouchakov (ibid, para 15), Reuter (ibid, paras 22–24), Tsuruoka (*YILC*, 1980, I, 1627th session, 7 July 1980, paras 1–2), Diaz Gonzalez (ibid, para 9), Barboza (ibid, para 14), Quentin-Baxter (ibid, para 17), Pinto (ibid, para 25), Tabibi (*YILC*, 1980, I, 1628th session, 8 July 1980, para 21), Sucharitkul (ibid, para 28).

[176] Comp Ouchakov (*YILC*, 1980, I, 1620th session, 26 June 1980, para 17) and Schwebel (*YILC*, 1980, I, 1621st session, 27 June 1980, para 2) or Barboza (*YILC*, 1980, I, 1627th session, 7 July 1980, para 11).

[177] *YILC*, 1980, II, part Two, 50 (art 34). See the same expression in the final text of 2001; *Report of the International Law* Commission, A/56/10, 2001, art 21; see also J Crawford, *Second Report on State responsibility*, A/CN.4/498/Add.2, 30 April 1999, para 301.

[178] *YILC*, 1980, II, part Two, 34, para 2.

[179] Mexico (A/C.6/35/SR.48, 13 November 1980, paras 22–23), Iraq (A/C.6/35, SR.51, 17 November 1980, para 62) Egypt (A/C.6/35, SR.52, 18 November 1980, para 54).

[180] A/C.6/35/SR.47, 12 November 1980, para 24.

[181] A/C.6/35/SR.49, 14 November 1980, para 16.

[182] A/C.6/35, SR.50, 17 November 1980, para 4.

[183] A/C.6/35, SR.51, 17 November 1980, para 56.

[184] A/C.6/35, SR.53, 19 November 1980, para 30.

[185] A/C.6/35, SR.56, 20 November 1980, para 26.

[186] A/C.6/35, SR.57, 21 November 1980, para 35.

[187] A/C.6/35, SR.58, 21 November 1980, para 17.

[188] A/C.6/35, SR.59, 24 November 1980, para 31.

[189] A/C.6/35, SR.50, 17 November 1980, para 15.

[190] See: USA (A/C.6/35, SR.51, 17 November 1980, para 4) and UK (A/C.6/35, SR.51, 17 November 1980, para 11).

Ultimately the practice that developed throughout the Cold War shows that a large majority of States always fought the idea of preventive war, whatever name it went by, and preferred to keep to the wording of article 51. Although a minority of States initially attempted to bend the meaning of that provision, complaints gradually abated and finally left no mark in the texts adopted. In any event, it seems very difficult to show that preventive self-defence was accepted by the international community of States as a whole during this period, but also, as shall be seen, in the years that followed.

c) The Discussions on UN Reform in the Organisation's 60th anniversary Year

The 1990s saw few debates on preventive self-defence.[191] However, several commentators emphasised certain stances taken up after 11 September 2001.[192] The positions of several States have been pointed out, whether allies of the US or not, and Security Council resolution 1368 (2001) from which one might deduce a progressive recognition of the right of preventive self-defence, including in a broader hypothesis than that of an imminent threat.[193] I do not feel such an argument is convincing for several reasons.[194] First because, upon scrutiny, some of the declarations cited are more political posturing than specifically legal lines of argument. Next because the number of States cited—ten or so at most—remains small in any event. Lastly and above all because a review of the discussion for the sixty years of the UN dispels any doubt on the matter: the States parties to the Charter have manifestly not accepted to loosen the wording of article 51.

Preventive self-defence was debated at length for the UN's sixty years, the Secretary-General having tasked a 'High-Level Panel' to draft a text dealing with various aspects of UN reform. This text, published in 2004, includes a section on self-defence that reads:

> [A] threatened State, according to long established international law, can take military action as long as the threatened attack is *imminent*, no other means would deflect it and the action is proportionate. The problem arises where the threat in question is not imminent but still claimed to be real: for example the acquisition, with allegedly hostile intent, of nuclear weapons-making capability. Can a State, without going to the Security Council, claim in these circumstances the right to act, in anticipatory self-defence, not just pre-emptively (against an imminent or proximate threat) but preventively (against a non-imminent or non-proximate one)?[195]

---

[191] But see: Korea; A/C.6/54/SR.25, 3 November 1999, para 98.

[192] M Reisman and A Armstrong, 'The Past and Future of the Claim of Preemptive Self-Defense' (2006) 100 *AJIL* 538–46.

[193] ibid, 538. See below and above, ch 3, s I.

[194] See also: T Christakis, 'Existe-t-il un droit de légitime défense en cas de simple "menace"? Une réponse au "groupe de personnalités de haut niveau" de l'ONU', above n 48, 218–19.

[195] *A more secured world: Our shared responsibility*, Report of the Secretary-General's High-level Panel on Threats, Challenges and Change, United Nations, 2004, A/59/565, paras 188–89.

In answering no to this last question, the Panel then clearly rules out the notion of 'unilateral preventive action', in the very broad sense.[196] *A contrario*, the Panel considers that self-defence is allowed in the event of an 'imminent or proximate threat', a position that can be found too in the March 2005 report by the UN Secretary-General:

> Imminent threats are fully covered by Article 51, which safeguards the inherent right of sovereign States to defend themselves against armed attack. Lawyers have long recognized that this covers an imminent attack as well as one that has already happened.[197]

These two passages rekindled the debate on preventive self-defence that had gone cold over the previous twenty years, at least in the context of the UN. It seems especially interesting to see how it has developed in what is presented as a thoroughly new context, that of the 'war against terrorism'.

All told, from the sources I have consulted, only ten States at most have clearly[198] supported the position defended by the Panel and then by the UN Secretary-General. That position was very bluntly dismissed though by other States, as shall be seen next, explaining why the only texts finally adopted by States as a whole seem to set aside the preventive self-defence argument.

We must begin by observing in this respect that, on the particular point of preventive self-defence, the excerpts from the foregoing reports appear purely and simply to consecrate the official US position as exposited in September 2002 in a document considered as expressing the Bush doctrine.[199] According to that document, 'For centuries, international law recognized that nations need not suffer an attack before they can lawfully take action to defend themselves against forces that present an imminent danger of attack'.[200]

---

[196] ibid, paras 190–92.

[197] *In larger freedom: towards development, security and human rights for all*, A/59/2005, 24 March 2005, 33, para 124. The Secretary-General simply mentions 'lawyers'. The High-level Panel Report (above n 195) quotes more precisely: O Schachter, 'The Right of States to Use Force' (1984) 82 *Michigan LR* 1633–65; W Friedmann, *The Changing Structure of International Law* (New York, Columbia UP, 1964) 259–60; L Henkin, *How Nations Behave*, 2nd edn (New York, Columbia Univ Press, 1979) 143–45. According to T Christakis, only O Schachter really supports anticipatory self-defence ('Existe-t-il un droit de légitime défense en cas de simple "menace"? Une réponse au "Groupe des personnalités de haut niveau" de l'ONU', above n 48, 200–01, n 11); see also P Hilpold, 'Reforming the United Nations: New Proposals in a Long-Lasting Endeavour' (2005) 52 *NILR* 396 and 399; *contra* L Boisson de Chazournes, 'Rien ne change, tout bouge, ou le dilemme des Nations Unies. Propos sur le rapport du Groupe de personnalités de haut niveau sur les menaces, les défis et le changement' (2005) 109 *RGDIP* 154.

[198] See also: GA, *Exchange of views on the President's draft outcome document of the High-level Plenary Meeting of the General Assembly of September 2005*, A/59/HLPM/CPR.1, Statement by the Argentine Delegation, Permanent Mission of the Argentine Republic to the UN, New York, June 22, 2005.

[199] M Reisman and A Armstrong, 'The Past and Future of the Claim of Preemptive Self-Defense', above n 192, 532–33.

[200] *The National Security Strategy of the United States of America*, September 2002, 15; www.whitehouse.gov/nsc/nss.html.

Those terms occur almost verbatim in the reports by the Panel and the UN Secretary-General.[201] Admittedly, as emphasised, those reports do not follow the aspirations expressed by the US, *de lege ferenda*, to extend further the concept of self-defence by admitting it in the event of a non-imminent threat, because of the particular dangers that terrorist activities would take on in the current context. Even so, *de lege lata*, the possibility of preventive self-defence is presented as an accepted thing. It will not be surprising then that Washington welcomed the two reports, noting that 'the Panel agrees that a threatened State does not have to wait until it is attacked to act in order to exercice its inherent right of self-defense, as recognized by Article 51 of the UN Charter',[202] since:

> The Secretary-General's report makes the key point that a State need not wait until it is actually attacked in order to use force in self-defence, which is to say that there is a right of anticipatory self-defence in appropriate circumstances. Anticipatory action is an element of the inherent right of self-defence that remains lawful under the United Nations Charter.[203]

The US takes up therefore the traditional argument that the expression 'inherent right' does indeed leave untouched an existing custom consecrating preventive self-defence.

This argument was unsurprisingly defended by several allies of the US. The UK representative asserted that 'the Charter does not limit a Member State to taking action in self-defence only after an armed attack has occurred',[204] which position was also taken by the representative for Australia.[205] Israel's representative declared that

> Israel notes the clear statements of the Panel and the Secretary General recognizing that a State may use force in self-defense in the event of both actual and imminent attacks, and *believes that this observation should also be explicitly included in the Outcome Document itself.* (emphasis added)[206]

---

[201] See above.

[202] *US Reactions to UN Secretary-General's High-Level Panel Report*, 'Contemporary Practice of the United States' (2005) 99 *AJIL* 495; see also, *Statement by Ambassador Patrick Kennedy, US Representative for United Nations Management and Reform, on the Report of the High Level Panel on Reform, in an Informal Meeting of the General Assembly, January 31, 2005;* www.un.int/usa/05_013htm; *The National Security Strategy of the USA,* March 2006, www.whitehouse.org; 'Contemporary Practice of the United States' (2006) 100 *AJIL* 690.

[203] USA, A/59/PV.87, 7 April 2005, 23; see also *Statement by M Adler, US Advisor, on Freedom From Fear, in the UNGA Discussion of Cluster II Issues for the High Level Panel, April 22, 2005,* www.un.int/usa/05print_083htm.

[204] A/59/PV.85, 5 April 2005, 26; see also 'United Kingdom Materials on International Law', 2001, 691; (2002) 73 *BYBIL* 853–55; (2003) 74 *BYBIL* 767 and 769; (2004) 75 *BYBIL* 822–23 and 825–26; (2005) 76 *BYBIL* 902.

[205] GA, 7 April 2005, Plenary Exchange on the Secretary-General's report, 'In Larger Freedom', *Statement by HE Mr John Dauth LVO Ambassador and Permanent Representative of Australia to the UN,* Australian Mission to the United Nations, www.AustraliaUN.org.

[206] Informal Meeting of the GA on the Draft Outcome of the High-Level Plenary Meeting of the GA (14–16 September 2005), *Statement by HE Ambassador Dan Gillerman, Permanent Representative of Israel to the UN*; see also *United Nations Reforms—Position Paper of the Government of Israel,* 1 July 2005, www.mfa.gov.il/gen_assembly.

Israel therefore proposes explicitly taking up the possibility of preventive self-defence in the final documents for the sixty years of the UN.

This possibility is defended again by other States that could not be classified as unconditional allies of the US. One thinks first of African States like Uganda, which also wishes the recognition of self-defence in the event of an actual or imminent attack to be expressly stated in the final text,[207] and Morocco, speaking through Mohamed Bennouna, then the country's permanent representative to the UN.[208] But one can also cite two States that traditionally are not very sensitive to an extensive interpretation of the prohibition of the use of force; Liechtenstein,[209] and above all Switzerland, the latter considering that self-defence can be invoked by a State when it is the victim of an armed attack or that such an attack is 'absolutely imminent'.[210] Let us mention too the case of Korea which states it shares the viewpoint that article 51 of the Charter applies also to imminent threats.[211]

Russia's position, which is sometimes cited as being similar to that of the US on this point,[212] ought to be mentioned at this stage. Upon analysis, it seems that the Russian position cannot be reduced to pure and simple acceptance of preventive self-defence. By the terms of the clarification made in February 2005 by Russia's foreign minister, 'Where a country has been subjected to a terrorist attack and there are serious grounds to believe that a repetition of this attack from an identified source is inevitable, the State by way of the exercice of its right to self-defense can take necessary measures to liquidate or reduce that lingering threat'.[213]

[207] 'With regard to security threats, a state is entitled to use force in self-defence in the event of actual or imminent attack. This principle is within the ambit of the Charter of the United Nations *and should be clearly reflected in the outcome document*' (emphasis added); *Statement by HE Mr Francis K Butagira, Ambassador and Permanent Representative of the Republic of the Republic of Uganda to the United Nations to the 10th Informal Meeting of the Plenary of the High-Level Plenary Meeting of the GA of September 2005*, New York, 1 July 2005, Permanent Mission of Uganda to the UN.

[208] *Echange de vues sur les recommandations contenues dans le rapport du groupe de personnalités de haut niveau sur les menaces, les défis et le changement*, New York, 31 January 2005, www.morocco-un.org.

[209] *Statement by HE Christian Wanaweser, 27 January 2005, informal meeting of the GA*, Permanent Mission of the Principality of Liechtenstein to the UN, para 9.

[210] Our translation; Permanent Mission of Switzerland to the United Nations, 59th session of the GA, informal consultations, points 45 and 55 of the agenda, Report of the Secretary-General: In Larger Freedom; Cluster II: Freedom from fear; *Declaration of HE Mr Peter Maurer, permanent représentative of Switzerland to the United Nations*, New York, 21 April 2005; see also 'La pratique suisse en matière de droit international public' (2002) 12 *RSDIE* 643; *contra*, 'La pratique suisse en matière de droit international public' (2001) 11 *RSDIE* 599; A/59/PV.86, 6 April 2005.

[211] Report of the Secretary-General: 'In Larger Freedom: Towards Security, Development and Human Rights for All: Cluster II (Freedom from Fear)', www.koreanconsulate.org/un.

[212] MC Wood, 'Towards New Circumstances in Which the use of Force May Be Authorized? The Cases of Humanitarian Intervention, Counter-Terrorism and Weapons of Mass Destruction', above n 92, 81, n 21; see also R Kolb, 'Chronique commentée de quelques faits internationaux. Deuxième partie' (2006) 16 *RSDIE* 405–08.

[213] *Ministry of Foreign Affairs of the Russian Federation, Information and Press Department, Russian MFA Information and Press Deparment Commentary Regarding a Russian Media Question Concerning Possible Preventive Strikes at Terrorits' Bases*, February 3, 2005; www.ln.mid.ru/.

Russia does not claim therefore that self-defence can be implemented even before a first act of armed attack can be established.[214] The situation evoked presupposes on the contrary that a first attack has indeed occurred. In such an event, Russia considers though that the riposte may consist not just in repelling an ongoing attack but also in preventing new attacks from occurring, especially when faced with terrorist acts perpetrated from abroad. This position calls for certain remarks relative to the traditional condition of necessity as a constituent component of self-defence, but it cannot be reduced to support for the preventive self-defence argument.

That argument has been very obviously criticised by a significant number of States, the first of which are traditionally refractory to the Bush administration doctrine. Evidence of this is the very clear position taken by Iran's representative:

> The report argues that 'Lawyers have long recognized that [Article 51] covers an imminent attack as well as one that has already happened.' (*A/59/2005, para. 124*) It is evident that, from a purely legal perspective, nothing can be further from the letter or the spirit of the Charter or the opinion of independent jurists. Various judgments of the International Court of Justice (ICJ) in various cases have emphasized that measures in self-defence are legitimate only after an armed attack occurs. Article 51 in no way covers imminent threats, and international law does not confer any legitimacy on the dangerous doctrine of pre-emption.[215]

Likewise for Algeria's representative:

> As to the use of force, the Secretary-General clearly endorses the Panel's logic regarding the interpretation of Article 51 of the Charter on legitimate self-defence. We do not share that reasoning. We believe that the wording of Article 51 is

---

[214] See also: 'Russian Minister of Foreign Affairs Sergey Lavrov's Interview with Mayak Radio Station on September 12, 2005; www.ln.mid.ru/; *Transcript of Interview Granted by Minister of Foreign Affairs of the Russian Federation Igor Ivanov to the Russian Television Channel RTR, September 13, 2002*, ibid; *Transcript of the Interview Granted by Minister of Foreign Affairs of the Russian Federation Lergey Lavrov to the Al-Jazeera TV Channel, Moscow, September 10, 2004*, ibid; 'Position of Russiana at the 61st UNGA', ibid: 'we consider inadmissible to undermine or weaken the above principle, for example through a broad interpretation of the right of states to an individual or collective self-defense under Article 51 of the UN Charter. That principle provides an adequate legal basis for establishing acceptable limits to the use of force in exercising the right of self-defense, including in the context of "new challenges and threats" such as terrorism, the spread of weapons of mass destruction, etc. Based on that norm, the right of self-defense shall arise if a state comes under an "armed attack", meaning an attack by armed forces or with the use of other means (subject to commensurability in terms of scale, intensity and potential consequences), for instance in case of a massive terrorist attack. In principle, to exercise the right of self-defense, the state is not supposed to wait for negative consequences of such an attack' (para 10).

[215] A/59/PV.87, 7 April 2005, 17; see also *Statement by Ambassador Mehdi Danesh-Yazdi, Permanent Representative of the Islamic Republic of Iran at the informal thematic consultations of the General Assembly in the Report of the Secretary-General, 'In Larger Freedom—Towards Development Security and Human Rights for All', Cluster II Issues (freedom from fear)*; *Statement by HE Dr M Javad Zarif, Permanent Representative of the Islamic Republic of Iran at the informal meeting of the Plenary of the High-level Plenary Meeting of the GA of September 2005, June 21, 2005*, www.reformtheun.org.

restrictive and that the legitimate right of self-defence can therefore be invoked and applied only in the case of armed aggression. Indeed, doctrine and jurisprudence teach us that Article 51 in no way covers imminent attacks.[216]

A similar position was defended by States like Belarus,[217] Indonesia,[218] Pakistan,[219] Egypt,[220] India[221] and Turkey.[222] We can cite China's position that 'Anticipatory self-defense or preventive use of military force is not advisable; the use of force must be authorized by the Security Council'.[223] Similarly, one can mention the Latin American States such as Costa Rica[224] and above all Mexico, whose representative methodically refuted the passages from the High-Level Panel and Secretary-General's reports by observing that preventive self-defence was contradicted by the wording of

[216] A/59/PV.86, 6 April 2005, 9–10.

[217] 'Belarus calls against any ambiguous interpretation of Article 51 of the Charter in order to justify by some states unilateral preventive use of force as actions in self-defense'; Ministry of Foreign Affairs of the Republic of Belarus, *Position of the Republic of Belarus for the 60th Session of the UN General Assembly*, http://mfa.gov.

[218] 'We feel that the recommendatons on certain important issues tended to introduce interpretations that are inconsistent with preceding explanations, such as on the issue of the "preemptive" right to self-defense. We do believe Article 51 shall be carefully considered, and that it would avoid any rewriting and reinterpretation'; *Statement by HE Mrs Adiyatwidi Adiwoso Asmady, Deputy Permanent Representative of the Republic of Indonesia to the UN at the Informal Consultations of the General Assembly*, New York, 22 February 2005, www.indonesiamission-ny.org/NewStatements/om022205.htm; see also A/59/PV.88, 7 April 2005.

[219] A/59/PV.86, 6 April 2005, 5; see also *Statement by Ambassador Munir Akram, Permanent Representative of Pakistan to the UN Informal Meeting of the GA on the Report of the High-Level Panel on Threats and the UN Millennium Project Report (23 February 2005)*; www.un.int/pakistan.

[220] A/59/PV.86, 6 April 2005, 12.

[221] 'With regard to the debate on use of force, we believe that Article 51 is clear enough. The framers of the Charter never intended this article to cover anything beyond its text. This view has the support of the decision and opinions of the principal judicial organ of the United Nations, the International Court of Justice. We believe that Charter gives full authority to the Security Council to preserve international peace and security from threats, whether they be latent or patent'; *Statement by Mr Nirupan Senn, Permanent Representative, on Report of the Secretary-General: 'In Larger Freedom: Towards Development, Security and Human Rights for All' at the 59th session of the UN GA on April 8, 2005*, www.un.int/india/.

[222] 'Article 51 of the UN Charter covers imminent attack and that the right of self-defence can be evoked accordingly' is not a universally accepted interpretation in international law. Therefore, in reaffirming this Article, we should be careful and avoid introducing a new and broad interpretation which might lead to certain complications'; *Statement by HE Ambassador Baki Ilkin, Permanent Representative of Turkey to the UN, Informal Thematic Consultations of the GA on the Report of the Secretary-General In Larger Freedom: Towards Development, Security and Human Rights for All, Cluster II: Freedom from Fear, New York, 22 April 2005*, www.un.int/turkey.

[223] *Statement by Ambassador Wang Guangya on the Report of the High-Level Group*, 27 January 2005, www.china-un.org/eng/; see also *Position Paper of the People's Republic of China on the United Nations*, 17 June 2005, www.chinaconsulate.org/nz; A/60/PV.13, 18 September 2005, 20.

[224] 'We welcome the Panel's recommendation that art. 51 of the Charter should not be rewritten. However, as some other delegations have done before, we must express our concern for the introduction of imminent threat. Such concept should be subject to various interpretations, creating a dangerous grey area on the possible use of force. We advocate for a strict textual interpretation of article 51'; *Statement during the Informal Consultations on the Report of the High Level Panel*, Bruno Stagmo, Ambassador, Permanent Representative of Costa Rica, January 31 2005, Mision permanente de Costa Rica ante las Naciones Unidas.

article 51 and had been rejected on several occasions in the debates that led
to the adoption of resolutions 2625 (XX), 3314 (XXIX) and 42/22.[225] The
case of Belgium is interesting too, since that State made a lengthy study of
the Panel's and the Secretary-General's reports, particularly on the issue of
self-defence before finally clearly dismissing the argument for preventive
self-defence.[226]

Alongside these positions by States from various regions of the world,
mention must be made of the position of the Non-Aligned Movement of
117 States that published several documents commenting on the reports
cited, taking up several times a passage about article 51 by which:

> The Non-Aligned Movement emphasizes that Article 51 of the UN Charter is
> restrictive and recognizes 'the inherent right of individual or collective self-defence
> if an armed attack occurs against a Member of the United Nations'. This Article
> should not be re-written or re-interpreted. This is supported by the practice of the
> UN and in accordance with international law pronounced by the International
> Court of Justice, the principal judicial organ of the UN, concerning this question.
> The Non-Aligned Movement stresses its deep concern over the intention of a
> group of States to unilaterally re-interpret or re-draft the existing legal instru-
> ments, in accordance with their own views and interests. NAM reemphasises that
> the integrity of international legal instruments must be maintained by Member
> States.[227]

This declaration, accepted and reiterated by the majority of UN Member
States, does not explicitly rule out the hypothesis of preventive self-defence,
but one could consider that it does so implicitly. In any event the insistence

[225] *Intervencion del embajador Juan Manuel Gomez-Robledo, Representante permanente alterno
de Mexico, en el debate sobre el informe del secretario general, Cluster II. Libertad para vivir sin
Temor, 22 de abril de 2005,* www.un.int/mexico/2005/ .

[226] Senate of Belgium, 'Rapport fait au nom de la Commission des relations extérieures par
Mme Annane et M. Galand', session of 2004–2005, 24 May 2005, 3-1028-1; Presentation of
Mrs Jihane Annane, co-rapporteur, Senate of Belgium, *Annales,* 16 June 2005, morning ses-
sion, La réforme des Nations Unies, Doc.3-1028, 3-117; 16 June 2005, afternoon session,
Annales, 3-118, 59; http://www.senate.be.

[227] *Comments of the Non-Aligned Movement on the Observations and Recommendations contained in the Report of the High-Level Panel on Threats, Challenges and Change* (A/59/565 and
A/59/565CORR.1), New York, 28 February 2005, paras 23–24; www.un.int/malaysia/NAM/;
see also *Statement by HE Ambassador Rastam Mohd Isa, Permanent Representative of Malaysia
to the United Nations, in his capacity as Chairman of the Coordinating Bureau of the Non-Aligned
Movement, on behalf of the NAM, at the Informal Thematic Consultations of the GA on the Report
of the Secretary-General entitled 'In larger freedom: towards development, security and human rights
for all' (A/59/2005) on Cluster II: Freedom from fear,* New York, Thurday, 21 April 2005, paras
15–16; Permanent Mission of Malaysia to the United Nations; Special Meeting of the
Ministers of Foreign Affairs of the NAM, Doha, Qatar, 13 June 2005, Declaration,
NAM/2005/SFMM/05, 13 June 2005, paras 16–17, www.un.int/malaysia/NAM/; *Statement by
Chairman of the Coordinating Bureau of the NAM on behalf of the NAM at the Informal Meeting
of the Plenary of the GA concerning the Draft Outcome Document of the High-Level Plenary Meeting
of the GA delivered by HE Ambassador Radzi Rahman Chargé d'affaire ai of the Permanent
Mission of Malaysia to the UN,* 21 June 2005; www.un.int/malaysia/NAM/; *14th Summit
Conference of Heads of State or Government of the NAM,* Havana, Cuba, 11–16 September 2006,
2006/Doc.1/Rev.3, para 20.2.

on the need to interpret article 51 strictly, the reference to the case law of the International Court of Justice, which we have seen was invoked by States very hostile to this hypothesis, and the circumstance that among these are some of the most influential members of non-aligned countries are all arguments in this direction.[228] Notice too that after recalling the document from which an excerpt has just been cited, the movement's representative asserted in the debates in the General Assembly that: 'The member countries of NAM, which represent almost two thirds of the membership of this Organization, have noted that generally the ideas and observations submitted by NAM have not been taken into consideration in the Secretary-General's report'.[229] This criticism applies perfectly well to the development of the report on article 51 of the UN Charter.[230]

All told, it is clear that the preventive self-defence argument the Secretary-General presented as being widely accepted is in fact far from being so. Many States from various parts of the world were frankly hostile to it.[231] Other States that were less prominent abstained from defending but also from directly contesting the disputed excerpts from the reports cited. Some merely referred back to article 51,[232] sometimes insistently so that it should not be conflated with the provision bestowing competence on the Security Council;[233] others considered that the question was not clearly decided[234] or that it required close scrutiny;[235] and others still remained completely silent on this particular point.[236] On the whole, the declarations

---

[228] See also: *Text of speech by Malaysia's Prime Minister Datuk Seri Abdullah Ahmad Badawi at the opening of the Ministerial Meeting of the NAM Coordinating Bureau on Monday at the Putrajaya International Convention Centre*, May 29, 2006, para 31; www.reformtheun.org.

[229] 5 April 2005, A/59/PV.85, 16.

[230] See also: Jamaica (on behalf of the G77); 5 April 2005, A/59/PV.85, 18.

[231] *Contra*; J Wouters and T Ruys, 'The Legality of Anticipatory Military Action after 9/11: the Slippery Slope of Self-Defense' (2006) 59 *Studia Diplomatica* 56.

[232] Ukraine, on behalf of the GOUAM (Georgia, Uzbekistan, Ukraine, Azerbaijan and Moldova), A/59/PV.88, 7 April 2005; see also Statement by the Delegation of Azerbaijan at the Informal Meeting of the Plenary on the High-Level Plenary Meeting of the General Assembly of September 2005, 1 July 2005, Permanent Mission of the Republic of Azerbaijan to the United Nations.

[233] Brazil (17 September 2005, A/60/PV.9), Sweden (Prime Minister's Office 21 September 2004, Speech at the opening of the UN General Assembly 59th Session, www.sweden. gov.se).

[234] Sierra Leone; *Statement by HE Mr Allieu Ibrahim Kanu, Ambassador/Deputy Permanent Representative on 6th Committee*, 60th session of the UNGA, 17 October 2005, Permanent Mission of the Republic of Sierra Leone to the United Nations, www.un.int/sierraleone/ documents/.

[235] Cameroon (8 April 2005, Press Release GA/10339), Ireland (September 2003; *Statement by Mr Bertie Ahern to the General Debate at the 58th GA of the UN*, New York, 25 September 2003, www.un.int/ireland/).

[236] France (*La France, les Nations Unies et l'année 2005*; www.diplomatie.gouv.fr); EU (*UK Statement on behalf of the EU by HE Sir Emyr Jones Parry, Permanent Representative of the United Kingdom to the United Nations, 28 July–2 August, 2005, GA; Statement on behalf of the European Union at the informal session of the UN Plenary Assembly on the September Summit, 21 June 2005*, www.europa-eu-un.org/articles/fr/article_4279_fr.htm.

of the Non-Aligned Movement weigh fully, though, when one seeks to compare the respective weights of groups that are for and against this idea.

In this context, it is not at all surprising in any event that the text ultimately adopted by UN Member States as a whole makes no mention of preventive self-defence and seems rather to condemn it indirectly. At the outcome of the World Summit of Heads of State and Government in New York City from 14 to 16 September 2005, a declaration was made that read, under the heading 'use of force':

> We reiterate the obligation of all Member States to refrain in their international relations from the threat or use of force in any manner inconsistent with the Charter . . . We reiterate the importance of promoting and strengthening the multilateral process and of addressing international challenges and problems by strictly abiding by the Charter and the principles of international law, and further stress our commitment to multilateralism. We reaffirm that the relevant provisions of the Charter are sufficient to address the full range of threats to international peace and security. We further reaffirm the authority of the Security Council to mandate coercive action to maintain and restore international peace and security. We stress the importance of acting in accordance with the purposes and principles of the Charter.[237]

The text underscores therefore that the Charter provisions are adequate and then insists on the Security Council's authority 'to address the full range of threats to international peace and security', with no exception or reservation in favour of a right to self-defence in the event of an 'imminent threat'. No reference or allusion to anticipatory self-defence arises from any part of the document which ultimately is the only text on which UN Member States as a whole have agreed.

Given the context in which it was drawn up, it seem to me that this omission is significant. The calls for preventive self-defence, first made by the US, then taken up by the Panel and the UN Secretary-General, then reiterated by a few States during the debates on the matter ran into such opposition that no record of them is to be found in the final document. The earlier drafts did not contain any reference to preventive self-defence either,[238] probably because it was so patently obvious that the concept could not be generally accepted. The text finally adopted seems, on the contrary, to have taken up the proposals from the Non-Aligned Movement, which we saw was far from being won over to preventive self-defence.[239] On this point one can only recall the claims from Israel and Uganda that the idea be explicitly taken up in the final document,[240] the rejection of

---

[237] *2005 World Summit Outcome*, A/RES/60/1, 24 October 2005, paras 77–79.

[238] See, eg: *Revised Draft outcome document of the high-level plenary meeting of the General Assembly of September 2005 submitted by the President of the General Assembly*, 10 August 2005, A/59/HLPM/CRP.1/Rev2.

[239] cp *Proposed Amendments by the NAM to the Draft Outcome Document of the High-Level Plenary Meeting of the GA*, 1 September 2005, A/59/HLPM/CRP.1/Rev.2, paras 54–55*bis*.

[240] See above.

which confirms the significant character of the insistence on the Security Council's competencies and on the existing provisions of the UN Charter that are adequate to cope with 'the full range of threats to international peace and security'.

In conclusion, the debates for the 60 years of the UN are significant. These debates provided an opportunity to some States to formulate a claim that had not been advanced for a long time so explicitly, on a world-wide scale at any rate. This new attempt is reminiscent of the position expressed in the 1950s and 1960s when several States insisted on there being new types of threat related to the advent of the nuclear era to justify the possibility of preventive self-defence. As observed above, the General Assembly at the time refused to consecrate the notion, with most States preferring to insist on the letter of article 51 and on a restrictive interpretation of that provision. That position prevailed again in 2005, even if this time around the threats were characterised as fundamentally new because of the 'war against terrorism'.

The Continuing Refusal of the International Community of States as a Whole to Accept the Idea of Preventive Self-Defence at the Time of Specific Precedents

A review of precedents in which preventive self-defence was evoked shows that the notion has never been accepted by the international community of States as a whole.[241] This observation is valid for the precedents discussed within UN political bodies (a) and is confirmed by existing international case law (b).

a) The Absence of General Acceptance of Preventive Self-Defence in Precedents Debated Within the UN's Political Organs

We shall cover below only what seem the most significant precedents in which the doctrine of preventive self-defence has been invoked, for one reason or another, setting them out in chronological order.[242] Cases where the idea of prevention is obviously related to a problem of riposte to an 'indirect' attack, as when South Africa and Israel in the 1960s and 1970s claimed to act within the territory of third States to prevent attacks but at the same time to put an end to armed actions already undertaken against them by armed bands supposedly operating from the territories of those States shall not be covered again.[243] It seems to me that in such instances we are no

---

[241] SA Alexandrov, *Self-Defense Against the Use of Force in International Law*, above n 14, 149; see also J Combacau, 'The Exception of Self-Defence in UN Practice' in A Cassese (ed), *The Current Legal Regulation of the Use of Force*, (Dordrecht, Martinus Nijhoff, 1986) 24–25.

[242] See also the war between Vietnam and Kampuchea (S/PV.2108, 11 January 1979, para 115 *ff*; S/PV.2110, 13 January 1979, para 29); and France in Tunisia; 'Pratique française du droit international' (1961) 7 *AFDI* 961–65.

[243] See below.

longer strictly in the situation of self-defence officially motivated by a riposte to a simple threat.

A first precedent invoked by doctrine is that of the 1962 Cuban missile crisis.[244] The US took quarantine measures against Cuba in October that year to prevent Cuba from receiving Soviet nuclear material liable to arm missiles that could strike US territory.[245] In this sense, the measures taken by the US might be likened to self-defence to avert a threat of armed attack.[246] There is no need for lengthy developments, though, to show the excessive character of such a claim, first, because the US itself did not invoke the doctrine of preventive self-defence.[247] The country's representative on the Security Council thought that 'since the end of the Second World War, there has been no threat to the vision of peace so profound'.[248] *A contrario*, the US did not claim there was an 'imminent threat' justifying the exercise of a right of self-defence. Legally, it referred rather to a threat to peace that supposedly entitled the Organisation of American States to recommend measures against Cuba.[249] As already reported, it was on the basis of a decision by a regional organisation, and therefore by a collective security mechanism, that the US decision was justified. Preventive self-defence, on the other hand, was not invoked.[250] This cannot be seen as a precedent in this area particularly since, as observed earlier, it cannot be asserted that the US argument was accepted by the international community of States as a whole.[251]

Another classical precedent is that of the Six Day War.[252] Insofar as Israel justified its going to war by the threat to its security further to the aggres-

---

[244] R Higgins, *The Development of International Law Through the Political Organs of the United Nations*, above n 41, 202–03; A Clark Arend and RJ Beck, *International Law and the use of Force* (London and New York, Routledge, 1993) 74–76; R Jennings and A Wattts, *Oppenheim's International Law*, vol 1, above n 74, 425; J Yoo, 'International Law and the War in Iraq' (2003) 97 *AJIL* 573; R Wedgwood, 'The Fall of Saddam Hussein: Security Council Mandates and Preemptive Self-Defense', above n 72, 584–85; T Franck, *Recourse to Force. State Action Against Threats and Armed Attacks*, above n 26, 99–101.

[245] See above, ch 2, s II, and ch 6, s II.

[246] MS McDougal, 'The Soviet-Cuban Quarantine and Self-Defence', above n 50, 597–604; CG Fenwick, 'The Quarantine Against Cuba: Legal or Illegal?' (1963) 57 *AJIL* 589–90; B MacChesney, 'Some Comments on the "Quarantine" of Cuba' (1963) 57 *AJIL* 595–96; CQ Christol, 'Maritime Quarantine: The Naval Interdiction of Offensive Weapons and Associated Matériel to Cuba, 1962' (1963) 57 *AJIL* 533–36 and 543.

[247] SA Alexandrov, *Self-Defense Against the Use of Force in International Law*, above n 14, 155; LA Sicilianos, *Les réactions décentralisées à l'illicite. Des contre-mesures à la légitime défense*, above n 61, 399; T Christakis, 'Vers une reconnaissance de la notion de guerre préventive?', above n 48, 27; RN Gardner, 'Neither Bush nor the "Jurisprudes"', above n 72, 587–88.

[248] S/PV.1022, 23 October 1962, 17, para 82.

[249] ibid, 15–17, paras 79–81; see above, ch 2 s II.

[250] CQ Christol, 'Maritime Quarantine: The Naval Interdiction of Offensive Weapons and Associated Material to Cuba, 1962' (1963) 57 *AJIL* 533–37. See also T Christakis, 'Existe-t-il un droit de légitime défense en cas de simple "menace"? Une réponse au "groupe de personnalités de haut niveau" de l'ONU', above n 48, 217.

[251] Above, ch 6, s II.

[252] *Keesing's Contemporary Archives*, 1967–1968, 22099–102.

sive behaviour of Egypt and of other Arab States and insofar as the Security Council did not condemn the State of Israel, one might see in this, some argue, a general acceptance of preventive self-defence.[253] Here again, the reasoning falls foul of the very terms used by the representative of the main State concerned on the UN Security Council. While it is true that this representative evokes provocative gesturing and a threat that endangered Israel,[254] he very clearly specifies on what basis Israel claimed to be acting in self-defence against Egypt:

> Thus, on the morning of 5 June, when Egypt engaged us by air and land, bombarding the villages of Kissufim, Nahal-Oz and Ein Hashelosha we knew that our limit of safety had been reached, and perhaps passed. In accordance with its inherent right of self-defence as formulated in Article 51 of the United Nations Charter, Israel responded defensively in full strength.[255]

Israel's representative then made similar pronouncements in respect of Syria and Jordan:

> To the appeal of Prime Minister Eshkol to avoid any further extension of the conflict, Syria answered at 12.25 yesterday morning by bombing Megiddo from the air and bombing Deganya at 12.40 with artillery fire and kibbutz Ein Hammifrats and Koordani with long-range guns. But Jordan embarked on a much more total assault by artillery and aircraft along the entire front, with special emphasis on Jerusalem . . .'.[256]

At the critical juncture, during the first debate on the issue in the Security Council, Israel therefore makes a clear distinction between threats and provocations on one side and material acts of aggression on the other. Plainly it is the latter and not the former that, for Israel, justified an action in self-defence within the meaning of article 51.[257] At no time was preventive self-defence invoked, whether by Israel or by the States that then supported it politically.[258] In any event, whatever the Israeli line of argument, the many condemnations of it mean it cannot be asserted that it would have been recognised by the international community of States as a

---

[253] T Franck, *Recourse to Force. State Action Against Threats and Armed Attacks*, above n 26, 101–05; see also SM Schwebel, 'Aggression, Intervention and Self-Defence', above n 115, 481; P Malanczuk, 'Countermeasures and Self-Defense as Circumstances Precluding Wrongfulness in the International Law Commission's Draft Articles on State Responsibility', above n 170, 762–64; J Nyamuya Maogoto, 'New Frontiers, Old Problems: The War on Terror and the Notion of Anticipating the Enemy', above n 40, 31.

[254] S/PV.1348, 6 June 1967, 17, para 178.

[255] ibid, 15, para 155.

[256] ibid, 15, para 158.

[257] See also: *UNYB*, 1967, 199–200.

[258] USA (S/PV.1348, 6 June 1967, 2–3, paras 8–18, and 11–14, paras 116–40; see also *Keesing's Contemporary Archives*, 1967–1968, 22115 and 22121, and A Constantinou, *The Right of Self-Defense under Customary International Law and Article 51 of the UN Charter*, above n 7, 121.

whole.[259] It is self-evident in this respect that the absence of any formal condemnation by the Security Council, which can be explained for obvious political reasons, cannot be construed legally as an *opinio juris* of all the UN's Member States.[260]

To justify the outbreak of war against Iran, Iraq's representative claimed

> my Government was left with no choice but to direct preventive strikes against military targets in Iran. There was, to borrow from the Caroline case, a 'necessity of self-defence, instant, overwhelming, leaving no choice of means and no moment for deliberation'.[261]

Even if it is often overlooked by doctrine, the Iran-Iraq war is one of the rare precedents in which the *Caroline* case is cited, and which we have seen was considered a classical argument for preventive self-defence. Upon examination, it turns out, though, that Iraq used a legally more orthodox conception of self-defence by claiming to have been the victim of an armed attack by Iran.[262] In any event, the legal argument advanced by Iraq is far from having convinced the international community of States as a whole.[263]

A more classical precedent is that of the Israeli bombing of the Iraqi nuclear reactor on 7 June 1981.[264] Having remained evasive about the legal basis for its action,[265] the State of Israel invoked extended preventive self-defence within the Security Council, as attested by this declaration:

> We have been reminded here of the *Caroline* affair. But that incident, as is well known—and the representatives of the United Kingdom and the United States will bear me out in this—occurred almost a century and a half ago. It occurred precisely 108 years before Hiroshima. To try and apply it to a nuclear situation in the post-Hiroshima era makes clear the absurdity of the position of those who

---

[259] USSR (S/PV.1348, 6 June 1967, 5, para 40 and 5–6, para 49; S/PV.1351, 8 June 1967, paras 35 and 121), Bulgaria (S/PV.1348, 6 June 1967, para 72; S/PV.1351, 8 June 1967, para 96), Mali (S/PV.1348, 6 June 1967, para 80), India (ibid, para 88), Iraq (ibid, para 105) Morocco (ibid, para 251), Syria (ibid, paras 201–02) and Jordan (S/PV.1351, 8 June 1967, 13, para 135); see also France; 'Pratique française du droit international' (1967) 13 *AFDI* 895–96.

[260] T Christakis, 'Existe-t-il un droit de légitime défense en cas de simple "menace"? Une réponse au "groupe de personnalités de haut niveau" de l'ONU', above n 48, 216; 'Vers une reconnaissance de la notion de guerre préventive?', above n 48, 25; SA Alexandrov, *Self-Defense Against the Use of Force in International Law*, above n 14, 154; J Wouters and T Ruys, 'The Legality of Anticipatory Military Action after 9/11: the Slippery Slope of Self-Defense', above n 231, 50–51; see also A Clark Arend and RJ Beck, *International Law and the use of Force*, above n 244, 77.

[261] S/PV.2250, 15 October 1980, 6, para 40; see also A/35/PV 22, 3 October 1980, para 104 and C Rousseau, 'Chronique des faits internationaux' (1981) 85 *RGDIP* 168–79.

[262] See : C Alibert, *Du droit de se faire justice dans la société internationale depuis 1945* (Paris, LGDJ, 1983) 110–11.

[263] SC Res 479 (1980) of 28 September 1980, 522 (1982) of 4 October 1982, 540 (1983) of 31 October 1983, 582 (1986) of 24 February 1986, 598 (1987) of 20 July 1986, 598 (1987) of 20 July 1987.

[264] *Keesing's Contemporary Archives*, 1981, 31908–09.

[265] *Letter dated 8 June 1981 from the Permanent Representative of Israel to the United Nations addressed to the President of the Security Council*, S/14510, 8 June 1981.

base themselves upon it. To assert the applicability of the *Caroline* principles to a State confronted with the threat of nuclear destruction would be an emasculation of that State's inherent and natural right of self-defence . . . the concept of a State's right to self-defence has not changed throughout recorded history. Its scope has, however, broadened with the advance of man's ability to wreak havoc on his enemies. Consequently the concept took on new and far wider application with the advent of the nuclear era.[266]

Thus self-defence is supposedly admissible henceforth in the event of a non-imminent threat because of the seriousness of the risk in the nuclear age. The argument was immediately denounced by the Security Council and then by the UN General Assembly, which condemned the Israeli action as incompatible with the Charter.[267] It is true, as some commentators have revealed, that some States have based their condemnation on the criticism of a broad conception of preventive self-defence,[268] without challenging the extended notion in its traditional sense.[269] Several States have, however, more fundamentally refused to caution any idea of preventive war, recalling that self-defence presupposed the existence of a prior armed attack.[270] Under the circumstances, this precedent can plainly not reveal an acceptance of the notion by the international community of States as a whole.[271]

To the best of my knowledge, preventive self-defence has since then no longer been invoked as such as an argument justifying a military intervention. This overview of the practice, however, might be ended with the 2002–2003 Iraq crisis. It should be recalled that, at least until the adoption of resolution 1441 (2002) of 8 November 2002, the US seemed to base its 'right' to intervene on the concept of preventive war.[272] The reasoning exposited by President Bush in the UN General Assembly was that Iraq had weapons of mass destruction (especially chemical and bacteriological ones)

---

[266] S/PV.2288, 19 June 1981, 8, para 80 and 9, para 85.

[267] SC Res 487 (1981) of June 1981; GA Res 36/27 of 13 November 1981 (109-2-34); see also Belgium (and EC States) ('La pratique belge en matière de droit international' (1984–1985) 18 *RBDI* 391), Canada ('Canadian Practice in International Law' (1982) 20 *CYIL* 306–07 and 318) and UK ('United Kingdom Materials on International Law' (1981) 52 *BYBIL* 510, 511 and 512).

[268] T Franck, *Recourse to Force. State Action Against Threats and Armed Attacks*, above n 26, 105–07; A Clark Arend and RJ Beck, *International Law and the use of Force*, above n 244, 77–79.

[269] Sierra Leone (S/PV.2283, 15 June 1981, paras 146–48), USA (S/PV.2288, 19 June 1981, para 157), France ('Pratique française du droit international' (1981) 27 *AFDI* 900).

[270] Brazil (S/PV.2281, 13 June 1981, 5, para 39), Pakistan (ibid, para 70), League of Arab States (ibid, para 98), Ireland (S/PV.2283, 15 June 1981, para 25), Yugoslavia (ibid, para 46), USSR (ibid, paras 63–64), Romania (ibid, para 117), Mexico (S/PV.2288, 19 June 1981, para 115) Uganda (ibid, para 141); see also J Wouters and T Ruys, 'The Legality of Anticipatory Military Action after 9/11: the Slippery Slope of Self-Defense', above n 231, 51.

[271] A Cassese, 'Article 51', above n 12, 1338; LA Sicilianos, *Les réactions décentralisées à l'illicite. Des contre-mesures à la légitime défense*, above n 61, 399–402; G Fischer, 'Le bombardement par Israël d'un réacteur nucléaire irakien' (1981) 27 *AFDI* 164–65; see also A D'Amato, 'Israel's Air Strike upon the Iraqi Nuclear Reactor' (1983) 77 *AJIL* 585.

[272] See above, ch 6, s II.

and that it had ties with terrorist organisations including Al Qaeda.[273] In this context there was every reason to fear that terrorist groups might procure weapons from Iraq for use in deadly attacks similar to those of 11 September 2001. The 'preventive war' was therefore justified, the disarming of Iraq being designed to avert a threat that weighed directly on the US and indirectly on all the States liable to be the target of new terrorist attacks.[274] However, a change in international law cannot be inferred from these declarations. While it was not clearly assumed in legal terms, this argument was dismissed by many States. The very day President Bush made his speech, the French foreign minister dismissed the idea of any unilateral preventive action.[275] More generally, it should be emphasised that the Non-Aligned Movement, which itself includes the majority of UN Member States was especially clear in this area. After recalling the need to respect Iraq's political independence, the Movement 'reiterate[d] its firm rejection of any type of unilateral action against any Member State of the United Nations'.[276] The Non-Aligned Movement then asked on several occasions to speak in the Security Council to reassert the central role of the UN and of multilateralism in maintaining international peace and security. Like the Islamic Conference Organisation (with its 57 States), it again condemned any use or threat of the use of force on the pretext of combating terrorism.[277] The preventive war argument does not seem to have convinced Western States any more in view of the positions of States like France, Germany or Belgium that constantly insisted on the need to maintain the Security Council's authority by opposing the very principle of preventive unilateral military action.[278] Even the States that lined up behind the US to fight the war did not do so by taking up the argument of preventive war or preventive self-defence.[279] It is interesting to observe in this respect that it is on the pretext of an authorisation that could be deduced from resolution 1441 (2002) that these States—and the US too for that matter—claimed that their military intervention was warranted.[280] This argument, we have seen, is far from convincing. The very reference to it despite everything shows, though, that the vast majority of States still prefers to interpret a

---

[273] A/57/PV.2, 12 September 2002.

[274] See: J Nyamuya Maogoto, 'New Frontiers, Old Problems: The War on Terror and the Notion of Anticipating the Enemy', above n 40, 9–13.

[275] A/57/PV.3, 12 September 2002, 31.

[276] *Declaration of the Meeting of Ministers of Foreign Affairs of the Non-Aligned Movement*, UN General Assembly, New York, 18 September 2002, para 12; www.nam.gov.za/media/02925un.htm.

[277] www.oic-oci.org.

[278] See: O Corten, 'Opération *Iraqi Freedom:* peut-on admettre l'argument de l'"autorisation implicite" du Conseil de sécurité? (2003) 36 *RBDI* 205–47.

[279] See, eg, the Vilnius Group (*Statement of the Vilnius Group Countries in Response To The Presentation by the United States Secretary of State to the UN Security Council concerning Iraq*, February 5, 2003).

[280] See above ch 6, s II.

classical cause of justification very broadly (in the case in point the Security Council authorisation) rather than resort to such a fuzzy and dangerous notion as preventive self-defence.[281] Lastly, it will be observed that many commentators, at the time of the conflict, reaffirmed their condemnation of the concept of preventive self-defence.[282]

Finally, a brief review of contemporary practice shows that the intervening States themselves only exceptionally invoke the concept of preventive self-defence and that the concept has never been accepted as a principle by States as a whole. Admittedly one might retort that the dismissal or absence of invocation of the notion is because of factual circumstances, with no precedent being comparable to the formula that arose from the *Caroline* case. Even so, as indicated at the outset, consideration of the ordinary meaning of article 51 implies that self-defence is presumed to require the existence of an armed attack. While it is methodologically possible to reverse this presumption, this can only be done by demonstrating the existence of a practice revealing an agreement of the international community of States as a whole.[283] In view of the foregoing, such proof is far from having been given.[284] The task proves that much harder because the few instances from international case law do not point in this direction, far from it.

b) The Reluctance of International Case Law to Admit Preventive Self-Defence

While there is no precedent dealing expressly with the doctrine of preventive self-defence, whether to accept or to dismiss it, it is difficult to remain silent about certain statements of the International Court of Justice.[285] Thus,

---

[281] A Cassese, 'Article 51', above n 12, 1339–41; T Christakis, 'Existe-t-il un droit de légitime défense en cas de simple "menace"? Une réponse au "groupe de personnalités de haut niveau" de l'ONU', above n 48, 218.

[282] See, eg: 'Appel de juristes de droit international concernant le recours à la force contre l'Irak': 'Self defence presupposes the existence of a prior armed attack; consequently, "preventive self defence" is not admissible under international law' (text published in (2003) 36 *RBDI* 272 and signed by, among others G Abi Saab, G Arangio-Ruiz, P Benvenuti, L Boisson de Chazournes, I Brownlie, J Cardona, M Chemillier-Gendreau, L Condorelli, R Daoudi, E David, C Dominicé, PM Dupuy, PM Eisemann, V Gowlland-Debbas, B Graefrath, P Klein, M Kohen, R Kolb, M Koskenniemi, S Laghmani, E Lagrange, Y Le Bouthillier, A Mahiou, JY Morin, G Palmisano, A Paulus, A Pellet, A Remiro Brotons, H Ruiz Fabri, J Salmon, D Simon, E Suy and U Villani); see also 'Statement by Japanese International Law Scholars on the Iraqi Issue', March 2003 in (2003) 36 *RBDI* 293–96; but see 'Coalition of the willing? Make that war criminals', *The Sidney Morning Herald*, Feb 26, 2003, in (2003) 36 *RBDI* 288).

[283] Above, ch 1, s II.

[284] Independent International Fact-Finding Mission on the Conflict in Georgia, *Report*, September 2009 (www.ceiig.ch/Report.html), vol II, 255. According to the Commission, 'there is no consensus whether self-defence against concrete imminent attacks os permitted'.

[285] Concerning the *Corfu Channel* case, see above, ch 2, s I and H Waldock, 'The Regulation of the Use of Force by Individual States in International Law', above n 92, 499–503; LA Sicilianos, *Les réactions décentralisées à l'illicite. Des contre-mesures à la légitime défense*, above n 61, 397–98.

—in *Military and Paramilitary Activities*, the Court specified on the issue of individual self-defence that 'the exercice of this right is subject to the State concerned having been the victim of an armed attack';[286]

—in its opinion on the *Legality of the Threat or Use of Nuclear Weapons*, the Court recalled that 'This prohibition of the use of force is to be considered in the light of other relevant provisions of the Charter. In Article 51, the Charter recognizes the inherent right of individual or collective self-defence *if an armed attack occurs*'; (emphasis added)[287]

—in the *Oil Platforms* case, after recalling the passage cited above in *Military and Paramilitary Activities*, the Court went on to say that it

> has simply to determine whether the United States has demonstrated that it was the victim of an 'armed attack' by Iran such as to justify it using armed force in self-defence and the burden of proof of the facts showing the existence of such an attack rests on the United States;[288]

—in its opinion on the *Legal Consequences of the Construction of a Wall in the Occupied Palestinian Territory*, after citing it *in extenso*, the Court recalled that 'Article 51 of the Charter thus recognizes the existence of an inherent right of self-defence in the case of armed attack by one State against another State';[289]

—lastly, in the matter of *Armed Activities on the Territory on the Congo*, the Court considered that:

> Article 51 of the Charter may justify a use of force in self-defence only within the strict confines there laid down. It does not allow the use of force by a State to protect perceived security interests beyond these parameters. Other means are available to a concerned State, including, in particular, recourse to the Security Council.[290]

All of these statements seem to denote a reluctant attitude of the Court, to say the least, in respect of any form of preventive war conducted without Security Council authorisation.[291] One can add this excerpt from a

---

[286] (1986) ICJ Rep 103, para 195; but see ibid, para 194.

[287] (1996) ICJ Rep 244, para 38.

[288] (2003) ICJ Rep 189, para 57; but see the Iranian position in the written proceedings: 'only such anticipatory self-defence as is legitimised under the *Caroline* formula can be considered lawful' (Reply, 154, para 7.57).

[289] (2004) ICJ Rep 194, para 139.

[290] ICJ, 19 December 2005, para 148; see also oral pleadings; Corten (CR 2005/3, 12 April 2005, paras 6 and 32) and Brownlie (CR 2005/7, 18 April 2005, 28–29, para 72).

[291] GM Danilenko, 'The Principle of Non-Use of Force in the Practice of the International Court of Defence' in WE Butler (ed), *The Non-Use of Force in International Law* (Dordrecht, Kluwer, 1989) 105–06; T Christakis, 'Existe-t-il un droit de légitime défense en cas de simple "menace"? Une réponse au "groupe de personnalités de haut niveau" de l'ONU', above n 48, 219–20; M Reisman and A Armstrong, 'The Past and Future of the Claim of Preemptive Self-Defense', above n 192, 533; G Palmisano, 'Determining The Law on the Use of Force: the ICJ and Customary Rules on the Use of Force' in E Cannizzaro and P Palchetti (eds), *Customary International Law On the Use of Force* (Leiden/Boston, Martinus Nijhoff, 2005) 217; Tribunal permanent des peuples, 'Le droit international et les nouvelles guerres', session de Rome, December 2002 (2003) 36 *RBDI* 262.

decision of the Eritrea–Ethiopia Claims Commission entered on 19 December 2005 by which 'As the text of Article 51 of the Charter makes clear, the predicate for a valid claim of self-defense under the Charter is that the party resorting to force has been subjected to an armed attack'.[292]

It is true that the preventive self-defence argument has not been expressly excluded from these precedents, the ICJ even specifying on two occasions that it was not ruling on that question.[293] It is difficult, though, not to interpret this case law[294] as confirming the letter of article 51 of the UN Charter. It will be observed besides that the latest statements were made after 11 September 2001 in the context of the renewed debate on the possibilities of preventive war. The general feeling among the judges seems to be reluctance, or even wariness of certain arguments that tend to erode the strict Charter regime on the prohibition of the use of force. In any event, and as already pointed out, it is for doctrine favourable to preventive self-defence to prove the existence of a practice attesting to its acceptance. The least that can be written is that the ICJ case law will be of no avail in this respect.

B. The Question of 'Indirect Aggression'

In the aftermath of 9/11, the US administration stated its intention to riposte to the attacks on New York City and Washington by affirming: 'We will make no distinction between the terrorists who committed these acts and those who harbor them'.[295] In an address of 18 September 2001, the President himself said that

> those who plan, authorize, commit or aid terrorist attacks against the United States and its interests—including those who harbor terrorists—threaten the national security of the United States. It is, therefore, necessary and appropriate that the United States exercise its right to defend itself and protect United States citizens both at home and abroad.[296]

And so the 'war on terror' could be materialised by a riposte not just against the perpetrators of the attacks but also against any States that supported them in any shape or form. In some sense, such States would be indirectly guilty of an armed attack justifying the US exercising its right of self-defence. It is in this perspective that some scholars claim that article 51

---

[292] *Partial Award*. Jus ad Bellum. *Ethiopia's Claims 1–8*, 19 December 2005, para 11.

[293] ICJ, *Military and Paramilitary Activities* (1986) ICJ Rep 103, para 194 and *Armed Activities* (2005) ICJ Rep, para 143. See also: JA Green, *The International Court of Justice and Self-Defence in International Law* (Oxford, Hart Publishing, 2009) 28–30.

[294] See also: *Japan v Shigeru Sakata and ors*, 16 December 1959, Japanese Supreme Court, Judge Shuyichi Ishizaka (*ILR*, vol 32, 58).

[295] S/PV.4370, 7–8; see also *President Signs Authorization for Use of Military Force bill*, Statement by the President, The White House, September 18, 2001, www.whitehouse.gov/.

[296] *President Signs Authorization for Use of Military Force bill*, Statement by the President, www.whitehouse.gov/; see also M Byers, 'Terrorism, the Use of Force and International Law After 11 September' (2002) 51 *ICLQ* 406–07.

justifies a riposte against States that, while they themselves have not carried out an armed attack, have supported private agents who were responsible for such an attack.[297] The argument is therefore that of self-defence in response to what one may designate an 'indirect aggression'.

Before evaluating the relevance of this argument, it should be clarified that it is situated in terms of the attribution of acts of war to a State and not of the extension of the scope of application of the prohibition of the use of force to non-State entities. This latter point has already been examined in chapter three. Certain claims were set out there by which self-defence within the meaning of article 51 could henceforth be exercised against not just other States but also private groups guilty of an act of aggression, especially in the context of the 'war against terrorism'. It has been shown that current international law does not admit such claims, the *jus contra bellum* remaining a legal regime applicable among States, which does not preclude States from combating terrorist activities in the name of maintaining public order, but through international cooperation in criminal matters and policing or the implementation of coercive measures in their own territory. This reluctance to extend the field of application of the rule does not prevent questioning about possible implication of a State's responsibility in the event of acts perpetrated by private groups. It is this question that shall be dealt with here, by examination of the 'indirect aggression' argument.

In my view, this argument does not correspond to existing international law even such as it has developed since 9/11. The Charter law posits an alternative: either a State is directly guilty of an armed attack because of the scale of its implication in the armed action conducted by private groups, and self-defence may be exerted against it without any need to evoke an 'indirect aggression', or a State is harbouring or aiding a private group that is engaging in armed actions against a third State, but without being substantially implicated in the group's activities. There is then a violation of international law, but not an 'armed attack' within the meaning of article 51. Self-defence cannot then be exercised as the Security Council alone is competent for deciding on the appropriate measures. Thus 'indirect aggression', which here shall mean simple support for the activity of irregular groups, has not been admitted in international law, whether in the applicable texts or through evolving practice.

---

[297] T Franck, *Recourse to Force. State Action Against Threats and Armed Attacks*, above n 26, 53 and *ff*; M C Wood, 'Towards New Circumstances in Which the Use of Force May Be Authorized? The cases of Humanitarian Intervention, Counter-Terrorism, and WMD', above n 92, 87; J Brumée and SJ Toope, 'The Use of Force: International Law After Iraq', above n 41, 794–95; see also Y Dinstein, 'International Legal Response to Terrorism' in *Mélanges R Ago. Le droit international à l'heure de sa codification*, t II (Milan, Giuffrè, 1987) 146; M Reisman, 'International Legal Responses to Terrorism', above n 42, 41–54.

The Non-Recognition of 'Indirect Aggression' in Legal Texts

The possibility of characterising a state that supposedly uses private groups to attack another state as an aggressor has long been evoked in the UN.[298] After long years of discussion,[299] the General Assembly drew up a provision that is still considered relevant, article 3*(g)* of the definition of aggression. Beyond this specific provision, one can take into account the texts bearing more generally on state responsibility. Lastly, a cursory review of the discussion for the 60 years of the UN is required. Upon examination, it shall be seen that none of these texts admitted the concept of indirect aggression as just defined.

a) Article 3(g) *of the Definition of Aggression and its Interpretation*

By application of its article 3*(g)*, the definition appended to General Assembly resolution 3314 (XXIX) defines aggression as:

> The sending by or on behalf of a State of armed bands, groups, irregulars or mercenaries, which carry out acts of armed force against another State of such gravity as to amount to the acts listed above, or its substantial involvement therein.[300]

Under this provision, a State shall only be held responsible for acts of armed force by irregulars on certain apparently very stringent conditions.[301] First, and as a precondition, it must be shown that the acts in question are 'of such gravity as to amount to' classical acts of aggression such as invasion or bombing of a territory, or an attack on a ship or aircraft.[302] It is a question here only of applying the criterion of gravity, which appears in article 2 of the definition, to the specific instance of armed actions by private persons. Assuming that, in a specific situation, this first condition were met, a second condition would still have to hold, which condition itself opens up two possibilities:

—either the State in question 'sent' the armed groups to perpetrate acts tantamount to a classical attack, which presupposes the groups were under the State's authority. The situation may be considered as a form of application in the area of *jus contra bellum* of certain mechanisms for informally

---

[298] See: O Corten and F Dubuisson, 'Lutte contre le terrorisme et droit à la paix: une conciliation délicate' in E Bribosia and A Weyembergh (ed), *Lutte contre le terrorisme et droits fondamentaux* (Bruxelles, Bruylant and Nemesis, 2002) 37–69.

[299] See: E Aroneanu, *La définition de l'agression. Exposé objectif* (Paris, éditions int, 1958).

[300] GA Res 3314 (XXIX), 14 December 1974.

[301] P Lamberti Zanardi, 'Indirect Military Aggression' in A Cassese (ed), *The Current Legal Regulation of the Use of Force* (Dordrecht, Martinus Nijhoff, 1986) 111–19; I Brownlie, *International Law and the Use of Force by States*, above n 47, 370 *ff*; 'International Law and the Activities of Armed Bands' (1958) 7 *ICLQ* 731–33; AM Rifaat, *International Aggression* (Uppsala, Almqvist&Wiksell Int, 1979) 274; L Condorelli, 'The imputability to States of acts of international terrorism' (1989) 19 *Israeli Yearbook on Human Rights* 233 and *ff*.

[302] AM Rifaat, *International Aggression*, above n 301, 273–74.

attributing to a State acts by individuals under international responsibility law.[303] Acts by individuals may be ascribed to the State because of the control the State exercises over the perpetrators of those acts, which relates to a problem that shall be contemplated below.

—or, even if the State has not sent irregular forces to perpetrate acts of aggression, the State is responsible for 'substantial involvement' in perpetrating those acts.[304] It is then directly responsible for the act constituting the engagement, without any need to impute to it actions by private persons.[305]

There is nothing, however, in the text of article 3*(g)* to specify the nature of such 'substantial involvement',[306] even if the effect of the expression implies that the position is other than that of sending in the forces.[307] One can imagine first that a State's forces participate in a combined attack with private groups, but that State will then be the author of a direct aggression under subsections *(a)* and following of article 3. The specific feature of article 3*(g)* seems to refer to the situation where, without participating on the ground in the attack as such, the State is engaged in preparing or carrying it out but in more logistical terms, by making available its infrastructure, its equipment or its services, for example, but without going as far as to conduct the armed actions itself. The substantial involvement seems therefore to take on a potentially broad scope, although it presupposes that the State concerned not only knew of the forthcoming perpetration of an act of aggression but also decided to participate in it in a substantial way, without however controlling the whole of the operation since, in such a case, we would be back in the situation where the State 'sends' in troops. *A contrario*, the mere fact that armed groups are operating from a State's territory without that State being willing or able to put an end to such an operation is not enough to bring us within the scope of article 3*(g)* of the definition of aggression.[308] Tolerating or harbouring irregular groups, while plainly an unlaw-

---

[303] A Cassese, 'The International Community Legal Response to Terrorism' (1989) 38 *ICLQ* 598; F Dubuisson, 'Le terrorisme, nouvelle forme d'agression armée au sens du droit international?' in P Calame, B Denis and E Remacle (eds), *L'art de la paix. Approche transdisciplinaire* (Bruxelles, Peter Lang, 2004) 295; A Randelzhofer, 'Article 51', above n 18, 800–01; A Nollkaemper, 'Attribution of Forcible Acts to States: Connections Between the Law on the Use of Force and the Law of State Responsibility' in N Blokker and N Schrijver (ed), *The Security Council and the Use of Force. A Need for Change?* (Leiden/Boston, Martinus Nijhoff, 2005) 148.

[304] O Schachter, 'The Lawful Use of Force by a State against Terrorists in Another Country' (1989) 19 *Israeli Yearbook on Human Rights* 216–19.

[305] J Verhoeven, 'Les 'étirements' de la légitime défense', above n 34, 56–57.

[306] J Stone, 'Hopes and Loopholes in the 1974 Definition of Aggression', above n 50, 237–39. LA Sicilianos, 'L'invocation de la légitime défense face aux activités d'entités non-étatiques' (1989) *Hague YIL* 152–57; F Dubuisson, 'Le terrorisme, nouvelle forme d'agression armée au sens du droit international?', above n 303, 297; P Lamberti Zanardi, 'Indirect Military Aggression', above n 301, 115.

[307] B Broms, 'The Definition of Aggression' (1977-I) 154 *RCADI* 354.

[308] P Lamberti Zanardi, 'Indirect Military Aggression', above n 301, 115.

ful act in regard of many provisions of the *jus contra bellum* already cited,[309] is not enough to characterise a situation as an armed attack entitling the victim State to make a unilateral military riposte. As such, the concept of indirect aggression seems incompatible with the ordinary meaning of article 3*(g)* as accepted at the time by UN Member States as a whole.

Beyond the text ultimately adopted, it is not without interest to look briefly at the position of States as it was being elaborated. Such a review confirms the idea that simple support for armed bands (or *a fortiori* mere tolerance of the presence of such bands in a territory) should be considered as an 'armed attack' within the meaning of article 51 was intentionally was set aside.[310]

Initially, in the 1950s, the idea of indirect aggression was taken up in several draft definitions.[311] Panama proposed characterising as aggression simply tolerating the organisation in one's territory of armed bands responsible for incursions against another State.[312] The proposal was criticised by the UK representative who thought it too dangerous.[313] Likewise Mexico feared that the notion of indirect aggression might have extremely serious effects on the interpretation of article 51.[314] At the time, the concept of indirect aggression ostensibly inspired marked reluctance among most States,[315] including the US.[316]

A divide was, however, to form in the late 1960s between certain Western States that were rather favourable to the concept of indirect aggression, and Socialist or Third World States that were generally more critical of it.[317] A

---

[309] Above, ch 3, s I.

[310] O Corten and F Dubuisson, 'Opération "Liberté immutable": une extension abusive du concept de légitime défense' (2002) 106 *RGDIP* 56–57; RA Müllerson, 'The Principle of Non-Threat and Non-Use of Force in The Modern World', above n 59, 33–35.

[311] *Special Committee on the Question of Defining Aggression*, 8 October–9 November 1956, GA, 12th session, Supp no 16 (A/3574), New York, 1957, paras 59–60; see also GA Res 380 (V), 17 November 1950 and A/C.6/SR.1483, 23 October 1974, para 28.

[312] A/C.6/SR.406, 20 October 1954, para 8; see also Panama and Iran (A/AC.77/L.9), Paraguay (A/AC.77/L.7), USSR (AC.77/L.4), China (A/C.6/SR.409, 26 October 1954, para 14; A/C.6/SR.412, 1 November 1954, para 25; A/C.6/SR.417, 8 November 1954, para 30).

[313] A/C.6/SR.412, 1 November 1954, para 8.

[314] A/C.6/SR.415, 4 November 1954, para 45; see also Netherlands (A/C.6/SR.417, 8 November 1954, paras 8–9).

[315] Peru (A/C.6/SR.418, 9 November 1954, para 28), France (A/C.6/SR.409, 26 October 1954, para 18), Greece (A/C.6/SR.409, 26 October 1954, para 18), Iran (A/C.6/SR.405, 18 October 1954, para 9), Belgium (A/C.6/SR.514, 7 October 1957, 9), USSR (A/C.6/SR.403, 14 October 1954, para 17 and A/AC.77/L.4), Syria (A/C.6/SR.517, 14 October 1957).

[316] According to the Secretary of State: 'if you open the door to saying that any country which feels that it is being threatened by subversive activities in another country is free to use armed force against that country, you are opening the door to a series of wars all over the world, and I am confident that it would lead to a third world war'; January 14, 1957, MM Whiteman (ed), *Digest of International Law*, vol 12 (Washington, Department of State Publ, 1971) 58.

[317] See: P Rambaud, 'La définition de l'agression par l'Organisation des Nations Unies' (1976) 80 *RGDIP* 869.

1969 draft definition by Australia, Canada, Italy, Japan, the UK and the US mentioned as an example of aggression:

(6) organizing, supporting or directing armed bands or irregular or volunteer forces that make incursions or infiltrate into another State;
(7) organizing, supporting or directing violent civil strife or acts of terrorism in another State; or
(8) organizing, supporting or directing subversive activities aimed at the violent overthrow of the Government of another State.[318]

In contradistinction to this text, the draft by 13 countries (Colombia, Congo, Cyprus, Ecuador, Ghana, Guyana, Indonesia, Iran, Mexico, Spain, Uganda, Uruguay and Yugoslavia), also from 1969, provided that:

When a State is a victim in its own territory of subversive and/or terrorist acts by irregular, volunteer or armed bands organized by another State, it may take all reasonable and adequate steps to safeguard its existence and its institutions, without having recourse to the right of individual or collective self-defence against the other State under Article 51 of the Charter.[319]

---

[318] A/AC.134/L.17, 25 March 1969; see also USA (A/C.6/SR.1080, 25 November 1968, para 74; A/C.6/SR.1169, 3 December 1969, para 22; A/AC.134/SR.19, 2 July 1968 in A/AC.134/SR.1-24, 198; A/AC.134/SR.31, 7 March 1969 in *Special Committee on the Question of Defining Aggression*, Second Session, A/AC.134/SR.25-51, 33–35; A/AC.134/SR.62, 24 July 1970 in A/AC.134/SR.52-66; A/AC.134/SR.63, 24 July 1970 in A/AC.134/SR.52-66; A/AC.124/SR.73, 6 August 1970 in A/AC.134/SR.67-78; A/AC.124/SR.74, 7 August 1970 in A/AC.134/SR.67-78), UK (A/C.6/SR.1166, 2 December 1969, para 24; A/AC.134/SR.32, 10 March 1969 in *Special Committee on the Question of Defining Aggression*, Second Session, A/AC.134/SR.25-51, 39; A/AC.134/SR.62, 24 July 1970 in A/AC.134/SR.52-66), Australia (A/C.6/SR.1166, 2 December 1969, para 37), Canada (A/AC.134/SR.56, 17 July 1970 in A/AC.134/SR.52-66; A/AC.134/SR.28, 27 February 1969 in *Special Committee on the Question of Defining Aggression*, Second Session, A/AC.134/SR.25-51, 19), Italy (A/AC.134/SR.55, 16 July 1970 in A/AC.134/SR.52-66), Japan (A/AC.134/SR.34, 13 March 1969 in A/AC.134/SR.25-51; A/AC.134/SR.67, 30 July 1970 in A/AC.134/SR.67-78); see also India (A/C.6/SR.1078, 22 November 1968, para 49) and Norway (A/AC.124/SR.74, 7 August 1970 in A/AC.134/SR.67-78).

[319] Article 8; A/AC.134/L.6, 24 March 1969, and Add 1 and 2. According to Mexico 'the right of self-defence was justified solely in the case of an armed attack. That sentence should be interpreted strictly, since under the Charter armed attack was the only justification for exercising the right of self-defence. Violation of international treaties or the rights or interests of other States, repudiation of debts, *acts of subversion and terrorism, military preparations which did not constitute armed attack*, danger to the life and property of foreigners and breaking of diplomatic relations should no longer be considered, as in the past, to justify the use of force in self-defence. *Although the proposal referred exclusively to direct armed aggression it did not overlook the question of the support increasingly being given by Governments to subversive or terrorist activities against the territorial integrity or political independance of other States. Since the right of self-defence under Article 51 of the Charter could not be invoked in such cases, the sponsors had included paragraph 5, which covered the matter*'; (emphasis added); A/AC.134/SR.15, 26 June 1968 in A/AC.134/SR.1-24, 147; see also A/AC.134/SR.30, 6 March 1969 in *Special Committee on the Question of Defining Aggression*, Second Session, A/AC.134/SR.25-51, 27; A/AC.134/SR.60, 22 July 1970 in A/AC.134/SR.52-66, 86; Uruguay; A/AC.134/SR.21, 4 July 1968 in A/AC.134/SR.1-24.

That position was shared by the USSR[320] and other Socialist States,[321] Third World countries,[322] and some Western States.[323] It was this majority position that finally weighed on the drafting of article 3*(g)* of the definition which, as seen, does not assimilate simple tolerance to an armed attack. This article must therefore be construed very restrictively, as the French delegation very clearly affirmed shortly before its adoption.[324] Yet other States made pronouncements along these lines,[325] which led several States favourable to the concept of indirect aggression to criticise article 3*(g)*.[326]

Finally, the consideration of the definition of aggression requires proceeding with all necessary caution when evoking the hypothesis of a simple tolerance of a State with regard to an irregular group.[327] In such cases, there is incontestably a violation of article 2(4) of the UN Charter, which prohibits very broadly any form of active or passive support for irregular forces. Conversely, States refused to liken passive support to an 'armed attack' within the meaning of article 51 of the Charter.[328] It is only in the hypothesis of active support, that will itself take the form either of sending in irregular bands by the State or of a substantial engagement in armed

---

[320] According to the text of the definition proposed by USSR: 'C. The use by a State of armed force by sending armed bands, mercenaries, terrorists or saboteurs to the territory of another State and engagement in other forms of subversive activity involving the use of armed force with the aim of promoting an internal upheaval in another State or a reverseal of policy in favour of the aggressor shall be considered an act of indirect aggression' (A/AC.134/L.12, 25 February 1969); see also A/C.6/SR.1206, 26 October 1970, para 4; A/C.6/SR.1272, 2 November 1971, para 7.

[321] Ukraine (A/C.6/SR.1274, 3 November 1971, para 25), Belarus (A/C.6/SR.1270, 28 October 1971, para 40), Yugoslavia (A/AC.134/SR.41, 24 March 1969 in A/AC.134/SR.25-51, 141; see also A/AC.134/SR.58, 21 July 1970 in A/AC.134/SR.52-66), Poland (A/C.6/SR.1346, 31 October 1972, para 6), GDR (A/C.6/SR.1441, 19 November 1973, para 16), Mongolia (A/C.6/SR.1274, 3 November 1971, para 46).

[322] Dahomey (A/C.6/SR.1075, 20 November 1968, para 34), Nigeria (A/C.6/SR.1351, 6 November 1972, para 20), UAR (A/AC.134/SR.22, 5 July 1968 in A/AC.134/SR.1-24), Sudan (A/AC.134/SR.22, 5 July 1968 in A/AC.134/SR.1-24), Guyana (A/AC.134/SR.33, 12 March 1969 in A/AC.134/SR.25-51), Uruguay (A/AC.134/SR.63, 24 July 1970 in A/AC.134/SR.52-66), Ecuador (A/AC.134/SR.58, 21 July 1970 in A/AC.134/SR.52-66), Syria (A/AC.124/SR.81, 3 February 1971 in A/AC.134/SR.79-91).

[323] Italy (A/C.6/SR.1205, 22 October 1970, para 16; GA/C.6/SR.1472, 9 October 1974, para 25), Cyprus (A/AC.134/SR.60, 22 July 1970 in A/AC.134/SR.52-66; A/AC.134/SR.63, 24 July 1970 in A/AC.134/SR.52-66; A/AC.134/SR.39, 21 March 1969 in A/AC.134/SR.25-51; A/AC.134/SR.44, 25 March 1969 in A/AC.134/SR.25-51).

[324] A/C.6/SR.1441, 19 November 1973, paras 45-46; A/C.6/SR.1474, 11 October 1974, para 29; A/C.6/SR.1204, 21 October 1970, para 13; A/C.6/SR.1271, 1 November 1971, para 30; A/C.6/SR.1348, 2 November 1972, para 19; A/C.6/SR.405, 18 October 1954, para 23.

[325] See: Sweden (GA/C.6/SR.1472, 9 October 1974, para 7) and Canada (H M Kindred *et al* (eds), *International Law Chiefly as Interpreted and Applied in Canada* (Emond Montgomery Publ Limited, 1987) 32).

[326] Israel, (A/C.6/SR.1480, 18 October 1974, para 59) and USA ('Contemporary Practice of the United States' (1990) 84 *AJIL* 726–27).

[327] I Brownlie, 'The Use of Force in Self-Defence', above n 47, 244–45.

[328] F Dubuisson, 'Le terrorisme, nouvelle forme d'agression armée au sens du droit international?', above n 303, 292–93 and 'La pratique suisse en matière de droit international public' (2000) 10 *RSDIE* 669.

action, that it can be concluded there is a situation of self-defence. In all other instances, the Security Council alone shall be competent to decide on any implementation of armed coercive measures.

b) Consideration of the General Principles of State Responsibility

It is perfectly possible when interpreting article 3*(g)* of the definition of aggression to turn to the mechanisms of international responsibility and more especially to the rules governing the imputation of wrongful acts to a State.[329] Such consideration, however, can only be subsidiary, since the right of responsibility must, as *lex generali*, take a back seat behind the *lex specialis* represented by the rules on the prohibition of the use of force.[330] The reference to the law of international responsibility can therefore only come into play for interpreting article 51 of the Charter and not to circumvent it or to challenge it.

Alongside the classical hypothesis of imputation by legal organs that covers typical examples of aggression such as the bombing of one State's territory by the forces of another, the law of responsibility opens up the way to two less formal mechanisms.[331] Under the first mechanism, the acts of an irregular group are as a matter of principle attributable to the State since the group is completely dependent on the authorities of the State, making it in some sense a '*de facto* organ'. Under the second mechanism, the acts of individuals, who cannot be assimilated to *de jure* or *de facto* organs of the State, are nonetheless attributable to the State because of the control it exerts *in casu* over the acts in question. Each of these mechanisms shall be detailed by referring to case law relating to international responsibility while provisionally ignoring case law more specifically about the definition of aggression, which will be set out later.[332]

The first option was evoked by the ICJ first in *Military and Paramilitary Activities*, where it indicated that it was for the Court

> to determine at this point . . . whether or not the relationship of the *contras* to the United States Government was so much one of dependence on the one side and control on the other that it would be right to equate the *contras*, for legal purposes, with an organ of the United States Government, or as acting on behalf of that Government.[333]

In the case of the *Crime of Genocide*, the Court cited this excerpt to deduce that

---

[329] LA Sicilianos, 'L'invocation de la légitime défense face aux activités d'entités non-étatiques', above n 306, 149 *ff*; see also G Gaja, 'In What Sense was there an "Armed Attack"?', www.ejil.org/forum; O Corten and F Dubuisson, 'Opération 'Liberté immuable': une extension abusive du concept de légitime défense', above n 310, 65–70.

[330] See: ICJ, *Crime of Genocide*, (2007) ICJ Rep, para 401.

[331] ICJ, *Crime of Genocide*, (2007) ICJ Rep, para 397.

[332] Below: II, B.

[333] (1986) ICJ Rep 62, para 109.

according to the Court's jurisprudence, persons, groups of persons or entities may, for purposes of international responsibility, be equated with State organs even if that status does not follow from internal law, provided that in fact the persons, groups or entities act in 'complete dependence' on the State, of which they are ultimately merely the instrument.[334]

It was on the basis of this legal criterion that the Court refused to consider the *contras* as organs of the US, then Serbian forces of Bosnia-Herzegovina as organs of the Yugoslav State, while the two States in question had supported the relevant entities politically, financially and to some extent militarily.[335] By application of this case law the armed actions of an irregular group could not be imputed to a State unless, in reality, the group is so dependent on the State that it is one of its instruments and legally one of its organs. In view of the two precedents just cited, the extent of control required must be particularly great; it cannot be inferred from simple support, even military support, and *a fortiori* not from simple tolerance of the irregular group.

Another possibility for imputing acts committed by an irregular group to a State is to show that in a specific instance (and no longer generally) an act was accomplished under the State's direction or control. This option was codified in article 8 of the draft adopted by the ILC in August 2001 directly aimed at the hypothesis of attributing acts of private persons to a State.[336] Entitled 'Conduct directed or controlled by a State', it lays down that:

> The conduct of a person or group of persons shall be considered an act of a State under international law if the person or group of persons is in fact acting on the instructions of, or under the direction or control of, that State in carrying out the conduct.[337]

The text clearly shows the stringency required at the point when one wishes to attribute the acts of a private group to a State.[338] A general loose control over the group is no longer enough to attribute to the State the doings of each of the group's members. As the Commission confirmed, 'Such conduct will be attributable to the State only if it directed or controlled the specific operation and the conduct complained of was an integral part of that operation'.[339] If this method is applied to the case that

---

[334] ICJ, *Crime of Genocide*, (2007) ICJ Rep, para 392.

[335] ICJ, *Military and Paramilitary Activities*, (1986) ICJ Rep 63, para 110; *Crime of Genocide*, (2007) ICJ Rep, para 394.

[336] ICJ, *Crime of Genocide*, (2007) ICJ Rep, para 298.

[337] ILC, *Responsibility of States for Internationally Wrongful Acts*, 2001, annexed to GA Res 56/83 of 21 December 2001.

[338] JA Gonzales Vega, 'Los atentados del 11 de septiembre. La operacion "Libertad duradera" y el derecho de legitima defensa' (2001) 53 *REDI* 254.

[339] *Draft articles on Responsibility of States for Internationally Wrongful Acts, with commentaries, YILC*, 2001, vol II, Part Two, 47, para 3.

concerns us, the imputation to a State of a military operation perpetrated by private persons presupposes that the State controlled or directed that specific operation. In other cases, the specific responsibility for an operation cannot be ascribed to a State, even if it tolerated the presence of the perpetrators of the operation in its territory. While it incontestably violated international law by its negligent behaviour, the State in question is not for all that the author of an armed attack within the meaning of article 51 of the Charter.

The stringency of the ILC's solution is that much more remarkable in that it follows a hesitation that for a time marked its work on the issue. Article 8 was drafted previously in a more general manner as it provided very broadly that a fact could be imputable to a State if 'it is established that such person or group of persons was in fact acting on behalf of that State',[340] which might cover the attribution of a deed to a State via its simply tolerating the activity of irregular groups. The new Special Rapporteur, James Crawford, pointed out this ambiguity and insisted on the need to remove it in one way or another.[341] It was therefore in full awareness of the situation that the final text was drawn up after observations had been made on the draft by governments and been further discussed in the Commission.[342]

This choice was explicitly based on State practice, but also on the part of the *Military and Paramilitary Activities* case specifically about the attribution to the US of violations of human rights by the *contras*. The ILC cites the passage in which the Court observes that, despite US involvement in certain activities of those forces:

> All the forms of United States participation mentioned above, and even the general control by the respondent State over a force with a high degree of dependency on it, would not in themselves mean, without further evidence, that the United States directed or enforced the perpetration of the acts contrary to human rights and humanitarian law alleged by the applicant State. Such acts could well be committed by members of the *contras* without the control of the United States. For this conduct to give rise to legal responsibility of the United States, it would in principle have to be proved that that State had effective control of the military or paramilitary operations in the course of which the alleged violations were committed.[343]

This excerpt does not concern the attribution of an armed attack to a State but, if it is transposed to this specific domain, we reach the same conclusion as that drawn from the interpretation of article 3(g) made by the ICJ.

---

[340] *YILC*, 1974, vol I, 152.
[341] *First report on State responsibility*, A/CN.4/490/Add.4, 26 May 1998, paras 200 and 215.
[342] See also: A/CN4./L.569, August 1998.
[343] ICJ, *Military and Paramilitary Activities*, (1986) ICJ Rep 65, para 115; see FA Boyle, 'Determining US Responsibility for Contra Operations under International Law' (1987) 79 *AJIL* 86–93.

In both instances, it must be shown that the State concerned controlled the wrongful acts that one is seeking to impute to it. A general control, even as extensive as that which the Reagan administration exercised over the anti-Sandinista forces does not satisfy the legal criteria for imputation, whether generally (it has been seen that that would suppose establishing the existence of a relation of 'complete dependence') or for specific acts.

The case law of the International Criminal Tribunal for the former Yugoslavia (ICTY) and in particular the appeal decision in the *Tadić* case has sometimes been invoked in contradistinction.[344] In this decision, entered on 15 July 1999, the Tribunal's Appeals Chamber considered that the overall control by the Yugoslav authorities of the Serb forces in Bosnia-Herzegovina was enough to internationalise the conflict, without the need to prove the imputation of specific behaviour to the Yugoslav State.[345] The Appeals Chamber revised the trial court decision on this point by affirming explicitly that the criterion stated by the ICJ 'does not seem to be persuasive'.[346] This reasoning clearly did not convince the ILC,[347] which was then in the final stage of its work on State responsibility. After noting that the majority of judges of the ICTY Appeals Chamber 'considered it necessary' to disapprove the ICJ approach, the ILC retorted that:

> The tribunal's mandate is directed to issues of individual criminal responsibility, not State responsibility, and the question in that case concerned not responsibility but the applicable rules of international humanitarian law. In any event *it is a matter for appreciation in each case whether particular conduct was or was not carried out under the control of a State, to such an extent that the conduct controlled should be attributed to it.*[348] (emphasis added)

Moreover, the ICJ was keen to set itself apart from the Criminal Tribunal in the *Crime of Genocide* case, the case law of which was invoked by the plaintiff State.[349] The Court cited article 8 of the ILC draft and applied the criteria of instructions and control over specific acts.[350] It then expressly declared that it had

---

[344] See: Y Dinstein, *War, Aggression and Self-Defense*, 4th edn, above n 7, 203–04.

[345] ICTY, Appeals Chamber, Aff IT-94-1-A, 15 July 1999, para 83 *ff*.

[346] ICTY, CA, Aff IT-94-1-A, 15 July 1999, 47 (ii); *contra*, ICTY, Trial Chamber, 7 May 1997, IT-94-1-T, para 585 *ff*.

[347] See also: Judge Shahabuddeen, ICTY, Appeals Chamber, Aff IT-94-1-A, 15 July 1999, dissenting opinion, para 7 *ff*.

[348] *Draft articles on Responsibility of States for Internationally Wrongful Acts, with commentaries*, YILC, 2001, vol II, Part Two, 48, para 5.

[349] See: Pellet (CR 2006/8, 3 March 2006, 32–39, paras 57–70; CR 2006/31, 18 April 2006, 39, para 73) and Condorelli (CR 2006/10, 6 March 2006, 11–12, paras 4–5 and 28–30, paras 40–43); cp Brownlie (CR 2006/16, 13 March 2006, 36–41, paras 38–41).

[350] According to the Court, 'it is not necessary to show that the persons who performed the acts alleged to have violated international law were in general in a relationship of "complete dependence" on the respondent State; it has to be proved that they acted in accordance with that State's instructions or under its "effective control". It must however be shown that this "effective control" was exercised, or that the State's instructions were given, in respect of each

given careful consideration to the Appeals Chamber's reasoning . . . but finds itself unable to subscribe to the Chamber's view . . . the ICTY was not called upon in the *Tadić* case, nor is it in general called upon, to rule on questions of State responsibility, since its jurisdiction is criminal and extends over persons only.[351]

In the end, international responsibility law can play a limited role since it is aimed only at the interpretation of article 3*(g)*, which plainly constitutes a *lex specialis*. By application of the ILC's works, of which the UN General Assembly took note, and of ICJ case law, an armed attack akin to aggression by an irregular group cannot be attributed to a State unless the group is under the 'complete dependence' of the State or if the specific attack was conducted under the instructions, directives or control of that State.[352] Conversely, any criterion of 'overall control' is 'unsuitable, for it stretches too far, almost to breaking point, the connection which must exist between the conduct of a State's organs and its international responsibility'.[353] These general principles, that were accepted as a result of work over decades, are still very much alive. They were not questioned during the discussion at the time of the 60 years of the UN.

c) The Absence of Challenge to Existing Law in the Debates for the Sixty Years of the UN

As has already been pointed out several times, the resolution adopted at the 2005 World Summit was intentionally orthodox as regards the non-use of force.[354] In the face of the sometimes more political than legal doctrines tending to call into question the current rules of the *jus contra bellum*, States were keen to reassert that 'the relevant provisions of the Charter are sufficient to address the full range of threats to international peace and security'.[355] No other passage of the declaration suggests that acts perpetrated by private groups might be imputed to a State, whether those groups are characterised as 'terrorists' or not for the sole reason that they are tolerated or even supported by that State. On the contrary, in its report the 'High-Level Panel on Threats, Challenges and Change' only evokes State support for irregular groups in the part on the Security Council's competences and

---

operation in which the alleged violations occurred, not generally in respect of the overall actions taken by the persons or groups of persons having committed the violations. ((2007) ICJ Rep, para 400); *contra;* Judge Al-Khasawneh (dissenting opinion, paras 36–39) and Judge *ad hoc* Mahiou (dissenting opinion, paras 113–17).

[351] ibid, para 403; see also paras 404–05.

[352] See: Independent International Fact-Finding Mission on the Conflict in Georgia, *Report*, September 2009 (www.ceiig.ch/Report.html), vol II, 259 *ff*; see also Institut de droit international Resolution on Self-defence, 27 October 2007, Santiago Session (www.idi-iil. org/idiE/navig_chon2003.html), para 10 ('instructions, direction or control').

[353] ICJ, *Crime of Genocide*, para 406.

[354] See above.

[355] *2005 World Summit Outcome*, A/RES/60/1, 24 October 2005, para 79.

not in that on self-defence.[356] In fact, and as detailed above, the controversies were over the concept of preventive self-defence;[357] as far as I know no proposals were made to modify or relax article 3(g) of the definition of aggression. There is no reason then to question the method that arises from reading this proposition, where necessary construed on the basis of the general principles of the law of international responsibility unless it can be shown that practice has led to an alteration of the *opinio juris* of the international community of States as a whole, which is far from obvious, as shall be observed next.

The Non-Recognition of Indirect Aggression from the Precedents on the Use of Force

As with the question of 'preventive self-defence' we shall begin by examining practice as it has been treated before the UN's political organs (a) before determining the lessons that can be deduced from international case law (b).

a) The General Non-Acceptance of Indirect Aggression in Precedents Debated within the UN's Political Organs

The first precedents touching upon the question of indirect aggression date from the 1940s and 1950s and no very clear conclusions can be drawn from them. They are mostly about situations in which self-defence, although invoked incidentally, was invoked only to justify measures that remained limited to the national territory with no military incursion into the territory of a third State. Thus,

—in the aftermath of the Second World War, Greece accused Albania and then other neighbouring States of supporting communist rebels, including by making part of their territories available to them; these accusations were intended to justify the British presence in Greece but not an armed action against any third State;[358] in any event, the UN General Assembly condemned the support given by some of Greece's neighbouring States to Greek irregular forces without, though, evoking a situation of self-defence within the meaning of article 51 of the Charter;[359]

---

[356] *A more secured world: Our shared responsibility*, Report of the Secretary-General's High-level Panel on Threats, Challenges and Change, United Nations, 2004, above n 195, 64, para 193; see also para 194; A Nollkaemper, 'Attribution of Forcible Acts to States: Connections Between the Law on the Use of Force and the Law of State Responsibility', above n 303, 138.

[357] Above.

[358] See: K Wellens, *Résolutions et déclarations du Conseil de sécurité (1946–1992). Recueil thématique* (Bruxelles, Bruylant, 1993) 23; AM Rifaat, *International Aggression*, above n 301, 219; see also above, ch 5, s II.

[359] See: GA Res 109 (II) ('Threats to the political independence and territorial integrity of Greece') of 21 October 1947; 193 (III) of 27 November 1948; 288 (IV) of 18 November 1949; 382 (V) of 1 December 1950 and 508 (VI) of 7 December 1951. See also R Higgins, *The Development of International Law Through the Political Organs of the United Nations*, above n 41, 191.

—in 1958 Lebanon and Jordan appealed to the US and the UK to support them in putting down a rebel movement allegedly backed by the United Arab Republic; self-defence was invoked[360] but not as a basis for action against that State,[361] but rather to bolster the argument of consent to the presence of US and British troops;[362] in any event, some States criticised the argument,[363] the UN not having taken any clear legal stance in the end.[364]

In the first two decades after the Charter's entry into force, no decisive precedent can therefore be invoked one way or the other.[365]

The 1960s, 1970s and 1980s, however, saw the indirect aggression argument condemned several times, it being often invoked in the period in situations of unresolved decolonisation. Three situations can be evoked along these lines.[366]

—On 28 March 1964 the UK bombed a Yemeni town supposedly in riposte to aid provided to Yemen by irregular forces operating in the Federation of South Arabia then under British rule. Self-defence was clearly invoked this time to justify an attack by a third State, held responsible for an 'indirect aggression'.[367] The argument did not convince the other States,[368] and the Security Council even adopted a resolution deploring the British action and condemning the reprisals as incompatible with the goals of the UN.[369]

—From the late 1960s Israel began to justify its bombings of and incursions into Lebanon and then Tunisia by invoking self-defence to riposte to

---

[360] Lebanon (S/PV.833, 18 July 1958, para 10), USA (S/PV.829, 16 July 1958, para 50); see also France (S/PV.828, 15 July 1958, paras 7–9), Canada (S/PV.828, 15 July 1958, para 16), China (S/PV.831, 17 July 1958, para 99), Jordan (S/PV.831, 17 July 1958, para 24), UK (S/PV.831, 17 July 1958, para 32; S/PV.834, 18 July 1958, paras 79 and 81; 'UK Contemporary Practice' (1959) 8 *ICLQ* 151 and 152.

[361] USA; S/PV.827, 15 July 1958, paras 34–35.

[362] See above, ch 5.

[363] See: UAR (S/PV.828, 15 July 1958, para 33; S/PV.830, 16 July 1958, para 4; S/PV.831, 17 July 1958, para 109), USSR (S/PV.829, 16 July 1958, para 40) and Sweden (S/PV.830, 16 July 1958, paras 47–48).

[364] See: K Wellens, *Résolutions et déclarations du Conseil de sécurité (1946–1992). Recueil thématique*, 70; R Higgins, *The Development of International Law Through the Political Organs of the United Nations*, above n 41, 193–94.

[365] See also 'Pratique française du droit international' (1957) 3 *AFDI* 803; (1958) 4 *AFDI* 806–09; (1959) 5 *AFDI* 888; (1960) 6 *AFDI* 1069; AC Kiss, *Répertoire de la Pratique française en matière de droit international public*, tome VI, (Paris, edn CNRS, 1969) 67–69.

[366] See also: (S/9781, 5 May 1970; 'Contemporary Practice of the United States' (1970) 64 *AJIL* 932–41; (1973) 67 *AJIL* 765–67; MM Whiteman (ed), *Digest of International Law*, vol 12, above n 316, 143–48, and 'Symposium on United States Actions in Cambodia' (1971) 65 *AJIL* 81–83.

[367] S/PV.1106, 2 April 1964, paras 34–35; S/PV.1109, 7 April 1964, paras 30 and 31; S/PV.1111, 9 April 1964, para 30.

[368] USSR (S/PV.1106, 2 April 1964, paras 72, 79 and 101), Iraq (S/PV.1106, 2 April 1964, para 64), UAR (S/PV.1106, 2 April 1964, paras 108 and 114), Bolivia (S/PV.1111, 9 April 1964, para 18).

[369] SC Res 188 (1964) of 28 March 1964 (9-0-2) and S/PV.1111, 9 April 1964.

alleged support by those States to irregular Palestinian fighters. The Israeli State presented a similar argument in the UN to that defended by the US after 11 September 2001: article 51 of the UN Charter supposedly legitimises any action against a State that harbours groups of irregulars or tolerates their activity, without it being necessary to demonstrate any authority, control or substantial involvement.[370] The line of argument failed to convince the UN Member States and was repeatedly condemned by the Security Council.[371]

—Likewise Portugal,[372] South Africa[373] and Southern Rhodesia[374] vainly claimed to be acting in self-defence against certain front-line States because of the aid they were allegedly providing to irregular forces operating from their territories. Here too the concept of indirect aggression is far from having been admitted by UN Member States as a whole, which on the contrary condemned the armed actions of the two racist regimes and of Portugal as being contrary to international law.[375]

It is true, especially in the context of debates involving Israel, South Africa and Southern Rhodesia, that the legitimacy of the national liberation movements was underscored by several States.[376] Other States criticised the military action for being disproportionate,[377] which might suggest *a contrario* that such action was not condemnable as a matter of principle. Even so, and what matters legally, a general acceptance of the possibility of

---

[370] See, eg: S/PV.1643, 26 February 1972, paras 39, 44 and 47; S/PV.1650, 26 June 1972, para 9; S/PV.2615, 4 October 1985, paras 193–94; see also RA Falk, 'The Beirut Raid and the International Law of Retaliation' (1969) 63 *AJIL* 415–43 and Y Blum, 'The Beirut Raid and the International Double Standard. A Reply to Professor Richard A Falk' (1970) 64 *AJIL* 73–105.

[371] SC Res 313 (1972) of 28 February 1972, 316 (1972) of 26 June 1972, 508 (1982) of 5 June 1982, 509 (1982) of 6 June 1982, 517 (1982) of 4 August 1982; see also France ('Pratique française du droit international' (1982) 28 *AFDI* 1050, (1986) 32 *AFDI* 1023), Canada ('Canadian Practice in International Law' (1986) 24 *CYIL* 441), UK ('United Kingdom Materials on International Law' (1985) 56 *BYBIL* 519 and 522; (1986) 57 *BYBIL* 620–21; (1988) 59 *BYBIL* 569), USA (*Digest of United States Practice* (Washington, Department of State Publication, 1979) 1749–51; 'Contemporary Practice of the United States' (1986) 80 *AJIL* 165–67 and J Nyamuya Maogoto, 'New Frontiers, Old Problems: The War on Terror and the Notion of Anticipating the Enemy', above n 40, 5–7).

[372] *Repertory of Practice of United Nations Organs*, Supp no 4 (1966–1969), vol 1—Art 2 (4), 55–60 and 68.

[373] See, eg: S/PV.2078, 6 May 1978.

[374] See, eg: S/PV.1985, 14 January 1977.

[375] A Cassese, 'Article 51', above n 12, 1343–46. See France ('Pratique française du droit international' (1984) 30 *AFDI* 1022), UK ('United Kingdom Materials on International Law' (1981) 52 *BYBIL* 509–11; (1982) 53 *BYBIL* 507; (1983) 54 *BYBIL* 528; (1984) 55 *BYBIL* 580; (1985) 56 *BYBIL* 520–22; (1086) 57 *BYBIL* 621–22 and 642; (1988) 59 *BYBIL* 569–70), and Belgium ('La pratique belge en matière de droit international' (1989) 22 *RBDI* 577–81).

[376] C Gray, *International Law and the Use of Force*, 3rd edn, above n 12, 138–40 and F Dubuisson, 'Le terrorisme, nouvelle forme d'agression armée au sens du droit international?', above n 303, 299.

[377] See, eg: France; S/PV.1650, 26 June 1972, paras 9–11.

self-defence in riposte to an indirect aggression cannot be shown on the basis of this practice. On the contrary, if there is any decisive lesson to be learned from these events, it is that there is a general tendency to dismiss this kind of argument.[378]

Sometimes cited in the opposite sense is the example of Soviet military intervention in Afghanistan which was supposedly justified by the fight against indirect infiltration into Afghan territory from certain neighbouring States.[379] However, upon examination, it proves difficult indeed to identify clearly the Soviet Union's legal position insofar as, while aid to irregular forces from abroad is characterised as an aggression warranting self-defence, it is above all the consent of the government in the territory of which the military action took place that is invoked, all in performance of a 1978 Soviet–Afghan treaty.[380] The USSR was not therefore claiming to be entitled to attack a State that was supporting subversive irregular groups, but to help a State that was supposedly a victim of such groups and that allegedly asked it for such help on the basis of a treaty providing for this possibility. In any event, it shall be noted that it is difficult to deduce any *opinio juris* from this isolated and contingent legal line of argument especially inasmuch as on other occasions Moscow has consistently spoken out against the notion of indirect aggression.[381] Moreover, it is clear that however it is interpreted the Soviet argument was resolutely dismissed by the vast majority of UN Member States that besides insisted on there being no legally valid consent from Afghanistan.[382]

The argument of self-defence for repelling an indirect aggression did not prosper either in the context of certain murderous conflicts that characterised the 1990s. The precedent of the Democratic Republic of Congo (DRC) is emblematic in this respect insofar as Rwanda and Uganda both

---

[378] A Cassese, 'Article 51', above n 12, 1346; JA Gonzales Vega, 'Los atentados del 11 de septiembre. La operacion "Libertad duradera" y el derecho de legitima defensa', above n 338, 256; O Corten and F Dubuisson, 'Opération "Liberté immutable": une extension abusive du concept de légitime défense', above n 310, 59–60.

[379] A Cassese, 'Return to Westphalia? Considerations on the Gradual Erosion of the Charter' in A Cassese (ed), *The Current Legal Regulation of the Use of Force* (Dordrecht, Martinus Nijhoff, 1986) 515; see also C Alibert, *Du droit de se faire justice dans la société internationale depuis 1945*, above n 262, 416–19.

[380] D Simon and LA Sicilianos, 'La 'contre-violence' unilatérale. Pratiques étatiques et droit international' (1986) 32 *AFDI* 71; see USSR, GDR, Bulgaria, Poland and Afghanistan (S/PV.2185, 5 January 1980; S./PV.2186, 5 January 1980; S/PV.2187–90, and C Rousseau, 'Chronique des faits internationaux' (1980) 84 *RGDIP* 829–31. See also above, ch 5.

[381] As underlined by Egypt; S/PV.2185, 5 January 1980.

[382] GA Res 40/12 of 13 November 1984; China, UK and Kampuchea (S./PV.2186, 5 January 1980); UK ('United Kingdom Materials on International Law' (1980) 51 *BYBIL* 472–74), France ('Pratique française du droit international' (1980) 26 *AFDI* 871–72), Switzerland ('La pratique suisse en matière de droit international public' (1980) 36 *ASDI* 227; (1981) 37 *ASDI* 276–77), Belgium ('La pratique belge en matière de droit international' (1981–1982) 16 *RBDI* 721–22; (1984–1985) 18 *RBDI* 390–91; (1986) 19 *RBDI* 567; (1987) 20 *RBDI* 471); see also PM Dupuy, 'Observations sur la pratique récente des "sanctions" de l'illicite' (1983) 87 *RGDIP* 506–07.

presented their occupation of part of Congolese territory as a riposte to general support the Congo authorities allegedly provided beforehand to irregular forces.[383] This argument was not accepted by the Security Council which, on the contrary, called for the withdrawal of foreign troops from the DRC and expressly stated that Rwanda and Uganda had violated the DRC's sovereignty and territorial integrity.[384] The Bosnia-Herzegovina precedent cannot be interpreted so readily. Despite reports of Yugoslav and Croatian involvement in the conflict in its early years, involvement which was reflected by increased support for irregular forces found guilty of criminal acts,[385] the Security Council invariably refused to characterise the actions of the two States as 'armed attacks'.[386] The General Assembly stated on several occasion the inherent right to self-defence of the Republic of Bosnia-Herzegovina but, from a reading of the resolutions adopted, it appears extremely difficult to determine whether the characterisation of aggression results solely from the support of the Yugoslav State for irregular Serb forces of the *Republika Srpska* or whether it takes account also of the direct participation of organs of the Yugoslav State.[387]

Similarly we can further mention these precedents that can be ranked in the category of the fight against terrorism:

—the US bombing of Libya, officially in the name of the 'inherent right of self-defence'[388] in riposte to Tripoli's alleged support for international terrorism, was condemned by the UN General Assembly;[389]
—after the 1991 Gulf War, Turkey entered Iraq to attack PKK troops by invoking the need to protect itself because the Iraqi authorities were

---

[383] See Uganda's representative in GA, 23 March 1999, 95th plenary meeting, A/53/PV.95, 14; see also written and oral pleadings in ICJ, *Armed Activities*.

[384] SC Res 1304 (2000) of 16 June 2000 and 1234 (1999) of 9 April 1999; see also T Franck, *Recourse to Force. State Action Against Threats and Armed Attacks*, above n 26, 66.

[385] *Situation of human rights in the territory of the former Yugoslavia: 6th periodic report on the situation of human rights in the territory of the former Yugoslavia / submitted by Tadeusz Mazowiecki, Special Rapporteur of the Commission on Human Rights, pursuant to paragraph 32 of Commission resolution 1993/7 of 23 February 1993*, E/CN.4/1994/110, 21 February 1994, para 117.

[386] SC Res 479 (1992) of 7 April 1992, 752 (1992) of 15 May 1992, 757 (1992) of 30 May 1992, 762 (1992) of 29 June 1992, 770 (1992) of 13 August 1992, 781 (1993) of 31 March 1993, 836 (1993) of 3 June 1993.

[387] GA Res 46/242 of 31 July 1992, 47/121 of 18 December 1992, 48/88 of 20 December 1993, 49/10 of 3 November 1994.

[388] S/PV.2674, 15 April 1986, 13; 'Contemporary Practice of the United States' (1986) 80 *AJIL* 632–36; *Digest of United States Practice* (Washington, Department of State Publication, 1981–1988) vol III, 3405–10; LA Sicilianos, *Les réactions décentralisées à l'illicite. Des contre-mesures à la légitime défense*, above n 61, 419.

[389] GA Res 38/41 of 20 November 1986 (79-28-33); see also Organization of Islamic Conference Res 21/5 'on the American aggression against the Jamahiriya', Fifth Islamic Summit Conference, 26–29 January 1987; Res 38/9 'on the right of the Great Socialist Peoples Libyan Arab Jamahiriya to receive reparations for losses resulting from US aggression in 1986', 12–13 November 2000 (www.oic-oci.org); see also Belgium 'La pratique belge en matière de droit international' (1987) 20 *RBDI* 472–73.

unable to control their own territory;[390] this justification was criticised by several Arab and European States;[391]

—the self-defence argument raised by the US to justify the targeted attacks on Sudan and Afghanistan in 1998 for the official purpose of riposting to the Dar Es Salam and Nairobi attacks[392] does not seem to have been accepted by other States, including European States.[393]

In short, until the eve of 11 September 2001, States never accepted the 'indirect aggression'[394] argument, an attitude that ultimately fits quite well with the position of UN Member States as a whole as reflected in article 3*(g)* of the definition of aggression.

The war against Afghanistan begun on 7 October 2001 seems from this standpoint to mark a change of direction.[395] The US immediately invoked self-defence to riposte to an indirect aggression. As seen, this argument went along with the formulation of a new doctrine that simply harbouring or tolerating the presence of a terrorist group in one's territory would suffice to count as an armed attack within the meaning of article 51 of the Charter.[396] Now in the aftermath of 9/11 very many States showed their

---

[390] 'As Iraq has not been able to exercise its authority over the northern part of its country since 1991 for reasons well known, Turkey cannot ask the Government of Iraq to fulfil its obligation, under international law, to prevent the use of its territory for the staging of terrorist acts against Turkey. Under these circumstances, Turkey's resorting to legitimate measures which are imperative to its own security cannot be regarded as a violation of Iraq's sovereignty' (*Letter dated 24 July 1995 addressed to the President of the Security Council*, S/1995/605, 24 July 1995; see also S/1997/552, 18 July 1998; C Gray, *International Law and the Use of Force*, 3rd edn, above n 12, 140–43; T Ruys, '*Quo vadit jus ad bellum?*: A Legal Analysis of Turkey's Military Operations Against the PKK in Northern Iraq' (2008) 9 *Melbourne JIL* 1–30 and above, ch 3, s I.

[391] France, quoted by A Laursen, 'The Use of Force and (the State of) Necessity' (2004) 37 *VdbJIL* 515, fn 144; see also Germany (*Keesing's Contemporary Archives*, 1995, 40563), Libya (*Letter dated 12 July 1995 1995 addressed to the President of the Security Council*, S/1995/566, 12 July 1995), the Arab League (*Letter dated 24 September 1996, addressed to the Secretary-General*, S/1996/796, 26 September 1996) and UE quoted by SA Alexandrov, *Self-Defense Against the Use of Force in International Law*, above n 14, 181; *contra*, UK ('United Kingdom Materials on International Law' (1997) 68 *BYBIL* 630–31; (1998) 68 *BYBIL* 586).

[392] *Letter dated 20 August 1998 from the Permanent Representative of the United States of America to the United Nations addressed to the President of the Security Council*, S/1998/780, 20 August 1998.

[393] Arab League (res 22/9 'on US attack on Al-Shifa pharmaceutical plant in Khartoum', 12–13 November 2000, www.oic-oci.org) NAM ('opposition to selective and unilateral actions in violation of principles and purposes of the United Nations'; Declaration of Durban of 3 September 1998, www.nam.gov.za, para 159); see also ' Contemporary Pratice of the United States' (1999) 93 *AJIL* 164–65, SC Res 193 (1998) of 28 August 1998 and C Gray, *International Law and the Use of Force*, 3rd edn, above n 12, 197.

[394] SD Murphy, 'Terrorism and the Concept of "Armed Attack" in Article 51 of the UN Charter' (2002) 43 *Harvard ILJ* 46 (cp 49–50); S Regourd, 'Raids 'anti-terroristes' et développements récents des atteintes illicites au principe de non-intervention' (1986) 32 *AFDI* 79–103; *contra:* H Labayle, 'Droit international et lutte contre le terrorisme' (1986) 32 *AFDI* 134–35.

[395] See above, ch 3, s I.

[396] See above.

support for and their agreement with the US administration.[397] Apart from individual stances,[398] we can mention resolutions of the Organisation of American States or of NATO that recognised the existence of a situation of self-defence.[399] This was also the case of the Security Council in its resolution 1368 (2001) adopted on 12 September 2001 recognising the US's right of self-defence.[400] If these points are combined with the absence, or at any rate the scarcity, of criticism of operation 'Enduring Freedom', one might be tempted to conclude that this reflects a change in the *opinio juris* of States as a whole in favour of the indirect aggression argument.[401]

However, such a conclusion would seem premature at this stage.[402] Several indications should prompt us to exercise the greatest caution before concluding there has been a substantial change in the definition of aggression. To understand this one need only take in turn the two factors determined as relevant in evaluating the birth of a customary rule: the existence of a claim by certain States and the acceptance of that claim by the international community of States as a whole.[403]

—First the legal argument of the States that supported military action against Afghanistan is not without ambiguity.[404] European States seemed to base this military action more on Security Council resolution 1368 (2001) than on the notion of self-defence envisaged autonomously.[405] In other words, in view of certain declarations, it is unclear whether article 51 supposedly justifies henceforth all actions in self-defence in riposte to

---

[397] MN Schmitt, *Counter-Terrorism and the Use of Force in International Law*, above n 55, 8; M Poulain, 'Les attentats du 11 Septembre et leurs suites. Quelques points de repères' (2002) 48 *AFDI* 31.

[398] Canada, Chile and Norway in October 2001 (www.un.org/terrorism/statements), UK ('United Kingdom Materials on International Law' (2001) 72 *BYBIL* 679–91).

[399] UE (*Statement by General Affairs Council of the EU, 8 October 2001*, www.europa.eu.int/; *Military operations in Afghanistan—Declaration by the EU Presidency*, 7 October 2001, www.eu2001.be/), OAS (CP/RES.796 (1293/01), 19 September 2001, www.oas.org/), NATO (12 September 2001, Press Release (2001) 124, www.nato.int/); see AF Fernandez Tomas, 'El recurso al Articulo quinto del tratado de Washington tras los acontecimientos del 11 de septiembre: mucho ruido y pocas nueces' (2001) 53 *REDI* 205–26.

[400] See above, ch 3, s I.

[401] T Franck, *Recourse to Force. State Action Against Threats and Armed Attacks*, above n 26, 67, SR Ratner, 'Ius ad Bellum and Jus in Bello after September 11' (2002) 96 *AJIL* 906–10; M Byers, 'Terrorism, the Use of Force and International Law after 11 September', above n 296, 409–10; see also ME O'Connel, *International Law and the "Global War on Terror"* (Paris, Pedone, 2007) 45; C Tams, 'The Use of Force against Terrorists' (2009) 20 *EJIL* 378 *ff*.

[402] G Cahin; 'Le rôle des organes politiques des Nations Unies' in Enzo Cannizaro and Paolo Palchetti (eds), *Customary International Law on the Use of Force: A Methodological Approach* (Leiden/Boston, Martinus Nijhoff, 2005) 168; A Remiro Brotons, 'Terrorismo, Mantenimiento de la paz y nuevo orden' (2001) 53 *REDI* 156–57; JA Gonzales Vega, 'Los atentados del 11 de septiembre. La operacion "Libertad duradera" y el derecho de legitima defensa', above 338, 265–66; D Kritsiolis, 'On the *jus ad bellum* and *jus in bello* of Operation Enduring Freedom', *ASIL Proceedings*, 2002, 37.

[403] Above, ch 1, s II.

[404] G Cahin, 'Le rôle des organes politiques des Nations Unies', above n 403, 171.

[405] EU Council, 21 December 2001, www.europa.eu.int/; see also above, ch 6, s II.

an indirect aggression or whether only action that might be based on Security Council resolution 1368 (2001) would be accepted.[406] The same kind of uncertainty prevails for Russia's official position.[407] What is clear, however, is that the US does not consider itself bound by any Council resolution and it invokes rather self-defence as such. Under these circumstances, at any rate, it is no easy matter to outline the new rule supposedly claimed by the intervening States or their allies.[408]

—More so as, and so we come to a second point, the *opinio juris* of States that are not close allies of the US is not easy to determine either.[409] First because some States did indeed display their reluctance to embrace the doctrine of indirect aggression,[410] while the 57 member States of the Islamic Conference Organisation adopted a resolution that is difficult to construe as an approval of the legal doctrine of the US administration.[411] Next because even those States that did support operation 'Enduring Freedom' did not necessarily attest a legal conviction fulfilling the criteria that one is entitled to demand in order to establish a new *opinio juris*.[412] Some of them were plainly under pressure that might make their position seem less than sincere in a context where the US affirmed that all those who did not support it should be considered allies of the terrorists.[413] Other States in the emotionally charged context of the aftermath of 9/11 provided political support that cannot readily be translated into legal terms.[414]

—It will be observed lastly that, in practice, the ties between Al Qaeda and the Afghan government before the outbreak of war were particularly close. The specific characteristics of this situation plainly mean that the Afghanistan precedent cannot be assimilated to mere tolerance or passive and diffuse support that are generally typical of what is called 'indirect

---

[406] A Nollkaemper, 'Attribution of Forcible Acts to States: Connections Between the Law on the Use of Force and the Law of State Responsibility', above n 303, 167.

[407] See above.

[408] M Kohen, 'The use of force by the United States after the end of the Cold War, and its impact on international law' in M Byers and G Nolte (eds), *United States Hegemony and the Foundations of International Law* (Cambridge, Cambridge University Press, 2003) 222; C Gray, *International Law and the Use of Force*, 3rd edn, above n 12, 200–01.

[409] F Dubuisson, 'Le terrorisme, nouvelle forme d'agression armée au sens du droit international?', above n 303, 309–11.

[410] Belarus, North Korea, Cuba, Iraq, Iran, Syria, Qatar and Malaysia (GA, October and November 2001, www.un.org/terrorism/statements/).

[411] *Final Communiqué of the 9th extraordinary session of the Islamic Conference of the Ministries of Foreign Affairs*, Doha, Qatar, 10 October 2001, www.oic-oci.org.

[412] M Kohen, 'The use of force by the United States after the end of the Cold War, and its impact on international law', above n 409, 224.

[413] See the interview by President Pervez Musharraf, mentioning serious threat from the USA against Pakistan, in *The Guardian*, September 22, 2006.

[414] M Kohen, 'The use of force by the United States after the end of the Cold War, and its impact on international law', above n 409, 224; see also *2001 ASEAN Declaration on Joint Action to Counter Terrorism*, 5 November 2001, www.aseansec.org/.

aggression'. If the Afghan precedent can be employed, it would therefore only be to evaluate comparable situations in which the ties between the private groups and the host State proved extremely close.[415]

In view of these factors, it can be considered that the war against Afghanistan, while it probably signals a certain questioning of the traditional definition of aggression as it is expressed in article 3(g)[416] does not as yet show the existence of a new agreement of the international community of States as a whole.[417] To become established, such agreement should therefore be based on other precedents that could clarify the legal situation.[418]

In this respect it has already been noted that in the 2000s several States had justified military interventions by evoking ties between the territories of States concerned and certain terrorist groups.[419] It has already been pointed out, though, that in each of these cases the legal arguments put forward by the intervening States fell well short of convincing the UN Member States as a whole. One cannot readily therefore deduce from this any confirmation or above all clarification in relation to the precedent of the war against Afghanistan.

As an illustration of this difficulty, one can mention the precedent of Israel's invasion of Lebanon in July 2006, which was officially presented as a riposte to several actions conducted by Hezbollah including the abduction of Israeli soldiers.[420] The Israeli military intervention was vigorously condemned by many States, but they emphasised above all the excessive and disproportionate use of force,[421] some of them recognising besides that Israel had a right to defend itself[422] or more vaguely 'to protect its territory

---

[415] O Corten and F Dubuisson, 'Opération "Liberté immutable": une extension abusive du concept de légitime défense', above n 310, 68–69.

[416] A Lagerwall, 'Kosovo, Afghanistan, Irak: le retour des guerres d'agression?' in O Corten and B Delcourt (eds), *Les guerres antiterroristes* (Brussels, Contradictions, 2004) 93.

[417] See: P Klein, 'Le droit international à l'épreuve du terrorisme' (2006) 321 *RCADI*, ch 4; A Nollkaemper, 'Attribution of Forcible Acts to States: Connections Between the Law on the Use of Force and the Law of State Responsibility', above n 303, 159 and 170; G Piero Buzzini, 'Les comportements passifs des Etats et leur incidence sur la réglementation de l'emploi de la force en droit international général' in Enzo Cannizaro and Paolo Palchetti (eds), *Customary International Law on the Use of Force: A Methodological Approach* (Leiden/Boston, Martinus Nijhoff, 2005) 104 and 113–116; see also G Guillaume, 'Terrorism and International Law' (2004) 53 *ICLQ* 546–47.

[418] See: N Schrijver, 'Responding to International Terrorism: Moving the Frontiers of International Law for 'Enduring Freedom' (2001) 48 *NILR* 286.

[419] Above, ch 3, s I.

[420] S/PV.5489, 14 July 2006, 6; see also *Letter dated 12 July 2006 addressed to the Secretary General*; www.israel-un.org/.

[421] Peru, Russia, Argentina, Qatar, Japan, Tanzania, Greece, France, Switzerland, Norway, Jordan, Morocco, New Zealand, Chile and Mexico; see S/PV.5488, 13 July 2006; S/PV.5489, 14 July 2006; S/PV.5493, 21 July 2006; S/PV.5493 (Resumption 1), 21 July 2006.

[422] ibid: USA, Peru, Ghana, Argentina, UK, Denmark, Greece, France, Brazil, Norway, Australia, Turkey, Djibouti, Canada and Guatemala; see also Finland (on behalf of the EU; Bulgaria, Romania, Turkey, Croatia, Macedonia, Albania, Bosnia and Herzegovina, Serbia, Iceland, Ukraine and Moldova aligning themselves with the statement); S/PV.5493 (Resumption 1), 21 July 2006, 16.

and its population'.[423] Should it be concluded that this right was accepted in principle as allowing a military action against a State allegedly harbouring or tolerating an irregular group?[424] The difficulty here resides in the specificities of the situation of fact that cannot be reduced to a classical case of 'indirect aggression'.[425] Hezbollah did indeed have close ties with the Lebanese State at the time of the Israeli action, some of the organisation's members being at the same time members of the government, as Israel pointed out in justifying its action.[426] Similarly Syria and Iran were denounced as 'sponsors' of Hezbollah, which was even presented as a simple agent of the two States.[427] One might therefore think that, in the view of Israel and of several of its allies, self-defence was applicable in the case in point because of the very close ties maintained between the irregular forces that supposedly launched a prior attack and certain States including Lebanon itself. It is true that these standpoints are highly ambiguous and so it seems a very difficult business to deduce from them any *opinio juris*.[428] From reading the arguments of the States that characterised the Israeli action as an aggression or as contrary to international law, it is not easy to determine whether this violation is solely because of the disproportionate character of the use of force[429] or whether its actual principle is to be condemned.[430] It is clear that, given the scale of the Israeli intervention and of the resulting damage and victims, many States could do nothing but condemn this intervention, without it being easy to determine what their position would have been had the military action been more targeted.

More conclusive are the reactions to the Colombian armed intervention against the FARC in Ecuadorian territory on 1 March 2008. As shown in chapter three of this book, it is not clear whether the self-defence argument was invoked only *vis-a-vis* the FARC or also *vis-a-vis* the Ecuadorian State.[431] What was perfectly clear, however, was the firm condemnation of the Columbian intervention (although very limited in scope and in time) by

---

[423] Switzerland, S/PV.5493 (Resumption 1), 21 July 2006, 18.

[424] See: Crossing the Thin Blue Line: An Inquiry into Israel's Recourse to Self-Defence against Hezbollah', (2007) 43 *Stanford JIL* 270 *ff.*

[425] A Zimmerman, 'The Second Lebanon War: *Jus ad bellum, jus in bello* and the Issue of Proportionality' (2007) 11 *Max Planck UNYB* 109–15.

[426] S/PV.5493, 21 July 2006.

[427] ibid and S/PV.5488, 13 July 2006; see also USA (ibid), UK and Canada (S/PV.5493 (Resumption 1), 21 July 2006, 6).

[428] F Dubuisson, 'La guerre du Liban de l'été 2006 et le droit de la légitime défense' (2006) 39 *RBDI* 529–64, and E Cannizaro, 'Entités non-étatiques et régime international de l'emploi de la force. Une étude sur le cas de la réaction israélienne au Liban' (2007) 111 *RGDIP* no 2.

[429] China, Jordan, Morocco, Indonesia, League of Arab States; S/PV.5489, 14 July 2006; S/PV.5493 (Resumption 1), 21 July 2006; see also NAM; S/2006/548, 19 July 2006, annex, paras 1 and 2).

[430] Qatar, Saudi Arabia, Congo, Syria, Iran, Venezuela, Cuba and Sudan; S/PV.5489, 14 July 2006; S/PV.5493 (Resumption 1), 21 July 2006.

[431] Above, ch 3, s II.

the Latin American States.[432] This precedent confirms the reluctance of these States to accept any weakening of the *jus contra bellum* regime under the pretext of fighting terrorism.

Moreover, one must emphasise that, in its September 2009 Report, the Independent International Fact-Finding Mission on the Conflict in Georgia reaffirmed the existing law. The Commission had to determine if Russia was responsible for an indirect aggression against Georgia before the military intervention of this State, which began on 7 August 2008. As a matter of fact, it was clear that Russia had close ties with the Abkhaz and Ossetian seperatist entities, including in the military field.[433] Yet, as a matter of law, the Commission stated that:

> North and South Ossetian military operations are attributable to Russia if they were sent by Russia and if they were under effective control by Russia. This follows from Art. 3 (g) of UN Resolution 3314 . . . For the purpose of determining the possible international legal responsibility of Russia, and also for indentifying an armed attack by Russia, the use of force by South Ossetians and other volunteers from North Caucasus, might be attributed to Russia under two headings. First, the other actors might have been *de facto* organs of Russia in the sense of Art. 4 ILC Articles. Under this first heading, the volunteer fighters could be equated with Russian organs only if they acted 'in complete dependence' of Russia of which they were ultimately merely the instrument. Second, South Ossetian or other acts are attributable to Russia if they have been 'in fact acting on the instructions of, under the direction or control of, that state' (Art. 8 ILC Articles). Under that second heading, the actions of volunteers were attributable to Russia also if they acted under control of Russia. In the law governing state responsibility, and arguably also for identifying the responsibility for an armed attack, control means 'effective control'.[434]

The Commission did not mention the Afghan or any other precedent as having modified the current state of international law on this particular topic. It concluded that an indirect Russian aggression could not be proven in law.

Finally, it is true that some precedents are difficult to interpret because of the division among States and the often very imprecise character of their discourses. In this context, it would seem to me to be overstating things to say that the international community of States as a whole had radically modified its legal position. Moreover, in view of the specific features of the Afghan and Lebanese precedents, especially in terms of the ties between the

---

[432] CP/RES.930 (1632/08), 5 March 2008 (www.oas.org/consejo/resolutions/res930.asp) and Declaration of the Heads of State and Government of the Rio Group on the recent events between Ecuador and Colombia, 7 March 2008, annex 2 of the Report of the OAS Commission, Annex 2 in Report of the OAS Commission that visited Ecuador and Columbia, OEA/Ser.F/II.25, 16 March 2008 (www.oas.org/CONSEJO/Docs/RC00089E01.DOC).

[433] Independent International Fact-Finding Mission on the Conflict in Georgia, *Report*, September 2009 (www.ceiig.ch/Report.html), vol II, 19.

[434] ibid, vol II, 259–60.

private groups characterised as terrorists and the local public authorities, it would be very tricky to determine from what point it would henceforth be acceptable to riposte in self-defence to acts perpetrated with the simple active or passive support of a foreign State. And it is difficult indeed to remove the uncertainty in view of international case law which, whether old-established or recent, remains consistent with law as it has been set out in the texts.

b) The Absence of Acceptance of Indirect Aggression in International Case Law

Beyond the passages analysed earlier on the law of international responsibility, the question of indirect aggression was dealt with as such in detail by the ICJ in 1986 in the case of *Military and Paramilitary Activities*. The ICJ was led to examine the argument raised by the US that El Salvador supposedly acted in self-defence in response to support from Sandinista Nicaragua for Salvadorian rebels.[435] The Court began by asserting that 'There appears now to be general agreement on the nature of the acts which can be treated as constituting armed attacks', before going on to specify that the definition in article 3(g) of the definition appended to resolution 3314 (XXIX) 'may be taken to reflect customary international law'. The world's highest court then specified that it 'does not believe that the concept of "armed attack" includes not only acts by armed bands where such acts occur on a significant scale but also assistance to rebels in the form of the provision of weapons or logistical or other support'.[436] Similarly it stated that

> while the concept of an armed attack includes the despatch by one State of armed bands into the territory of another State, the supply of arms and other support to such bands cannot be equated with armed attack. Nevertheless, such activities may well constitute a breach of the principle of the non-use of force and an intervention in the internal affairs of a State, that is, a form of conduct which is certainly wrongful, but is of lesser gravity than an armed attack.[437]

In another passage of the decision, the Court distinguishes 'the most grave forms of the use of force (those constituting an armed attack) from other less grave forms'. It also mentions notably the breach of the principle that 'Every State has the duty to refrain from organizing, instigating, assisting or participating in acts of civil strife or terrorist acts in another State or acquiescing in organized activities within its territory directed towards the

---

[435] See: JN Moore, 'The Secret War in Central America and the Future of World Order' (1986) 80 *AJIL* 43–127.

[436] ICJ, *Military and Paramilitary Activities*, ICJ Rep (1986) 103–04, para 195; see JP Rowles, '"Secret Wars", Self-Defense and the Charter—A Reply to Professor Moore' (1986) 80 *AJIL* 579 and fn 45; *contra:* JL Harsgrove, 'The *Nicaragua* Judgment and the Future of the Law of Force and Self-Defense' (1987) 81 *AJIL* 139–40; JN Moore, 'The *Nicaragua* Case and the Deterioration of World Order' (1987) 81 *AJIL* 154–55.

[437] ICJ Rep (1986) 126–27, para 247.

commission of such acts'.[438] These positions of principle were to be very concretely applied by the Court to the specific circumstances of the case, the Court ruling out the self-defence argument made by the US. The Court considered that, supposing it were real, any support from the Nicaraguan government to the Salvadorian rebels could not be likened to an actual 'armed attack' that alone could have legitimated a use of force.[439] Alongside this, it abstained from characterising as aggression the albeit particularly strong support from the US for the Nicaraguan *contras*. The Court preferred to characterise US support as intervention in matters within Nicaragua's national jurisdiction or, for some of its aspects, as an unlawful use of force.[440] *A contrario*, and pursuant to the positions of principle set out previously it avoided characterising such support as an armed attack.

Some commentators in the specific domain of the use of force, and not only in the general area of international responsibility, have criticised this judgment relying on the decision of the ICTY in the *Tadić* case.[441] And yet, as pointed out above, the case does not concern the definition of armed attack or, consequently, that of self-defence or more generally the question of the imputation to States of acts constituting a use of force.[442] At most it is relevant for understanding the problem of characterisation of an international conflict within the meaning of the law of armed conflict or as the case may be for getting a grasp of more general questions of international responsibility. On the specific point of the relevance of the interpretation of article 3*(g)* of the definition of aggression, the decision in *Military and Paramilitary Activities* has therefore not called into question the *Tadić* decision.[443] In any event, we have already noted that the ILC and the ICJ in the *Crime of Genocide* case wanted to distance themselves from this decision in terms of the law of international responsibility and more especially of the criteria surrounding the issue of attributing an act to a State.[444]

A decision of the Court after the events of 11 September 2001 confirms the lessons of the *Military Activities* case. In *Armed Activities*, Uganda relied on its right of self-defence to riposte to attacks by Ugandan rebels—essentially of the Alliance of Democratic Forces (ADF)—from Congolese territory and with the active and passive support of the DRC authorities.[445]

---

[438] ICJ Rep (1986) 101, para 191.

[439] ICJ Rep (1986) 118 *ff*, para 227 *ff*; separate opinions of Judges Nagendra Singh (ibid, 154) and Ruda (ibid, 175–76); *contra*, dissenting opinion of Judge Schwebel, ibid, 231 *ff*; see also K Highet, 'Evidence, the Court and the Nicaragua Case' (1987) 81 *AJIL* 1–56.

[440] ICJ Rep (1986) 146–47, paras 3 and 4.

[441] T Franck, *Recourse to Force. State Action Against Threats and Armed Attacks*, above n 26, 60–63; see also A Randelzhofer, 'Article 51', above n 18, 801.

[442] See above.

[443] O Corten and F Dubuisson, 'Opération "Liberté immuable": une extension abusive du concept de légitime défense', above n 310, 66–68.

[444] Above.

[445] Uganda's Counter-Memorial, 21 April 2001, chs 3 and 17.

The DRC replied that in fact no support or even tolerance could be demonstrated and that in law Uganda could not then impute to the DRC any act of aggression on the basis of the criteria set out in article 3(g) of the definition of aggression as interpreted by the Court in *Military and Paramilitary Activities*.[446] Even if the gist of the debates was about the proof of Uganda's allegations,[447] a legal controversy opposed the parties, with the defendant State arguing that these criteria had been relaxed somewhat, especially in the context of the fight against terrorism.[448] In its decision, the Court approved the Congolese party, emphasising that

> while Uganda claimed to have acted in self-defence, it did not ever claim that it had been subjected to an armed attack by the armed forces of the DRC. The 'armed attacks' to which reference was made came rather from the ADF. The Court has found above (paragraphs 131–135) that there is no satisfactory proof of the involvement in these attacks, direct or indirect, of the Government of the DRC. The attacks did not emanate from armed bands or irregulars sent by the DRC or on behalf of the DRC, within the sense of Article 3 (g) of General Assembly resolution 3314 (XXIX) on the definition of aggression, adopted on 14 December 1974. The Court is of the view that, on the evidence before it, even if this series of deplorable attacks could be regarded as cumulative in character, they still remained non-attributable to the DRC.[449]

Even if the Court did not think it useful to develop its argument further, several lessons can be deduced from this statement.

—First, as already pointed out, the lawfulness of an action in self-defence in the territory of a third State presupposes that a prior armed attack can be attributed to that State; attacks by private groups are not enough in themselves to justify a riposte against another State without proof of its implication.[450]
—Secondly, to settle this issue of the attribution of acts by private groups to a State, the reference instrument remains article 3(g) of the definition of aggression. Recent practice, including after 9/11, has not called into question the relevance of this provision.
—Thirdly, the Court's interpretation of article 3(g) seems fully consistent with its case law in *Military Activities*. The Court wonders whether the irregular groups were sent by the State and checks whether the State is not implicated in attacks perpetrated by these groups. The criterion of sending groups in is applied, with merely tolerating or harbouring groups not being evoked as sufficient factors. This is a significant omission given that Uganda tried to attenuate the effects of this case law along these lines

---

[446] Reply of the DRC, May 2002, ch 3, ss 1 and 2.
[447] See: CR 2005/14 and CR 2005/15, 27 April 2005 and CR 2005/16, 29 April 2005.
[448] Uganda's Counter-Memorial, 21 April 2001, ch 17.
[449] ICJ Rep (2005) para 146.
[450] Above, ch 3, s II.

before the Court.[451] The Court does not take up either the argument of substantial diffuse involvement, relating not to the armed attacks by the irregular groups but to the operation and activities of the groups in general. In actual fact, the Court does not even cite the criterion of 'substantial involvement', and simply evokes that of sending in troops. No grounds are given in this decision for this omission that is somewhat surprising in that it further reduces the legal possibilities of attribution.

After entering the decision just cited, the Court asserts somewhat enigmatically that it 'has no need to respond to the contentions of the Parties as to whether and under what conditions contemporary international law provides for a right of self-defence against large-scale attacks by irregular forces'.[452] To the best of my knowledge, the only pertinent arguments of the parties referred to the relevance of article 3(g) of the definition of aggression and its interpretation in respect of the case law of *Military and Paramilitary Activities*. In this respect, it does seem that the Court actually answered the question affirmatively, as the DRC had hoped.[453] In actual fact, the Court confirmed its earlier case law and at a time when it might have been sensitive to the arguments challenging it. In the context in which the decision was entered, one cannot help thinking it was a deliberate judicial policy to reaffirm the relevance of the UN Charter rules about the non-use of force in general and of self-defence in particular.[454]

Ultimately, it shall be recalled that article 51 does not specifically settle the question of the involvement of private groups in armed attacks. Initially a good many States construed this silence as meaning self-defence might not be evoked in such an event. Progressively a compromise has emerged leading to the drafting of article 3(g) of the definition of aggression, stating very stringent criteria by which an unlawful use of force crosses the threshold allowing it to be characterised as an armed attack. Thus a State that sends irregular groups to operate in another State's territory is directly responsible for the armed actions carried out. Moreover, a substantial engagement in such actions means it can be considered there is a situation of self-defence. After 11 September 2001, it might have been thought that we were heading towards a very broad conception of 'substantial involvement', as covering no longer direct State participation in an armed action but any tolerance a State might be guilty of in respect of the activities of irregular groups operating in or from its territory. Upon examination, it

---

[451] Uganda's Counter-Memorial, 21 April 2001, 211, para 359; I Brownlie, CR 2005/7, 18 April 2005; see also R Vansteenberghe, 'L'arrêt de la Cour internationale de Justice dans l'affaire des activités armées sur le territoire du Congo et le recours à la force' (2006) 39 *RBDI* 671–02.

[452] ICJ Rep (2005) para 147.

[453] See also above, ch 3, s I.

[454] See also: JA Green, *The International Court of Justice and Self-Defence in International Law*, above n 293, 44–51.

seems excessive though to affirm that the doctrine developed along these lines by the US administration has been accepted by the international community of States as a whole. It has often been difficult to identify any clear legal conviction in the discourse on the war against terrorism, especially when speaking of specific instances that are often highly controversial, as in the Israeli–Palestinian conflict. However, one is forced to observe that the criteria set out in article 3(g) have never been formally challenged by States. The opportunity arose for the 60 years of the UN to think about the relevance of the Charter provisions for managing new threats. However, no challenge was made. Similarly, those criteria still seem relevant in the view of the ICJ which did not hesitate to make adjudications along these lines both in 1986 and in 2005. At the time of writing, it seems therefore that each individual situation must still be gauged against the definition of aggression as accepted by the international community of States as a whole. In this perspective, there would be nothing to prevent interpreting the criterion of 'substantial involvement' as covering massive support for armed bands operating from the territory of the State in question, without that State actually participating in the armed actions as such.[455] The future will tell whether such a development is to be accepted by the international community of States as a whole.

II Necessity and Proportionality

Article 51 of the UN Charter does not explicitly refer to the need for proportionality as a condition for the lawfulness of self-defence. It might be thought, however, that by referring to 'defence' in the event of an 'armed attack' this provision suggests that the measure must be necessary to repel the attack and proportionate to the intended objective. This interpretation is confirmed by the clarification that no provision of the Charter affects self-defence 'until the Security Council has taken measures necessary to maintain international peace and security'. The expression clearly shows that in order to be consistent with international law self-defence must be necessary, which is no longer so if the Security Council fulfils its responsibilities by supervising the collective use of force. The criteria of necessity and proportionality have been expressly stated in case law too. In *Military and Paramilitary Activities*, the ICJ notes that the parties agree in affirming that 'whether the response to the attack is lawful depends on observance of the criteria of the necessity and the proportionality of the measures taken in self-

---

[455] A Randelzhofer, 'Article 51', above n 18, 801; A Nollkaemper, 'Attribution of Forcible Acts to States: Connections Between the Law on the Use of Force and the Law of State Responsibility', above n 303, 170; see also J Brumée and SJ Toope, 'The Use of Force: International Law After Iraq', above n 41, 805; T Ruys and S Verhoeven, 'Attacks by Private Actors and the Right of Self-Defence' (2005) 10 *Journal of Conflict & Security Law* 289–320.

defence'.[456] In the case of the *Legality of the Threat or Use of Nuclear Weapons*, the ICJ states that:

> The submission of the exercise of the right of self-defence to the conditions of necessity and proportionality is a rule of customary inter-national law . . . This dual condition applies equally to Article 51 of the Charter, whatever the means of force employed.[457]

These conditions were to be recalled and appraised again in the *Oil Platforms*[458] and *Armed Activities* cases[459] to which we shall return. They were also accepted unanimously by doctrine,[460] and recognised by the ILC in its work on international responsibility.[461] These conditions are not or are no longer fundamentally challenged by States.[462] Moreover, it can be noted from the outset that necessity is systematically associated with the condition of proportionality with which it seems to maintain close ties.[463]

Before saying anything about the nature of those ties, one thing must be made quite clear. In theory, necessity or proportionality appear to be accessory or even subsidiary criteria. It is only once the aggressor State has been designated that one looks in a limited way into the question of observance of the criteria of necessity or of proportionality. The three decisions entered by the ICJ in this field confirm this. Whether in the *Military and*

---

[456] ICJ Rep (1986) 103, para 194.

[457] ICJ Rep (1996) 245, para 41.

[458] ICJ Rep (2003) paras 43, 51, 74 and 78.

[459] ICJ Rep (2005) para 147.

[460] Institut de droit international Resolution on Self-defence, 27 October 2007, Santiago Session (www.idi-iil.org/idiE/navig_chon2003.html), para 2. See also R Higgins, 'The Legal Limits to the Use of Force by Sovereign States. United Nations Practice' (1961) 37 *BYBIL* 1961, 298; *The Development of International Law Through the Political Organs of the United Nations*, above n 41, 198–99; A Randelzhofer, 'Article 51', above n 18, 804–05; A Cassese, 'Article 51', above n 12, 1333; R Jennings and A Watts (eds), *Oppenheim's International Law*, above n 74, 420–23; F Berman, J Gow, C Greenwood, V Lowe, A Roberts, P Sands, M Shaw, G Simpson, C Warbrick, N Wheeler, E Wilmshurst and M Wood, 'The Chatham House Principles of International Law on the Use of Force on the Use of Self-Defence', above n 20, 967–69; C Alibert, *Du droit de se faire justice dans la société internationale depuis 1945*, above n 262, 688; P Malanczuk, 'Countermeasures and Self-Defense as Circumstances Precluding Wrongfulness in the International Law Commission's Draft Articles on State Responsibility', above n 170, 796–98; J Nyamuya Maogoto, 'New Frontiers, Old Problems: The War on Terror and the Notion of Anticipating the Ennemy', above n 40, 19.

[461] See below.

[462] But see: France (A/AC.134/SR.72, 6 August 1970 in A/AC.134/SR.67-78), Ghana (A/C.6/SR.1205, 22 October 1970, para 40; A/C.6/SR.1270, 28 October 1971, para 6), Austria (A/C.6/SR.1208, 27 October 1970, para 55), Belarus (A/C.6/SR.1270, 28 October 1971, para 42), Mongolia (A/C.6/SR.1274, 3 November 1971, para 38), Hungary (A/C.6/SR.1275, 3 November 1971, para 42), Cuba (A/C.6/SR.1273, 2 November 1971, para 32; A/C.6/SR.1349, 3 November 1972, para 29), Czechoslovakia (A/C.6/SR.1273, 2 November 1971, para 42) and Ukraine (A/C.6/SR.1274, 3 November 1971, para 28).

[463] J Gardam, *Necessity, Proportionality and the Use of Force by States* (Cambridge, Cambridge University Press, 2004); 'Proportionality and Force in International Law' (1993) 87 *AJIL* 391–413; R Ago, Addendum to the eight report on State responsibility, A/CN.4/318, Add.5-7, *YILC*, 1980, II, part One, para 120. See also Independent International Fact-Finding Mission on the Conflict in Georgia, *Report*, September 2009 (www.ceiig.ch/Report.html), vol II, 247–48.

Paramilitary Activities, Oil Platforms or *Armed Activities* cases, the Court each time dismissed the argument of self-defence primarily because the State invoking it had failed to prove that it had previously been the victim of an armed attack, and only incidentally because its riposte did not prove 'necessary' or 'proportionate' under the circumstances of the case.[464] This impression is confirmed in part by a more general examination of practice: the essential issue often remains that of identifying the aggressor State and not taking account of a general criterion of necessity or proportionality.

To try to clarify somewhat the meaning these criteria may take on, we shall begin by saying something about the relations between self-defence and Security Council action (A). As indicated from the outset, it follows directly from article 51 of the Charter that self-defence cannot be considered necessary if the Security Council itself has already taken appropriate measures. Then we shall go on to consider other situations in an attempt to define the meaning and the relationship of the conditions of necessity and proportionality in the absence of Security Council action (B).

A. The Limit of Necessary Measures Adopted by the Security Council

As already pointed out, article 51 states that no provision of the Charter affects the right of self-defence 'until the Security Council has taken measures necessary to maintain international peace and security'. Similarly:

> Measures taken by Members in the exercise of this right of self-defence shall be immediately reported to the Security Council *and shall not in any way affect the authority and responsibility of the Security Council under the present Charter to take at any time such action as it deems necessary in order to maintain or restore international peace and security.* (emphasis added)

Thus self-defence can only be considered lawful if and to the extent that the Security Council has not itself decided to take measures it deems necessary in respect of the situation in question.[465] Keeping to the text of the Charter, 'necessary actions' may or may not consist in adopting enforcement measures to end such aggression.[466] It is for the Security Council to decide on the measures to be taken.[467] Pending the adoption of such measures, the very purpose of self-defence appears to be to offset, given the urgency and gravity of the situation, the absence of appropriate collective security measures.[468] If such measures have indeed been decided on by the

---

[464] C Gray, *International Law and the Use of Force*, 3rd edn, above n 12, 151–54.

[465] See: Institut de droit international Resolution on Self-defence, 27 October 2007, Santiago Session (www.idi-iil.org/idiE/navig_chon2003.html), para 9.

[466] H Kelsen, 'Collective Security and Collective Self-Defense under the Charter of the United Nations' (1948) 42 *AJIL* 793.

[467] ibid; see also above, ch 6, s I.

[468] LA Sicilianos, 'Le contrôle par le Conseil de sécurité des actes de légitime défense' in SFDI, *Le chapitre VII de la Charte des Nations Unies* (Paris, Pedone, 1994) 72; see also AC Kiss, *Répertoire de la Pratique française en matière de droit international public*, tome VI (Paris, edn CNRS, 1969) 70, no 95.

competent organ for deciding on the use of force, no unilateral measure has cause to be, even if taken in self-defence.[469] This is the same rationale as underpins self-defence in municipal law: the institution authorises a reaction to an exceptional situation during such time as the forces of law and order are unable to react.[470] This situation ends when the use of force can be ensured by the public authorities, private violence being by definition limited and provisional only.[471]

This pattern has been illustrated many times in practice with the Security Council not hesitating to adopt resolutions limiting the exercise of certain States' right to self-defence. In the conflict between Iran and Iraq, for example, the Council requested and then demanded that both sides observe a ceasefire and 'discontinue all military actions on land, at sea and in the air, and withdraw all forces to the internationally recognized boundaries without delay'.[472] Likewise the Council tried to end the war raging in the DRC by requesting and then demanding that all sides observe a ceasefire.[473] The demand to cease hostilities was made again in more limited international armed conflicts such as the Falklands War[474] and the territorial dispute between Ethiopia and Eritrea.[475] The logic is the same in all these precedents: the Security Council takes up the issue and considers it necessary to call for an end to hostilities, either because it has not been able—or willing—to determine who the aggressor was or because it considers that the legal consequences of the aggression must be examined in a pacified setting and not further to an armed action, whether carried out in self-defence or not. The Security Council decision is clear and all UN Member States are bound to comply with it under article 25 of the Charter. The text of article 51 confirms that no State can claim to eschew this decision in the name of its natural right to self-defence. Even if a State has been the victim of a prior armed attack, the military riposte can no longer, by application of a Security Council decision, be considered 'necessary' in the circumstances of the case.

This very clear superiority of a Security Council decision over the exercise of a natural right of self-defence is confirmed by the precedent of the

---

[469] See: DW Greig, 'Self-Defence and the Security Council: What Does Article 51 Require?' (1991) 40 *ICLQ* 366–402, and N Schrijver, 'Responding to International Terrorism: Moving the Frontiers of International Law for "Enduring Freedom"', above n 419, 281.

[470] R Ago, Addendum to the eight report on State reponsibility, A/CN.4/318, Add.5-7, above n 464, 51, para 84 and R Ago, *YILC*, 1980, I, 1619th session, 25 June 1980, para 3; see also H Kelsen, 'Collective Security and Collective Self-Defense under the Charter of the United Nations' (1948) 42 *AJIL* 784–85.

[471] SA Alexandrov, *Self-Defense Against the Use of Force in International Law*, above n 14, 104; Nguyen Quoc Dinh, 'La légitime défense d'après la Charte des Nations Unies' (1984) 52 *RGDIP* 232–34.

[472] SC 598 (1987) of 20 July 1987, para 1.

[473] SC Res 1258 (1999) of 6 August 1999, para 4, 1279 (1999) of 30 November 1979, para 1, 1291 (2000) of 24 February 2000, para 1, 1304 (2000) of 12 June 2000, paras 1 and 12.

[474] SC Res 502 (1982) of 3 April 1982.

[475] SC Res 1177 (1998) of 26 June 1998, para 1.

war in Bosnia-Herzegovina in the 1990s. It will be recalled that from
September 1991 the Security Council had adopted a resolution establishing
an arms embargo for the whole of Yugoslavia,[476] that it saw fit to maintain
after the creation of new States including Bosnia-Herzegovina.[477] This
State, however, thought it was in a situation of self-defence further to an
armed attack allegedly by the FRY and for a while the Republic of Croatia.
A situation of self-defence would have authorised it to call for and obtain
support, including military support, from third States despite the embargo
laid down by the Security Council. Bosnia-Herzegovina argued that the
'inherent' character of its legitimate right of self-defence meant that this
right could not be impeded by the Security Council resolution, which would
either have to be interpreted as not opposing the exercise of that right or be
considered invalid as *ultra vires*. This argument was laid before the ICJ,[478]
but was also disseminated more widely.[479] However, it cannot be affirmed
that it won over the international community of States as a whole.[480] While
the General Assembly adopted several resolutions inviting the Security
Council to modify its policy,[481] it was the Council that continued to be considered responsible for maintaining international peace and security.[482] In
this way the Security Council deemed it necessary, while deciding to maintain the arms embargo until the end of the conflict,[483] to authorise the use
of force with a view to pursuing specific objectives, essentially of a humanitarian order.[484] It is on the strength of these resolutions, and not by invoking collective self-defence that might have been exercised beyond or even
against the Council resolutions, that some States conducted military actions
on the ground.[485]

The primacy of Security Council resolutions should not be understood
as *putting an end to* the right of self-defence. Despite what the terms of certain resolutions might suggest,[486] article 51 does not imply that self-defence

---

[476] SC Res 713 (1991) of 25 September 1991.

[477] SC Res (1992) of 8 June 1992, preamble, 761 (1992) of 29 June 1992, preamble, 764
(1992) of 13 July 1992, preamble, 770 (1992) of 13 August 1992, preamble, 787 (1992) of
16 November 1992, preamble; see also S/PV.3247.

[478] See: Application instituting proceedings, 20 March 1993 and Boyle, CR 1993/12, 1
April 1993, 41 *ff* and CR 1993/13, 2 April 1993, 47.

[479] C Scott, F Chang, A Qureshi, P Michell, J Kalajdzic and P Copeland, 'A Memorial for
Bosnia: Framework of Legal Arguments Concerning the Lawfulness of the Maintenance of the
United Nations Security Council's Arms Embargo on Bosnia and Herzegovina' (2004) 16
Michigan JIL 1-140.

[480] See also: (1994) 43 *ICLQ* 714 and 'United Kingdom Materials on International Law'
(1994) 65 *BYBIL* 691–92.

[481] GA Res 47/121 of 18 December 1992 (102-0-57), 48/88 of 29 December 1993 and
49/10 of 8 November 1994.

[482] See: T Christakis, *L'ONU, le Chapter VII et la crise yougoslave* (Paris, Montchrestien,
1996) 48 and *ff*.

[483] SC Res 1021 (1995) of 22 November 1995, 1031 (1995) of 15 December 1995, para 22.

[484] SC Res 836 (1993) of 4 June 1993, para 10.

[485] See below, ch 8, s II.

[486] See: SC 225 (1968) of 19 June 1968.

vanishes whenever the Security Council has taken the 'necessary measures'; the provision merely indicates that these measures can 'impair' the exercise of this right. Thus the adoption of collective security measures by the Council limits the exercise of the right of self-defence by the State concerned but without stripping it in its essence of this 'inherent' right. This right is aimed at 'the very survival of a State',[487] which explains why it cannot disappear by definition and only the way it is exercised may be affected, as the case may be, by Security Council action.

Practice very clearly confirms this theoretical schema. When on 6 August 1990, just a few days after Iraq's invasion of Kuwait, the Security Council decided on an embargo to restore international peace, at the same time it 'affirm[ed] the inherent right of individual or collective self-defence, in response to the armed attack by Iraq against Kuwait, in accordance with Article 51 of the Charter'.[488]

This resolution was to be recalled on several occasions, including in resolution 678 (1990) authorising the use of force if by 15 January 1991 Iraq had not put an end to its aggression and all of its consequences.[489] It is observed that, according to the Security Council itself, the adoption of measures necessary to maintain international peace and security does not put an end to the right of self-defence, only the exercise of this right can be affected by such measures.[490] Along these lines, in the case of *Armed Activities*, the Court affirmed that

> any military action taken by the DRC against Uganda during this period [after 7 August 1998, when the Ugandan armed attack began] could not be deemed wrongful since it would be justified as action taken in self-defence under Article 51 of the United Nations Charter'.[491]

The conclusion is significant insofar as the Court makes no mention of the Security Council's adoption during this period of resolutions calling for a ceasefire between the parties.[492] It can therefore be deduced that the RDC's right of self-defence did not disappear with the adoption of these resolutions, and article 51 could still be invoked after the Security Council had

---

[487] ICJ, *Legality of the Threat or Use of Nuclear Weapons*, ICJ Rep (1996) 266 (E).

[488] SC Res 661 (1990) of 6 August 1990, preamble; see also SC Res 546 (1984) of 6 January 1984.

[489] SC Res 678 (1990) of 29 November 1990, para 2.

[490] See: O Schachter, 'United Nations Law in the Gulf Conflict' (1991) 85 *AJIL* 452–73; C Dominicé, 'La sécurité collective et la crise du Golfe' (1991) 2 *EJIL* 103; T Franck and F Patel, 'UN Police Action in Lieu of War: "The Old Older Changeth" ', ibid, 63–74; EV Rostow, 'Until What? Enforcement Action or Collective Self-Defense?', ibid, 506–16; BH Weston, 'Security Council Resolution 678 and Persian Gulf Decision Making: Precarious Legitimacy', ibid, 516–35; see also P Weckel, 'Le Chapitre VII de la Charte et son application par le Conseil de sécurité' (1991) 37 *AFDI* 188–92.

[491] ICJ Rep (2005), para 304.

[492] SC Res 1234 (1999) of 9 April 1999, para 3; SC Res 1258 (1999) of 6 August 1999, para 4, and 1304 (200) of 16 June 2000, para 1.

taken the measures it deemed necessary. For that matter Uganda never contested this.[493]

If self-defence can still be invoked even when the Security Council has taken the necessary measures, what exactly is the meaning of the order of precedence inscribed in article 51? In principle it means that the exercise of a right of self-defence cannot justify the violation of resolutions validly adopted in application of Chapter VII of the Charter. So Iran, even if it had been attacked initially, could not continue the armed conflict once the Security Council had demanded its suspension and Iraq itself had declared it was ready to cease hostilities.[494] Similarly no State could aid Bosnia-Herzegovina militarily in violation of the arms embargo, even in the name of collective self-defence. This seemingly simple principle may, however, become complicated in certain situations as in the three cases below.

First it may sometimes be difficult to determine whether the Security Council has indeed taken the 'measures necessary to maintain international peace and security' within the meaning of article 51.[495] Things are straightforward enough if no resolution is adopted, which was a common occurrence throughout the Cold War when the use or threat of the veto blocked the Security Council leaving intact the exercise of self-defence by aggressed States.[496] But it is not sufficient for the Council to take up the question and for a resolution to be adopted for it to be considered that the condition set out in article 51 has been fulfilled.[497] In resolution 1368 (2001), adopted in the aftermath of the attacks of 11 September 2001, the Security Council, 'recognizing the inherent right of individual or collective self-defence in accordance with the Charter', 'unequivocally condemns' these 'terrorist attacks', 'expresses its deepest sympathy and condolences to the victims', 'calls on all States to work together to bring to justice' those responsible for them and 'calls also on the international community to redouble their efforts to prevent and suppress terrorist acts'. Then, before deciding to remain seized of the matter, it '*Expresses* its readiness to take all necessary steps to respond to the terrorist attacks of 11 September 2001, and to combat all forms of terrorism, in accordance with its responsibilities under the Charter of the United Nations'. (emphasis added)[498] If the Council 'expresses its readiness' to take necessary measures, then *a contrario* it has not yet taken

---

[493] See written and oral pleadings.

[494] E David, 'La guerre du Golfe et le droit international' (1987) 20 *RBDI* 160; see also 'Pratique française du droit international' (1983) 29 *AFDI* 909; (1984) 30 *AFDI* 1012–13.

[495] TD Gill, 'Legal and Some Political Limitations on the Power of the UN Security Council to Exercice its Enforcement Powers Under Chapter VII of the Charter' (1995) 26 *NYIL* 92 ff; A Constantinou, *The Right of Self-Defense under Customary International Law and Article 51 of the UN Charter*, above n 7, 196; R Bermejo Garcia, *El marco jurídico internacional en materia de uso de la fuerza: ambigüedades y limites* (Madrid, Ed Civitas, 1993) 313.

[496] J Combacau, 'The Exception of Self-Defence in UN Practice' in A Cassese (ed), *The Current Legal Regulation of the Use of Force* (Dordrecht, Martinus Nijhoff, 1986) 16–17.

[497] SA Alexandrov, *Self-Defense Against the Use of Force in International Law*, above n 14, 146.

[498] Resolution 1368 (2001) of 12 September 2001, para 5.

them.[499] It can more generally be deduced that a simple condemnation or expression of sympathy, a simple appeal or the fact of being or remaining seized of a question do not constitute of themselves 'measures necessary to maintain international peace and security'.[500] Should it be considered on the other hand that such measures were taken by the Council when, after reaffirming the right of self-defence and characterising the attacks of 11 September as a threat to international peace and security, it decides on the basis of Chapter VII on general measures of fighting terrorism?[501] In absolute terms, certainly, but one cannot obviously deduce from this anything about the US's exercise of its right of self-defence in the context of the war against Afghanistan engaged a few days after the resolution was adopted. The aforecited resolution does not refer specifically to the situation in Afghanistan, which was only addressed by the Security Council after the beginning of military action officially in the name of self-defence.[502] In this context, it can be considered that the Security Council has never taken the necessary measures that might preclude the US from exercising its right of self-defence.[503] The question of whether the war against Afghanistan was necessary to this end has therefore never been decided by the Council.

A second possible problem is where the Council has plainly adopted measures necessary for maintaining peace but it cannot readily be determined to what extent it has meant to impede a State exercising its right of self-defence.[504] The Second Gulf War is a good illustration of this situation. In its resolution 678 (1990) of 29 November 1990, the Security Council authorises States co-operating with the Government of Kuwait 'to use all necessary means to uphold and implement' its resolutions 'unless Iraq on or before 15 January 1991 fully implements' those resolutions.[505] It seems plain that, under the circumstances, Kuwait and its allies cannot in any event use force against Iraq before the date indicated, even by virtue of their right to collective self-defence.[506] It is not easy, however, to determine from

---

[499] See: N Schrijver, 'Responding to International Terrorism: Moving the Frontiers of International Law for 'Enduring Freedom', above n 419, 284.

[500] PM Eisemann, 'Attaques du 11 Septembre et exercice d'un droit naturel de légitime défense' in K Bannelier et al (eds), Le droit international face au terrorisme (Paris, Pedone, 2002) 239.

[501] SC Res 1373 (2001) of 28 September 2001.

[502] O Corten, 'Vers un renforcement des pouvoirs du Conseil de sécurité dans la lutte contre le terrorisme?' in K Bannelier et al (eds), Le droit international face au terrorisme (Paris, Pedone, 2002) 264–65.

[503] T Franck, 'Terrorism and the Right of Self-Defense' (2001) 95 AJIL 841; M Byers, 'Terrorism, the Use of Force and International Law After 11 September', above n 296, 412.

[504] See also: O Schachter, 'United Nations Law in the Gulf Conflict', above n 492, 457–60.

[505] SC Res 678 (1990) of 29 November 1990, para 2; see J Verhoeven, 'Etats alliés ou Nations Unies? L'ONU face au conflit entre l'Iraq et le Koweït' (1990) 36 AFDI 178–79 and 187.

[506] See the views expressed by France (S/PV.2963, 29 November 1990, 68; 'Pratique française du droit international' (1991) 37 AFDI 1014–16), UK (S/PV.2963, 29 November 1990, 82), USSR (ibid, 96), Canada ('Canadian Practice in International Law' (1991) 29 CYIL 496), USA ('Contemporary Practice of the United States' (1991) 85 AJIL 340–41) and Netherlands ('Netherlands State Practice' (1992) 23 NYIL 367).

when and to what extent this right was limited. One might *a priori* consider that from 6 August 1990, that is four days after the invasion of Kuwait, the Council had taken enforcement measures under Chapter VII of the Charter by opting for the embargo, which *a contrario* excluded the option of immediate military intervention.[507] This conclusion would seem correct to me. It is hard to imagine, when the Security Council decides to opt for a peaceful means of settling a crisis, that States might circumvent its choice by engaging in an armed action in the name of their right to self-defence. An examination of Security Council debates of the time confirms for that matter that no State affirmed it was entitled to make war on Iraq without authorisation, which explains the adoption of the aforecited resolution 678 (1990).[508] It is true that the US and several of its allies relied on self-defence as recalled in resolution 661 (1990) to deploy military forces in the Gulf as from August 1990,[509] but with limited intent: to prevent any attack by Iraq upon other States in the region,[510] and to implement minimum measures of constraint to enforce the Security Council embargo.[511] In the first instance, no problem of compatibility arises with the Security Council resolutions, as the Council clearly left the States of the region free to call on aid from foreign armies for their defence. In the second, it could be considered that the stopping and searching of vessels were necessary measures of self-defence that did not contradict but reinforced the embargo option chosen by the Council.[512] This situation would have been entirely different if States had begun a war to drive Iraq from Kuwait by force while the Security Council was seized of the question and had clearly decided not (yet) to use force. In such a case, the measures of self-defence implemented could certainly not have been characterised as 'necessary'.[513] That this assumption was not materialised confirms besides that this was what most States believed at the time.[514]

Thirdly, is the case where it is the aggressor State that refuses to abide by a Security Council resolution imposing a cessation of hostilities by pursu-

---

[507] SC Res 661 (1990) of 6 August 1990.

[508] See: S/PV.2933, 6 August 1990; S/PV.2934, 9 August 1990; S/PV.2937, 18 August 1990.

[509] ND White and Ö Ülgen, 'The Security Council and the Decentralized Military Option: Constitutionality and Function' (1997) 44 *NILR* 391–92.

[510] S/PV.2934, 9 August 1990, 7, 17, and 46; see also S/PV.2937, 18 August 1990, 29 and *Letter dated 9 August 1990 addressed to the President of the Security Council*, S/21492, 10 August 1990; S/PV.2963, 29 November 1990, 101; 'Pratique française du droit international' (1990) 36 *AFDI* 1046–47.

[511] SC Res 665 (1990) of 25 August 1990, para 1 and S/PV.2938, 25 August 1990, 28; 'Pratique française du droit international' (1990) 36 *AFDI* 1047–48.

[512] See: S/PV.2938, 25 August 1990, 29/30 and 48/50.

[513] S/PV.2943, 25 September 1990, 28/30; S/PV.2951, 29 October 1990, 88.

[514] But see: 'United Kingdom Materials on International Law' (1990) 60 *BYBIL* 627–31, 631; (1991) 62 *BYBIL* 702; (1992) 63 *BYBIL* 820; cp *Letter dated 17 January 1991, addressed to the President of the Security Council*, S/22097, 17 January 1991; 'United Kingdom Materials on International Law' (1991) 62 *BYBIL* 704–08; S/PV.2977, 25 February 1991, 377; see also C Warbrick, 'The Invasion of Kuwait by Iraq' (1991) 40 *ICLQ* 486–88.

ing its aggression and as the case may be its invasion or occupation of the territory of the aggressed State. Might that State not exercise its right of self-defence because of the Council resolution? To exclude this possibility would have the absurd and unreasonable result of depriving the aggressed State of any right of self-defence, with its possible disappearance as a consequence. In such a case, it must indeed be considered that a riposte is necessary. On this assumption the Security Council would not have sanctioned the initial aggression—it would just have made a general call to both parties for an end to hostilities—nor the aggressor State's violation of its own resolution—the Security Council not having reacted to the failure to comply with this request. At the time of the riposte it would therefore not have taken the measures 'necessary to maintain international peace and security', which would authorise the State to exercise its right of self-defence. The conclusion seems to be borne out by practice. In the Congo conflict, the Security Council—like the ICJ as just recalled[515]—carefully abstained from condemning the DRC for its defensive military actions against Rwanda and Uganda and even after the adoption of certain resolutions calling for a ceasefire. It is Rwanda and Uganda rather that were condemned, especially at the time of the events in Kisangani.[516] Thus the aggressed State can exercise its right of self-defence in the event that the aggressor State continues its aggression in spite not only of article 2(4) of the Charter but also of the specific requirements of the Security Council.[517]

Finally each situation must be decided in view of the Security Council's intent. As pointed out, it may be that the Security Council has not taken specific measures or that the measures taken do little if anything all to impede a State's exercise of its right of self-defence. Such a hypothesis obviously does not imply that self-defence is always 'necessary' within the meaning of international law. It supposes rather that the need for it be verified by appealing to more general criteria that refer, in my view, to considerations of effectiveness and of proportionality.

B. The General Meaning of Conditions of Necessity and Proportionality

In what follows I shall begin with the meaning of necessity before setting out how this ties in with proportionality. If one keeps to its ordinary meaning, 'necessity' may be used in a narrower or broader sense. The first assimilates it to 'an indispensable thing'.[518] What is necessary here seems to be likened to necessity as a circumstance precluding wrongfulness, codified by

---

[515] ICJ, *Armed Activities*, ICJ Rep (2005), para 304; see above.

[516] SC Res 1304 (2000) of 16 June 2000, para 2.

[517] See also the *Falklands* case; 'Netherlands State Practice' (1983) 14 *NYIL* 330 and 'United Kingdom Materials on International Law' (1982) 53 *BYBIL* 500–02.

[518] *The Oxford English Reference Dictionary* (Oxford, Oxford University Press, 1996) 968.

the ILC as supposedly 'the only way' of achieving an objective.[519] However, 'necessity' also includes an attenuated meaning when it is related to 'a state of things or circumstances enforcing a certain course'.[520] The term relates here to the meaning discerned by the European Court of Human Rights for which necessity stands apart from the term 'indispensable' in leaving more leeway to interpretation.[521]

In the case of self-defence, we shall see that necessity has not been understood either in its first narrow sense nor in its looser meaning. In practice, appreciating this criterion presupposes combining the criteria of effectiveness and proportionality, which are to be appraised depending on the specific circumstances of each case.

Dismissal of Overly Narrow or Overly Broad Conceptions of Necessity

At first sight one might think that necessity has been apprehended in the primary ordinary meaning of the notion as relating to a very strict condition of exclusivity of means. In his 1980 report on international responsibility, Professor Ago considered that:

> The reason for stressing that action taken in self-defence must be *necessary* is that the State attacked (or threatened with imminent attack, if one admits preventive self-defence) must not, in the particular circumstances, *have had any means of halting the attack other than recourse to armed force*. In other words, had it been able to achieve the same result by measures not involving the use of armed force, it would have no justification for adopting conduct which contravened the general prohibition against the use of armed force . . . In fact, the requirements of the 'necessity' and the 'proportionality' of the action taken in self-defence can simply be described as two sides of the same coin. Self-defence will be valid as a circumstance precluding the wrongfulness of the conduct of the State *only if that State was unable to achieve the desired result by different conduct involving either no use of armed force at all or merely its use on a lesser scale.* (emphasis added)[522]

This conception seems to be shared by many scholars.[523] It has also been defended by certain States in the context of procedures before the ICJ.

---

[519] ILC, Responsibility of States for Internationally Wrongful Acts, 2001, Article 25 § 1a), annexed to GA Res 56/83 of 21 December 2001; see above ch 4, s II.

[520] *The Oxford English Reference Dictionary*, above n 520, 968.

[521] ECHR, *James and others*, 21 February 1986, Series A no 98, para 51; *Handyside*, 7 December 1976, Series A no 24, para 48.

[522] *YILC*, 1980, vol II, Part One, 69, paras 120–21; see also *YILC*, 1980, vol I, 1619th session, 25 June 1980, para 24.

[523] According to R Higgins, self defence is 'an exceptional right which may only be exercised if no other means are available' (*The Development of International Law Through the Political Organs of the United Nations*, above n 41, 205); see also Y Dinstein, *War, Aggression and Self-Defence*, 4th edn, above n 7, 237; F Berman, J Gow, C Greenwood, V Lowe, A Roberts, P Sands, M Shaw, G Simpson, C Warbrick, N Wheeler, E Wilmshurst and M Wood, 'The Chatham House Principles of International Law on the Use of Force on the Use of Self-Defence', above n 20, 967; C Alibert, *Du droit de se faire justice dans la société internationale depuis 1945*, above n 262, 688; see also Judge Schwebel, dissenting opinion, ICJ, *Military and Paramilitary Activities*, ICJ Rep (1986), paras 201 and 204.

France, in the context of the opinion on the *Legality of the Threat or Use of Nuclear Weapons*, has thus interpreted necessity as a condition of self-defence by expressly citing the words of Rapporteur Ago that we have just set out.[524] No State has contradicted it on this point.[525] In the *Oil Platforms* case, Iran also defended this conception by considering that the US could have taken measures other than the armed actions, which were not 'necessary', and so could not be characterised as self-defence.[526] The defendant State replied essentially on the facts by claiming that there was no alternative under the circumstances of the case in point. In strictly legal terms, however, the criterion of exhaustion of peaceful means was not contested.[527]

However, these assertions of principle should not mislead us. In practice I know of no precedent where an act of self-defence has been condemned for the sole reason that its author failed to prove that it had not first exhausted all possible peaceful means. Case law is very instructive on this point.

—In *Military and Paramilitary Activities*, the Court observed that the US measures could not be considered as a 'necessity' for the defence of El Salvador in the context of collective self-defence. Indeed, those measures 'were only taken, and began to produce their effects, several months after the major offensive of the armed opposition in El Salvador had been completely repulsed'.[528] The Court did not therefore condemn the US because it failed to prove it had first exhausted all peaceful means before turning to the military option. It observed rather that, at the moment it took the measures, they could hardly be characterised as necessary to a riposte that had already produced its effects.

—In the *Oil Platforms* case, the Court devoted several pages of its judgment to the condition of necessity without ever naming or applying the criterion of exhaustion of peaceful means. In the case in point, it considered that some of the US military actions were unnecessary by observing that first it was not proved that the targets had any military function and above all that the US had not officially complained to Iran of the military activities conducted on the oil rigs, 'which does not suggest that the targeting of the platforms was seen as a necessary act'.[529] The Court does not rely on the fact that the US did not supposedly first try to settle the dispute

---

[524] Perrin de Brichambaut, CR 95/23, 1 November 1995, 66.

[525] According to the UK, 'States should only use force in self-defence as a matter of last resort'; June 1995, para 3.37 (and 'United Kingdom Materials on International Law' (1995) *BYBIL* 726).

[526] Memorial of the Islamic Republic of Iran, 98 and paras 4.18–19.

[527] Counter-Memorial of the USA, 137, s 1 and Matheson, CR 2003/12, 26 February 2003, 53–54, para 18.63.

[528] ICJ Rep (1986) 122, para 237.

[529] ICJ Rep (2003) 198, para 76.

by means other than military ones; it deduces that the US itself did not consider this option was a 'necessity', while citing as a relevant objective criterion 'the nature of the target of the force used avowedly in self-defence'.[530]

—In the *Armed Activities* case, the DRC insisted particularly on the exhaustion of peaceful means criterion to affirm that the measures taken by Uganda did not meet the condition of necessity of an action in self-defence.[531] The defendant State challenged this criterion, considering that 'the concept of necessity simply implies that the conduct remains within the appropriate purpose'.[532] In its judgment, while asserting that, in view of the absence of prior armed attack, it did not have to adjudicate on the criterion of necessity, the Court

> cannot fail to observe, however, that the taking of airports and towns many hundreds of kilometres from Uganda's border would not seem proportionate to the series of transborder attacks it claimed had given rise to the right of self-defence, nor to be necessary to that end.[533]

The only criterion used in considering that certain measures are not necessary seems to be, as in *Oil Platforms*, the absence of any military benefit from the action undertaken in respect of its stated aim. The fact, though, that Uganda had not used other peaceful means before opting for military action was not evoked by the Court.

These three precedents, which are, as far as I know, the only ones in which a court or tribunal has condemned a State by observing an absence of necessity of an action officially conducted in self-defence seem to indicate that the concept should not be understood in its first sense as requiring proof that all other possible measures have been exhausted.[534]

Does this mean that necessity should be understood in its looser sense? In view of existing case law it is clear that necessity is a notion that is not left entirely to the appreciation of the State that may be acting in self-defence.[535] In the *Oil Platforms* case, the US affirmed that it sincerely believed that the attacks against the platforms were necessary for its security and that 'A measure of discretion should be afforded to a party's good faith application of measures to protect its essential security interests'.[536] In the *Armed Activities* case, Uganda claimed that 'If the concept of necessity of self-defence is to be applied on the basis of effectiveness and common

---

[530] ibid, 196, para 74.

[531] Memorial of the DRC, 206–07, para 5.28; Reply of the DRC, 230, para 3.159; see also Klein, CR 2005/3, 12 April 2005, 47–48, para 3 and 48–52, paras 5–16.

[532] Brownlie, CR 2005/7, 18 April 2005, 31, para 82; see also 32, para 89.

[533] ICJ Rep (2005), para 147.

[534] See: USA, 'Contemporary Practice of the United States' (2004) 98 *AJIL* 600.

[535] Independent International Fact-Finding Mission on the Conflict in Georgia, *Report*, September 2009 (www.ceiig.ch/Report.html), vol II, 248.

[536] ICJ Rep (2003), para 73; see Matheson, CR 2003/12, 26 February 2003, 54, para 18.64.

sense, it is surely the view of the victim State and its nationals which must prevail'.[537]

Such assertions appear to rely on a certain logic. If it is indeed established that a State is the victim of an armed attack, it is the victim State that is best placed to appreciate the appropriateness and scale of the riposte.[538] It might seem excessive to condemn it when it merely reacted to a particularly serious violation of international law on the pretext that the reaction was, in the eyes of a third party led to adjudicate on it *a posteriori*, inopportune or exaggerated. Such reasoning is far from having convinced the ICJ, however, which plainly insisted on the objective character of any determination as to what is necessary. Already in the case of *Military and Paramilitary Activities*, the ICJ had pointed out that whether a measure is necessary or not is not 'purely a question for the subjective judgement of the party'.[539] This is reiterated in *Oil Platforms*[540] and the Court even added to refute the US claim that 'the requirement of international law that measures taken avowedly in self-defence must have been necessary for that purpose is strict and objective, leaving no room for any "measure of discretion"'.[541]

As seen, such stringency did not lead the Court to sanction a State for the sole reason that it had not shown it had exhausted all peaceful means. Such stringency indeed led to the observation, which is in itself incompatible with the argument of absolute freedom of appreciation, that the behaviour of that State did not obey the criterion of necessity that conditions the lawfulness of a measure of self-defence.

To conclude on the subject of this case law, it should be recalled that the Court has never been confronted with a situation where the State that invoked self-defence had been able to show it had been the victim of an armed attack. In each of the precedents considered, it was *both* because it had not been proved that it had been the victim of a prior armed attack *and* as its reaction appeared unnecessary and disproportionate that the State was condemned.[542] At this stage it can be observed in any event that the criterion of necessity cannot be construed either too narrowly as this would liken it to what is absolutely essential or too loosely as this would only refer back to the appreciation of each State concerned. If one recalls the original meaning of necessity, it is in its second sense rather, relating to what is more than useful but less than essential, that it seems to be consecrated here. Again one might ask how one can concretely adjudicate on this subject, which leads us to look for more specific criteria able to refine the meaning of the notion.

---

[537] Brownlie, CR 2005/7, 18 April 2005, 34, para 92.

[538] See dissenting opinion of Judge Schwebel, ICJ, *Military and Paramilitary Activities*, ICJ Rep (1986) 293–94, para 69.

[539] ICJ Rep (1986) 141, para 282.

[540] ICJ Rep (2003) 24, para 43.

[541] ICJ Rep (2003) 196, para 73.

[542] JA Green, *The International Court of Justice and Self-Defence in International Law*, above n 293, 106.

Necessity: Exclusivity of the Ultimate Purpose, Effectiveness and Proportionality

The condition of necessity refers us to the very essence of self-defence: the true test of the measure in question is to check that it is indeed a genuinely defensive measure, that is, designed to put an end to an armed attack.[543] This condition of purpose was well expressed by Roberto Ago who, as Special Rapporteur on international responsibility, in evoking self-defence specified that 'the objective to be achieved by the conduct in question, its raison d'être, is necessarily that of repelling an attack and preventing it from succeeding and nothing else'.[544]

It was on this basis, in the *Armed Activities* case, that the DRC accused Uganda of pursuing other purposes than riposting to an armed attack, by citing in support several statements by top Ugandan officials mentioning broader objectives such as humanitarian concerns or very vague concerns about security in the region.[545] The DRC argued that the Ugandan measures could not then be considered as 'necessary' for the purposes of self-defence.[546] In its judgment the Court seems to have consecrated this position by asserting that:

> Article 51 of the Charter may justify a use of force in self-defence only within the strict confines there laid down. It does not allow the use of force by a State to protect perceived security interests beyond these parameters. Other means are available to a concerned State, including, in particular, recourse to the Security Council.[547]

This *dictum* suggests that, if the objective of a State exceeds that of a riposte to an aggression and extends to the simple defence of its security, then by definition one can no longer consider a measure as 'necessary' or, what amounts to the same thing, that it is 'proportionate' within the meaning of article 51 of the Charter.[548]

Necessity depends therefore on a criterion of exclusive purpose.[549] If other objectives than self-defence may be detected (such as a change in a border, the appropriation of resources, the overthrow of a government, the destruction of infrastructure, the punishing of a State, etc), the measure

---

[543] See: J Kammerhofer, 'Uncertainties of the Law on Self-Defence in the United Nations Charter' (2004) 35 *NYIL* 200–02.

[544] *YILC*, 1980, II, Part One, 69, para 119. See also Independent International Fact-Finding Mission on the Conflict in Georgia, *Report*, September 2009 (www.ceiig.ch/Report.html), vol II, 248.

[545] Reply of the DRC, 232–36, paras 3.160–64.

[546] Klein, CR 2005/3, 12 April 2005, 48–52, paras 5–16.

[547] ICJ Rep (2005), para 148.

[548] J Gardam, *Necessity, Proportionality and the Use of Force by States*, above n 464, 156; see also D Simon and LA Sicilianos, 'La "contre-violence" unilatérale. Pratiques étatiques et droit international', above n 381, 75–78.

[549] See also: 'La pratique suisse en matière de droit international public' (2002) 12 *RSDIE* 644.

shall by definition no longer be a 'defence' and shall no longer be 'necessary'. It will be at most a sort of punitive expedition akin to armed reprisals and by definition contrary to international law.[550] Even so it must be specified that the exclusive purpose must be understood in the meaning of main or ultimate aim, as indicated in the expression 'raison d'être' used by Professor Ago. If under the particular circumstances of a case the only way to put an end to an attack is to overthrow the government that decided on it, the purpose of changing a government is admissible insofar as it remains subordinate to the ultimate—and exclusive in these terms—purpose of self-'defence'.[551] This criterion may obviously be difficult to apply. In the Second World War, for example, it is difficult to contest that the aim of overthrowing the Nazi regime was clearly connected with—and subordinate to—that of ending the aggression that had begun in the late 1930s. However, in the case of Vietnam's invasion of Cambodia in 1979, begun in the name of self-defence, one can doubt whether the measures taken were necessary and proportionate insofar as it was in theory only a matter of putting an end to limited incursion along the border, which could hardly justify overthrowing the government in place.[552] Beyond the variety of the instances, it is important in any event to ask whether the measures implemented are indeed 'necessary' to the pursuit of one and just one goal, which is to put an end to an attack even if other intermediate objectives may be pursued by the State acting in self-defence.

Another clarification must be made at this point concerning a question of timing. By definition, the essential objective of self-defence is 'repelling an attack' and 'preventing it from succeeding', which presupposes *both* stemming the effects of a present and past situation *and* preventing the occurrence of a future situation which would be the pursuit of the attack. Self-defence cannot therefore be exclusively future oriented, insofar as it would be aimed only at preventing any future attack: it must involve repelling an attack which by definition is underway. But this same requirement implies that self-defence cannot be exclusively past-oriented, in the sense that it is designed only to reprimand or punish a behaviour that is no longer current. The first clarification entails all the debates about the question of 'preventive', 'preemptive' and 'anticipatory' self-defence to which we shall not return at this point except to observe that even the commentators most favourable to a broad conception of self-defence claim that this consists in reacting to behaviour that has already been observed (whether actually aggressive or merely threatening).[553] The second refers to another debate about the immediate character of self-defence and requires we dwell on it for an instant.

---

[550] Above, ch 4, s II.
[551] Judge Schwebel, dissenting opinion, ICJ, *Military and Paramilitary Activities*, ICJ Rep (1986) 270, para 9.
[552] See below, ch 8, s II.
[553] Above, s I.

For doctrine, self-defence would only be admissible if begun while the attack was ongoing, and not once it had ended.[554] In the latter case we would no longer be dealing with a 'necessary' measure of self-defence but an actual punitive expedition, which should rather be characterised as reprisals.[555] The reasoning is perfectly correct in itself but it directly raises the question of how to determine whether an attack is or is not 'in progress' at the time of the riposte. The problem is very easily solved if dealing with an invasion followed by occupation of territory which constitutes an ongoing unlawful act under the rules of international responsibility.[556] But this is not always so. One might be faced with a series of targeted military attacks, whether air strikes, land operations or particularly serious attacks against a third State. Should one in this case separate each attack and require an immediate riposte to each of them, or can one on the contrary consider that the aggression is made up of these attacks as a whole with as a consequence the possibility of riposting after a specific attack has ended. In the *Oil Platforms* case, Iran opted for the first part of the alternative, asserting that the US military actions could not be necessary because they took place after the end of the attacks to which the actions were purported to respond.[557] The US favoured the second part of the alternative, replying that it would be contrary to the very essence of self-defence to force a State to wait for the next attack before reacting.[558] Even if the Court did not explicitly decide between the parties on this point, it can be considered that, as a matter of principle, it seems difficult to accredit the Iranian argument. To reason otherwise would prevent a State that was the victim of a missile attack from reacting once the missile had reached its target as the attack would then be completed; this would be a plainly absurd and unreasonable interpretation in respect of the very objective of self-defence. For that matter, if one admits that necessity implies some attempted recourse before turning to peaceful means—as shall be seen below—it is paradoxical to require at the same time an immediate reaction after each particular act that constitutes a use of force.[559]

---

[554] See: Y Dinstein, *War, Aggression and Self-Defence*, 4th edn, above n 7, 242–43; A Constantinou, *The Right of Self-Defense under Customary International Law and Article 51 of the UN Charter*, above n 7, 159–61; M Forteau, *Droit de la sécurité collective et droit de la responsabilité internationale de l'Etat* (Paris, Pedone, 2006) 417–18.

[555] See: A/C.6/S.R.886, 1 December 1965, para 42; A/AC.119/SR.9, 3 September 1964; A/AC.125/SR.66, 1 August 1967; A/C.6/S.R.1095, 13 December 1968, para 36.

[556] R Ago, A/CN.4/307 and Add.1 and 2, YILC, 1978, II, Part One, para 28; *Report of the International Law Commission*, A/56/10, 2001, GA, 56th session, Supp no 10 (A/56/10), art 14, para 3.

[557] Reply of Iran, 149–51, paras 7.47–50; Bothe, CR 2003/7, 19 February 2003, 31 *ff*.

[558] Rejoinder of the USA, 164, para 5.33; Matheson, CR 2003/12, 26 February 2003, 49.

[559] Judge Schwebel, dissenting opinion, ICJ, *Military and Paramilitary Activities*, ICJ Rep (1986) 366, para 209; see also J Gardam, *Necessity, Proportionality and the Use of Force by States*, above n 464, 150.

The understanding of aggression as a set of facts has been indirectly established by the ICJ in *Legality of Use of Force*, at the stage of protective measures. For reasons of jurisdiction, Yugoslavia claimed that the military attack by NATO States should be characterised as 'instantaneous wrongful acts' under the law of responsibility.[560] The Court in its order considered rather that there was a general dispute that related to the bombings 'taken as a whole'[561] and also considered that 'the use of force in Yugoslavia'— which it here too also considered generally—'raises very serious issues of international law'.[562] Even if it was drawn up in a specific context related to problems of competence, this precedent is significant: an aggression or a use of force must be envisaged as a set of acts connected by the same logic and not as a succession of separate acts.[563] Consequently the 'immediate' character of self-defence must not be taken in too narrow a sense: it is a matter of requiring that the riposte is aimed at behaviour that is still current, even if the material effects of its latest manifestation have already disappeared. It will be important to check therefore on a case by case basis whether the purpose of the act of self-defence is indeed to put an end to an aggression that is 'underway', which may perfectly well be reflected by the probability of a new attack further to a number of others.[564] As Rapporteur Ago stated: 'If, however, the attack in question consisted of a number of successive acts, the requirement of the immediacy of the self-defensive action would have to be looked at in the light of those acts as a whole'.[565]

It is clear, however, that the simple assertion that a permanent 'state of war' exists between two States and that justifies self-defence many years after the end of actual military operations cannot be admitted, as shown by the condemnation of several Israeli military operations conducted on this pretext.[566] Similarly, it will be recalled that the ICJ deemed that the US military intervention was not 'necessary' because of the overly long delay— 'several months' in the Court's terms—that had elapsed after the Salvadorian rebels' offensive that was allegedly supported by Nicaragua and to which the US claimed it was riposting.[567]

---

[560] Corten, CR 99/25, 12 May 1999, 17–23.

[561] ICJ, *Legality of Use of force*, ICJ Rep (1999) Order of 2 June 1999, para 28.

[562] ibid, para 17.

[563] See also: *Military and Paramilitary Activities*, ICJ Rep (1986) 146, para 3; *Armed Activities*, Reply of the DRC, 11 and 13, para 1.20; ICJ Rep (2005), paras 164–65.

[564] See: Y Dinstein, *War, Aggression and Self-Defence*, 4th edn, above n 7, 202.

[565] Addendum to the eight report on State reponsibility, *YILC*, 1980, vol II, Part One, 70, para 122; see also Judge Schwebel, dissenting opinion, *Military and Paramilitary Activities*, ICJ Rep (1986) 368–69, para 213.

[566] SC Res 111 (1956) of 19 January 1956; LA Sicilianos, *Les réactions décentralisées à l'illicite. Des contre-mesures à la légitime défense*, above n 61, 412; see also C Greenwood, 'The Concept of War in Modern International Law' (1987) 36 *ICLQ* 290 *ff* and above, ch 4, s II.

[567] See above and J Gardam, *Necessity, Proportionality and the Use of Force by States*, above n 464, 152.

It is in accordance with all these clarifications about the purpose of the riposte that we can envisage another aspect of necessity relating to a criterion of effectiveness of the measure. A measure that is utterly ineffective could not be characterised as 'necessary' within the meaning of international law. In *Oil Platforms* the parties clashed on this issue, with Iran claiming that the platforms attacked had no military function,[568] a point that the US contested.[569] The Court found in favour of Iran on this point and so indirectly enshrined a criterion of effectiveness that was missing in the case in point: if the target has no military role, its destruction cannot prove effective and therefore necessary in repelling an attack.[570] The same reasoning can explain the Court's judgment in the *Armed Activities* case, when it observed that 'the taking of airports and towns many hundreds of kilometres from Uganda's border would not seem proportionate to the series of transborder attacks it claimed had given rise to the right of self-defence, nor to be necessary to that end'[571]. It is hard to see, and the DRC did not fail to emphasise it,[572] how the taking of an airport located more than 1000 kilometres from a border is effective in securing that border. The criterion of effectiveness here brings into play a technical aspect over which military or strategic experts may argue. However, it should be specified that only obvious inefficacy will be sanctioned in practice, the State acting in self-defence not having to prove that each aspect of its action was effective in an overly narrow sense. As pointed out at the outset, while necessity cannot be construed by leaving an absolute margin of appreciation to States, it cannot be interpreted too stringently either.[573]

That being so, not every effective measure for repelling an aggression should be considered as a 'necessity' within the meaning of self-defence. Necessity must be contemplated conjointly with the criterion of proportionality that is the other side of the same coin.[574] Their association is entirely logical. What is a disproportionate measure if not a measure that goes beyond what its purpose requires, that is, which is not necessary for the pursuit of that same purpose? To illustrate this issue we can return to Israel's invasion of Lebanon in 2006.[575] As said, the Israeli State claimed to be riposting to the abduction of some of its soldiers by Hezbollah and to recurrent rocket launches by that group from Lebanese territory.[576] Most

---

[568] Bothe, CR 2003/15, 26 February 2003, 59, para 17.

[569] Matheson, CR 2003/12, 26 February 2003, 52, para 18.59

[570] ICJ Rep (2003), para 74.

[571] ICJ Rep (2005), para 147.

[572] Klein, CR 2005/3, 12 April 2005, para 19.

[573] See above.

[574] Addendum to the eight report on State reponsibility, *YILC*, 1980, vol II, Part One, 69, para 121.

[575] See: F Dubuisson, 'La guerre du Liban de l'été 2006 et le droit de la légitime défense', above n 429; E Cannizaro, 'Entités non-étatiques et régime international de l'emploi de la force. Une étude sur le cas de la réaction israélienne au Liban', above n 429.

[576] Above, s I.

of the States that spoke in the Security Council condemned the Israeli military action underscoring its disproportionate character especially in view of the scale of the damage inflicted on the infrastructure of the Lebanese State and the number of civilian victims. Plainly many had serious trouble understanding in what way these radical measures were necessary to end Hezbollah's activities.[577] Proportionality thus seems to be one way to evaluate whether a measure is necessary and especially after the measure has wrought its effects. Thus even if it proves effective—in that it actually puts an end to the attack in progress—a military riposte that entails disproportionate effects—say the annihilation of the aggressor State—should not be considered as 'necessary'.[578] The disproportionality seems here to be the mark that the State supposedly acting in self-defence was pursuing some other end than merely riposting to an attack, which refers us back to the question of multiple aims. So proportionality invariably implies comparing the military action justified by self-defence with its essential objective, which is to repel an attack that is underway.[579] Proportionality must not, however, be understood as a simple comparison of the material damage caused.[580] It is true that in *Oil Platforms* the Court seems to operate in this way by noting the disproportion between the destruction of several Iranian frigates, oil platforms and vessels by the US army and the explosion of a mine that allegedly damaged a US vessel without sinking it or killing any of its crew.[581] But the comparison of the material damage should not be understood here as the sign of any more fundamental disproportion between the action and 'the attack to which it was said to be a response'[582] or to the 'transborder attacks it claimed had given rise to the right of self-defence'.[583] It is indeed the attacks that must be compared and beyond them the behaviours of the two States in question in respect of the purpose of acting in self-defence.[584]

A further clarification can be made as to the notion of proportionality. The common association of the criterion of necessity and that of exhaustion of peaceful means was mentioned above. Even if it was then ruled out in its strict sense as requiring a State acting in self-defence to prove it had first exhausted all other means before being able to make its riposte, this criterion remains relevant in its more flexible sense. If it is manifest that other means were, given the circumstances, appropriate for responding to an

---

[577] See, eg: Russia; S/PV.5493 (Resumption 1), 21 July 2006, 2.

[578] See, eg: Malaysia in the context of the Gulf war; S/PV.2963, 29 November 1990.

[579] R Ago, Addendum to the eight report on State reponsibility, above n 464, 69, para 121; see also Judge Schwebel, dissenting opinion, *Military and Paramilitary Activities*, ICJ Rep (1986) 367–68, para 212; Judge Higgins, Legality of the Threat or Use of Nuclear Weapons, ICJ Rep (1996) 586–87.

[580] J Gardam, *Necessity, Proportionality and the Use of Force by States*, above n 464, 160–61.

[581] ICJ Rep (2003) 198, para 77.

[582] ibid.

[583] ICJ Rep (2005), para 147.

[584] See: R Ago, *YILC*, 1980, I, 1619th session, 25 June 1980, para 25.

armed attack and that those other means were not used voluntarily, it might be thought that the military reaction is disproportionate and therefore not 'necessary'. On this issue we may return briefly to the relations between self-defence and Security Council action.[585] Assuming that a State that is attacked has the means to ask the Security Council to take appropriate measures to end an aggression and knowingly chooses not to do so, preferring to start a unilateral riposte, one might ask whether self-defence is proportionate to the circumstances and therefore necessary. This is what Professor Ago seems to indicate when he specifies that self-defence presupposes that an 'extremely urgent situation obviously leaves it no time or means for requesting other bodies, including the Security Council, to undertake defensive action'.[586] The requirements must obviously be adapted to the specifics of each case, which is no easy matter. The war begun against Afghanistan by the US and its allies in October 2001 attests to this, since this war has been condemned by few States although it does seem to illustrate the situation just evoked.[587] The US had the possibility of going to the Security Council and did so.[588] But rather than asking the Council to take the necessary measures to respond to the unlawful acts perpetrated by the Afghan State—possibly by authorising a military riposte—it preferred to act on the fringe of the UN which was confined to a more general role of fighting terrorism.[589] This precedent is difficult to interpret, though, and it seems a tricky business to deduce any very precise legal lessons from it. First because some States—especially European ones—seemed to consider that the war had actually been accepted, if not authorised, by the Security Council;[590] a position which, if true, would settle the problem of necessity. Next, and as pointed out above,[591] because the extremely emotional context in which events occurred is hardly amenable to the expression of any true *opinio juris*. In the domain of necessity as in others, the Afghan precedent should only be used therefore in conjunction with others if one wishes to see in it the mark of a practice and beyond that of a customary rule.

Lastly an especially involved hypothesis is worth evoking. Assuming a State that has actually been the victim of a prior armed attack exercises its

---

[585] See above.
[586] R Ago, Addendum to the eight report on State reponsibility, above n 464, 70, para 123.
[587] J Gardam, *Necessity, Proportionality and the Use of Force by States*, above n 464, 145.
[588] See: SC Res 1368 (2001) of 12 September 2001, above.
[589] A Remiro Brotons, 'Terrorismo, Mantenimiento de la paz y nuevo orden' (2001) 53 *REDI* 150–60; J Alcaide Fernandez, 'La "guerra contra el terrorismo": una "OPA hostil" al derecho de la comunidad internacional' (2001) 53 *REDI* 300–01; JI Charney, 'The Use of Force Against Terrorism and International Law' (2001) 95 *AJIL* 836–37; VS Mani, '"Humanitarian" Intervention Today' (2005) 313 *RCADI* 241–49; O Corten, 'Vers un renforcement des pouvoirs du Conseil de sécurité dans la lutte contre le terrorisme?', above n 504, 260 *ff*; O Corten and F Dubuisson, 'Opération "Liberté immuable": une extension abusive du concept de légitime défense', above n 310, 74–75; Y Sandoz, 'Lutte contre le terrorisme et droit international: risques et opportunités' (2002) 12 *RSDIE* 336–40.
[590] See above, s I, and ch 6.
[591] Above, s I.

right of self-defence in a disproportionate manner; can its action *as a whole* be deemed unlawful, or should only a *part* of that action be characterised as such; that part that caused the disproportion? To my mind, it is the first part of the alternative that should take precedence.[592] First because the other option, that advocating the separation between the various aspects of the same use of force hardly seems feasible. How might one measure exactly the excess or disproportion, given that necessity or proportionality are measured by very broad criteria that are not only quantitative (such as the area of territory occupied) but also qualitative, the decisive criterion remaining the suitability of the measure relative to the objective of self-defence? It seems both easier and more consistent with legal logic to consider that if the condition of necessity or proportionality is not met then the action as a whole should be deemed contrary to international law. Along these lines we have observed above that case law seems to consider the use of force as an overall behaviour rather than a succession of separate military actions. Secondly, the settling of this issue requires that a distinction be drawn between the criteria of necessity and proportionality within the meaning of *jus in bello* on the one hand and of *jus contra bellum* on the other.[593] Within the context of the law of armed conflict, it can readily be considered that a particular action that does not correspond to the requirements of military necessity be unlawful without that affecting the lawfulness of the military operation of which that action is part in respect of the UN Charter. Thus the bombing of a civilian objective by a State acting in self-defence may be characterised as contrary to international human rights law without that entailing a violation of article 2(4) of the Charter. The specific character of the conditions of necessity and proportionality in respect of the *jus contra bellum* implies by contrast that if it is not proportionate to the armed attack to which it is supposed to be a riposte, a measure can no longer be considered as self-defence within the meaning of the Charter. 'Defence' presupposes, as seen, a measure that is proportionate to the pursuit of an essential purpose of riposting. *A contrario* a disproportionate measure may be considered as exceeding this essential purpose and so by definition can no longer be characterised as self-defence but as akin rather to a punitive expedition or reprisals. As Roberto Ago indicates 'self-defence could not justify a genuine act of aggression committed in response to an armed attack of limited proportions'.[594] In this perspective, case law[595] like practice[596] makes no distinction between the different aspects of one and the same

---

[592] See: R Kolb, *Ius contra bellum. Le droit international relatif au maintien de la paix*, 2nd edn, above n 25, 293.
[593] See: J Gardam, *Necessity, Proportionality and the Use of Force by States*, above n 464, 16–17.
[594] *YILC*, 1980, I, 1619th session, 25 June 1980, 188, para 25.
[595] See above; see also *Weizaecker and others*, ILR, vol 16, 349.
[596] See: J Gardam, *Necessity, Proportionality and the Use of Force by States*, above n 464, 181.

military operation: it is characterised as a whole as necessary or not—and so as self-defence or not—in the light of the circumstances of the case.

It is true that, as said, there is no precedent where it has been held that a State that was actually the victim of an armed attack has exercised its right of self-defence unlawfully.[597] However, this possibility cannot be excluded in principle and it is perhaps worth evoking a few theoretical possibilities that might arise.[598] Generally we shall work on the assumption that a State A, that commits an initial attack, suffers a disproportionate riposte from a State B.

—A first instance is that where State B engages in action against State A although the armed attack by State A has already ended. State A, which made the initial attack, is now in a position of acting in self-defence against what must be characterised as a fresh attack attributable to State B.

—A second instance is one where, whereas troops from State A have entered State B's territory, State B replies by restoring its authority over its territory and then by invading and occupying the territory of State A, none of which is necessary. State B's riposte could no longer be considered as self-defence with as a consequence that it is A that finds itself in turn acting in self-defence. State A could then take only measures necessary to end B's wrongful action. Concretely, that could justify, for example, State A repelling State B's armed forces from its territory but without following up by occupying part of State B's territory or *a fortiori* invading it.

—In a third instance, State A attacks State B by bombarding it from its territory (or again by being implicated in attacks carried out from its territory) and State B reacts disproportionately by invading the entire territory of State A. Here again, State A is in a position of self-defence and may repel State B's forces, which does not mean it is not responsible for all of the initial acts of aggression against State B.

This entire array of possibilities does not exclude the possibility of considering that, in the circumstances of the case, B's disproportionate reaction, while a violation of article 2(4) of the UN Charter, is not serious enough to be characterised as an aggression, meaning that A consequently is not in a situation of self-defence. Besides, nothing would prevent any court tasked with determining the amount of any reparations from allowing for the fact that State A was the first to commit an armed attack, with all the consequences that might entail in terms of the causal connection between the unlawful act perpetrated and the damage caused. Thus State

---

[597] Above, and J Gardam, ibid, 158.

[598] See also: O Corten and A Lagerwall, 'La violation d'un cessez-le-feu constitue-t-elle nécessairement une violation de l'article 2 § 4 de la Charte des Nations Unies?' (2008) 61 *RHDI* 118–21.

B might consider it need not compensate the damage to State A (for example damage further to the riposte in its territory) by showing that, had A not initially mounted an armed attack it would not have suffered any damage.

In its report on State responsibility, the ILC considered it need not enter into any detailed examination of the conditions of proportionality and necessity of a measure in self-defence, arguing that 'These are questions which in practice logic itself will answer and which should be resolved in the context of each particular case'.[599]

This affirmation has the merit of emphasising the very relative character of the appreciation of these ideas in a given case. Even so necessity and proportionality are legal criteria and as such they may be interpreted by legal methods. In this perspective, it shall be recalled first of all that it is the State that is the victim of an armed attack that shall be the first judge of the measures to be taken.[600] Its judgment shall be made, though, at its own risk, its leeway being limited by that of other States and possibly of certain international political or legal organs.[601] On the substance of the matter, evaluating compliance with the condition of necessity will presuppose first checking whether the Security Council has not itself taken the measures 'necessary to maintain international peace and security' that would impede the State concerned in exercising its right of self-defence. If this is not the case and to that extent, it will be important to check whether the official purpose of the action is indeed essentially to riposte to an armed attack in progress. Beyond this official objective, the question will then be whether the measures actually implemented have been effective. If so, there will remain the question of the proportionality of the action that can be appraised in view of its effects. All in all, as a general criterion for guidance, the more limited the choice of means of the State concerned, the more its action will appear necessary within the meaning of self-defence.

Conclusion

Self-defence is probably one of the most controversial institutions in contemporary international law. From the time the UN Charter was first adopted, discussions have borne primarily on the prior condition for the existence of an armed attack, the principle of which has been questioned by application of theories of 'preventive self-defence'. We have seen that from the 1950s to the present, the balance of power has remained unchanged: a majority of States has preferred to abide by the wording of article 51 of the Charter. That text is still the essential reference point that is supplemented by consideration of the definition of aggression adopted by the General

---

[599] 'Report of the ILC on the work of its 32nd session (5 May–25 July 1980)', A/35/10, YILC, 1980, II, Part Two, 60, para 22.

[600] R Ago, Addendum to the eight report on State reponsibility, above n 464, para 123.

[601] ibid.

Assembly in 1974. In this respect, article 3*(g)* allowing under certain circumstances an act of aggression to be ascribed to a State without that State itself having used its armed forces in international relations is still used by present-day international case law. Attempts to call it into question by likening mere support or tolerance to an indirect armed attack liable to engender a right to self-defence have been unsuccessful to date. While a degree of confusion may have been observed in the case of the war against Afghanistan begun by the US in October 2001, it is difficult to deduce from this any new agreement of the international community of States as a whole. Patently the idea of indirect aggression has not been enshrined in legal texts, including the most recent ones; it has also been the subject of condemnations in actual fact, especially further to Israeli military action against Syria and Lebanon. It is true that, in this last case, discussions related also to the conditions of necessity and proportionality which we have seen take on legal signification, even if these conditions must be specifically related to the features of each individual case.[602] All told, it seems that as a specifically legal concept self-defence must be stringently interpreted by application of the criteria set out in the UN Charter.

---

[602] O Schachter, 'Self-Defense and the Rule of Law' (1989) 83 *AJIL* 267.

8

A Right of Humanitarian Intervention?

T
HE ARGUMENT THAT military action to save human lives is not contrary to international law is a very old one.[1] It is found in classical writings[2] and has been regularly used by States, especially in the second half of the nineteenth century.[3] The argument became more difficult to support after the adoption of the UN Charter and the subsequent strengthening of the prohibition of the use of force, but it still subsists in the notion of 'humanitarian intervention', not forgetting the persistent justification of the protection of nationals.[4] The advent of a 'New World Order' that supposedly provides better guarantees for human rights has seen a revival of this idea, especially in some areas of French doctrine that forged the concepts of a 'right' (*droit*) or a duty of interference (*devoir d'ingérence*)[5] which, like the previous concepts, remain highly contested.[6] The 1999 Kosovo war marked a new step in this old debate that was to give rise to the concept of 'responsibility to protect', the latest terminological manifestation of humanitarian military action.[7]

Before evaluating it further it is essential to define clearly the concept under study because it is the subject of so many diverging interpretations and conceptions. The expression 'right of humanitarian intervention' that shall be used in this chapter may be defined by taking each of its terms in turn.

[1] SD Murphy, *Humanitarian Intervention. The United Nations in an Evolving World Order* (Philadelphia, Univ of Pennsylvania Press, 1996) 32 *ff*; see also A Pellet (ed), *Droit d'ingérence ou devoir d'assistance humanitaire?* (Paris, La documentation française, Problèmes économiques et sociaux, dossiers d'actualité mondiale, Nos 758–59, 1995) 49–56.

[2] See, eg: Suarez (*De bello*, S.5, nos 5–8) or de Vitoria (*De Jure Belli*, 1, 22, 26).

[3] See: G Rolin-Jacquemyns, 'Note sur la théorie du droit d'intervention' (1876) 8 *RDILC* 673–82; A Rougier, 'La théorie de l'intervention d'humanité' (1910) 14 *RGDIP* 468–526.

[4] F Teson, *Humanitarian Intervention. An Inquiry into Law and Morality* (New York, Transnational Publishers, 1st edn, 1988, 2nd edn, 1997).

[5] B Kouchner, *Le malheur des autres* (Paris, Odile Jacob, 1991); M Bettati, 'Un droit d'ingérence?' (1991) 95 *RGDIP* 639–70; see M Bettati and B Kouchner (eds), *Le devoir d'ingérence* (Paris, Denoël, 1987).

[6] O Corten and P Klein, *Droit d'ingérence ou obligation de réaction?* (Bruxelles, Bruylant, 1st edn 1992, 2nd edn 1996); O Paye, *Sauve qui veut? Le droit international face aux crises humanitaires* (Bruxelles, Bruylant, 1996).

[7] See: L Feinstein and AM Slaughter, 'A Duty to Prevent' (2004) 83 *Foreign Affairs* 136.

—In the first place, by using the term 'right' rather than, say, 'duty', we situate ourselves within the legal sphere and not in the realms of ethics or politics. Many studies investigate the conditions under which such a notion can arise in today's international society and endeavour to come up with an ideal definition with the help of theories of justice.[8] Others envisage the question by emphasising the balance of power that accounts for and limits the advent of humanitarian interference,[9] or the representations conveyed by the notion.[10] For my own part and in keeping with the approach taken throughout this book, I shall simply evaluate the question within a clearly marked out frame of reference, that of the positive international legal order.[11] The term 'right' also denotes the idea of an autonomous legal basis: a 'right' of humanitarian intervention, it can be surmised, would justify a military action independently of the classical foundations for such justification such as the host State's consent, Security Council authorisation, or even self-defence.[12] In this perspective it is *unilateral* military action alone that shall come in for appraisal here.

—In the second place, the term 'intervention' relates to a military and not, say, economic or diplomatic action conducted by one or more States and not by non-governmental organisations, for example.[13] For an association like *Médecins Sans Frontières* to enter a State's territory without its consent shall not be considered as a case of 'intervention'.[14] This choice seems logical enough remembering that the prohibition of the use of force is a rule that governs relations among States, while the possible use of violence by individuals relates rather to rules of municipal law and so to each State's exercise of its sovereign police powers.[15] Conversely, military action by one State in another State's territory will be the typical situation of intervention to be dealt with here.

---

[8] See, eg: M Walzer, *Just and Unjust Wars* (New York, Basic Books, 1977) or D Sanchez Rubio, 'Interventions humanitaires: principes, concepts et réalités' in *Interventions humanitaires? Points de vue du sud*, (2004) 11 *Alternatives sud* (Paris, Syllepse, 2004) 7–52; see also BD Lepard, *Rethinking Humanitarian Intervention. A fresh legal approach on fundamental ethical principles in international law and world religions* (Pennsylvania, Pennsylvania Univ Press, 2002); A Roberts, 'Legality Verses Legitimacy: Can Uses of Force be Illegal but Justified' in P Alston and E MacDonald (eds), *Human Rights, Intervention and the Use of Force* (Oxford, Oxford University Press, 2008) 179.

[9] O Corten, 'Droit, force et légitimité dans une société internationale en mutation' (1996) 37 *Revue interdisciplinaire d'études juridiques* 71–112; P Moreau Defarges, *Droits d'ingérence dans le monde post-2001* (Paris, Presses de la fondation nationale des sciences politiques, 2006).

[10] A Orford, *Reading Humanitarian Intervention. Human Rights and the Use of Force in International Law* (Cambridge, Cambridge University Press, 2003).

[11] Above, ch 1, s II.

[12] Above, chs 5, 6 and 7.

[13] See: J Salmon (ed), *Dictionnaire de droit international public* (Bruxelles, Bruylant, AUF, 2001) v° 'intervention humanitaire (ou d'humanité)' 610; see also P Bringuier, 'A propos de l'ingérence humanitaire' in *Mélanges Gilbert Apollis* (Paris, Pedone 1992) 21–23.

[14] O Corten and P Klein, 'L'assistance humanitaire face à la souveraineté des Etats' (1992) *Revue trimestrielle des droits de l'homme* 343–64.

[15] Above, ch 3.

—In the third place is the question of determining the 'humanitarian' character of the intervention. Traditionally the concept has been criticised because of the unavowed designs pursued by some States when officially conducting humanitarian actions.[16] Here we shall not go down the road of somehow checking the sincerity of declared motives in each individual case. The simple official mention of humanitarian objectives shall be enough for us to characterise a military action as a 'humanitarian intervention'. Operations officially to protect nationals in danger shall be included in this framework.

The question to be asked then shall be whether the intervening State invokes a legal basis capable of justifying its action and whether the international community of States as a whole has in some way or other accepted the validity of that legal basis.[17]

Framed in this way, the question seems to me, despite the doctrinal controversies it still raises, one of the least complex in contemporary international law. First of all because the 'right of humanitarian intervention' has no basis in any of the relevant legal texts, whether the UN Charter or other treaties or non-treaty instruments (section one). Then because examination of the precedents that are generally evoked in support of such justification reveals that States are very reluctant to accept it in positive international law, even and perhaps above all after the Kosovo war that closed the last century (section two).

I Non-Recognition in Legal Texts

Neither article 2(4) nor any other provision of the UN Charter expressly reserves the possibility of intervening militarily in the territory of a third State without its consent in the absence of Security Council authorisation and if not acting in self-defence. This observation is beyond contention and remains uncontested. Doctrine in favour of humanitarian intervention considers, though, that the right may be deduced *implicitly* from existing texts which, without referring to it directly, supposedly do not go against it. Such a claim, however, hardly stands up to scrutiny whether in respect of classical texts (A) or of more recent debates (B).

---

[16] See, eg: *Le droit d'ingérence est-il une nouvelle légalisation du colonialisme?*, Actes du colloque organisé par l'Académie du Royaume du Maroc, Rabat, 14–16 October 1991; M Bennouna, 'De l'ingérence humanitaire à la tutelle internationale. La sécurité collective en question' in *Sécurité collective et crises internationales*, Actes des Journées d'études de Toulon (Paris, La documentation française, 1994) 312–13; *contra:* Ryan Goodman, 'Humanitarian Intervention and Pretexts for War' (2006) 100 *AJIL* 107–41.

[17] See above, ch 1, s II.

A. The Dismissal of the Right of Humanitarian Intervention in Classical Legal Texts

In the absence of any express or direct recognition—but also prohibition[18]—of any right of humanitarian intervention in the Charter, doctrine favourable to it bases its entire argument on an *a contrario* interpretation of the final part of article 2(4):

> All Members shall refrain in their international relations from the threat or use of force *against the territorial integrity or political independence of any State, or in any other manner inconsistent with the Purposes of the United Nations.* (emphasis added)

So the prohibition supposedly relates only to uses of force directed at certain objectives, whether to impinge upon the territorial integrity or the political independence of a State or to infringe some other purpose of the UN. Since, by definition, the right of humanitarian intervention purportedly has as its aim to enforce human rights and since observance of these rights is one of the acknowledged purposes of the UN, it supposedly follows that this right is not incompatible with article 2(4) of the Charter.[19]

Even if at first sight it is founded on a form of logic, such an interpretation does not seem convincing. The argument does not stand up to scrutiny in terms of the principles of interpretation expressed in the Vienna Convention. Such *a contrario* reasoning has besides invariably been dismissed by a large majority of States in debates about the use of force within the UN.

The Weakness of the *a contrario* Interpretation of Article 2(4) in Terms of the Principles of the Vienna Convention on the Law of Treaties

The first problem raised by the argument for the right of humanitarian intervention is that it goes against the essential criterion of interpretation of taking account of the ordinary meaning of the terms of the treaty.[20] It seems excessive indeed to claim that an armed action conducted on the territory of a State without its consent would not be contrary to its territorial integrity

---

[18] I Brownlie, *International Law and the Use of Force by States* (Oxford, Clarendon Press, 1963) 342.

[19] J Stone, *Aggression and World Order. A Critique of United Nations Theories of Aggression* (London, Stevens & Sons Limited, 1958) 95; F Teson, *Humanitarian Intervention. An Inquiry into Law and Morality*, above n 4, 1st edn 1988, 130–31, 2nd edn, 1997, 150–51; B Lepard, *Rethinking Humanitarian Intervention* (Pennsylvania, Pennsylvania Univ Press, 2002) 344–45; E Perez Vera, 'La protection d'humanité en droit international' (1969) 5 *RBDI* 415; CF Amerasinghe, 'The Conundrum of Recourse to Force—to Protect Persons' (2006) 3 *Int Org LR* 49–51; M Bettati, 'Un droit d'ingérence?' (1991) 95 *RGDIP* 649–50; S Sur, 'L'affaire du Kosovo et le droit international: points et contrepoints' (1999) 45 *AFDI* 286; see also C Chinkin, 'The Legality of NATO's Action in the Former Republic of Yugoslavia (FRY) under International Law' (2000) 49 *ICLQ* 917–18.

[20] Article 31(1) of the Vienna Convention on the Law of Treaties.

or to its political independence, or performed in a manner incompatible with the UN's purposes.

—For the first of these points, it has been claimed that the idea of infringement of territorial integrity should be understood in a narrow sense, as contrary to any attempt to appropriate or annex a State's territory in part or in full, but not as contrary to a purely humanitarian action leaving recognised international borders unchanged.[21] Such a claim is already subject to caution because the expression territorial integrity is sometimes used to criticise any violation of borders in practice and in doctrine alike.[22] Above all it tends to isolate the notion of territorial integrity from that of political independence, which is directly associated with it. Conducting military action on the territory of a State without its consent by definition comes down to calling into question its political independence, a notion that implies at the very least that each State exercises full executive power in its territory without external interference.[23] And so, even if a humanitarian intervention were not aimed at overthrowing the government of a State or at changing its political regime, it would still be incompatible with the concept of independence in what is most fundamental about it.[24] For these reasons alone, the *a contrario* interpretation of article 2(4) does not seem readily reconcilable with contemporary international law.[25] The only form of military action that is neither contrary to a State's territorial integrity nor to its political independence is one which has that State's consent on conditions that have been set out before.[26]

—In any event, the final words of the provision do not concern, as claimed in the doctrine favourable to the right of intervention, the *objective* of an armed action. They refer very generally to any use of force conducted in a '*manner* inconsistent with the Purposes of the United Nations'. (emphasis added) Thus, whatever its purpose, an armed action that is not

---

[21] E Perez Vera, 'La protection d'humanité en droit international', above n 19, 420–21.

[22] R Higgins, *The Development of International Law Through the Political Organs of the United Nations* (London/New York/Toronto, Oxford University Press, 1963) 182–83.

[23] J Zourek, 'Enfin une définition de l'agression' (1974) 20 *AFDI* 21 and O Schachter, 'The Legality of Pro-Democratic Invasion' (1984) 78 *AJIL* 649.

[24] N Ronzitti, *Rescuing Nationals Abroad Through Military Coercion and Intervention on Grounds of Humanity* (Dordrecht, Martinus Nijhoff, 1985) 8; M Akehurst, 'Humanitarian Intervention' in H Bull (ed), *Intervention in World Politics* (Oxford, Clarendon Press, 1984) 105.

[25] S Chesterman, *Just War or Just Peace? Humanitarian Intervention and International Law* (Oxford, Oxford University Press, 2001) 48–52; O Corten and P Klein, *Droit d'ingérence ou obligation de réaction?*, 2nd edn, above n 6, 163–64; O Paye, *Sauve qui veut? Le droit international face aux crises humanitaires*, above n 6, 130–31; X Pacreau, *De l'intervention au Kosovo en 1999 à l'intervention en Irak de 2003* (Paris, LGDJ, 2006) 140–44; see also TD Gill, 'Humanitarian Intervention: Legality, Justice and Legitimacy' in *The Global Community YIL & Jurisprudence 2004* (New-York, Oceana Publications, 2004) 57–58.

[26] See above, ch 5.

consented to infringes the maintenance of international peace and security and therefore the essential objective of the UN.[27] In the case of an action authorised by the Security Council or carried out in self-defence, the purpose cannot be considered infringed precisely because there are provisions that expressly govern the way to pursue the objective. In other cases of military intervention, however, the absence of any explicit legal basis makes them incompatible with the fundamental general purpose of maintaining international peace.

Thus there is hardly room for doubt that the argument of the right of humanitarian intervention is counter to the very text of article 2(4) of the Charter.

Some commentators believe, however, that they can avoid this pitfall by claiming that the pursuit of one of the UN's purposes, in particular the defence of human rights, would justify a use of force even if it went against the purpose of maintaining international peace and security.[28] The argument is not readily compatible with the actual text of article 2(4), nothing in which indicates that it authorises infringement of any of the UN's purposes. In any event, the actual aim of the provision is to replace a rationale of unilateral use of force by mechanisms instigating collective security. It is along these lines that the Charter enshrined the abandoning of classical conceptions whereby each State decided unilaterally to initiate an armed action in the name of what it considered fair or appropriate.[29] To consider that each State could weigh up the different purposes of the UN that consist in maintaining peace, defending human rights but also in economic development and in the right of peoples to self-determination,[30] and conduct a military intervention against another State in the name of that assessment would be plainly to bring into question the very foundations of the prohibitive regime established in 1945.[31] Thus the *a contrario* interpretation of the final words of article 2(4) seems incompatible with the object and purpose of this proposition.[32] One might admittedly make out an argument based on the effect of these final words, which could only open up possibilities of military action that might not have existed had they not been added. It will

---

[27] M Virally, 'Panorama du droit international contemporain' (1983) 183 *RCADI* 102; see also WD Verwey, 'Humanitarian Intervention' in A Cassese (ed), *The Current Legal Regulation of the Use of Force* (Dordrecht, Martinus Nijhoff, 1986) 68; S Chesterman, *Just War or Just Peace? Humanitarian Intervention and International Law*, above n 25, 52–53.

[28] F Teson, *Humanitarian Intervention. An Inquiry into Law and Morality*, above n 4, 1st edn, 131, 2nd edn, 151.

[29] O Corten, 'Droit, force et légitimité dans une société internationale en mutation', above n 9.

[30] Art 1 of the UN Charter.

[31] O Schachter, 'Is There A Right to Overthrow an Illegitimate Regime?' in *Mélanges Virally* (Paris, Pedone, 1991) 427; VS Mani, '"Humanitarian" Intervention Today' (2005) 313 *RCADI* 163.

[32] D Simon and LA Sicilianos, 'La "contre-violence" unilatérale. Pratiques étatiques et droit international' (1986) 32 *AFDI* 65–66.

be replied that the reference to the UN's purposes has the effect of reserving the other provisions of the Charter that enshrine the possible use of force by means of Security Council action or the institution of self-defence. Moreover, in actual fact, we shall see that historically this wording was devised to strengthen and not weaken the stringency of the prohibition.[33]

Allowance for context argues along the same lines. First because no provision of the Charter provides for a right of humanitarian intervention, whether in its parts on armed action or those on human rights. Then because article 2(3) of the Charter very generally compels States to settle their disputes peacefully.[34] As a humanitarian intervention invariably follows from a disagreement between the intervening State and the State that is the target of allegations about human rights' violations, and so from a 'dispute' in the legal sense of the term,[35] such an intervention can hardly be considered compatible with the UN Charter.

This conclusion is confirmed by allowance for the broader context of the Charter constituted by any relevant rule of international law applicable between the parties.[36] Conventions on the protection of human rights include mechanisms for peaceful settlement of disputes without ever opening up the way for unilateral military actions.[37] In the case of the Convention prohibiting genocide, resort to 'competent organs of the United Nations'[38] is provided for, suggesting that the Security Council could take appropriate measures, including military ones, but not that States could act of their own initiative. In the case of humanitarian international law, States are bound to respect it and 'to ensure respect' of it, but it is then stipulated that 'in situations of serious violations of the Conventions or of this

[33] See below.

[34] O Corten and P Klein, *Droit d'ingérence ou obligation de réaction?*, 2nd edn, above n 6, 166–67; O Paye, *Sauve qui veut? Le droit international face aux crises humanitaires*, above n 6, 129–30.

[35] CPJI, *Mavromatis Palestine Concessions*, Series A no 2, 11.

[36] Art 31(3)(c) of the Vienna Convention on the Law of Treaties.

[37] According to art 56 of the UN Charter, 'All Members pledge themselves to take joint and separate action in co-operation with the Organization for the achievement of the purposes set forth in Article 55'. Article 2 § 2 of the *Institut de droit international* resolution on 'The Protection of Human Rights and the Principle of Non-intervention in Internal Affairs of States' states that 'Without prejudice to the functions and powers which the Charter attributes to the organs of the United Nations in case of violation of the obligations assumed by the members of the Organizations, States, acting individually or collectively, are entitled to take diplomatic, economic and other measures towards any other State which has violated the obligation set forth in Article 1, *provided such measures are permitted under international law and do not involve the use of armed force in violation of the Charter of the United Nations*' (emphasis added, 13 September 1989 (1990) 63/2 *AIDI* 286; www.idi-iil.org).

[38] According to art VIII of the Convention, 'Any Contracting Party may call upon the competent organs of the United Nations to take such action under the Charter of the United Nations as they consider appropriate for the prevention and suppression of acts of genocide or any of the other acts enumerated in article III'; see also art IX; JL Holzgrefe, 'The Humanitarian Intervention Debate' in JL Holzgrefe and Robert O Keohane (eds), *Humanitarian Intervention. Ethical, Legal and Political Dilemmas* (Cambridge, Cambridge University Press, 2003) 43–44.

Protocol, the High Contracting Parties undertake to act, jointly or individually, *in co-operation with the United Nations and in conformity with the United Nations Charter*' (emphasis added)[39], the International Committee of the Red Cross having besides made clear its objection to any right of unilateral intervention.[40] The same rationale is found in international criminal law or the fight against terrorism, with certain provisions specifying that 'Nothing in this Convention shall be construed as justifying the violation of the territorial integrity or political independence of a State in contravention of the Charter of the United Nations'.[41] We have shown earlier that the right of intervention evoked in article 4(h) of the Constituent Act of the African Union was to be construed as requiring prior Security Council authorisation if an intervention involved implementing enforcement measures within the meaning of article 53(1) of the Charter.[42] In short, examination of the relevant conventional sources shows that States did not intended to derogate from article 2(4) and the resolutely collective system of international security underpinning it.

This impression is confirmed by a reading of the resolutions adopted by the General Assembly on the use of force and that reveal on this point a 'subsequent agreement between the parties regarding the interpretation of the treaty or the application of its provisions'.[43] Particularly significant in this respect is resolution 2625 (XXV) by which 'Every State has the duty to refrain from the threat or use of force to *violate the existing international boundaries of another State* or as a means of solving international disputes . . .'. (emphasis added)

The italicised expression shows that any forcible crossing of an international border is prohibited as a matter of principle, with that prohibition not covering just the occupation or appropriation of territories. Moreover, the definition of aggression appended to General Assembly resolution 3314 (XXIX) defines this notion as 'the use of force by a State *against the sovereignty,* territorial integrity or political independence of another State, or in any other manner *inconsistent with the Charter of the United Nations* . . .'. (emphasis added) Two terminological differences have therefore been introduced compared with the initial wording of article 2(4): first the introduction of the very broad concept of sovereignty alongside the concepts of

---

[39] Art 89 of Protocol 1 Additional to the Geneva Conventions; see E David, *Principes de droit des conflits armés*, 3rd edn (Bruxelles, Bruylant, 2002) 564.

[40] A Ryniker, 'The ICRC's position on "humanitarian intervention"' (2001) 842 *IRRC* 527–32.

[41] Art 14 of the International Convention Against the Taking of Hostages, 17 December 1979, A/34/46.

[42] Above ch 6, s I; but see A Peyro Llopis, 'L'Union africaine, un système de sécurité régionale pour la paix civile' in *L'Union africaine face aux enjeux de Paix, de sécurité et de défense* (Paris, L'Harmattan, 2003) 111, fn 99.

[43] Art 31(3)(a) of the Vienna Convention on the Law of Treaties. See C Gray, *International Law and the Use of Force*, 3rd ed (Oxford, Oxford University Press, 2008) 34–35.

territorial integrity and political independence; then the incompatibility with the actual Charter and not with its purposes. These two clarifications make it even more difficult to affirm that a humanitarian intervention conducted in a State's territory without its consent is not prohibited by the Charter.[44] The concept of sovereignty extends even more clearly than that of political independence to the exclusive exercise by the State in question of control over its territory. The definition then stipulates that 'No consideration of whatever nature, whether political, economic, military or otherwise, may serve as a justification for aggression',[45] which again can only be construed as strengthening the prohibition and condemning any unilateralist excess.[46] It further gives as examples of aggression the bombing by a State or the attack by the armed forces of a State against the forces of another without requiring any intention to violate its territorial integrity. Similarly too resolution 42/22 very generally lays down that 'States have the duty to abstain from armed intervention and all other forms of interference or attempted threats against the personality of the State or against its political, economic and cultural elements',[47] a formulation whose scope leaves little room for any potential *a contrario* reasoning. Lastly, it shall be emphasised that the resolutions adopted by the General Assembly from the late 1980s governing humanitarian assistance and aimed at setting up a 'new international humanitarian order' remain very classical in terms of the non-use of force.[48] The sovereignty of the State in whose territory humanitarian dramas arise is reasserted and, while that State's duty to accept help is affirmed in certain circumstances, the prospect of a unilateral right of armed intervention by a third State is never evoked, even indirectly or implicitly. On the contrary, it is the pathway of cooperation and peaceful settlement of disputes that is reasserted, it being understood that 'The sovereignty, territorial integrity and national unity of States must be fully respected in accordance with the Charter of the United Nations'.[49]

---

[44] N Ronzitti, *Rescuing Nationals Abroad Through Military Coercion and Intervention on Grounds of Humanity*, above n 24, 8.

[45] Art 5(1) of the Definition; see also below.

[46] I Brownlie and CJ Apperley, 'Kosovo Crisis Inquiry: Memorandum on the International Law Aspects' (2000) 49 *ICLQ* 886, para 40.

[47] Principle I, 7 of the Declaration on the Enhancement of the Effectiveness of the Principle of Refraining from the Threat or Use of Force in International Relations.

[48] See: GA Res 43/131 of 8 December 1988; 45/100, 45/101 and 45/102 of 14 December 1990 and M Bettati, 'Souveraineté et assistance humanitaire. Réflexions sur la portée et les limites de la résolution 43/131 de l'Assemblée générale de l'ONU' in *Mélanges René-Jean Dupuy* (Paris, Pedone, 1991) 38–42; M Torelli, 'De l'assistance à l'ingérence humanitaire' (1992) 795 *RICR* 241–42; MJ Domestici-Met, 'Aspects juridiques récents de l'assistance humanitaire' (1989) 35 *AFDI* 132–33; C Zorgbide, *Le droit d'ingérence* (Paris, PUF, 1994) 107–12.

[49] GA Res 46/182 of 19 December 1991, annex, I.3; see O Corten, 'Nouvel ordre international humanitaire ou droit d'ingérence?' in O Corten *et al* (eds), *A la recherche du nouvel ordre mondial*, t I (Bruxelles, Complexe, 1993) 161 *ff*; O Paye, *Sauve qui veut? Le droit international face aux crises humanitaires*, above n 6, 107–12; PM Eisemann, 'Devoir d'ingérence et non-intervention: de la nécessité de remettre quelques pendules à l'heure' (1991) 3 *Relations internationales et stratégiques* 72–73; G Guillaume, 'L'ingérence humanitaire. Inventaire du

One final classical means of interpretation may be used as a supplementary way of dismissing the *a contrario* reasoning argument, that of the *travaux préparatoires* of the Charter.[50] The Dumbarton Oaks proposals included a prohibition adressed to Members 'to refrain in their international relations from the threat or use of force in any manner inconsistent with the purposes of the Organization'.[51] The inclusion of a reference to territorial integrity, political independence and to 'in any other manner inconsistent with the Purposes of the United Nations' stems from the desire of several States to protect explicitly these values against the use of force and not, *a contrario*, to open up the way to the acceptance of military interventions that did not infringe them.[52] In the course of debate, certain fears were voiced as to whether this wording might not justify certain uses of force because of the claimed legitimacy of their objectives. The Drafting Committee was keen to address these concerns by explicitly stating that 'It was furthermore clear that there will be no legitimate wars in any sense'.[53] This assertion failed to reassure all States, with some considering that no doubt should be left about the stringency of the prohibition. The US representative then pointed out that 'The intention of the authors of the original text was to state in the broadest terms an absolute, all-inclusive prohibition; the phrase "or in other manner" was designed to insure that there should be no loopholes'.[54]

In short, it is clear that the aim of the drafters of the Charter was to prohibit any use of force in international relations, except insofar as this possibility was provided for in some of its provisions.[55] This initial intention was, for that matter, never contradicted subsequently. This has already been observed in analysing the texts on the subject after the Charter came into force. And the conclusion is confirmed by examination of the debates on the topic prior to the adoption of certain texts.

---

droit positif' (June 1993) *Revue des deux mondes* 107; O Russbach, *ONU contre ONU. Le droit international confisqué* (Paris, La découverte, 1994) 34–35.

[50] E Giraud, 'L'interdiction du recours à la force. La théorie et la pratique des Nations Unies' (1963) 67 *RGDIP* 512–13; CHM Waldock, 'The Regulation of the Use of Force by Individual States in International Law' (1952) 81-II *RCADI* 493; S Chesterman, *Just War or Just Peace? Humanitarian Intervention and International Law*, above n 25, 49 *ff*; I Brownlie, 'The Use of Force in self-Defence' (1961) 64 *BYBIL* 233–36; JF Murphy, *The United States and the Rule of Law in International Affairs* (Cambridge, Cambridge University Press, 2004) 159; I Brownlie and CJ Apperley, 'Kosovo Crisis Inquiry: Memorandum on the International Law Aspects', above n 46, 884–85, paras 33–36.

[51] *UNCIO*, vol 3, 3.

[52] See the Australian amendment text, at the origin of article 2 § 4 text, *UNCIO*, vol 3, 443.

[53] *UNCIO*, vol 6, 721.

[54] *UNCIO*, vol 6, 335. See also the intervention of the representative of Belgium, ibid.

[55] See also above, ch 4, s II.

Dismissal of the *a contrario* Interpretation of Article 2(4) in the Context of UN Debates on the Use of Force (1945–1999)

We have just observed that the texts on the major resolutions of the General Assembly governing the use of force seemed to exclude any right of humanitarian intervention. That impression is confirmed upon examination of the debates that preceded their adoption, which showed great reluctance by the international community of States as a whole to admit such a justification in contemporary international law. Five points should be set out in this respect.

First, an impressive number of States from all regions of the world were keen to emphasise that the use of force knew of only two exceptions: self-defence or military action under the aegis of the Security Council.[56] It could admittedly be retorted that, by the argument of the *a contrario* interpretation of article 2(4), the right of humanitarian intervention is not an 'exception' to the prohibition of the use of force, but is simply not covered by the prohibition. Careful examination of States' declarations shows, however,

---

[56] France (A/C.6/S.R.1179, 24 September 1970, para 9; A/C.6/SR.1077, 22 November 1968, para 19; A/C.6/SR.1077, 22 November 1968, para 19), Spain (A/C.6/S.R.813, 18 November 1963, para 8), Cuba (A/C.6/S.R.820, 27 November 1963, para 22; A/C.6/S.R.893, 8 December 1965, para 36; A/C.6/S.R.1091, 10 December 1968, para 41), Philippines (A/C.6/S.R.823, 2 December 1963, para 4), India (A/AC.119/SR.3, 31 August 1964), Argentina (A/AC.119/SR.3, 31 August 1964), Czechoslovakia (A/C.6/S.R.871, 8 November 1965, para 35), Mali (A/C.6/S.R.882, 24 November 1965, para 28), Mexico (A/C.6/S.R.886, 1 December 1965, paras 34 and 37; A/C.6/32/SR.65, 7 December 1977, para 5), Cyprus (A/C.6/S.R.892, 7 December 1965, para 18), Bolivia (A/C.6/S.R.1004, 21 November 1967, para 25), Australia (A/C.6/S.R.1178, 23 September 1970, para 38), Portugal (A/C.6/S.R.1182, 25 September 1970, para 3), Guatemala (A/AC.119/SR.14, 8 September 1964), Nigeria (A/AC.119/SR.4, 31 August 1964; A/AC.119/SR.7, 2 September 1964), Iran (A/C.6/SR.329, 19 November 1952, para 43; A/C.6/SR.416, 5 November 1954, para 34), Sweden (A/C.6/SR.332, 22 November 1952, para 9), Netherlands (GA, Supp no 16 (A/3574), New York, 1957, para 208), Iraq (A/AC.77/L.8/Rev.1), Mexico, Paraguay, Peru and Dominican Republic (A/AC.77/L.11), Belgium (A/C.6/SR.514, 7 October 1957), Syria (A/C.6/SR.517, 14 October 1957), Guatemala (A/C.6/SR.520, 22 October 1957), Ecuador (A/AC.134/SR.58, 21 July 1970 in A/AC.134/SR.52-66), Bulgaria (A/C.6/SR.519, 18 October 1957), Guyana (A/AC.134/SR.65, 28 July 1970 in A/AC.134/SR.52-66), Italy (A/AC.134/SR.18, 1 July 1968 in A/AC.134/SR.1-24; A/AC.134/SR.64, 27 July 1970 in A/AC.134/SR.52-66), Ghana (A/AC.134/SR.37, 18 March 1969 in A/AC.134/SR.25-51; A/C.6/SR.1169, 3 December 1969, para 45), Canada (A/AC.134/SR.45, 26 March 1969 in A/AC.134/SR.25-51), Afghanistan (A/C.6/SR.1206, 26 October 1970, para 49), Greece (A/C.6/SR.1208, 27 October 1970, para 3), Uruguay (A/AC.134/SR.95, 1 March 1972 in A/AC.134/SR.79-91), Romania (A/C.6/SR.1207, 27 October 1970, para 25), Egypt (A/C.6/SR.1269, 27 October 1971, para 13), Haiti (A/C.6/SR.1443, 20 November 1973, para 17), FGR (A/C.6/SR.1478, 16 October 1974, para 19), Brazil (A/C.6/32/SR.65, 7 December 1977, para 28), Bangladesh (A/C.6/34/SR.21, 18 October 1979, para 13), Algeria (A/36/415, 8 September 1981), DRC (A/C.6/37/SR.35, 3 November 1982, para 1), Jordan (A/C.6/37/SR.39, 8 November 1982, para 67), Cape Verde (A/C.6/38/SR.17, 17 October 1983, para 88), Kenya (A/C.6/39/SR.17, 11 October 1984, para 68), Chile (A/C.6/42/SR.18, 9 October 1987, para 27), Botswana (A/C.6/42/SR.21, 13 October 1987, para 47). See also Switzerland, then a non-Member State; 'La pratique suisse en matière de droit international public', *ASDI* 1983, 248).

that what they had to say was plainly intended to dismiss the arguments based on the legitimacy of the purpose of a military intervention, whether humanitarian or other. The term 'exception' is not used in a technical sense but in its very general meaning, the idea being quite simply to identify the situations in which a use of force would be countenanced.[57] The dismissal of a third possible exception must therefore be understood in a broad sense as countering any justification or argument legitimising a use of force that is not expressly provided for in the UN Charter.[58]

As a second point, it shall be underscored that the *a contrario* interpretation from which the expression 'against the territorial integrity or political independence . . .' was regularly raised and dismissed from the 1950s to the 1980s. This is hardly surprising for States that were traditionally careful to maintain the full stringency of the prohibition of the use of force, such as the Third World States,[59] Socialist States[60] and Latin-American States.[61] However, several Western States too took up the same positions, as attested to for example[62] by statements from the representatives of Australia:

> There seemed to be general agreement that the expression 'against the territorial integrity or political independence of any State' did not imply any qualification of the prohibition of the threat or use of force;[63]

and of the US:

> [I]f the Members of the United Nations must refrain in their international relations from the threat or use of force against the territorial integrity of any State, it was obvious that they were bound to respect the frontiers of other States.[64]

[57] See, eg: Bahamas (A/C.6/36/SR.10, 2 October 1981, para 23), Ecuador (A/C.6/S.R.1003, 20 November 1967, para 53), Israel (A/C.6/S.R.767, 27 November 1962, para 15), Yugoslavia (A/C.6/S.R.753, 5 November 1962, para 31), China (A/C.6/S.R.818, 21 November 1963, para 6), Colombia (A/C.6/S.R.929, 11 November 1966, para 8) or Panama (A/C.6/SR.403, 14 October 1954, para 27; A/C.6/SR.406, 20 October 1954, para 8).

[58] See also France, 'Pratique française du droit international' (1964) 10 *AFDI* 950 and Institut de droit international, *Declaration on the use of force*, 2 September 2003 (2003) 36 *RBDI* 573–74, and commentaries by J Salmon, ibid, 566–72.

[59] According to Madagascar, 'the words "against the territorial integrity or political independence" in no way limited the scope of the prohibition' (A/AC.119/SR.9, 3 September 1964, 17–18); see also India (A/C.6/SR.418, 9 November 1954, para 13), China (A/C.6/SR.417, 8 November 1954, para 31).

[60] See, eg: USSR (A/AC.119/SR.43, 2 October 1964).

[61] Chile (A/C.6/S.R.1092, 11 December 1968, para 31; A/AC.125/L.23, 24 March 1966, e) and A/AC.125/SR.22, 23 March 1966, para 31), Mexico (A/C.6/S.R.806, 6 November 1963, para 17; A/C.6/42/SR.17, 8 October 1987, para 8) Ecuador (A/C.6/S.R.1183, 28 September 1970, para 35), and Brazil (A/C.6/34/SR.18, 16 October 1979, para 41).

[62] See also: UK (A/C.6/S.R.805, 5 November 1963, para 8); Netherlands (A/C.6/SR.410, 28 October 1954, para 32) and Israel (A/C.6/SR.412, 1 November 1954, para 35).

[63] A/AC.119/SR.10, 3 September 1964, 10; see also the statement of the representative of Cyprus; A/C.6/S.R.822, 29 November 1963, 238, para 7.

[64] A/AC.119/SR.42, 2 October 1964, 7; see also A/C.6/S.R.808, 11 November 1963, para 19; A/AC.119/SR.3, 31 August 1964; A/AC.134/SR.59, 22 July 1970 in A/AC.134/SR.52-66; MM Whiteman, *Digest of International Law*, vol 13, (Washington, Department of State Publ, 1968) 358.

Such declarations can be explained in part by the concern to rule out arguments based on the legitimacy of national liberation struggles that were then regularly advanced, or by a challenge to the 'Brejnev doctrine'.[65] Against this backdrop, Western States preferred to insist on the prohibition set out in article 2(4), condemning any argument based on the legitimacy of motives. In doing so they indirectly but clearly dismissed any idea of a right of humanitarian intervention.

As a third point, the dismissal of the right of humanitarian intervention arises too from examination of the proposal that finally led to article 5 of the definition of aggression whereby 'No consideration of whatever nature, whether political, economic, military or otherwise, may serve as a justification for aggression'. This wording seems to stem from a 1956 draft filed by the Soviet Union by which:

> The attacks . . . may not be justified by any considerations of a political, strategic or economic nature . . . In particular, the following may not be used as justification.
>
> A. The internal situation of a State, as for example:
>
>   a) Backwardness of any people politically, economically or culturally;
>   b) Alleged shortcomings in its administration;
>   c) Any danger which may threaten the life or property of aliens;
>   d) Any revolutionary or counter-revolutionary movement, civil war, disorders or strikes;
>   e) Establishment or maintenance in any State of any political, economic or social system . . .[66]

This list has been taken up in part or in full by other States.[67] Criticism of it was not because of its constituent parts but because of its underlying principle. By listing such justifications, it could be understood that other justifications that were not explicitly stated would *a contrario* be admissible, whereas only an armed attack could justify a riposte under article 51 of the UN Charter.[68] Likewise, in the draft definition presented in 1969 by Australia, Canada, Japan, the UK and the US, it is asserted that an aggression is a use of force the objective of which is not only to call into question an international border or demarcation line but also to:

---

[65] See above ch 2, s II, and the views expressed by the UK (*Report of the Special Committee on Enhancing the Effectiveness of the Principle of Non-Use of Force in International Relations*, Supp no 41 (A/36/41) 1981, para 161).

[66] Draft resolution of the USSR, A/AC.77/L.4, art 6, reproduced in the 1956 Report of the Special Committee on the question of defining aggression, 8 October–9 November 1956, GA, Off Doc, 12th session, Supp no 16 (A/3574), New York, 1957 (see also BB Ferencz, *Defining International Aggression. A Documentary History and Analysis* (New York, Oceana Pub, vol II, 1975, 244). The formula already appears in the draft definition of 4 November 1950, A/C.1/603.

[67] Syria, A/C.6/SR.517, 14 October 1957.

[68] 1956 Report of the Special Committee on the question of defining aggression, 8 October–9 November 1956, GA, Off Doc, 12th session, Supp no 16 (A/3574), New York, 1957, 10, para 77.

(3) disrupt or interfere with the conduct of the affairs of another State;

(4) secure changes in the Government of another State; or

(5) inflict harm or obtain concessions of any sort (par. IV A).[69]

This very broad formula seems indeed to exclude any idea of a right of humanitarian or democratic intervention,[70] for example, even if some States were critical of it, fearing it would open up the road to military interventions that were officially justified by purposes other than those listed.[71] In commenting upon this draft, France's representative asked whether a military intervention to enforce international law or to respond to an unlawful act might not be considered an aggression.[72] Referring also to an intervention by the representative for Cyprus about the protection of nationals,[73] the US representative answered that

> he had heard no cases mentioned which he would not regard as being designed to obtain some form of concession or at least to inflict harm, which was the language of paragraph IV A (5). That sub-paragraph was very broad and made clear the illegality of certain uses of force which, before the adoption of the Charter, could be claimed to be legal because of the purpose for which they alleged to be carried out.[74]

He further affirmed that the list was by no means exhaustive,[75] as did Canada's representative who 'could not conceive a case of the kinds mentioned which was not covered by paragraph IV A (5). If that paragraph was not broad enough then it should be broadened'.[76] He went on:

> [I]f one of the acts listed in paragraph IV B was carried out by a State for the purpose of enforcing a treaty or protecting its nationals it was difficult to see how that would not be intended to 'inflict harm or obtain concessions of any sort'. It was precisely to avoid the type of situation mentioned by the representative of Cyprus

---

[69] A/AC.134/L.17, 25 March 1969, para IV A.

[70] See also paragraph III, *a contrario*: 'The use of force in the exercise of the inherent right of individual or collective self-defence, or pursuant to decisions of or authorization by competent United Nations organs or regional organizations consistent with the Charter of the United Nations, does not constitute aggression' (A/AC.134/L.17, 25 March 1969, para III).

[71] Mexico (A/AC.134/SR.60, 22 July 1970 in A/AC.134/SR.52-66), Cyprus (A/AC.134/SR.60, 22 July 1970 in A/AC.134/SR.52-66), Cuba (A/C.6/SR.1167, 3 December 1969, para 46).

[72] A/AC.134/SR.47, 27 March 1969 in A/AC.134/SR.25-51.

[73] A/AC.134/SR.47, 27 March 1969 in A/AC.134/SR.25-51, 208; see also A/AC.134/SR.68, 31 July 1970 in A/AC.134/SR.67-78, 24 and A/AC.134/SR.69, 3 August 1970 in A/AC.134/SR.67-78, 44; A/AC.134/SR.47, 27 March 1969 in A/AC.134/SR.25-51, 211.

[74] A/AC.134/SR.47, 27 March 1969 in A/AC.134/SR.25-51, 210.

[75] A/AC.134/SR.69, 3 August 1970 in A/AC.134/SR.67-78, 41. According to the USA, '[t]he extension of the right of self-determination to oppressed peoples would mean that a democratic State was entitled to overthrow the Government of a dictatorial State whose people seemed to be oppressed. *Such a doctrine was false, both in law and politics, and it had never been recognized by the United Nations*' (emphasis added; A/AC.134/SR.73, 6 August 1970 in A/AC.134/SR.67-78, 98).

[76] A/AC.134/SR.47, 27 March 1969 in A/AC.134/SR.25-51, 210.

that sub-paragraph (5) had been included. Furthermore, it was clearly stated that the list was not exhaustive.[77]

As for the UK, in responding to the fears that attacks that were not justified by the objectives mentioned might be considered as not coming within the definition of aggression, it specified: 'The cases listed in paragraph IV A were merely examples, perhaps the most obvious, and no more. This list was not exhaustive'.[78] In the end, the controversies were smoothed by the drafting of article 5(1) of the definition of aggression. Clearly this provision was drawn up in a particularly broad manner so as to exclude the lawfulness of any armed action based on the legitimacy of its objective. It shall be recalled on this point that some States' defence of the criterion of intent in the definition of aggression was aimed rather to exclude the possibility of error or to maintain a distinction between a use of force that did not constitute an aggression and a true armed attack.[79] In view of all of the debates preceding the adoption of resolution 3314 (XXIX), and in particular of the excerpt reproduced above, it is in any case obvious that the international community of States as a whole was very far from accepting the excuse of a right of humanitarian intervention. This excuse was evoked again, to be dismissed forthwith, in the 1980s in the context of debates that led to the adoption of resolution 42/22. At most that period marks the emergence of the idea that serious violations of human rights may degenerate into a threat against peace conferring competence on the Security Council.[80] *A contrario*, no unilateral right of intervention is recognised.

As a fourth point, it should be noted that on the fringe of the debates with the UN, some States spoke out resolutely against any right of intervention. Thus, according to a legal study drawn up by the UK civil service in 1984

the overwhelming majority of contemporary legal opinion comes down against the existence of a right of humanitarian intervention, for three main reasons: first, the UN Charter and the corpus of modern international law do not seem specifically to incorporate such a right; secondly, State practice in the past two centuries, and especially since 1945, at best provides only a handful of genuine cases of humanitarian intervention and, on most assessments, none at all; and finally, on prudential grounds, that the scope for abusing such a right argues strongly against its creation.[81]

---

[77] A/AC.134/SR.47, 27 March 1969 in A/AC.134/SR.25-51, 211; see also USA (A/AC.134/SR.47, 27 March 1969 in A/AC.134/SR.25-51, 211).

[78] A/AC.134/SR.68, 31 July 1970 in A/AC.134/SR.67-78, 27.

[79] Above, ch 2, s I; see also: 'Contemporary Practice of the United States' (2004) 98 *AJIL* 599.

[80] Report of the Special Committee on Enhancing the Effectiveness of the Principle of Non-Use of Force in International Relations, A/39/41, 4 April 1984, para 76; Report of the Special Committee on Enhancing the Effectiveness of the Principle of Non-Use of Force in International Relations, A/40/41, 10 June 1985, paras 90, 117 and 118.

[81] Planning Staff of the Foreign and Commonwealth Office, 'Is Intervention ever justified?', July 1984; 'United Kingdom Materials on International Law' (1986) 57 *BYBIL* 618–19; see

Likewise in a memorandum of 13 November 1996 the Canadian Legal Bureau mentioned the controversial character of the right of humanitarian intervention before adding that:

> For its part, Canada has never endorsed humanitarian intervention as an exception to the principle of non-intervention in the domestic affairs of States unless carried out collectively under the auspices of the UN Security Council's Chapter 7 powers.[82]

France adopted a similar position.[83]

As a fifth point, it shall be observed that the protection of nationals was not admitted either as a legitimate objective that could set aside the applicability of article 2(4). This has already been noted in the debates on article IVA of the Western States' draft definition of aggression.[84] This does not mean that all States dismiss this possibility but rather that, when they do support it, it is by reference to the concept of self-defence. The UK thus claimed that

> by mistreating foreigners on its own territory, a State committed an act of aggression against the country of which the foreigners were nationals: and in defending itself, the State concerned was exercising its right of self-defence.[85]

This assertion was vehemently criticised by several other States for which a simple infringement of foreign nationals' rights cannot be equated to an armed attack within the meaning of article 51 of the Charter.[86] We shall not delve further into this debate at this point; suffice it to say that as a matter of principle there is nothing to rule out characterising the armed attack on part of a population of a State as an aggression[87] but that in practice this justification is often invoked abusively as shall be observed later.[88] All of this explains why the UK representative's statement fell well short of being accepted by the international community of States as a whole. In any event, the protection of nationals was not recognised as a self-standing cause, with its own justification, stemming from an *a contrario* interpretation of article 2(4) of the

---

also this declaration of the Minister of Foreign Affairs: '[. . .] any armed intervention could not be regarded as lawful unless the state in which intervention took place gave a genuine invitation for the intervening state or the intervention could be justified in accordance with the principle of self-defence, confirmed by Article 51 of the United Nations Charter'; 'United Kingdom Materials on International Law' (1984) 55 *BYBIL* 581.

[82] 'Canadian Practice in International Law' (1997) 35 *CYIL* 362.

[83] 'Pratique française du droit international' (1971) 17 *AFDI* 1077–78; see also E Spiry, 'Interventions humanitaires et interventions d'humanité: la pratique française face au droit international' (1998) 102 *RGDIP* 421–33.

[84] See above.

[85] A/C.6/SR.292, 19 January 1952, 239, para 38.

[86] Iran (A/C.6/SR.293, 21 January 1952, para 20), Greece (A/C.6/SR.292, 19 January 1952, para 7) and Mexico (A/AC.125/SR.66, 1 August 1967).

[87] Above, s I, B and ch 7, s I.

[88] Below, s II.

Charter.[89] As seen, that interpretation was clearly condemned by very many and very diverse States. Only the consent of the State, self-defence or Security Council authorisation could theoretically, if the requisite legal conditions were met, justify a humanitarian intervention in the narrow sense (if limited to the protection of nationals alone) or in the broad sense (if the objectives go beyond that). States' positions on this point have been unchanging and did not change in the debates that received new impetus in the late 1990s.

B. The Persistent Refusal to Accept a 'Right of Humanitarian Intervention'

To the best of my knowledge the right of humanitarian intervention was no longer generally debated in the early and mid 1990s.[90] While the proclamation of a 'New World Order' gave rise to the adoption of General Assembly resolutions on humanitarian assistance, it has already been seen that those texts were highly classical, emphasising the need to respect State sovereignty.[91] Moreover, it shall be seen that this period was marked by several precedents showing that humanitarian action could be carried out not unilaterally but under the auspices of the Security Council and with its authorisation.[92] In 1999 the war against Yugoslavia was to give fresh impetus generally to the debate about the possibilities of military intervention without Security Council authorisation. This is how the concept of 'responsibility to protect' arose in the 2000s. In scrutinising the context in which it emerged, its contents and then the way it was received by States, one can only conclude that the prohibition of the use of force has been strengthened and not relaxed.[93] A similar conclusion can be drawn from examination of the debates over diplomatic protection that revealed persistent reluctance to countenance unilateral military operations. Finally, far from emerging as a new customary rule, the right of humanitarian intervention has been very firmly and regularly condemned since the close of the last century.

The Context in Which 'Responsibility to Protect' Emerged:
Condemnation on Principle of the Right of Humanitarian Intervention

At the opening of the 54th session of the General Assembly, while affirming that 'enforcement actions without Security Council authorization

---

[89] cp Thailand (A/C.6/S.R.763, 20 November 1962, 164, para 14) and Mexico (A/C.6/S.R.806, 6 November 1963, para 12), Syria (A/AC.134/SR.59, 22 July 1970 in A/AC.134/SR.52-66) and Ecuador (A/AC.134/SR.10, 17 June 1968 in A/AC.134/SR.1-24).

[90] But see: A Koroma, 'Humanitarian Intervention and Contemporary International Law' (1995) 5 *RSDIE* 409–16.

[91] Above.

[92] Below, s II.

[93] *Contra*: JG Castel, 'The Legality and Legitimacy of Unilateral Armed Intervention in an Age of Terror, Neo-Imperialism, and Massive Violations of Human Rights: Is International Law Evolving in the Right Direction?' (2004) 42 *CYIL* 22–24.

threaten the very core of the international security system founded on the Charter of the United Nations',[94] the Secretary-General evoked a

> developing international norm in favour of intervention to protect civilians from wholesale slaughter . . . Any such evolution in our understanding of State sovereignty and individual sovereignty will, in some quarters, be met with distrust, scepticism and even hostility. But it is an evolution that we should welcome.[95]

In his Millennium Report, the Secretary-General went on to say:

> Humanitarian intervention is a sensitive issue, fraught with political difficulty and not susceptible to easy answers. But surely no legal principle—not even sovereignty—can ever shield crimes against humanity'[96].

He then considered that 'In essence the problem is one of responsibility: in circumstances in which universally accepted human rights are being violated we have the responsibility to act'.[97] On reading these declarations one perceives a degree of uneasiness in the Secretary-General's mind, an uneasiness that is reflected too by what he terms the dilemma of the need to uphold respect of human rights while respecting State sovereignty and maintaining the security system provided for in the UN Charter. In this context one can understand the creation of an International Commission on Intervention and State Sovereignty in September 2000 at the initiative of the Canadian government.[98] In December 2001 the Commission published a report official entitled 'The Responsibility to Protect'.[99] Before specifying the scope of the concept, it should be underscored that it was drawn up in a climate of reluctance or even of open hostility. The caution in the terms of the Secretary-General, who was careful to emphasise the need to maintain the system set up by the Charter, was not enough to appease opposition from a very large majority of States.

The right of humanitarian intervention was first criticised in the 54th and 55th sessions of the General Assembly in the aftermath of the war against Yugoslavia. In view of those debates, States can be arranged into five categories whose positions show that the international community of States as a whole is far from consecrating the right of humanitarian intervention.

—A first category brings together the many States that have directly and forcefully condemned the right of humanitarian intervention, often in the name of respect of State sovereignty and maintenance of the system for

---

[94] *Report of the Secretary-General on the work of the Organization*, A/54/1, 1999, 8, para 66.

[95] AG, A/54/PV.4, 20 September 1999, 4. *Report of the Secretary-General on the work of the Organization*, A/54/1, above n 94, 8, para 62.

[96] K Annan, *We the Peoples. The role of the United Nations in the 21st Century* (UN, 2000) 48 (www.un.org/millennium/sg/report/full.htm).

[97] *Report of the Secretary-General on the work of the Organization*, A/55/1, 2000, 5, para 37.

[98] See: Canada; A/55/PV.6, 7 September, 16–17; A/55/PV.15, 14 September 2000, 1–5.

[99] International Commission on Intervention and State Sovereignty, *The responsibility to protect* (December 2001), www.iciss.ca/report-en.asp.

centralising the use of force established by the UN Charter. Countries adopting this stance include Algeria,[100] Belarus,[101] Bolivia,[102] North Korea,[103] China,[104] Cyprus,[105] Colombia,[106] Costa Rica,[107] Cuba,[108] Ecuador,[109] Egypt,[110] Ethiopia,[111] Guatemala,[112] India,[113] Iran,[114] Iraq,[115] Jordan (on behalf of the NAM),[116] Libya,[117] Mexico,[118] Mongolia,[119] Mozambique,[120] Namibia,[121] Nepal,[122] Norway,[123] Papua New Guinea,[124] Russia,[125] Senegal,[126] Syria,[127] Tunisia,[128] Turkmenistan,[129] Ukraine,[130] Uruguay[131] and Vietnam.[132]

[100] A/54/PV.32, 8 October 1999, 15–16; see also A/54/PV.4, 20 September 1999, 14; A/C.4/54/SR.12, 26 October 1999, 6–7, para 58.

[101] A/C.4/54/SR.12, 26 October 1999, 2, para 1.

[102] A/54/PV.33, 11 October 1999, 12.

[103] A/55/PV.30, 27 September 2000, 5; see also A/54/PV.14, 25 September 1999, 9; A/55/PV.17, 15 September 2000, 27.

[104] A/54/PV.27, 6 October 1999, 12–13; see also A/54/PV.35, 20 October 1999, 12–13; A/55/PV.29, 27 September, 17.

[105] A/55/PV.29, 27 September 2000, 8.

[106] A/C.4/54/SR.10, 18 October 1999, 14, para 105; see also A/54/PV.5, 20 September 1999, 8–11.

[107] A/55/PV.35, 17 October 2000, 27; see also A/54/PV.9, 22 September 1999, 9.

[108] A/54/PV.32, 8 October 1999, 2; see also A/54/PV.12, 24 September 1999, 15; A/55/PV.16, 15 September 2000, 18; A/55/PV.30, 27 September 2000, 25–26.

[109] A/55/PV.26, 21 September 2000, 19; see also A/C.4/54/SR.13, 27 October 1999, 3, para 10; A/55/PV.29, 27 September 2000, 14.

[110] A/54/PV.29, 7 October 1999, 17; see also A/C.4/54/SR.10, 18 October 1999, 12, para 85.

[111] A/C.4/54/SR.13, 27 October 1999, 2, para 5.

[112] A/C.4/54/SR.12, 26 October 1999, 12, para 97.

[113] A/54/PV.27, 6 October 1999, 19–20; see also A/C.4/54/SR.11, 26 October 1999, 3, para 18; A/55/PV.30, 27 September 2000, 20.

[114] A/54/PV.29, 7 October 1999, 11–12; see also A/C.4/54/SR.12, 26 October 1999, 10, para 78.

[115] A/54/PV.12, 24 September 1999, 28; see also A/54/PV.29, 7 October 1999, 15–16; see also A/55/PV.5, 7 September 2000, 43; A/55/PV.31, 28 September 2000, 3–4.

[116] A/C.4/54/SR.10, 18 October 1999, 8, para 53; see also A/54/PV.4, 20 September 1999, 33.

[117] A/54/PV.19, 30 September 1999, 16–17; see also A/54/PV.29, 7 October 1999, 21–22.

[118] A/54/PV.11, 23 September 1999, 31–32; see also A/54/PV.27, 6 October 1999, 2–3.

[119] A/54/PV.27, 6 October 1999, 10–11; see also A/54/PV.35, 20 October 1999, 6; A/55/PV.36, 18 October 2000, 10.

[120] A/C.4/54/SR.12, 26 October 1999, 4–5, para 39.

[121] A/55/PV.24, 20 September 2000, 12; see also A/55/PV.31, 28 September 2000, 18.

[122] A/C.4/54/SR.13, 27 October 1999, 4, para 21.

[123] A/54/PV.55, 17 November 1999, 14.

[124] A/C.4/54/SR.13, 27 October 1999, 6, para 40.

[125] A/54/PV.6, 21 September 1999, 14; A/54/PV.29, 7 October 1999, 1–2; A/C.4/54/SR.12, 26 October 1999, 5–6, para 49; A/55/PV.20, 18 September 2000, 7; A/55/PV.29, 27 September 2000, 30.

[126] A/54/PV.36, 20 October 1999, 10–11; see also A/55/PV.35, 17 October 2000, 15.

[127] 3rd committee, 27 October 2000, Press Release, GA/SHC/3609; see also A/54/PV.18, 30 September 1999, 17.

[128] A/55/PV.6, 7 September 2000, 12; A/55/PV.21, 18 September 2000, 14–15; see also A/C.4/54/SR.13, 27 October 1999, 5, para 29.

[129] A/55/PV.23, 19 September 2000, 7.

[130] A/54/PV.29, 7 October 1999, 7; see also A/C.4/54/SR.13, 27 October 1999, 7, para 51.

[131] A/55/PV.31, 28 September 2000, 26.

[132] A/55/PV.35, 17 October 2000, 22.

—A second category of States, that is very close to the first, comprises States that were insistent on the need to obtain Security Council authorisation to implement armed action outside of instances of self-defence. This was true of Barbados,[133] Brazil,[134] Burkina Faso,[135] Ivory Coast,[136] Jamaica,[137]   Kazakhstan,[138]   Laos,[139]   Malaysia,[140]   Moldova,[141] Pakistan,[142] the Philippines[143] and Spain.[144]

—A third category is of States that have less directly condemned the right of humanitarian intervention, often insisting more generally on the need to abide by the UN Charter and maintain the UN's role. Such positions have been taken by the Czech Republic,[145] France,[146] Gambia,[147] Germany,[148] Indonesia,[149] Italy,[150] Kenya,[151] Mali,[152] Mauritius,[153] Oman,[154] Peru,[155] Qatar,[156] Romania,[157] Sierra Leone,[158] Singapore,[159] Slovak Republic,[160] Sri Lanka,[161] Sudan[162] and Venezuela.[163]

---

[133] A/54/PV.18, 30 September 1999, 28.

[134] A/54/PV.36, 20 October 1999, 7; see also A/54/PV.4, 20 September 1999, 7; A/55/PV.35, 17 October 2000, 18.

[135] A/54/PV.14, 25 September 1999, 13.

[136] A/54/PV.35, 20 October 1999, 22.

[137] A/54/PV.17, 29 September 1999, 3.

[138] A/54/PV.12, 24 September 1999, 21.

[139] A/54/PV.21, 1 October 1999, 4; see also A/55/PV.6, 7 September 2000, 27; A/C.4/54/SR.11, 26 October 1999, 5, para 32.

[140] A/54/PV.32, 8 October 1999, 10; see also A/55/PV.16, 15 September 2000, 7; A/55/PV.29, 27 September, 26–27; A/C.4/54/SR.11, 26 October 1999, 7, para 43.

[141] A/54/PV.32, 8 October 1999, 17.

[142] ibid, 18.

[143] A/55/PV.30, 27 September 2000, 3; see also A/C.4/54/SR.10, 18 October 1999, 12, para 92.

[144] A/54/PV.32, 8 October 1999, 25–26.

[145] A/54/PV.9, 22 September 1999, 49–50.

[146] According to France, 'we must uphold the principle of international intervention, *under United Nations auspices*, to assist the victims' (emphasis added; A/54/PV.4, 20 September 1999, 27); see also 'Pratique française du droit international' (1999) 45 *AFDI* 917–18.

[147] A/54/PV.13, 24 September 1999, 9.

[148] According to the German Minister of Foreign Affairs, 'A practice of humanitarian interventions could evolve outside the United Nations system. This would be a very probematic development' (A/54/PV.8, 22 September 1999, 12).

[149] A/55/PV.31, 28 September 2000, 12; see also A/54/PV.11, 23 September 1999, 36.

[150] A/54/PV.8, 22 September 1999, 20–21.

[151] A/54/PV.15, 25 September 1999, 22; see also A/C.4/54/SR.13, 27 October 1999, 5, para 33.

[152] 3rd Committee, 7 November 2000, Press Release, GA/SHC/3619.

[153] A/54/PV.18, 30 September 1999, 8.

[154] A/55/PV.31, 28 September 2000, 33.

[155] A/55/PV.35, 17 October 2000, 18.

[156] A/55/PV.22, 19 September 2000, 19.

[157] A/54/PV.11, 23 September 1999, 39–40.

[158] 6th Committee, 15 October 1999, Press Release GA/L/3110.

[159] A/54, PV.27, 6 October 1999, 15.

[160] A/54/PV.7, 21 September 1999, 7–8.

[161] A/55/PV.21, 18 September 2000, 25.

[162] A/54/PV.19, 30 September 1999, 29–30.

[163] A/54/PV.27, 6 October 1999, 24.

—A fourth category comprises a few States that have taken a 'wait and see' position, happy to call for debate without coming down clearly on either side. These include Australia,[164] Canada,[165] Liechtenstein,[166] Macedonia (FYROM)[167] and the Republic of Korea.[168]

—Lastly seven States seem to have defended the idea of the right of humanitarian intervention. Of these the Netherlands,[169] Poland,[170] Sweden[171] and the United Kingdom[172] have settled for making very general declarations with imprecise legal outlines, such as saying that the international community cannot remain inactive when confronted with serious violations of human rights. Only Denmark,[173] Lithuania[174] and Slovenia[175] have made clearer commitments, although from a careful reading of their declarations it cannot be affirmed with certainty that they consider they are dealing with existing law, their proposals seeming to be more *de lege ferenda*.

So at the time the 'International Commission on Intervention and State Sovereignty' is set up and sets to work, the balance of power is clear. Only a tiny minority of States seems to defend the idea of a right of intervention without any Security Council authorisation. It is even doubtful that any one of them has affirmed that a right of humanitarian intervention, which is recognised rather as a moral duty, is admitted in positive international law,

---

[164] 3rd Committee, 10 November 1999, Press Release, GA/SHC/3554.

[165] A/54/PV.10, 23 September 1999, 17.

[166] A/54/PV.13, 24 September 1999, 33–34.

[167] A/54/PV.29, 7 October 1999, 10.

[168] A/54/PV.29, 7 October 1999, 19–20.

[169] A/54/PV.13, 24 September 1999, 22–23.

[170] A/54/PV.17, 29 September 1999, 6.

[171] A/54/PV.7, 21 September 1999, 32–34.

[172] A/54/PV.5, 20 September 1999, 34–36; see also 'United Kingdom Materials on International Law' (1999) 70 *BYBIL* 567–68. The UK will clearly invoke a right of humanitarian intervention later; 'United Kingdom Materials on International Law', (2000) 71 *BYBIL* 643–44 and 646–50; (2001) 72 *BYBIL* 695–96; (2002) 73 *BYBIL* 850 and 871; (2004) 75 *BYBIL* 816; see also (2005) 76 *BYBIL* 904.

[173] 'As a last resort, the international community must have the ability to act in the face of organized mass murder or ethnic-cleansing, even if the Security Council is blocked. The challenge is to keep open the option of humanitarian intervention without Security Council authorization in extreme cases, but to do so without jeopardizing the international legal order' (A/55/PV.13, 13 September 2000, 33).

[174] 'The newly evolving concept of humanitarian intervention is a real fact now. It has already taken place in practice, and is likely to be repeated. The concept lags behind reality, and has aroused controversy, which could have been avoided had a consensus been worked out by UN Member States beforehand [. . .]; there is an obvious need to establish rules legitimizing such interventions, as well as mechanisms to uphold such rules' (A/54/PV.35, 20 October 1999, 19).

[175] 'It is imperative to elaborate a doctrine for humanitarian intervention based on a modern interpretation of the United Nations Charter in line with new international relations and norms, which in certain conditions give priority to the protection of human rights' (A/55/PV.5, 7 September 2000, 26; see also A/55/PV.18, 16 September 2000, 16; A/55/PV.30, 27 September 2000, 24).

whether through an *a contrario* interpretation of article 2(4) or through some other legal reasoning. By contrast, a very large majority of States that have spoken has excluded this possibility by condemning unilateral military action.

This evaluation of positions is confirmed by a review of declarations made at the time outside of the UN. The Group of 77, an organisation that speaks for 132 UN Member States,[176] adopted a foreign ministers' declaration on 24 September 1999 by which:

> The Ministers stressed the need to maintain clear distinctions between humanitarian assistance and other activities of the United Nations. *They rejected the so-called right of humanitarian intervention, which has no basis in the UN Charter or in international law.* (emphasis added)[177]

Some months later, another declaration reiterated this condemnation in similar terms.[178] It will be noticed that there is an intent to speak both in terms of treaty law ('the UN Charter') and international customary law ('or in international law'). Declarations of the sort were also adopted by the 115 States of the Non-Aligned Movement, whose foreign ministers declared in April 2000:

> We also reiterate our firm condemnation of all unilateral military actions including those made without proper authorization from the United Nations Security Council . . . which constitute acts of aggression and blatant violations of the principle of non-intervention and non-interference.[179]

[176] Given the importance of this stance we shall take the liberty of recalling the identities of the States concerned: Afghanistan, Algeria, Angola, Antigua and Barbuda, Argentina, Bahamas, Bahrain, Bangladesh, Barbados, Belize, Benin, Bhutan, Bolivia, Bosnia and Herzegovina, Botswana, Brazil, Brunei Darussalam, Burkina Faso, Burundi, Cambodia, Cameroon, Cape Verde, Central African Republic, Chad, Chile, China, Colombia, Comoros, Congo, Costa Rica, Ivory Coast, Cuba, Cyprus, Democratic People's Republic of Korea, Democratic Republic of Congo, Djibouti, Dominica, Dominican Republic, Ecuador, Egypt, El Salvador, Equatorial Guinea, Eritrea, Ethiopia, Fiji, Gabon, Gambia, Grenada, Guatemala, Guinea, Guinea Bissau, Guyana, Haiti, Honduras, India, Indonesia, Iran, Iraq, Jamaica, Jordan, Kenya, Kuwait, Lao People's Democratic Republic, Lebanon, Lesotho, Liberia, Libyan Arab Jamahiriya, Madagascar, Malawi, Malaysia, Maldives, Mali, Malta, Marshall Islands, Mauritania, Mauritius, Micronesia, Mongolia, Morocco, Mozambique, Myanmar, Namibia, Nepal, Nicaragua, Niger, Nigeria, Oman, Pakistan, Palestine, Panama, Papua New Guinea, Paraguay, Peru, Philippines, Qatar, Romania, Rwanda, Saint Kitts and Nevis, Saint Lucia, Saint Vincent and the Grenadines, Samoa, Sao Tome and Principe, Saudi Arabia, Senegal, Seychelles, Sierra Leone, Singapore, Solomon Islands, Somalia, South Africa, Sri Lanka, Sudan, Suriname, Swaziland, Syrian Arab Republic, Thailand, Togo, Tonga, Trinidad and Tobago, Tunisia, Turkmenistan, Uganda, United Arab Emirates, United Republic of Tanzania, Uruguay, Vanuatu, Venezuela, Vietnam, Yemen, Zambia, Zimbabwe.

[177] Paras 69 and 70; Declaration given on the occasion of the 35th anniversary of the creation of the 'Group of 77'; www.g77.org/DoSC/Decl1999.html.

[178] *Declaration of the South Summit*, Havana, 14 April 2000, annex I to the letter dated 5 May 2000 from the Permanent Representative of Nigeria to the UN addressed to the President of the GA, A/55/74, 12 May 2000, para 54.

[179] Final Document, Ministerial Conference, Cartagena (Columbia) 8–9 April 2000, para 11; www.nam.gov.za/xiiiminconf/; see also Declaration of Durban: 'humanitarian assistance should be neutral and impartial, be provided at the request of the country concerned, and fully respect its territorial integrity and sovereignty' (Declaration adopted after the XIIth summit in Durban, 3 September 1998, para 63, www.nam.gov.za/xiisummit/index.html).

Mention must also be made of the 57 Member States of the Islamic Conference Organisation,[180] that took up very clear positions along these lines. Thus on 30 June 2000 at the outcome of its Kuala Lumpur Conference:

> It affirmed its rejection of the so-called right to humanitarian intervention under whatever name or from whatever source, for it has no basis in the Charter of the United Nations or in the provisions of the principles of the general international law.[181]

The expression 'under whatever name' seems to be aimed at the concept of responsibility to protect, which is manifestly perceived as an unavowed form of right of humanitarian intervention. The heads of State of those countries made declarations along these lines a few months later at Doha,[182] and then on 27 June 2001 at Bamako.[183] In a word, a very clear majority of States forcefully and repeatedly condemned the idea of a right of humanitarian intervention. It is hardly surprising then that no such notion is to be found in the report instituting the concept of the 'responsibility to protect'.

The Absence of a Unilateral Right of Intervention in the Concept of 'Responsibility to Protect'

The concept of 'responsibility to protect' was forged by an International Commission on Intervention and State Sovereignty that drafted a report after more than a year's work. Its objective was to come up with a text that could both meet the aspirations for a better capacity to intervene in cases of massive violations of human rights and to comply with the wishes of UN Member States to maintain a strict legal framework to prevent any risk of misuse. This balancing act between idealism and realism led the Commission to put its proposals to the representatives of several States in the course of the many meetings and consultations. It is in this context that its report, which advocates maintaining a relatively traditional stance in strictly legal terms, can be understood.[184]

Admittedly the Commission begins by noting that State sovereignty is no longer considered a concept opposing any action:

> The Commission found in its consultations that even in States where there was the strongest opposition to infringements of sovereignty, there was general acceptance that there must be limited exceptions to the non-intervention rule for certain kinds of emergencies. Generally expressed, the view was that these

---

[180] www.oic-oci.org/oicnew/member_states.asp.

[181] Final Communiqué of the 27th session of the Islamic Conference of Foreign Ministers, Kuala Lumpur, Malaysia, para 79; www.oic-oci.org/index.asp.

[182] Final Communiqué of the 9th session of the Islamic Conference of Heads of States, Doha (Qatar), 12–13 November 2000, para 88; www.oic-oci.org/index_french.asp.

[183] ICFM/28-2001/FC/Final, Final Communiqué of the 28th session of the Islamic Conference of Foreign Ministers, Bamako (Republic of Mali), 25–27 June 2001.

[184] X Pacreau, *De l'intervention au Kosovo en 1999 à l'intervention en Irak de 2003*, above n 25, 152–55.

exceptional circumstances must be cases of violence which so genuinely 'shock the conscience of mankind', or which present such a clear and present danger to international security, that they require coercive military intervention.[185]

When examining the criteria of what it designates as a 'just cause', the Commission emphasises, though, the central question of the proper authority to evaluate in each specific instance the presence of each of these criteria. And in this respect the Commission 'is in absolutely no doubt that there is no better or more appropriate body than the Security Council to deal with military intervention issues for human protection purposes'. It adds:

That was the overwhelming consensus we found in all our consultations around the world. If international consensus is ever to be reached about when, where, how and by whom military intervention should happen, it is very clear that the central role of the Security Council will have to be at the heart of that consensus. The task is not to find alternatives to the Security Council as a source of authority, but to make the Security Council work much better than it has.[186]

The prospect of unilateral military action seems indeed to be excluded as another excerpt from the report confirms:

Interventions by ad hoc coalitions (or, even more, individual States) acting without the approval of the Security Council, or the General Assembly, or a regional or sub-regional grouping of which the target State is a member, do not—it would be an understatement to say—find wide favour. Even those countries involved in the Kosovo intervention, and prepared to passionately defend its legitimacy by reference to all the threshold and precautionary criteria we have identified in this report, for the most part acknowledge its highly exceptional character, and express the view that it would have been much preferable to have secured the Security Council's—or failing that the General Assembly's—endorsement.[187]

At most the Commission evokes as a hypothesis the possibility of some subsidiary competence of the General Assembly, which we have observed was not accepted by the international community of States as a whole.[188] In the end, however, the Commission confined itself to existing law: no military action can be undertaken without prior authorisation from the Security Council.[189]

---

[185] International Commission on Intervention and State Sovereignty, *The responsibility to protect* (December 2001), above n 99, para 4.13.

[186] ibid, para 6.14.

[187] ibid, para 6.36.

[188] Above, ch 6, s I.

[189] International Commission on Intervention and State Sovereignty, *The responsibility to protect* (December 2001), above n 99, para 6.15; according to the Commission, 'As a matter of political reality, it would be impossible to find consensus, in the Commission's view, around any set of proposals for military intervention which acknowledged the validity of any intervention not authorized by the Security Council or General Assembly' (ibid, para 6.37). *Contra:* VS Mani, ' "Humanitarian" Intervention Today', above n 31, 297–300; JG Castel, 'The Legality and Legitimacy of Unilateral Armed Intervention in an Age of Terror, Neo-Imperialism, and Massive Violations of Human Rights: Is International Law Evolving in the Right Direction?', above n 93, 24); see also J Brumée and SJ Toope, 'The Use of Force: International Law After Iraq' 53 (2004) *ICLQ* 800–03.

By application of Chapter VII of the UN Charter and as confirmed by practice in the 1990s,[190] the Council may perfectly well authorise a humanitarian type action provided that it is related to an objective of maintaining or restoring peace.

Admittedly, beyond the strictly legal point of view, the Commission seems to reserve the hypothesis of an exceptional situation in which a military action not authorised by the Security Council might be considered *morally* justified.[191] It dwells on the need, in particular for permanent members, to take account of political reality that might lead States that were particularly anxious to intervene in especially serious instances to circumvent the UN if the veto were misused. Maintaining the credibility of the UN and the Charter would entail the Security Council effectively exercising its responsibility to protect threatened populations in the event a State could not or would not do so. These considerations, though, are clearly in a different dimension to positive international law: they are issues rather of political legitimacy and appropriateness. It is clear from the Commission's report that in law military action is accepted only under the circumstances provided for by the UN Charter: Security Council authorisation or in certain instances self-defence under article 51 of the Charter.[192] However, even with so strict a definition, the concept of 'responsibility to protect' has been received with great circumspection and even reluctance by some UN Member States.

Reluctance of States over the Concept of 'Responsibility to Protect'

The concept of the responsibility to protect was amply debated for the sixty years of the UN. A record of it is found in the 2005 World Summit declaration, especially in the excerpt:

Responsibility to protect populations from genocide, war crimes, ethnic cleansing and crimes against humanity

138. Each individual State has the responsibility to protect its populations from genocide, war crimes, ethnic cleansing and crimes against humanity. This responsibility entails the prevention of such crimes, including their incitement, through

---

[190] International Commission on Intervention and State Sovereignty, *The responsibility to protect* (December 2001), above n 99, para 4.23; L Boisson de Chazournes and L Condorelli, 'De la "responsabilité de protéger", ou d'une nouvelle parure pour notion déjà bien établie' (2006) 110 *RGDIP* 13.

[191] 'But that may still leave circumstances when the Security Council fails to discharge what this Commission would regard as its responsibility to protect, in a conscience-shocking situation crying out for action. It is a real question in these circumstances where lies the most harm: in the damage to international order if the Security Council is bypassed or in the damage to that order if human beings are slaughtered while the Security Council stands by' (*The responsibility to protect*, above n 99, para 6.37).

[192] Against this background, the Commission stated also that: '[. . .] as to the use of military force by a state to rescue its own nationals on foreign territory, sometimes claimed as another justification for "humanitarian intervention," we regard that as being again a matter appropriately covered under existing international law, and in particular Article 51 of the UN Charter' (ibid, para 4.27).

appropriate and necessary means. We accept that responsibility and will act in accordance with it. The international community should, as appropriate, encourage and help States to exercise this responsibility and support the United Nations in establishing an early warning capability.

139. The international community, through the United Nations, also has the responsibility to use appropriate diplomatic, humanitarian and other peaceful means, in accordance with Chapters VI and VIII of the Charter, to help to protect populations from genocide, war crimes, ethnic cleansing and crimes against humanity. In this context, we are prepared to take collective action, in a timely and decisive manner, through the Security Council, in accordance with the Charter, including Chapter VII, on a case-by-case basis and in cooperation with relevant regional organizations as appropriate, should peaceful means be inadequate and national authorities are manifestly failing to protect their populations from genocide, war crimes, ethnic cleansing and crimes against humanity . . .[193]

These two paragraphs enshrine the concept of responsibility to protect. The first underscores the rights and duties of each State, which must not only abide by but also enforce human rights in its territory. The second paragraph then contemplates, as a supplementary and subsidiary consideration, the role of the 'international community'. That community must first implement all peaceful means 'to help to protect populations'. As a final resort it may undertake 'a collective action' but 'through the Security Council, in accordance with the Charter, including Chapter VII'. These paragraphs were 'reaffirm[ed]' by the Security Council in its resolution 1674 (2006) on the protection of civilians in times of armed conflict.[194] The Council reaffirms its attachment to 'Article 2 (1–7) of the Charter' and to the 'principles of the political independence, sovereign equality and territorial integrity of all States',[195] while declaring it is ready to take 'appropriate steps' in the event of 'flagrant and widespread violations of international humanitarian and human rights law in situations of armed conflict', which 'may constitute a threat to international peace and security'.[196]

The scheme thus proposed appears to be a codification of existing law which saw the emergence in the 1990s of Security Council practice and right to authorise military action to put an end to dramatic humanitarian situations characterised as threats to peace within the meaning of the Charter.[197] *A contrario*, the document recognises no right of humanitarian intervention

---

[193] A/RES/60/1 of 24 October 2005; see also *A more secure world: Our shared responsibility*, Report of the Secretary-General's High-level Panel on Threats, Challenges and Change, (UN, 2004) 65–66, para 199–203) and *Report of the Secretary-General, In larger freedom: towards development, security and human rights for all*, A/59/2005, 24 March 2005, A/59/2005, 24 March 2005, 39, para 125.

[194] SC Res 1674 (2006) of 28 April 2006, para 4.

[195] Preamble of the resolution.

[196] SC Res 1674 (2006) of 28 April 2006, para 26, and S/PV.5430, 28 April 2006.

[197] Above, ch 6, s I.

outside of the hypothesis of an authorisation.[198] It also abstains from taking up the considerations of the International Commission on Intervention and State Sovereignty about a possible abusive veto, about the possibility of legally questionable but morally justified action, and about *realpolitik* that might consecrate the practice of circumventing the Security Council if it is inactive.[199] The 2005 World Summit document remains drafted in classical legal fashion, a conclusion that is that much more inescapable as the excerpt just cited must be tied in with those dealing specifically with the use of force in a way that, as we have seen, remains consistent with the ordinary meaning of the relevant provisions of the Charter.[200]

A review of the debates over the adoption of the text further confirms the extreme reluctance of States to admit the possibility of a right of humanitarian intervention.[201] Upon examination it can be observed that the balance of power at the turn of the century has not only not been challenged but has become accentuated in the sense of insistence on compliance with the collective security mechanisms provided for by the Charter. The 115 Member States of the Non-Aligned Movement reiterated in 2005 and then in 2006 their 'rejection of the "right" of humanitarian intervention, which has no basis either in the UN Charter or in international law';[202] the Rio Group has more generally considered that the Charter provisions were still relevant for governing all situations that threatened peace,[203] while for the Georgia, Uzbekistan, Ukraine, Azerbaijan and Moldova (GUUAM) Group, coercive measures to protect a population 'can be taken only as a last resort and under the explicit mandate of the Security Council',[204] an affirmation that was taken up almost as it stood by the European Union.[205] Alongside

---

[198] *Contra:* C Stahn, 'Responsibility to Protect: Political Rhetoric or Emerging Legal Norm?' (2007) 101 *AJIL* 109 and 119–20.

[199] L Boisson de Chazournes and L Condorelli, 'De la "responsabilité de protéger", ou d'une nouvelle parure pour notion déjà bien établie', above n 190, 17.

[200] A/RES/60/1 of 24 October 2005, paras 77–80.

[201] See also C Gray, *International Law and the Use of Force*, 3rd ed, above n 43, 51–55.

[202] *Statement by Rastam Mohd Isa, Permanent Representative of Malaysia to the UN, in his capacity as Chairman of the Coordinating Bureau of the NAM, on behalf of the NAM, at the 4th Informal Meeting of the Plenary of the 59th Session of the General Assembly*, 27 January 2005, para 16, www.int/malaysia/NAM; see also *Special Meeting of the Ministers of Foreign Affairs of the NAM*, Doha, Qatar, 13 June 2005, Declaration, NAM/2005/SFMM/05, para 18, www.un.int/malaysia/NAM/, and *Statement by Chairman of the Coordinating Bureau of the NAM on behalf of the NAM*, 21 June 2005, para 4 g), www.int/malaysia/NAM/; *Ministerial Meeting of the Coordinating Bureau of the Non-aligned Movement*, Putrajaya, Malaysia, 27–30 May 2006, Final Document, para 208, www.un.int/malaysia/NAM/.

[203] UNGA, Exchange of views on the President's draft outcome document of the High-level Plenary Meeting of the General Assembly of September 2005 (A/59/HLPM/CPR.1), *Statement by the Argentine Delegation (on behalf of the Rio Group)*, www.reformtheun.org.

[204] A/59/PV.88, 7 April 2005, 22.

[205] 'The international community has the responsibility to decide and to act case by case through a comprehensive range of measures, including collective action through the Security Council, and in extreme cases, and out of necessity, by use of force, authorized by the Security Council' (*UK Statement on behalf of the EU*, 28 July–2 August 2005, GA, www.reformtheun.org).

these collective stances, States generally spoke out along the same lines individually, whether Asian,[206] African,[207] Latin American[208] or European[209] and Western[210] States. In presenting the document to the US Senate, the US ambassador to the UN affirmed that:

> We were successful in making certain that language in the Outcome Document guaranteed a central role for the Security Council. We were pleased that the Outcome Document underscored the readiness of the Council to act in the face of such atrocities, and rejected categorically the argument that any principle of non-intervention precludes the Council from taking such action.[211]

---

[206] Azerbaijan (*Statement by the Delegation of Azerbaijan At the Informal Meeting of the Plenary on the High-Level Plenary Meeting of the General Assembly of September 2005*, 1 July 2005, www.reformtheun.org), China (*Position paper of the People's Republic of China on the UN Reform*, 7 June 1965, point 7; www.china-un.org), India (*Statement by Mr Nirupam Sen, Permanent Representative of India*, April 8, 2005, www.un.int/india/; see also *Statement by Mr Nirupam Sen, Permanent Representative of India*, April 22, 2005; *Statement by Mr Nirupam Sen, Permanent Representative of India*, April 8, 2005, and *Statement by Mr A Gopinathan, Deputy Permanent Representative*, November 25, 2002; ibid), Indonesia (*Statement by the Indonesian Delegation at the Informal Thematic Consultations of the General Assembly on Cluster III of the SG's Report*, New York, 20 April 2005, www.indonesiamission-ny.org/), Iran (A/59/PV.87, 7 April 2005, 18; *Statement by Mr Javad Zarif, Permanent Representative of Iran*, June 21, 2005, www.reformtheun.org), Malaysia (Text of speech by Malaysia's Prime Minister at the opening of the Ministerial Meeting of the NAM Coordinating Bureau, para 31, www.reform theun.org), Pakistan (*Statement by Ambassador Munir Akram, Permanent Representative of Pakistan*, 23 February 2005, www.un.int/pakistan/; A/59/PV.86, 6 April 2005, 5), Turkey (www.un.int/turkey/).

[207] Algeria (A/59/PV.86, 6 April 2005, 9), Egypt (ibid, 13), Morocco (*Déclaration de SE M Mohamed Bennouna, Représentant Permanent du Royaume du Maroc: 'Echanges de vues sur les recommandations contenues dans le rapport du groupe de personnalités de haut niveau sur les menaces, les défis et le changement, 31 January 2005*, marocco-un.org), Uganda (A/59/PV.88, 7 April 2005, 8).

[208] Chile (A/59/PV.86, 6 April 2005, 20) and Costa Rica (*Statement during the Informal Consultations on the Report of the High Level Panel, Bruno Stagmo, Ambassador, Permanent Representative of Costa Rica, January 31 2005*, Mission permanente de Costa Rica ante las Naciones Unidas).

[209] Belarus (www.mfa.gov), France (*La France, les Nations Unies et l'année 2005*, 20, www.diplomatie.gouv.fr), Norway (A/59/PV.88, 7 April 2005, 13), Russia (A/59/PV.87, 7 April 2005, 6), San Marino (A/59/PV.86, 6 April 2005, 24), Switzerland (Permanent Mission of Switzerand to the United Nations, 59th session of the GA, informal consultations, points 45 and 55 of the agenda, Report of the Secretary-General: In a larger freedom; Cluster II: Freedom from fear; *Statement by HE Mr Peter Maurer, permanent Representative of Switzerland to the Nations Unies*, New York, 21 April 2005; 'La pratique suisse en matière de droit international public' (1994) 4 *RSDIE* 624–27; (2002) 12 *RSDIE* 636–42, Ukraine (A/60/PV.11, 18 September 2005, 18–19).

[210] Canada (December 2, 2004, Canada welcomes report on UN reform, www. pco-bcatgc.ca; see also *Statement by the Prime Minister on a UN Report*, March 21, 2005, ibid).

[211] US Permanent Representative to the UN, testimony before the Senate Foreign Relations Committee, 'Contemporary Practice of the United States' (2006) 100 *AJIL* 464; see also ibid, 463. But see *Letter from Ambassador Bolton to UN Member States Conveying US Amendments to the Draft Outcome Document Being Prepared for the High Level Event on Responsibility to Protect*, August 30, 2005, www.un.int/usa/reform-un-jrb-ltr-protect-8-05.pdf and C Stahn, 'Responsibility to Protect: Political Rhetoric or Emerging Legal Norm?', above n 198, 109.

Conversely I know of but a few rare declarations made in the UN[212] by which a military action might take place without Security Council authorisation. At most, some States have spoken out very generally in favour of the responsibility to protect, without recalling—but without denying either—that the concept implied Security Council authorisation to make a military intervention lawful.[213] Even *de lege ferenda*, manifestly one no longer dares to call for the introduction of a right of humanitarian intervention from fear of stirring up opposition and causing the failure of the idea, however modest it may be legally, of the responsibility to protect. This concern to maintain the existing legal framework[214] is confirmed again in view of the debates that at the same time related to certain arrangements for diplomatic protection.

The Refusal to Admit of a Right to Armed Action to Rescue Nationals in the Context of Debates on Diplomatic Protection

The question of a right of armed intervention to rescue nationals was incidentally addressed in the context of the works of the International Law Commission on diplomatic protection. In his preliminary report Mohammed Bennouna had stated that:

> The State retains, in principle, the choice of means of action to defend its nationals, while respecting its international commitments and the peremptory norms of international law. In particular, it may not resort to the threat or use of force in the exercise of diplomatic protection.[215]

This affirmation was to be challenged by John Dugard in his first report which contained a draft article 2 whereby:

---

[212] Outside the UN, UK stated that: 'under international law, force may be used provided that its use is in exercise of the inherent right of individual or collective self-defence as recognized in Article 51 of the UN Charter; or is authorized by the United Nations Security Council under Chapter VII of the UN Charter; or—in exceptional circumstances—is the only way to avert an overwhelming humanitarian catastrophe' (Parliamentary Under-Secretary of State, FCO, 18 March 2004, (2004) 75 *BYBIL* 852–53); see also A/59/PV.85, 5 April 2005, 26–27; cp *Déclaration de Ouagadougou du XXe sommet de la Francophonie*, 27 November 2004; text and list of these States on www.diplomatie.gouv.fr/.

[213] Australia (A/59/PV.88, 7 April 2005, 4), Israel (*United Nations Reforms—Position Paper of the Government of Israel*, 1 July 2005, www.mfa.gov.il/MFA/Foreign+Relations/Israel), Liechtenstein (*Statement by HE Christian Wanaweser, 27 January 2005, informal meeting of the GA*, Permanent Mission of the Principality of Liechtenstein to the UN, para 10; A/59/PV.88, 7 April 2005, 19), New Zealand (A/59/PV.88, 7 April 2005, 9), USA (*Letter from Ambassador Bolton to UN Member States Conveying US Amendments to the Draft Outcome Document Being Prepared for the High Level Event on Responsibility to Protect*, August 30, 2005, above n 211).

[214] B Delcourt, 'The Doctrine of 'Responsibility to Protect and the EU Stance: Critical Appraisal' (2006) 59 *Studia Diplomatica* 70–77.

[215] Mohammed Bennouna, *Preliminary Report on Diplomatic Protection*, A/CN.4/484, 4 February 1998, 4, para 11. Similarily, according to the Base of Discussion VIII (3) proposed by Garcia Amador, 'In no event shall the direct exercise of diplomatic protection imply a threat, or the actual use, of force or any other form of international in the domestic or external affairs of the respondent State' §A/CN.4/96, *YILC*, 1956, vol II, 221, para 241.

The threat or use of force is prohibited as a means of diplomatic protection, except in the case of rescue of nationals where:

(a) The protecting State has failed to secure the safety of its nationals by peaceful means;

(b) The injuring State is unwilling or unable to secure the safety of the nationals of the protecting State;

(c) The nationals of the protecting State are exposed to immediate danger to their persons;

(d) The use of force is proportionate in the circumstances of the situation;

(e) The use of force is terminated, and the protecting State withdraws its forces, as soon as the nationals are rescued.[216]

The Rapporteur considered that, in view of 'the practice of States',[217] 'it is difficult to contend that the Charter's prohibition on the use of force extends to the protection of nationals abroad'.[218] Dugard seemed to base this type of military action on self-defence.[219] He stated in this respect that the action to rescue its nationals was distinct from the controversial notion of humanitarian intervention. While admitting from the outset to doubts about the acceptance of the draft article 2, he preferred that the Commission make a pronouncement on this point.[220]

As he himself expected the draft article 2 of the Special Rapporteur raised a number of criticisms: the broad interpretation of self-defence that it implied was called into question as was the tendency to extend exception to the prohibition of the use of force;[221] it was observed that the UN's failure to condemn certain operations by political organs did not amount to a general acceptance of the lawfulness of those operations;[222] it was also asked whether such a question was indeed within the Commission's remit,[223]

---

[216] A/CN.4/506, 7 March 2000, 16–17.

[217] ibid, 18, para 52 (mentioning the Entebbe raid, 21, para 59).

[218] ibid, 20, para 58.

[219] ibid, 22, para 60; see also *YILC*, 2000, vol I, 2617th session, 9 May 2000, 39, para 26 ('the threat or use of force in the exercise of diplomatic protection could be justified only if it could be characterized as a kind of self-defence').

[220] The rapporteur precised that: 'He had been reluctant to devote too much space to the matter in his comments, particularly as there was a prospect of article 2 being rejected by the Commission' (ibid, 39, para 23).

[221] Baena Soares (ibid, 43, para 58), Economides (ibid, 44, paras 65–68), Illueca (*YILC*, 2000, vol I, 2618th session, 10 May 2000, 47–48, paras 5–10), Kabatsi (ibid, 48–49, paras 17–18), Pellet (ibid, 50, para 25), Idris (ibid, 51, para 32), Rodriguez Cedeno (ibid, 54, para 61), Kateka (ibid, 54, para 68), Hafner (ibid, 55, para 75), Galicki (*YILC*, 2000, vol I, 2619th session, 11 May 2000, 56, paras 3–4), He (ibid, 58, para 23), Pambou-Tchivounda (ibid, 58, para 29), Candioti (ibid, 59–60, paras 40–42), Brownlie (ibid, 60, para 51), Opertti Badan (*YILC*, 2000, vol I, 2620th session, 12 May 2000, 64, para 2), Goco (ibid, 65, para 11), Kamto (ibid, 69, para 43).

[222] M Brownlie; *YILC*, 2000, vol I, 2617th session, 42, para 50.

[223] M Brownlie; ibid, 42, para 49; see also MM Gaja (ibid, 44, para 62), Tomka (ibid, 49, paras 73 and 76), Pellet (*ACDI*, 2000, vol I, 2618th session, 10 May 2000, 50, para 24), Idris (ibid, 51, para 32), Rosenstock (*ACDI*, 2000, vol I, 2619th session, 11 May 2000, 56–57, para 8), Addo (ibid, 57, para 11), He (ibid, 58, para 23), Sreenivasa Rao (ibid, 63, para 75), Simma (*ACDI*, 2000, vol I, 2620th session, 12 May 2000, 66–67, para 22), Momtaz (ibid, 68, para 29).

which was to lead to the removal of any reference to the use of force.[224] To my knowledge, of all those who have spoken on the matter, just one member of the Commission has not challenged maintaining article 2.[225]

The same trend could be observed within the Sixth Commission of the UN General Assembly. Many States supported the Commission's decision to do away with draft article 2, denying that a military action to protect nations could be justified in respect of article 2(4) of the Charter.[226] To the best of my knowledge just one State has declared itself in favour of the principle set out in draft article 2[227] while yet other States considered that the matter was not one of diplomatic protection.[228]

It was further to this debate that not only was the old article 2 deleted but article 1 of the draft was drawn up so as to challenge its contents. Under this provision, in effect, 'Diplomatic protection consists of resort to diplomatic action or other *means of peaceful settlement* by a State . . .'. (emphasis added)[229] This text, which adopts a similar formulation to that initially chosen by Rapporteur Bennouna,[230] was adopted by the Drafting Committee at the first reading,[231] and was then the subject of observations by 11 States, with none of them calling into question the expression underscored.[232] Article 1 was then amended for pure form and adopted at the second reading, still with a reference to the peaceful character of

---

[224] See *YILC*, 2000, vol I, 2619th session, 11 May 2000, 56 *ff.*

[225] Lukashuk (*YILC*, 2000, vol I, 2618th session, 10 May 2000, 52–53, paras 54–56).

[226] Spain ('Diplomatic protection should be viewed as the initiation of a procedure for the peaceful settlement of a dispute. Article 2, paragraph 4, of the Charter of the United Nations was categorical in rejecting the threat or use of force, and no exceptions should be formulated that might cast doubt on that basic principle of international law'; A/C.6/55/SR.19, 13 November 2000, 2, para 5). See also China (ibid, 5–6, para 30), India (ibid, 8, para 39), Norway, speaking on behalf of the Nordic countries (ibid, 9, para 48), Bosnia and Herzegovina (ibid, 9, para 51), Poland (ibid, 10, para 56), Germany (ibid, 11, para 64), Russia (ibid, 11, para 68), Republic of Korea (ibid, 12–13, para 76), Czech Republic (A/C.6/55/SR.20, 14 November 2000, 3, para 14), Slovenia (ibid, 3, para 16), Mexico (ibid, 7, para 47), Argentina (ibid, 8–9, para 52), Venezuela (ibid, 11, para 78), Iran (ibid, 12, para 86), Iraq (ibid, 13, paras 90–91), Greece (ibid, 13–14, para 97), Jordan (A/C.6/55/SR.21, 14 November 2000, 3, para 7), Bahrain (ibid, 4, para 15), Switzerland (ibid, 5, para 20), Brazil (ibid, 5, para 26), Libya (A/C.6/55/SR.22, 6 November 2000, 9, paras 53–55), Colombia, speaking on behalf of the 'Rio Group' ('The Rio Group rejected the use of force as a means of exercising diplomatic protection'; A/C.6/55/SR.23, 14 November 2000, 2, para 5), Romania (ibid, 10, para 69), Burkina Faso (A/C.6/55/SR.24, 16 November 2000, 9–10, para 55), and Cuba (ibid, 11, para 71).

[227] 'Draft article 2 should state explicitly that the use of force by a State in the protection of its nationals should be limited to highly exceptional circumstances in which their lives were in immediate danger' (Italy; A/C.6/55/SR.19, 13 November 2000, 3–4, para 15).

[228] See, eg: UK (A/C.6/55/SR.19, 13 November 2000, 4, para 23) Cyprus (A/C.6/55/SR.21, 14 November 2000, 2, para 2), Japan (A/C.6/55/SR.23, 14 November 2000, 11, para 80), Portugal (A/C.6/55/SR.24, 16 November 2000, 5, para 22).

[229] A/CN.4/L.613/Rev.1, 7 June 2002, Art 1 § 1.

[230] See the text above.

[231] A/CN.4/L.647, 24 May 2004.

[232] A/CN.4/561, 27 January 2006; see also A/CN.4/561/Add.1, 3 April 2006; A/CN.4/561/Add.2, 12 April 2006; A/CN.4/575, 18 August 2006.

dispute settlement.[233] In its commentary on article 1, the Commission specified that:

> Diplomatic protection must be exercised by lawful and peaceful means . . . The use of force, prohibited by Article 2, paragraph 4, of the Charter of the United Nations, is not a permissible method for the enforcement of the right of diplomatic protection.[234]

On 18 December 2006 the General Assembly took note of the draft article and asked governments to say whether it was appropriate to draw up a convention on diplomatic protection.[235]

This episode clearly shows that, as a matter of principle, States do not accept that military intervention can be justified by the sole argument of rescuing threatened nationals. The failure of draft article 2 drawn up by Special Rapporteur John Dugard is significant. Although he had based the text on an institution like self-defence and not any self-sustained or autonomous justification, the text was rejected by a great number of States.

Ultimately the debates in the UN since 1999 seem to have marked the failure of the doctrine of the right of humanitarian intervention, whether taken in its general sense or restricted to the protection of nationals. Further to the Kosovo war, the UN General-Secretary was eager to begin the debate in the perspective of possible reforms for the UN's 60 years. A very large number of States spoke out on this issue on several occasions and almost systematically along the same lines: apart from in self-defence, to be lawful, any military action must be grounded on a Security Council authorisation. The concept of 'responsibility to protect' merely expresses the ordinary law of the UN Charter, even if it is by giving precedent to a flexible interpretation by which the Security Council can characterise grave violations of human rights as threats to peace and authorise a coercive action on this basis. In this sense, the consecration of the concept is a codification of the practice that has developed progressively since the early 1990s. At the same time it attests to the refusal of a very great majority of States to go any further and open up the way to unilateral actions in the name of the legitimacy of their motives—a refusal that may also be deduced from a review of the precedents generally evoked to illustrate the right of humanitarian intervention.

II The Non-Existence of Decisive Precedents

Although the notion is not enshrined in the relevant texts, on the basis of a number of precedents, doctrine in favour of the right of humanitarian inter-

---

[233] A/CN.4/L.684, 2 June 2006.

[234] *Report of the International Law Commission*, 58th session, 1 May–9 June and 3 July–11 August 2006, A/61/10, 26–27, para 8.

[235] A/RES/61/35 of 4 December 2006.

vention has taken the view that a customary rule could be established.[236] These shall be considered chronologically and divided into two periods: before 1990[237] and after 1990. That date marks the advent of what some have hailed as the 'New World Order', an order in which there is supposedly a questioning of the concept of sovereignty to the benefit of better protection of human rights, which might extend to taking the form of 'humanitarian interference'.[238] And yet, upon examination, neither the first (A) nor the second period (B) reveals a challenge to or a new interpretation of the prohibition of the use of force as set out in article 2(4) of the Charter.

A. The Absence of Consecration of a Right of Humanitarian Intervention before 1990

We shall envisage below what might be considered the most relevant precedents in chronological order but beginning by those that involve the right of humanitarian intervention in the broad sense and then look at the more specific question of the protection of nationals.

The Absence of Acceptance of a Right of Humanitarian Intervention in State Practice

We shall consider in turn the cases of Biafra (1968–1970), Bangladesh (1970), Cambodia (1978–1979), Uganda (1979), the Central African Republic (1979) and Nicaragua (1981–1990).[239] It will be observed that for each of these precedents the right of humanitarian intervention was not invoked by States, including the intervening States. Intervening States referred rather to classical legal arguments such as self-defence or the consent of the States in whose territory the military operation was conducted. It is somewhat contestable, though, to claim that the line of argument advanced by the intervening States, whatever its content, was accepted by the international community of States as a whole.

The Biafran precedent is a good illustration of the state of positive international law prevailing at the time.[240] This secessionist conflict claimed

---

[236] CF Amerasinghe, 'The Conundrum of Recourse to Force—to Protect Persons', above n 19, 37–341.

[237] Concerning cases prior to 1945, see S Chesterman, *Just War or Just Peace? Humanitarian Intervention and International Law*, above n 25, 24–44; U Beyerlin, 'Humanitarian Intervention' (1982) 3 *EPIL* 212; I Pogany, 'Humanitarian Intervention in International Law: the French Intervention in Syria Re-Examined' (1986) 35 *ICLQ* 182–90; R Kolb, Ius contra bellum. *Le droit international relatif au Maintien de la paix*, 2nd edn (Bâle, Helbing & Lichtenhahn/ Bruxelles, Bruylant, 2009) 304–05.

[238] O Corten *et al*, *A la recherche du nouvel ordre mondial*, t I (Bruxelles, Complexe, 1993).

[239] See also other cases, eg the intervention in Burundi in 1972: 'La pratique belge en matière de droit international' (1974) 10 *RBDI* 271–72 and 328–32; see also (1975) 11 *RBDI* 326; 'Pratique française du droit international' (1973) 19 *AFDI*.

[240] See also the Suez Crisis, the USA's representative stating that: 'If [. . .] we were to agree that the existence in the world of injustices which this Organization has so far been unable to

several tens of thousands of victims, including many civilians.[241] It is in this context that some asserted they began to defend a right of humanitarian interference, precisely because of the extremely stringent conception of sovereignty that then prevailed.[242] It is on the basis of this principle and on that of non-intervention, that the attempted secession was expressly condemned by the OAU[243] and by the UN Secretary-General,[244] who plainly thought their respective roles should be confined to simple mediation. Only four States recognised the independence of the Republic of Biafra between 1967 and 1970, without for all that evoking a right of military intervention to protect the victims of the conflict.[245] The others did not consider they were authorised to recognise the secessionist entity.[246] The US considered the conflict as purely internal to Nigeria.[247] The UK proclaimed its neutrality while continuing to supply arms to the government authorities, as did the Soviet Union.[248] France seemed to recognise the situation as one where the right of people to self-determination applied and it evoked a 'genocide'[249] but contemplated nothing other than diplomatic action and a suspension of arms shipments rather than military action.[250] The position of the Belgian foreign minister is fairly typical of the legal conviction of States at the time: the Security Council could not be seized by its own motion of what was supposedly an internal affair within the meaning of article 2(7) of the Charter.[251]

Conversely no State invoked a right of humanitarian intervention either indirectly or implicitly. Humanitarian aid was provided in part through the ICRC, always in cooperation with the authorities in Lagos.[252] In short, Biafra's failed secession testifies to a singularly narrow interpretation of the

cure means that the principle of the renunciation of force should no longer be respected, [. . .] then I fear that we should be tearing this Charter to Shreds' (1956, UNGA, 1st Emergency Special Session 652nd meeting, 23, quoted in TJ Farer, 'Humanitarian Intervention before and after 9/11: legality and legitimacy' in JL Holzgrefe and RO Keohane (eds), *Humanitarian Intervention. Ethical, Legal and Political Dilemmas*, (Cambridge, Cambridge University Press, 2003) 60–61.

[241] C Rousseau, 'Chronique des faits internationaux' (1968) 72 *RGDIP* 228–31; see also P Mertens, 'Les modalités d'intervention du Comité international de la Croix-Rouge dans le conflit du Nigéria' (1969) 15 *AFDI* 183–209.

[242] B Kouchner, *Le malheur des autres* (Paris, Odile Jacob, 1991); M Bettati and B Kouchner (eds), *Le devoir d'ingérence*, (Paris, Denoël, 1987).

[243] See the texts in J Salmon, *La reconnaissance d'Etat. Quatre cas: Mandchoukouo, Katanga, Biafra, Rhodésie du sud*, (Paris, Armand Colin, 1971) 161–62.

[244] ibid, 168–69.

[245] ibid, 163–64 and 192–94.

[246] C Rousseau, 'Chronique des faits internationaux' (1969) 73 *RGDIP* 193.

[247] C Rousseau, 'Chronique des faits internationaux' (1968) 72 *RGDIP* 233.

[248] ibid, 233–34.

[249] See also: F Wodie, 'La sécession du Biafra et le droit international public' (1969) 73 *RGDIP* 1029–32.

[250] 'Pratique française du droit international' (1970) 16 *AFDI* 945–47.

[251] 'La pratique belge en matière de relations internationales' (1971) 7 *RBDI* 271; see also (1970) 6 *RBDI* 595–97; (1972) 8 *RBDI* 284–86; (1973) 9 *RBDI* 279–80.

[252] C Rousseau, 'Chronique des faits internationaux' (1969) 73 *RGDIP* 196–97.

UN Charter that supposedly prevents not just States but also the Security Council from intervening in an internal conflict, even in the event of grave breaches of human rights.

Although it was ultimately successful, the secession of Bangladesh does not give rise to a different conclusion in terms of a hypothetical right of humanitarian intervention.[253] First because India, which conducted a military action in December 1971 against Pakistan, did not clearly claim such a right.[254] While referring to the dramatic humanitarian situation that characterised the crisis,[255] in strictly legal terms the Indian authorities resorted to the classical argument of self-defence. The declaration by India's representative on the Security Council is highly instructive in this respect:

> We did it because we had no option. The Pakistan Army puts its cannons on the frontier and started shelling our civilian villages . . . But after having killed their own people they now turn their guns on us. Eight hundred and ninety complaints of border violations have been made to Pakistan since 25 March. What was the response to these? They rejected them all. They continued to shell our villages, kill our civilians. What was the remedy left to us? . . . We decided to silence their guns, to save our civilians . . . We have suffered at the hands of Pakistan four aggressions, and we are not going to take it any more . . .[256]

Likewise the Indian prime minister had declared on the day the intervention was launched that there was no other choice than to 'face up to the aggression'.[257] In view of these stands and of other declarations of Indian representatives it is clear that it is not the right to rescue war victims alone that was invoked as a legal basis to justify the intervention.[258] In any event, and this is a second decisive factor, no *opinio juris* of the international community

---

[253] See: *Keesing's Contemporary Archives*, 1972, 25053–58; C Rousseau, 'Chronique des faits internationaux' (1972) 76 *RGDIP* 538–47; *Yearbook of the UN*, 1971, 143–46.

[254] According to M Akehurst, India had 'realized that humanitarian intervention was an insufficient justification for the use of force'; 'Humanitarian Intervention' in Hedley Bull (ed), *Intervention in World Politics* (Oxford, Clarendon Press, 1984) 96; see also SA Alexandrov, *Self-Defense Against the Use of Force in International Law* (The Hague/London/Boston, Kluwer, 1996) 208; VS Mani, ' "Humanitarian" Intervention Today', above n 31, 237, fn 281 and 'The 1971 War on the Indian Sub-Continent and International Law' (1972) 12 *Indian Journal of International Law* 83–99; *contra* F Teson, *Humanitarian Intervention. An Inquiry into Law and Morality*, 2nd edn, above n 4, 200–10.

[255] S/PV.1606, 4 December 1971, 17, para 175; see also C Alibert, *Du droit de se faire justice dans la société internationale depuis 1945* (Paris, LGDJ, 1983) 287–91.

[256] S/PV.1606, 4 December 1971, 15, para 163 and 17, para 175; AG, A/PV.2003, 7 December, para 169. India refers to a 'refugee aggression'; S/PV.1606, 4 December 1971, paras 160–61; see also AG, A/PV.2003, 7 December, paras 165–205.

[257] Our translation; C Rousseau, 'Chronique des faits internationaux' (1972) 76 *RGDIP* 547.

[258] LA Sicilianos, *Les réactions décentralisées à l'illicite. Des contre-mesures à la légitime défense* (Paris, LGDJ, 1990) 486; see also N Ronzitti, *Rescuing Nationals Abroad Through Military Coercion and Intervention on Grounds of Humanity*, above n 24, 96–97; W Verwey, 'Humanitarian Intervention' in A Cassese (ed), *The Current Legal Regulation of the Use of Force* (Dordrecht, Martinus Nijhoff, 1986) 63.

of States as a whole in favour of such a right can be established,[259] far from it. The few States that supported India did not do so by taking up this argument,[260] and above all a large number of States condemned India's military intervention.[261] Pakistan itself replied legally to India on the basis of self-defence, claiming that it had only taken 'all reasonable and adequate steps' to end subversive or terrorist acts by irregular groups organised by India.[262] Several States characterised the Indian action as an aggression contrary to international law,[263] with some insisting on the need to respect Pakistan's territorial integrity however serious the internal situation.[264] In the end, the General Assembly adopted a resolution calling for the withdrawal of the armed forces of both States within their own borders, pursuant to the UN Charter and its article 2(4), which plainly did not evolve during this crisis.[265]

The dismissal of the notion of the right of humanitarian intervention is clearer still in the case of Vietnam's military intervention in Cambodia in December 1978.[266] Even though the Khmer Rouge regime was responsible for very many deaths, the Vietnamese authorities justified their intervention by the argument of self-defence, claiming it had merely repelled

> the border war started by the Pol Pot-Ieng Sary clique against Viet Nam . . . The Pol Pot-Ieng Sary clique strove to intensify the war against Viet Nam. Of the 23 divisions which the Kampuchean Army had at the time, the Pol Pot-Ieng Sary clique massed 19 on the border between Viet Nam and Kampuchea . . . Like any other country in a similar situation, Viet Nam is determined to exercise its right of

---

[259] S Chesterman, *Just War or Just Peace? Humanitarian Intervention and International Law*, above n 25, 73 (and n 202); SD Murphy, *Humanitarian Intervention. The United Nations in an Evolving World Order*, above n 1, 98–100; T Franck, *Recourse to Force. State Action Against Threats and Armed Attacks*, (Cambridge, Cambridge University Press, 2002) 140–43; T Franck, 'Interpretation and Change in the law of humanitarian intervention' in JL Holzgrefe and Robert O Keohane (eds), *Humanitarian Intervention. Ethical, Legal and Political Dilemmas* (Cambridge, Cambridge University Press, 2003) 216–17; T Franck and N Rodley, 'After Bangladesh: The Law of Humanitarian Intervention by Military Force' (1973) 67 *AJIL* 297; N Ronzitti, *Rescuing Nationals Abroad Through Military Coercion and Intervention on Grounds of Humanity*, above n 24, 97; M Akehurst, 'Humanitarian Intervention', above n 24, 96–97.

[260] See, eg: USSR, S/PV.1606, 4 December 1971, 25–26, paras 267–68.

[261] See also: AM Weisburd, *Use of Force. The Practice of States Since World War II* (Pennsylvania, Pennsylvania Univ Press, 1997) 149.

[262] S/PV.1606, 4 December 1971, 9, para 99.

[263] China (S/PV.1606, 4 December 1971, 23, para 241 and AG/PV.2003, 7 December 1971, paras 311 and 324), and Albania (ibid, para 115).

[264] Jordan (AG/PV.2003, 7 December 1971, para 141), Sweden (ibid, para 302), Togo (ibid, para 202; see also para 204), Mauritania (ibid, para 307); see also USA (S/PV.1606, 4 December 1971, 18–19, para 194), France ('Pratique française du droit international' (1972) 18 *AFDI* 1027), Belgium ('La pratique belge en matière de droit international' (1973) 9 *RBDI* 279–80; see also ibid, 248–49), (1974) 10 *RBDI*, 1974, 237–38; see also GA, 2002nd and 2003rd meetings (LA Sicilianos, *Les réactions décentralisées à l'illicite. Des contre-mesures à la légitime défense*, above n 258, 587, n 299).

[265] GA Res 2793 (XXVI) of 7 December 1971 (104-11-10); O Schachter, 'General Course in Public International Law', (1982) 178 *RCADI* 144 and CF Amerasinghe, 'The Conundrum of Recourse to Force—to Protect Persons', above n 19, 31.

[266] *Keesing's Contemporary Archives*, 1979, 29613–21; C Alibert, *Du droit de se faire justice dans la société internationale depuis 1945*, above n 255, 307–10.

legitimate defence recognized by the Charter of the United Nations and by international law to defend its independence, sovereignty and territorial integrity . . . Viet Nam is determined to repel aggression and to punish the aggressors . . .[267]

Vietnam further claimed not to have been involved in the overthrow of the Cambodian government of the time, which was allegedly the work of Cambodian forces acting independently.[268] To this extent, it had supposedly not interfered in another State's internal affairs. It cannot be said that this argument won over the international community of States as a whole, since a large majority of UN Member States, on the contrary, condemned the Vietnamese military intervention.[269] Only a few Socialist Bloc States supported Vietnam but none justified the intervention by a right of humanitarian intervention, even if the violations of human rights by the Khmer Rouge government were occasionally mentioned.[270] It is particularly significant in this respect that although it had not been evoked, the argument of a right of humanitarian intervention was explicitly rejected by several States as is evidenced by these declarations by France, Norway, Australia and the UK, respectively, the latter speaking for the ten EC Member States:

—The notion that because a régime is detestable foreign intervention is justifiable and forcible overthrow is legitimate is extremely dangerous. That could ultimately jeopardize the very maintenance of international law and order and make the continued existence of various régimes dependent on the judgement of their neighbours;[271]

—The Norwegian Government and public opinion in Norway have expressed strong objections to the serious violations of human rights committed by the Pol Pot régime. However, the domestic policies of that Government cannot—we repeat, cannot— justify the actions of Viet Nam over the last days and weeks;[272]

—Like other Governments, we cannot accept that the internal policies of any Government, no matter how reprehensible, can justify a military attack upon it by another Government;[273]

—The history and record of that Pol Pot regime is no justification, in our view, for invasion and occupation.[274]

---

[267] S/PV.2108, 11 January 1979, 12, paras 115 and 120, and at 13, para 126; see also *Keesing's Contemporary Archives*, 1979, 29613.

[268] S/PV.2108, 11 January 1979, 13–14, paras 130–36.

[269] See, eg: *Joint Statement of the special meeting of the ASEAN Foreign Ministers held on 12–13 January 1979 in Bangkok*, S/13025, 12 January 1979.

[270] USSR (S/PV.2108, 11 January 1979, 2, paras 10 and 14, para 146 *ff*), Czechoslovakia (ibid, 3, para 26 *ff*), GDR (S/PV.2109, 12 January 1979, 7–8, para 66 *ff*), Hungary (ibid, 9, para 81 *ff*), Poland (S/PV.2111, 15 January 1979, 8, para 78 *ff*), Bulgaria (ibid, 10, para 109 *ff*).

[271] S/PV.2109, 12 January 1979, 4, para 36.

[272] S/PV.2109, 12 January 1979, 2, para 18.

[273] S/PV.2111, 15 January 1979, 3, para 25.

[274] 'United Kingdom Materials on International Law' (1981) 52 *BYBIL* 375; see also 'United Kingdom Materials on International Law' (1987) 58 *BYBIL* 629–30 and S/PV.2110, 13 January 1979, para 65.

And so a large majority of States condemned the Vietnamese intervention,[275] leading the General Assembly to adopt resolutions calling for the withdrawal of foreign forces from Cambodia.[276] Clearly this is a precedent that very sharply called into question any idea of a right of humanitarian intervention.[277]

In this context it seems problematic to claim, at the same time, that States supposedly recognised this right at the time of Tanzania's military intervention in Uganda in February 1979 resulting in the overthrow of the regime of president Idi Amin Dada.[278] Once again it must be noted that it is not violations of human rights that were invoked as the legal ground for intervention but self-defence.[279] For the Tanzanian government 'The war between Tanzania and Idi Amin's regime in Uganda was caused by the Ugandan army's aggression against Tanzania and Idi Amin's claim to have annexed part of Tanzanian territory. There was no other cause for it'.[280]

It is true, as some commentators have pointed out,[281] that this action was not condemned either within the UN or the OAU. This complacent attitude cannot be interpreted, though, as a general acceptance of a right of humanitarian intervention that was not invoked by any official authority, the debates having focused rather on the responsibility of one or other State in

---

[275] China (S/PV.2108, 11 January 1979, 10, para 100), Kuwait (S/PV.2109, 12 January 1979, 2, paras 8–9), USA (S/PV.2110, 13 January 1979, 6–7, paras 74–76), Portugal (ibid, 3, para 29), Yugoslavia (S/PV.2111, 15 January 1979, 12, para 132), Japan (ibid, 2, para 18), Belgium ('La pratique belge en matière de droit international' (1986) 19 *RBDI* 155), Netherlands ('Netherlands State Practice' (1980) 12 *NYIL* 254).

[276] GA Res 34/22 of 14 November 1979, 35/6 of 22 October 1980, 36/5 of 21 October 1981, 37/6 of 28 October 1982; see also EC's position in 'La pratique belge en matière de droit international' (1981–1982) 16 *RBDI* 717–18.

[277] LA Sicilianos, *Les réactions décentralisées à l'illicite. Des contre-mesures à la légitime défense*, above n 258, 489; see also S Chesterman, *Just War or Just Peace? Humanitarian Intervention and International Law*, above n 25, 79–81; T Franck, *Recourse to Force. State Action Against Threats and Armed Attacks*, above n 259, 145–51; N Ronzitti, *Rescuing Nationals Abroad Through Military Coercion and Intervention on Grounds of Humanity*, above n 24, 98–101; M Akehurst, 'Humanitarian Intervention', above n 24, 97–98; SD Murphy, *Humanitarian Intervention. The United Nations in an Evolving World Order*, above n 1, 103–04; A Clark Arend and RJ Beck, *International Law and the Use of Force* (London and New York, Routledge, 1993) 121–23; AM Weisburd, *Use of Force. The Practice of States Since World War II*, above n 261, 42–44; R Kolb, 'Note on humanitarian intervention' (2003) 85/849 *IRRC* 125.

[278] *Keesing's Contemporary Archives*, 1979, 29669–74.

[279] WD Verwey, 'Humanitarian Intervention', above n 27, 61; see also A Tanca, *Foreign Armed Intervention in Internal Conflict* (Dordrecht/Boston/London, Martinus Nijhoff, 1993) 174–75; SD Murphy, *Humanitarian Intervention. The United Nations in an Evolving World Order*, above n 1, 105–07; A Clark Arend and RJ Beck, *International Law and the Use of Force*, above n 277, 125.

[280] (1979) 16 *Africa Research Bulletin (Political, Social and Cultural Series)* 5328, quoted in LA Sicilianos, *Les réactions décentralisées à l'illicite. Des contre-mesures à la légitime défense*, above n 258, 490; see also *Keesing's Contemporary Archives*, 1979, 29669–71.

[281] F Teson, *Humanitarian Intervention. An Inquiry into Law and Morality*, 2nd edn, above n 4, 179–95 and 185–87; T Franck, 'Interpretation and Change in the law of humanitarian intervention', above n 259, 219–20; CF Amerasinghe, 'The Conundrum of Recourse to Force—to Protect Persons', above n 19, 32.

the outbreak of the conflict.[282] It can be understood rather as a sign of the difficulty in determining which of the two States was first to resort to force against the other.[283]

No general acceptance of a right of humanitarian intervention can be deduced either from the case of French military intervention in the Central African Republic in September 1979.[284] As already pointed out[285] this action was presented as a response to a call from the authorities of the Central African Republic[286] and therefore an action legally based on the State's consent and not on some hypothetical right of humanitarian intervention. While criticised by a few States, the French military intervention prompted few reactions.[287] In any event, it would be excessive, to say the least, to see in it any agreement by the international community of States as a whole as to a new interpretation or revision of article 2(4) of the UN Charter.[288]

We shall end this short review by recalling the precedent of the US intervention in Nicaragua in the 1980s. While denouncing the Sandinista regime as a 'totalitarian Communist dictatorship' guilty of numerous human rights violations, the US justified its action in law not on the strength of a right of humanitarian or democratic intervention but on the ground of self-defence.[289] This argument did not convince either the majority of UN Member States, or the International Court of Justice, which noted in a famous *obiter dictum* on respect for human rights that 'the use of force could not be the appropriate method to monitor or ensure such respect'.[290]

---

[282] *Keesing's Contemporary Archives*, 1979, 29669; see SA Alexandrov, *Self-Defense Against the Use of Force in International Law*, above n 258, 210–12; S Chesterman, *Just War or Just Peace? Humanitarian Intervention and International Law*, above n 25, 77–79 and AM Weisburd, *Use of Force. The Practice of States Since World War II*, above n 261, 40–42.

[283] M Akehurst, 'Humanitarian Intervention', above n 24, 98–99; see also 'La pratique belge en matière de droit international' (1978–1979) 14 *RBDI* 586–97; (1981–1982) 16 *RBDI* 665–66.

[284] *Keesing's Contemporary Archives*, 1979, 29933–35.

[285] Above, ch 5, s I.

[286] 'Pratique française du droit international' (1979) 25 *AFDI* 909–10.

[287] LA Sicilianos, *Les réactions décentralisées à l'illicite. Des contre-mesures à la légitime défense*, above n 258, 491; AM Weisburd, *Use of Force. The Practice of States Since World War II*, above n 261, 227.

[288] M Akehurst, 'Humanitarian Intervention', above n 24, 98; A Clark Arend and RJ Beck, *International Law and the Use of Force*, above n 277, 126; S Chesterman, *Just War or Just Peace? Humanitarian Intervention and International Law*, above n 25, 81–82; C Alibert, *Du droit de se faire justice dans la société internationale depuis 1945*, above n 255, 264–67; *contra*: SD Murphy, *Humanitarian Intervention. The United Nations in an Evolving World Order*, above n 1, 108; see also F Teson, *Humanitarian Intervention. An Inquiry into Law and Morality*, 2nd edn, above n 4, 196–200; CF Amerasinghe, 'The Conundrum of Recourse to Force—to Protect Persons', above n 19, 32–33.

[289] See ICJ, *Military and Paramilitary Activities*, ICJ Rep (1986) 70, para 126 and S/PV.2525, 30 March 1984, para 81.

[290] ICJ, *Military and Paramilitary Activities*, ICJ Rep (1986) 134, para 268; see also 133, para 263 and SD Murphy, *Humanitarian Intervention. The United Nations in an Evolving World Order*, above n 1, 129–30; NS Rodley, 'Human Rights and Humanitarian Intervention: the

A review of precedents characteristic of the Cold War clearly show that States remain attached to a classical conception by which violations of human rights cannot justify military actions from outside.[291] Initially, as observed in the case of Biafra, this conception seemed even to be opposed to any stance or action being taken by the UN itself.[292] As observed previously, it was only in the 1990s that States as a whole admitted an extended competence of the Security Council to deal with situations that had formerly been considered as purely internal, including by authorising an outside military intervention.[293] *A fortiori*, no unilateral right of action was accepted, nor called for, before the 1990s,[294] a conclusion that might be extended to the specific case of the protection of foreign nationals.

The Absence of Acceptance of a Right of Intervention in Favour of Nationals in State Practice

I know of no precedent in which a right of intervention in favour of nationals has been invoked in itself and autonomously outside of any connection with a classical legal ground. The Suez Crisis has sometimes been mentioned.[295] Upon examination it turns out, though, that the protection of nationals was barely evoked in the Security Council,[296] the main argument of the UK and France relating to 'provisional' or 'preventive' measures in the interest of maintaining peace[297] and adopted to protect their 'vital interests'[298] while self-defence was also evoked.[299] It is interesting too to observe that the two States claimed that because of the lawful character of the objectives officially pursued they were not infringing the sovereignty or territor-

---

Case Law of the World Court' (1989) 38 *ICLQ* 327–28 and 331–32; F Teson, 'Le peuple, c'est moi! The World Court and Human Rights' (1987) 81 *AJIL* 123–83 and *Humanitarian Intervention. An Inquiry into Law and Morality*, 2nd edn, above n 4, 267–312.

[291] As M Byers and S Chesterman wrote, 'the history of the second half of the 20th century is one of non-intervention for humanitarian purposes'; 'Changing the rules about rules? Unilateral humanitarian intervention and the future of international law' in JL Holzgrefe and Robert O Keohane (eds), *Humanitarian Intervention. Ethical, Legal and Political Dilemmas* (Cambridge, Cambridge University Press, 2003) 183; see also WD Verwey, 'Humanitarian Intervention under International Law' (1985) 32 *NILR* 405 and TD Gill, 'Humanitarian Intervention: Legality, Justice and Legitimacy', above n 25, 59–60.

[292] See also another example in 'Pratique française du droit international' (1990) 36 *AFDI* 1056–58.

[293] Above, ch 6, s I.

[294] See: X Pacreau, *De l'intervention au Kosovo en 1999 à l'intervention en Irak de 2003*, above n 25, 146–47.

[295] MM Whiteman (ed), *Digest of International Law*, vol 12 (Washington, Department of State Pub, 1971) 200–03.

[296] S/PV.749, 30 October 1956, para 141; cp S/PV.751, 31 October 1956, paras 45 and 63.

[297] Above, ch 6, s II.

[298] See: R Higgins, 'The Legal Limits to the Use of Force by Sovereign States. United Nations Practice' (1961) 37 *BYBIL* 315.

[299] G Marchton, 'Armed Intervention in the 1956 Suez Canal Crisis: The Legal Advice tendered to the British Government' (1988) *ICLQ* 777 *ff*.

ial integrity of Egypt.[300] At any rate, their argument plainly did not convince the international community of States as a whole.[301]

This absence of any mention of a right of military intervention to protect nationals explains why all of the precedents generally cited in this area have already been examined in other chapters of this book. Here we shall simply recall three hypotheses.

—As a first hypothesis, the protection of nationals has been invoked only in relation to the consent of the government of the State in whose territory the litigious military operation took place.[302] In the case of Lebanon in 1958 the US based its argument essentially on this justification,[303] which it adopted again in 1965 when intervening in the Dominican Republic.[304] Belgium did likewise in the case of the Congo in 1964[305] as in 1978.[306] The Belgian argument made out in 1960 was more ambiguous but it was pointed out that it consisted mainly in a reference to a treaty by which the young Congolese State is said to have accepted Belgian military action.[307] France too invoked the consent of the local authorities in justifying actions to protect its nationals in Mauritania, Zaire and Chad in the 1970s[308] and in Gabon in May 1990.[309]

—A second situation is where the intervening State justifies its action to protect its nationals on the ground of self-defence.[310] This is what Israel claimed at the time of the Entebbe raid in 1976,[311] and the US claimed first in 1980 in the failed military operation in Iran,[312] and then in 1989 when it invaded Panama.[313]

[300] UK; S/PV.750, 30 October 1956, para 67; S/PV.751, 31 October 1956, para 50.

[301] See above, ch 2, s II and ch 6, s II.

[302] See above, ch 5, and RJ Zedalis, 'Protection of Nationals Abroad: Is Consent the Basis of Legal Obligation?' (1990) 25 *Texas IL Journal* 209 ff.

[303] See the USA's position; S/PV.827, 15 July 1958, para 43; see also para 44 and paras 34–35.

[304] *Letter dated 29 April addressed to the President of the Security Council*, S/6310, 29 April 1965; S/PV.1196, 3 May 1965, paras 67–68); see also CG Fenwick, 'The Dominican Crisis: Intervention or Collective Self-Defense' (1966) 60 *AJIL* 64; RT Bohan, 'The Dominican Case: Unilateral Intervention' (1966) 60 *AJIL* 809–10.

[305] *Letter dated 21 November 1964 addressed to the President of the Security Council by the representative of Belgium*, S/6055, 22 November 1964; *Letter dated 24 November 1964, addressed to the President of the Security Council by the representative of the USA*, S/6062, 24 November 1964, annex I.

[306] 'La pratique belge en matière de droit international' (1969) 5 *RBDI* 636; (1980) 15 *RBDI* 632; see also C Alibert, *Du droit de se faire justice dans la société internationale depuis 1945*, above n 255, 253–59.

[307] Above, ch 2, s I.

[308] 'Pratique française du droit international' (1978) 24 *AFDI* 1085–93; A Manin, 'L'intervention française au Shaba' (1978) 24 *AFDI* 166.

[309] 'Pratique française du droit international' (1990) 36 *AFDI* 1058.

[310] CF Amerasinghe, 'The Conundrum of Recourse to Force—to Protect Persons', above n 19, 19–22 and above, ch 7.

[311] S/PV.1939, 9 July 1976, para 115.

[312] *Letter addressed to the President of the Security Council by the representative of the USA*, S/13908, 25 April 1980, and ch 4, s II.

[313] See: VA Nanda, 'The Validity of United States Intervention in Panama under

—A third option is to rely on an action conducted in the name of collective security, pursuant to Chapter VIII of the Charter. This is how the US and its allies justified the 1983 military action in Grenada.[314]

In each of these cases, the protection of nationals was not a self-standing legal basis for justifying a military intervention.[315] The relevant legal basis is as such much more classical, even if the arguments of consent of the State, of self-defence or of collective security are very broadly interpreted for the purposes of covering the military operation under consideration.

In any event, we have already pointed out that none of the arguments made out to legitimate the aforecited military intervention was accepted by the international community of States as a whole. Generally most of these precedents brought reprobation from most States, whether the Congo, Entebbe, Grenada or Panama.[316] More specifically I have found records of few stances in favour of a distinctive right of military intervention intended to protect nationals.[317] By contrast several States have insisted on condemning this doctrine even though it was not clearly relied upon by the intervening States.[318]

Practice seems, then, to confirm that outside of assumptions that supposedly come within the scope of justifications admitted for the use of force, the protection of nationals is not considered an appropriate basis for justifying a military intervention.[319] While certain claims have sometimes been made along these lines, they have not been accepted by States as a whole.[320] Here too, we have not departed from the ordinary meaning of the terms of

International Law' (1990) 84 *AJIL* 494 *ff*; see also TJ Farer ('Panama: Beyond the Charter Paradigm' (1990) 84 *AJIL* 505 *ff*) and A D'Amato ('The Invasion of Panama Was a Lawful Response to Tyranny' (1990) 84 *AJIL* 516–24).

[314] S/PV.2487, 25 October 1983, 22, paras 191–93; see also F Teson, *Humanitarian Intervention. An Inquiry into Law and Morality*, 2nd edn, above n 4, 210–21 and L Doswald-Beck, 'The Legality of the United States Intervention in Grenada' (1984) 31 *NILR* 360–66.

[315] 'Is Intervention ever justified?', in 'United Kingdom Materials on International Law' (1986) 57 *BYBIL* 617–18; (1993) 64 *BYBIL* 732; see also T Meron, *The Humanization of International Law* (Leiden/Boston, Marinus Nijhoff, 2006) 517; A Tanca, *Foreign Armed Intervention in Internal Conflict*, above n 279, 120; SD Murphy, *Humanitarian Intervention. The United Nations in an Evolving World Order*, above n 1, 92–94, 109–11 and 112–15; I Brownlie, 'General Course of Public International Law' (1995) 255 *RCADI* 203; 'The UN Charter and the Use of Force, 1945–1985' in A Cassese (ed), *The Current Legal Regulation of the Use of Force* (Dordrecht, Martinus Nijhoff, 1986) 497; 'The Principle of Non-Use of Force in Contemporary International Law' in WE Butler (ed), *The Non-Use of Force in International Law* (Dordrecht, Kluwer, 1989) 23–24.

[316] See above and WD Verwey, 'Humanitarian Intervention', above n 27, 62.

[317] See: France (S/PV.873, 13 July 1960, para 144 and 'Pratique française du droit international' (1960) 6 *AFDI* 1070) and UK (in M Akehurst, 'Humanitarian Intervention', above n 24, 100).

[318] USSR (S/PV.830, 16 July 1958, para 16), UAR (S/PV.831, 17 July 1958, para 110), Tunisia (S/PV.878, 21 July 1960, para 23), and Nigeria (S/PV.1176, 15 December 1964, para 7).

[319] LA Sicilianos, *Les réactions décentralisées à l'illicite. Des contre-mesures à la légitime défense*, above n 258, 458–62.

[320] M Akehurst, 'Humanitarian Intervention', above n 24, 103–04.

article 2(4) of the UN Charter, which, we have seen, opposed such a possibility.[321] This behaviour was not to change fundamentally after the end of the Cold War despite the changes wrought by the advent of what has been called a 'New World Order'.

B. The Absence of Consecration of a Right of Humanitarian Intervention since 1990

In the idealistic outlook that broadly characterised the end of the Second Gulf War, the US President affirmed he could see emerging 'a new world order, a world where the rule of law, not the law of the jungle, governs the conduct of nations', a new order in which human rights were also to be guaranteed.[322] It was in this context that calls for the emergence of a 'right of humanitarian interference' developed. It shall be seen that in legal terms these calls were not consecrated by practice, whether for humanitarian intervention in general or in the specific case of protection of nationals.

The Continuing Absence of an 'Right of Humanitarian Intervention' in State Practice

Since 1990 there have been many precedents of military operations conducted essentially in the context of internal conflicts formally motivated by humanitarian considerations. In this sense, humanitarian intervention has without contest taken on a new dimension compared with the Cold War years. Legally, the advent of a *right* of intervention would presuppose, however, showing that this practice is accompanied by reference to a distinctive legal basis that has been accepted by the international community of States as a whole.[323] Such a demonstration has proved troublesome in view of the stances taken by States that have consisted essentially in debating the existence of a clear (a) or presumed (b) authorisation from the Security Council to use force, with State consent or self-defence being used occasionally (c).

a) The Reference to Clear Authorisation From the Security Council to Justify a Humanitarian Intervention

As indicated earlier, the 1990s saw the development of Security Council activity in the domain of maintaining international peace and security. It was observed in particular that the Security Council relied on a broad

---

[321] Above, s I.

[322] G Bush, 'Operation Desert Storm Launched', Address to the Nation from the White House, 16 January 1991, *US Department of State Dispatch* (21 January 1991), 38 (findarticles.com); see also *Déclaration du gouvernement français*, 19 March 1991; 'Pratique française du droit international' (1991) 37 *AFDI* 1011 and 1022, and P Herman, 'Le monde selon Bush: genèse d'un nouvel ordre mondial' in O Corten *et al*, *A la recherche du nouvel ordre mondial*, t I (Bruxelles, Complexe, 1993) 16.

[323] Above, ch 1, s II.

interpretation of the notion of threat to peace to intervene frequently in internal conflicts.[324] This interpretation of the Charter was quite broadly accepted by States provided certain conditions, that we shall not go over again here, were observed. It will be recalled, however, that humanitarian grounds were used to characterise certain threats to peace and to assign specific objectives to military operations, especially in Somalia, Bosnia-Herzegovina and Rwanda.[325] These three precedents, when a codification of a right of inference[326] was sometimes invoked, testify in fact to the possibility of conducting humanitarian interventions in the context of a classical justification of a use of force: Security Council authorisation under Chapter VII of the UN Charter.[327] *A contrario*, it would be going too far to deduce from this a possibility of using force in the absence of any such authorisation. The same is true of further precedents such as the military operations in East Timor in 1999 or in the Côte d'Ivoire in 2003, again on the basis of Security Council resolutions.[328]

It will be noticed that when the intervening States were led to justify their action in law, they clearly invoked the entitlement given by the relevant Security Council resolutions, without generally or independently evoking any right of humanitarian intervention. For the case of Somalia, we can cite as particularly characteristic the UK position as expressed by the Foreign Secretary Douglas Hogg in a House of Commons debate on the role of the United Nations in British policy:

> I think the powers under the Charter are perfectly adequate. Although the United Nations is prohibiting in intervening in the internal affairs of Member States, Article 2.7 of the Charter speaks of matters which are 'essentially' internal affairs, and humanitarian matters are, of course, now matters of international concern. The prohibition of interference by the United Nations in internal affairs has also an important exemption: if you take action under Chapter VII, the prohibition does not apply. But to take action under Chapter VII, as is presently being considered by the Council, does require a determination that the situation or the dispute is a threat to international peace and security. In the case of Somalia the Council has already reached that determination some months ago when it imposed an arms embargo because the lack of stability in the country was, of course, a threat to its neighbours, as was the refugee situation.[329]

---

[324] Above, ch 6, s I.

[325] See, eg: SC Res 770 (1992), 794 (1992) and 949 (1994), above, ch 6, s I.

[326] See: O Corten, 'Nouvel ordre international humanitaire ou droit d'ingérence?', above n 49, 159.

[327] O Corten and P Klein, 'L'autorisation de recourir à la force à des fins humanitaires: droit d'ingérence ou retour aux sources?' (1993) 4 *EJIL* 506–33; see also TG Weiss, 'UN Security Forces in Support of Human Values' (1994) *ASIL Proceedings* 329–31.

[328] Above, ch 6, s I and 'Pratique française du droit international' (1999) 45 *AFDI* 895.

[329] 'United Kingdom Materials on International Law' (1992) 63 *BYBIL* 823; see also 'Pratique française du droit international' (1993) 39 *AFDI* 1021; 'Canadian Practice in International Law' (1993) 31 *CYIL* 364–65; (1994) 32 *CYIL* 329.

The French army's operation in Rwanda was justified by a similar line of legal argument. The prime minister of the time spoke out clearly on the issue in the National Assembly:

[This is a] humanitarian operation intended to save threatened populations [and it is subject to a] number of conditions or specific principles governing this humanitarian intervention.

First principle: France will act only with a mandate from the UN Security Council. The Government considered that action of this type, responding to a humanitarian duty, ought despite its urgency to be authorized by the international community.[330]

The NATO bombings of Serb forces in Bosnia-Herzegovina from 1994 to September 1995 were again supported by the Security Council resolutions cited above. On 9 August 1993 the North Atlantic Council approved the possibility of air strikes, confirming that:

NATO's actions take place under the authority of the United Nations Security Council, within the framework of the relevant UNSC resolutions, including UN Security Council resolutions 770, 776 and 836, and in support of UNPROFOR as it carries out its overall mandate.[331]

A few weeks earlier the French foreign minister had evoked possible bombings, insisting on 'saying very solemnly that in any event such a decision would require a formal resolution from the UN Security Council'.[332] The French authorities later took the view that 'the North Atlantic Council's decisions need not be submitted to the Security Council for a fresh decision' since they 'are *clearly and unambiguously* within the ambit of Security Council resolutions 824 and 836 on safe areas'. (emphasis added)[333]

Despite the diversity of the situations involved it will be noted that the statement of the humanitarian objective is accompanied by a mention of a clear legal basis constituted by one or more explicit authorisations previously given by the Security Council.[334] As the declarations cited well

---

[330] Our translation; 'Pratique française du droit international' (1994) 40 *AFDI* 1032; see E Spiry, 'Interventions humanitaires et interventions d'humanité: la pratique française face au droit international' (1998) 102 *RGDIP* 429–30.

[331] Text in: (1993) 19 *DAI* 420–21; see also the decisions taken by the Council authorising recourse to the NATO air strike force to support the action of UNPROFOR, specifically at Sarajevo, of 9 February 1994; text in: (1994) 6 *DAI* 118, and the Declaration on the situation in former Yugoslavia by the North Atlantic Council, of 30 May 1995; text in: (1995) 14 *DAI* 426 (see www.nato.int/).

[332] Our translation; 'Pratique française du droit international' (1993) 39 *AFDI* 1023.

[333] Our translation; 'Pratique française du droit international' (1994) 40 *AFDI* 1039; see also 'Pratique française du droit international' (1995) 41 *AFDI* 942; 'Netherlands State Practice' (1994) 25 *NYIL* 458 and 'Contemporary Practice of the United States' (1994) 88 *AJIL* 522–25.

[334] This does not mean that none of these military actions raises problems of interpretation, especially as regards NATO actions in Yugoslavia; see R Higgins, 'Some Thoughts on the Evolving Relationship Between the Security Council and NATO' in Boutros Boutros-Ghali, *Amicorum Discipulorumque Liber* (Bruxelles, Bruylant, 1998) 523 *ff*.

reflect, the moral concerns are deployed in a legal framework constituted by principles everyone agrees to reaffirm as relevant. One might of course cite other discourses that do not take up this legal justification. But the fundamental thing to point out at this stage is that where a legal argument is raised it refers to a UN Security Council resolution.

The general acceptance of arguments made by the intervening States in the context of these precedents, to which one might add others such as East Timor (1999) or the Côte d'Ivoire (2003), must therefore be clearly understood. What the international community of States as a whole has accepted is the possibility of a humanitarian intervention in an internal conflict under the aegis of the Security Council pursuant to the Charter.[335] This is a marked development compared with the Cold War period where this possibility was used not only for political reasons but also in the name of a very broad conception of the principle of non-intervention that supposedly opposed any outside action in civil wars even by the UN. Such a conception is no longer legally tenable. This does not mean, though, far from it, that States have accepted military operations without any authorisation, and without clear authorisation, from the Security Council.[336]

b) Reference to Presumed Authorisation From the Security Council to Justify Humanitarian Interventions

In chapter six we checked off various precedents in which interventions were legally justified by what was no longer a clear and established but an indirect or presumed Security Council authorisation.[337] We cited military operations in Kurdistan (1991) and against Yugoslavia (1999) and in Iraq (2003).

We shall not go back into the detailed facts and relevant legal positions. However, for each of these precedents a few remarks can be made that confirm that the right of humanitarian intervention is far from having been accepted by States as a whole.

The case of Iraqi Kurdistan does not call for long developments, even if it is sometimes evoked as a precedent underpinning an emerging right of humanitarian intervention.[338] It shall be recalled simply that, with the

---

[335] SD Murphy, *Humanitarian Intervention. The United Nations in an Evolving World Order*, above n 1, 241–42.

[336] C Chinkin, 'The Legality of NATO's Action in the Former Republic of Yugoslavia (FRY) under International Law' (2000) 49 *ICLQ* 919.

[337] Above, ch 6, s II.

[338] N Schrijver, 'Challenges to the Prohibition to Use Force: Does the Straitjacket of Article 2 (4) of the UN Charter Begin to Gall to Much?' in N Blokker and N Schrijver (eds), *The Security Council and the Use of Force. Theory and Reality. A Need for Change?* (Leiden/Boston, Martinus Nijhoff, 2005) 38; see also M Wood, 'Towards New Circumstances in Which the Use of Force May Be Authorized? The Cases of Humanitarian Intervention, Counter-Terrorism and Weapons of Mass Destruction' in ibid, 82; B Roth, 'Bending the Law, breaking it or developing it? The US and the humanitarian use of force in the post-Cold War area' in M Byers and G Nolte (eds), *United States Hegemony and the Foundation of International Law*

exception of the UK,[339] the intervening States preferred to resort to an extremely broad interpretation of Security Council resolution 688 (1991) in claiming to justify their action.[340] This attitude is significant. Whereas in the context of the time it might have been expected that a right of humanitarian intervention should be claimed as characteristic of the 'New World Order', this was not so. The need to be able to rely on Security Council authorisation was not fundamentally challenged.[341]

The case of Kosovo might *a priori* generate more debate since, beyond the deep ambiguity characterising the statements made in justification on this occasion,[342] some intervening States clearly claimed a right of humanitarian intervention without Security Council authorisation.[343] The UK thought that 'In the exceptional circumstances of Kosovo it was considered that the use of force would be justified on the grounds of overwhelming humanitarian necessity, *without Security Council authorisation*'.[344] The Netherlands evoked a right of intervention to prevent 'genocide' or 'to avert

---

(Cambridge, CUAT, 2003) 241; T Franck, 'Interpretation and Change in the law of humanitarian intervention', above n 259, 220; C Greenwood, 'International Law and the NATO Intervention in Kosovo' (2000) 49 *ICLQ* 929–30; R Dumas, 'La France et le droit d'ingérence humanitaire' (1991) 3 *Relations internationales et stratégiques* 57–64.

[339] 'The states taking action in northern Iraq did so in exercise of the customary international law principle of humanitarian intervention' (A Aust, Legal Counsellor, FCO, 'United Kingdom Materials on International Law' (1992) 63 *BYBIL* 827). See C Gray, *International Law and the Use of Force*, 3rd edn, above n 43, 36–37.

[340] SD Murphy, *Humanitarian Intervention. The United Nations in an Evolving World Order*, above n 1, 187–92.

[341] J Currie, 'NATO's Humanitarian Intervention in Kosovo: Making or Breaking International Law?' (1998) 36 *CYIL* 312–13; C Ero and S Long, 'Cases and Criteria: the United Nations in Iraq, Bosnia and Somalia' in R Williamson (ed), *Some Corner of a Foreign Field* (New York, St Martin's Press, 1998) 158–59; A Tanca, *Foreign Armed Intervention in Internal Conflict*, above n 279, 113–14; NE Ghozali, 'Heurts et malheurs du devoir d'ingérence humanitaire' (1991) 3 *Relations internationales et stratégiques* 88–89; TD Gill, 'Humanitarian Intervention: Legality, Justice and Legitimacy', above n 25, 60–61.

[342] L Weerts, 'Droit, politique et morale dans le discours justificatif de l'Union européenne et de l'OTAN: vers une confusion des registres de légitimité' in O Corten and B Delcourt (eds), *Droit, légitimation et politique extérieure. L'Europe et la guerre du Kosovo* (Bruxelles, Bruylant, 2001) 85–122; see also D Kritsiotis, 'The Kosovo Crisis and NATO's application of Armed Force against the Federal Republic of Yugoslavia' (2000) 49 *ICLQ* 340; I Brownlie and CJ Apperley, 'Kosovo Crisis Inquiry: Memorandum on the International Law Aspects', above n 46, 882, para 22; C Gray, *International Law and the Use of Force*, 3rd edn, above n 43, 40.

[343] See: J Currie, 'NATO's Humanitarian Intervention in Kosovo: Making or Breaking International Law?', above n 341, 305; TM Franck, 'What Happens Now? The UN After Iraq' (2003) 97 *AJIL* 615–16; BR Roth, 'Bending the Law, breaking it or developing it? The US and the humanitarian use of force in the post-cold war area', above n 338, 258; R Bermejo Garcia, 'Cuestiones actuales referentes al uso de la fuerza en el Derecho Internacional' (1999) 15 *AnnDI* 64; D Kritsiotis, 'The Kosovo Crisis and NATO's application of Armed Force against the Federal Republic of Yugoslavia', above n 342, 357–58.

[344] 'United Kingdom Materials on International Law' (1998) 69 *BYBIL* 593; see also (1999) 70 *BYBIL* 571–98; (2000) 71 *BYBIL* 640–42, and T Meron, *The Humanization of International Law*, above n 315, 522; D Kritsiotis, 'The Kosovo Crisis and NATO's application of Armed Force against the Federal Republic of Yugoslavia', above n 342, 340–45.

large-scale and massive violation of basic human rights in the framework of a humanitarian emergency situation'.[345] Germany declared over the need to secure authorisation that 'derogation from this principle could only be exceptional: to prevent humanitarian catastrophes and grave violations of human rights, when an immediate intervention is absolutely necessary for humanitarian reasons'.[346] Belgium argued in the International Court of Justice for a 'right of humanitarian interference'.[347] These stances cannot suffice, though, for it to be asserted that we are dealing with a precedent attesting to the emergence of a right of humanitarian intervention[348] for two reasons.

First, it would be overstating things to claim that all intervening States have invariably based their actions on such a right.[349] Some of them, including France, have dismissed it from the outset.[350] Germany itself had asserted before the outbreak of war that 'the use of force, if it becomes the extreme resort, *requires a mandate from the UN* and from international law.' (emphasis added)[351] As observed earlier, a review of the positions of the various Member States of NATO reveals a recurrent desire to refer to a presumed authorisation from the Security Council.[352] In other words, as in the case of Kurdistan, States often prefer to interpret broadly an existing legal basis rather than invoke a new one, a form of behaviour already observed during the Cold War.[353] Moreover, and this is a decisive factor, some intervening States insisted that the case of Kosovo should not be construed as a precedent in legal terms.[354] The declaration of the German foreign

---

[345] 'Netherlands state practice' (2000) 31 *NYIL* 190; see also 198.

[346] Our translation; *DAI*, 1999, doc No 142, 306.

[347] ICJ, *Legality of the Use of Force (Yugoslavia v Belgium)*, Ergec, CR 1999/15, 10 May 1999.

[348] C Gray, 'From Unity to Polarization: International Law and the Use of Force against Iraq' (2002) 13 *EJIL* 13–16; A Peters, 'Le droit d'ingérence et le devoir d'ingérence—Vers une responsabilité de protéger' (2002) 79 *RDIDC* 300–01.

[349] J Stromseth, 'Rethinking humanitarian intervention: the case for incremental change' in JL Holzgrefe and Robert O Keohane (eds), *Humanitarian Intervention. Ethical, Legal and Political Dilemmas* (Cambridge, Cambridge University Press, 2003) 234–40; F Dubuisson, 'La problématique de la légalité de l'opération "Force alliée" contre la Yougoslavie: enjeux et questionnements' in O Corten and B Delcourt (eds), *Droit, légitimation et politique extérieure. L'Europe et la guerre du Kosovo* (Bruxelles, Bruylant, 2001) 174; Y Nouvel, 'La position du Conseil de sécurité face à l'action militaire engagée par l'OTAN et ses Etats membres contre la République fédérale de Yougoslavie' (1999) 45 *AFDI* 301–02. Concerning the UK, see also the *4th Report of the House of Commons Foreign Affairs Committee*, according to which, 'to justify its action the British Government relied not just upon a defence of humanitarian intervention, but a defence of humanitarian intervention in support of the Security Council, if not specifically endorsed by the Security Council' (HC28-I (2000) 49 *ICLQ* 876).

[350] 'Pratique française du droit international', (1998) 44 *AFDI* 738.

[351] Our translation; AFP, 5 November 1999.

[352] Above, ch 6, s II.

[353] F Dubuisson, 'La problématique de la légalité de l'opération "Force alliée" contre la Yougoslavie: enjeux et questionnements', above n 349, 176.

[354] International Commission on Intervention and State Sovereignty *The responsibility to protect* (December 2001), above n 99, para 6.36.

minister in the General Assembly in September 1999 is particularly characteristic in this respect:

> The intervention in Kosovo, which took place in a situation where the Security Council had tied its own hands after all efforts to find a peaceful solution had failed, was intended to provide emergency assistance and, ultimately, to protect the displaced Kosovo Albanians. The unity of the European States and the Western Alliance, as well as various Security Council resolutions, were of crucial significance here. However, this step, which is only justified in this special situation, must not set a precedent for weakening the United Nations Security Council's monopoly on authorizing the use of legal international force. *Nor must it become a licence to use external force under the pretext of humanitarian assistance. This would open the door to the arbitrary use of power and anarchy and throw the world back to the nineteenth century.* (emphasis added)[355]

Similarly, for the Belgian foreign minister:

> We hope that resorting to force without the Council's approval will not constitute a precedent. The world needs an international legal order that prevails over the law of the jungle. In this respect, we all hope that resolution 1244 (1999) signals a return to international legality.[356]

And the French foreign minister stated that 'we French, we have declared it was an exception, this Kosovo matter, and not a precedent'[357] In view of these declarations, it would be excessive to say the least to consider that the States that intervened in Yugoslavia in 1999 intended to promote the emergence of a right of humanitarian intervention.

Next and in any event we have already observed that the military operation against Yugoslavia had been condemned by a large number of States, including allies of the intervening States.[358] The ICJ itself affirmed that it was 'itself profoundly concerned with the use of force in Yugoslavia, which under the present circumstances raises very serious issues of international law'.[359]

---

[355] A/54/PV.8, 22 September 1999, 12.

[356] A/54/PV.14, 25 September 1999, 17; see also 'La pratique belge en matière de droit international' (2002) 35 *RBDI* 252.

[357] Our translation; Minister of Foreign Affairs, 18 February 2000, *Base documentaire des déclarations françaises depuis 1990*, www.diplomatie.fr; see also M Albright, Secretary of State of the USA in V Lowe, 'International Legal Issues Arising in the Kosovo Crisis' (2000) 49 *ICLQ* 938.

[358] See, eg: the 'Rio Group' declaration, 25 March 1999 (GRIO/SPT-99/10; A/53/884-S/1999/347, 26 March 1999), above, ch 6, s II; see also M Byers and S Chesterman, 'Changing the rules about rules? Unilateral humanitarian intervention and the future of international law', above n 291, 184; M Kohen, 'The Use of Force by the US after the end of the Cold War, and its impact on International Law' in M Byers and G Nolte (eds), *United States Hegemony and the Foundation of International Law* (Cambridge, CUAT, 2003) 219; C Gray, *International Law and the Use of Force*, 3rd edn, above n 43, 47; 'La pratique suisse en matière de droit international public' (2000) 10 *RSDIE* 671.

[359] ICJ, Legality of Use of Force, ICJ Rep 1999, orders of 2 June 1999, (*Yugoslavia v Belgium*), para 17; (*Yugoslavia v Canada*), para 16; (*Yugoslavia v France*), para 16; (*Yugoslavia v Germany*), para 16; (*Yugoslavia v Italy*), para 16; (*Yugoslavia v Netherlands*), para 17; (*Yugoslavia v Portugal*), para 16; (*Yugoslavia v United Kingdom*), para 16; (*Yugoslavia*

The Kosovo precedent was rather a precedent for recalling the need to abide by the UN Charter and especially by the provision of its article 53 making the lawfulness of any enforcement operation by a regional organisation conditional upon it having prior authorisation from the Security Council. We have already set out the stages in the debate on principles within the UN at the instigation of the Secretary-General on the concept of 'responsibility to protect' and observed the near-unanimous maintenance of an orthodox interpretation of the Charter.[360] Historically Kosovo was the first opportunity for States to take up a position as to the possibility of generally recognising a right of humanitarian intervention. And this possibility was very firmly set aside, not only *de lege lata* but also *de lege ferenda*.

Similarly again, it shall be noticed that the overthrow of Saddam Hussein's regime, which was pointed up as being a particularly repressive and criminal one, was not justified by the existence of a right of humanitarian or democratic intervention.[361] As specified, the argument of the US and its allies was to presume a Security Council authorisation on the basis of various existing resolutions.[362] *A contrario*, no State thought that the need to enforce human rights in Iraq could legitimise unilateral military action.[363] Besides, although the argument was not actually invoked, it was dismissed expressly by several States that denounced the war against Iraq.[364] To take just one example, Malaysia's representative declared that:

> The focus in the Council should be on promoting United Nations diplomacy to resolve the problem through effective inspections and weapons destruction, not on legitimizing war against Iraq to effect 'regime change'. Removing the head of State or Government of a sovereign State is illegal and against the Charter, and it must never be a project that has the endorsement of this Council. The provisions of the Charter on this matter are very clear and unambiguous, as has been underscored by many speakers in this debate.[365]

---

v Spain), para 16; (*Yugoslavia v USA*), para 16; see also G Palmisano, 'Determining The Law on the Use of Force: the ICJ and Customary Rules on the Use of Force' in E Cannizzaro and P Palchetti (eds), *Customary International Law On the Use of Force* (Leiden/Boston, Martinus Nijhoff, 2005) 215.

[360] Above, s I.

[361] L Condorelli, 'Vers une reconnaissance d'un droit d'ingérence à l'encontre des 'Etats voyoux'?' in K Bannelier *et al* (eds), *L'intervention en Irak et le droit international* (Paris, Pedone, 2004) 47–48; see also J Brumée and SJ Toope, 'Slouching Towards New "Just" Wars: International Law and the Use of Force After September 11th' (2004) 51 *NILR* 382 and 384–85.

[362] Above, ch 6, s II.

[363] See: S Spiliopoulou Akermark, 'Storms, Foxes and Nebulous Legal Arguments: Twelve Years of Force against Iraq, 1991–2003' (2005) 54 *ICLQ* 222–23.

[364] Iran (S/PV.4625 (Resumption 1), 16 October 2002), Viet Nam (S/PV.4625 (Resumption 2), 17 October 2002), League of Arab States (S/PV.4709, 18 February 2003), India and Zimbabwe (S/PV.4709 (Resumption 1), 19 February 2003), Germany (S/PV.4714, 7 March 2003), South Africa, League of Arab States and Libya (S/PV.4721, 19 March 2003), cp Germany, S/PV.4717 (11 March 2003).

[365] S/PV.4625 (Resumption 2), 17 October 2002, 7.

c) Reference to the Classical Argument of State Consent or Self-Defence to Justify Humanitarian Intervention

At this stage, we can evoke briefly the three precedents already examined above: the military action in Liberia and Sierra Leone by ECOWAS troops and that in Afghanistan by the US and its allies. In each of these instances, humanitarian concerns or concerns for the defence of human rights have not been absent from the justificatory discourse, which is why some commentators cite them in support of the argument for the emergence of a right of humanitarian intervention.[366] In each case, however, it has been seen that the legal argument, insofar as it can be made out, has remained fairly classical in its principle. ECOWAS could rely on the consent of government authorities and present its action as a peace-keeping operation.[367] *A contrario*, no right of humanitarian or democratic intervention justifying military action against the governments in question without Security Council authorisation was invoked.[368] In the case of Afghanistan, it was self-defence that was invoked.[369] However, violations of the rights of man, and of woman, perpetrated by the Taliban regime were not mentioned as relevant legal grounds.[370] In short, even if these precedents raise questions as to the evolution of international law, it is in terms of the interpretation of articles 53 and 51 of the UN Charter and not in terms of the emergence of a right of humanitarian intervention outside of the Charter system.

Finally, the Russian intervention in Georgia, in August 2008, deserves some attention. Justifying this military action, President Medvedev denounced human rights abuses commited by the Georgian government which, according to him, 'opted for genocide to accomplish its political objectives'.[371] Yet, Russia did not invoke any 'right of humanitarian intervention', but rather self-defence under article 51 of the Charter.[372] Commenting on these events in its September 2009 Report, the Independent International Fact-Finding Mission on the Conflict in Georgia stated that, even if Russia had invoked humanitarian objectives:

---

[366] T Franck, 'Interpretation and Change in the Law of Humanitarian Intervention', above n 259, 221–23; C Greenwood, 'International Law and the NATO Intervention in Kosovo', above n 338, 929; J Lewitt, 'The Evolving Intervention Regime in Africa: From Basket Case to Market Place?' (2002) *ASIL Proceedings* 138.

[367] Above, ch 6, s II.

[368] I Brownlie and CJ Apperley, 'Kosovo Crisis Inquiry: Further Memorandum on the International Law Aspects' (2000) 49 *ICLQ* 907–08.

[369] Above, ch 7, s I.

[370] R Falk, 'What Future for the UN Charter System of War Prevention?' (2003) 97 *AJIL* 596–97; M Byers, 'Terrorism, the Use of Force and International Law After 11 September' (2002) 51 *ICLQ* 404–05.

[371] *Statement by President of Russia Dmitry Medvedev*, August 26, 2008, eng.kremlin.ru/speeches/2008/08/26/1543_type82912_205752.shtml.

[372] Letter dated 2008/08/11 from the Permanent Representative of the Russian Federation to the United Nations addressed to the President of the Security Council, S/2008/545, 11 August 2008.

State practice and opinio iuris do not support the claims scholars have made in favour of a rule on humanitarian intervention without a Security Council mandate, and the law has not developed in the direction of the experts' proposals, however morally desirable such a rule might be. The cautious endorsement of the concept of 'responsibility to protect' by international actors barely affected the law on unilateral interventions, because the 'responsibility to protect' was quickly limited to UN-authorized operations. So the potentially emerging international principle of a 'responsibility to protect' only allows humanitarian actions authorized by the Security Council, (if at all).[373]

Ultimately, review of the practice that has developed since the 1990s yields two lessons. First, States as a whole refuse to invoke—and all the more so to accept—a right of humanitarian intervention that might constitute a distinctive and autonomous legal basis for justifying a use of force. Certain precedents in which States refused to intervene without Security Council authorisation could be cited in support of this.[374] As such, a certain continuity can be observed compared with the Cold War period. Second, it seems that certain scope for humanitarian action may be deduced from the use of classical legal grounds: consent from the government involved, Security Council authorisation and, in exceptional cases, actions in self-defence that lead to the overthrow of a government responsible both for an armed attack and for serious violations of human rights. The connection between humanitarian considerations and these legal bases does not seem to be called into question as such with States debating rather the application in each instance of traditionally recognised legal mechanisms. There has unquestionably been an evolution compared with the period before 1990, which we have seen was marked by reluctance as a matter of principle to engage in any outside military action in an internal conflict.

The Persistent Absence of Acceptance of a Right of Intervention in Favour of Their Nationals in State Practice

In this specific domain I know of no precedents to challenge the conclusions we came to in view of the practice that developed during the Cold War. The protection of nationals is invariably invoked in conjunction with some other legal ground when it comes to justifying a use of force. The US invoked self-defence to justify actions that were motivated besides by the protection of its nationals, whether in the military operation against Iraq in June 1993 or the bombings of Sudan and Afghanistan conducted officially in riposte to attacks against the embassies in Kenya and Tanzania.[375] Belgium insisted on the consent of the government in place when it conducted an operation

---

[373] Independent International Fact-Finding Mission on the Conflict in Georgia, *Report*, September 2009 (www.ceiig.ch/Report.html), vol II, 284.
[374] See, eg: 'La pratique belge en matière de droit international' (1997) 30 *RBDI* 285–86.
[375] Above, ch 4, s II.

to evacuate its nationals from Rwanda in 1994.[376] It is worthwhile too recalling the case of rescue in Monrovia in 1990 that illustrates the possibility of conducting a coercive action of such limited scope (both in time and materially, no fighting having occurred) that it was not considered as a use of force within the meaning of article 2(4) of the Charter.[377] This is an exceptional instance insofar as, more often than not, the rescue of nationals is denounced as a pretext for interfering in a conflict alongside one or other of the parties. It must, however, be kept in mind as a possibility that does not come within the field of application of the prohibition of the use of force. *A contrario*, in all cases where there is a genuine use of force, the protection of nationals cannot be considered as a distinctive argument but must be connected up with others such as the consent of the State in question, self-defence or Security Council authorisation.

Close scrutiny of the debates that surrounded the preparation of the Second Gulf War could cast doubt on this conclusion. In the context of debate that preceded the Security Council's adoption of resolution 674 (1990) demanding that Iraq end the hostage-taking of foreign nationals, the US representative affirmed that:

> I want to leave no doubt on this issue. We join the Council in this demand and we urge the Government of Iraq to comply. But I want to underscore one point very clearly. Every nation has the duty to protect its citizens. This is a fundamental obligation. The United States will do that which is necessary to meet its obligations to its own citizens.[378]

Likewise when resolution 678 (1990) was adopted authorising a possible use of force as from 15 January 1991, the French representative stated that

> this undertaking is without prejudice to any and all rights of my Government under the Charter, including its rights in the event the Government of Iraq allows any harm to come to foreign nationals held against their will by that Government.[379]

The same was said by the representatives of the UK,[380] the USSR[381] and the USA.[382] It was not contested, though, by any State. Now, this statement makes it plain that military action would be justified if Iraq were to harm foreign nationals. However, I find it difficult to interpret this precedent as a general acceptance of a right of protection of foreign nationals in the absence of more specific evidence. It will be recalled in this respect that

---

[376] 'La pratique belge en matière de droit international' (1997) 30 RBDI 286. See also the British intervention in Sierra Leone; 'United Kingdom Materials on International Law' (2000) 71 BYBIL 645.

[377] Above, ch 2, s I.

[378] S/PV.2951, 29 October 1990, 91.

[379] S/PV.2963, 29 November 1990, 68.

[380] ibid, 82.

[381] ibid, 96.

[382] ibid, 103.

the States concerned thought that the collective action conducted in the Security Council context had not ended States exercising their right of self-defence.[383] Insofar as these States specify that the resolutions in question would not prevent them from intervening, it may be thought that they contemplate such possible intervention as the exercise of their right of self-defence, should they be the object of an armed attack via an attack against their nationals.[384]

A final precedent is worth mentioning.[385] In August 2008, Russia intervened militarily in Georgian territory in South Ossetia claiming its right to protect its nationals meaning both its troops stationed on the ground as 'peace-keeping forces' and Georgian civilians to whom Russia had also granted its nationality.[386] Russia thus claimed to be reacting to a genocidal type of military action previously engaged by the Georgian army.[387] However, one cannot consider these events as the sign of recognition of a right to protect nationals. First because Russia did not invoke this right as such but officially relied on a right of self-defence under article 51 of the Charter. Second because in any event its line of argument was criticised by many States, which seemed far from convinced.[388] Likewise, according to the Independent International Fact-Finding Mission on the Conflict in Georgia, 'the protection of one's own nationals does not, according to the prevailing opinion of writers, constitute an autonomous, additional justification for the use of force. There is probably not one single instance in state practice where a state invoked an independent, stand-alone entitlement to rescue its nationals, without relying on one of the classic grounds of justification'.[389]

Once again the episode illustrates the reluctance of the international community of States as a whole to admit the arguments intended to justify military intervention by the protection of nationals.

Conclusion

The question of humanitarian intervention raises awkward question in ethical terms and may give rise to highly problematic situations on the ground that depend on the circumstances of each case. In terms of positive

---

[383] Above, ch 7, s II.

[384] See: 'Pratique française du droit international' (1990) 36 *AFDI* 1043.

[385] See: O Corten, 'Déclarations unilatérales d'indépendance et reconnaissances prématurées: du Kosovo à l'Ossétie du sud et à l'Abkhazie' (2007) 111 *RGDIP* 749–51.

[386] *Letter dated 11 August 2008 addressed to the President of the Security Council by the Permanent Respresentative of Russia*, S/2005/545, 11 August 2008.

[387] S/PV.5969, 28 August 2008, 7. See also above.

[388] S/PV.5952, 8 August 2008; S/PV.5953, 10 August 2008; S/PV.5961, 19 August 2008; S/PV.5969, 28 August 2008, and en.wikipedia.org/wiki/International_reaction_to_the_2008_South_Ossetia_war.

[389] Independent International Fact-Finding Mission on the Conflict in Georgia, *Report*, September 2009 (www.ceiig.ch/Report.html), vol II, 286.

international law, however, it seems that we are faced with a relatively straightforward problem in respect of the many stances taken by a large majority of States, especially since the late twentieth century. The advent of the concept of 'responsibility to protect' has consecrated in the texts the possibility of acting in the humanitarian domain through the Security Council and under its aegis. *A contrario*, any intention to intervene unilaterally has been very clearly dismissed in legal terms. As for the case of action to protect nationals, no trace of it is to be found in the texts, which invariably invoke only collective action or self-defence as possible justifications for the use of force against a State's consent. A review of practice confirms that in almost all precedents States acting militarily for humanitarian reasons or to rescue their nationals do so by relying legally on a classical justification and not on any independent rule conferring a right of intervention. In this respect, it shall be recalled lastly that no circumstance precluding lawfulness may be invoked in the domain of the use of force, even if we are in the presence of a humanitarian type of action. As observed before, at the time of the works of the International Law Commission on international responsibility, the UK had suggested that it might be possible to invoke distress in this type of situation.[390] As seen too, this attempt failed further to objections it gave rise to among the Commission members and among States. There could therefore be no trying to reintroduce the right of humanitarian intervention which we have just seen had been rejected by States, in the context of exceptional justificatory circumstances. In conclusion, one can only recall the full stringency required when trying to establish the existence of a customary rule by echoing the words of a UK lawyer speaking in the International Court of Justice:

> This Court has on many occasions set out the real requirements of custom. There must be a coherent body of State practice. That practice must be of sufficient generality to show widespread support among States. The practice must embody a positive belief that it is required by law. Support for the existence of the rule must be evident . . . Custom is not something which can be conjured from the air . . . It is not something which can be assumed, or deduced from appeals to general principles of humanity.[391]

---

[390] Above, ch 4, s II.
[391] ICJ, Legality of the Threat or Use of Nuclear Weapons, N Lyell, CR95/34, 15 November 1995, 50.

Conclusion

I N CONCLUSION IT can be affirmed at the end of this study that the hypothesis that has been the thread running through it is validated in view of the practice and stances taken by the international community of States as a whole: the legal regime of the UN Charter instituted a 'law against war' the principle of which has never been called into question by a significant majority of States. The stringency of this *jus contra bellum* implies, first, that only certain arguments are legally admissible when a State attempts to justify a use of force. These are the consent of the State in whose territory the intervention takes place (which, under certain circumstances, means we are no longer dealing with a use of force against a State within the meaning of article 2(4) of the Charter), Security Council authorisation or self-defence.[1] Conversely, circumstances excluding unlawfulness—whether a state of necessity, extreme distress or counter-measures—cannot be used to elude this peremptory legal rule.[2] Likewise, one cannot attack a State on the pretext that it is not the State as such that is the target but private groups located in its territory: the rule prohibiting the use of force 'in international relations' remains a rule protecting the territorial integrity and political independence of all States, even after the events of 11 September 2001.[3] Secondly, the concern to maintain the stringency of this rule entails the failure of attempts to add new justifications (such as the 'right of humanitarian intervention')[4] or to construe very broadly the legally admitted exceptions (as is the case with the notions of 'preventive self-defence' or presumed Security Council authorisation).[5]

The scope of these lessons must admittedly be relativised, on two counts. First because they are grounded on a positivist legal method involving reliance on existing texts and on the interpretation made of them by the international community of States as a whole.[6] This is a choice, or even a postulate, that others are not forced to share.[7] Second, and in any event,

---

[1] Above, chs 5, 6 and 7.
[2] Above, ch 4.
[3] Above, ch 3.
[4] Above, ch 8.
[5] Above, chs 6, s II and 7, s I.
[6] Above, ch 1, s II.
[7] Above, ch 1, s I.

because our conclusions relate only to coercive acts of some gravity and that may therefore be characterised as a use of 'force' within the meaning of the UN Charter. The question of the lawfulness of minor coercive acts such as international abductions or even very limited police operations remains open, though, and must be appraised depending on treaty law and the very general principle of respect for State sovereignty.[8] If, however, one works within the bounds of a true use of force and abides by the method followed by the International Court of Justice in particular, I think the claim that the 'law against war' is maintained is largely borne out by the positions taken by States.

But beyond this conclusion which derives from existing law, ought new possibilities for the use of force not to be envisaged *de lege ferenda*? This issue has not been addressed in this book. First because, to my mind, the creation of new rules of law is a job for political decision makers and not for lawyers, unless they are following an approach based on the philosophy of international law to come up with proposals for reform. Then because, in any event, existing doctrinal thinking seems to me unable to revise the prohibition of the use of force as it is laid down in the Charter while maintaining a legal regime that can be characterised as *jus contra bellum*. To illustrate this, one might evoke the many studies that, as their authors see it, come up with new concepts to improve existing law. This was the case in the domain of preventive war or even more so in that of the 'right of humanitarian intervention'. As an example, further to the war against Yugoslavia in 1999, it was proposed that a military action might be justified in an exceptional situation characterised by:

1. Serious violations of human rights amounting to a crime against humanity.
2. Systematic refusal by the State concerned to cooperate with the UN.
3. Deadlock in the Security Council that could not otherwise have failed to condemn or deplore the situation, while characterising it as a threat to international peace and security.
4. The exhaustion of all peaceful means of dispute settlement.
5. The implementation of a collective intervention led by a group of States and not by a hegemonic power.
6. Limitation of this intervention to what is strictly necessary to the pursuit of humanitarian objectives.[9]

This conceptualisation largely takes up criteria traditionally used by a certain doctrine.[10] As such it is open to the criticism that is often made of it,

---

[8] Above, ch 2, s I.

[9] Antonio Cassese, '*Ex iniuria ius oritur*: Are We Moving towards International Legitimation of Forcible Humanitarian Countermeasures in the World Community?' (1999) 10 *EJIL* 27.

[10] See, eg: WD Verwey, 'Humanitarian Intervention under International Law' (1985) 32 *NILR*, 418; A Bonde, *Traité élémentaire de droit international public* (Paris, Dalloz, 1926) 245; Elisa Perrez-Vera, 'La protection d'humanité en droit international', (1969) 5 *RBDI* 418;

especially in terms of the excessive power of characterisation left to intervening States to apply these general criteria to particular given circumstances.[11] The originality lies here, however, in the formulation of the third
criterion that confers on the Security Council the power to prevent abusive
unilateral interpretations. Upon examination and contrary to what its
designer intended, it seems to me though that this criterion does not really
make it possible to overcome the alternative of strict observance of existing
law and the risk of a return to subjectivity that characterised the *jus ad
bellum* of before the Charter.[12] It must be clearly understood that, if the six
criteria listed were to form the legal rule of reference tomorrow, each
Security Council Member State would be fully aware that by voting for a
resolution condemning a State or deploring the situation, by characterising
the situation as a threat to peace, it would in fact be accepting to authorise
a military intervention. The problem of the veto of certain States such as
China or Russia and therefore of the 'deadlock'[13] of the Security Council is
therefore not at all settled by this proposal; it is simply shunted upline, to
the time the Council deals with the question without explicitly contemplating the use of force. Unless of course it is considered that the will of the
Council can be circumvented in the name of what are held to be higher
moral values . . . which would amount to eliminating the third criterion
above without further ado. In other words, it seems difficult indeed, unless
one is to call into question the continuation of a legal regime of *jus contra
bellum,* to circumvent the rules of the Charter conferring on the Security
Council the power to authorise or, in the specific case of self-defence, to
supervise the use of force.[14]

Finally this book could not end without emphasising the very limited
character of the legal rule in a domain so closely tied to sovereignty and to
power as the decision to wage war. While it is undeniable, as has been seen
from the many precedents set out above, that States develop a 'foreign legal

---

Romualdo Bermejo Garcia, *El marco jurídico internacional en materia de uso de la fuerza:
ambigüedades y límites* (Madrid, editorial civitas SA, 1993) 401; see also more recently,
A Peters, 'Le droit d'ingérence et le devoir d'ingérence—Vers une responsabilité de protéger',
(2002) 79 *RDIDC* 306–07.

[11] See, eg: Mohammed Bedjaoui, 'La portée incertaine du concept nouveau de "devoir
d'ingérence" dans un monde troublé: quelques interrogations' in Actes du colloque organisé
par l'Académie royale du Maroc, *Le droit d'ingérence est-il une nouvelle législation du colonialisme?* 1991, 232–63; Jean-Marc Sorel, 'Le devoir d'ingérence: longue histoire et ambiguïté
constante', (1991) 3 *Relations internationales et stratégiques,* 95-107 and more recently
B Kingsbury, 'Sovereignty and Inequality' (1999) 9 *EJIL* 618–20.

[12] See the developments in the present author's 'Peut-on définir un nouveau droit d'intervention humanitaire?', (1999) 31–32 *Dialogues. Revue internationale d'arts et de Sciences* 200–17.

[13] The term 'deadlock' is very much a value judgement in that it implies that the Security
Council is refusing to take a decision that is subjectively thought desirable.

[14] See the developments in the present author's 'La référence au droit international comme
justification du recours à la force: vers une nouvelle doctrine de la guerre juste?' in Anne-Marie
Dillens (ed), *L'Europe et la guerre* (Bruxelles, FUSL, 2001) 69–94.

policy',[15] its scope should not be exaggerated. First because it is more than likely that States base their decisions on factors other than law, especially when they have the means to do so. Next, and even if one chooses to stay within the realms of words and not deeds, because law is only one register among others,[16] that may be used in a more or less sustained way to legitimate a military operation depending on the circumstances of the day. Alongside this legal register, States will often play on a political register, openly based on their interests or on the interests they claim to be those of the 'international community'.[17] A moral register, consisting in an appeal to peremptory and higher values, will be drawn on occasionally, for example by States claiming to be conducting a 'humanitarian intervention'. It is possible for that matter in one or other particular case to study the respective proportions of these justificatory registers and analyse their interactions in States' official pronouncements.[18] This is a particularly interesting approach but one that is situated more in the perspective of the political sciences than of the classical legal method to which we have confined ourselves in this book. It is only if one follows this classical method that one can affirm, without being accused of idealism or even of naivety, that there is still, in this day and age, a 'law against war'.

---

[15] From the expression that is the title to the reference work by G de la Charrière, *La politique juridique extérieure* (Paris, Economica, 1983).

[16] See the developments in the author's 'La persistance de l'argument légaliste. Eléments pour une typologie contemporaine des registres de légitimité dans une société libérale', (2002) 50 *Droit et société. Revue internationale de théorie du droit et de sociologie juridique*, 185–203.

[17] For details see O Corten and B Delcourt, 'Droit, légitimation et politique extérieure: précisions théoriques et méthodologiques' in O Corten and B Delcourt (eds), *Droit, légitimation et politique extérieure. L'Europe et la guerre du Kosovo* (Bruxelles, éd Bruylant, 2001) 19–30.

[18] This is the perspective explored in the book just cited of the war against Yugoslavia in 1999; see the present author's 'Les ambiguïtés de la référence au droit international comme facteur de légitimation. Portée et signification d'une déformalisation du discours légaliste' ibid, 223–60.

Selected Reading

The bibliography that follows is truly and even radically 'selective'. I have abandoned all hope of giving full references to all the documents and studies cited in the main text (with full references for the first citation in each section) so as not to make the book even heavier reading, both literally and figuratively.

As stated in the introduction, the book relies essentially on positions taken up by States and therefore on a number of documents in which they are expressed (I). Doctrine has only been used as supplementary material (II).

I Documents

Many of the texts consulted in writing this book are reproduced in part or in full at the following electronic address: www.ulb.ac.be/droit/cdi/, under 'dossiers'.

Many documents are from the UN. Useful links include:

www.un.org/depts/dhl/dhlf/unbisnet/indexf.htm;
documents.un.org/default.asp
untreaty.un.org/French/treaty.asp
www.un.org/law/ilc/
www.icj-cij.org/
www.un.org/french/aboutun/fmissions.htm

The texts consulted, for which a precise reference is given each time in the main text, are essentially:

—documents that preceded the adoption of the major resolutions of the UN General Assembly on the prohibition of the use of force: resolutions 2625 (XXV), 3314 (XXIX), 42/22, 60/1; these documents include the committee, special group or Secretariat-General reports and the minutes of debates within the relevant committees or the General Assembly itself (Sixth Commission or Plenary Session);
—works of the International Law Commission on the various subjects relating directly or indirectly to the prohibition of the use of force: rights and duties of States, code of crimes against the peace and security of mankind, law of treaties, international responsibility, responsibility of international organisations, diplomatic protection; apart from the works

of the Commission itself (that can be found on the web site above or in the *Yearbooks of the International Law Commission*), the positions of States were consulted, especially on the Sixth Commission of the UN General Assembly;

—positions of States or groups of States on the fringes of the UN; web sites of a number of these groups were consulted, whether international organisations or otherwise (Group of 77, Non-Aligned Movement, Islamic Conference Organisation, African Union, Organization of American States, European Union, NATO, etc) and sites specific to States (especially the permanent missions within the UN);

—digests of practice published in certain international law journals since 1945: *American Journal of International Law, Annuaire français de droit international, Annuaire suisse de droit international/Revue suisse de droit international et de droit européen, British Yearbook of International Law, Canadian Yearbook of International Law, Netherlands Yearbook of International Law, Revue belge de droit international* and certain classical works such as A-C Kiss, *Répertoire de la pratique française en matière de droit international public* (Paris, ed CNRS) and *Digest of United States Practice* (Washington, Department of State Publication) (several volumes, cited in the main text);

—minutes of Security Council debates on precedents involving an interpretation of the rule prohibiting the use of force; a selection of these precedents is on the web site cited; the index of this book directs readers to where each of these precedents is examined;

—positions States have expressed in the International Court of Justice in all cases relating to the prohibition of the use of force; the written and oral proceedings can be consulted on the Court's web site;

—the *travaux préparatoires* of the UN Charter published as: *Documents of the United Nations Conference of International Organization (UNCIO)* (San Francisco, London, New York, UN Information Organizations, 1945);

—for factual material, reference was made above all to *Keesing's Contemporary Archives*, Record of World Events (London, Longman) and to 'Chronique des faits internationaux' in *Revue générale de droit international public.*

II Doctrine

There is a wealth of books and studies about the prohibition of the use of force; in writing this book I systematically consulted the following journals since 1945: *American Journal of International Law (AJIL), Annuaire français de droit international (AFDI), Annuaire suisse de droit international (ASDI)/Revue suisse de droit international et de droit européen (RSDIE), British Yearbook of International Law (BYBIL), Canadian Yearbook of International Law (CYIL), International & Comparative Law Quarterly (ICLQ), European Journal of International Law (EJIL), Netherlands International Law Review*

(NILR), Netherlands Yearbook of International Law (NYIL), Revue belge de droit international (RBDI), Revue générale de droit international public (RGDIP).

Other journals and books consulted are cited in the main text.

The following books on the prohibition of the use of force were especially useful:

Y Dinstein, *War, Aggression and Self-Defence*, 4th edn (Cambridge, Cambridge University Press, 2005) xxv and 349.

T Franck, *Recourse to Force. State Action Against Threats and Armed Attacks* (Cambridge, Cambridge University Press, Hersch Lauterpacht Memorial Lectures, 2002) xii and 205.

R Kolb, Ius contra bellum. *Le droit international relatif au maintien de la paix*, 2nd edn (Bruxelles, Bruylant, Bâle, Helbing Lichtenhahn, 2009) xiv and 435.

C Gray, *International Law and the Use of Force*, 3rd edn (Oxford, Oxford University Press, 2008) xvii and 455.

L-A Sicilianos, *Les réactions décentralisées à l'illicite: des contre-mesures à la légitime défense*, foreword by Nicolas Valticos, preface by Denys Simon (Paris, LGDJ, 1990) xxix and 532.

Other works that were most useful in dealing with more specific aspects are cited in the relevant chapters or sections.

Index

Lightning Source UK Ltd.
Milton Keynes UK
UKHW02f0608210518
322936UK00002B/26/P

9 781849 463584